A MOST UNIQUE
MACHINE

The Michigan Origins
of the American Automobile Industry

by
GEORGE S. MAY

WILLIAM B. EERDMANS PUBLISHING COMPANY

Library of Congress Cataloging in Publication Data

May, George Smith, 1924-
　　A most unique machine.
　　Bibliography: p. 349
　　1. Automobile industry and trade — Michigan — History.
I. Title.
HD9710.U53M434　　　338.4'7'629209774　　74-19230
ISBN 0-8028-7032-5

To Tim and his Nana

Contents

Illustrations

Introduction

Actually, of course, there was nothing *unique* about the machine that moved along a Detroit street, under its own power, late one winter evening in 1896. Numerous other vehicles, propelled by variations on what was essentially the same engine, had appeared at many places in Europe and the United States during the preceding decade. A few had even been produced commercially. But in one sense, the reporter was correct in using the term "a most unique machine" to describe the motor wagon piloted by Charles B. King on the night of March 6, 1896. As nearly as can be determined, this was the first gasoline-powered road vehicle to appear on the streets of Michigan's largest city, and, as present evidence indicates, probably the first such vehicle successfully driven anywhere in the state.

Nevertheless, the event received only passing notice in a state where bicycles, streetcars, interurbans, railroads, steamships, and the antics of an occasional balloonist seemed to be providing sufficient variety to the age-old modes of transportation. The possibilities of manufacturing these vehicles also received little consideration in a state whose well-balanced economy — a blend of farming, lumbering, mining, and a growing amount of manufacturing — was just beginning to recover from the severe shock and dislocation of the depression that had begun in 1893. No one in 1896 could possibly have conceived of the impact — the unique impact — that King's machine and its successors would soon have. At the time, Michigan was a young state, only six decades old. Many inhabitants still recalled when it was an undeveloped territory, living off the fur trade, with only a half dozen or so small, widely scattered settlements precariously perched at the water's edge around the rim of two great peninsulas. Yet ten years after 1896, that frontier heritage, which had seemed so real amidst the small town, rural atmosphere of the nineties, was fast being shoved aside. In ten years the gasoline automobile and Michigan had joined in an unbeatable combination to move the state out in front of any other area in the world in this new industry. In the process, everything was being reshaped, transforming Michigan's image to one of a fast-paced, urban, industrialized area. The turn-of-the-century image, the small-town frontier heritage, was rendered obsolete by the automobile.

A few years later, in 1922, the Detroit businessman and historian, Clarence M. Burton, noted that historians had thus far paid little heed to what had been happening in the state in the twentieth century, particularly with regard to the growth of the auto industry. Burton quoted one writer as observing:

> In all of the books on Michigan history, copious treatment is given the money represented by our agriculture, our lumber interests, our salt industry, our furniture output, our mining product; yet this giant industry, which far overtops them all, not only in money values but in its far-reaching influence, is dismissed in this manner: "Automobiles are made in many cities, etc., etc."

Burton, who had had a small part in the organization of one or two Detroit automobile companies and was well acquainted with many of the leaders of the industry in Michigan, tried to correct this imbalance in histories of Detroit and Wayne County that he directed; but half a century later there is still truth in what Burton stated in 1922: "the automobile industry awaits its historian."[1]

Historians, who are supposedly furnishing the means whereby mankind's progress is revealed in a well-balanced, meaningful manner, often seem to lose sight of this goal. Instead, many devote their time to whatever interests them, regardless of its importance. This writer, for example, pleads guilty to having contributed a number of titles to the already very extensive literature available on the history of the Mackinac area in the seventeenth, eighteenth, and early nineteenth century. Although that history is exciting and picturesque, it has almost nothing to do with present-day conditions in Michigan. Nevertheless, the books, pamphlets, and articles dealing with that region's history are more abundant than those dealing with most aspects of Michigan's automobile industry, the pre-eminent influence that has shaped modern Michigan. Again, it is regrettably true that there are more full-length biographies and other published works available on the life of James J. Strang than there are on the life of any automobile figure with the exception of Henry Ford. Strang, it is true, is a fascinating subject, but can anyone argue that this red-haired Mormon rebel, who was the religious leader of a few thousand people on Beaver Island for less than a decade in the mid-nineteenth century and whose followers today number only in the hundreds, is as deserving of serious attention as Ransom Olds or William C. Durant or Walter P. Chrysler, whose work affects the daily lives of millions of people throughout the world?

This is not to say that histories of the automobile industry have not been written. A few minutes with the card catalog in any reasonably large library will quickly turn up the titles of scores of books that have appeared on the industry, the automobile, automotive leaders, individual companies, and assorted special topics. Today, interest in the automobile and its history may well be at its highest peak ever in both the United States and Europe. Unfortunately, there is little correlation between the quantity of material that has and is appearing and the quality that one would desire. With the exception of occasional works, such as Sidney Fine's studies of the auto industry during the depression years of the thirties and the three-volume study of Henry Ford and the Ford Motor Company, by Allan Nevins and a team of associates, one searches in vain for the kind of studies, based on an extensive examination of the available sources, that seem in comparison to be so much more common in the literature, for example, on the railroad and oil industries. As for overall histories of the auto industry, John B. Rae's brief, 245-page text in the Chicago History of American Civilization series, published in 1965, is, as the publisher's blurb says, the only work that can be described as a "scholarly treatment of the whole span of the automobile industry."

As one turns to the vast quantity of literature that remains after the works of a few such as Rae, Fine, Nevins, and the earlier studies of Lawrence Seltzer and Ralph Epstein have been winnowed out, one is left with a mass of material: it is frequently good reading, it is frequently the result of considerable research on the part of the author and contains much valuable information, but, at the same time, it is often characterized by a limited or even distorted emphasis and, most serious, by a general tendency to accept as fact what frequently, upon closer inspection, turns out to be not factual at all. It is, in short, popular history at its best and at its worst. It seemingly offers the automobile buff, for whom so much of it is apparently written, the background information that will add to his interest in old cars, but by not digging deeply enough beyond the rib-tickling anecdote and the hearsay evidence, it misses the real drama and excitement, as well as the true significance of this great subject.

The present work deals with what is unquestionably the most important aspect in the history of the American automobile industry — the rise of automobile manufacturing in Michigan during the period from its inception in the mid-nineties to about 1909. By then, companies in Detroit, Flint, Lansing, and several other southern Michigan communities had made the state by far the leading auto manufacturing center in the world. The activities of such non-Michigan pioneers as the Duryeas, Elwood Haynes, Hiram Maxim, George Pierce, and Alexander Winton, which have received so much attention in previous studies, cannot obscure the fact that the end result of these activities did not prove as lasting as those of their contemporaries who developed and built the Oldsmobile, Cadillac, Ford, and Buick. While giving full attention to the somewhat familiar (though, as I try to make clear, not always accurate) stories about Olds, Ford, Leland, and Durant, I have attempted to place them in the proper perspective of their time and locality, dealing also with the host of other individuals and forces that contributed to the industry's growth in the state. The overall intent is to suggest not only why Detroit, and in a larger sense Michigan, forged ahead of all other areas, but what is perhaps even more to the point, to answer such questions as why Ford succeeded and so many other Michigan mechanics with equal or superior abilities and opportunities failed, and why Flint developed as a major automobile center while a city like Jackson did not. I had expected to devote much attention also to the enormous impact that the automobile and its manufacture had upon the entire state, but the necessity of giving so much space to a clarification of the manufacturing and business developments of the story made it impossible to deal with these other matters in this volume.

Sources for this book are discussed in the bibliographical essay following the text. These sources are so diverse and voluminous that a really definitive study of this subject would require far more time and a much greater degree of patience than is granted me. What I have tried to do in this book, through an extensive sampling of such primary materials as manuscript and archival records, newspapers, trade journals, and memoirs, as well as the relevant secondary sources, is not only to present the story in as clear a manner as possible, but hopefully to demonstrate the great opportunities and untapped resources that await the diligent researcher. Such a one would find, as I have, that when the myths and half-truths are stripped away, the result is not a loss but a great gain in the interest and fascination this topic holds.

My indebtedness to various people for the help they have given is acknowledged elsewhere, but here I would like to mention my debt to my students, most of them from the Detroit area, who first made me realize the need for more information on the auto industry than was available for their use and mine, thereby launching me on this project; to my publisher for going along with my idea for a book on this subject; and finally to my wife, who helped extensively in the research and typing that were required to bring this book to completion.

GEORGE S. MAY
Ypsilanti, Michigan

A MOST UNIQUE MACHINE

Charles King and Oliver Barthel *on their first public test of King's experimental horseless carriage.*

CHAPTER 1

"OF CARRIAGES AND KING" *

At 11 p.m. on the night of March 6, 1896, Charles Brady King, twenty-eight years old, a Detroit engineer and manufacturer, and his young assistant, Oliver E. Barthel, seated themselves in an open carriage. In appearance, this carriage was little different from many others driven daily on the streets of Detroit in that period, except that King's carriage was horseless. The vehicle began to move along Woodward Avenue in downtown Detroit with no visible assistance from its occupants aside from King's trifling efforts to guide it with a steering lever. The event "caused a deal of comment" from the scattered pedestrians who were still out at that late hour along the city's main thoroughfare. A crowd assembled in the street, hampering further progress by the strange vehicle.

King had held road tests prior to March 6, but under circumstances that would guarantee privacy. His public debut, on the other hand, attracted the attention not only of some night owls but also of the city's newspapers who next day reported the event. The *Journal* gave King the most extensive coverage and tried to explain what made his carriage move.

*The chapter title is from a United States Treasury Department war bond radio program that featured the career of Charles King.

It consists of a four-cylindered engine, the connecting rods of which drive a shaft, at which at the opposite ends are respectively the fly wheel and the belt wheel. The belt wheel connects by a belt with a drum situated just back of the driver's seat and half under the bottom of the vehicle. Inside the drum is arranged an equalizing gearing, that when turning corners equal power shall be given to each set of wheels, but allowing the wheels on one side to run as much faster than the other, as the curve requires.

The fuel used to set this mechanism in motion was gasoline, and, the *Journal* declared, "when in motion, the connecting rods fly like lightning, and the machine is capable of running seven or eight miles an hour." In short, it was "a most unique machine."

Unique it was to Detroit, where Charles King had staged that city's first public exhibition of a gasoline-powered horseless carriage. The event also may have been the first of its kind anywhere in Michigan; but, as King pointed out at the time, such vehicles were no longer a complete novelty in Europe or in some other parts of the United States. Furthermore, he went on, "I am convinced they will in time supersede the horse."

Recognizing the commercial possibilities that were inherent in such a development, King announced his intention to produce and sell motor carriages. Although he had very little luck in this venture, King's actions in the spring of 1896 were among the first slight stirrings of a movement that, within a decade, would carry Michigan to world leadership in an industry that did not exist in the state at that time.[1]

* * *

Contrary to popular conceptions, Detroit did not invent the automobile nor did the manufacturing of such motor vehicles originate there or at any other point in Michigan. European inventors, mechanics, engineers, and businessmen were well 'ahead of Americans in both developments. By the 1880's, several Europeans had solved the basic problems of powering a vehicle with an internal-combustion gasoline engine, the type of vehicle that would prevail in the future. By 1890, commercial production of these horseless carriages had already begun, with France seizing and holding leadership in the industry throughout the decade.[2]

Although considerable experimental work had been carried on in the United States prior to this time in an effort to develop various kinds of self-operating road vehicles, the spark that ignited truly successful efforts came from Chicago. It all began on May 1, 1893, as the sun began to disperse the dark clouds, chilling mist, and swirling fog which earlier had threatened to cancel the long-awaited ceremonies scheduled for that morning in the city's Jackson Park. Uniformed soldiers and cavalrymen signaled the start of the proceedings and the arrival of the distinguished guests to the speaker's platform. Finally the preliminaries were over and the President of the United States, Grover Cleveland, was telling the assembled thousands: "As by a touch, the machinery that gives life to this vast exhibition is set in motion, so at the same instant let our hopes and aspirations awaken forces which in all time to come shall influence the welfare, the dignity, and the freedom of mankind." With that he pressed a button and instantly water spurted from fountains, cannons boomed, chimes rang out, whistles tooted, and engines sputtered and vibrated. The World's Columbian Exposition, better known as the Chicago World's Fair, opened to the public.

In the next six months, the millions of visitors to the fair saw and experienced many things that would effect changes far exceeding anything Cleveland or his listeners could possibly have envisioned that spring morning. There were hints of impending change in such diverse areas as architectural styles, the uses of electricity, and even women's rights. But among the various influences, probably the one least appreciated at the time was the impact that Chicago's great "White City" had on the development of a new means of transportation which did not yet have even a commonly accepted name.[3]

As early as 1890, the commission established to set up the international fair had offered rewards to exhibitors of "steam, electric and other road vehicles propelled by other than animal power." Charles Duryea, one of the foremost American automotive pioneers, recalled later that this announcement encouraged him and many fellow experimenters "who had been discouraged by ridicule and pity [to take] a fresh hitch at their trousers." Duryea, a resident of Peoria, Illinois, intended to exhibit a horseless carriage but was unable to do so. Later in 1893, however, on September 21, in Springfield, Massachusetts, his younger brother Frank drove what is usually cited as America's first successful gasoline-powered automobile, which Charles had designed and Frank had then carried through to completion.[4]

The failure of the Duryeas to exhibit a road vehicle at Chicago was less surprising than the absence of several others who had already built such vehicles and who, one would think, would have welcomed the opportunity to publicize their accomplishments. Among these absentees were such notable figures (in automobile history) as Sylvester H. Roper of Roxbury, Massachusetts, who between 1859 and 1895 built ten operable steam cars, Ransom E. Olds of Lansing, Michigan, who had put together two steam-powered horseless carriages and received national recognition in a magazine in May 1892, and William Morrison of Des Moines, Iowa, who is credited with constructing America's first electric vehicle in 1891 and driving it on the streets of Chicago a year later.[5]

Morrison's vehicle was well displayed at Chicago in 1893 by Harold Sturges, its new owner and head of the Chicago firm that had supplied Morrison with the batteries used to power the carriage. Sturges exhibited the vehicle in the Electrical Building at the fair and had it driven frequently around the exhibition grounds, giving a few fair-goers their first thrilling ride in a horseless carriage. Those who rode later recalled riding in the Sturges Electric, as Harold Sturges brazenly labeled his purchase;

unfortunately, he thereby deprived William Morrison of the fame right-fully due to him as the builder of the car.

Also on view in the Electrical Building was a battery-operated, three-wheeled rolling chair, the Keller-Dengenhart, which carried as many as three riders down the aisles of the building but was probably not in-tended to be a road vehicle. A London company was also listed as an exhibitor of electric vehicles.

As for steam-powered carriages, a type that had been in existence for over a century, only one may have been exhibited. This was a steamer patented in 1892 by Achille Philion, a circus performer at the fair, who intended to use the car in his act. Whether he did or not is uncertain. The vehicle is still in existence and was driven in the 1951 Red Skelton comedy about the horseless carriage days, *Excuse My Dust*.

The only gasoline-powered motor vehicle at the Columbian Expo-sition was a quadricycle exhibited by the Daimler Motor Company of Long Island, New York, a firm established by the American piano manu-facturer, William Steinway. He had acquired the American rights to prod-ucts patented in Germany by Gottlieb Daimler. Steinway hoped to manu-facture the Daimler automobile but initially he concentrated on manufac-turing the Daimler gas engine for use in motor launches.[6]

The impact that this handful of self-operating vehicles had on those who attended the fair was minimal also because of the vast and amazing assemblage of other attractions that competed for the visitor's attention. On the midway was the gigantic wheel, 250 feet high, designed by George Washington Gale Ferris and intended to be the focus of attention just as the Eiffel Tower had been at the Paris Exposition in 1889. In the section called the *Streets of Cairo* was the immortal "Little Egypt," whose "genu-ine native muscle dance" was viewed with awe by millions. Elsewhere, one could contemplate other awesome sights: a monstrous engine in Machinery Hall that could generate fourteen thousand horsepower, and a thirty-foot replica of a stove, exhibited by Detroit's Michigan Stove Company.[7]

Little wonder that a few puny and primitive horseless carriages were relatively unnoticed. Even the *Scientific American* magazine, which in the past had informed its readers of some of the European and Ameri-can efforts to develop practical motor vehicles, completely neglected the topic in the many columns that it devoted to the fair and its attractions. Railroad locomotives, a variety of marine vessels, Turkish sedan chairs, phaetons (four-wheeled horse-drawn carriages), tally-ho coaches, Abraham Lincoln's state carriage, bicycles, and other modes of transportation on view at the fair were described in the magazine — but not a mention of motor cars. Chris Sinsabaugh, one of the most famous writers for automo-tive trade publications in the twentieth century, visited the fair as a young man and knew that there was at least one horseless carriage on exhibition; at the time, however, he was not interested enough to look at it; and years later he could not even remember the car's name.[8]

A few visitors to the exposition were more observant. George Forsyth and Olaf Nelson of Franklin, Minnesota, were inspired by what they saw to go out and buy two gasoline engines which they used in vehicles they built between 1894 and 1897. Of more lasting impact on American automotive developments was the effect that a visit to the fair had on Elwood Haynes of Kokomo, Indiana. He was inspired to complete his famous horseless carriage of 1894 quite directly by what he saw in Chicago.

Another visitor interested in motor vehicles was Henry Ford, a thirty-year-old mechanic taking a brief holiday from his job in Detroit to visit the fair. He almost certainly must have seen the New York Central's new locomotive, the "999," one of the most popular sights in the Transportation Building. Nine years later, Ford's most famous racing car, named after the locomotive, began to approach on land the speed records the original "999" had set on rails. Also, Ford may well have studied the extensive display of gas engines, particularly the Otto engine, a type that he had known about and worked on since the middle of the previous decade. But the attraction that Ford remembered best was "a small gasoline engine that had been mounted on a wide two-wheeled horsecart, and used for pumping water," possibly a motorized fire engine that is said to have been part of the Daimler Motor Company's exhibit. Ford reportedly felt that this engine was much like the one he had been attempting to build, and he returned to Detroit, therefore, inspired to resume his work with the added knowledge he had acquired in Chicago.[9]

Another Detroiter who was at the fair, but in a different capacity, was Charles B. King. Of all the individuals who contributed to the development of the automobile industry in Michigan, few, if any, were more capable in their chosen field than King. None, it is safe to say, was as diversified in his interests, for King was not only interested in all things mechanical. He also developed into a first-class artist whose etchings were widely exhibited. As a musician he could perform creditably on numerous instruments; and he was a long-time student of spiritualism and psychic phenomena, and a self-taught architect. The home that he designed and built for himself in Larchmont, New York, was viewed with considerable awe by a *New Yorker* writer in 1946. Earlier, in 1915, another writer had described King's home in Detroit as "an 'Old Curiosity Shop' of art objects, relics, and mechanical devices from everywhere." The same writer described King as "another man of the seer type, a rare sort of genius, half artist, half mechanic, and altogether a gentleman," whose well-developed aesthetic interests were, he felt, a key to King's noticeable disinterest in the commercial, money-making applications of his inventions.[10]

Charles B. King's roots in Detroit were deep. His mother, Matilda Davenport, was a Detroit girl; one of his grandmothers had been born in the city when it was still a stockaded fort; and one of his grandfathers, King claimed, operated the first steam ferry between Detroit and Windsor. King, however, was born in 1868 on Angel Island in San Francisco Bay, California, where his father, John H. King, an army colonel, was stationed. His boyhood was one of constant movement from one army post to another until the family settled in Detroit at his father's retirement in 1882.

Five years later, young King enrolled as an engineering student in Cornell University, but his father's death in 1888 forced him to leave college soon thereafter and return home. He was then twenty years old, a confident, good-looking young man, "full of ideas." He took a job as a draftsman with the Michigan Car Company, one of the leading manufacturers of railroad cars in the country. After about two years he went to work for another Detroit manufacturer, the Russel Wheel and Foundry Company. King was the Russel Company's representative at Chicago in 1893 where it won an award for its logging cars. In addition, however, King had on exhibition a pneumatic hammer which he had designed in 1890 and which he had successfully used for riveting and caulking purposes. The device was the only one of its kind on display and won for King the exposition's highest award — a bronze medal and a diploma. A steel brake beam that King had invented was also used on several refrigerator cars that were on exhibit.[11]

Although still in his mid-twenties, King had begun to make his mark in engineering circles. It was not surprising, therefore, that by the time he came to Chicago, he had already begun to take a look at one of the newest areas of interest to engineers, the automotive field. Nevertheless, it seems to have been due only to his exploration of other exhibits at the fair that King developed a real interest in experimenting with a horseless carriage of his own design. He saw and even rode in the Sturges Electric, but like nearly all of Michigan's automobile men of his generation, King never regarded electricity as a practical means of propelling the kind of vehicle he had in mind. He made little effort, therefore, to become better acquainted with Harold Sturges or his electric car.

A short distance from the Russel exhibit in the Transportation Building was one that King studied with some care, the exhibit of the Daimler Motor Company. Oddly enough, the gasoline-powered car, which seems to have been one of the items in this display, made so little an impression on King that he could not even recall it in later years. But Daimler's engines interested him, and as he came to know the company's representative, Mr. Weinman, the latter proposed that King's company manufacture these engines under a license issued by the New York company. Nothing came of Weinman's proposal, partly, King said, because of difficulties he foresaw in manufacturing the Daimler engines, and, perhaps more importantly, because the royalty that Russel would have had to pay Weinman's firm was regarded as too high. Had this deal been closed, the Russel Wheel and Foundry Company might have achieved fame as Detroit's first auto-parts manufacturer.[12]

King's inspiration to build a gasoline-powered vehicle came not from the work of Gottlieb Daimler but from that of a more obscure source, the Sintz Gas Engine Company of Grand Rapids, Michigan. Clark Sintz had been born in Springfield, Ohio, around 1850. As early as 1862 he was developing an interest in steam engines, which led him to begin their manufacture in 1873. A visit to the Philadelphia Centennial Exposition of 1876, however, was for Clark Sintz and for many other mechanically minded Americans an eye-opener, because it introduced him to the internal-combustion gasoline engine. By 1885, Sintz had developed an advanced gasoline engine and the following year he organized the Sintz Gas Engine Company in Springfield. In 1891 he patented a two-cycle engine which he then manufactured and sold as a marine engine. He moved his company to Grand Rapids late in 1892, by which time his sons Guy and Claude were also in the business. Addison A. Barber of Grand Rapids, who had persuaded Sintz to make the move, became treasurer of the company.

A few months later, *Scientific American* gave extended notice to a discussion of the Sintz exhibit at Chicago, where the "well known" Sintz engine was on display. Although the engines were known for their marine uses, at least one of the one-cylinder engines had already been used in 1892 to power a horseless carriage built in Milwaukee by Gottfried Schloemer and Frank Toepfer. Theirs was a crude vehicle that did, however, work, after a fashion, and survives today in the Milwaukee Public Museum. Schloemer and Toepfer failed in their efforts to manufacture the Milwaukee car, one of several predecessors of the Duryea; theirs was a fate that would unfortunately be common to almost all of the numerous Sintz-powered automobiles in the future.[13]

Whether Charles King knew of the use that Schloemer and Toepfer had already made of the Sintz engine is not known, but as he studied the engine in Chicago, he too came to the conclusion that it could be used in a road vehicle as well as in a boat. In July, therefore, he ordered, "for experimental purposes," a one-cylinder, one-horsepower Sintz two-cycle engine, to be delivered to him in Detroit where, later that year, King struck out on his own to form the Charles B. King Company. His goal was to market some of his inventions and to work on other products, such as a horseless carriage, which he might seek to market in the future. The initial funds to start this business came from King's sale, in 1894, of his patent rights for his brake beam invention to the American Brake Beam Company of Chicago, which proceeded to manufacture the device and in succeeding years made it standard equipment on thousands of railroad cars. King rented office space on the second floor of John Lauer's Machine Shop on St. Antoine Street in Detroit. For the next few years, King and Lauer worked together closely. Lauer, who King always maintained was at that time "the best mechanic in Detroit," not excluding the more famous Henry M. Leland, was a Prussian immigrant in his fifties. He had been in business in Detroit since 1881 contracting to do machine shop jobs and manufacturing special machinery and tools. He gave King the run of the shop and did all of the actual manufacturing work involved in King's business, at a modest cost to King. Lauer even allowed King to oversee the men in his shop when they were working on a job for King. Basically, however, the arrangement permitted King to be free from the cares of the factory, enabling him to devote his full attention to sales and new products.[14]

In this period, King never had more than one or two assistants. Of these, the most important was Oliver E. Barthel who, as a seventeen-year-old boy, was hired by King late in 1894. Barthel had been fired from his first job as a draftsman with the Frontier Iron Works of Detroit, manufacturers of marine steam engines, who felt he was too inexperienced. Barthel, who would later figure prominently in a number of early automotive activities, was a Detroit native who, like King, had been forced by the death of his father to give up his engineering studies and go to work. King took time to give Barthel practical training which, as the younger man later recalled, "I could not have gotten in any college." Barthel learned quickly and ultimately contributed much to the success King achieved during the six years the two men worked together — and work together they did, sometimes at the same drafting board, an arrangement that was possible because King was righthanded and Barthel lefthanded. In addition, Barthel, who had spent four years of his childhood in Europe where his father had represented the Michigan Stove Company, could speak German fluently and was able to help King in communicating with Lauer's predominately German work force.[15]

Initially, the Charles B. King Company concentrated on manufacturing King's pneumatic hammer, on which he was granted a patent in January 1894. It was the first of more than forty patents he would be awarded during his lifetime. But from the outset, King intended also to begin producing motor vehicles. In the fall of 1893 the engine he had ordered from Sintz was delivered, and King began planning its application to a vehicle. By October 27 he had completed plans for a "motor tricycle," showing an interest similar to that of other automotive pioneers, including Ransom E. Olds, in a horseless vehicle that was halfway between a bicycle and the later automobile. By December, however, he had completed the drawings for a four-wheeled "Road Carriage," an open vehicle with a single seat, beneath which the Sintz engine was to be located. In these details, King's car did not differ from other horseless carriages of that day, but instead of a tiller, which most builders of this period used for steering purposes, King planned to use a wheel. He had gotten his idea, he claimed, from the wheels that fire departments used to guide their hook-and-ladder units. An additional change was that the driver of the vehicle would sit on the left, in contrast with the right-hand drive that was customary in American motor vehicles until the second decade of the twentieth century.[16]

The Sintz company followed with interest King's efforts to develop a new use for its engines. In January 1894, the company received a letter from a Frenchman, G. Cheminais, who wanted to represent the Grand Rapids firm in Europe. In his letter he mentioned that a Paris newspaper,

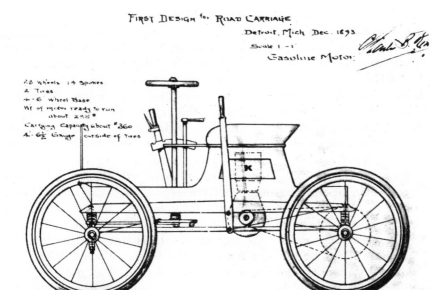

First Design for Road Carriage.
Detroit, Mich. Dec. 1893
Scale 1 - 1
Gasoline Motor:

28 Wheels 14 Spokes
2 Tires
4 - 6 Wheel Base
Wt of motor ready to run
about 258 #
Carrying Capacity about #360
4 - 6½ Gauge outside of Tires

Charles King's December 1893 plan for a four-wheeled motor vehicle, which he published in 1945 in his autobiographical volume, A Golden Anniversary, *from the original drawing that is now in Detroit's Automotive History Collection. As King points out in his caption, the steering wheel and left-hand drive were most unusual automotive features for that day.*
Courtesy University of Michigan Graduate Library

Le Petit Journal, was promoting what was hailed as the world's first automobile race, to be run in July over a route from Paris to Rouen. Thinking that Sintz might want to enter the competition, Cheminais asked: "Are you able to apply your [engine] to a four place wagon?" The manager of Sintz sent the letter on to King, who, he apparently felt, would be in a better position to answer this question.

King corresponded with Cheminais and received more information about the race, including a copy of the rules, which told those who had a vehicle to enter: "That it runs is all we want, improvement will come later." Despite such anything-goes standards, King ultimately gave up any idea of submitting an entry. The time factor alone made his participation in the race impossible. As late as April he was still working on the design of his car, completing revised plans that were still based on the Sintz engine but were slightly different in details from those he used in his earlier specifications for a four-wheeled rig. By this time, he could not have built the car, tested it, and shipped it to France by the July deadline. But then, during this same period, he decided that any immediate plans to build a motor vehicle would have to be shelved. One reason was that after putting the Sintz engine through some severe tests, King concluded that it was too unreliable to be used in a motor vehicle. "It had a tendency to backfire," was one defect he later recalled. In addition, however, "and, frankly stated," he admitted, "I did not have the funds for such an ambitious venture."[17]

Although Frank Duryea also became disillusioned with the Sintz engine when he experimented with it later in 1894, it was probably King's lack of funds and not the inadequacies of the Sintz engine that was the major reason why he had to delay the completion of his automotive plans. In support of this view is the fact that a third automotive pioneer, Elwood Haynes, successfully employed the Sintz engine in his first car. Haynes, of Kokomo, Indiana, an engineering graduate of Johns Hopkins University and Worcester Polytechnic Institute, began working on a horseless carriage as early as 1891. After seeing the Sintz exhibit at the Chicago World's Fair, he was convinced that the engine was what he had been looking for. He placed an order with the company's representative and received delivery of the engine in November 1893. According to King, a Sintz engineer went to Kokomo to break in the engine. For the test, the engine was placed on two saw horses in the Haynes kitchen. When the engine was started, however, it shook loose and jumped all over the floor spilling gasoline. Since there was a fire in the nearby kitchen stove, the testers hurriedly evacuated the room. Fortunately, the gasoline did not ignite, but Mrs. Haynes would not allow the men back in her kitchen. Nevertheless, on July 4, 1894, a vehicle designed by Elwood Haynes and built by the Riverside Machine Works of Kokomo, owned by the brothers Elmer and Edgar Apperson, made a test run in the Indiana city. A single-cylinder, two-cycle Sintz supplied the power. Although the car was scarcely satisfactory by any subsequent standards of operation, the fact that it ran at all provided Haynes and the Appersons with the initial publicity that started them on their way to automobile manufacturing careers. Reliable or not, the Sintz engine from Grand Rapids enabled Elwood Haynes, not Charles King, to go on record in automobile annals as the designer of America's second successful gasoline car.[18]

King, meanwhile, did not let his initial setback discourage him from continuing to work toward his goal of building his own motor vehicle. To learn more about the Paris — Rouen race and to broaden his knowledge about automotive developments in Europe, King took out a subscription to Le Petit Journal, and within a year he was paying a New York clipping service to send him any story it found that dealt with horseless carriages, motorcycles, and related subjects. Thus he began to collect information about what others in the field were doing, a start toward breaking down the atmosphere of isolation and ignorance in which these automotive pioneers labored.[19]

By the end of 1894, King had done considerable work in developing both two-cylinder, two-cycle and four-cylinder, four-cycle engines to provide the kind of power plant for his vehicle which he had not found in the smaller Sintz engine. Information on the exact nature of his work in 1894 and 1895 is of a technical and somewhat contradictory character, but it appears that by the summer of 1895 Charles King had largely overcome the engineering problems and that further delays in completing a gasoline-powered vehicle were caused by other problems such as a lack of certain parts and by his recurring financial difficulties.

At this point, King received the extra incentive he needed to try to push his work to completion. The Chicago *Times-Herald* announced that it would sponsor America's first automobile race over a route between Chicago and Milwaukee, with substantial cash rewards. The origins of this race are by no means clear. Herman H. Kohlsaat, a prominent Chicago businessman who had bought the *Times-Herald* early in 1895, claimed he got the inspiration for the race in May 1895, when he read an account of the Paris — Bordeaux race, which various newspaper figures in France were sponsoring. He called in Frederick Upham Adams, a Chicago writer with considerable mechanical interests and abilities, who was known to his newspaper colleagues as Grizzly Adams. Kohlsaat saw an opportunity for the *Times-Herald* to sponsor a race and gain the same kind of attention that the Paris—Rouen and the Paris—Bordeaux competitions had brought to their French newspaper sponsors. Adams, Kohlsaat declared, agreed with the idea enthusiastically and prepared the plans for the event. Another account, however, credits Adams with having originated the idea in 1894 and then selling Kohlsaat on the proposal. Kohlsaat also claimed later that they had originally planned to stage the race on July 4, 1895, and that they received sixty entries by that date, but since Elwood Haynes was the only one ready with a car, the race was postponed until Labor Day, and then finally to November. Actually, however, although Kohlsaat and Adams may have first thought in terms of a July 4 race date, no announcement concerning the race seems to have appeared until July 9, at which time the *Times-Herald* declared that it would offer a total of five thousand dollars in prizes to "the successful competitors in a horseless carriage or vehicle motor race between Milwaukee and Chicago." The contest would be held "not far from the 1st of November." Shortly thereafter November 2 was selected.

The initial *Times-Herald* story of July 9 made it clear that the sponsors, like other road-racing promoters of that era, viewed the event not simply as a sporting spectacle. The race was being held "with a view of stimulating invention and rousing an interest" in this new form of transportation. The rules and regulations set forth a few days later clearly indicated this serious intent. The competition was limited to "vehicles having three or more running wheels, and which derive all their motive power from within themselves. No vehicle shall be admitted to competition which depends in any way on muscular exertion, except for purposes of guidance." Each vehicle must be able to carry "comfortably" at least two persons throughout the race. Judges would eliminate any vehicle deemed to be unsafe to operate, and they could also bar any entry which they felt was not of "practical utility." The criteria for awarding the top prize of $2000 and the other lesser prizes would include the practical nature of the machine, its cost, its economy of operation, and its general appearance and design, in addition to the speed with which the vehicle completed the race. As further evidence of his desire to make the race a serious test of the effectiveness of the motor vehicles, Kohlsaat appointed a panel of judges with impressive scientific and mechanical qualifications. He also had a testing device constructed to provide information concerning the fuel consumption and efficiency of every machine entered in the contest.[20]

To milk additional publicity from the race, Kohlsaat and Adams also sponsored a contest to choose an appropriate generic name for these vehicles to replace the awkward and rather negative "horseless carriage," the term most commonly employed in the United States at that time. The general manager of the Public Telephone Company of New York won the prize of $500 for his entry of "Motocycle," but although the term was used extensively in stories and correspondence relating to the *Times-Herald* race, it aroused little enthusiasm and after November went into general disuse, leaving the field wide open for several years until "automobile," a term of French origin, won general favor everywhere but in Great Britain.[21]

Within ten days after plans for the race were published, more than twenty entries had been received by the *Times Herald,* and by mid-October the list had swollen to eighty-three, with several of these indicating they intended to have more than one motocycle in the field. The New York *Times* called the response "astonishing." As the date of the race approached, a spokesman for the *Times-Herald* declared that with one motocycle "equipped with an aluminum bronze gas engine" that could develop six horsepower, and with several other entrants claiming ratings as high as four and five horsepower for their engines, "there is no estimating the results that will be attained."[22]

Among the eighty-three contestants listed in October, three were from Michigan: R. W. Elston of Charlevoix, J. D. Hagaman of Adrian, and, a familiar name, the Sintz Gas Engine Company. Subsequently, at least one more Michigan entry was submitted, that of A. Baushke & Brothers, a Benton Harbor carriage manufacturer. None of the four Michigan entrants was among the handful that ended up competing in the race, because none of them had been able to complete their machines in time. Two other more famous Michigan auto pioneers also did not compete. Ransom E. Olds of Lansing, who may have been working on a gasoline-powered vehicle and later claimed to have operated it as early as 1893, considered submitting his name but then decided that he could not take the time away from his engine business to bring his vehicle up to competitive standards. Henry Ford, who also claimed later that he had built and driven his first car as early as 1893, was not even a spectator at the race. He told Kohlsaat in 1914: "I never wanted anything so badly in my life as to go to that race, but I could not get anyone to loan me the carfare to Chicago."[23]

Charles King made it to Chicago, but not, as he had hoped, as the driver of his own car. On August 15, he had written to Frederick Adams notifying him of his intention to enter a motocycle which would "have four wheels and a 4 H.P. gasoline engine. Its capacity will be four persons, but it is probable that in the race but two persons will ride." Later in the month King described the vehicle he was building as "the first motocycle which is of light weight" and could nevertheless seat four. It would weigh 675 pounds "and will probably be sold for about $600.00." Thus, after two years, King's efforts seemed to be nearing a climax. He was building a car not simply to compete in a race but to place a model in production and to sell at a low price. In doing so he anticipated the direction the Michigan automobile industry would later take under the leadership of Olds and Ford.

Soon, however, it became apparent that King was not as far along in his work as his letters of August had implied. On September 5, he informed a wheel company in New York that he would order four wheels "when drawing is completed and everything is definitely settled." Nearly two weeks later he was requesting a price on tires from the Chicago firm of Morgan and Wright, but since he asked prices on tires of two different sizes he had apparently not yet decided on the wheel dimensions of his motocycle. During the same period he was writing to Clark Sintz about a carburetor, and to other companies inquiring about chains for the transmission.

On September 11, King advised the Chicago *Times-Herald* that although he was "using all haste," it did not seem likely he could complete his motocycle by November 2. He joined others who were requesting the paper to postpone the race to allow them more time to finish their cars. Two weeks later, King sent Adams a photograph of his completed four-horsepower engine, which weighed only a hundred pounds and, King said, incorporated ideas which had "never been used in gas engines before." But he confessed that it was now impossible for him to complete the carriage in the time remaining before the race. Therefore King asked that his name be withdrawn as a contestant and offered his services as a judge or umpire in the race. Later, he would blame his withdrawal on his difficulties in getting pneumatic tires for his car. Another explanation came in 1940 when he confessed to an interviewer: "I didn't have money enough to get it through."[24]

The fact that King had no car to drive in the *Times-Herald* race proved to be a source of embarrassment to him later when he, like Ford, Charles Duryea, Haynes, Olds, and other American automobile pioneers, claimed to have completed a gasoline motor vehicle at a date earlier than the evidence seemed to indicate. Early advertisements of the King Motor Car Company, which Charles King helped to establish in 1910, used a photograph of King and Oliver Barthel seated in a vehicle identified as King's first automobile which, the ads declared, was driven on the streets of Detroit in 1894. Actually, the photograph was taken in 1896, and the vehicle pictured is the one King drove for the first time in March of that year. In 1915, Peter Clark Macfarlane wrote in *Collier's* that King had tested his first motor vehicle early in 1894, but the runs were made at night and were "so successfully concealed that now Mr. King has some difficulty in establishing the fact that he actually made them." But, as Dr. Milo M. Quaife of Detroit's Burton Historical Collection asked King in 1940, if it were true that he had a car built and running in 1894, "wouldn't you have been able and ready to go to the race at Chicago a year later?" The 72-year-old pioneer, obviously puzzled, replied: "That is a thought." Some explanation for this discrepancy may have been provided by King's assistant, Oliver Barthel, who recalled that when he came to work for King in November 1894, King's first car "was practically completed." Barthel indicates that problems with the engine, a lack of certain parts, and the overall expensiveness of the project prevented King from finishing the vehicle. His explanation may suggest why 1894 later came to be thought of as the date of King's first car, especially since King claimed that the loss of certain business records in a fire in 1901 made it impossible for him to check his recollections of all the events of earlier years.[25]

In asking that his name be withdrawn as a contestant in the race, King showed greater consideration than most of the others who had sent in their names; when November 2 arrived, the *Times-Herald* found to its embarrassment that only two contestants were ready to race their cars. One was a Benz gasoline vehicle, imported from France and owned by Hieronymus Mueller, a manufacturer of brass goods in Decauter, Illinois. He and his twenty-four-year-old son, Oscar, had made enough alterations in the vehicle so that they felt justified in calling it the Mueller-Benz. Oscar was to drive it in the race. The other vehicle was a Duryea, entered by the Duryea Motor Wagon Company, recently organized in Springfield, Massachusetts, to produce the gasoline buggy that the Duryea brothers had developed. Frank Duryea was to drive the car, with Charles as a passenger. When this paucity of contestants became evident on the eve of the day set for the race, Herman Kohlsaat reluctantly agreed to postpone the event until Thanksgiving Day, November 28, in hopes that others would be ready by that time. But to fend off the catcalls this announcement was bound to elicit from his newspaper rivals, he persuaded Oscar Mueller and Frank Duryea to stage an exhibition run on November 2 from Chicago to Waukegan and back, with a prize of $500 to the one who finished first. An accident disabled the Duryea, allowing the Mueller-Benz to win the prize. The European import averaged about eight miles an hour, compelling two reporters covering the race on a tandem bicycle to back pedal at times in order to avoid passing the motorists.[26]

Delaying the race for twenty-six days did not greatly increase the number of cars on hand for the event at the rescheduled time. Among the new arrivals were two more imported Benz automobiles, owned by the De La Vergne Refrigerating Machine Company of New York and the R. H. Macy Department Store, also of New York, both of whom were undoubtedly encouraged by the showing that the Mueller-Benz had made on

November 2. The Macy Company even tried to drive its Benz from New York to Chicago, but snow and bad roads finally made it necessary for the car to finish the trip in a freight car. Also at the starting line in Jackson Park on the morning of November 28, joining the repaired Duryea and the others, were two electric vehicles, the well-known one owned and driven by Harold Sturges and another one, called the Electrobat, entered by Henry C. Morris and Pedro G. Salom of Philadelphia, and driven by Morris. Another entrant, Elwood Haynes, was enroute to Jackson Park with his gasoline vehicle when he smashed a wheel and was put out of commission. Several other vehicles were withdrawn at the last minute for a variety of reasons.[27]

During the preceding three days heavy snows, driven by winds up to sixty miles an hour, created driving conditions that would cause many motorists even today to hesitate to take their cars out on the road. In 1895, these conditions might have brought on a postponement of the race had not one postponement already been made. Kohlsaat did, however, agree to reduce the race from the original Chicago — Milwaukee route to a fifty-three-mile route from Jackson Park to Evanston and back. Having done this he insisted that the race must be held, to save the *Times-Herald* from becoming the laughing-stock of the newspaper world. Shortly after 8:30 a.m., therefore, the three judges told the assembled drivers to prepare their vehicles, and at 8:55, the Duryea, driven by Frank Duryea, was the first car across the starting line. Within the next ten minutes the De La Vergne-Benz, the Macy-Benz, the Sturges Electric, and the Morris and Salom Electrobat also got underway.

Each car had been assigned an umpire who rode with the driver to insure that all rules were respected and a record kept of the fuel that was used. Charles King had been assigned to be the umpire in the Mueller-Benz entry, but this vehicle was late in arriving at the park and did not finally get started until more than an hour and ten minutes after the Duryea was already on the road. Oscar Mueller again did the driving, and, in addition to King, Charles G. Reid came along as a passenger. Cheers and assorted snowballs greeted the three men as Mueller hurried along the route in a desperate effort to make up lost time. Shortly after eleven they spotted the Electrobat ahead of them and in a few minutes moved past it on Lake Shore Drive. Ten minutes later, in the vicinity of Lincoln Park, Mueller steered around Harold Sturges. Both electric vehicles soon withdrew from the competition, their batteries run down from the heavy going over the snow-covered streets. They joined on the sidelines the De La Vergne-Benz, which had been forced out shortly after the start of the race.

By noon the race was a close one between the Duryea and the Macy-Benz; the lead changed hands several times as one or the other entry had to stop for repairs. At 2:39 p.m., the Mueller-Benz made the turn in Evanston and started the return trip, now an hour and fifty minutes behind the Duryea and Macy entries. After a short delay caused by a problem with a clutch, Mueller got going, and as the road conditions improved, King reported, "the fast speed clutch was thrown in and we went bowling along at sixteen miles an hour." However, barring accidents to the front runners, it was too late now for Mueller's entry to duplicate its earlier win in Chicago.

Late in the afternoon, the strain began to tell on the three men. They had been riding in freezing temperatures in an uncovered vehicle for six hours, with almost nothing to eat since breakfast. Charles Reid fell unconscious and had to be lifted into a passing cutter. Then, shortly before eight in the evening, as the Benz proceeded along Garfield Boulevard near Halsted Street, Oscar Mueller fainted. King grabbed control of the steering lever and stopped the car. Since Mueller was the starting driver, the rules required him to accompany the car to the finish. King, therefore, moved the unconscious man over into the passenger's seat, and climbed into the driver's seat. Holding onto Mueller to keep him from falling out, King then drove the rest of the way, reaching Jackson Park at 8:53 p.m. There he learned that the Duryea had come in over an hour and a half earlier, but the Macy-Benz had been unable to finish, thus giving the Mueller-Benz, as the only other surviving entry, second-place money.

Oscar Mueller was taken away in a hack to a hospital where he recovered from his ordeal. For several years after the race he and his father harbored ambitions of becoming automobile manufacturers, but although they had to give these up, later, during the First World War, Oscar left the family business in Decauter to establish a metals company in Port Huron, Michigan, which manufactured auto parts, among other things.

King, meanwhile, after seeing that Mueller was taken care of, walked over to the nearby Del Prado Hotel to get a late dinner. In the lobby, the desk clerk, mistaking the wet and dirty motorist for some tramp, called out: "You don't belong here; you belong down-the-line!" When King explained that he had just brought the Mueller-Benz in second in the *Times-Herald* race, the clerk's face brightened and he told King, "You will have the best we have in the house and it won't cost you a cent!" King cleaned up, went into the dining room, and enjoyed "the most sumptuous Thanksgiving Dinner" he ever had, a fitting end to the most memorable day in his life. He refused the Muellers' offer to share half of their second-place earnings with him, but he did accept the gold medal they had also received, a medal to go along with the one he had won in Chicago two years before.[28]

Critics declared that about all the *Times-Herald* race had demonstrated was how unreliable the horseless carriages of that day really were. But others felt, to the contrary, that the race had shown that these vehicles could perform successfully under the most wretched of conditions. To be sure, the race had highlighted the limitations of the electric vehicle, but at the same time the advantages of the gasoline carriage had been widely publicized. Even more important for the future, the victory of the Duryea over the imported European vehicles began to establish the reputation of the American-built car as the equal, if not the superior, of the foreign products.[29]

Beyond all this, however, the true importance of what Kohlsaat had done lay not in what happened in the race but simply in the announcement that the race would be held. Prior to this time, those who were working on horseless carriages had little or no knowledge of what others were doing. Hiram Maxim, a New England auto pioneer, declared that when he began his work in 1892, he "was blissfully ignorant" of the work others had done or were doing in Germany, France, Great Britain, and the United States. "As I look back," he wrote in the 1930's, "I am amazed that so many of us began work so nearly at the same time, and without the slightest notion that others were working on the problem." In the fall of 1895, this situation suddenly changed as the names of entrants in the Chicago race revealed the large number of individuals engaged in more or less serious efforts to build self-propelled road vehicles. When many of these men assembled for the race in Chicago, either as owners, drivers, officials, or spectators, they began to exchange data and ideas. A sense of fellowship and comradeship began to develop among these inventors, mechanics, and tinkerers, who now saw that they were not alone in their ambitions to create horseless carriages.[30]

To foster this development, the first trade publications devoted to subjects of common interest for this emerging automotive fraternity appeared at this time. In mid-October, Edward E. Goff of Chicago published the first issue of *Motocycle,* whose title was obviously inspired by the *Times-Herald* race. The following month the more famous monthly, *Horseless Age,* often erroneously called the first automobile journal, appeared in New York, published by E. P. Ingersoll. The fact that both magazines continued to be published in the following months, although *Motocycle* did not survive for very long, provided striking testimony that interest in motor vehicles was not confined to just a handful of crackpots, as some were contending.[31]

Simultaneously with the appearance of these pioneering automotive magazines came a movement to form the first automotive organization, a movement initiated on October 8, 1895, by Charles King when he sent the following letter to the editors of several publications including the Chicago *Times-Herald* and a professional journal, *Electrical Engineering:*

> Realizing the fact that we have already a large number of people in this country interested in the coming revolution, the motor vehicle, and in order to pave the way for the early success of this vehicle of the future, it is proposed to form a National Organization which will have as its object the furtherance of all details connected with this broad subject, and to hold stated meetings, when papers can be read and discussions follow as to the respective merits of all points in question. Such an organization is needed now, and upon its formation would meet with the hearty co-

operation of the newspapers, the friends of good roads and the public at large. It is therefore proposed that such an organization be now formed and have as its name the American Motor League. This title is broad and it is well suited to survive any change that the future may bring.[32]

The response to King's suggestion was favorable and led to a meeting in Chicago on the evening of November 1 of twenty-two individuals, most of them in the city for the race that had been scheduled for the following day. Charles King was the only one from Michigan in attendance. Also present were the Duryea brothers and two other officers of the Duryea Motor Wagon Company, Henry Morris and Pedro Salom of Philadelphia, Elwood Haynes, publishers Ingersoll and Goff, and others from such scattered points as Pasadena, California, Salt Lake City, Utah, and Hamilton, Ontario. The American Motor League was organized, the first automobile association in the United States, and, King claimed, the first one in the world, since comparable organizations in France and Great Britain were not formed until later in 1895. At the second meeting of the league, held in Chicago on November 29, the day after the *Times-Herald* race, Charles Duryea was elected president, King was elected treasurer, and H. D. Emerson, a Cincinnati carriage manufacturer, Henry Morris, and Hiram Maxim were elected vice-presidents of the organization.

The league continued in existence for a number of years, ultimately having members in more than six hundred cities and towns. One of its first actions was to petition Chicago officials, in December 1895, to remove the prohibitions on the use of motor vehicles on city streets. The prohibitions had been suspended for the races in November, but led, nevertheless, to a scene where a policeman ordered Elwood Haynes to take his horseless carriage off the streets. The city acceded only partially to the league's request, declaring that motor vehicles were not yet sufficiently advanced to be entitled to the same privileges that were accorded other vehicles. The inconclusive result of this first lobbying action by the league perhaps helps to explain why it gave way in later years to other organizations which proved to be more effective spokesmen for automotive interests.[33]

King was one of the most active members in the new organization. As treasurer he took a special interest in organizing a campaign to recruit members. Among the members whom he signed up was Hiram Maxim, an engineer with the Motor Carriage Division of the Pope Manufacturing Company in Hartford, Connecticut. Like King, he had served as an umpire in the Thanksgiving Day race. By March 1896, King had also enlisted his wealthy Detroit friends, Henry Joy and John and Truman Newberry. In addition, King used his position with the league to lend weight to statements he sent to such publications as *Horseless Age* regarding various automotive subjects. Through these activities, King was promoting the American Motor League, but at the same time he was making valuable new contacts which were promoting himself and also, for the first time, drawing attention to Detroit as a city active in automotive developments.[34]

By the latter part of 1895, King could see that a motor vehicle industry was emerging. Correspondents in London and Paris kept him informed of the activities of European automobile companies. He had personal knowledge of what the Duryea Motor Wagon Company and the Pope Manufacturing Company in New England were doing. All this, he told a correspondent in Toledo, Ohio, provided "convincing proof" that the manufacturing of motor vehicles had become "a reality." As a manufacturer, King intended to take advantage of this new business opportunity.[35]

In November 1895, the first issue of *Horseless Age* carried an advertisement for Charles B. King of Detroit, "manufacturer of King's Patent Gas Engines for Vehicles, Launches, Etc." King also began writing to a lengthy list of potential customers for his engines. For example, he wrote to Joseph G. Shaver of Milwaukee, who had gained some publicity as the builder of a steam car. King hoped to interest Shaver in his gasoline engine, "designed exclusively for vehicle use," which he hoped to have on the market in about two months. In December, he described this two-cylinder engine to his fellow experimenter, Hiram Maxim. His experience with one-cylinder engines, King told Maxim, indicated that they were "hard to start. . . . Perhaps you will think I am on the wrong track, but so many are accomplishing this result (and they claim successfully) that I am willing to burn a few dollars for the cause." Of course he was hoping to make money in the venture, and prospects seemed promising; he told another correspondent that he was receiving three inquiries about his engine each day.[36]

Late in December 1895, or very early in January 1896, King received a letter from one of the Duryeas asking if he would be interested in manufacturing their engine. The Duryea Motor Wagon Company, capitalizing on the fame that had come to it as a result of its victory in the *Times-Herald* race, was now pushing ahead with plans to manufacture its vehicle. The first Duryeas were produced in February 1896, and later that month were exhibited at the Boston Mechanics Fair where Frank Duryea made two sales. About a dozen Duryeas may have been sold that year, marking the beginning of American automobile production. Aware of the Duryea company's plans, King recognized the value of this opportunity to produce an engine whose reliability had been thoroughly proven in competition, a far different thing from trying to market an untested engine of his own design. On January 4, 1896, therefore, King wrote to "Dear Friend Duryea" (probably Frank, although the copy of his letter does not indicate which brother he was addressing) that the "suggestion that your engine be turned out here meets with my favor. We are in a first class condition to do this work, have fine tools and skilled workmen and are in a position to make the engine on *an interchangeable plan* [King's emphasis]. . . ." Here in a few words King summarized some of the basic reasons for Detroit's subsequent advance to the forefront in the automobile industry — the presence of skilled workers with the tools and ability

to produce parts with such slight variance as to be capable of use inter-
changeably, an essential prerequisite to the mass production of automobiles. The Duryea proposal was that King should manufacture their
engines for other users of gasoline engines, but King also offered to supply
the Springfield company with the engines "at a very low figure" if, as it
got into vehicle production, it found itself unable to handle its own
engine needs.[37]

In the middle of January, King traveled to Springfield where he
spent a week completing the manufacturing arrangements. Under an
agreement signed on January 18 by King and George Henry Hewitt, president of the Duryea Motor Wagon Company, King was granted a two-year
license "to manufacture at his factory in Detroit, Michigan, and in no
other place or places" engines containing certain improvements made by
James Frank Duryea, on which a patent application had been filed June
7, 1895. These engines were to be sold under the name of the "Duryea-
King Gas Engine," indicating that the contract negotiations had been
by no means one-sided. King agreed to sell as many engines as possible,
"in all sizes and for such purposes as may be demanded by the public,
throughout the United States and the Dominion of Canada." The contracting parties would agree on a minimum selling price, with the Duryea
company getting ten per cent of the net on every engine that King manufactured and sold.

This contract was probably, as Frank Duryea asserted, "the first
licensing agreement in America for the manufacture of a proved gasoline
automobile engine." The linking of Charles King's name to their engine
was important to the Duryeas, Frank said, because this "was our first recognition by one who really knew engines." As for King, he had contracted
to become Detroit's first automobile parts manufacturer.[38]

He lost no time publicizing his connection with the Duryea company. The February 1896 issue of *Horseless Age,* with whose publisher,
E. P. Ingersoll, King was now well acquainted, noted this development
and declared that King was "a mechanical engineer who has entered
heart and soul into the motor business, and with his thorough knowledge
of the subject, and facilities of manufacture, he will undoubtedly turn
out reliable motors and plenty of them." Immediately upon his return
from the East, King began to drum up business by writing letters. He
wrote to Joseph Shaver, whom he had earlier sought to interest in his own
engine, and informed Shaver that he was "about to enter into the manufacture of the Duryea-King Motor for carriages. This is the motor that
took first place in the *Times-Herald* contest and it probably represents the
most perfect type of vehicle on the market today." At about the same time,
the Wayne Sulkeyette and Road Cart Company of Decauter, Illinois, asked
King's advice about using a two-horsepower engine in a motor vehicle;
he urged them to consider instead the heavier, five-horsepower Duryea-
King motor that he could shortly offer them. Writing in *Horseless Age,*
King declared that a five-horsepower motor was best suited for American

motor carriages in view of the bad road conditions that existed in the country.

By mid-February, King was far enough along in his manufacturing preparations to be able to offer to supply the Packard brothers of Warren, Ohio, future developers of the Packard car, his new engine within twenty days of the receipt of their order. "The price of this five horsepower motor, complete with batteries, coil, starting handle and muffler, is $410.00." In another letter, a few weeks later, he accompanied this price with a term that would become world famous: "F.O.B. Detroit."[39]

To publicize the Duryea Motor Wagon, and to stimulate interest in the motor that powered it, King arranged to have the winning entrant of the *Times-Herald* competition on display at the Detroit Riding Club's annual horse show in April. He informed Charles Duryea that several Detroit individuals "representing considerable capital" had expressed an interest in investing money — whether in the Duryea company or in King's firm was not clear — "if the wagon was as represented." Duryea shipped the vehicle to Detroit by train. It was King's later recollection that they had problems starting the wagon when they got it off the freight car, and, as a result, had to haul it away in a horse-drawn dray. The ignition problem was solved, and each day of the show King drove the horseless carriage around the indoor ring; its presence created mixed, it not outright hostile, emotions among the assembled horse-lovers, especially because the fumes from the car's exhaust provided a good deal of coughing among the occupants of ringside seats. Nevertheless, on the last night of the show, in a gesture of good sportsmanship, the riding club presented Duryea with special gold and leather medals, perhaps in recognition of the fact that vehicles such as Duryea's would have little effect on the genteel uses of the horse that were favored by the members of such clubs, while at the same time these vehicles would free the horse of the hardships of the beast of burden.[40]

Despite King's promotional efforts, his high hopes for a large demand for Duryea-King motors were never realized. All that came out of John Lauer's shop was one motor which had been ordered by the Emerson and Fisher Company of Cincinnati. H. D. Emerson's carriage firm had been hired by the Robinson and Franklin Brothers Circus to build a motor carriage as a circus attraction, following the lead of Barnum and Bailey, which had begun featuring a Duryea Motor Wagon among its other freaks. The Duryea-King motor was shipped to Cincinnati on April 13, and King left sometime later to help in assembling and testing the horseless carriage. After a week of concentrated effort, the job was completed and an exhausted King returned to his hotel room where he slept several hours past the time of his scheduled departure by train for Detroit. "I am somewhat recovered today," he wrote to his future wife, Grace Fletcher, the next morning, "having had pie for breakfast and an introduction to two actresses." He described John Robinson, the circus boss, as "a strange genius," a millionaire who "expresses his kindest thoughts in very strong language." When King had cautioned him against attempting to operate the heavy carriage on any very steep hills, Robinson replied: "Never mind that, I will have my biggest elephant behind it and it will go over any hill down that way." Robinson tried to persuade King to join the circus as the driver of the carriage, with the assistance of the circus's Albino man, who was, Robinson said, "a first class mechanic." With some regret, the Detroiter turned down the job and "the alluring social life" which Robinson held out as one of its main attractions.[41]

King's work with the Emerson and Fisher Company on the motorized circus wagon was not his first association with that firm. A short time earlier the company had turned over to King an iron-tired wagon for use in his horseless carriage experiments. King removed the four-cylinder engine from the still incomplete car he had been working on in 1894-95 and installed it in the new wagon, along with a gas tank, water tank, muffler, bearings, and foot-operated speed controls. He retained the wagon's tiller-operated steering mechanism, rather than installing the steering wheel he had designed for his own car since he felt it was not practical to make such a major change in what was to be just a testing vehicle anyway. However, the driver was seated on the left side of the vehicle, as contemplated in King's earlier plans in 1893-94. It was this unique machine, very literally a horseless carriage, weighing twice as much as the vehicle King had been building, that King drove on the historic trip along Woodward Avenue on the night of March 6, 1896.[42]

According to Oliver Barthel, a freeze-up cracked King's four-cylinder engine later in March, and he subsequently sold it, together with the blueprints and patterns, to Charles Annesley, a fellow Detroiter who was also interested in automobiles, but who later manufactured this engine for marine uses at a plant he was associated with in Buffalo. King's experimental vehicle was reconstructed in 1956, on the sixtieth anniversary of the original's appearance in Detroit, and this reconstruction is now displayed in the Detroit Historical Museum. King returned to work on a new two-cylinder engine of his own making. Promises of additional orders for the Duryea-King had not been fulfilled, and King had decided that the Duryea engine, although satisfactory, was not powerful enough. By August, he was testing this new motor, again in the Emerson and Fisher wagon. King reported to W. G. Walton, an Ontario colleague in the American Motor League, that his motor was propelling the vehicle at speeds of up to eighteen and twenty miles an hour and up hills with as much as a twenty per cent grade. King's latest success was noted by the Detroit *Free Press,* which found in it further evidence that Detroit was gaining recognition for its efforts in this fast-developing new transportation field. However, as King complained to E. P. Ingersoll, the authorities in Detroit were restricting his use of Belle Isle as a testing site to the morning hours only and at speeds that could not exceed three miles an hour. He declared he would fight these restrictions, comparing them to the infamous Red Flag Law in Great Britain which earlier in the century had stifled promising efforts to employ steam vehicles on Britain's high-ways.[43]

King's two-cylinder engine was praised by *Horseless Age* as "un-doubtedly one of the simplest and most efficient motors yet produced" for horseless carriages. By November 1896, King claimed to have received "a large number of orders" for the motor. One buyer was W. G. Walton, the horseless carriage enthusiast from Hamilton, Ontario, who early in 1897 announced the development of a new form of transmission for motor vehicles, designed to be used with the King Motor. Another motor was shipped off to Professor William H. Pickering, a Harvard astronomer, for a carriage he was building. King also installed one of his engines in the first car he had been working on in 1894 and which he now completed but apparently never used. Subsequently he sold the vehicle and its engine to Byron J. Carter of Jackson, future developer of the Cartercar, the most famous of the friction-drive cars that generated some interest in the early years of the twentieth century. Still another King Motor was sold to the Kalamazoo Railway Velocipede Company, which built what may have been the first gasoline-powered hand car in the United States. King went to Kalamazoo for a test run, during the course of which the water tank, located under the floor of the car, blew up, showering scalding hot water on King and his companions, who could not jump off because they were traveling over a high trestle at the time. It was, King said, "an exciting ride." Despite the mishap, the company was satisfied with the performance of King's engine, although it thought the $400 price tag was rather high.[44]

In February 1897, King expanded his line of automotive parts to include "a suspension tangent wheel, specially designed for motor ve-hicles," which was said to be much sturdier than the standard spoke wheel. A month later he was also selling an automatic cylinder oil cup, and his advertisements now referred to his "Vehicle Motors and Sundry Parts." But the market for these products was still a limited one and sales were discouragingly few, too few for King, who always seems to have been short of cash in this period.

In March 1896, King wrote to John Brisben Walker, urging him to increase the amount of the prize money that would be awarded in the motor competition that Walker's *Cosmopolitan* magazine was sponsoring. King estimated that it cost at least a thousand dollars to build a motor vehicle, and the prizes Walker was offering were not enough to cover this expense plus the added expenses involved in shipping a vehicle to the site of the race in New York. "This art is at present in a crude state," King observed, "and is mainly in the hands of the inventor, who has not as yet been encouraged by capital." King did not compete in the *Cosmo-politan* race in May; and although his name was included among the early entrants for a race that was to be held in Providence, Rhode Island, in September 1896, he was not among the participants on the day of the race. In view of the knowledge and experience that King now possessed in the area of motorized vehicles, the most likely assumption is that financial considerations dictated his withdrawal from the field. "The times are too hard at present for any development in the motor industry," he told his one-time racing companion, Oscar Mueller, in August. "I can see no other alternate except to wait until the clouds pass over and the people have money enough to enter into this new field."[45]

By the summer of 1897, therefore, King was turning his attention to the development of a gasoline engine for marine uses, for which there was a ready market in the Great Lakes region. This was an industry that interested his wealthy Detroit friends, Henry Joy and John and Truman Newberry, and they provided him with some financial help. By October, a marine engine was on the market, and prospective buyers could see it on an exhibition launch that King had built and was operating on the Detroit River. An article in *Scientific American* in January 1898 described the "simple, compact, quiet running" engine as weighing seven hundred pounds and developing up to seven and a half horsepower.[46]

But King had not abandoned the automotive field entirely. Early in 1898 he was selling a four-horsepower engine, priced at $375, "amply sufficient for Motor Wagon purposes, unless it is desired for heavy trucking." Another engine, built for the Martin Motor Wagon Company of Buffalo, sold for just $275. King also seems to have been doing some more work in the building of a complete automobile.[47]

Then the Spanish-American War broke out. The Michigan Naval Reserve, of which King, along with Joy, the Newberrys, and other Detroit socialites were members, was called into active service. While King was functioning as a chief petty officer on the *U. S. S. Yosemite,* the vessel to which all of these Michigan sailors were assigned, Oliver Barthel looked after King's engine and pneumatic tool business. Upon their return from the war, however, King's financial partners disposed of their interest in the company, so King had to carry on alone. In 1899, he took on the job of designing and building a $10,000, seventy-foot yacht for J. A. Vanderpoel of Boston, but when he finished, he had difficulty getting paid for the job. Late in January 1900, he wrote to Mrs. Vanderpoel, asking that the amount still owing be paid at once. "I am badly in need of funds and have stood off my creditors regarding the yacht as long as possible," King declared.[48]

It is at this time that King sold his marine engine business to the Olds Motor Works of Detroit and joined that company as an engineer. Although Olds was developing and manufacturing automobiles, this was not in King's department. As he told E. P. Ingersoll, he was "too busy at present to think of anything outside of getting [marine] engines built." Barthel took care of King's pneumatic tool sales, but in May 1901 King sold that business, too. Never again would he have the kind of freedom that came from being his own boss, as he had been when he was conducting his automotive experiments in the mid-nineties. He still was to make many important contributions to the automobile industry, but they would be the contributions of a subordinate, not a leader of the industry. Perhaps that was as he wanted it to be. In 1946 he told a reporter of a reflector device he had designed for his car. Friends were urging him to manufacture the gadget, but King had obviously decided that the pleasures of inventing a product were enough satisfaction for him. "I don't want to put anything into production," he confided to the reporter. "Just want to go on making things."[49]

CHAPTER 2

"A SUBJECT OF RIDICULE AND A SPECTACLE OF FOLLY"

Late in November 1895, the development of a Michigan automobile industry took a surprising turn with an announcement from Benton Harbor, on the opposite side of Michigan's lower peninsula from Detroit, that "a full-fledged factory for the manufacture of [horseless] vehicles" was about to be established in that city. What Charles King had thus far failed to accomplish in the future motor capital of the world, a small carriage manufacturing company in the heart of Michigan's lush fruit belt claimed to have done — it had built a gasoline-powered motor vehicle, which it would now proceed to manufacture "extensively."[1]

The carriage company, which had been doing business for a decade or more, was operated by two brothers, Albert and Louis Baushke. The Baushke company was a small concern whose work force never varied much from the ten or so employees it had late in 1895. It was similar to most of the approximately 125 establishments in the state at this time that were manufacturing horse-drawn vehicles. The wagons and buggies the Baushkes produced were probably designed primarily for the local market, in contrast to a few large vehicle manufacturers in Flint, Pontiac, Grand Rapids, Detroit, Jackson, and Kalamazoo who had their sights set on a much more far-ranging sales territory.[2]

Some time prior to November 1895, the Baushkes had been approached by William O. Worth who, on June 17, 1895, had applied for a patent on a gasoline engine that could be used, he told the two brothers, to power a horseless carriage. At least two sources indicate that either the Baushkes or Worth, or possibly both, had been working on the development of a horseless carriage as far back as 1884. Worth proposed that he and the Baushkes collaborate on the construction of a gasoline-powered vehicle. Worth's "ideas were so exalted, his theories so plausible and his zeal and confidence so great," it was later reported, that the brothers agreed not only to build the carriage at their own expense, but they also advanced Worth the money he needed to finance his part of the project.[3]

Work on the machine proceeded "quietly" for several weeks until November 26, 1895, when the Benton Harbor *Palladium* broke the news that the vehicle had been completed and was "ready for tests of speed, safety, convenience, and practicability." By the next day newspapers elsewhere were picking up the story, with emphasis on the claim that the Benton Harbor vehicle was "different from horseless carriages of other makes in this and other countries." William Worth provided the motor, Albert Baushke handled the metal work on the carriage, and brother Louis crafted the wooden parts; together they constructed a two-seat vehicle with the gasoline engine "concealed in the body of the carriage." The noise of the engine was eliminated, the *Palladium* asserted, by "an ingenious arrangment," and, when in motion, the vehicle was said to be able to go "in any direction and at any speeds desired." The Baushkes were enthusiastic. They announced they were forming the Benton Harbor Motor Carriage Company, which would take over the business and the three-story frame factory of A. Baushke & Brothers to manufacture motor carriages and other types of road vehicles. The *Palladium* was equally excited by the news, hailing these plans as bound to bring new fame to Benton Harbor "when these motor carriages are turned out in quantities for the market."[4]

There are dramatic contradictions in the various accounts of what happened to this venture of the Baushkes and their associate, Worth. The initial announcement of the building of their first vehicle had stated that it was being entered in the Chicago *Times-Herald* race on Thanksgiving Day, two days later. Subsequently, the *Times-Herald,* in its account of that race, reported that the Baushke entry had arrived in Chicago, but too late to take part in the race. How the vehicle reached Chicago is not stated, but the implication is that the Baushke gasoline vehicle was operable and only the lateness of its arrival prevented it from competing against the Duryea Motor Wagon, the Mueller-Benz, and the other vehicles that started the race. This account implies that the Baushkes and Worth had built and operated a gasoline-powered motor vehicle months before King, Henry Ford, and Ransom Olds tested their first gasoline vehicles. Most histories

William Worth's and the Baushke brothers' Benton Harbor Motor Carriage,
as it appeared in later years on exhibition in Indianapolis.
Courtesy Benton Harbor News-Palladium

credit only the Duryeas and Elwood Haynes for accomplishing this feat
prior to November 1895.[5]

In the week following the race, the Detroit *Journal* printed positive
confirmation that the Baushke vehicle was operating; its Benton Harbor
correspondent reported the machine "rolling along the street without the
aid of man or beast" and amazing the citizenry "at the easiness with which
the carriage is operated and the remarkable good speed obtained." Other
newspapers in Michigan reportedly carried similar stories in the following
weeks. Then in January 1896, both *Horseless Age* and *Motocycle* carried
reports on the "Benton Harbor Motor Carriage," complete with a photograph of the vehicle which clearly showed that the Baushkes were skillful
builders of carriages. The gasoline motor, which was not visible, was said
to generate seven and a half horsepower, as much as Charles King later
claimed for his heavier marine engines. It could propel the vehicle "over
any ordinary country road at a speed of from 1 to 23½ miles an hour." The
weight of the machine, with enough fuel and water for a 300-mile trip, was
said to be about 1050 pounds. In Benton Harbor, according to reports, the
carriage company had "fitted up" a factory to manufacture two models:

"one of the finest materials and workmanship, the other of substantial construction but less elegant finish." The company, it was reported, would be "ready to fill orders in the near future." Although something obviously intervened to upset these plans, the Benton Harbor Motor Carriage Company and its vehicle are duly recorded in various lists of automobiles and automobile manufacturers, accompanied by the date 1896, which makes it the first automobile manufacturer in Michigan and gives the company a claim to second place in the country behind the Duryea Motor Wagon Company of Massachusetts.[6]

Unfortunately, however, much of the above is largely fantasy. There is no good evidence that the Benton Harbor Motor Carriage Company was ever actually established, and if it was not, the reason undoubtedly is that the motor carriage the company had planned to manufacture never operated successfully. Despite the report of the Chicago *Times-Herald* that the Benton Harbor entry actually came to Chicago, the Benton Harbor *Palladium* clearly indicates that it did not. On Thanksgiving Day, the paper reported that round-the-clock efforts by the Baushkes and Worth to get their vehicle ready had failed, and that they had been forced to give up on the afternoon before the race. The vehicle was not yet in running condition. Far from being in Chicago on the next day, the Baushke-Worth machine had apparently not even left the shop in Benton Harbor.[7]

Following their failure to complete their horseless carriage by Thanksgiving, Benton Harbor's embryo auto manufacturers then announced that they expected to test their machine on the city's streets during the first week in December; it was during that week that the Detroit paper reported the astonishment of the city's residents at the sight of the carriage moving along effortlessly without benefit of horses. The local *Palladium*, however, was more astonished at the reporter's "truly wonderful" powers of prophecy since "the motocycle mentioned is not as yet completed."[8]

On December 17, it was reported that the Baushke-Worth vehicle would probably be tested on Friday, December 20. The illness of one of the mechanics working on the carriage was given as the reason these tests had not taken place earlier as promised. On December 20, however, the tests were once more cancelled, this time because of "the bad weather and the state of the roads." The excuse at least sounded plausible, since unseasonably heavy rains had caused an eighteen-inch rise in the St. Joseph River, resulting in extensive flooding in Benton Harbor and numerous washouts of roads and bridges.[9]

Finally, at the end of January, 1896, the *Palladium* reported that the "Benton Harbor 'horseless carriage'" had actually been driven a short distance "the other night," but the editor labeled as "slightly premature" the optimistic reports on the success of these tests that were appearing in other publications. "We will give the inventors a chance to perfect [the machine] before writing it down a success, although we all join in sincere hope that it will be made practical." He praised Worth and the Baushke brothers for their "persistence" and "ingenuity," but he said that as yet the vehicle "had too much of the nature of a steam engine to be serviceable," a remark that, unfortunately, does little to explain the precise nature of the problems that needed to be corrected to make the gasoline-powered vehicle a success.[10]

Then, on February 8 the bubble burst. "Motor-Carriage a Failure" was the heading of a story in the *Palladium,* less than two and a half months after that paper's heady assessment of the boost that this carriage was going to provide for Benton Harbor's reputation. The glib Mr. Worth, declared the Baushkes, had failed to live up to his promise to produce a practical motor to propel their carriage. The newspaper gave the impression that its earlier report of the vehicle having been driven some distance may have been false and that the machine had simply remained in the factory, "a subject of ridicule and a spectacle of folly." Albert Baushke, announcing that he and his brother had given up on Worth, declared they were looking for another motor that would prove workable, so that the money they had sunk into this venture would not be a total loss.[11]

In the weeks immediately following this announcement, no word appeared in the local newspaper concerning progress the Baushkes were making in finding a mechanic to replace W. O. Worth. It is clear that they soon decided to concentrate on the kind of work they understood. During the next quarter of a century, the annual reports of the state factory inspector continued to list the firm of Baushke Brothers, but buggies and wagons, never automobiles, were listed as the firm's products. Sometime after 1896, the one motor vehicle the Baushkes had built, imperfect as it was, was purchased by the Haynes Motor Car Company of Kokomo, Indiana. In 1944, a photograph of this rare vehicle appeared in the Benton Harbor *News-Palladium,* which reported that the car was on display in Indianapolis. In addition to this vehicle, the Baushkes were said to be building a second machine, of a different body style. What happened to it is not known; probably it was never completed.[12]

As for Worth, his automobile career was not concluded when the breakup with the Baushkes occurred. He was granted a patent on his gasoline engine in April 1897, and five months later, now listed as a resident of Chicago, he had returned to the patent office to apply for a patent on a complete motor vehicle. When the patent was granted on July 12, 1898, the first of seven automobile-related patents awarded to Worth between 1898 and 1902, he assigned two-thirds of his patent rights to William R. Donaldson of Louisville, Kentucky, and Henry W. Kellogg of Battle Creek.

The latter, like his distant relatives, Dr. John Harvey Kellogg and W. K. Kellogg, who were about to make Battle Creek famous for another product, was a member of the Seventh-day Adventist denomination, whose headquarters at this time were in Battle Creek. Beginning in 1870, when he was thirty years old, Henry Kellogg had been connected with the Adventists' publishing house, both in Battle Creek and as one of its representatives in Europe. His European travels, beginning in 1885, may have awakened in Kellogg the interest in automotive developments which would lead him to become associated with William Worth in the late nineties. Worth, too, seems to have been an Adventist, or "Sabbath-keeper," and was depicted by one of the brethren in the church as having been victimized by "some professed Sabbath-keepers, and some who are not Sabbath-keepers, [who] have tried to take advantage of him, and have done so, and in that way have tried to rob him of his invention, which in every case has left him very poor." Henry Kellogg had then come to his assistance, and by 1899 they felt they had solved the problems of building horseless carriages that had stymied Worth in his earlier venture in Benton Harbor. After seeking the advice of Mrs. Ellen G. White, the spiritual leader of the Adventists, the Chicago Motor Vehicle Company was incorporated at a million dollars, with offices in Chicago and a factory in the suburb of Harvey, Illinois. Worth was the president and chairman of the firm, Kellogg was treasurer and superintendent, and William Donaldson, who was apparently also an Adventist, was secretary and sales manager. (A fourth individual, J. E. Keith, had the title of general manager.) The Worth, a "rapid delivery" commercial vehicle, was depicted on the company's letterhead but whether it or any other vehicles were ever produced by the company is doubtful. By 1902, Worth was engaged in obtaining engines for river boats that the Adventists were planning to use for missionary work among Negroes in remote areas of the South. A Worth car was produced by another Chicago company in 1902, and a Worth high-wheeler and a Worth truck were produced in Evansville from 1907 to 1910. Whether William Worth was connected with these companies is not presently known. As for Henry Kellogg, his obituary in 1918 makes no mention of what was apparently his short-lived career as an automobile manufacturing executive.[13]

*　　*　　*

Albert and Louis Baushke, as well as William Worth and Henry Kellogg, deserve attention and sympathy as among the first in a long list of unfortunate Michiganians who failed in the automobile business. But, on a more positive note, their activities in 1895 and 1896 serve to demonstrate the very considerable interest in horseless carriages that existed at that time in Michigan outside of Detroit. Important as Charles King's work was in the genesis of the auto industry in the state, the fact remains that the first successful experiments with horseless carriages in Michigan were not those of the Detroit pioneers but of outstate experimenters. The subsequent emergence of Detroit as the capital of the motor industry has led to a tendency to overemphasize the role Detroit has played and to overlook the influence that other areas in the state have always exerted in making Michigan the dominant force in the development and manufacturing of autombiles.

In western Michigan some activity had occurred several years before the Baushke-Worth effort of 1895-96. An unsubstantiated report states that in 1891 Marshall McCluer of Spring Lake built and operated a motorized buggy that attained speeds of up to twenty miles an hour.

Of a more definite nature are reports of the patent Homer L. Boyle of Grand Rapids received in 1892 on a vehicle that used either a steam engine or a gasoline engine. There are no records indicating whether Boyle built this vehicle, but three years later two other promising experiments in the automotive line were underway in Michigan's second largest city. The Sintz company announced late in 1895 that it would produce gas engines "for the carriage and wagon trade." In addition, the company's intention of building its own motor vehicle was evidenced by entries it submitted in both the *Times-Herald* and *Cosmopolitan* races in 1895 and 1896. In neither case, however, did the company have a finished vehicle to drive in the contests. But then in the summer of 1897, Sintz achieved its goal. The company manager, H. A. Winter, the same individual who had passed on to Charles King the idea of entering a vehicle in the Paris — Rouen race in 1894, announced that Sintz had completed and tested its motor vehicle and found that it surpassed its "most sanguine expectations." Powered by a six-horsepower, two-cylinder Sintz engine, the vehicle, Winter said, had been driven about a thousand miles by September 1897, and "We have yet a hill to find that we cannot climb or a street so crowded that we cannot traverse it." A photograph of the machine reveals an interesting design feature: the driver operated the car from the rear seat. Passengers sat in the front seat of the carriage. The vehicle was apparently built by the Sintz company in collaboration with Milton O. Reeves of Columbus, Indiana, who is famous for an automobile of an even more unusual design — his eight-wheeled Octoauto, built in 1911, a car that failed to capture the public's fancy.[14]

Meanwhile, in 1894 Clark Sintz had sold his interest in the company that bore his name and, with his sons, Guy and Claude, had formed the Wolverine Motor Works, also located in Grand Rapids. This company manufactured a gasoline engine patented by the nineteen-year-old Claude, and in November 1895 was reported to be "placing one of their motors on a carriage" which, it was said, would "undoubtedly" be operating by the following year. Some accounts claim that three years later, in 1898, a gasoline motor vehicle that took part in a parade for Grand Rapids' returning Spanish-American War veterans was built by Clark Sintz's Wolverine Motor Works, but since writers in later years found it difficult sometimes to distinguish between the original Sintz company and Clark Sintz's later Wolverine Motor Works, this 1898 Grand Rapids car may have been simply another version of the 1897 Sintz-Reeves effort.[15]

Elsewhere in Michigan, others were busily building their own versions of the vehicle that would replace the horse. One such individual was Robert W. Elston, a retired carriage builder living in the northern Michigan resort community of Charlevoix. In March 1895, a reporter for a local paper visited Elston in his home workshop and was shown "an electric wagon that has in it the elements of revolution in road transit." Elston declared that he had perfected the vehicle after two years of work. He claimed that the batteries would run the wagon for nine hours and that on level roads it could attain speeds of twelve miles an hour. No demon-stration showing the vehicle in motion seems to have taken place, but the reporter left with the hope "that the manufacturing of the Elston Electric Road Wagon will, ere long, be a Charlevoix industry." In May, Elston applied for a patent on his "self-propelling vehicle," but he had appar-ently scrapped his storage batteries as the means by which the vehicle was to be propelled. In the summer of 1895, Elston went to Racine, Wis-consin, and ordered a "Hot Air Engine," which was then much in the news. It had been designed by Edward Joel Pennington, supposedly as a revolu-tionary new type of engine running on either gasoline or kerosene. Elston entered his horseless creation in the *Times-Herald* race and submitted a photograph with his entry, even though the engine had not yet been delivered. A sketch of the two-seater carriage appeared in the November issue of *Horseless Age,* along with a story in which Elston claimed the vehicle would go as fast as twenty-five miles an hour. Elston, of course, did not make it to Chicago, but during the month of the Chicago-to-Evanston race his vehicle was on public exhibition in a Charlevoix store. How it got there is not clear, but the Charlevoix *Sentinel,* with the same nice poetic touch, expressed confidence that Elston's machine "will, ere long, be heard from."

At that point, the trail of this automotive venture, especially inter-esting because it is one of the very few such developments outside of the industrialized southern part of Michigan, begins to fade. Elston was eventually granted his patent in February 1897, and in that same period he was also reported to have taken out a patent on "an improved differ-ential or 'balance' gear for motor vehicles." For some years he operated a hotel which he built in Charlevoix, but what became of his automobile is not known. Old-timers in the area recall hearing him talk about the car and one remembers seeing it, "but I can't say for sure if I ever saw it run." Probably it never did if Elston was depending on the Pennington motor to power it, for Edward Pennington was one of the great con men of all time. In the 1890's he was the center of one automobile promotion scheme after another, both in the United States and Great Britain, none of which ever seemed to produce what Pennington promised. Robert Elston was not the only one to be taken in by this smooth talker. Whether Elston's wagon would have gone twenty-five miles an hour with the Pennington Hot Air Motor will never be known since few if any such engines were ever manufactured.[16]

Elsewhere, in the small central-Michigan town of Fowlerville, Her-bert A. Sprague was reported in November 1895 to be "preparing to build both two and four-wheeled vehicles." He would employ "the most approved methods . . . to secure lightness, strength and the reduction of friction in both motor and vehicles," worthy objectives all, as was his announced intention to use the well-tested Otto four-cycle engine. His niece recalls being told that her uncle succeeded in developing a gasoline-powered vehicle, but that his plans ended when "the man who was to back him backed out of the deal."[17]

Even scantier reports are available on the work of two other Michigan automotive pioneers of this period. In December 1895, G. A. Kennedy, a locksmith and bicycle repairman in the southeastern Michigan town of Blissfield, was said to be working on a motor vehicle. Apparently more modest than some of his contemporaries, Kennedy did not claim success as yet but expressed his hope that he would complete his machine by the following spring. Another would-be inventor, George L. Roby, whose residence was listed as Albion, Michigan, applied for a patent on a motor vehicle a year later. The fact that he finally received his patent in February 1899 does not prove that he actually built and operated the vehicle. American automobile history is replete with examples that attest to the fact that such practical considerations did not enter into the patent office's decision to award, or not award, a particular patent.[18]

For the most part, few of these endeavors in outstate Michigan — and there undoutedly were others — proved any more successful than those of the Baushkes. The question as to who was the first to achieve real success in building and running a motor vehicle in Michigan can never be answered with complete certainty. In 1949, the most famous early Michigan auto pioneer, Ransom Eli Olds, then eighty-five years old and speaking through his official biographer, confidently declared that not only had he built the first horseless carriage in Michigan but prior to him "there had been no successful inventors of horseless vehicles" anywhere. The inaccuracy of such sweeping claims, if not apparent to the aging Lansing industrialist or his dutiful Boswell, should be obvious to anyone having even a nodding acquaintance with the literature of the automobile and its history. Not only was Olds, who built his first motorized vehicle in 1887, preceded by a goodly number of "successful' inventors of horseless vehicles" in Europe and the United States; he was not even the first in his adopted state of Michigan.[19]

If by the term horseless carriage one is simply referring to a self-propelled road vehicle, then there had been a number of such vehicles on Michigan's roads since well back into the nineteenth century. "The biggest event" of Henry Ford's boyhood years, he always maintained, occurred in 1876, shortly before his thirteenth birthday, when he and his father came upon a portable steam engine on the road into Detroit. These engines were used to operate threshing machines, among other things, but those that Ford had seen previously had been moved from farm to farm by horses. This machine, however, had no horses. Instead, a chain connected the engine and the rear wheels, under the boiler, enabling it to move about under its own power. The ponderous vehicle, manufactured by the Nichols and Shepard Company of Battle Creek, left an enduring impression on the young boy; in later years, a photograph of this machine hung on the wall of Ford's office. In the mid-eighties, Ford's understanding of this type of mechanized vehicle was greatly enlarged when he handled the setting up and repairing of a road engine, manufactured by the Westinghouse Company, which could travel as fast as twelve miles an hour.[20]

Obviously, these two-ton monsters, although self-propelled, are not what normally comes to mind when the term horseless carriage is mentioned. However, these steam engines had undoubtedly been present on Michigan's roads for some time. Joseph McCune, a farmer in Jefferson County, Ohio, was operating possibly the first such machine in America, in the 1850's. Ford, therefore, was certainly not the only individual who might have been inspired by the sight of them to consider a lighter vehicle, designed specifically to transport passengers. In fact, such a steam vehicle was constructed in the winter of 1884-85 in Memphis, Michigan, a few miles west of Port Huron, by John Clegg and his son, Thomas, who operated a machine shop. Their vehicle carried four passengers and reached speeds of up to twelve miles an hour with its single-cylinder steam engine. In the summer of 1885, Thomas Clegg drove the steamer in and around Memphis for a total of perhaps five hundred miles. His longest trip was one of eighteen miles to Emmet, where Clegg appeared in the Fourth of July parade, with a local priest as his passenger. John Clegg was from Great Britain where steam omnibuses had been operated on the highways earlier in the century; this may explain the origins of the Cleggs' interest in this form of locomotion. It was also the recollection, though otherwise unconfirmed, of a ninty-five-year-old man, who had known the Cleggs as a youth, that Thomas Clegg had worked with Olds on the steam vehicle Olds was trying to build in this same period.

The Cleggs' steamer was, aside from such road engines as those built by Nichols and Shepard, Michigan's first horseless carriage of which there is any record. (This excludes a vehicle patented in 1870 by Frederick J. Forsyth of Bay City, who claimed it would run on springs. Over fifty such spring cars were accepted by the patent office between 1866 and 1897, but none of them were ever proven to work very effectively.) It is quite likely, given the widespread knowledge of steam power by the last half of the nineteenth century, that others in Michigan had built steam vehicles, perhaps earlier than 1884, but that their efforts went unrecorded or lie buried in obscure newspaper files. Interesting as such discoveries would be, they nevertheless would probably have no real significance for the history of the Michigan automobile industry. For that matter, the work of John and Thomas Clegg is only of antiquarian interest. After 1885 their carriage stood around for years, rusting. Although Ransom Olds began his automotive career in 1887 with a three-wheeled steam vehicle that seems to have been far inferior to the work of the Cleggs, completed two years earlier, it is with Olds, not the Cleggs, that the Michigan automobile industry originated.[21]

Although virtually every writer who has dealt with the history of the American automobile industry has acknowledged that Olds was one of the most important figures—possibly, in fact, the *most* important one — in determining the direction the industry would follow as it grew and devel-

Ransom E. Olds, *the hint of a twinkle in his eyes; when this photo was taken, Olds was at the height of his fame as an automaker.*
Courtesy Motor Vehicle Manufacturers Association

oped in the twentieth century, little serious attention has been given to a study of his life. His only biographies of any length are one by Duane Yarnell, copyrighted and published by Olds in 1949 and which was, according to one of Olds' daughters, virtually ghost-written by her father,[22] and the second, a more scholarly and objective biography by Glenn Niemeyer, published in 1963, which, though a great improvement over the Yarnell work, shows the usual deficiencies of a doctoral dissertation rushed into print. As Ransom Olds' family turns over more and more of his papers to the Historical Collections at Michigan State University, the time may yet arrive when a biography can be written that is truly worthy of this path-breaking automaker.

On his eightieth birthday, Ransom Olds told a reporter that he got started on the development of an automobile "because I didn't like the smell of horses on the farm." Such sentiments are reminiscent of Henry Ford's remark that his interest in mechanical, labor-saving devices was first aroused by his dislike of the hard physical labor to which he had been subjected as a farm boy. Unlike Ford, however, Olds was not born on a farm. He was born on June 3, 1864, in Geneva, Ohio, a village of some eighteen hundred inhabitants, where his father, Pliny Fisk Olds, had a blacksmith and machine shop. The mechanical interests that became the central focus of Ransom's life were thus a natural outgrowth of the knowledge he gained of machines and their operation from his father.[23]

When Ransom, the youngest of five children, was six years old, the Olds family moved to Cleveland where Pliny Olds had accepted a position with an iron works. Four years later, the father's declining health led the family to abandon the city for an Ohio farm where they lived for another four years. His experiences during those years may account for Ransom Olds' expressed aversion to farm life. His father failed as a farmer, and when Pliny Olds had an opportunity to return to the kind of work for which he was trained, he went back to Cleveland, while the family stayed on the farm, which he had been unable to sell.

In September 1880, the Olds family was reunited once more when they moved to Lansing, Michigan, where, according to his granddaughter, Pliny Olds had learned of a machine shop for sale. He worked out a deal whereby he exchanged his farm property for a house and two lots in Lansing, where in the fall Olds once again went into business for himself. With his son Wallace as his partner, the firm took the name P. F. Olds & Son. During the next seventy years Lansing was home for Ransom Olds, except for a brief period at the turn of the century when he moved to Detroit. In the last five decades of his life he was Lansing's most famous citizen, and the individual most responsible for the great changes that came about in his town during his lifetime.[24]

For the enterprising individual interested in going into business, Lansing had some distinct attractions in 1880. A young city, barely thirty years old, Lansing's population of 8326 was small by any standard, even in Michigan where urbanization was still in a preliminary stage of development. What distinguished the city from all other Michigan communities, however, was the fact that it was the headquarters of the state's government, the growth of which had been signaled in 1879 by the dedication of a new capitol building. Although not as large as some others that were erected at this same time, Michigan's new capitol, built at a cost of $1,500,-000, was a giant in contrast with the modest wood frame structure that had served the state previously. Important as Lansing's position as the state capital may have been, it is probable that Pliny Olds was more interested in the fact that the city lay in the center of a rich and still growing agricultural region; the numerous farming operations, as they became ever more mechanized, would require his services in repairing machinery. Lansing was also the site of a surprising variety of industrial firms. Some of them, such as several grist mills, and E. Bement and Sons, manufacturers of farm implements, were adjuncts of the region's agrarian economy, while others, such as the Lansing Chair, Handle and Furniture factory, A. Clark & Company, carriage manufacturers, a foundry, two breweries, and several sawmills, brick yards, and assorted other businesses dealt with a broader spectrum of the population. Small as most of these enterprises were, they nevertheless represented potential customers for Olds' machine shop.[25]

For young Ransom Olds, the early years of the family's residence in Lansing are said to have been spent at Lansing's high school, although a search of local school records has failed to confirm this. He rose at five in the morning, built the home fires, and fired up the boiler in the shop nearby before eating breakfast and hiking off to school. After school, on Saturdays, and during vacations he worked in the shop, receiving no pay for two years, he later recalled, after which his father began paying him fifty cents a day. In 1882-83, Olds reportedly enrolled in a local business school for six months to prepare himself to handle the company's books, which were becoming more complex as the business grew. In 1885, upon reaching the age of twenty-one, Ransom purchased his brother Wallace's interest in the machine shop and became his father's partner.[26]

Until the mid-eighties, the Olds shop had been engaged principally in repair work, although it had also built a few wood- or coal-burning steam engines. But when Ransom joined the partnership, he is said to have taken the initiative in developing and manufacturing a small steam engine of one or two horsepower that used a gasoline burner to heat the water, thereby achieving the desired steam pressure more quickly than was possible with engines using other types of fuel. The Olds steam engine soon became popular with businesses that required only intermittent power, and therefore were attracted by the fast buildup provided by the Olds engine. To meet the demand for its new engines, the Olds company in 1887 moved from its original shop, which measured eighteen by twenty-six feet, into a large two-story plant, twenty-five feet by a hundred feet in length. Within two years more space was acquired. The payroll, too, increased, from twelve employees in 1887 to twenty-three by 1893, a figure that remained constant during the next four years, despite rising sales.

Between 1887 and 1892, over two thousand engines were reportedly sold, and by the latter year, sales totaled more than $20,000, in contrast with the annual income of about $7000 in 1885. Despite a severe economic depression, sales continued to increase after 1892, reaching $29,000 in 1896.[27]

Further indication of the growth of the Olds company is found in its incorporation on July 31, 1890. Several writers have declared that this action was taken in order to secure outside capital and that this goal was accomplished with the resources of Edward W. Sparrow and Samuel L. Smith, who would later play the dominant roles in financing the first two Olds automobile companies. But neither the newspaper account reporting the filing of incorporation papers nor state records support this claim. The corporation's first annual report, filed with the Secretary of State, declared that as of January 2, 1892, its total capitalization was $30,000, of which amount $15,000 was actually paid in. Of the three thousand shares issued, Pliny Olds held 1450, Ransom had an equal amount, and Wallace Olds owned the remaining hundred shares. It seems unlikely that Sparrow and Smith would have put any money into a company without receiving stock in return. In 1894, the holdings of Pliny Olds were reduced to 1150, while Wallace's share increased to 250, and Ransom's to 1600, giving him now a majority control of the firm. By early 1897, Pliny's holdings had been reduced to only fifty shares and Wallace's cut back to two hundred; Ransom Olds now held 2600, and Madison F. Bates, an employee of the company, became the first stockholder outside the Olds family, with 150 shares. It was not until the end of 1897, when the company was reorganized and recapitalized at $50,000, that significant outside investment funds became evident.[28]

The growth of P. F. Olds and Son as an increasingly well-known manufacturer of engines in the period from 1885 to 1897, therefore, seems to have been accomplished by the Olds family without any loss of control to outsiders. Within the family, Ransom Olds ran the company during most, if not all of this period, first as general manager, then finally as president. Although his father held the title of president when the firm was incorporated and was an equal shareholder with the son for several years, it is clear that Ransom was in charge. If we may believe the official biography of Ransom Olds, his father, who was sixty-two in 1890, took his reduced influence in the business gracefully, admitting that he lacked the business sense needed to run this growing concern and expressing his confidence that Ransom had the necessary abilities to do so. By the mid-nineties, Pliny Olds had ceased to take an active part in the affairs of the business, and by the end of the decade he had retired to California.[29]

The increasing prosperity of P. F. Olds & Son after 1885 and the control that R. E. Olds exercised over it was of primary importance to his subsequent successful move into the automobile industry. The national reputation that the Olds name acquired for its engines, and the company's impressive growth rate had occurred under his direction. His later attempts to acquire the additional capital he needed to manufacture automobiles thus were made much easier for him than for an individual who had developed a motor vehicle but did not have evidence of his business and manufacturing abilities; these interested investors as much if not more than evidence of mechanical capabilities. Then, too, the money Olds was making and his access to the company's equipment and the services of its workmen enabled him to carry on his experiments with the horseless carriage with fewer of the problems that frequently delayed the similar efforts of men like Charles King.

Olds' mechanical interests centered on engines and the uses to which they could be put. Having developed the small Olds steam engine, he sought to adapt it for use in a carriage, an idea which he claimed first came to him when the Olds family moved from Cleveland to Detroit via lake steamer and then by train to their new home in Lansing. In both cases they were conveyed by steam-powered means of transportation in far less time than it would have taken for a comparable trip by carriage behind Old Bess, the family horse.

The results of Olds' first attempts to build a steam-driven road vehicle were crude — a three-wheeled box with a tiller steering the front wheel in the same way that a child's tricycle is steered. A two-horsepower Olds steam engine in the rear of the car propelled the vehicle at speeds of from five to ten miles an hour. In later years, Olds told in great and picturesque detail of having tested this vehicle in 1886, taking it out before dawn so as not to attract attention, but, he said, the machine made such a racket that it awakened the entire neighborhood. Evidence, however, indicates that these tests were not made until the summer of 1887.[30]

Pliny Olds apparently did not entirely approve of what his son was doing. He told Dr. Frank Kedzie of Michigan State College, who had come into the shop to see about a repair to a steam engine: "Ranse thinks he can put an engine in a buggy and make the contraption carry him over the roads. If he doesn't get killed at his fool undertaking, I will be satisfied." In his old age, Ransom Olds cited other instances of the opposition and ridicule that he said greeted his attempt to build a steam vehicle. One wonders if he may not have exaggerated the degree of this reaction somewhat. After all, the possibility of a vehicle powered by steam should not have seemed so absurd at a time when steam locomotives, steamships, steam launches, and steam road engines had become commonplace.[31]

Nevertheless, Olds had to admit that his first steam-powered carriage was not a success. Sometime around 1890, he dismantled the three-wheeler and began work on a four-wheeled machine, incorporating the axle and rear wheels from his earlier carriage. The two front wheels of the new vehicle were larger than the rear wheels and were placed close together, giving the body greater stability than his first vehicle had had but still retaining something of the tricycle look. To provide the additional power that the first vehicle had lacked, Olds used two steam engines, which, with the boiler, were placed on a platform at the rear. Two passengers plus the operator could be accommodated on a seat placed in front of the engines and boiler. A fringed canopy top gave the vehicle a surrey-like appearance. However, as Olds explained in 1892 to a reporter from the *Scientific American* magazine, the "great advantages" his vehicle had over a surrey and other horse-drawn carriages were "that it never kicks or bites, and never tires out on long runs, and during hot weather [the driver] can ride fast enough to make a breeze without sweating the horse." Then, no doubt recalling the chores of caring for the family horse, Olds pointed out that his invention "does not require care in the stable, and only eats while it is on the road, which is no more than at the rate of 1 cent per mile." On good roads, the twelve-hundred-pound vehicle reportedly could travel at speeds of fifteen miles an hour, a marked improvement over Olds' first steamer, and without the noise that had announced its approach well in advance. Although he did not publicize it at the time, Olds was still not satisfied with his second effort. There was no way to put it into reverse, and it was no hill climber. "I dreaded the sight of a hill," Olds declared later. On steep hills, legend has it that he had his wife Metta follow behind with a large block of wood to put under the rear wheels in case the engine stopped, in which case the brakes might not be able to keep the carriage from rolling downhill. (Olds' daughters stated that their mother did indeed sometimes assist their father in this manner, although, they claim, the assistance was rendered in connection with some of Olds' later gasoline-powered cars.)[32]

Exactly when Ransom Olds completed and tested his second steam-powered horseless carriage is even less certain than the facts regarding his first effort. However, that it was operating by 1892 is evidenced by an article on his "gasoline steam carriage" which appeared in *Scientific American* for May 21, 1892. An accompanying engraving, made from a photograph of the vehicle, was, from all appearances, taken in late fall or early spring. This article was probably the first indication the outside world received concerning any automotive activities in the state of Michigan, although there may have been some newspaper accounts of Olds' work prior to this time. That this information was carried in *Scientific American* is particularly significant since this weekly periodical, founded in 1848, had by the 1890's attained a circulation of nearly fifty thousand. The magazine claimed it had the largest circulation of "any scientific paper in the world." It also had a solid reputation as the most widely read and influential general publication for inventors (for whom it provided special services regarding patents, copyrights, and trademarks), businessmen, and others who were interested in the latest developments in nearly all areas of science. The magazine had always followed closely the progress that was made in developing horseless carriages and now, in the nineties, as this progress was advancing from the experimental into the commercial stage, *Scientific American* was a major source of technical information on automobiles.[33]

Olds, speaking through his official biographer in 1949, professed to have been "considerably surprised" that *Scientific American* had heard about his steam carriage and thought it sufficiently important to send a staff member to Lansing to see it. "R. E. was quick to sense the publicity value that would come from a favorable writeup about his new invention." This last statement is no doubt true, but it also seems quite possible that Ransom Olds, who was already demonstrating great understanding of the importance of publicity to the success of his business, had something to do with planting the story in *Scientific American*. At least as early as May 1891, P. F. Olds & Son had been running occasional advertisements in this magazine. A month before the article on the Olds steam carriage was published, one ad boasted that the "Olds' Gasoline Engine" (a bit of deception, actually, since it was a gasoline-heated steam engine) provided the "Best small power in the world." The advertisement was repeated in the May 21, 1892, issue within three pages of the description of the Olds vehicle. One suspects this was no coincidence. *Scientific American* may have been less prone than other early automotive trade journals to giving special attention to the products of companies that provided steady advertising revenues; however, it is hard to believe that, for example, the magazine's highly favorable report on the Sintz Gas Engine Company's exhibit at the Chicago World's Fair was not related to the fact that Sintz was one of its regular advertisers, or that the highly laudatory story on the Olds Steam Engine which appeared in *Scientific American* for June 9, 1894, had no connection with an observable increase in P. F. Olds & Son's ads earlier in 1894. It seems logical, at least, that, in the spring of 1892, when Olds sent in his advertising copy to *Scientific American,* he would have mentioned the carriage that he had recently built; he was aware of the interest the publishers had shown in this subject over the years. In 1910, one writer traced the phenomenal growth of the Michigan automobile companies to the fact that they knew how to advertise. The evidence from *Scientific American* in the 1890's indicates that Ransom Olds had learned the basic elements of advertising and publicity early in his business career.[34]

Although Olds regarded the story about his second steam carriage primarily as another means of promoting the Olds engine and not as a means of selling the vehicle itself, the article did have the incidental effect of eliciting an offer from an English patent medicine firm, the Francis Times Company of London, to purchase the vehicle. Olds offered to sell it for $400, and the company accepted. In the spring of 1893, the Olds steamer was shipped, as directed, to the firm's branch office in Bombay, India. Depending on which account one reads, the vehicle either arrived in India and was used there for several years, or it was lost at sea when the ship carrying it sank. Whatever may have been the fate of this steam car, a good many writers, including not only Olds enthusiasts, but the scholarly student of the auto industry, James Flink, writing as recently as 1970, have claimed that this was the first sale of an American-made horseless carriage. This is demonstrably not true. It is true that the Olds sale preceded by three years the sale of the first Duryea Motor Wagon in February 1896. The Duryea had been manufactured for the purpose of being sold, and its sale, therefore, is rightfully regarded as marking the beginning of commercial auto production in the United States. The sale of the experimental Olds steam carriage, on the other hand, was preceded in 1892 by William Morrison's sale of his experimental electric car and quite probably by the sales of other experimental vehicles. Nevertheless, there does seem to be substance to the claim that the Olds steamer was the first American car sold to a foreign buyer.[35]

The real importance of the two steam carriages that Olds built, however, is that these were the only ones of this type that he did build. While a number of other automotive pioneers continued work on the development of a practical steam car, Olds began thinking in terms of a vehicle powered by an internal combustion gasoline engine. He began focusing his efforts, as did his fellow Michiganians Charles King and Henry Ford, on the type of car that would prove to be the overwhelmingly popular choice when automobile-buying habits were fixed a few years later. This change in Olds' thinking was the logical outgrowth of the move of P. F. Olds & Son away from steam engines into the field of gas and gasoline engines. The current growth of this trend was indicated by the large number of such engines exhibited at the Columbian Exposition in 1893 in contrast to their scarcity at the Centennial Exposition in Philadelphia only seventeen years earlier.

Unfortunately, as in other aspects of the early business career of Olds, it is not possible to document in a very satisfactory manner this vital shift in his interests from steam to gasoline engines. For one thing, Olds was a man with a number of interests. This fact, already observable in the 1890's, became more evident later when he began to devote far more time to land developments, power lawn mowers, travel, yachting, and other interests than he did to automobiles, although they continued to be the main source of his public recognition. In July 1895, when we would expect that Olds was spending every waking moment thinking and working on engines and motor vehicles, he, together with another Lansing resident, was applying for a patent on an elevator gate. Some sources suggest that Olds began working on a gasoline engine at the time of the incorporation of P. F. Olds and Son in 1890. However, if such was the case, real progress was not made for several years. The first patent awarded to Olds was one in 1891 for a governor to be used in steam engines. In 1894 Ransom Olds and his brother Wallace patented a "multiplex vapor-burner," presumably to be used in a steam engine.[36]

It was not until August 24, 1895, that a patent application for a "gas or vapor engine" was filed by Ransom Olds and Madison F. Bates, an employee who assigned his rights to P. F. Olds and Son. There were those in Lansing who said that Bates deserved the main credit as the designer of the engine. Olds no doubt had a hand in the project, but it is likely that his father, his brother, and perhaps other workers beside Bates also made contributions. As the dominant individual in the company, Ransom Olds should be credited for authorizing the move into the gasoline engine field, but to credit him with the sole responsibility, as some have done, for this and other mechanical developments is to ignore the help that he, like other automobile pioneers, had in implementing his ideas.[37]

Commercial production of the new engine did not begin until 1896. Prior to March of that year, the Olds steam engine was the only product that P. F. Olds and Son advertised, but beginning in March 1896, the company also began promoting the Olds Safety Gas and Vapor Engine. That month also saw the appearance of articles in *Scientific American* and *Horseless Age* concerning this new engine. The stories and the advertisements both emphasized the simplicity, efficiency, and safety in the engine's operation — features that were said to make it a superior product.[38]

The new Olds engine was a commercial success. Gas and gasoline engines with ratings of as much as fifty horsepower were soon being manufactured and shipped to customers throughout the United States and abroad. Sales figures for the company rose from $29,000 in 1896 to $42,000 in 1897. By May of 1897 the company was referring to "The Engine that Built a 10,000 square ft. addition last year," and on November 22, 1897, the company's name was changed to the Olds Gasoline Engine Works. Capitalization of the firm was increased from $30,000, where it had been since 1890, to $50,000, of which $41,000 was paid in, an increase of $11,000 in the amount of capital invested in the company within one year's time. In the same period, new equipment and enlarged plant facilities had increased the company's productive capacity by fifty per cent.[39]

The success of the Olds Gasoline Engine Works touched off a boom that made Lansing a center of the industry in the next few years. Madison Bates and James P. Edmonds, another Olds associate, formed the Bates and Edmonds Gas Engine Company in 1899. They were the first of many Olds alumni, as they became called, to strike out on their own and whose influence ultimately extended into all aspects of automotive developments. The New-Way Motor Company, Hildreth Manufacturing Company (later the Novo Engine Company), and the Ideal Air-Cooled Engine Company were among other Lansing manufacturers who entered this field. By 1910 there were seven gasoline engine manufacturers in the city. The largest was the Seager Engine Works, the successor of the Olds company.[40]

In the initial development and promotion of the Olds gasoline engine there was little indication of its potential use in a road vehicle. Apparently, the first use that the Olds family made of the engine was in powering several launches that they operated for their own pleasure on Lansing's Grand River, just as Olds, a decade earlier, had tested his steam engine in a skiff before trying it on the road. As Charles King was discovering, there was a constant demand for marine engines at this time, which probably explains why the publicity concerning the Olds engine that appeared in the automobile journal *Horseless Age* in March 1896, mentioned only the motor's marine application. Company advertisements were less specific, indicating simply that the engine could be adapted to a variety of uses.[41]

Exactly when Olds and his men began working on a gasoline-powered vehicle is difficult to say. Part of the confusion of dates that one finds in various sources stems from the tendency to refer to the earlier Olds steam engine as a gasoline engine since a gasoline burner was used to heat the water. As a result, in 1904, Henry Ford's attorney, who was about to call Olds to testify for the defense in the Selden Patent case, was confused when he discovered one source referring to the Olds vehicle of 1887 as a gasoline car while another one called it, correctly, a steam car. Ransom Olds added to the confusion when he, like others of his automotive contemporaries, sometimes played fast and loose with dates in order to make his earlier work appear as innovative as possible. We may dismiss as totally unfounded his claim to having built his "first usable gasoline vehicle" in 1893, since at that time work on the Olds gasoline engine was still in a preliminary stage. Similarly, there is no evidence to support the claim made by automobile historians such as Arthur Pound and others that Olds completed a gasoline car in 1895. There is, on the other hand, no reason to doubt that by the latter part of 1895, with the gasoline engine perfected, the Olds organization was giving active consideration to its use in a vehicle. Ransom Olds apparently did give some thought to building such a vehicle for the *Times-Herald* race, but did not do so, probably because plans for the vehicle were not yet complete and because of the necessity to give all his attention to the task of gearing up the plant to manufacture the new engine. By the following spring, with the gasoline engine in production, and with the greater knowledge of gasoline buggies gained from studying the well-publicized efforts of the Duryeas, King, and even the Baushkes, the time was right, as Olds himself declared in a paper he read in 1897, for him to resume horseless carriage experiments.[42]

On this occasion, instead of trying to build the entire vehicle through his own efforts and those of his workers, as he had done in the case of his steam cars, Olds sought outside assistance in the area where he was least knowledgeable. An arrangement was made with Frank G. Clark, the young assistant superintendent of Lansing's largest carriage manufacturers, Clark and Son, whereby Clark would provide the body of the vehicle while Olds supplied the engine and transmission. By the first part of August, eight months after the unsuccessful Baushke-Worth attempt and six months after Charles King drove his test wagon in Detroit, Olds and Clark and several of their men had completed and successfully tested Lansing's first gasoline-powered motor carriage. As it turned out, neither Olds nor Clark stayed many years with the automobile manufacturing firm that had its inception with their vehicle, but over forty years later, Clark's blacksmith, Charles Blade, who had hammered out the front axle for the 1896 car, was still, at age eighty, employed by the Oldsmobile division of General Motors.[43]

On August 11, 1896, Olds invited a local newspaper reporter to take a ride in the new car. The newsman was immediately struck by "the beauty of the vehicle." The body was painted a dark green "with dainty red trimmings" and "leather furnishings of the latest pattern." There were two seats, with the one in the rear being adjustable so that passengers could face backward. Beneath the body was a five-horsepower engine, not attached directly to the body, so that passengers were protected from the motor's vibrations; this feature was later hailed as one of the carriage's most advanced qualities. The wheels were fitted with cushion tires, and ball bearings were used throughout. The weight of the complete vehicle was one thousand pounds, which Olds felt could be reduced by at least twenty per cent.[44]

There has been some controversy surrounding the method Olds used to start the engine in this vehicle. The Olds gasoline engine, as it was described in March 1896, was designed for either the hot tube or the electric method of ignition. It appears, then, that Olds was already familiar with the latter system, one that had been employed by Benz in his engines for a decade and a half. It had also been described in an article in *Motocycle* in 1895 which cited the advantages of electric ignition over the "dangerous" hot tube method. In 1949, however, Olds declared that he used the primitive hot tube technique in his first gasoline-powered car until an electrician at New York's Sing Sing Prison sent him an early version of a spark plug he had designed. Olds declared that this device gave him and his men the idea of igniting the gasoline with an electric spark rather than with the method they had been employing, It made a good story, with, of course, a reference to the electric chair that was one of the Sing Sing technician's responsibilities. Contrary to his later report, however, when Olds applied for a patent on his vehicle on September 18, 1896, he referred to the use of "an electric ignitor for the engine," indicating that Olds and his staff, like nearly all the American automobile experimenters at this time, did not need a stranger to tell them of the electric ignition system. Perhaps the Sing Sing story had some connection with later work which led to Olds' application in 1898 for a patent on an electric starter for a gas engine.[45]

At any rate, at the time of his public demonstration in August 1896, Olds put the machine through its paces for the Lansing reporter, demonstrating its hill-climbing abilities and subjecting it to other severe tests, all of which were passed successfully. He operated the vehicle from the right side of the front seat. With his right hand he advanced the engine by means of successive quarter turns of a lever from low gear, with a speed of four miles, on up to high gear, with a maximum speed of eighteen miles an hour. (A day after this information appeared in Lansing, the Detroit *News* reported that the vehicle had a top speed of twenty-five miles an hour.) Another turn put the car into reverse, a feature conspicuously absent from the earlier Olds steam cars. The steering was done with another lever on the left-hand side of the driver.

The newsman was impressed. "There is no doubt," he wrote the following day, "that the much mooted question of the horseless carriage has been successfully solved by Messrs. Olds & Clark." Olds was equally satisfied. The vehicle was "noiseless and light running, yet perfect in every detail as regards wear, stability and carrying capacity," he declared. He was certain that with this vehicle he could have won first place in the *Times-Herald* race the previous year, and as proof of his confidence he sent in an entry for the horseless carriage competition that was to be held in September at Providence, Rhode Island. However, the Olds machine was not one of the participants in that race, one of the most boring on record. (The expression "Get a horse!" is said to have originated here.) Olds probably was absent because he decided the rewards were not worth the expense and the damage to his reputation that a loss would have entailed. His official excuse was that he had objected to the rules set forth by the event's sponsors.[46]

The clearest statement of what Olds was seeking to achieve with this first gasoline motor vehicle is found in the opening paragraph of the description that he prepared for his patent application in September 1896.

> My invention relates to that type of motor-carriage in which the motive power is produced by a gasolene-motor; and the object of my invention is to produce a road-vehicle that will meet most of the requirements for the ordinary uses on the road without complicated gear or requiring engine of great power and to avoid all unnecessary weight.

A simple, lightweight automobile with enough power to meet the normal needs of the average driver — this seems to have been what Charles King had had in mind in 1895. It was certainly the approach that Henry Ford would pursue until he achieved his spectacular success with the Model T in 1908. Twelve years before that great turning-point in automotive history, however, Ransom Olds had fixed his sights on that same goal, and although he later went off in a different direction, he eventually returned to his original objective with the curved-dash Oldsmobile in 1900. The success that that model was to enjoy began to mold the public's image of the Detroit and Michigan auto industry as one basically devoted to the production of practical, utilitarian automobiles for the masses. The evolving image portrayed an industry that, with a few obvious exceptions, was willing to allow the big, fancy, high-powered, hand-made, and expensive machines so dear to the hearts of the automobile buffs — the Pierce-Arrows, the Mercers, the Duesenbergs, the Rolls-Royces, the Bugattis, and the host of other honored names — to be produced elsewhere.[47]

In August 1896, news of the latest gasoline motor carriage spread quickly beyond the immediate confines of Lansing. On August 13, the Detroit *News* reported the success of R. E. Olds who, "after six years experimenting," had completed a horseless carriage. By August 14, a Grand Rapids paper was quoting "friends" of Olds, who declared that his vehicle, "that is said to work to perfection . . . will come into general use." At about the same time a Canadian acquaintance of Charles King questioned him about the Olds vehicle, and King replied:

> I can only state that I have not seen his carriage or the motor, but know that the Olds's [sic] company experimented five or six years ago with a steam carriage. This, however, proved to be too bulky; and upon taking up

the manufacture of the gasoline engine which they have done recently they have experimented farther [*sic*] with the horseless carriage problem.

By September, a communication from P. F. Olds & Son describing the vehicle was published in *Motocycle,* with an accompanying photograph. Similar coverage appeared in *Horseless Age* in October and *Scientific American* in November, the latter referring to this "compact and well proportioned vehicle which has been giving good service during the past few weeks on the country roads of Michigan." Oddly, these stories, all of which were obviously based on information supplied by the Olds company, contained no mention of the role Frank Clark had played whereas the hometown newspaper had made it clear that this was a joint venture of Olds and Clark. But outside of Lansing, it was the "Olds Motor Carriage," which "was invented by Mr. R. E. Olds." It was his name alone that appeared on the application to the United States Patent Office in September 1896, although eight of the twelve claims made to support the patentable character of this motor carriage dealt with the supporting frame, which was presumably supplied by Frank Clark.[48]

When he was asked if he intended to manufacture this vehicle, Olds answered without equivocation: "Certainly." His days of experimenting were over. He had no illusions of cutting deeply into the business of the carriage manufacturers, but there were, he said, "a great many persons in this country and Europe [who were] waiting for someone to make a vehicle of this character that is a success." Olds thought he had a product that was superior to any other motor vehicle of the time in terms of lightness, economy of operation, and its ability to seat four people. Sometime in the late summer or fall of 1896, therefore, advertisements appeared for what Olds first called his Motor-Cycle, with a price tag of $1000. The manufacturing was to be done in the shop of P. F. Olds and Son, where, by the end of 1896, work was said to have been underway to fill several orders that had already come in.[49]

Modest as it was, this first attempt at automobile manufacturing in Michigan soon foundered. The need to keep up with the rapidly growing market for its gasoline engines made it impossible for the Olds company to spare any of its energies for other products. Readers of *Horseless Age* in January 1897 were advised of P. F. Olds and Son's inability thus far to manufacture any motor vehicles. Although it announced its intention "to do so soon," the possibility that it could go ahead with its existing facilities and financial resources became ever less likely in the succeeding months. It was at this time that the Olds automobile enterprise was saved by outside financial sources.[50]

The central figure in this rescue operation was Edward W. Sparrow, a fifty-year-old native of Ireland who, since settling in Lansing in 1858, had built up a great fortune based on extensive land holdings in Lansing, and on investments in mineral lands and vast tracts of timber. He had long been a promoter of Lansing's economic development, having served as secretary-treasurer of the Lansing Improvement Association in 1873 when that group published a book intended to attract more business to the capital city. Sparrow had been one of the founders as well as being the president of the City National Bank and one of the principal owners of the Lansing Wheelbarrow Company, one of the city's largest manufacturing firms. Whether Olds approached Sparrow or, as Olds claimed, Sparrow made the first overtures, discussions led to a meeting in Sparrow's Lansing office on Saturday afternoon, August 21, 1897. At that time the Olds Motor Vehicle Company was organized for the purpose of "manufacturing and selling motor vehicles." This is apparently the first such company actually to have been formed in Michigan, if, as seems likely, the Benton Harbor Motor Carriage Company, announced twenty-one months earlier, never got beyond the talking stage.[51]

The men who assembled in Sparrow's office and others listed as stockholders when the distribution of the $50,000 in capital stock was announced some two weeks later constituted a cross-section of the Lansing business community. All of them undoubtedly had seen the gasoline vehicle that Olds had been demonstrating around town during the past year. Their interest in this "invention" was later expressed by Eugene F. Cooley, a leading Lansing businessman for a quarter of a century, who recalled:

> I am sure I did not see any great future for the invention, and I do not think others did, but we felt that, if developed, the power vehicle would have some sale and that a business possibly could be developed which would show a profit. I am free to say that I had not the faintest vision of what has eventuated in the automobile business.

Cooley, besides being one of the organizers and the manager of the Lansing Wagon Works, was a close friend and business associate of Edward Sparrow. In 1884 the two had gone on a month-long trip west and in 1886 they had been two of the principal organizers of the City National Bank, where they were now officers. When Sparrow was selected to be the president of the Olds Motor Vehicle Company, therefore, it was not surprising that his friend Cooley was chosen vice-president, although he owned only one share of stock in the company. Sparrow's influence can also be detected in the election of Arthur C. Stebbins as secretary of the vehicle company, for Stebbins was an officer in the Lansing Wheelbarrow Company, another of Sparrow's interests. Almost certainly Sparrow was also responsible for interesting a former Lansing resident living in Detroit, Samuel L. Smith, in investing in the company.[52]

The paths of Samuel Latta Smith and Edward Sparrow had crossed many times, not only in Lansing, where Smith had lived in the 1880's, and where he, too, had helped found the City National Bank, but in Michigan's Upper Peninsula, where both had extensive investments, including some in the Michigan Land and Lumber Company, of which Smith was the president in the 1890's while Sparrow served as secretary-treasurer. Unlike Sparrow, Smith was a native of Michigan, having been born in Algonac in 1830. His older brother, Angus, became a prominent figure in the Great Lakes grain trade, first at Sandusky, Ohio, then at Milwaukee. Samuel's

Samuel L. Smith *in 1911. At the time the photograph was taken and published,
it seemed appropriate to describe the aging financial angel of the Olds Motor
Works as a "capitalist"; it was an accurate description that did not have quite
the opprobrious connotations that it would later acquire.*
Courtesy Burton Historical Collection

business career, on the other hand, had taken him in 1859 to the northern
part of the Great Lakes, to the Copper Country where he made his fortune.
He became one of the leading merchants in Houghton, but he made his
money by helping to organize a half dozen copper mining companies
including Copper Range, the only successful Michigan copper mining

company still in business in the 1970's. Through other investments, Smith was fortunate also to have had a tie-in with the Calumet and Hecla, for many years the giant among Michigan copper mining operators. In the 1870's, Smith had played important roles in the construction of two railroads into the Copper Country and in the completion of the Portage Lake and Lake Superior Ship Canal, vital to the transportation needs of the booming mining industry. In addition, Smith had found time to be active politically. Like many businessmen of his generation, he was a Democrat, and had served a term in the state House of Representatives from St. Clair County, just prior to moving north. In the 1860's he had twice been the party's candidate for other major political offices. Now in 1897, it was perhaps not surprising that the aging but still active millionaire began to develop still another interest, putting up what was for him a paltry sum of money for five hundred shares of stock in a new company that gave some promise of meeting the transportation needs of the future. Sparrow and Stebbins matched Smith's investment at this time, but within less than two years he had acquired the dominant financial position in the enterprise.[53]

In return for only $10,000 of paid-in capital, which he apparently felt would enable him to manufacture his vehicle, Ransom Olds was forced to trade away the kind of administrative independence he enjoyed in the family-owned P. F. Olds and Son. At the moment, it was true, he was on at least equal footing in the motor vehicle company with Sparrow and the other outsiders. Olds controlled exactly half the stock, and with Frank Clark's 125 shares, the two men who had built the company's prototype vehicle were the majority stockholders. Olds was elected to be the manager of the firm, which placed him in charge of production, and he was also elected to the post of treasurer, which gave him an influential voice in other aspects of the company's operations. Then, too, he still controlled P. F. Olds and Son, which, for the present, would be manufacturing the motor vehicle until the new company had its own facilities. Three months after the incorporation of the auto company the need to expand the engine company led to its reorganization as the Olds Gasoline Engine Works. Eugene Cooley represented Sparrow's group of businessmen in the new firm; he bought a thousand shares of the new stock and in return was elected vice-president of the engine works. Olds, who still held on to a substantial majority of the stock, was elected president. In running the company, however, he could hardly afford now to alienate a stockholder with the kind of influence Cooley had in the community.[54]

Thus, by the end of 1897, in any decision Ransom Olds made he had to consider and, in some cases at least, be guided by the views of his fellow officers and stockholders, who may have lacked his knowledge of the two companies' products, but who, on the other hand, had the money he needed to produce them. The problems inherent in this division of knowledge and authority was illustrated at the first directors' meeting of the motor vehicle company on August 21. President Sparrow reportedly turned to his production chief and said, "Olds, we want you to make one perfect horseless carriage." Olds, who had not hesitated to claim perfection for his vehicle in 1896, now replied that Sparrow's request was impossible to carry out, adding, "You shouldn't even expect it." Olds' view prevailed and, in his minutes, Secretary Stebbins crossed out the word *perfect* and inserted the words *nearly perfect* in the motion as finally adopted. Unfortunately for Ransom Olds, he would not always find it so easy to win approval for his viewpoint.[55]

By October, the company reported that orders were coming in for the Olds vehicle faster than they could be handled. Ten vehicles were under construction, and in the next few months several motor vehicles were apparently produced and sold. It would be interesting to know the names of those who bought these first Michigan-manufactured automobiles, but all that is known is that one car supposedly went to a buyer in Grand Rapids, another was shipped to Chattanooga, Tennessee, and a third to Florida. A fourth, which eventually wound up in the Smithsonian Institution, was first thought to have been the original Olds gasoline vehicle of 1896, but later research identified it as another vehicle, almost identical to the first, dating probably from 1898. It is apparently the only one of several horseless carriages built by Ransom Olds between 1887 and 1898 that still survives. In addition to the cars mentioned above, one or more of these Olds gasoline cars were exhibited at county fairs in 1898 and 1899, a promotional device that originated with the use of a Duryea in the Barnum & Bailey Circus in 1896 and made the automobile a popular attraction on the fair circuit for a number of years.[56]

Even if the Olds Motor Vehicle Company sold no more than four cars in 1897-98, it was doing better than most of the companies that were formed in this period and which, despite grandiose plans, never produced anything more substantial than some exquisite stock certificates. The records of the few that got cars into production are scarcely impressive. The Duryea Motor Wagon Company of Springfield, Massachusetts, after turning out thirteen vehicles in 1896, broke up shortly thereafter as a result of discord between the Duryea brothers. By 1897, three years after their success with their experimental gasoline buggy, Elwood Haynes and the Apperson brothers from Kokomo, Indiana, had still not gotten a vehicle into production. In Cleveland, Alexander Winton, who had completed his first gasoline automobile in 1896, a short time after Olds and Clark completed theirs, established the Winton Motor Car Company in 1897. Despite the publicity he had gained in the summer of that year by driving one of his cars from Cleveland to New York, an unprecedented feat which he carried out in a mere ten days, he did not begin to achieve commercial success until 1898. The first of the famous steamers developed by the identical twins, Francis and Freelan Stanley, appeared in 1897 in Newton, Massachusetts; although they may have produced as many as a hundred of these cars in the next few months, they shortly sold the business and did not return to production on their own until 1901. The leading automaker of the period was another New England firm, the Pope Manufacturing Company of Hartford, Connecticut; its total output in 1897 and 1898 was only 540 cars — nearly all of them electric vehicles — a figure that indicates the embryonic state of the industry at this time.[57]

Olds and his colleagues probably had only a limited appreciation for what was happening to the industry as a whole, but they did know what was going on in their company. Some of them, including Frank Clark, became so disappointed at the snail-like progress that they unloaded their stock even though probably at a considerable loss. Ransom Olds still had confidence in the future of the motor vehicle, but it was becoming evident to him that without additional capital the future of the Olds Motor Vehicle Company was, to say the least, uncertain.

What saved the anemic Olds automobile venture at this time was the robust Olds engine company and its ability to attract investors, who, in order to get this money-maker, were willing to adopt its weak sister. In the fall of 1897, Ransom Olds, in order to devote his attention to building motor vehicles, had turned over the management of the engine business to his brother Wallace. The latter is an obscure figure, receiving little or no mention in the Olds annals, mainly because of certain events in 1898. At that time an organizing drive by the machinists' union had been quite successful in recruiting employees of the engine works. The union then began negotiating with the company on wages and working conditions. When Ransom Olds, who was willing to accept some but not all of these demands, discovered that his older brother was supporting the union and not carrying out the management's decisions, he fired Wallace. In March, the twenty-eight-year-old, Canadian-born Richard H. Scott was brought in by Olds from the Toledo Machine and Tool Company, where he had been factory manager, to take over Wallace's position at the Olds Gasoline Engine Works. Some of the workers went on strike, demanding Scott's removal and Wallace Olds' reinstatement. It was several months before Scott was able to restore peace and get the plant back into full production. During the next thirty years, Olds and Scott were the closest of business associates until differences over company policy in the late 1920's permanently wrecked their friendship.[58]

The labor troubles in the early part of 1898 only briefly slowed the remarkable growth of the engine works. Sales increased from $42,000 in 1897 to nearly $72,000 in 1898. To meet the demand for its engines, the company's work force rose from around 22 in 1897 to 49 in 1898; the expansion of the plant and its equipment rose at a comparable rate. Considering these dramatic signs of growth, it was not surprising that when the capital stock was increased from $50,000 to $150,000 in October 1898, not only did Olds, Cooley, and several others almost double their personal investments in the company, but blocks of five hundred shares of stock each were purchased by three newcomers: Frederick Thoman, whose business connections linked him with the Sparrow-Cooley forces; Reuben Shettler, another

Lansing businessman; and, most significant, Frederic L. Smith, son of the charter investor in the Olds Motor Vehicle Company.[59]

Smith's investment confirms his later recollections that it was "the sure field for the gas engine" and the good dividend record of the Olds Gasoline Engine Works that attracted the attention of the "cold-nosed wealthy." Two such cold-nosed types from Detroit approached Olds in the summer of 1898. John T. Holmes, secretary-treasurer of the Michigan Portland Cement Company, and John M. Nicol, listed as being in the investment business, suggested a merger of the motor vehicle and engine companies into a million-dollar corporation and moving the business to Detroit. An agreement signed by Olds, Holmes, and Nicol in July clearly suggests that the two Detroiters were willing to subsidize the automobile enterprise in order to secure the engine works. While $40,000 in cash and stock was to be paid to the motor vehicle company, $75,000 in cash and $125,000 in stock in the new company was the agreed-upon price for the engine company. Even though Ransom Olds backed out of the deal, claiming later that the method by which Holmes and Nicol proposed to finance the company would not have been sufficiently rewarding to him, it must have given him renewed confidence, as one biographer points out, to know that financial interest in his endeavors was not confined solely to Edward Sparrow's Lansing group of investors.[60]

Early in 1899, a second proposition came from an even more distant source. Olds reportedly received a feeler from eastern capitalists who had ideas of financing an automobile factory in the New York area. This was a period when there was a sudden upsurge of interest in the speculative possibilities offered by the automobile. Writing in *McClure's Magazine* in July 1899, Ray Stannard Baker declared that in the first four months of that year "companies with the enormous aggregate capitalization of more than $388,000,000 have been organized in New York, Boston, Chicago and Philadelphia for the sole purpose of manufacturing and operating these new vehicles." For a time Olds thought he might be part of one of the companies Baker wrote about. He went to Newark, New Jersey, and picked out a site for a plant, but when the unnamed capitalists who had contacted him failed to proceed with their financial plans, Olds gave up and returned home, leaving to future historians the fruitless task of speculating as to what might have happened to the automobile industry in Michigan if Olds had actually moved his manufacturing activities to the East in 1899.[61]

In later years, Olds had the satisfaction of knowing that all of the multi-million-dollar stock promotions of the late nineties, with such high-sounding names as the Anglo-American Rapid Vehicle Company and the Automobile Company of America, soon passed into oblivion. But a much more modest venture capitalized at a mere half million dollars, the Olds Motor Works lived on to become the Oldsmobile Division of the General Motors Corporation. This newest of the several firms that bore the Olds name, born on May 8, 1899, apparently developed out of talks Olds held in Detroit on his return from the East. One version is that Olds met with

John Holmes and John Nicol, who repeated their offer of the previous summer; a second story is that it was Samuel L. Smith with whom Olds discussed the need for more money to set the motor vehicle company on its feet. Smith was a kindly and courteous gentleman who by the nature of his personality would have listened sympathetically to what the younger man had to say. In the end he agreed to provide the financial transfusion that saved the auto company from a lingering death. When it came to money, however, the old copper king was no angel of mercy, but a canny businessman. Motor vehicles by themselves were too risky a gamble, so he covered his bet by insisting that the highly profitable engine works be included in the reorganized company. It may be true, of course, as is often reported, that Smith agreed to put up the additional funds because of his interest in finding a business in which his sons Frederic and Angus could become involved, but it seems doubtful to this writer that sentiment played a very large part in his decision.[62]

The details of the financing of the new company have never been dealt with very thoroughly despite the enormous impact the Olds Motor Works exerted in the development of the automobile industry. Of the $500,000 in stock that the corporation was authorized to issue, initially only $350,000 was distributed in the form of shares with a par value of ten dollars each. The first distribution of twenty thousand shares went entirely to Samuel Smith, with the exception of forty shares which were divided equally among Olds, Edward Sparrow, Frederic Smith, and a fourth individual, James H. Seager, who, unlike the others, apparently did not previously hold any stock in the Olds companies. Although Seager's hometown was Hancock, Michigan, hundreds of miles away from the Lansing-Detroit base of the other investors, and although within a few years the Seager family would own more Olds stock than any other group except the Smiths, no one has determined how Seager came to be involved in this southern Michigan venture. The answer seems obvious. James Henry Seager was a brother-in-law of Samuel Smith, having originally come to the Copper Country in 1871 as Smith's business associate. Seager, like Smith, had been one of the organizers of the Copper Range Mining Company, and by 1899 he was one of the leading businessmen in his area. He had interests in such wide-ranging fields as railroads, hotels, foundries, banks, electric power, and newspapers. Basically, however, Seager, like Smith (and Sparrow to a lesser extent), owed his wealth to Michigan's copper. The Michigan automobile industry owes a great deal to the extractive economy that prevailed in the state in the nineteenth century.[63]

The 19,960 shares of Olds stock that Samuel Smith received in May 1899, came to him in return for the money he pumped into the new company. This cash investment, according to his son, was $200,000, of which amount $50,000 went to the original stockholders in the Olds Motor Vehicle Company and the Olds Gasoline Engine Works, and the remaining $150,-000 was placed in the treasury of the new company. Smith did not, however, retain control of all the stock. The remaining fifteen thousand of the origi-

nal thirty-five thousand shares were distributed to the shareholders in the
two companies that were being absorbed as compensation for the assets of
these firms. In addition, Samuel Smith sold many of his shares to business
associates and friends. Thus, the first annual report of the Olds Motor
Works filed with the state in 1900 showed that on February 21st of that
year the company's stock was dispersed rather widely. Individuals with the
largest holdings were Samuel Smith with 12,085, a drop of nearly eight
thousand shares since the previous May, Ransom Olds with 7500, and
Eugene Cooley with 2750. Edward Sparrow now owned a thousand shares
of stock in the new company; Frederic Smith, Frederick Thoman, and
Reuben Shettler each held 625; Arthur Stebbins had 250, and Pliny Olds,
the founder of the original Olds company, owned 125 shares.[64]

The list of new investors was especially interesting. With fifteen
hundred shares Schuyler Seager Olds (no relation to Pliny or Ransom) had
the fourth largest investment in the company. A resident of Lansing, he had
made the Olds name well known as a prominent attorney and politician
long before Pliny Olds brought his family to town. S. S. Olds had common
business interests linking him to Sparrow, Cooley, and Stebbins, who may
have been responsible for persuading him to invest in the Olds Motor
Works. It seems more likely, however, that he was brought in through his
connections with James Seager. Not only had his father and Seager's father
been close friends, which accounts for Schuyler Olds' middle name, but
Olds had married James Seager's sister. Through marriage, S. S. Olds was
thus also related to Samuel Smith. The fact that "Sky" Olds was the chief
lobbyist in Lansing for the railroad interests as well as having served as
a counsel for the Michigan Central Railroad no doubt explains how Henry
Russel of Detroit, for many years general counsel for the Michigan Central,
came to purchase a thousand shares of Olds stock. Russel's entry in turn
helped to widen the circle of investors to include several other wealthy
and highly influential Detroiters: Russel's brother George, a Detroit banker
and the immediate past president of the American Bankers Association;
Henry Ledyard, long-time president of the Michigan Central; and Henry
M. Campbell, Russel's law partner. Each of the three men obtained five
hundred shares of Olds stock.[65]

Through such intricate family and business connections, control of
the new Olds company was firmly in the hands of investors outside the
Olds family. The power among these outside interests now lay not with
Edward Sparrow and his Lansing group, as had been the case in the Olds
Motor Vehicle Company, but with the Smith family and their Detroit-
based associates. All in all, these investors, both old and new, were an
exceedingly potent collection of men whose power was based not entirely
on wealth. Russel's father, Dr. George B. Russel, had been one of Detroit's
most respected medical doctors and businessmen; Cooley's father, Thomas
M. Cooley, and Campbell's father, James V. Campbell, were generally
regarded as Michigan's most distinguished jurists of the nineteenth century;

Ledyard's grandfather was Michigan's greatest political leader of the century, Lewis Cass.

Where did Ransom Olds fit into this picture? At the age of thirty-five he had certainly come a long way since his twenty-first birthday when he had had difficulty scraping together a few hundred dollars to become his father's partner. Nevertheless, the wealth and social standing that he had achieved since that time were dwarfed when placed against the similar attainments of Samuel Smith, Henry Russel, or Edward Sparrow. However, Olds still had one thing these men lacked — the mechanical knowledge needed to make their investments pay off. Aware of his ability, the investors shortly proceeded to give tangible proof that they recognized his importance.

Initially, Samuel Smith was president of the Olds Motor Works, and Olds held the positions of vice-president and general manager; but sometime after the formation of the company, a change occurred so that the annual report of the company in February 1900 lists Ransom Olds as president and general manager, Samuel Smith as vice-president, and his son Frederic as secretary. These three officers were joined on the board of directors by Henry Russel and Eugene Cooley. Olds would remain as the president until the following year, but clearly he would have to get along with his fellow directors, whose personal stockholdings alone were more than double those of Olds, not to mention the thousands of other shares held by their relatives and friends.[66]

It was announced that the operation of the Olds Motor Works would be carried on in Lansing while a search, which had been underway well before the official formation of the company, continued for a permanent location. Site offers reportedly came from Chicago, Toledo, Cleveland, Indianapolis, Buffalo, and even Muskegon, Michigan, but the only move that seems to have been considered seriously was to Detroit. In April, Walter S. Campbell, head of the Merchants and Manufacturers Exchange in Detroit, and Edward I. Stimson, a Detroit realtor, discussed with the Olds organization possible locations for a factory. On April 19th, *Horseless Age* reported that the Olds company would move to Detroit. In May, less than a week after the incorporation of the company, the purchase of nearly five acres of land, located between the Detroit River and Jefferson Avenue, next to the Detroit Stove Works and near the Belle Isle Bridge, was announced. The corporation also announced plans to begin immediate construction of several buildings to house the firm's various engine and automobile manufacturing activities. It is quite probable that the fact the Smiths lived in Detroit was a factor in this decision, but the advantages that a city of Detroit's size offered in terms of skilled labor, suppliers, and shipping facilities were certainly the important considerations.[67]

Before the end of the year, the new plant in Detroit was open, although operations were also continuing at the engine plant in Lansing. The transfer of the main office to Detroit meant that the Olds family had to leave its home and friends in Lansing. Seven decades later, Mrs. Gladys

Olds Anderson, one of Ransom's two daughters, recalled that by December of 1899 they had moved, and on New Year's Eve she related: "I remember Father got all of us children out of bed just before midnight, explaining that we would not have the chance ever again to see a new century born and he didn't want us to miss it. We saw the old century out in our home in Detroit." In actuality, what they were witnessing was not just the passing of another century, but the end of a whole way of life, one that would never be regained.[68]

CHAPTER 3

"DETROIT, THE BEAUTIFUL"

At the time the Olds family and the Olds enterprises were moving to Detroit, that city was making plans to celebrate its birthday — the two-hundredth anniversary of Detroit's founding, on July 24, 1701, by the Frenchman, Antoine de la Mothe Cadillac. Hopes of hosting a world exposition on that occasion were dashed when Buffalo pre-empted those honors by announcing it would stage the Pan-American Exposition in 1901. Late in 1899, therefore, a group of Detroit citizens, headed by Mayor William C. Maybury, a Democrat, and United States Senator James Mc-Millan, Michigan's most influential Republican, initiated a drive for the construction of an impressive memorial to Detroit's past, the dedication of which during the bicentennial might be of more lasting importance than an exposition. At the urging of a wealthy Detroit art collector, Charles L. Freer, an advisory committee of outsiders, headed by the famous architect Stanford White and including the sculptor Augustus Saint Gaudens, was engaged to recommend the design and location of the memorial.

The plans that White unveiled at the Detroit Museum of Art in February 1900 called for the construction on Belle Isle of a colossal monument in the classical tradition centering around "a great Doric column, the highest in the world — surrounded by groups of sculpture in the water, . . . and supporting a tripod which would assume a torch-like character at night by the use of electricity and by a great flame of natural gas. . . ."[1]

Many citizens responded with enthusiasm to White's proposal, which was to be carried out at a cost of a million dollars, the funds to come from private donations. There were some dissenters, however, among whom was David Dunbar Buick, a former manufacturer of bathtubs, toilets, and other plumbing supplies, now working on gasoline engines, who outlined his concept of an appropriate monument: it would be "taller than any skyscraper" with "the outward appearance of a human figure," a hundred feet across the shoulders and with other parts of the anatomy of proportionate dimensions. Inside this facade was to be housed an art museum, an observatory, a convention hall, and much, much more.[2]

Detroit did indeed observe its bicentennial on July 24, 25, and 26, 1901, with three great parades, much pageantry, many speeches, and general frivolity. But the event did not quite live up to earlier expectations. A memorial was dedicated, but it was a stone chair, seven feet tall, scarcely of monumental proportions, which was somehow supposed to symbolize Cadillac. Stanford White had nothing to do with this commemorative piece, because the money for Detroit's answer to Giotto's Campanile in Florence failed to materialize. Freer's disgust at the lack of local support for White's plans is said to have been the major cause of his later decision to place his priceless Oriental art collection in a museum in Washington, rather than in his own home town.[3]

David Buick, too, failed to win support for his proposed memorial, but by the summer of 1901 he was well along in the work that would shortly lead to the appearance of the first of the many vehicles that have borne his name. During the bicentennial parades Buick observed that amidst numerous horse-drawn parade entries, including the star attraction Mrs. William Crosby, "a very handsome woman of superb figure," who received the loudest acclaim by driving a Roman chariot, pulled by four large white horses — amidst such eye-catching spectacles were a few automobiles. The judges of the entrants in the floral parade singled out for high praise an auto owned by Mrs. Henry B. Lewis, wife of a local manufacturer. With "her coachman in blue livery at the lever," Mrs. Lewis' entry, lavishly embellished with two peacocks and masses of yellow asters, "drew universal admiration and brilliantly presented the prophecy that the horseless carriage can be an affair of beauty as well as speed." Other awards went to an automobile entered by the man who reputedly invented the ice-cream soda, Detroit candy-maker Fred Sanders, and another owned by William E. Metzger, famous in automotive history as America's as well as Detroit's pioneer independent auto dealer. Non-prize-winners, but very

*From left to right: Ransom Olds, Frederic Smith, Mrs. James H. Dono-
van, and Mrs. Marguerite Beaubien pose amidst four shades of purple
flowers that covered an Oldsmobile (whose outline was definitely not
that of the curved-dash Olds runabout) in Detroit's bicentennial floral
parade.*
Courtesy University of Michigan Graduate Library

much in evidence, were Ransom Olds (a relatively unknown businessman
whom the Detroit *News* identified as C. Olds) and Frederic Smith, the
only auto manufacturers in the parade, driving their own creation.
With two officers of the Woman's Bi-Centenary Committee as passengers,
Olds and Smith were complimented on providing proof "that the horseless carriage with twentieth century ladies, could be made a lovely vision
of beauty and worth."[4]

Cadillac's Chair was a grave disappointment to those Detroiters who
had been hoping for a more impressive memorial to the city's past, and
after only forty years it was taken down and removed from the public's
view. By that time, it had long since become apparent that although this
piece of stone furniture had not said much about Detroit's past, there
could not have been more appropriate symbols of Detroit's future than
the handful of motor vehicles that were also a part of those civic observances at the beginning of the twentieth century.[5]

* * *

At the turn of the century, Detroit was, as it always has been,
Michigan's largest city. With a population of 285,704, it was the thirteenth
largest city in the United States, ranking ahead of such places as Louisville and Jersey City, with which it had vied for population honors in

the latter part of the nineteenth century. But Detroit still lagged behind Buffalo and Cleveland, its perennial rivals across Lake Erie. This was galling to the ardent civic boosters, who had hoped for a much larger increase during the nineties than the thirty-nine per cent gain achieved in that decade. It was the smallest percentage of advance since the earlier years of the century when Detroit first began to be transformed from a remote frontier outpost into the commercial center for a rapidly growing region of farms and towns.[6]

As Detroit was built and then rebuilt from the 1820's onwards, the last physical vestiges of the eighteenth-century French community that had survived the fire of 1805 had disappeared. By 1900, little remained other than a few ancient fruit trees planted by the French settlers and some quaint street names to remind visitors that Detroit was older than New Orleans, older, in fact, than nearly every American city west of the Atlantic coastal regions. The presence of such families as the Beaubiens, Campaus, Ducharmes, Girardins, Morans, and others whose names and ancestry harked back to that early period lent a definite stabilizing character to Detroit society that contrasted sharply with the upstart atmosphere so frequently observed by visitors to other midwestern cities. Henry Utley, head of the Detroit Public Library at the end of the nineteenth century, claimed that not only society but also Detroit business was under the influence of the conservative, thrifty, rather plodding spirit of the old French *habitant,* resulting in Detroit gaining a reputation in some circles as a "rather slow and unenterprising city." In the city's defense, Utley said, Detroit had flourished in its own modest, "eminently safe and reliable" way as much or more than other communities that had been addicted to more spectacular and speculative business philosophies.[7]

Most Detroiters in 1900, however, were as much newcomers to the area as the average residents of Chicago, Toledo, or Indianapolis. The Anglo-Saxon element had begun to appear with the coming of the British in the late eighteenth century, followed in the first half of the nineteenth century by a huge influx of Americans from New York and New England who indelibly stamped on all aspects of life in the city the distinctive characteristics of the Yankee. These influences were still much in evidence in 1900, but they had now been much diluted through the subsequent introduction into the city of peoples of differing backgrounds. From within the United States, migration from the neighboring areas of the Midwest now exceeded that from the Northeast; from the more distant southern states, a few Negroes had found their way to Detroit after the upheaval of the Civil War, joining others of their race who had been a part of the migration from the East some years earlier. To this mixture of native-born peoples there had been added since the middle years of the nineteenth century an ever widening variety of foreign immigrant groups. In numbers, the Irish had been the early leaders, although their neighbors from the British Isles, along with a large group from Britain's North American possession on the other side of the Detroit River, were also frequently counted among the new arrivals. From continental Europe came the Germans, who soon far outnumbered the Irish and all other nationality groups, and the Poles, who by the nineties were becoming a sizable element in the city's population (more so than the census figures indicate, since many Poles were counted as Germans, Austrians, or Russians, after the nations that had absorbed their homeland). A number of Italians and other Europeans were also represented in Detroit's cosmopolitan population, where, by the nineties, individuals of foreign birth, or one or both of whose parents were immigrants, constituted the overwhelming proportion of the residents.

If Detroit's appearance in 1900 reflected the more recent period of its development, it was, nevertheless, in the view of many, an appearance that reflected much beauty and charm. "Detroit, the Beautiful," in fact, was a popular term employed in the tourist brochures. One brochure, prepared for members of the National Education Association which met in Detroit in 1901, went so far as to claim that it was "generally conceded" that among all the cities of the United States, "Detroit stands without a peer, the most happily located and most beautiful of all." The writer's enthusiasm could not be curbed, for he went on to declare that of all the great cities of the world, "perhaps" only Paris surpassed Detroit in charm.[8]

The city's most attractive asset was the "noble Detroit river," which, more than anything else, enabled the city in this era to be touted as "par excellence, a summer home," the center of mid-America's greatest resort area. For starters, a visitor could ride a ferry to Belle Isle for a dime and enjoy, within sight of a modern city, the "pristine glory" of a "genuine natural forest"; he could relax in the Casino, with its "matchless view down the river" and "refresh the inner man"; he could take a carriage or bike ride around the island, or hire a canoe and go out on the lakes and shallow canals of the city-owned island park. There were also numerous excursion boats that provided frequent, inexpensive trips down the river all the way to Put-in-Bay, or up river, past Belle Isle, through Lake St. Clair, into the delta of the St. Clair River ("The Little Venice of America"), and on to Port Huron, "a veritable ride of delights and summer comfort." For those with more time, and only a little more money, there was ample opportunity to board one of several steamers leaving daily for Cleveland, Buffalo, Georgian Bay, Mackinac Island, Sault Ste. Marie, Duluth, and other points around the Great Lakes.[9]

Not only tourists were drawn to Detroit, but, it was claimed, the city's pleasant surroundings were an important inducement in persuading workers who were needed in the city's shops and industries to come and make this their permanent home. And for these people, Detroit had much to offer besides the opportunities for boat trips. Despite its population of over a quarter of a million, the city in the 1890's still retained something of the small town atmosphere with its tree-lined streets, its numerous parks, its business district where a ten-story building was still a novelty, and its residential neighborhoods, in which Detroit took special pride.

Calling itself the "city of homes," Detroit pointed not simply to the man-
sions of the rich, but also to the "comfortable homes of merchants, arti-
sans, and mechanics," and even to the small houses of the laborers, "which,
as a rule, are trimly kept." Few cities anywhere, Detroit boasted, could
claim such a high percentage of citizens who owned their own homes.[10]

Many of the vestiges of village life still survived, one reporter discovered in the summer of 1896. Outside many homes, a tin cup still hung
by the well, the source of water for many families, and any passerby, friend
or stranger, who was welcome to slake his thirst. In vacant lots in some of
the best parts of town cattle could be seen grazing, driven there daily by
hired hands. Regardless of their social standing, the reporter declared,
"all good householders believe it their duty to keep chickens, spade a small
garden, and maintain a small orchard." This still was possible when the
demand for city land had not yet made such use of property economically
impractical. Interestingly, the newsman also found that there were still
many businessmen who went home at noon to eat "dinner" with their
families. "Time with them, as with the village craftsman, is a bountiful
commodity, and the cheerful jest goes round, the food is passed and re-
passed, and the delights of life in the family circle enjoyed to their full.
It may be," the writer speculated, "that this is a good, if not the best way
to live, and that, in our struggle for money, we are sacrificing much of
the good fellowship of life, and that when we think the home-going business man wasting too much time, we are misguided mortals and our
boasted city progress is a step backward."[11]

Whether it was good or bad, there could be no doubt that by the
beginning of the twentieth century Detroit was growing up, and the signs
of the village would soon be lost forever as a metropolis spread across the
landscape. Already in the 1880's the older oil and gas lamps that had lit
the streets had begun to give way to electricity as arc lights, mounted on
towers a hundred feet or more in height, provided a new and spectacular
approach to the after-dark lighting problem. In 1893, electricity for home
use became available. By this time, also, communications between the
ever larger number of businesses and homes in the city were being conducted increasingly over the telephone, a medium first introduced to Detroit in 1878.[12]

Along the river ran one of the city's two principal thoroughfares,
Jefferson Avenue, whose eastern sections were still the preferred address
for many of the older wealthy families, such as the McMillans and the
Newberrys, whose stately homes, beautifully landscaped, stood well back
from the street. In the middle of the nineteenth century, life in the city
had still been confined to a narrow strip running from Jefferson and the
river inland to West Fort Street, which ran parallel to Jefferson and was
favored by the Chandlers and some of the other prominent political families. Later in the century, however, the growth of the city forced expansion northward along Woodward Avenue, the other main city artery,
which strikes off at right angles from Jefferson. For the first few blocks

inland, Woodward constituted the heart of the business district. Beyond Grand Circus Park, however, it changed to a street of churches and the magnificent residences of a newer class of rich families such as the Freers and the Heckers. Their homes, long since put to different uses, are among the few examples of Victorian opulence to survive the commercial developments that enveloped this area, once Detroit's showplace.[13]

At the end of the nineteenth century, horses, like cattle and chickens, were a common sight in Detroit. One tourist publication included a photograph of Detroit's "White Wing Brigade who keep our avenues spotless." Like the college marching bands of later years, the uniformed men spelled out the initials of the Department of Public Works before moving on with their push-brooms to clean up after the city's ten thousand horses. Huge quantities of manure were carted out into the surrounding countryside and were put to good use by the farmers who supplied the city's vegetable, fruit and dairy needs. But, although this was the horse-and-buggy era, relatively few Detroit families could afford the luxury of owning their own horse. To get around the city, they might, on special occasions, avail themselves of the services of one of the seventy-five livery, sale, and boarding stables in Detroit. More commonly, they walked or rode the streetcars, which were horse drawn until public pressures in the nineties forced the traction companies to modernize their equipment.

By the end of the decade, electric interurban lines were fanning out of the city: down river to Wyandotte and Toledo; up river to Grosse Pointe, where the rich had their summer cottages, and on to Mt. Clemens, with its mineral baths, and Port Huron; inland out Woodward Avenue to Highland Park, Birmingham, Bloomfield Center (today's Bloomfield Hills), and Pontiac; or out Michigan Avenue, through open country to the tiny farm village of Dearborn and beyond to the college communities of Ypsilanti and Ann Arbor. In that age of the ten-hour day, six-day work week, the working-man and his family could, for a few cents, enjoy an occasional Sunday outing in the country.[14]

Again in the nineties, additional mobility was provided by the bicycle, which in Detroit, as everywhere in the country, suddenly achieved enormous popularity. Enthusiasts joined clubs and bicycled for the fun of it, wheeling around Belle Isle or on organized caravans to nearby communities. In their travels these wheelmen became uncomfortably conscious of the horrible conditions not only of the country roads but of most of Detroit's streets. By 1899, after years of agitation by these bicyclists and others, some improvements had occurred. There were 270 miles of paved streets in the city, but much of this pavement was in the form of cedar blocks, a picturesque carryover from old Detroit, charming one and all with the distinctive clip-clop effect produced by horses' hooves, and with the pleasant smell of burning tar and wood, a frequent occurrence during hot, dry spells. In the rainy season the pavement reportedly had a tendency to float. However, under the prodding of good-roads' advocates and civic leaders such as Mayor Hazen Pingree, notable progress had been achieved in the nineties in providing asphalt or brick pavements for the city's main arteries. Some claimed that Detroit, for a city of its size, had the best streets in the country, a condition that Ransom Olds later claimed was a major reason in the decision to move his automobile manufacturing activities from Lansing to Detroit.[15]

The primary function of Detroit's streets, with their bicycles, carriages and streetcar lines, whose tracks ran down the center or along the side of the major thoroughfares, was to get the city's workers to their jobs. For a very large percentage of these workers, men and women, that meant a job in a factory. This brings us to another side of Detroit, one not quite so pretty and therefore dwelled on only briefly, if at all, in the tourist literature. This was a side discovered by J. Horace McFarland, president of the American Civic Association, as he approached Detroit in the fall of 1908 on a bright, clear day — bright and clear, that is, until he got into the city and found the sun disappearing "into a cloud of sooty gloom." The soot emanated from scores of factory chimneys; he found that soft coal was "burned as smokefully, wastefully, and shamefully as in most other cities in this land . . . with the result that the carbon thereby wasted into the air is blown and breathed into the homes and lungs of the populace." Pollution — that bane of an industrial society — is no newcomer to Detroit, nor can the automobile industry be blamed for having introduced it to the Detroit area, no matter what its responsibility may be for other changes that have long since removed the adjective "beautiful" from any realistic description of Detroit. While it is true that by 1908 auto plants were contributing their fair share of pollutants to the atmosphere of what McFarland had found to be, on the whole, an attractive community, ten years earlier, before any automobiles were being manufactured in Detroit, one prominent businessman was writing individuals in the city seeking support for an anti-smoke suit that he was instituting. "If you have suffered damage to property or personal discomfort and annoyance from the unnecessary smoke nuisance from shops, factories, etc. between Jefferson Avenue and the River," he declared, "you may be interested in my effort to have it abated." Earlier still, in 1891, the Detroit *News* had commented on the manner in which residential areas were being disrupted and destroyed by the advance of industry in the city. "When a manufacturing business pokes its greasy nose among the fine houses . . . then good-bye to green lawns and quiet life."[16]

By the 1890's, forty thousand or more Detroiters were employed in that city's factories, and the annual value of the products was estimated to be one hundred million dollars by 1899. The variety and diversity of these products is surprising. In the industrial floats that participated in one of the bicentennial parades, not one was from an automobile manufacturer. Nevertheless, over seventy Detroit manufacturers were represented in the parade; in many cases, the firms had been in business for years and, as one automotive writer noted in 1913, had "more than put Detroit 'on the map'" long before the city was associated with the production of motor vehicles. At the beginning of the twentieth century, Detroit boasted that it had the largest seed house, stove factories, chemical laboratory, varnish factory, and parlor and library table factory in the world, and the largest paint factory and railroad car works in the United States.[17]

Gardeners and farmers everywhere knew of Dexter M. Ferry's seed company, which, before the end of the nineteenth century, seems to have gained general recognition as the largest business operation of its kind in the world. Even better known among cigar smokers, pipe smokers, and the laboring man who chewed when factory regulations forbade him to smoke was Detroit's tobacco industry; the value of its products in the 1880's exceeded that of any of the city's other manufactured goods. Prior to that time, John J. Bagley, two-term governor of Michigan in the seventies, made a fortune with his Mayflower brand chewing tobacco, causing him to remark one day to a Detroit clergyman: "You and I thrive on the sins of the people." (Another Detroiter, Hiram Walker, thrived on profits made from catering to what many of his generation regarded as an even more sinful human craving, but he at least located his distillery across the river in Canada.)

Although Detroit continued to be noted for its tobacco products, sometimes being referred to as the "Tampa of the North," other products had surpassed tobacco in value and fame by the 1890's. Among these were stoves; Detroit had the largest stove manufacturer in the world in the Michigan Stove Company. Only slightly smaller was the Detroit Stove Works, whose Jewel stoves competed with Michigan Stove's Garland throughout the world. These two companies, plus a third, Peninsular Stove Company, together employed over 2500 workers in 1899 and produced over 215,000 stoves, about sixty per cent of the total production of the twenty-one major stove companies in Detroit and elsewhere in Michigan.[18]

Beginning about the time of the Civil War, when the stove industry had first arisen, the pharmaceutical industry had begun to take root in Detroit. The Parke-Davis Company emerged as the largest of the firms engaged in this work in Detroit and one of the largest pharmaceutical houses anywhere. Shipbuilding, dating back to the early years of the British period in the 1760's, was another major industrial activity. The Detroit Drydock Company and several other shipyards in Detroit and its immediate environs launched more ships annually in the early 1890's than the shipyards of any other area in the United States. This industry in turn helped to spawn the development in Detroit of engine works, machine shops, foundries, and companies specializing in brass and bronze products, and paints and varnishes.

In the 1890's a chemical industry began to develop, first in neighboring Wyandotte, where Captain J. B. Ford founded the Wyandotte Chemical Corporation, and then in Detroit with the location there of a plant of the Belgian-based Solway Process Company. Both companies drew on the underground salt resources of the Detroit River area as the raw material for their products, a fact which caused members of Captain Ford's family in the twentieth century to be referred to on society pages as the "Salt" Fords, to distinguish them from that other Detroit Ford family.

But in the closing years of the nineteenth century, the unquestioned leader of the Detroit industrial community was the car industry — the manufacturing of railroad freight cars and other pieces of railroad equipment. In 1899, six thousand men were employed in this industry, turning out eighty to a hundred cars a day, for an annual product worth at least fifteen million dollars. The foremost of the companies in this field had been the Michigan Car Company, established in 1864 by James McMillan and John Newberry. Twenty-one years later, Frank J. Hecker and Charles Freer established the Peninsular Car Company, which soon rivaled the McMillan-Newberry firm in size. Also in the field was the Russel Wheel and Foundry Company, founded by Henry Russel's father in the 1850's, plus a number of smaller firms making wheels and other parts. The number of companies was greatly reduced in the early 1890's when the Michigan and Peninsular companies, plus some of the smaller establishments, merged; later, in 1899, this consolidated company was absorbed into the giant American Car and Foundry Company.

These varied industrial enterprises had helped to create a substantial group of wealthy Detroit citizens by the late nineties, only a quarter century after the death of Eber Brock Ward, widely touted as Michigan's first home-grown millionaire. The basis for this wealth varied. Railroads were the foundations of the McMillan, Joy, and Newberry fortunes, lumber was the basis of the Alger, Murphy, and Palms money, and mercantile activities fostered the wealth of the Ducharmes and Buhls. But, as in the case of Samuel L. Smith, whose money had come from still another source, mining, these men, whose fortunes were modest in comparison with those of such contemporaries as Rockefeller, Carnegie, or the Vanderbilts, showed a marked willingness to gamble with some of their money, hoping to increase their wealth by investing in new enterprises. The willingness of the Smiths to bankroll the Olds Motor Works was but one sign of the interest that part of Detroit's well-to-do class now began to show in the auto industry. Their interest was probably the single most important factor behind Detroit's rise to the top in this new industry, creating new fortunes that dwarfed those made in seeds, tobacco, stoves, and railroad cars.

CHAPTER 4

"A GREAT MANY PEOPLE SPEAK ABOUT FORD'S RIG"

In September 1899, an anonymous reporter writing in *Motor Age* examined the scarcely observable progress that the fledgling auto industry had thus far achieved in Detroit, and came to the astounding conclusion that the city "promises to become a center of motor vehicle manufacture. The preparations bear the earmarks of systematic effort and strong financial backing — the first requisites for success." How one wishes he could learn the identity of this writer. If he had showed the same astuteness in sizing up prospects in only a few other instances, he would be ranked with the greatest business analysts of all time, for in 1899 production from Detroit's auto plants was neglible and automobiles of any kind were still a novelty on the city's streets.[1]

In September 1897, a year and a half after he had tested his own horseless carriage, Charles King reported to E. P. Ingersoll of *Horseless Age* that "three or four motor carriages" were "running about the streets here." None of them, however, according to King, were worthy of special notice. It is likely that these vehicles, like those King had operated, were all of the homemade, one-of-a-kind variety. Several Detroiters were now receiving some attention as automotive experimenters. According to Oliver Barthel, King had not been the only Detroiter whose interest in horseless carriages had been stimulated by the Chicago *Times-Herald* race in 1895. Reminiscing in the 1950's, when old age and poor health may have affected his memory, Barthel claimed that Barton Peck and Charles Annesley (or Ainsley, as Barthel or his interviewer incorrectly spelled the name), like King, had been working on four-cylinder engines at that time and had actually built cars that worked, after a fashion, in the early months of 1896. There is little other evidence indicating that either Peck or Annesley had succeeded in developing motor vehicles as early as Barthel claimed, but both were definitely among the many Americans during these years who were enamored with this new mode of transportation; they were also among that multitude who never quite succeeded in doing what they had hoped to do with the automobile.[2]

Peck's career was a bizarre one. His father, George Peck, was a successful Detroit dry-goods merchant who had become a close business associate of James McMillan; in the 1890's, he was serving simultaneously as the president of the Michigan Savings Bank and the Edison Illuminating Company of Detroit. Young Peck apparently had no interest in following in his father's conventional business footsteps. Instead, he was fascinated with speed. At first he was attracted to bicycles, but he soon turned to automobiles. With an ample allowance from his father, who also provided him with a shop for his experiments, Barton Peck began developing a motor vehicle; by March 1897, he was far enough along to apply for a patent on the vehicle, an application that the Patent Office obligingly approved the following December. In the summer of 1898, Peck reported to *Horseless Age* that while testing his vehicle at 2 a.m. one morning, he had gotten up to "the breakneck speed of thirty miles an hour"; he was forced, he reported, to revamp the mechanism to hold the four-cylinder engine down to a safer speed of twenty miles an hour. Even that was too fast for the authorities who, Peck declared, no doubt with considerable pride, had arrested him one night for speeding on one of Detroit's main streets. His is undoubtedly one of the earliest traffic violations on record. Peck also claimed at this time to have formed a company, the Detroit Horseless Carriage Company, which, if his claim was true, would have been Detroit's first auto company; by the fall of 1898 Peck announced he was ready to go into production. A photograph of the Peck automobile showed it to be "designed after the ordinary Victoria, having two seats facing each other. It is painted black, with dark green running gear and nickel plated trimmings."

Although Peck was working on a second vehicle in February 1899, his interest in automobiles began to wane for reasons that are partially apparent from a newspaper interview in August of that year. At that time, Peck denied that he had any intention of manufacturing an automobile. The work he had been carrying on over the past two years had been, he claimed, of an experimental nature, experiments that led him "to the conclusion that the gasoline motor of to-day, like the one on my carriage, is not a success." To be sure, the motor operated up to his expectations,

> but there is one great obstacle that must be overcome and that is the offensive odor from the gasoline that had been burned and that is discharged into the air. It is a sickening odor and I can readily see that should there be any number of them running on the streets, there would be an ordinance passed by the council forbidding them.

He still had some hopes of correcting this problem, but if he did not, he said, it would be pointless to continue further because the one defect of smell would lead to a public condemnation of these vehicles. Perhaps because he was not satisfied with the progress he was making in his automotive experiments, Peck soon turned his attention to manufacturing electrical furnace supplies. He even became involved with a hair-restorer before again returning to his old love of speed; this time he took up aviation. He bought up large amounts of Florida flat lands to use as landing fields, and eventually sold these lands for a fortune, enabling him to retire to Arizona with riches reportedly far exceeding those his father had accumulated.[3]

Charles G. Annesley is a more shadowy figure who is best remembered as the man who bought Henry Ford's first car. In the Detroit city directories for the mid-1890's Annesley is listed as an electrician, an occupation that perhaps proved to be his introduction to Ford, chief engineer for a local power company at the time. According to Ford, Annesley did not haggle over the price, but agreed readily to pay two hundred dollars for the slightly used Ford quadricycle. (Annesley was not, as some have called him, the purchaser of the first used car, since other pioneers, such as William Morrison and Ransom Olds, had earlier sold the experimental vehicles they had built and driven.) Annesley later sold this car, but before he did he no doubt got ideas from it for the machine or machines that he was working on. By September 1899, with financial backing from M. L. Marr of Saginaw, Annesley was seemingly on his way to success as an automobile manufacturer. At that time he was said to have built four electric vehicles, as befitted his electrician's background, but his main interest had centered on gasoline-powered vehicles, of which he built three. Seven automobiles, if Annesley really built that many, was a remarkable accomplishment. In Michigan perhaps only Ransom Olds had thus far surpassed it. But Annesley's career as an automaker was an abbreviated one. Possibly one reason was that his cars were not very good. That was, in fact, Oliver Barthel's evaluation of his first one. Possibly, too, the financial backing was inadequate to maintain Annesley's budding enterprise. In any case, Annesley had left Detroit by 1900 and was next reported in Buffalo in 1901 as a superintendent at the Buffalo Gasoline Motor Company. In addition to engines, the company was beginning to produce automobiles, quite likely because of the influence of Annesley, whose enthusiasm for cars was undiminished by his personal setbacks. The last that is heard of

Annesley, he was involved in manufacturing marine engines, still in Buffalo, using designs he had purchased from Charles King.[4]

Annesley's name does not appear in a Detroit *News* story in mid-July 1899, which, predicting that the city was "on the edge of a genuine surprise in the use of automobiles," mentioned the names of several other individuals in the city developing horseless carriages of either the gasoline or electric varieties. None of the experimenters had completed their work at that time but all expected to be finished in a few weeks. The only individual willing to discuss his work was C. W. Koch, described as a Detroit carriage builder with over twenty years' experience, who was engaged in building four electric vehicles of the three-wheeled design for an outside firm. He did not name the firm but it might have been Annesley's, since the number of electrics Koch was building corresponds to the number that Annesley would shortly be credited with having constructed. As a carriage builder, however, Koch had a personal interest in the new horseless carriage since he felt that this was a field that might revive the business of carriage manufacturers, many of whom, he said, were barely making ends meet because of greatly reduced profits in the production of horse-drawn vehicles.

In addition to Koch, the *News* at this time also listed Barton Peck, Henry W. Koehler, James Rogers, and several unnamed individuals as engaged in automotive experiments in the city. One of the unnamed experimenters may have been Henry C. Hart, a manufacturer of cabinet hardware, who, after developing and patenting a gasoline motor, had been reported in October 1898 to be attempting to apply his engine to a vehicle.[5]

Most of the Detroit auto experimenters of this period — King, Peck, Annesley, and Hart, at least — like such outstate contemporaries as Olds, Worth, and Sintz, had one thing in common. Their interest in motor vehicles seems in all cases to have stemmed from an earlier interest in gasoline engines. Their automobiles can be viewed as a natural outgrowth of their desire to develop new uses and applications for their engines. King, Annesley, and Worth eventually went from automobiles back to the production of engines, while Olds continued the manufacturing of engines and automobiles side by side for a number of years.

The same line of development — first the engine, then the automobile — is evident in the career of still another Detroit pioneer of this same period. Henry Ford, whose chances of success initially seemed no brighter than those of the others, ultimately succeeded to a degree that no one could possibly have foreseen. Ford received his first national publicity in the columns of *Horseless Age* in November 1898. The journal noted that Ford had "built a number of gasoline vehicles which are said to have been successfully operated. He is reported to be financially supported by several prominent men of the city, who intend to manufacture the Ford vehicle." Although the Detroit *News* summation of automotive activities in Detroit in mid-July 1899 did no more than mention "John Ford" (accuracy does not seem to have been a strongpoint of Detroit papers in this period) as one of these experimenters, by the end of that month both the *News* and the Detroit *Journal* had stories and photographs of the "Ford automobile," which, the *News* reported, could attain a speed of thirty miles an hour and could "carry the passengers from Detroit to Ann Arbor for four cents worth of gasoline." Within a few days, the formation of a company to manufacture this car was announced, but it would be another four years before the public would actually see a Ford-manufactured automobile.[6]

* * *

With the exception of possibly two or three political leaders, no American since Abraham Lincoln has had more written about him than Henry Ford. For a man some have charged was barely literate, Ford contributed a surprising amount to this verbiage during his lifetime. The Library of Congress printed catalog of its card files lists fourteen books and pamphlets authored by Ford. Little, if any, of the content of these publications was written by Ford, but in the case of the more substantial works, he at least had the honesty to give equal billing to his collaborator; as Ford's defenders have pointed out, this is more than can be said for many public figures who never acknowledged their use of ghost writers.

In addition to these volumes and a number of articles that have appeared under Ford's name, the number of published works that have been devoted solely or principally to Henry Ford, could some bibliographer succeed in compiling a complete listing, would very likely deserve the adjective astronomical. *Books in Print* listed twenty-two biographies or monographs devoted to Ford in print in 1971. Several of the biographies were designed for young people, but one can quickly compile a list of over twenty full-length biographies, most now out of print, that have appeared over the past six decades intended for adult audiences. Of magazine articles there is almost no end. Volume twenty-six of the *Reader's Guide to Periodical Literature*, covering the period from March 1966 to February 1967, nearly twenty years after Ford's death, was the first volume since volume one, covering the years 1900 to 1904, not to index at least one article by or about Henry Ford. In the volumes covering the decade of the 1920's two or three columns were required to list all of the Ford articles, even with the small type and abbreviated forms of citation that *Reader's Guide* employs. Furthermore, this does not account for the many articles indexed under the heading Ford Motor Company, most of which probably contained some reference to the head of the firm. Nor does it include articles about Ford that appeared in periodicals of a more limited circulation than those scanned by *Reader's Guide* — the specialized magazines, the scholarly journals, foreign magazines, and automotive trade publications. It seems logical to assume that the sampling of Ford articles listed in *Reader's Guide* constitutes only a fraction of this total literature.

Nor was this attention that was lavished on Ford in the twenties the result of the general popularity that businessmen are assumed to have enjoyed during that prosperous decade. In contrast to the 150 lines that were required to index all the articles by or about Ford that were listed under his name in the *Reader's Guide* for 1925-28, only sixteen lines were required to index all the articles that were listed under the heading John D. Rockefeller, Sr., while a mere seventeen lines took care of the entire DuPont family. Fifty-two lines were devoted to articles by or about Andrew Mellon, but nearly all this attention stemmed from Mellon's political role as a leading member of Calvin Coolidge's cabinet. Among well-known auto industry leaders, besides Ford, twenty-seven lines were all that it took to record the articles by or about William C. Durant, Alfred P. Sloan, Jr., and Walter P. Chrysler, combined, while the name of Ransom Olds does not even appear. Clearly, Henry Ford was regarded by most magazine editors as a name with marketing appeal far exceeding that of other men with equal wealth or business rank.

As for other publications in which Ford appears but is not the center of the discussion, none of the numerous works on the auto industry published after about 1914 would have been considered complete without some extended discussion of Henry Ford's role in the development of the industry, but more surprising is the regularity with which Ford appears in other non-fiction works, many of which have not the remotest connection with automobiles or the auto industry. In addition, such writers as Upton Sinclair, Aldous Huxley, and John Dos Passos have written Ford into some of their fiction.

The attitudes toward Ford in this vast literature have run from extremely adulatory to highly critical; on the one hand is the almost worshipful tone of the distinguished American economist, John R. Commons, in "Henry Ford, Miracle Maker" (*The Independent*, May 1, 1920), while on the other there are the scathing criticisms of a later American economist, John Kenneth Galbraith, who, in an essay in his *The Liberal Hour*, published in 1960, refused to credit Ford even with having been a good mechanic. The appearance between 1954 and 1963 of the supposedly definitive three-volume biography by Allan Nevins and associates failed to stem the tide of Fordiana. In recent years, Booton Herndon's *Ford, An Unconventional Biography of the Men and Their Times*, published in hardcover in 1969 and in paperback in 1971, entertainingly served up warmed-over stories about Ford, considerable new material about Ford's jet-setting grandson, and a rather stupefying amount of detail concerning Booton Herndon. In 1970, Dr. Anne Jardim's *The First Henry Ford: A Study in Personality and Business Leadership* tried a new approach to a familiar subject by figuratively putting the old billionaire on the couch in the interest of the fashionable psychological-biography technique. In 1972 came Reynold W. Wik's *Henry Ford and Grass-roots America*, a most scholarly work, but one which, considering earlier books that dealt with Ford and the Selden Patent, and Ford's philanthropies, raised the possibility that the consuming interest in Henry Ford may be reaching ridiculous lengths. Oddly enough, despite this immense outpouring of words, there remain significant gaps in our knowledge of Ford, not to mention nearly complete disagreement among authors concerning overall interpretation of Ford and his career. What should probably have been a relatively simple, uncomplicated story has been so muddied by so many attempts to provide answers to questions nobody asked that the picture of Henry Ford that has been created may very well be that of an imaginary character. Much as we lament the paucity of biographical studies of other automotive pioneers, this very fact may enable us to examine these men in a more judicious fashion than is now possible regarding Henry Ford.

The basic outlines of Ford's life, of course, are incontestable. He was born on a farm within what are now the city limits of Dearborn, Michigan, on July 30, 1863. As a boy he received the kind of rudimentary education common to the rural schoolhouse of that day. He disliked the drudgery of work on his father's farm, so the first chance he got, at age sixteen, he escaped to the big city, Detroit, to develop his mechanical abilities and earn a living. Nothing unusual in any of this. Nor is there any mystery in the details of the next decade of young Ford's life as he went from job to job, went back to the farm, married, and then finally returned to Detroit in 1891 to take a position with the Edison Illuminating Company. At age twenty-eight, Ford may have thought he had found his niche. His work with the Edison company was apparently satisfactory, for within a couple of years he had advanced to the position of chief engineer (the term *engineer* being used not in the professional sense but in the mechanical sense, as in "locomotive engineer"). That Ford may have been thinking of a career in the power industry is evidenced by his unsuccessful bid in 1893 to be named superintendent of Detroit's new municipal power plant. But shortly thereafter he was hit hard by the horseless carriage bug, and the direction of Ford's life was radically altered.[7]

Just when Henry Ford built his first automobile is still a source of confusion, although authorities in the field now agree that the year in which it was completed and tested was 1896. In the fall of 1901, *Motor Age,* in the first extended notice concerning Ford that appeared in that Chicago journal, reported: "Mr. Ford began to dabble in autos 5 years ago," that is, in 1896. Two years later, however, in December 1903, the magazine *Automobile* initiated a series of inaccuracies by declaring that Ford had "turned his attention to automobile construction" in 1891 "and built a two-cylinder gasoline machine after his own designs." In 1895, the magazine continued, Ford had constructed a second vehicle. David T. Wells, in a review of the auto industry that he wrote in 1907, listed 1892 as the year Ford started work on a car and 1893 as the year he "came into the industry." In 1909, however, the *Cycle and Automobile Trade Journal* returned to 1891 as the date of Ford's first car, and compounded the error by labeling it the first car built in Detroit. By 1916, when James Rood Doolittle's history of the automobile industry appeared, 1893 had become the accepted date, which led Doolittle to credit Ford with having been the second American to build an operable gasoline vehicle; Doolittle had arrived at that conclusion after taking as gospel Charles Duryea's equally fictitious claim to having completed such a vehicle in 1892. (Further confusion was added at this time when Peter Clark MacFarlane declared that the car Ford completed in 1893 had been a steam car, a claim that Eugene Lewis was repeating as late as 1947.) Although Edward D. Kennedy was still using the 1893 date in his study of the industry published in 1941, the facts were being sorted out by that time; by 1943, William Simonds, in his authorized biography of Ford, placed this event in 1896. Unsuspecting authors in other fields, however, continued to use the erroneous information.[8]

This confusion of dates originated with the Ford Motor Company, which, a month and a half after its incorporation in June 1903, made the advertising claim:

> We are the pioneers of the GASOLINE AUTOMOBILE. Our Mr. Ford made the first Gasoline Automobile in Detroit and the third in the United States. His machine made in 1893 is still in use.

As we have seen, by the end of 1903 the date of this first car had been pushed back to 1891. Then in 1904, in sworn testimony, Ford stated that he had completed this automobile sometime in the winter of 1891-92, but had not driven it until 1893; these statements were presented in a more formal manner in his autobiography in 1922. At that time, Ford declared that he drove the machine, "the first and for a long time the only automobile in Detroit," for a total of about a thousand miles between 1893 and 1896.[9]

There is absolutely no creditable support for these claims. The newspaper stories concerning Charles King's test drive in March 1896 make it clear that no other gasoline motor vehicle at that time was known to have preceded King's on the streets of Detroit, certainly none that was driven as openly and as frequently as Ford claimed to have driven his. Ford's distortions of the truth must have been intentional at the outset, although perhaps later in life, like Charles King, he began to believe the story he had been repeating for so many years. Pre-dating his work was no doubt part of the new Ford Motor Company's effort to prove to the public that the man responsible for the company's cars had as much or more experience in building automobiles as any other designer in the country. The assertion that Henry Ford was successfully operating a gasoline-powered vehicle prior to the time that George B. Selden was granted his patent on November 5, 1895, certainly did have something to do with strengthening Ford's position in the suit that was begun against the company in 1903 by the holders of the Selden Patent. Whatever their origins, however, Ford's actions have had serious consequences for the historian who seeks to deal with this aspect of automotive history. Since Ford's recollections are the main source, and, in many instances, the only source of information on his activities prior to 1896, the demonstrably false nature of his claims regarding his first automobile cannot be excused or passed off as of little importance, as biographers such as Allan Nevins have

done; if we cannot believe what Ford says in this instance, we must likewise doubt the accuracy of other statements not corroborated by reliable
sources.[10]

After examining the record of Henry Ford's earlier work with due
skepticism, therefore, it seems plausible to assume, as Anne Jardim has
done, that Ford's initial interest was in engines, not vehicles. He had had
experience in operating, repairing, and, if he is to be believed, in building
steam engines, and he claimed that he had repaired an Otto gas engine
at the Eagle Iron Works in Detroit by 1885, and to have built such an
engine from scratch in 1887 (or was it 1890, as Ford said on another
occasion). He was sufficiently knowledgeable about engines in 1891 to be
hired by the Edison company and, later, to be given the chief responsibility for keeping its engines in operating condition. According to Ford and
others associated with him during these years (whose recollections, it
should be noted, were not recorded until fifty or sixty years later), Ford
experimented with gasoline engines in his spare time on the job at Edison
in a portion of the plant that he had appropriated.

In his experiments, Henry Ford demonstrated one of his most valuable talents — getting others to work for him. Whatever his personality
may have become in later years, in his younger days Ford had a friendly,
engaging nature that drew fellow workers to him like a magnet, as one
of them put it, and made them want to help on his projects. Even as a
boy, his sister recalled, Henry had only to tell his schoolmates of his
ideas for a water wheel and primitive steam turbine to get them to pitch
in and build it "very willingly." Similarly, a constant theme running
through stories concerning the mature Ford is of others busily engaged
in working on one of Ford's newest ideas, while Ford himself sits and
watches. "I never saw Mr. Ford make anything," recalled one blacksmith
who worked with Ford in the 1890's. "He was always doing the directing."
Some of those who knew him depict Ford as essentially nothing but an
idea man who required the skills of others to make his ideas a reality.
This view, which foreshadows that of such critics as John Kenneth Galbraith, overlooks other evidence that Ford possessed real mechanical ability;
even more important, the description obscures the fact that this is the
same role that Ransom Olds came to play in his automobile companies,
and, in fact, is one that any executive must come to if he is not to be
overwhelmed by the burden of carrying out a myriad of detailed tasks
that could be turned over to assistants. This characteristic was, in fact,
William C. Durant's greatest weakness as an administrator, one that prevented him, more than anything else, from fully mobilizing the resources
of General Motors; Henry Ford, however, showed real adeptness in the
early years of the Ford Motor Company in locating able assistants and in
giving them the responsibility of implementing his ideas. This had as
much to do with the success of the Ford company in these years as Durant's desire to be the decision-maker on all matters had to do with G.M.'s
failure for many years to live up to its potential.[11]

With the advice and assistance not only of his fellow Edison workers, but of others, especially Charles King and Oliver Barthel whom Ford came to know when he took Edison repair work to John Lauer's machine shop, Ford had succeeded by the early part of 1896 in building a gasoline engine that could be used in a road vehicle. One story, which was related by Ford late in life and has become the accepted tradition in the Ford family, has it that he first tested this two-cylinder engine on Christmas Eve, 1893, in the kitchen of the house that he, his wife Clara, and seven-week-old son Edsel had recently moved into at 58 Bagley Avenue. If Ford was correct in his recollection of the date of the test, it seems to rule out any possibility that he had had a gasoline motor vehicle operating in the spring of 1893, as he had earlier claimed. However, Barthel and King insisted in their reminiscences that Ford did not build this engine until the winter of 1895-96. Both declared that Ford received some inspiration from an engine designed by Edward Joel Pennington, the individual on whom Robert Elston of Charlevoix was relying in 1895 to furnish the source of power for the vehicle he had built. Barthel believed that Ford did not begin work on an engine until early in 1896, using as a guide an article published in January of that year describing Pennington's engine. King told Charles Duryea in 1915 that Ford had built his engine sometime around the end of 1895; in 1940 King recalled in detail how he had helped test Ford's engine one evening in his kitchen, much to Clara Ford's annoyance. Edsel, who was around two years old at that time, King said, was sleeping in a bedroom directly off the kitchen, and Mrs. Ford feared the effects that the noise and the gasoline fumes would have on the baby. King and Ford persevered in the test until about three in the morning, and the noise finally did awaken Edsel, but, as Clara laughingly told the men, the boy, not apparently realizing what had disturbed him, and thinking instead that he was keeping himself awake, had said to his mother, "Ain't Edsel a terror?" The similarities in the accounts of the kitchen experiments as given by Ford and King suggest that they were referring to the same event. However, if Edsel Ford was old enough to talk, the test must have taken place about the date King recalled and not in 1893, as Ford contended.[12]

Having found a suitable power plant, probably in 1896, Ford proceeded with the construction of a motor vehicle. Again he drew upon King for help and materials. Ford also followed closely King's progress on a gasoline-powered machine. According to Barthel, when King and Barthel made their test drive in March 1896, Ford followed them on a bicycle. According to claims and reports, Ford also had a half dozen or more men who assisted in various ways on his motor vehicle, which was put together in a shop behind Ford's Bagley Avenue home. As it finally emerged, the vehicle was a lightweight machine, weighing only five hundred pounds, considerably lighter than either Charles King's or Ransom Olds' vehicles that also had their debuts in 1896. Ford referred to the car as a quadricycle, an appropriate term since in its construction he drew more on the

Henry Ford — *a handsome, self-assured figure in his 1896 quadricycle around 1902.*
Courtesy Motor Vehicle Manufacturers Association

arts of the bicycle maker and far less on those of the carriage maker than was customary among American auto pioneers. Tiny as the finished car was, however, it was too wide to get through the door of the shed for the test drive Ford and his chief assistant, Jim Bishop, planned for the pre-dawn hours of June 4. Undeterred by his apparent miscalculation, Ford took an axe and knocked out enough of the brick wall to allow the quad-ricycle to pass out into the dark, rainy night. With Bishop out ahead on his bicycle, Ford started up the engine, took hold of the steering lever, and moved down the cobblestone alley and around a couple of blocks to Washington Boulevard where the car stopped dead. Ford and Bishop located the source of the problem, got the part they needed from the Edison plant just down the street, got the car going again and drove back to Bagley Avenue where Clara Ford served the men breakfast.[13]

Although the newspapers, if they knew of the event, ignored Ford's trial run, others were soon aware of what Ford had accomplished since he continued to drive the vehicle about town. Early in July, while Charles King was away on vacation, his secretary wrote to him: "A great many people speak about Ford's rig. Causing quite a show." In August, King mentioned Ford in correspondence he had with E. P. Ingersoll, although the latter at this time made no mention of Ford or his automobile in the columns of *Horseless Age.* King also went with Ford when he gave the car its first long-distance test, a drive of nine miles out to visit Ford's father on his farm in Dearborn. The father was not impressed, King recalled, nor, apparently, were the neighbors who came over to see what William Ford's son had built.

> I could see that old Mr. Ford was ashamed of a grown-up man like Henry fussing over a little thing like a quadricycle. We'd gone and humiliated him in front of his friends. Henry stood it as long as he could, then he turned to me and said, in a heartbroken way, "Come on, Charlie, let's you and me get out of here."

Henry's sister, recalling a visit during this period, remembered that her father refused to get in the car or to allow his son to take him for a ride. The conservative farmer, she said, "saw no reason why he should risk his life at that time for a brief thrill from being propelled over the road in a carriage without horses."[14]

Despite such evidence that William Ford still disapproved of his son's decision to abandon the life of a farmer for that of a mechanic, Sidney Olson in his *Young Henry Ford* contends that this was not the case at all. "The facts are that William constantly jogged in to Detroit . . . to see what his son was up to; and he followed the progress of the car with the keenest interest." Anne Jardim goes further and asserts that it was Henry Ford who, for a reason she believes is the key to understanding his inner psychological workings, circulated what she also thinks are false stories of the father's alleged hostility toward his son's work.[15]

Ford's resentment at his father's attitude, whether real or imagined, perhaps explains the almost filial way in which Ford came to idolize Thomas Edison. At the annual convention of the Association of Edison Illuminating Companies, held in New York City in August 1896, Ford first met the great inventor and received from him strong encouragement to proceed with his work on gasoline motor vehicles. Ford had gone to the convention as one of three delegates sent by the Edison Illuminating Company of Detroit. At a dinner on August 12, Alex Dow, the new general manager of the Detroit plant, mentioned to the others seated around the table, including Edison: "This young fellow here has made a gas car." It may be that Dow was hoping that the reaction this information would stir up among the assembled advocates of electric power would induce Ford to give up this hobby and concentrate his attention upon what could obviously have been a promising career in the electric light industry. Instead of ridiculing Ford's work, however, Thomas Edison expressed an immediate interest in hearing more from Ford about what he was doing. After the Detroiter had given him a detailed explanation, Edison reportedly slammed his fist on the table and cried: "Young man, that's the thing; you have it. Keep at it!" Ford declared later: "That bang on the table was worth worlds to me. No man up to then had given me any encouragement . . . [but] here . . . out of a clear sky the greatest inventive genius in the world had given me complete approval."[16]

Ford himself, however, was not satisfied with what he had thus far accomplished. He continued to make changes in his first car, particularly in its body. To further these ends, he used his hiring authority as chief engineer at Edison to bring into the plant a Scotsman, David Bell, apparently because he learned that Bell was an experienced carriage blacksmith. Ford immediately took Bell to a basement shop next to the Edison plant where Ford had brought the quadricycle. Bell spent several weeks, he recalled, rebuilding parts of the vehicle (whether on company time or Ford's time is not clear). By the end of 1896, however, Ford had apparently sold the quadricycle to Charles Annesley and was beginning to develop a second vehicle. At this time, however, no matter how much he tried to cut corners by persuading others to work for him voluntarily, by getting scrap parts from the Edison shop, and in other ways saving money, Ford's experiments were putting a severe strain on him financially. His job paid well, but the expenses involved in building a car, which had caused similar delays in Charles King's work, took all that was left from Ford's pay after the family's living expenses, and soon the cost of his automotive work was eating up the family's savings. Fortunately, before long Ford found his financial angel in the person of William Cotter Maybury.[17]

Thousands of individuals each day pass by a statue of Maybury in Detroit's Grand Circus Park. Few, if any of them know who Maybury was, but the statue attests to the affection in which he was held by an earlier

William C. Maybury (*his mustache was not always as untidy as in this picture*), *whose support was crucial to the subsequent success of Henry Ford's automotive plans.*
Courtesy Burton Historical Collection

generation of Detroiters who remembered him primarily for his service as mayor of the city from 1897 to 1905. His political career, his highly successful law practice, and his activities as a Mason and an Episcopal layman dominate the biographical sketches of Maybury. In retrospect, however, nothing that Maybury did as city attorney, two-term Congressman, or mayor remotely approaches in importance the boost that he gave, at relatively little cost to himself, to the career of Henry Ford.[18]

The interest that William Maybury, Detroit's most popular Democrat, showed in Ford was a result of family connections. William Ford and Maybury's father, Thomas, were from the same town in Ireland, had migrated to Michigan in the 1830's within two years of each other, and had maintained close contact thereafter. It was in Thomas Maybury's Detroit home that William Ford and Mary Litogot were married in 1861. Young William Maybury, who was then either twelve or thirteen years old (biographies disagree as to his birthdate), very likely attended the wedding. Years later, therefore, when Henry Ford first arrived in Detroit, both Thomas Maybury, who had become quite wealthy through fortunate land investments, and his son William, already well known and liked in the city and being "retained as counselor by important business corporations and representative capitalists," probably gave what help they could to their old friend's son. For example, in 1893, William Maybury wrote a letter of recommendation on Ford's behalf when he was seeking a position with the city power plant.[19]

Exactly how or when Maybury became interested in Ford's automotive activities is not clear. A story in the Detroit *Journal* in 1899 reviewing these activities stated that Ford had "explained his ideas to William C. Maybury. The mayor saw that Ford was working along promising lines and he encouraged the inventor." Ford has related the help he received from Maybury to the time of the mayor's political career. He told one biographer, William Simonds, that Maybury came around to see the quadricycle at a time when he must have been running for mayor, Ford recalled, "for we had a picture of him in the window." Ford also declared that when he got into difficulties with the police over the operation of his quadricycle, Mayor Maybury gave him a driving permit, which Ford claimed gave him "for a time . . . the distinction of being the only licensed chauffeur in America." Ford's biographers have assumed that these events, marking the start of Maybury's interest in Ford's work, occurred in 1896, when Ford was still operating the quadricycle, but this is not possible. The only election in which Maybury was a candidate in this period was in November 1897, when he was elected to his first full term as mayor. By then, however, Ford had long since disposed of his quadricycle. Moreover, since his second car was still incomplete, there was not much to show candidate Maybury if he had come around at that time. Although Maybury had been serving as mayor of Detroit since April 10, 1897, when he was named to fill the unexpired term of Hazen S. Pingree, and thus could have given Ford official permission to drive his car as early as April 1897, Ford probably had no car to drive at that time.[20]

However, there is solid evidence that Ford was getting tangible help from Maybury before the latter's mayoral career had begun. This help was related to Maybury's business career, on which the Maybury biographies are unaccountably silent. On January 9, 1897, Maybury, using the stationery of the Standard Life and Accident Insurance Company, of which he was the managing director, wrote to the proprietor of the Detroit Motor Company, in which Maybury also had a business interest, asking that "Mr. Ford" be loaned a lathe for some work Maybury said Ford was doing for him. A receipt from the Detroit Motor Company two days later shows that Ford picked up the lathe, plus numerous accessories. Despite what Maybury said, the equipment was not for anything Ford was doing for Maybury, but for the work in progress throughout Detroit on Ford's second motor vehicle. As the expenses mounted, Maybury also began paying some of the bills. It is reported that regularly each Saturday a check from Maybury was received by the J. Allan Gray Carriage Company, which did blacksmithing work on the second car and which refused to extend Ford any credit for work he wanted done. Maybury, we know, also paid the costs involved in the first patent that Ford obtained, the rights to which were then assigned to Maybury.[21]

At the latest in 1898, and very probably sometime in 1897, Maybury was getting together a group of individuals on an informal basis to provide increased financial support for Ford's experiments, with the ultimate goal of manufacturing Ford's automobile and thereby getting a tidy return. The group included Everett A. Leonard, an officer with Maybury in the Standard Life and Accident Insurance Company, and a local doctor, Benjamin Rush Hoyt, reportedly a personal friend of Maybury's. The fourth member of the group and the most interesting of those whom Maybury recruited was Ellery I. Garfield. Garfield's involvement in the early efforts to manufacture a Ford automobile is not in itself a new revelation. His name appears in the list of stockholders of the Detroit Automobile Company, formed in 1899, the first of three auto companies with which Henry Ford was associated. One or two Garfield letters, along with other materials in the Ford Archives, enabled Allan Nevins and Sidney Olson, Ford biographers, to discuss Garfield's role in the activities preceding the incorporation of this company.[22] However, neither they nor other Ford researchers seem to have examined a collection of the papers of William Maybury, preserved in Detroit's Burton Historical Collection, in which are found a series of letters from Garfield in the years 1898 and 1899 that add significantly to our knowledge of this individual and of the events in this period.

Garfield was connected with the Fort Wayne Electric Corporation, one of the major manufacturers of electrical equipment in the country. How Maybury came to be acquainted with Garfield cannot be determined for certain, but since the Fort Wayne firm had been deeply involved for nearly a decade with both public and private power interests in Detroit, Garfield might well have made the initial approach. Maybury's influence in the political and business world in Detroit would certainly have made him a good friend for the Fort Wayne company to have. In promoting such a development, Garfield might well have sought to humor Maybury by agreeing to put a few dollars into the Ford kitty. If so, however, he soon began to develop what was obviously a serious interest in the vehicle Ford was building.[23]

Sometime in 1898, Maybury, Garfield, Leonard, and Hoyt replaced an earlier oral agreement with a written contract (the surviving copy is not signed or dated) whereby each of the four men promised to provide five hundred dollars to help finance Ford's "motor-wagon," in addition to funds that they had "collectively advanced" previously to meet Ford's expenses. In return the four sought to obtain contractual control over Ford and the products of his labor. Ford's patents and the vehicles that he built were to be shared on a basis of one-third to Ford and two-thirds to his backers. If a corporation were formed "to manufacture the inventions of said Ford, Ford's employment on a fair compensation by said company shall enter into any agreement made." Ford agreed not to "sell or transfer any right or invention, or construct wagons, or any part thereof, for any person or persons in contravention of this contract."[24]

Ellery Garfield was the only non-Detroiter involved in this first formal step in support of Ford's work. Nevins and Olson assumed that Garfield was from Fort Wayne, Indiana, the headquarters of the Fort Wayne Electric Corporation. This would place him in the ranks of a host of other midwesterners whose willingness to take a chance on an unproven product has been cited as a major reason why the production of automobiles came to be centered in the Middle West rather than in other sections of the country. But Garfield was not operating out of Fort Wayne; his connections with that far-flung electrical firm were with its operations in Boston, Massachusetts. His letters, both in the Ford Archives and in the Maybury Papers, help to document not the venturesomeness of the midwesterner, which supposedly nurtured the growth of the auto industry in that area, but the cautiousness of the easterner that reputedly is a main reason for the failure of the industry in the East. In addition, Garfield's letters point to some of the quirks in Ford's personality that delayed for so long the dream of getting his car into the marketplace.

Garfield apparently first talked with Ford early in 1898 and then again when he was in Detroit in June of that year. In a letter to Maybury on August 1, which Nevins quotes, Garfield declared that he shared with Maybury the confidence the latter had expressed in Ford's ability. Furthermore, Garfield said, "I believe he has faith in himself and that is a great deal," an interesting contemporary evaluation that exactly parallels what William Simonds later described as one of Ford's principal assets. However, Garfield then tempered his optimism with the assertion that because of "all the failures there have been in experimenting with gasoline," Maybury and his associates should carefully examine other motor vehicles and compare them with Ford's to "see wherein his excels, and to what extent. I believe it would be money well invested. It might save us a heap of money hereafter, or it might give us such faith and confidence that we should go ahead and push the business and make ten times as much as what it would cost us."[25]

Other Garfield letters not previously used by students of Ford reveal that from this time on there was a noticeable increase in Garfield's dissatisfaction with Ford. On August 18, after another trip to Detroit, he wrote to Maybury from Boston and declared he had great reservations concerning Ford's motor wagon. He preferred electric or steam power, a preference that had been backed up by "Alex" (Garfield had a penchant for not revealing the full identity of his acquaintances), a friend in Paris, who Garfield claimed was an expert on automobiles. When he was queried by Garfield on the practicability of Ford's vehicle compared with an electric or steam vehicle, Alex had cabled back: "Do not advise Motor Wagon."[26]

Another letter from Garfield on October 26, 1898, is important because it indicates that a few days prior to that date Ford had his second car in some kind of operating condition, a fact about which there has previously been no certainty. Garfield, who had seen the car, was by no means happy with its performance, expressing the hope that Ford would eliminate "that horrible noise of the motor and . . . also get rid of that smell of the Gasoline," two criticisms of the gasoline automobile, incidentally, that were most widely voiced by opponents of this type of vehicle. Garfield speculated that some of the misgivings he now had concerning Ford's work might have been "brought about by the unfortunate frame of mind that [Ford] is in," a puzzling and otherwise unexplained reference to Ford's mental state, which could well have been affected by the pressures and strain that bore down on him during these months when he seems to have worked harder than at any other time in his life.

In November, as noted earlier, news of Ford's successes first reached a wider audience with the brief mention of his work in *Horseless Age,* which reported that Ford was financially backed by "several prominent" Detroiters who intended to manufacture the car, a subject on which Ford, the magazine said, had no comment to make. Two months later, in letters to Maybury dated January 16 and 21, 1899, Garfield, despite his expressed reservations about Ford's work, reported that he was seeking to interest "moneyed friends" in the East to add their weight to the group backing Ford. However, he urged Maybury to use all of his persuasive powers to get Ford to speed up his tests of the vehicle. "I think you cannot have any true idea of the number of Motor Wagon Co's that are starting up," Garfield wrote, six months before Ray Stannard Baker dwelled on the automotive boom of 1899 in *McClure's.* "A week does not pass by," Garfield declared, "that I do not learn of two or three companies." Further delays on Ford's part, Garfield feared, could lead his eastern friends to turn their attention to one of the other numerous automobile ventures.

These letters were followed by one on January 27 of eight pages, typed on the letterhead of the Boston Electric Light Company, in which Garfield entered into his most extended discussion of the merits of Ford's new car, an examination that caused him to feel "a little worried about the prospect." He also refused to honor an appeal from Everett Leonard, "which I presume," Garfield told Maybury, "was written by your request," asking for a fifty-dollar contribution to help replenish the Ford experimental support funds, which had almost been exhausted. From this letter we learn that Maybury had talked with Ford about the tests that Garfield wanted him to conduct, but that Ford, "sanguine as ever," had made no definite commitments. Garfield meanwhile had gone ahead on his own, obtaining independent appraisals of Ford's machine from outside experts, whose identities he again chose not to divulge completely. It is clear from the quotations that he gives from one expert, Mr. H., that he was referring to R. W. Hannington, an engineer from Denver who worked for Charles Duryea for several months in 1897 and then, after breaking off that association, had made an effort "to see every motor wagon that was then being attempted." In Detroit he had an hour's talk with Ford and, without Ford's knowledge, had also carefully examined the latter's second car. His report, dated December 28, 1898, is in the Ford Archives[27] and is generally quite favorable, as were the other three reports that Garfield discussed in his letter of January 27. Both Hannington and another of Garfield's consultants, however, mentioned that there was nothing novel in Ford's machine.

The lack of novelty seemed to bother Garfield somewhat, but what upset him far more was Ford's failure to complete his work. "The report to us is that the wagon is all ready, except some one little thing, and when this is fixed it will be all right. When this little thing is fixed, there is something else, and so it goes, and has been going for a long time." Garfield declared that when he was last in Detroit Ford had told him there were two things remaining to be fixed on the car, and that when these adjustments were finished, which Ford had assured him would take only a few days, "he would be ready to start for Boston with the carriage, and would go clear through without a break down." Now, however, Ford was telling Everett Leonard that as soon as he finished with some other improvements "he will have the best wagon in existence." Garfield fumed: "It is the same old story."

Garfield's proposal was that within thirty days Ford turn his wagon over to Maybury with a statement that it was ready to be used. Ford was also to consent to an impartial outside appraisal by "some good honest mechanic" who would drive the car fifty miles a day for several days and report at the end of each day on the vehicle's performance. If Ford refused to consent to these tests, Garfield favored withdrawing support. The Winton company, he noted, was selling its vehicles, which were spoken of favorably. "If Mr. Ford has something that is better than anything in the field, he certainly should be willing to put it out, even if it is no better than the Winton carriage. If we wait until it is perfect," Garfield declared, "we never will see it." This sentiment was to be repeated, in one form or another, time and again by Ford's various backers in the next four and a half years.

Ellery Garfield concluded his long letter to Maybury with the expression of his confidence that if the tests he proposed were conducted and the results were satisfactory, it would take him, in Boston, no more than forty-eight hours to raise the money needed to form a company to manufacture the vehicle. On the other hand, Garfield said, perhaps "it would be a good idea for all hands to sell out to those people about whom we talked when I was in Detroit, and get our money back." A few months later, on June 2, Garfield may have regretted that he had not pushed harder for the latter course of action. The best months of the year for selling automobiles had slipped by, and still they were no nearer to manufacturing Ford's wagon. "You must realize," he told Maybury, "that I am in a very awkward fix here with my friends. I have made so many promises that have not materialized that they are losing faith in the carriage and me too, I am afraid."

If there was a real possibility in the first half of 1899 that the incipient Ford auto enterprise would be taken over by Garfield's eastern business friends, that possibility was eliminated during the summer by a powerful group of Detroit capitalists, perhaps the people mentioned by Garfield in his letter of January 27; these businessmen moved in to form and seize control of the Detroit Automobile Company, which was organized a few weeks after another group of Detroiters had obtained the major stock interest in the Olds Motor Works. Thus the East, which reportedly had had a chance to control the Olds company, lost a second chance to control what would eventually be a much more important automobile enterprise.

The Detroit Automobile Company filed articles of incorporation with the secretary of state in Lansing on July 31, 1899. It was capitalized at $150,000, a modest enough figure when one considers the multi-million-dollar stock companies that were being formed elsewhere at this time to manufacture automobiles, or, closer to home, the half-million-dollar Olds Motor Works. On the same day that the Detroit company's papers were filed, papers were also filed for the Omega Portland Cement Company in Jonesville, with an authorized capitalization of $350,000. A boom in the cement industry was attracting great attention at this time in Michigan, and it is probable that shrewd investors would have leaned toward the Jonesville firm rather than toward a company proposing to manufacture a product whose permanent appeal was still in some doubt.[28]

The one aspect of the Detroit Automobile Company that would likely have impressed the business world was its list of stockholders. In addition to Maybury, Leonard, Hoyt, and the long-suffering Garfield, who were among the charter investors, the list was headed by Colonel Frank J. Hecker, one of Detroit's best-known and wealthiest businessmen, whose fortune had been made in the manufacture of railroad cars. Hecker was closely associated with another railroad car manufacturer, Senator James McMillan, particularly after the two merged their companies, which consolidation was absorbed in 1899 by the American Car and Foundry Company. It is McMillan, indeed, who provided the main tangible link between most of the auto company's stockholders. Although the aging senator was not listed as owning any stock, his son William, who managed his father's affairs in Michigan, was down for a hundred shares. One hundred shares each were also purchased by Hecker, Frank W. Eddy, a director of several McMillan-controlled companies, and by Albert E. F. White, one of the four founders of the great D. M. Ferry seed company, of which James McMillan was vice-president. Smaller amounts of stock were obtained by Lem W. Bowen, treasurer of the Ferry company, and by Safford S. DeLano, whose father had been associated with McMillan in the railroad car industry since the 1860's. Other stockholders included an insurance salesman, Frank R. Alderman, Frederick S. Osborne, the head of the Detroit brokerage firm of Cameron, Currie & Company, Clarence A. Black, head of a wholesale hardware company and a power in the local Republican party, who was elected president of the new company, Mark Hopkins of St. Clair — all the other new investors were from Detroit — a close political ally of Senator McMillan and a founder of the Diamond Crystal Salt Company, and two men whose fortunes originally came from lumber, Patrick A. Ducey and William H. Murphy. Henry Ford was also given a small amount of stock, for which he put up no money. In addition to Black, other officers included White as vice-president, Murphy as treasurer, and Alderman as secretary; Ford, Eddy, and Bowen, along with these officers, comprised the board of directors.[29]

Few of the men who put money into this company were sticking their necks out very far. Only $15,000 in cash was paid in, representing 1500 shares of stock priced at ten dollars a share. For men like Hecker, McMillan, or Murphy, the thousand dollars that their one hundred shares presumably cost each of them was nothing but petty cash. Had they so desired, almost any of the stockholders could easily have put up the entire $15,000. Although they must have been familiar with the much larger investments that such neighbors and acquaintances as Samuel Smith, Henry Russel, and Henry Ledyard had made in the Olds automobile enterprise, Ford's backers had obviously not benefitted from the experience of Smith, who had learned that the few thousand dollars put into the Olds Motor Vehicle Company in 1897 was not an adequate base from which to begin manufacturing automobiles. Probably, however, most of the wealthy investors in Ford's company in 1899 did not give much serious thought to the matter. For them it was simply an interesting speculation which might pay off. If it failed, they would not be losing much.

Who it is that deserves credit for assembling this impressive cross-section of Detroit's influential business and political leaders is not clear. As in the case of the Olds companies, where one can discern a definite link between Edward Sparrow's group that supplied most of the initial outside backing and Samuel Smith's group that came into dominance in 1899, one can also find certain connections between Maybury's group, which had nursed Ford's experiments along for two years, and the larger new group of investors. A somewhat tenuous business relationship can be seen in the Standard Life and Accident Insurance Company, where the fathers of both William Murphy and Lem Bowen were officers with Maybury and Leonard. More important, however, during his career in law, politics, and business extending back to 1871, Maybury had come to know all or nearly all of the new investors. The fact that Maybury and the McMillan forces were in opposite political camps was no impediment. It is clear that both groups were careful to keep political preferences from interfering with the continued prosperity of their business interests. The fact that Maybury was now mayor and at the height of his political career and influence may well have been an asset to him in persuading some of his business acquaintances to invest in the company. This is only speculation, but from Ellery Garfield's letters we know that in the fall of 1898 Maybury was discussing with his associates a proposition from another group that was interested in putting money into a company to back Ford. Whether this was the same group that invested in the Detroit Automobile Company in the summer of 1899 we cannot say, nor do we know for certain what Maybury's role in these negotiations may have been. It appears, however, that William Maybury deserves the major share of credit for having carefully fostered this automobile venture from its tentative beginnings in 1896 until its full-fledged emergence three years later.

Some writers have concluded that Henry Ford, besides developing the automobile, had something to do with gathering the needed support from investors. Ford was no outcast, Sidney Olson declares. "Doors did not slam on him; they were opened to him." Ford, he believes, had been as successful in making friends among businessmen as he had been among his fellow workers, and he had been just as successful in getting the former to open their wallets as he had been in getting his less affluent friends to take up a wrench on his behalf. If this is true, it effectively demolishes any thoughts that Ford was the typical lonely inventor — ahead of his time, laughed at and scorned by all but his wife and a few devoted followers. Although it may be true that Ford does not conform to that particular stereotype, neither is there any solid evidence to show that he had anything to do with persuading anyone except Maybury to support the new enterprise. Indeed, Ford never claimed that he had done so. In his autobiography, he devoted only a paragraph to the Detroit Automobile Company, which, he said, was organized by "a group of men of speculative turn of mind . . . to exploit my car," an accurate enough description, and he made no mention of any efforts he himself may have made to secure the support of these individuals. His most sympathetic biographer, William

Simonds, much of whose information came directly from Ford, likewise depicts the company as developing not through Ford's initiative, but through that of others; the "chief promoter," Simonds asserts, was Frank Alderman. Whether this is what Ford told Simonds is not clear. It is quite likely that this is a conclusion Simonds arrived at through reading the newspapers from the period 1899-1900 where Secretary Alderman was often referred to as the spokesman for the company.[30]

Actually, the only new inventor in 1899 whose name has definitely been tied with Ford is William H. Murphy, who succeeded Maybury as Ford's most faithful supporter. Murphy's father, Simon J. Murphy, a prosperous Maine lumberman, had come to Michigan in the mid-sixties, when his son was about ten years old, to take charge of his lumber holdings in the state. Later, Simon Murphy extended his lumber operations to Wisconsin and California, and then broadened his multi-million-dollar business interests through investments in iron and copper mining, electric power, oil, cattle ranching, fruit growing, and real estate, especially in Detroit. In addition, he had been one of the original large investors in the Edison Illuminating Company as well as serving on the board of the Standard Life and Accident Insurance Company.[31]

Murphy's son William was given increasingly more important responsibilities in the management of the family's numerous businesses, but he still found time for other interests. Music became a life-long love, despite a severe impairment of hearing that had afflicted him since childhood. William Murphy also developed a fascination with horseless carriages; he once purchased a steam-powered fire engine for the Detroit Fire Department, but, as Murphy recalled, it was discarded when the operators found that sparks from the engine's exhaust were starting more fires than the engine and its crews were extinguishing. (Murphy's recollections may not have been entirely accurate. The Detroit historian, Silas Farmer, writing in the mid-eighties, reported that Detroit had purchased in 1874 the third self-propelled steam fire engine produced in the country. If this was the machine that Murphy had acquired for the city, it was not abandoned after a short time but was still in use a decade later.) No doubt Murphy had followed closely the progress of Henry Ford's experiments with vehicles, but it was not until 1899 that Ford is said to have discussed his work with Murphy. The latter reportedly told Ford that if his car was good enough to drive Murphy from his home in Detroit out to Farmington. over to Pontiac, and back home again, he would be interested in helping to establish a company to manufacture it. Sometime later Ford came around and took Murphy for that ride, with Murphy keeping a log in which he noted how the vehicle performed all along the way. Satisfied with the results, Murphy then supposedly told Ford: "Well, now we will organize the company."

Murphy's son-in-law, J. Bell Moran, who inherited this undated log, assumed that the trip was made in 1899, preceding the formation of the Detroit Automobile Company. However, an entry in a diary kept by

Clara Ford in 1901 shows that Ford and Murphy made a trip over the very same Detroit-Farmington-Pontiac route one afternoon in April of that year, by which time the Detroit Automobile Company had been dissolved. It is possible, of course, that Ford and Murphy took the same trip together twice, in 1899 and 1901. But there is an added complication: the information Moran gives regarding the number of associates who joined Murphy in the company that was formed following the trip, the amount of money they invested, and the amount of stock assigned to Ford, corresponds closely to what is known concerning the organization of the Henry Ford Company, which Murphy did indeed form later in 1901. The same details, as Moran gives them, do not jibe at all with those surrounding the formation of the Detroit Automobile Company. It seems likely, therefore, that the trip Murphy logged took place in the spring of 1901, and that his remarks at the conclusion of the trip, as Moran heard them repeated years later, referred to the action that would lead to the formation of the second, not the first, auto company with which Ford was affiliated.[32]

Like all of these early automobile enterprises, the Detroit Automobile Company started off with great expectations that, as was also all too frequently the case, were never realized. Once the company was safely established, Ford resigned his position with the Edison company to accept the job of mechanical superintendent with the auto company at a salary of $150 a month, equal to what he had been receiving at the power company. Alex Dow valued Ford's services and offered him a better job in an effort to keep him on with Edison. For his part, Ford is said to have twice tried to persuade Dow to invest in the automobile company. Each refused the other's proposal and went his separate way. By August 19, Ford and a few workmen had begun to occupy a building on Cass Avenue, formerly occupied by William Maybury's Detroit Motor Company. The auto firm took a three-year lease on the building. Secretary Frank Alderman announced that before the end of the year from 100 to 150 men would be employed manufacturing cars, the first of which he predicted would be ready by October 1. Ford's car was praised highly, especially by the Detroit Journal, which, in a lengthy illustrated story on July 29, referred to the automobile as a "novel machine" (something Ellery Garfield's experts had failed to detect earlier). Among other features, Ford was said to have eliminated the bothersome problems of smell and noise that Garfield had complained about the previous fall.[33]

The first of October came and went, without any cars appearing from the Cass Avenue factory. By the end of 1899 no passenger cars had yet been produced, although sketches of the company's surrey and its "hydrocarbon Phaeton" appeared in the December 14 issue of Motor Age. By this time, however, Ford and his handful of men, closer to ten in number than the one hundred or more talked of earlier, had about completed a tall, narrow, rather awkward-looking delivery wagon, on which Ford had apparently been working for close to a year. A Detroit newsman reported that winter on a rather harrowing drive he took in the vehicle with Ford, who seems to have found it amusing to scare the wits out of his passengers. Although the wagon was reportedly produced for one of the larger stores in Detroit, the only use to which it seems to have been put was an experimental mail run by the Detroit Post Office, a test that was pronounced a success but which did not lead to any demand for additional wagons.[34]

Frank Alderman explained in January 1900 that his company had held off taking orders for its vehicles until their "reliability and trustworthiness" had been thoroughly proven. These tests had been virtually completed, apparently, and he could, therefore, promise that they would soon have on the market a surrey, runabout, trap, phaeton, and physician's stanhope. But in February, a somewhat chastened Alderman, admitting that the fulfillment of his promises had again been postponed, remarked to one reporter: "You would be surprised at the amount of detail about an automobile." The following month, an unidentified official, noting the company's past practice of trying to set a date when automobiles would be available, declared that "we have concluded to stop that nonsense. We are making a machine that is easily controlled, solidly and perfectly constructed, and generating the greatest power with the least expense." Superintendent Ford and his staff, now numbering thirty men, were continuing to test the machine under all conditions, even on streets piled with two or three feet of snow, in which instance Ford reportedly "had no difficulty at all" in operating the car. Manufacturing would begin only after these tests had been satisfactorily completed.[35]

A report in *Horseless Age* in April 1900 that the company had twelve vehicles under construction would seem to have indicated that the manufacturing stage of the operations had finally commenced. It is doubtful, however, if any of these cars was ever completed, although there are conflicting reports as to whether the Detroit Automobile Company completed and sold any vehicle besides the one delivery truck. Regardless, the company's prospects obviously took a turn for the worse sometime in the spring of 1900. In a move clearly intended to cut expenses, part of the building that the company had rented was sub-leased to the C. R. Wilson Body Company. Finally, however, with almost nothing to show for over a year's work and with the costs of the operation approaching $86,000, the directors held a meeting to discuss their next move. Ford ducked the meeting, telling Fred Strauss, one of his workers, to answer any inquiry with the statement that Ford had gone out of town. Strauss relayed the message to the directors and recalled, a half century later, that there had been some disagreement among the directors and other stockholders present about what they should do. "Colonel Hecker," Strauss declared, "wanted to throw in the sponge. He said everything was going too slow." Frank Alderman, no longer the sunny optimist, apparently sided with Hecker. On the other hand, William Murphy and Mark Hopkins wanted to keep going, but to reduce the operations to an experimental basis again. Their view prevailed. When the question arose as to what to do with the vehicles that were then in various stages of construction, Hopkins said: "Throw all that stuff out, burn it, get rid of it." Accordingly, the next day Strauss and Charlie Mitchell, a blacksmith, "took sledge hammers and busted all these beautiful bodies. Then we burned them under the engine-room boilers." Although Henry Ford shortly came out of hiding and began tinkering in the small experimental shop in the front of the building that was all the company now occupied, the destruction of the unfinished vehicles really marked the end of the Detroit Automobile Company. It was probably at this time that the state factory inspector came around and found only five men on the payroll. Some stockholders began selling out for whatever they could get. William Maybury still had some faith in Ford, for he added to his stockholdings at this time. But finally a majority of the remaining investors decided, as Colonel Hecker had advised earlier, "to throw in the sponge." In January 1901, notice of the dissolution of the company was filed in Lansing.[36]

A number of reasons can be cited for the failure of the Detroit Automobile Company. The inexperience of the workers and the failure of suppliers to come up with the required parts at the expected time were the causes of some of the delays. The initial outlay of cash had not been adequate, but this was not a real deterrent to progress since individual stockholders, particularly, it appears, William Murphy, had been willing to take care of the bills during the period when there was still no income to offset the production costs. Clearly, the overriding cause of the company's lack of success was Henry Ford. By the summer of 1899, he had apparently developed his second automobile to the point where it was a reasonably good product by the standards of its day. Those who agreed to back him at this time must have received some assurance from Ford as to the acceptability of the vehicle and that, in Ford's opinion, it could be manufactured and sold. On this understanding Ford was hired to supervise the manufacturing operation. Some delay could be expected while Ford learned how to produce more than one automobile at a time, but the delays that occurred seem to have been the result of Ford's second thoughts about the adequacy of the vehicles. Preston M. Hulbert, a member of the Detroit patent law firm that handled Ford's patent applications as well as those of many other auto pioneers, including Olds, Buick, King, and Benjamin Briscoe, was a frequent visitor to the Detroit Automobile plant in the winter of 1899-1900 and watched the progress of the Ford commercial vehicle.

> After working about a week in getting the car together, adding a part here and there and cutting off other parts, it was finally ready for trial. . . . I remember Henry Ford getting in the seat, starting the motor and driving around the room, dodging the posts and incidentally a black cat that happened to be in the way. At the end of a short time something went wrong and he got out to look things over. He had a very serious expression on his face, but after a few minutes turned to his workmen and said, "Come on, boys, we'll have to try it over again."

Thus it was that new reasons were continually advanced by Ford to justify additional tests before production could proceed. The new stock-holders began to fret at the same kind of delaying tactics that had proven so annoying to Ellery Garfield a year earlier. Ford fooled his backers for a time, according to Fred Strauss, by having his men busily engaged in making parts which were actually not intended to be used for anything. Subsequently, in 1900, when some of Ford's backers became impatient at the lack of progress and began to pressure Ford, he apparently persuaded himself that by refusing to allow him enough time to develop an improved car, the stockholders had shown themselves to be nothing but money-grubbers, caring nothing for the quality of the product so long as it sold. Consequently, Ford seems to have felt absolved from the commitments he had made when he accepted the job of superintendent. Thus, accord-ing to the view that Ford expressed later in his autobiography, the re-sponsibility for the dissolution of the Detroit Automobile Company rested not with him but with the short-sighted investors whose "main idea seemed to be to get money."[37]

The remarkable part of this story, and the part that Ford's detrac-tors cannot explain adequately, is that after losing the support of such men as Frank Hecker, Mayor Maybury, and William McMillan, Ford was not finished in the automobile business. The reason seems to have been that his confidence in himself was undiminished. No matter what the truth may be as to the actual abilities and talents possessed by Ford, it was the impression he gave of a confident man, sure of himself and cer-tain that the wisdom of his principles would ultimately be recognized, that enabled him to retain the support of Murphy, Black, Bowen, White, and Hopkins after the Detroit Automobile Company went by the boards. When these five also lost faith in him in 1902, that same image enabled him to attract support from still another group of investors who financed the Ford Motor Company in 1903.

By 1903, however, Ford had a long way to go to catch up with other Detroit automobile companies which were making that city the talk of the motor world. Among these companies, the most famous was the Olds Motor Works, and no one in the industry was better known than the man who was regarded as responsible for that company's remarkable success — Ransom E. Olds.

CHAPTER 5

"THE OLDSMOBILE — BUILT TO RUN, AND DOES IT!"

In the winter of 1899-1900, with the opening of its factory in Detroit, the reorganization of the various Olds enterprises was completed. The Olds Motor Vehicle Company officially went out of existence on February 29, 1900. In the same period steps were also taken to bring the management of the Olds Gasoline Engine Works more clearly under the control of the Olds Motor Works by moving the offices of the engine operation to Detroit, although the Lansing plant continued to manufacture engines. By the middle of March 1900, the Detroit Olds plant had over a hundred men involved in the various tasks related to vehicle construction. When the assembling of the vehicles begins, "by and by," *Motor Age* reported, it will be "an easy matter to put a goodly number on the market each week." (Actually, since the Detroit plant was also engaged in manufacturing the Olds gas and gasoline engines, this Chicago automotive journal probably exaggerated the emphasis that was being given to the construction of automobiles.)[1]

Unfortunately the details of the company's operations during this

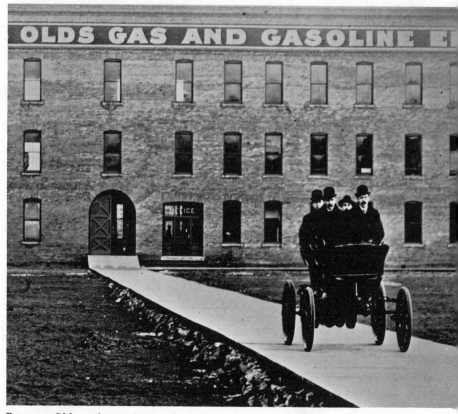

OLDS GAS AND GASOLINE E

Ransom Olds and associates *take an early model Oldsmobile out of the new Jefferson Avenue Olds plant.*
Courtesy Motor Vehicle Manufacturers Association

period cannot be documented adequately, but it is clear that Olds and his staff were still experimenting, seeking the model or models that would have the most commercial appeal. Olds later recalled that their plans were to "put out a model which would sell for $1250. I had it fitted up with some very up-to-the minute improvements — pneumatic clutch, cushion tires, electric push-button starter. We thought we had quite a car, but we soon found that it was too complicated for the public." This gasoline vehicle, however, was only one of eleven different cars that the company worked on in 1899 and 1900. A considerable amount of time was spent experimenting with electric cars, one of which, "a handsome electric stanhope," was the only automobile the company exhibited in September 1900, at a show in Chicago's Washington Park. Ransom Olds thus seems to have been the only one of the major auto pioneers to have explored all of the options available at that time to the builder of motor vehicles — steam, gasoline, and electric power.[2]

By 1900 the company had decided to call its motor vehicles Oldsmobiles, a trade name that followed in the wake of the Gasmobile, the Locomobile, the Mobile, and the Steamobile that other companies since

1898 had named the cars they were producing. One advertisement in 1900, although emphasizing the Olds engines, made reference to the "electric and gasoline Automobiles, Motor Trucks, Etc." that the company was also manufacturing, including a photograph of the Oldsmobile four-passenger "trap." Another advertisement from the same period indicated that most of the Oldsmobile models bore price tags ranging considerably beyond the $1250 price that Olds later recalled had been asked for his "up-to-the-minute" model. The electric stanhope sold for $1650, with an electric phaeton costing a hundred dollars extra. Gasoline models ranged all the way up to a four-passenger brougham model that was priced at $2750. How many of these vehicles were sold is not known. Edward D. Kennedy, in his history of the automobile industry written in 1941, stated that Olds sold four hundred cars between mid-1899 and the close of 1900, but this figure appears to be grossly inflated. Both Ransom Olds and Fred Smith in later years agreed that in this early period there were few sales for the vehicles they produced. The ledger for the automotive side of the business showed an outlay of $80,000 for the development of an acceptable product with little, if anything, to show in the way of income from sales to balance these expenses. The models that had been produced did not attract attention either because they were too expensive, or, if they were built at less cost, were not sufficiently durable. (It was perhaps one of the sturdier, more expensive Oldsmobiles of 1900 that was awarded a prize in 1922 by the National Automobile Chamber of Commerce as the second oldest car still in operation in the United States, being surpassed in age only by an 1899 Locomobile.) However, it seems certain that virtually all of the increase in sales — from $120,000 in 1899 to $186,000 in 1900 — was accounted for by the gasoline engine division. Although Fred Smith declared in 1928 that the profits gained from the sales of engines far offset the losses from automobiles, which, he said, were only "side issues" in 1900, the situation may not have looked so promising at the time to Smith, his father, Ransom Olds, and their fellow stockholders. How long could engine sales continue to subsidize the red-ink operations of the automobile department without jeopardizing the stability of the entire company?[3]

In the fall of 1900, therefore, "after a long sleepless night," Ransom Olds decided to return to the lightweight, relatively inexpensive type of motor vehicle he had been aiming at in 1896. He came into the office and told one of his engineers, Horace Loomis, according to the latter's account, "what we want to build is a small low down runabout that will have a shop cost around $300 and will sell for $650." Olds himself later claimed that he had wanted to develop a car that weighed five hundred pounds and would sell for $500. Actually, they finally came up with the curved-dash Oldsmobile that weighed seven hundred pounds and sold for $650. His "whole idea," Olds said, was to build a vehicle that would be so simple to operate "that anyone could run it and the construction such that it could be repaired at any local shop."[4]

Loomis took the sheets on which Olds had roughed out his ideas, and went to work on the final plan for the runabout; Milton Beck designed the engine, and Jonathan D. Maxwell, who, in 1894, had helped build the first Haynes-Apperson car, worked with Loomis on the transmission. By October the machine had been built and was being tested. In November Ransom Olds wrote to a correspondent in Texas that in addition to the $1200 Oldsmobile trap, "We are making a light Gasoline Runabout," not shown in the company's current catalogue. Olds said the new car would weigh about five hundred pounds and would sell for $600. That same price was quoted in the caption for a photograph of the runabout that appeared in a company brochure otherwise devoted to the Olds gasoline engine and published sometime in 1900. A special catalogue describing the runabout was distributed early in 1901. *Motor World* of February 7, 1901, reproduced from the brochure three photographs of what the magazine referred to as "the younger and more drylandish brother of the famous Olds marine motor." A somewhat similar story appeared in *Horseless Age* later that month and in *Motor Age* on March 6.[5]

With the debut of its gasoline runabout, Olds had introduced the car that not only would soon become the most popular car of its day, but would also have an impact on the American automobile industry and on the public that would be surpassed only by the Ford Model T. In February 1901, however, it would have been a far-sighted individual indeed who could have predicted such a future for this new car out of Detroit. In appearance this Oldsmobile was typical of the American automobile of the period in that it was, like such ancestors as the Duryea of 1893 and the King experimental wagon of 1896, literally a horseless carriage. Its most distinctive feature was its body, which, together with its frame and the rest of the motor vehicle, was patented by Ransom Olds later in 1901. The Oldsmobile body, however, was nothing but a copy of one of the standard horse-drawn carriage styles, as had been the case with the earlier Oldsmobile trap, stanhope, and brougham. Because of its curved front, the model for the Olds runabout is usually said to have been the cutter or sleigh body, but actually a runabout was a standard wheeled carriage style. The model was advertised in this period by various carriage manufacturers such as the Union Buggy Company of Pontiac, although its runabout had a straight, not a curved dash. The Oldsmobile curved-dash runabout may not have been the first runabout put out by the Olds Motor Works. An Oldsmobile ad that Floyd Clymer reproduces in his *Treasury of Early American Automobiles,* which, although it is not dated, must have appeared in 1899-1900, lists an Oldsmobile runabout at a price of $1000, $350 more than the list price of the curved-dash model when it was introduced. What this earlier runabout looked like is not known, but the 1900 Olds trap, although a larger vehicle, was quite similar in design to the 1901 curved-dash runabout, the major difference in the latter being that the curve in the dash that gave it its nickname was more pronounced than it had been in the trap.

Ransom Olds included these body design details in the rough plans for the new car that he turned over to his staff. Also included were the plans for the unusual suspension system; it provided the same comparatively vibration-free ride that had been one of the more advanced features of the first Olds gasoline vehicle in 1896. Like that earlier car, too, the runabout was powered by a one-cylinder gasoline engine, housed beneath the vehicle. (A few of the early curved-dash Oldsmobiles were electric-powered.) A crank on the right side, the driver's side, started the engine, which led the company to claim in ads for the car that it could be started by the operator while he was seated in the vehicle. Some have misinterpreted this claim as meaning that Olds had developed some kind of self-starting device a decade before Charles Kettering's invention of the first practical self-starter. The Oldsmobile was steered with a tiller that curved up from the floor towards the single seat that was provided in the runabout model. Initially, wire wheels with pneumatic tires were used, a change from the artillery-type wheels, with wooden spokes, which appear in the photograph of the 1900 Oldsmobile trap. The latter type of wheel, however, reappeared on later runabout models.[6]

At a time when some forward-looking European automobile manufacturers were turning out vehicles whose design was distinctive to the motor car, with the motor plainly evident at the front of the vehicle under a hood, the lines of the curved-dash Oldsmobile, like those of most American cars of that day, were distinctly reactionary. The bodies imitated the traditional designs of horse-drawn vehicles while trying to disguise as much as possible the fact that these were machines rather than horse-propelled carriages. Even among American automobiles, the curved-dash Oldsmobile blazed no new trails. The idea that Olds pioneered in developing lightweight, inexpensive automobiles at a time when motor cars were big, heavy, and expensive is completely erroneous. In France, the DeDion-Bouton firm had begun producing a small, lightweight, one-cylinder rear-engine automobile in 1899. Called a voiturette in Europe, and a motorette when it began to be sold in the United States, about 1500 of the little French cars had been purchased by April 1901. In the opinion of European automobile historians, it was this DeDion-Bouton that should be credited with popularizing the small car. The lesson was not lost on American automakers. The historian Ralph Epstein was told in the 1920's of at least one American auto pioneer, whom Epstein does not name, who bought one of the voiturettes in France in 1900 and had it shipped to his factory in the United States. There he planned to tear it apart, study it, and put out a copy. A runabout, as the voiturette model was generally called in the United States, was one of the models that Henry Ford's Detroit Automobile Company announced in January 1900 it would "soon" have on the market. Although that car never materialized, by 1900 there were a number of runabouts being put out by American companies.

All of them, including the Oldsmobile, which was by no means the first to appear, offered essentially the same features — a two-passenger, lightweight vehicle, powered, in the case of gasoline runabouts, by a one-cylinder engine housed at the rear of the body. Even the curved dash of the Olds was closely approximated by such rivals as a gasoline model unveiled by the People's Automobile Company of Cleveland in September 1900, and a steam runabout, manufactured by the Kidder Motor Vehicle Company of New Haven, Connecticut. The steam model, almost a dead ringer for the Olds, was made public early in 1901 at the same time as the first information concerning the Michigan-made runabout received general distribution. Nor was the price of the curved-dash Oldsmobile remarkable. The statement that it was "the first cheap car on the market" is simply not true. The People's runabout was similar to the Olds in weight, appearance, and power, and its price of $650 was identical to that of the Oldsmobile when it appeared a few months later. By 1900 some of the lightweight Locomobile steamers were being sold for $600, and in 1901 the Crestmobile, manufactured by the Crest Manufacturing Company of Cambridge, Massachusetts, was advertised for only $550. By 1902, there were several runabouts on the market priced at $600, all under the price for which the Oldsmobile continued to be sold, and in 1903 one could buy the Orient Buckboard from Waltham, Massachusetts. Its manufacturer boasted that it was "The Cheapest Automobile in the World," selling for $375, $275 less than the Oldsmobile. The Detroit runabout also faced competition from runabouts that were only slightly more expensive than the Oldsmobile. The Keystone Wagonette, the National electric runabout, and the Elmore two-cylinder gasoline runabout were advertised in 1900 and 1901 at a price of $750; several other models, including the DeDion-Bouton Motorette, a 450-pound vehicle, were in the $800 to $850 bracket. The very fact that Oldsmobile ads frequently failed to quote the car's price suggests that the company did not regard price as one of the car's unique selling points.[7]

The success that Ransom Olds and his associates enjoyed with their runabout is all the more striking, therefore, in view of the competition they had to overcome. Although they had what was for its time a reasonably good product, it was probably no better than some of the other runabouts. The strength of the Olds company and the key to its success lay in the company itself. It had solid financial backing, and, due to the booming market for its engines, was not solely dependent on the sales of its automobiles to stay in business. These were qualities that the People's Automobile Company, the Kidder Motor Vehicle Company, and most of the other competitors of the Olds Motor Works apparently did not possess. As a result, these firms vanished from sight before they could put many of their cars on the market. The relatively strong Olds company, on the other hand, was able to produce its runabout in sufficient quantities to profit enormously (thereby further strengthening itself) from the public's growing interest in a light, inexpensive car. Others had recognized the interest but had not always been able to capitalize upon it.

The solid character of the Olds organization was dramatically demonstrated in 1901 when it was hit by a disaster that would have been, and indeed in later years was, enough to drive weaker automakers out of business. Early Saturday afternoon, March 9, a fire, apparently the result of a gas or gasoline explosion, was discovered in the Detroit plant of the Olds Motor Works. Within about a half hour after a young timekeeper, James J. Brady, had turned in the alarm, the factory that had been completed only a little over a year earlier was reduced to rubble. One reporter described the fire as "a spectacle of rare magnificence." In spite of the efforts of the fire department, including a fire boat brought up in the river, the blaze "spread as though burning a house of cards." Only the foundry, detached from the rest of the factory, escaped relatively undamaged. Several workers were injured as they jumped from third-floor windows, but most employees fortunately had left for the day after completing their regular half-day shift at noon on Saturday. Property damage amounted to about $72,000, including the building, which was an almost total loss, and the machinery and supplies inside, which were also almost entirely unsalvageable. Only a part of the loss was covered by insurance.[8]

This fire has come to be enshrined in automobile history as one of the major turning points in the development of the industry, and, more specifically, in Detroit's emergence as the center of the industry. The essential features of the story, as related in countless chronicles, are as follows: The fire destroyed all the work that the Olds staff had done on automobiles, except for one completed curved-dash runabout which James Brady managed to rescue from the burning factory. In order to get back into business as soon as possible, Olds had no choice but to proceed with production of the only survivor of the eleven models. By taking the runabout apart, the plans and patterns that had been burned were replaced. With most of its production facilities knocked out, Olds was forced to sub-contract the production of the various parts of the runabout, which were then assembled in the make-shift temporary quarters the company was able to put together after the fire. In a short time, hundreds of Olds runabouts were being sold, the Olds Motor Works was the country's leading automobile manufacturer, and its success induced a number of its parts suppliers to decide to manufacture their own cars. This development resulted ultimately in the appearance of such well-known automobiles as the Cadillac, Maxwell, and Dodge. All of this, we have been told, because of a fire at 1308 Jefferson Avenue, Detroit, on March 9, 1901.[9]

Although there is an element of truth running through this tale, taken as a whole it is an inaccurate, highly over-simplified account of what actually happened. To begin with, the fire did not destroy the company's automobile plans. On the night after the fire, Ransom Olds, who had only learned of the disaster late Saturday afternoon upon his return from a California trip, admitted that the fire was a great blow to the company, particularly with the busy season for automobiles coming up, "and we expected to put machines on the market in a few days." But he declared that "in two or three weeks time we shall be running as though nothing had happened." This was possible, he explained, because "all of our plans and drawings" were discovered "uninjured in the vault in the building where they were kept." It is true that a curved-dash runabout was the only survivor of twenty or so automobiles that were in various stages of assembly in the factory at the time of the fire. Among the vehicles lost was a two-seat electric stanhope that fell through from an upper floor on to the steel safe in Fred Smith's office. It is also true that Willis Grant Murray, manager of the automobile department, was quoted right after the fire as saying that the company, after two years of experimentation, was just beginning to get into the production of electric vehicles at the time of the fire. Indeed, the previous January, a new company had been reported as about to open in Cleveland to handle "the line of electric and gasoline vehicles built by the Olds Motor Co. of Detroit." Thus the fact that, when the Olds company got back into production a few weeks after the fire, its efforts were entirely concentrated on the gasoline runabout appears to support the thesis that the fire forced Olds to abandon the other models on which the company had been working.

No doubt the fire did have some effect. As Olds' biographer Glenn Niemeyer theorizes, with the limited mechanical resources that Olds had right after the fire, the curved-dash runabout, the least complicated of the several models, would have been the easiest one to put on the market. This was an important consideration if Olds was to sell any cars during the spring and summer, the peak period in those years for auto sales. If he had wanted to produce the other models, Olds had the plans. He also could have obtained some of the vehicles that had been built and sold before the fire if they had been needed to rebuild the patterns. In fact, the "handsomely decorated" Oldsmobile that Ransom Olds and Fred Smith drove in the floral parade during Detroit's Bicentennial celebration four and a half months after the fire was not a curved-dash runabout but a larger, two-seat vehicle, apparently one of the earlier models that had been developed in 1899 and 1900.[10]

Other evidence seems to point clearly to the conclusion that the decision to emphasize the runabout had been made before the fire. An article on the Olds Motor Works in the annual report of the Michigan Bureau of Labor for 1904 makes no mention of the fire as a factor in this decision. It states simply that after an initial effort to offer the public almost any kind of model it would demand, the company "thought in order to make a success of the business it would be necessary to throw away all the patterns and commence anew and devote their whole energy to one style and finish." Sometime in 1900, after the curved-dash runabout had been developed, a decision was reached to try to produce a thousand of the cars before the winter of 1901-1902, an almost unheard of production goal for that time, and one that would certainly have left little time for the Olds workers to produce any other models. Advertisements for the runabout that appeared by February 1901, before the fire, showed a picture of that car and the accompanying text made no mention of other

models, gasoline or electric. "The Oldsmobile is a marvel to most people,"
one ad declared. "It is only a simple fact, however. Runs 40 miles on one
gallon gasoline [actually, a highly inflated claim]. Starts at will from seat.
Fully guaranteed." It was even safe enough for a child to operate, the ad
claimed.

Thus, well before the fire of March 9, the attention of the company seems to have been already centered on the little runabout. By
March 9, Olds officials claimed, orders for 334 of the little cars were on
hand. With this kind of interest developing, there can be no question
that the days of the stanhope and the trap, which had never generated
any appreciable buyer enthusiasm, were numbered, fire or no fire. Ransom
Olds and his associates deserve credit for having made the right decision
in a calm, orderly manner; it should not appear that the decision to stake
everything on the runabout was a desperation move forced on them by
a quirk of fate.[11]

Similarly, the March 9 fire was not the major factor, as it has cus-
tomarily been depicted, in turning Olds to outside suppliers of parts in
order to produce the runabout. Actually, at this stage in the industry's
development, few automobile companies could hope to be in a position
to make most of the parts that went into their cars; there were many at
this time and for years to come who argued that they should not even try
to do so. In March 1900, exactly a year before the Olds fire, *Motor Age*
noted that a manufacturer could

> now buy almost everything that goes to make up a motor-vehicle and can
> assemble it, which is a sufficiently difficult task, and devote the rest of his
> time to the selling of the product. This course requires the least invest-
> ment, involves the least risk, gives the most rapid turn-over of what money
> is invested, and finally, leads to success by the straightest and easiest road.

Without the facilities and the skills of these parts manufacturers, contended Eugene W. Lewis, long connected with the Timken Roller Bearing
Company, the auto industry's development would have been delayed
many years, since in this early period "many so-called motor car manufacturers in reality owned nothing but a name plate and an assembly
building." Eventually, as the larger auto makers began producing a larger
proportion of their own parts, the term "assembled car" began to be used
in a derogatory sense, but as late as 1912, the short-lived Standard Electric Car Company of Jackson, Michigan, was boasting in its ads that it
made virtually nothing. "Behind most of the units of its construction are
great concerns whose names are household words in this industry," the
company declared. "Westinghouse makes the motor and controller, Par-
rish and Bingham the frame, Hayes the wheels, Goodyear or Motz the
tires; Batteries, Exide or Ironclad as desired."[12]

At least as early as 1896, when Olds had turned to a Lansing carriage manufacturer to make the body for his first gasoline car, he had
been relying on outside firms for most of his parts. In 1900, the Cleveland
firm of Sipe and Sigler, manufacturers of storage batteries, announced on

July 16 the closing of "a noteworthy contract" to supply batteries for the line of electric cars Olds was preparing to manufacture. It was also in the summer of 1900, as nearly as Alfred P. Sloan, Jr., could later recall, that Sloan had received a long-distance call from Peter Steenstrup, Sloan's partner in the Hyatt Roller Bearing Company of Newark, New Jersey. Steenstrup told Sloan that he was coming back from Detroit with an order from Olds Motor Works for 120 bearings, four for each rear axle in thirty of the new runabouts the company was developing. But this was only the beginning. Steenstrup had been advised that Olds might build a thousand of these cars in the next year, which would mean, if Hyatt's bearing proved satisfactory, an enormous contract. "Pete was beside himself," Sloan declared, "and so was I." Hyatt continued to supply bearings for the Oldsmobile as large-scale production ultimately did begin the next year. At the same time, a process of development was initiated that led, in a few years, to the Hyatt company's move to Detroit, and then to its absorption into General Motors; these moves introduced Sloan to the corporation that, under his leadership, would take over the number one position in the industry in the 1920's. (Sloan's recollections give some indication that work on the curved-dash Olds may have begun earlier than the fall of 1900, which is when Horace Loomis dated the development.)[13]

Another manufacturer who received an order for parts from Olds sometime in 1900, again for the runabout, was Charles Stewart Mott, superintendent of the Weston-Mott Company in Utica, New York. This firm manufactured wire wheels, and in September 1900 it was working overtime to fill its orders, over fifty per cent of which were now from automobile companies. Olds gave Mott an order for five hundred sets of wire wheels. Later, in 1901 and 1902, the total number of wheels ordered by Olds rose to three thousand sets, "which was enormous business for that time," Mott later recalled. But then in 1902, following the lead of other auto companies, Olds switched from wire wheels to wooden artillery wheels, which Mott did not make. Or so Mott claimed in later years. However, in December 1902, Ransom Olds received a letter from Weston-Mott confirming an order for fifty sets of artillery wheels and fifty steering knuckles. Perhaps Mott's men had difficulty with this kind of wheel. At any rate, in 1903 Olds seemed to get its wheels mostly from the Prudden company of Lansing, and Mott, who says his firm was on the brink of ruin, went out and secured orders for axles, a product about which he knew nothing at the time, and proceeded to re-coup the company's fortunes. Like Sloan, his dealings with Olds in 1900 were among the first in a series that led to the removal of his company to Michigan and its ultimate absorption into General Motors. (At the time of his death on February 18, 1973, at age ninety-seven, Mott was still serving as a member of the board of directors of General Motors, a position he had held since 1913.)[14]

During the months prior to the fire of March 1901, Olds had apparently been buying parts from both Henry M. Leland, of the well-established Detroit machine shop of Leland and Faulconer, and from the proprietors of a new machine shop, two brothers, John and Horace Dodge. Leland had first been approached when the Olds staff had been unable to solve a problem with the runabout's transmission, which made an ungodly noise when the vehicle was in operation. Leland and his men found and corrected the difficulty, and his company was then given a contract to produce this part. At about the same time, the Dodges received a contract to produce the engines for the runabout, even though this would seem to have been the one part that Olds could have produced as well and less expensively than an outside firm. However, the Olds company had its hands full keeping up with the orders for the various gas and gasoline engines, which, in 1900, were the mainstay of the business. The company did not have the capability for producing a quantity of engines for the runabout, especially if the production goal of one thousand cars was to be met. On June 27, 1901, Leland and Faulconer also took on the job of producing engines for Olds, signing a contract for two thousand engines, a huge order for that day although apparently not a record, since the French firm of DeDion, Bouton et Cie is reported to have produced 20,000 engines for automobiles between 1895 and 1901.[15]

For bodies, Olds turned to the C. R. Wilson Carriage Company, a Detroit firm that had been making carriages for about twenty years before it began to experiment with the production of bodies for automobiles in the late nineties. Wilson had supplied parts for Henry Ford's early experimental vehicles and he now did the same thing for Olds. At the time of the Jefferson Avenue fire in March 1901, Wilson was reported to have "done considerable business" with Olds in the previous months. The Wilson firm, which changed its name to the C. R. Wilson Body Company and had been advertising its services regularly in automobile journals in 1900, continued to supply Oldsmobile bodies in the months after the fire as part of a business that made it by 1903 the largest supplier of auto bodies in the industry. Olds also bought bodies in the period after the fire from H. Jay Hayes of Cleveland and from Byron F. Everitt, who, after learning the carriage trade under the veteran Detroit carriage manufacturer, Hugh Johnson, established his own company in 1899. It was also in this later period of development, in 1902, that Olds and Jonathan Maxwell went to Detroit's largest sheet metal shop, the Briscoe Manufacturing Company, owned by the Briscoe brothers, Benjamin and Frank, with a sample of the radiator for the Oldsmobile. Benjamin Briscoe recalled that in his ignorance he at first mistook what Olds called a cooler for some kind of "antiquated band instrument." But he agreed to produce it, and shortly got a contract for 4400 radiators, plus fenders, gas tanks, and other sheet metal parts.[16]

"This order and other orders given by the Olds Motor Works at the same time to other concerns around Detroit," Briscoe maintained, "marked the beginning in a real way of the automobile manufacturing business in the city of Detroit." He was quite right, and the point worth making again is that these orders were going to be placed whether the Detroit plant of the Olds Motor Works was destroyed by fire or not. Olds had been buying parts increasingly from outside suppliers as the company got more and more into automobile work. Additional suppliers became involved as full-scale production of automobiles began to become a reality in 1901. A company as far distant as Brooklyn, New York, had produced a "considerable quantity" of drop forgings for Olds by the fall of 1901. With the emphasis in both the Lansing and Detroit Olds plants placed on the manufacture of engines, there was little the automobile department could do beyond simply assembling parts that were manufactured elsewhere. This was true as much before the fire as it was afterward, and conditions were still not much different in 1902, even though by this time Olds had available far greater manufacturing facilities than the company had had before the fire. The company was still buying parts from its old suppliers but it was also turning to such new ones as the Briscoes and H. Jay Hayes of Cleveland, rather than attempting to manufacture these parts itself. The idea, presented in many accounts of the auto industry, that it was the fire that caused Olds to farm out the manufacturing of the runabout's various parts simply does not hold up under inspection.[17]

The fire, however, did have its positive effects on the Olds Motor Works. For one, it was instrumental in bringing about the return of the company to its original home base of Lansing, where it has remained ever since. Less than three weeks after the fire, rumors were circulating that Olds, instead of rebuilding its Detroit plant, might leave that city for a location elsewhere, "if the right kind of inducements are offered." The rumor appears to have been one planted by the Olds company itself, as part of a technique frequently used by automobile companies and promoters. The strategy, as it would have been applied in this case, was to employ a none too subtle form of blackmail against Detroit, threatening that city with the loss of a promising business establishment if it did not offer the company some kind of benefit or special privilege. At the same time, other communities were invited to top Detroit's bid. It was a technique that the Jackson auto pioneer, Byron J. Carter, had used earlier in 1901, drumming up supposed backing from investors in Grand Rapids, South Bend, and Elkhart, Indiana, as a means of arousing support at home in Jackson. In the years ahead, no one would employ this refined form of a shakedown more masterfully than William C. Durant, who time and time again used the threat of moving one or more of his numerous automobile endeavors some place else as a means of wringing concessions from his home town of Flint.[18]

Within a week after word was leaked that Olds had developed a roving eye, Pontiac was reported to have formed a committee to try to persuade the firm to move to that city. The move would have made considerable sense, since there was already located in Pontiac a carriage industry second in Michigan only to Flint's. For Olds, it would have meant ready access to many of the skills and facilities needed in the building of its horseless carriages. However, the rumor plus an announcement after the fire that Olds, no matter what happened, would enlarge its existing engine plant in Lansing so that it might take on some of the work done in Detroit, was perhaps a clue to the businessmen of Lansing that now would be an appropriate time to try to bring back all of the operations of the city's prodigal son.[19]

The Lansing Business Men's Association took the initiative in inviting Olds to return by offering an attractive land site as Lansing's special inducement. Fifty-two acres in southwestern Lansing were available at one hundred dollars an acre from the Central Michigan Agricultural Society, which had previously used the land for its annual fair. The Business Men's Association raised the money to buy the land; the deed was made out to the Olds Motor Works. Some indication of the relatively low esteem in which the auto industry was generally held at this time, however, may be seen in the fact that efforts to raise the money by soliciting donations succeeded in raising only $1800. The remaining $3400 had to be borrowed. One of the two men who loaned the association this money was Fred Thoman, an Olds stockholder of several years' standing. Harris E. Thomas, an officer in the association, was officially delegated to present the offer to Olds, but behind the scenes another Olds stockholder, Reuben Shettler, was apparently the key figure in the negotiations.[20]

In 1936, Shettler wrote a five-page account detailing the role that he claimed to have played in arranging financing for the automobile companies with which Ransom Olds had been involved. At that time, 1936, the Lansing *State Journal,* according to Shettler, refused to print his article, either in the form of a news story or as a paid advertisement. Since the overall tone of Shettler's narrative was hostile toward Olds and Richard H. Scott, long-time associate of Olds, the implication is that the *Journal's* management either doubted the accuracy of the information or did not wish to antagonize these two most influential Lansing citizens. The general accuracy of what Shettler wrote in 1936, however, is attested to by contemporary documents that indicate that he was indeed the central figure in the events that led to the return of Olds to Lansing in 1901 and the subsequent organization in 1904 of the Reo Motor Car Company.[21]

Shettler himself is a rather mysterious figure. He was listed in the Lansing City Directory for 1894 as a jobber of threshing machinery, so his business interests could well have brought him into contact with P. F. Olds and Son, since that firm's engines were used on farms as well as in industry. Shettler had invested in stock of the Olds Gasoline Engine Works, although he claimed in 1936 that he had simply loaned Ransom Olds $5000. Upon the organization of the Olds Motor Works, Shettler received $5000 in cash plus an equal amount of stock. Because of these past relationships with Olds, he said he was urged by Lansing citizens in the spring of 1901 to use his influence to get the company to move back to Lansing. Shettler said he agreed to undertake the task "for the benefit of Lansing, which was then but a small town suffering from serious bank and factory failures." However, the wording of a report that he sent to the Olds Motor Works on August 14, 1901, in which he used such terms as "our machinery," "we can openly state," and "concessions granted us," indicates that Shettler was acting as an agent of the company rather than the town; thus the eight hundred dollars he claimed to have spent out of his own pocket during the several months he devoted to the negotiations were not spent entirely for Lansing's benefit but out of the expectation that the move would be a profitable one for the Olds company and, therefore, for its stockholders as well. The origins of the bad feelings that subsequently developed between Shettler and Olds may, in fact, be found in Shettler's reported bitterness later in 1901 at the failure of the Olds Motor Works to reimburse him for the expenses he had incurred on its behalf, although Fred Smith claimed that when the matter of compensation was discussed with Shettler at the time the deal for the land in Lansing was about to be closed, Shettler had brushed aside any suggestion that he should be paid.[22]

A letter from Samuel Smith to Ransom Olds, dated July 19, reveals that by the 19th the Olds company was in favor of the move to Lansing, with only details remaining to be worked out. Smith, who was vacationing at Harbor Springs in northern Michigan, instructed Ransom Olds: "I wish this matter to be closed at Lansing as soon as possible or before the offer lapses & gets away from us." He assured Olds that he would see that all the money that would be needed to build the new Lansing plant would be made available. "Our interest in this business is so large I favor making all that is warranted by demand of our product." He had talked with Henry Russel, who agreed with Smith that no time should be lost in starting the first Lansing building, with completion hopefully by December; a second building should be started later in the year, "so we can be certain of both buildings for use in the Spring when the demand will be large on us." He was insistent that the engine business be maintained, and he also saw a "fine business" developing for a pump that the company had perfected and suggested that the pump could be manufactured for the time being in Detroit "to keep up the appearance of using the present plant until we can get a fair price for it."[23]

The principal obstacle delaying final approval by the Olds directors of the offer made to them by the Lansing Business Men's Association was their desire to obtain certain concessions from the Grand Trunk Western Railway, the sole railroad serving the proposed new factory site in Lansing. Reuben Shettler conferred at length with Grand Trunk officials, who came to Lansing on several occasions, and, finally, he met with the president of the company in Montreal, Canada. In dealing with the requests of the Olds company, the railroad apparently was willing to gamble on its future growth, for it gave the Michigan firm much more than the current business of the company would seem to have warranted. Shettler, in fact, in his report to the Olds company on these arrangements emphasized that the Grand Trunk wanted them kept "strictly confidential." Grand Trunk agreed to bear all the expenses of putting in side tracks at the factory, to move machinery and other material for the new plant, and to move employees and their furniture from Detroit to Lansing at nominal rates to be paid by Olds, but with part of this charge to be rebated by the railroad to the company. As "leverage" for use in buying bricks and lumber to build the new Lansing plant, the Olds Motor Works was authorized to "state that the Grand Trunk System will bring us material for nothing." Finally, the Grand Trunk agreed to bring freight in and out of the Lansing plant twice a day and to see that these movements were coordinated to meet their local freight schedules; it was an arrangement, as Shettler pointed out, that "will practically give us a local station at the factory," a concession that the railroad officials were particularly anxious should not be publicized, even among the Olds staff.[24]

Another concern of the Olds company dealt with the availability of parts in Lansing. A local firm established by William K. Prudden, who, as a harness-racing enthusiast, had developed a rubber-tired sulky, was manufacturing wheels, which it supplied in increasing quantities to Olds and other automobile companies. To avoid costly shipping charges for bodies, the Auto Body Company was formed in the summer of 1901 by Lawrence Price, Harris Thomas, and other Lansing businessmen who had been involved in the drive to get Olds to move to the city. At the time of the announcement of the company's formation it was reported that Olds would purchase a substantial amount of the body company's output, but the new firm sought to discount the idea that it had been formed only as a supplier for Olds by stating that it would seek business on a national scale; the statement was shortly backed up by an order for three thousand bodies from a carriage company in Jackson.[25]

Finally, on August 12 the announcement was made that the Olds Motor Works had accepted the offer of the Lansing Business Men's Association. The formal transfer of the property to Olds took place in September. Work was to begin immediately on an assembly plant, with completion and final removal of the Olds operations from Detroit to Lansing to take place in January 1902. Construction would begin on a foundry when the assembly plant was completed, and a third building would be added in the spring.

Two reasons were given for the decision of the company to leave Detroit. One was "labor trouble" — machinists at the Detroit Olds plant had gone out on strike on May 20, joining union machinists throughout the country in a demand for a nine-hour day at the going rate for a ten-hour day. On May 31, only the intervention of police averted a possible pitched battle between company men and several hundred strikers from various shops who had gathered near the Olds plant with the intention of rushing the plant to get at the non-union workers inside. There was no further attempt to disrupt the work at the plant in the days that followed. The second reason that was alleged to have influenced the decision to move to Lansing was the shortage of skilled labor in Detroit, "a condition which," it was said, though not very logically, "would be a rarity in a small town."[26]

It seems unlikely that either of these official reasons actually had much bearing on the company's decision. The strike at the Olds Lansing plant in 1898 was an indication that the company could not expect to escape labor troubles now simply by returning to Lansing. As for the other reason, one need only recall that in 1899 the Olds Motor Works had announced it was moving from Lansing to Detroit in part because of the larger number of skilled workers found in the latter city. These conditions could not have changed greatly in the space of two and a half years. However, one element in the labor situation that may have helped Lansing's cause was the very noticeable difference in wage rates that had developed between the company's Detroit and Lansing plants. According to the state factory inspector, the average worker at the Olds plant in Detroit at the time it was inspected sometime in 1901 was getting $1.86 a day, while in Lansing the average daily wage was only $1.33, whereas the comparable figures for 1900 had been $1.25 in the Detroit plant as against the slightly higher Lansing rate of $1.27.[27]

As it developed, none of these factors caused Olds to turn its back on Detroit completely. At the time the company announced its plans to move to Lansing, the Merchants and Manufacturers Exchange of Detroit was reportedly trying to persuade the company to reverse this decision. Whether these efforts were responsible or not, the company did announce in November that it had decided to rebuild its plant in Detroit and operate it in conjunction with its new facilities in Lansing. The explanation that the company gave this time was that the scarcity of housing in Lansing made it impossible for it to move all of its working force to that city. The production of the curved-dash Oldsmobile accelerated rapidly, requiring an ever larger work force; the housing shortage, which already in the fall of 1901 had forced Olds to convert some of the buildings on the old fairgrounds into bunkhouses for the transferred workers, could very well have been a major reason for the decision to keep part of the operations in Detroit.[28]

By the end of 1901, therefore, Olds had taken care of its need for greatly expanded plant facilities to meet the demand for the Oldsmobile. Even with the temporary setup, the Olds forces had managed to produce around four hundred runabouts in 1901 (there is some dispute as to the exact figure). Although it was not the figure of one thousand cars that had been mentioned the previous spring, it was still an extraordinary production figure at a time when a survey in *Horseless Age* of sixteen of the best-known automobile companies in the country (not including Olds) showed that apparently only Locomobile (which claimed to have produced six thousand motor vehicles since its founding in 1899) and Winton (which had produced about seven hundred automobiles since 1897) had turned out as many cars in their entire history as Olds had in one year. Olds had not approached the goal of ten cars a day that it had set for itself in the spring, but by the end of October the company was aiming at a new production goal of twenty-five runabouts per day. During the year, total sales of the Olds Motor Works increased from $186,200 in 1900 to $410,400. For the first time, the automotive division, not the engine department, may have accounted for the largest share of these sales.[29]

Although Olds had begun to publicize and advertise its runabout prior to the fire of March 9, there is no doubt that the event helped greatly to draw attention to the company and its product. Automotive journals gave far greater attention to the company and its new car than they would have in more ordinary circumstances. The curiosity of those following the news of the automobile industry must have been aroused as they read of the feverish efforts of the Olds organization to resume production in makeshift quarters. In turn, this curiosity led to an eagerness for a glimpse of the curved-dash Oldsmobile. By the summer of 1901, as a few of the cars began to appear around the country, there was no longer much doubt that the company had a winner on its hands. When the Olds dealer in Chicago put his first Olds runabout on display early in June, *Motor Age* reported without any hesitancy that the car

> attracted more comment and more visitors, in a short time, than any other vehicle that ever came into the city of Chicago. The store was the objective point, apparently, of every automobilist in the city, for it was well filled all day with men who knew a good vehicle when they see one.

In spite of the fact that this particular vehicle "showed signs of haste in preparing it for shipment," the magazine declared that the claims Olds had made for the vehicle, particularly as to its relatively noiseless, vibration-free qualities, were impressively supported as the runabout was driven "up and down the store the greater part of the day." The following month, in response to a letter from a reader in New York who wondered if the things he had read about the Oldsmobile were really true, the editor of the magazine reported that although few samples had yet reached Chicago, "judging from personal observation and from the opinions expressed by other users, they have been quite satisfactory."[30]

The establishment of a dealer outlet for the Olds in Chicago, along with those announced earlier in 1901 in such other large cities as Cleveland and Detroit, together with a concerted advertising campaign not only in trade journals such as *Motor Age* and *Motor World* (although, strangely enough, apparently not in *Horseless Age*), aimed primarily at dealers, but also, in 1901, in some more general circulation magazines, such as *Review of Reviews* — all this is evidence of a well-planned program by Olds to promote the sales of the Oldsmobile.[31]

One market that was essential to the success of the car but still remained untapped, however, was the big eastern market, particularly New York City. A friend of Ransom Olds, who had just moved from Detroit to New Jersey, advised him in May 1901 that "there might be quite a sale for your machines here now. I find many more automobiles in town

One of Olds' test drivers, probably Roy D. Chapin, puts a curved-dash runabout through a rugged test of its hill-climbing capabilities. The site of the test was probably Belle Isle, where mounds of dirt thrown up in the construction of canals provided driving conditions that were generally lacking on Detroit's flat terrain.   Courtesy Michigan Historical Collections

than I expected to. When I left here — three years ago — an automobile was a rare sight. Now many may be seen."[32]

At about the same time, John Wanamaker approached Olds about handling sales for the car in New York and New Jersey, pursuing an interest similar to that of a rival department store, the R. H. Macy Company, which had imported the Benz in 1895. For some reason, however, Wanamaker failed to get a contract, and in the fall of 1901 Olds still did not have a dealer in New York City. To promote its car in the East, the Olds Motor Works bought space at the second annual national auto show to be held in New York City in November. Olds had exhibited at a show in Chicago in 1900 and had planned to exhibit there in March 1901, before the fire forced the company to cancel out, but this was the company's first appearance at the show that was already recognized as the most important annual promotional event in the industry. Such a show was not only a means of acquainting the public with a company's vehicles, but, at this stage in the industry's development, a means also of lining up new retailers for these vehicles.[33]

Seeking to squeeze as much publicity as possible from the Oldsmobile's debut in New York City, the company staged what has become one of the most famous incidents in automobile history. On October 29, Roy D. Chapin, a twenty-one-year-old test driver for Olds, started out from Detroit in a curved-dash runabout. Seven and a half days later he arrived at New York's Waldorf-Astoria Hotel, where Ransom Olds was awaiting him. When Chapin died in 1936, the Detroit *Times* compared the impact that his ride of 1901 had had on the auto industry with "Lindbergh's in aviation" and "Paul Revere's in history." By this daring deed, the public, the business world, and Chapin himself had all had their eyes opened to what the automobile could mean for them. "This drive," the paper declared, "is credited by authorities as the real turning point in the industry." Chapin's biographer, John Long, a veteran newspaperman and automotive trade association official, called the trip "the greatest motor transportation story up to that time, and one of the significant stories of all time." Another more impartial writer, Roger Burlingame, one of the foremost students of the history of technology, stated that "road conditions and the possibilities of new frontiers in the interior were brought sensationally to public attention in the exploit of Roy Chapin." Like so many aspects of the early history of Olds, these later assessments of the importance of this event are more a testimony to the image-building ability of the Olds company than the result of a careful study of the event itself.[34]

Whether Ransom Olds or Chapin was responsible for the original idea of the Detroit-to-New York endurance test is not clear. Olds claimed the credit and said he picked Chapin to drive the car because he was one of the company's chief test drivers. Others, however, believe that Olds simply placed his stamp of approval on an idea that originated with Chapin, who, in the years following, revealed an expert's awareness of what was good publicity. In any event, the concept had obviously been borrowed from Alexander Winton, the Cleveland auto maker who had had great success in using two long trips, from Cleveland to New York, in 1897 and 1899, as a means of advertising the merits of his car.[35]

Chapin's experiences during the week that it took him to drive from Detroit through Ontario, across western New York, and down the Hudson Valley to New York City, where he arrived on November 5, have been recounted in great detail on a number of occasions. At the conclusion of the 820-mile trip, during which the little runabout had consumed thirty gallons of gasoline and an astounding eighty gallons of water, and required numerous repairs, Chapin had proved, if anything, how risky such a motor trip was in that day, considering the abysmal road conditions and the still-primitive character of the automobile.[36]

What Chapin had not done, despite the claims of such well-informed automotive writers as Chris Sinsabaugh, was set an American long-distance automobile record, nor, as is more commonly asserted, was Chapin the first person to drive a car between Detroit and New York. In the summer of 1899, Mr. and Mrs. John D. Davis had started out from New York attempting a trans-continental trip to San Francisco in a gasoline vehicle specially built for them by the National Motor Company of Hartford, Connecticut. A month and a half and twenty-five breakdowns later, they reached Detroit; later in the fall they were reported to have limped into Chicago, greatly exceeding the distance covered by Chapin two years later. Their repair bills, however, were so great that *Scientific American* concluded that such trips "do more harm to the automobile industry than they do good."[37]

Far more impressive than the Davises' achievement, and also surpassing Chapin's distance record, were the accomplishments of Elwood Haynes and the Apperson brothers. They successfully piloted one of their Haynes-Apperson automobiles from Kokomo, Indiana, to Brooklyn, New York, in the summer of 1899, and again from Kokomo to New York City in the summer of 1901, with, it was claimed, a minimum of difficulty insofar as repairs were concerned. In the spring of 1901, an eight-horsepower French automobile was driven from New York to Chicago, and in May of that year, Alexander Winton, the pioneer in this kind of endurance venture, had attempted to cross the country, starting from San Francisco. He was, however, forced to abandon the attempt when he reached Nevada.[38]

It may not be correct even to state, as some have done, that Chapin had set a distance record for lightweight vehicles. The previous year, C. G. Wridgway had driven a DeDion-Bouton Motorette, an even lighter car than the Oldsmobile, from New York to Toledo, a distance only slightly less than that between Detroit and New York. Likewise, a relatively light automobile was used in the summer of 1901 by that pioneer American motor tourist, Arthur Jerome Eddy, in the remarkable odyssey that he described in his book, *Two Thousand Miles on an Automobile,* published in 1902 under the pseudonym of "Chauffeur." Eddy, a Chicago corporation lawyer who had been born in Flint, Michigan, in 1859, set out from Chicago on August 1 in his car, which he identified only as "an ordinary twelve hundred dollar single-cylinder American machine," with a nominal rating of 8½ horsepower. By the time he returned to Chicago on September 28, he had covered over 2600 miles in the course of a leisurely journey through the Middle West, the Northeast, and Ontario. Although a number of repairs to the car had been necessary during the trip, Eddy was quite satisfied with the vehicle's performance. "A number of little things were done," he reported upon bringing the car into the garage in Chicago, "but the mechanic spent only forty hours' time all told in making the machine quite as good as new. A coat of paint and varnish removed all outward signs of rough usage." Motoring was not inexpensive, Eddy had to admit, but the pleasures more than outweighed the expense.[39]

Thus, there was ample precedent for the kind of trip Olds and

Chapin planned. Nor were they the only ones to think of such a thing as a means of publicizing their car at the 1901 auto show. A Toledo manufacturer of steam cars displayed at its exhibit telegrams that had been sent from each stopping point along the route followed by one of its cars that was driven from Toledo to New York just prior to November. After the show was underway, the New York *Times* reported, "every day brings some one from a distance who had made a run of several hundred miles" to attend the auto show. As a result of the relatively routine nature of these occurrences, Chapin's arrival caused hardly a ripple of excitement in the press. The New York *Tribune* on November 7 briefly mentioned the bare facts of the trip, without mentioning the names of either the vehicle or the driver, along with the "owner's" comment that "his experience has showed that the lightweight automobiles are well adapted for such tours." The New York *Times* carried not a single word about the trip. Even in Detroit itself, as an examination of the issues of the *News* and the *Free Press* for the days just before and after Chapin reached New York shows, in 1901 neither of today's surviving Motor City papers considered the event worth any mention at all, let alone giving it front-page, headline coverage. (For that matter, neither paper showed interest in anything connected with the New York auto show.) Among trade journals, *Motor World* had a fifteen-line story detailing the achievements of the driver, whom it identified as D. N. Chapin. Like the New York *Tribune*, *Motor World* found that the chief importance of the feat was its demonstration of the ability of the inexpensive, light vehicle to maintain a pace that imported cars costing up to $20,000 would have been unable to maintain on the roads Chapin had to navigate. On the other hand, *Motor Age* gave very little notice to Chapin's trip in its extensive coverage of the New York show, and other accounts of the exhibition contained no mention at all of the supposedly sensational odyssey of the Olds runabout.[40]

Although we can recognize that Chapin's ride was not a record-setting deed that had the nation agog, its importance to the Olds company still remains. The company hastily included the news in its advertisements for the runabout, citing the trip "as a sample" of the car's "efficiency." Accuracy was of little concern to the copy writer who referred to Roy D. Chapin as "O. H. Chapin," and blithely ignored the truth, stating that throughout the trip there had been: "No break. No trouble." Of more immediate value to the company, there is evidence that visitors to the auto show stopped by the Olds exhibit in large numbers to see the runabout, perhaps attracted by reports of Chapin's trip, or, as *Horseless Age* thought, by the car's low price. The curved-dash Oldsmobile was one of a large number of one-cylinder cars exhibited at the New York show by sixteen companies. Although one auto writer speculated at the time that the "disuse" of this kind of vehicle in favor of multiple-cylindered cars was already becoming evident, others thought that the "great interest" shown in the Oldsmobile was evidence of a popular demand for this type of automobile.[41]

It seems to be a reasonable assumption that the attention the Olds-mobile received from show-goers helped Olds to get a dealer lined up in New York. Either during the show or shortly before it opened, a contract was signed with the sporting goods firm, A. G. Spaulding and Company; while the show was still in progress, however, company officials told Olds that its board of directors wanted to withdraw from the agreement because they saw no likelihood that Spaulding could sell one hundred Olds-mobiles in New York during the next year, as they had agreed to do in the contract. As it turned out, however, a far more satisfactory arrangement from Olds' standpoint was worked out before the end of the New York show with Ray M. Owen, an Oldsmobile dealer from Cleveland, and his financial backer, Roy Rainey. The latter agreed to back Owen in New York City if Olds would give him an exclusive agency. Ransom Olds agreed, setting the quota for the first year's sales at five hundred cars, an astronomical figure for that time. Later, as the three men were drawing up the contract, Olds reportedly suggested that Rainey and Owen order one thousand Oldsmobiles. "Then the public would drop its jaw," Olds said, "and take notice." Owen agreed, and although he did not achieve this quota in 1902, his success in selling seven hundred and fifty of the little runabouts during that year helped greatly to make the curved-dash Olds the most talked-about car in America.[42]

Probably no one benefited more from the successful Detroit-to-New York trip in the fall of 1901 than Roy Chapin himself. He was a native of Lansing, where his father, Edward Chapin, was a prominent attorney. The Chapins, like other Lansing residents, had been aware of the activities of Ransom Olds during the 1880's and 1890's, but Chapin's biographer thinks it unlikely that there is much truth to the story that Roy Chapin, as a boy, became interested in automobiles from his knowledge of the experiments Olds was conducting. Chapin's biographer also questions the story that the job Roy received from the Olds Motor Works in the spring of 1901 had any connection with an alleged talk between Ransom Olds and young Chapin some years earlier in which Olds had promised the eager boy a position in the Olds factory when he grew up. Actually, Chapin, who was a student at the University of Michigan at the time, received his job with Olds through the efforts of another Lansing resident, Horace Loomis, a graduate of Michigan Agricultural College and an old acquaintance of Chapin. At a salary of $35 a month, Chapin, a highly proficient amateur photographer, was at first assigned the duty of taking photographs of the Oldsmobile for advertising and other promotional uses. Within a few months, however, he had moved from this to the position of test driver, and then, by 1902, to a top position in the sales department. He attracted the attention and seems to have become a protégé of Fred Smith, who wrote to Chapin's mother early in the summer of 1902 "that of all the young men we have had around us in a similar capacity, he promises to be the best, and I have great confidence in his good sense and sound judgement." In a letter to Ransom Olds a month later, Smith suggested that Olds was not as enthusiastic about Chapin as Smith was. "Chapin," Smith wrote, "does *good* work in the office. You don't perhaps realize it, but he is posted thoroughly on the business being done in the various agencies . . . I don't think you do the boy Justice, quite." Smith then predicted that Chapin, who eventually became president of the Hudson Motor Car Company, one of the foremost leaders in the drive for good roads, and Secretary of Commerce under Herbert Hoover, would "make a tip top strong man anywhere before he gets through."[43]

This letter is one of the earliest indications of a breach between Ransom Olds and the Smiths, a rift that led ultimately, some eighteen months later, to the departure of Olds from the company that bore his name. The clash was perhaps inevitable, but during the first two years after the establishment of the Olds Motor Works, there were no visible signs of friction between Olds and the Smiths. Although Samuel Smith had initially been the president of the company, early in 1900, as noted previously, Ransom Olds moved up into that position. At the time of the fire on March 9, 1901, Olds was still referred to in news accounts as the president and chief spokesman of the company. The firm's annual report, however, listed Samuel Smith as president as of March 31, with Olds back in the post of vice-president. The elder Smith's stockholdings in the company had dropped to 5625 shares, making Olds, with 7500 shares, the largest single stockholder. But adding the holdings of Fred and Angus Smith to those of their father, the Smiths still retained the largest block of stock in the company (not even including the two thousand shares owned by Samuel Smith's brother-in-law, James Seager). The tone of Samuel Smith's letter to Olds in the summer of 1901 concerning the need to push ahead as fast as possible with the Lansing proposition was still friendly. Smith, although obviously exerting influence on company policy, as would be expected of one with his financial investment in the company, nevertheless couched his directives in a manner that left much room for Olds to exercise his own initiative. The letter concluded in a most friendly way with Smith expressing concern about Olds' health, which had not been good for some months. "If you will consent to going off for a rest now 1 or 2 weeks to a month I think it will improve your health and you will come back better prepared for the fall strain."[44]

As long as the company's headquarters and automobile work was located in Detroit, Ransom Olds and the Smiths seem to have worked together well. The Smiths, insofar as the manufacturing operations were concerned, deferred to Olds' judgment, based on his years of experience in manufacturing engines. But as the firm expanded, the necessity arose to hire additional personnel, among whom were some remarkably talented individuals. Joining the company in 1900 was Jonathan D. Maxwell, a native of Indiana, who was the same age as Olds. He had begun to learn the machinist's trade when he was fourteen years old. In 1894 he had helped build Elwood Haynes' first gasoline-powered vehicle and had continued working for Haynes and the Appersons until 1899 when he was engaged by a syndicate in Montreal, Canada, to build a gas engine, after which he joined Olds in Detroit. Charles King also became a member of the Olds staff in 1900, and although he was involved with the marine engine side of the business, he, like Maxwell, came to the company with a wealth of experience in the area of gasoline engines and automobiles. Two years later, the forty-two-year-old Charles D. Hastings, who had wide experience in sales and the details of office management, was brought in as office manager; he later became the foreign sales manager.

In 1901, the Olds Motor Works began advertising for workers in out-of-state papers, and particularly after the announcement of plans to build a large new factory in Lansing, the company was flooded with applications for jobs, many from other parts of the Midwest and Canada. Some of these were from men with considerable experience, for example, an applicant from Wheeling, West Virginia, who was the head of the trimming department in a carriage company; another, from Chicago, had fifteen years' experience in the machinist trade. The president of the National Automobile and Electric Company of Indianapolis, L. S. Dow, asked for a job in the commercial department of Olds, explaining that although he had helped organize the Indianapolis company two years earlier, he was being forced out of the firm because of its precarious financial condition. Others who were hired had little experience but were obviously very talented. Robert C. Hupp, who went to work as a common laborer at Olds in 1902, had formed his own company within six years and begun putting out the Hupmobile, a car whose production would later be directed by Charles Hastings. Still others were fresh out of college, again lacking the experience of Olds, Maxwell, King, or Hastings, but eager to learn — men like Chapin, Loomis, and Howard E. Coffin. The ablest engineer of the lot, Coffin was an Ohioan whose family had moved to Ann Arbor, Michigan, where in the 1890's Coffin attended the university. In 1898-99, in the university's engineering shops, he had built an internal-combustion gasoline engine and a steam-powered motor vehicle. He drove the latter around Ann Arbor for several years, and it is preserved today in the Henry Ford Museum in Dearborn. In 1902, just prior to graduation, Coffin was hired by the Olds company, where he ultimately headed the experimental engineering activities at the Detroit plant. A friend and fellow student of Chapin's and Coffin's, Roscoe B. Jackson, was also hired and before long became the Smiths' secretary. Frederick O. Bezner, six months younger than Chapin, was brought into the Olds purchasing staff from the National Cash Register Company; he was perhaps the first of an amazing number of employees of this Dayton company to move into the auto industry. Before the decade was out, Chapin, Coffin, Jackson, and Bezner, together with several other Olds alumni, including James Brady, would strike out on their own, emerging as the founders and top executives of the Hudson Motor Car Company of Detroit. For forty-five years that company was one of the most respected smaller auto companies in the business before becoming part of the merger in 1954 out of which the American Motors Corporation was created.[45]

With men such as these on the staff, the Smiths no longer needed to feel as dependent on Ransom Olds' judgment as they had earlier, and it seems clear that this was an important cause of the ill will between Olds and Fred Smith, in particular, that was coming into the open by the summer of 1902. Olds, who had been manufacturing and selling machines for nearly two decades, was objecting to the decisions and ideas of younger men without the same kind of practical experience. Nor was Olds the only one who felt that way. A firm from Binghamton, New York, that had been selling Olds engines for some years and was now interested in selling the Olds automobiles expressed outrage at the manner in which "this Kid C," apparently referring to Roy Chapin, had treated them "and many other of your customers," treatment that "we believe . . . will not win many friends for the Oldsmobile." The New Yorkers were being asked to accept Oldsmobiles on consignment from the dealer who had the franchise for their area. Although this was a marketing practice that would eventually become universal in the auto industry, the Binghamton company wanted to continue to operate under the more relaxed conditions that had existed when they had dealt directly with Ransom Olds.[46]

As long as the Olds operations were centered in Detroit, differences between Ransom Olds and Fred Smith were minimized by the fact that they were in daily personal contact with each other. When the operations were split between Detroit and Lansing a different arrangement had to be worked out. Smith stayed in Detroit, and in addition to his duties as secretary-treasurer took on the job of overseeing the work in the Detroit plant. Ransom Olds moved his family back to Lansing in 1901 so that he could assume active supervision of the new Lansing works while continuing to serve as general manager of all company activities. The result of this change seems to have been an increasing involvement by Smith in all aspects of the business, manufacturing as well as financial. By the spring of 1902, Smith was apparently having doubts about Olds' competence as manager of the manufacturing operations. Olds was taking a rather easygoing approach to the idea of quality control, telling Roy Chapin on one occasion "that it was time to correct a fault when the fault made itself evident on the road." By the summer of 1902, complaints from owners about defects in their Oldsmobiles led to a growing insistence by Smith and his father that Olds turn his attention to correcting these faults. In one letter, undated but apparently written in this period, Fred Smith spoke of the need for a meeting to discuss revamping the runabout. "The repair items are a fright and the black eye our runabout will get from breakage complaints will grow worse the deeper we get in." The same letter indicates an additional area of conflict. Smith expressed his disappointment at the failure of Olds to proceed with work on a new engine. He and his father did realize how busy Olds was, so they were thinking of naming an assistant who could relieve Olds of some of his work load.

Furthermore, if Olds did not proceed with the development of an improved engine, Smith threatened to take up the job at the Detroit plant. "I haven't any great doubt of being able to push it through and get something the trade really wants," Smith declared. "The old model is too weak and flimsy and none of our agents want it — I can't see any point in puddling away with that old batch of stuff — and I tell you quite frankly, that you are laying yourself open to future criticism in having your brother waste time and money on what you know is an insufficient engine." (This seems to indicate that Wallace Olds, whom Olds had fired in 1898, was now back in the company.) In the months following, Smith kept asserting the necessity to establish a large staff that would be engaged in designing and engineering changes in the company's automobiles. Those changes that had been made, Smith complained in April 1903, had been those forced on the company. There had been no initiative by the company to design something new to keep ahead of the public's demands. Finally, at the end of April, Smith carried out his earlier threat to establish an experimental shop under his supervision in the Detroit plant.[47]

From the standpoint of later standards in the auto industry, Fred Smith was quite correct in the criticisms he leveled at the runabout and Ransom Olds' manufacturing techniques. Smith, of course, did not publicly criticize the company's car. Late in 1902 he announced that the Oldsmobile for 1903 would be "just as good as the Oldsmobile of 1902." In light of what Smith had been saying about the 1902 Oldsmobile in private, this was faint praise indeed. The company's policy, Smith declared, was not to tinker with a good product, or make changes each year simply for the sake of change. However, if a way was found to improve the runabout, that improvement was added immediately, rather than being held off for twelve months to be included on a so-called new model.[48]

In the year 1902, the reasons for Fred Smith's criticisms of the curved-dash Oldsmobile and company operations in his private communications to Ransom Olds may not have been so evident to the average observer as they are to historians. Arthur Jerome Eddy declared in 1902 that there was not an automobile made at that time that did not develop "many crudities and imperfections in construction which could be avoided by care and conscientious work in the factory." The need for many repairs, of course, resulted from the poor condition of the roads and the carelessness or inexperience of the drivers, but, Eddy contended, "ninety per cent of the stops and difficulties are due to defective construction." The Oldsmobile may have been no worse than the average car in this regard, but there is evidence that Fred Smith and his father had reason for their concern about the number of complaints regarding the car. There were jokes, which may or may not have been good natured. One of the slogans used in advertising the car declared: "Built to Run, and Does It!" The mere fact that an automobile worked was still felt to be worthy of attention, but Alfred Reeves, who was engaged in automobile publicity work at the time, claimed that someone wrote in and declared that Olds should use a question mark, not an exclamation mark, after that line. Another slogan boasted: "The Oldsmobile — Nothing to Watch but the Road." A common retort was: "Yes, but you get damned tired watching the same piece of road all the time!"

In a more specific vein, James B. Seager, a member of the family that was one of the largest holders of stock in the Olds Motor Works, sent Fred Smith a thirteen-page letter from the southwestern part of the United States, setting forth in infinite detail the changes that would have to be made in the company's runabout for it to be able to perform satisfactorily in that rugged part of the country. The hill-climbing capabilities of the early curved-dash models were questionable even in the flat Detroit area. Ransom Olds sometimes tried to impress people by backing the car up a hill, but in fact this was perhaps the only way the car would make it up the grade. His daughters assert that they well recall that in this period their mother had the job of putting a block of wood under the rear wheels of the car if it stopped on a hill. Legend has always assigned this task to Mrs. Olds in connection with the earlier well-known tendency of the Olds 1892 steam car to balk at ascending a hill, but it may have been true of the later models as well.[49]

Complaints regarding the runabout were sufficiently widespread in the spring of 1902 to cause at least one potential buyer, Henry B. Westinghouse, vice-president of the Westinghouse Air Brake Company, to decide to wait another year before making a purchase, in the hope that by then a more reliable product would be available. It is reasonable to assume that this is not an isolated instance of negative reactions from potential Oldsmobile customers. Nevertheless, those who decided to purchase the car were numerous enough to make the little Olds the hottest-selling car of its day. Production rose from around four hundred cars in 1901 to at least twenty-five hundred in 1902 (one source claims that 3299 Oldsmobiles were "built and sold" that year) and four thousand in 1903. By the summer of 1902, Olds ads listed selling agents for the car in New York City, Washington, D.C., Philadelphia, Boston, Pittsburgh, Cleveland, Detroit, Chicago, Indianapolis, Omaha, Buffalo, Plainfield, New Jersey, St. Louis, Kansas City, Denver, Houston, Toronto, San Francisco, Minneapolis, and Milwaukee. The New England agent in December 1902 testified that although he handled seven other well-known makes of cars in addition to the Oldsmobile, he would drop all of them except the Olds if he had to, "so highly do we prize the agency." He candidly admitted that there were those who were critical of the car, "but let me tell you that there is no vehicle that is giving less trouble or more satisfaction." Since he had sold about two hundred Oldsmobiles, he felt that he "ought to know" what he was talking about. On a smaller scale, the Lockwood Brothers, who handled Oldsmobile sales in Jackson, Michigan, began advertising during the summer of 1902 in the Jackson *Daily Citizen,* a paper that had carried very little automobile advertising prior to this time. The following winter, apparently as their business picked up, the Lockwoods began placing ads more regularly, about once a week. One such ad referred to the "sterling merits" of the Oldsmobile as "testified to by 5000 satisfied users [referring of course to the total national sales figures]."[50]

The advertising and promotional campaign conducted by the Olds Motor Works was on a scale with few, if any, precedents in the industry up to that time. The company continued and expanded the policy begun in 1901 of placing ads in general circulation magazines such as *Harper's Weekly* and the *Saturday Evening Post*. The first Oldsmobile ad in the *Post* appeared on February 15, 1902. Despite the claims of Oldsmobile enthusiasts, this was not the first advertisement for an automobile to appear in the pages of the *Post*, let alone the first in a "national magazine." A year earlier an ad for the Skene, a steamer produced in Springfield, Massachusetts, was carried in the magazine, while occasional notices for other cars also preceded the first Olds ad. In April 1903, an Oldsmobile ad appeared in the *Ladies Home Journal*, the magazine with the largest circulation of that day. An illustration showed a woman leaving a millinery store and getting into a curved-dash runabout parked outside. The text emphasized features that would interest a woman, such as the car's reliability and its simplicity of operation. It was, the ad declared: "The ideal vehicle for shopping and calling — equally suitable for a pleasant afternoon drive or an extended tour." Other advertisements that aimed specifically at potential customers such as physicians testified further to the ingenuity of the Olds advertising campaign. Unlike some of its competitors who repeated the same message over and over, the Olds company continually revised its copy and frequently tailored it to fit the specific medium in which it was to be carried. The origins of this practice may perhaps be found in the constantly changing copy Olds had used in the 1890's to advertise his engines.[51]

In promoting the runabout, the company also continued to encourage public demonstrations of the Oldsmobile's endurance and reliability. In 1902, Milford M. Weigle drove an Oldsmobile to victory in the nation's first one-hundred-mile non-stop endurance race, and between 1902 and 1904 he gained additional publicity for the Olds by winning three gold medals and twelve silver cups at various events for light cars on dirt tracks. In 1903, Horace T. Thomas, a young engineer from Michigan Agriculture College who was on the Detroit staff of Olds, drove the Oldsmobile *Pirate* over a measured mile at Ormond Beach, Florida, in the time of 1:06.2, which was said to have been a new American record for cars under a thousand pounds in weight. The *Pirate* was a specially built 825-pound racing vehicle, but the same year the sturdy qualities of the standard runabout were given their most severe testing when Eugene Hammond and L. L. Whitman drove one of the cars from California to Detroit on a trip that took them more than sixty days. Two years later, Dwight B. Huss, with Milford Weigle as his mechanic and relief driver, took only forty-four days to pilot *Old Scout*, another Olds runabout, from New York City to Portland, Oregon, winning a thousand-dollar prize for making the first transcontinental trip in a light car. Huss repeated the trip in the same vehicle in 1931, and two years later he climbed back into the venerable *Old Scout* to deliver a message from the governor of Michigan to the governor of Illinois at the opening of the General Motors building at the 1933 Century of Progress Exposition in Chicago.[52]

Walter C. Morley, an Olds executive, declared in the fall of 1902 that the "large and rapidly increasing demand" for the Oldsmobile that these stunts and advertisements helped create "keeps our facilities for producing them at the utmost tension, and we are facing conditions never before known in America." To meet this challenge, the Olds organization pioneered in improving auto manufacturing practices in order to increase output. Cars that were being assembled were moved along from station to station in a crude version of the modern production line. Parts were placed in bins wherever they were needed along this line.

Some writers, such as John K. Barnes, have credited Olds with being the first to introduce mass production techniques to the industry, but this is an exaggeration, based, in the case of Barnes at least, on incomplete data regarding early production statistics. He compared Olds' production of 4000 cars in 1903 with Winton's production that same year of "about 700"; the 297 cars produced in Buffalo by George N. Pierce (predecessors of the later Pierce-Arrow); 200 vehicles manufactured by E. R. Thomas, another Buffalo auto maker; approximately the same number turned out by Elwood Haynes and the Apperson brothers, now representing two separate firms in Kokomo; 77 Locomobiles; and "a handful" of cars manufactured by several other concerns, including the Thomas B. Jeffery Company of Kenosha, Wisconsin. In actuality, however, the Jeffery company was turning out far more than a handful of its Ramblers, a runabout with a one-cylinder engine that cost more but also generated more power than the Oldsmobile's engine. Nearly three thousand Ramblers were produced in 1902 and 1903, equaling the production figures of the Olds during its first two years. Barnes also overlooked entirely Locomobile's reported production of six thousand lightweight steam cars in a two-year period beginning in 1899, a figure that nearly equaled the later output of the Oldsmobile for 1902 and 1903. In looking at the auto industry's production for 1903, Barnes also forgot the record of a new Detroit company which turned out about seventeen hundred Cadillacs that year, more than three times the first-year production figures rung up by Olds in 1901. Finally, Barnes, like most American writers since him, has blithely ignored the earlier achievements of such French auto manufacturers as Alexandre Darracq, who produced over 1200 automobiles in 1901, and DeDion, Bouton et Cie, which by April 1901 had turned out 1500 of its voiturette model in about a year and a half and by the end of that year was said to be producing at the very respectable rate of 200 cars a month.[53]

Thus, by 1903, several automobile concerns on both sides of the Atlantic had been or were being faced with the necessity of altering and streamlining their manufacturing techniques in order to achieve large-scale production. On the other hand, although these problems were not uniquely those of the Olds Motor Works, as Barnes and others have assumed, there is no reason to deny Olds the leadership among these large producers to which the company was obviously entitled by its production record. By 1903, Locomobile, the earlier volume leader, had fallen far to the rear among auto manufacturers as it abandoned its popular but frail steam car for gasoline vehicles; production figures for the Rambler in 1903 were down slightly from those of 1902, and no one could yet be sure if Cadillac would equal or surpass its initial production figures for 1903. Among American companies, Olds had certainly had the most impressive and continuous growth record since 1901. Sales that had totaled $410,401 in 1901 increased to $1,626,475 in 1902, and to $2,325,580 in 1903, nearly a six-fold increase in two years. By the summer of 1903, the sales of Oldsmobiles were great enough to persuade the management of the Olds Motor Works to sell the profitable Olds gasoline engine business to the Seager family, thus completing a move out of the engine field that had begun two years earlier with the sale of Charles King's marine engine division. In 1903, as Ransom Olds later told the Detroit broker, F. M. Delano, the company's net earnings were about $900,000, out of which dividends of over $327,000 had been paid, with the remainder used to pay for plant improvements. During the busy period of the year, the plant produced over thirty cars a day and sales ran in excess of $400,000 a month, "which," Olds said, "was nearly half clear profit." 1904 was certain to be another banner year; the plant's capacity had almost doubled and a bank balance of $400,000 made it unnecessary for the company to borrow money to purchase materials. So important had the company become that it was singled out by *Scientific American* in January 1904 as an example of the kind of advanced manufacturing operation that had enabled a few American auto manufacturers to emerge as leaders after the ordeal of the industry's formative years.[54]

Ironically, at the time this article appeared, at a time when the Olds Motor Works was producing more automobiles than any other company in the world, Ransom Olds was in the process of severing all connections with the firm that bore his name. The reason for his departure has in the past been alleged to have resulted from a conflict between Olds and the Smiths over what kind of car they should produce. Olds, it has been said, favored continuing with the popular little runabout, but the Smiths wished instead to abandon that car in favor of a larger, more expensive model. Without access to board minutes, other company records, and far more personal papers than have so far turned up, the full story cannot be written; the materials that are available, however, indicate that the determining factor behind Olds' decision to get out of the company was not simply a question of a low-priced versus a high-priced car. The major question was: who was going to run the company, Olds or Fred Smith?[55]

The annual report for the year 1902 that was filed with the state by the Olds Motor Works showed that as of the end of that year Henry Russel was president. In electing Russel to this position, which had previously been passed from Samuel Smith to Olds and then back to the elder Smith, the directors were passing over several others whose stock-holdings in the company were larger than Russel's, including Olds, who owned the largest single block of shares. However, the report also showed that Olds' stockholdings were down to sixty-five hundred shares, a thousand less than they had been previously. Early in January 1903, Olds was discussing with Ray M. Owen the possibility of selling more of his stock, and by the following April he was trying to unload some of his holdings on Henry Russel, who wrote to Olds that he was willing to buy as many as a thousand shares. He did purchase at least 500 shares at that time at $30 a share, and in August he notified Olds that he was ready to buy more shares. By late January 1904, Olds had informed a Detroit broker that he had sold 3600 shares at the $30 price.[56]

Some, if not all of the motivation behind this desire of Olds to reduce his stockholdings stemmed from his growing unhappiness with the way things were going in the company. Since the formation of the Olds Motor Works in 1899 he had never controlled the firm in the same sense that he had controlled the earlier family engine company, but as long as he had the determining voice in how the company was operated he had been able to live with the fact that the Smiths had financial control. Regarding the determination of company policy, Olds later claimed that he was regularly outvoted by the Smith forces on the board of directors. For example, he declared that he had opposed the company's entry, in March 1903, into the Association of Licensed Automobile Manufacturers, of which Fred Smith had been one of the principal architects; Olds had been unable to persuade a majority of the directors to vote against membership in this powerful trade association. Olds' authority in the company was more directly threatened when Fred Smith began meddling in the manufacturing details of the business. The first clear indication of Olds' reaction to this kind of interference in his special sphere of influence came in a letter that he wrote to Smith on May 1, 1903. Olds declared that he had just learned "by a round about way that you were putting in an experimental room at Detroit." Olds, who usually gave the impression of being mild-mannered, made no effort on this occasion to disguise his anger at Smith's actions. "Now if this is your policy to do business underhanded and un-beknown to me, as you have several other things," he told Smith, "I do not care to be associated with you. I am Vice President and Manager of this company and such things should not be taken up without my consent or the consent of the board. I have had all I want of this treatment." Olds did not resign, however, but stayed on in his position until the first part of January 1904. After the annual meeting, at which the stockholders re-elected Olds to the board of directors, the board, including Samuel, Fred, and Angus Smith, James H. Seager, Henry Russel and Eugene Cooley, refused to retain Olds in his executive capacity as vice president and general manager. They replaced him with Fred Smith. "It was a hard thing for me," Olds told a friend a few months later, "when I had been manager since 1885, besides working day and night to develop the business to a wonderful success."[57]

Olds blamed his ouster on Fred Smith's personal ambition to become manager and his desire thereby to gain the credit that had previously been accorded to Olds. No doubt ambition was involved, but there was more to it than that. As the company grew, its management became more complex. Olds seems to have had little interest in the day-to-day details of managing such a concern, or in the innovations that were required to do the job successfully. Subsequently, in his Reo Motor Car Company, he was perfectly happy to dump these managerial burdens into the lap of Richard Scott. It is only fair to Fred Smith to acknowledge that he saw these deficiencies in Olds and that he moved in to fill the need for strong direction from the top. Certainly he was correct in insisting on the need for more attention to quality control and for the establishment of an engineering research staff. Certainly, too, Smith was correct in feeling that the company needed to develop a new, larger model to take the place of the one-cylinder runabout.

There are facts, however, that indicate that the question of whether or not to develop a larger model was no longer a major issue by January 1904. As early as the spring of 1902, work on a two-cylinder car was underway at the Lansing plant, and Smith was cautioning Olds to "keep this thing under cover — as far as opening it up to visitors." By the end of November, the work had progressed sufficiently for Smith to express to Olds the hope that the latter, if he was satisfied with what had been done, might complete two of the new cars for display purposes at the upcoming New York auto show. Although this was not done, a public announcement was made in February 1903 of the intention of the Olds Motor Works to put such a car on the market. However, at the very same time, in direct contrast to the view of Fred Smith, who was enthusiastic about the potential market demand for a two-cylinder Oldsmobile, Ransom Olds was quoted as opposing the trend in the industry away from the inexpensive models, such as the curved-dash Olds, toward bigger, more lavish automobiles. In a conversation with Henry Russel in mid-April, Olds apparently argued that they should stick with the runabout since it was a money-maker. Russel, no doubt reflecting the views of the Smiths, replied that "while as you say, there is no harm against making as much money as we can, we must sustain the reputation of the concern as well as make profits." He reported a discussion he had had with a group of Detroit's "important and intelligent business men," none of whom at the outset of the meeting was aware of Russel's connection with the Olds company. Russel reported that in the opinion of these men the Olds Motor Works

> was *not* a *good permanent* business. They said it was banking on a temporary popularity & selling a cheap made machine. . . . A good many of them seemed to know all about the machine & what they were talking about. . . . We must take the lesson to heart . . . & put out a machine

which, even at a larger cost, will give us a big profit & which will be worthy of its name & establish a good will for the business which will last during the long time in which I hope we will be associated.[58]

In April 1903, Fred Smith wrote to Olds to express his disappointment at their failure to produce the touring car. As a consequence, he said, they had received angry letters from Olds' agents who were demanding a car with "more power, stiffer construction, and a more conventional dash — say french 'bonnet.'" Late in 1903, Reuben Shettler, who had moved to Los Angeles where he was the Oldsmobile agent, was voicing these same sentiments, urging on Olds the necessity for the company to come out with a big machine if it was not to lag behind its competitors. By this time, Olds himself seems to have been convinced, for he claimed a few months later that in the fall of 1903 he was thinking of designing a heavier touring car, in keeping with the trend in the industry away from the lightweight buggy construction of the runabout. Significantly, it was this new type of automobile, complete with a French-style bonnet or hood in the front, rather than another version of the curved-dash runabout, that Olds emphasized in the fall of 1904 when he came back into the industry with the Reo. Just as significant is the fact that Fred Smith, in his comments to Olds in April 1903, emphasized that the first priority of Olds and his staff should be the development, not of a larger car, but of an improved runabout model. "As I have always claimed," Smith wrote, "the *big* work is still ahead in planning a campaign to lead the trade with something new, practical & cheap." This is not what one would expect from a businessman committed, as he has been depicted, to the production of a big and expensive car to replace the runabout. It is apparent, however, that such was not the immediate goal of Fred Smith in 1903, nor of his father or brother, who seem to have deferred to him in managerial decisions. Nor did this become their overriding ambition in 1904, since when they dumped Olds they did not at the same time jettison the curved-dash Oldsmobile. The little car continued to be the mainstay of the Olds Motor Works in 1904, as production reached 5500, although some of this total represented the new two-cylinder touring car that began appearing in the last half of the year. In 1905, as production topped 6500, the touring car, selling for $1250, appeared in greater numbers, but in volume the low-priced, revamped one-cylinder runabout was apparently still the company's pace-setter. (Also in 1905, the curved-dash Olds received its biggest boost to immortality in the words and music of Vincent Bryan and Gus Edwards, whose song, "In My Merry Oldsmobile," is the only one of many songs about automobiles to have had lasting popularity.) Even in 1906, when the emphasis in the Olds plant was definitely on two- and four-cylinder models, a few runabouts were still produced. The contention that the break between Ransom Olds and the Smiths arose out of an unshakable commitment on the part of each to divergent types of cars is simply not accurate.[59]

Although it had been announced officially in January 1904 that Olds had stepped down in order to take a much-needed vacation, but that he would retain his interests in the firm, he immediately placed his stock on the market. Reportedly, Fred Smith agreed to help him in selling some of this stock at a good price. Olds felt that $30 a share was a reasonable figure, although Henry Russel, in agreeing to buy some of Olds' stock at that price the previous year, had indicated that he would do it as a favor to Olds and would not pay others as high a price for their stock. As it turned out, Olds was forced to sell most of his stock for as little as $10 a share. Olds blamed this on Fred Smith, who, instead of helping Olds to sell his stock at a high price, drove the market price down by circulating reports that he felt stock in the Olds Motor Works was a good investment at par value, that is, $10. Olds overlooked the fact that he himself had helped depress the value of his stock by trying to dump all of his large holdings at one time, thereby glutting the market for the issue.[60]

The upheaval in the executive ranks of the Old Motor Works in 1904 left bitter feelings that were not forgotten. A quarter of a century later when Fred Smith wrote his reminiscences about his activities in the auto industry, particularly the Olds Motor Works, he never once mentioned Ransom Olds by name. Similarly, in interviews that Olds gave in later years, he studiously avoided mention of Fred Smith. Both men still had roles to play as the auto industry developed, but their roles would not be as dominant as they had been when the two men were working together. In addition, the brilliant group of assistants that they had assembled was also broken up. Some stayed with the Olds Motor Works. Others left to join Olds in his new automobile venture, while others were hired away by other companies or left to seek to organize new auto companies. In later years, efforts would be made to organize annual reunions of the "Old Crew," or "Olds Alumni," a distinguished group of men in the auto industry whose prominence, as a group, was not equaled or surpassed until the emergence of the later "Ford Alumni," composed of individuals whom Henry Ford had fired.[61]

Thus the days of glory, although never forgotten, were soon over for the Olds Motor Works; but during its brief period of dominance, it had established a pattern in the auto industry that proved to be an enduring one. The early leaders in the industry in the United States had been firms such as the Duryea Motor Wagon Company of Springfield, Massachusetts, the Pope Manufacturing Company of Hartford, Connecticut, the Locomobile Company of America, located first in Massachusetts and then in Bridgeport, Connecticut, and the Winton Company of Cleveland. After the sudden emergence of the Olds Motor Works and its curved-dash Oldsmobile in 1901-1902, a non-Michigan automobile manufacturer would never again achieve sales leadership in the industry.

CHAPTER 6

"THE CAR THAT JOHN DOLSON BUILT," AND OTHER LOSERS

By 1904, several of the more prominent Olds employees, including Charles King and Jonathan Maxwell, had already moved on to other automobile ventures over which they no doubt hoped to exercise greater control. One of the first of these Olds graduates to attempt such a step up, and probably the first of them to see his name on a car that was being manufactured, was Willis Grant Murray. At the time of the fire in the Detroit Olds plant in March 1901, he had been referred to as the manager of the Olds automobile department. The September following the fire he surfaced in Adrian, Michigan, and provided the spark for a new automobile manufacturing effort, one of many that appeared in the first years of the new century throughout southern Michigan. He thereby helped regenerate outstate interest in the auto industry which had suffered from such abortive schemes as those of William Worth in Benton Harbor in 1895-96, and from the transfer of the more promising Olds business from Lansing to Detroit in 1899.

Murray is one of that host of lesser automobile pioneers about whom we know unfortunately little. Aside from the brief period of perhaps a year and a half that he was with the Olds Motor Works, no information is available regarding his experience in the automotive field before coming to Adrian. All that is known of his previous employment record prior to going to work for Olds is that Murray was listed in the Detroit city directory for 1899 as a traveling agent for the Arc Welding Company. When he arrived in Adrian in 1901 he was hailed as "the inventor and patentee," one who was "recognized as an expert in the production and operation of automobiles," whose automobile designs, "invented and patented" by him, were to be the basis for the car soon to be manufactured in that southeastern Michigan town. An inventor Murray was, but the only patent awarded to him during those years is one for a packing machine, the rights to which he had assigned to three Canadians. He may have had other patents pending when he came to Adrian, but if so, they were never approved by the patent office. This, plus subsequent developments, suggests that there was more than a touch of the old blarney in Willis Grant Murray.[1]

Adrian, at first sight, would have seemed to be as unlikely a place to launch an automobile manufacturing company as Benton Harbor had been six years earlier when William Worth arrived in that city. Like Benton Harbor, Adrian was located in the heart of one of Michigan's most productive agricultural areas, but, also like Benton Harbor, in addition to serving the farmers of the surrounding countryside, Adrian was the site of some sizeable manufacturing concerns that provided employment for more than 2000 of the city's 9654 residents. A furniture factory, an electric fuse works, a piano manufacturer, a knitting mill, and one or two companies making rural mail boxes were located in Adrian; but the largest manufacturers by far were two factories which together employed six to eight hundred workmen and produced woven wire fencing, a product that the Page Woven Wire Fence Company, the larger of the two, claimed to have pioneered in developing in the 1880's.[2]

Among Adrian's smaller manufacturers was the Church Manufacturing Company, incorporated in 1891, and engaged originally in making pumps, water supply goods, steel land rollers, and certain other items. By the summer of 1901, the company was still small, employing only twenty-seven men, but its main product was now gasoline engines. The newly elected president of the company was Walter Clement, who had earlier been manager of the Page Woven Wire Fence Company before becoming president and manager of Adrian's Bond Steel Post Company, a job that he now held concurrently with his position at the gasoline engine company. It was to the Church Manufacturing Company that Willis Murray came with his ideas about automobiles. It was a choice that may have been influenced by his knowledge of the origins of the Olds Motor Works. Although it was a small firm, Church was no smaller than P. F. Olds and Son had been in the mid-nineties. The manufacture of gasoline engines was an obvious parallel, but even more important, Church, through Walter Clement's ties with Adrian's larger manufacturing concerns, seemed to offer the same possibilities for obtaining the additional outside financial investment that had enabled Olds to get into the production of automobiles.[3]

Murray was not the first automobile experimenter that Adrian had seen. J. D. Hagaman, an Adrian resident, was among the many no-show entrants in the *Times-Herald* race in 1895; two other Adrianites who appear to have had more successful auto experiments were H. R. Lamb, secretary of the Lamb Wire Fence Company, and Walter F. Vedder, a local wagonmaker. Early in 1901 these men were reported to have built an automobile driven by a four-and-a-half horsepower gasoline engine. These experiments had not as yet led to any manufacturing activity when Murray hit town.[4]

On September 5, 1901, in a contract signed by Murray and Walter Clement, Murray agreed "to furnish complete detailed working drawings for the construction of a gasoline motor-car, to be known as the Murray Motor-Car, and to personally oversee and direct the making of patterns, the machine work, assembling and finishing of an experimental car" to be built in the shop of and at the expense of the Church Manufacturing Company. If this experimental car passed its tests satisfactorily, Murray agreed "to devote his entire time and energy to the selling and introduction of the car to the trade." He also bound himself to assign a half-interest "in any patents procured on said vehicle or parts thereto, it being mutually agreed that [the Church company] shall pay all expenses of obtaining . . . all such patents," a clause that suggests that Murray had not yet received or applied for any automotive patents. The Church company agreed to pay Murray a salary of two hundred dollars a month while he was supervising the construction of the car and to continue to pay him the same salary while he was finding a market for the vehicle. If the need arose subsequently to establish a separate firm to build and sell the automobile, Murray would be given half the stock in that company. It was also agreed that at the end of each year, the profits, after all expenses "chargeable to the manufacture and sale of the gasoline motor-car" had been deducted, were to be equally divided between Murray and Church.[5]

Within a week, news of these plans appeared in *Motor Age,* and within a month the Adrian *Daily Times* was reporting that progress had been made in constructing the experimental car. By mid-November, the Church company announced that the automobile had been completed, that the various tests to which it had been subjected showed "it to be all right," and that this result would "doubtless lead to the manufacture of more and probably a regular line of work." A few days later, more definite word was forthcoming that several orders for the car had already been received, with production expected to commence within sixty days. "The success of the experiments," the Adrian *Daily Times* declared, "insures its future manufacture here as a permanent business." Before long the paper was enthusiastically expounding the benefits to the city that would result from the money and the new workers that this business would bring into Adrian. These predictions, as it turned out, proved to be only slightly more accurate than the Benton Harbor *Palladium's* predictions concerning the Baushke-Worth motor vehicle's impact on Benton Harbor's economy had been in 1895.[6]

The Murray car was remarkably reminiscent of the curved-dash Oldsmobile, which was perhaps not surprising considering Willis Murray's background. The Murray, a light, gasoline runabout, was reported to have a fourteen-horsepower engine, which, although probably a gross exaggeration, led to its being advertised as "the most powerful car of its kind in America." Although normally a one-seat vehicle, additional seating arrangements were available, at an extra charge, and were said to provide "for as many passengers and in as great a degree of comfort as in many of the large vehicles of the tonneau type." Normally, the car was finished in black and red, but one that was exhibited at the Chicago motor show in March 1902 was "finished in ivory, white and gold, with russet leather upholstery, which, in connection with the nickel-plated trimming, makes a remarkably handsome machine, causing much favorable comment, particularly on the part of the ladies." In addition to its attractive appearance, however, the basic Murray model was also one of the cheapest cars, with a retail price of $600, $50 under the price of the least expensive Oldsmobile. As for mechanical features, Grant Snedeker, a life-long Adrian resident who was familiar with the car as a boy and then decades later restored two of the few Murrays known to have survived, declared that because the body was attached to the frame in only three places, riding in the car was much like riding in a rocking chair. In tests of the car on the streets of Adrian, the Church company announced that the Murray had demonstrated its ability to "climb a hill or sail through a mud drift with perfect ease, while its speed on a paved street is almost unlimited." Subsequent use seemed to indicate that the Murray was, for its day, a sturdy, reliable car. Two were entered in the Chicago one-hundred-mile, non-stop endurance competition in the summer of 1902 and were among only twenty-seven out of eighty entrants to finish the race. In another instance, a satisfied Murray owner reported he had driven the vehicle 1650 apparently trouble-free miles in one six-week period.[7]

Encouraged by the results of their tests and the reported interest in the car of unnamed "experts" and auto dealers "from the large cities," Murray and the Church company proceeded with plans to put the runabout into production, announcing that they intended to turn out between three and five hundred of the cars in 1902. While Willis Murray lined up parts suppliers, the Church company attempted to expand its facilities, "for it is well known," the local paper observed, "that the greatest economy in production can only be secured through the employment of the finest machinery and the most systematic equipment." To accomplish this end, plans were disclosed on December 20, 1901, to form a new corporation with a capitalization of $100,000 to succeed the Church Manufacturing Company. Over half of the stock was reported already sub-scribed by men connected with several local "money-making concerns." However, the completion of this reorganization was long delayed. Accord-ing to the city directory for 1903, the Church company still was capital-ized at only $42,000, unchanged from the figure given in 1901. By 1905, the $100,000 figure had been reached, but by then the Church company was washed up as an automobile manufacturer. The failure to obtain a large infusion of new capital in the winter of 1901-1902 seems to have been the leading cause of the ultimate failure of this auto venture. Lacking this kind of help, Church gambled on virtually abandoning its existing busi-ness in order to devote its facilities to the production of the Murray. Un-fortunately, production of the car did not proceed as easily as company officials had first thought possible.[8]

Early in December 1901, the Church company reported that it ex-pected to complete ten cars by the middle of January. But late in January, these ten cars were still "in process of construction," with completion now probable by mid-February. One Murray was exhibited at the Chicago show that began on March 1, where it was praised as "one of the most attractive vehicles on exhibition," but at the end of March, the first batch of ten runabouts was still not completed. The newspaper accounts indi-cate that shortages of materials and especially the inexperience of the workers were the prime causes for the failures in meeting the various dead-lines. Early in April, the company announced the receipt of the needed materials and declared that its workers "have now gained considerable insight into the work, and construction will be much more rapid than in the past. Everything is in excellent shape and the company now feels qualified to compete with any car in point of usefulness and durability."[9]

Finally, on April 25, 1902, came the first report of a Murray being completed and shipped out, in this case to Columbus, Ohio. In the next three months other reports were published of one, or in one case two, cars being shipped to Chicago and Danville, Illinois, Logansport, Indiana, an unidentified destination in Iowa, a town in Missouri, and another in Mis-sissippi. Although other cars were no doubt sold in the Adrian area, the fact that Church's publicity specifically mentioned these individual out-of-town sales seems to indicate that earlier expectations that shipments would proceed at an average of one a day had been far from fulfilled. By the end of August, the company was admitting that it had been "a little slow in making shipments," but once again was voicing confidence that the orders, which were said to be coming in from all over the country, would be filled more promptly in the future.[10]

From the available evidence, admittedly incomplete, a picture emerges of a small company, almost totally inexperienced in the as yet poorly developed art of making automobiles, trying to operate on a shoe-string and to sell its cars in the face of competition from comparatively well-financed, talent-rich firms such as the Olds Motor Works.

Church had tried. At the end of May 1902, it hired twenty more men; its work force now numbered fifty-four. Assuming the men knew their jobs, this force would have been large enough to assemble the Murray from parts produced elsewhere; but if many of the parts had to be turned out in the Church plant, the manpower would have been stretched too thin. The plant was remodeled in an attempt to transform the buildings from their previous uses to that of manufacturing automobiles; machinery was added, and the old pump storeroom became the finishing room for Murrays; a quarter-mile cinder track was built outside for testing, and the old method of making brass castings was discarded in favor of one that was optimistically declared to be an improvement. Through all the efforts, however, ran the persistent problems of inexperienced workmen awkwardly learning new jobs, and of suppliers who failed to deliver materials on time.[11]

Then in September came the clearest sign that the company was having real troubles when it informed Willis Grant Murray that "his services were no longer desired." A circular was sent out advising interested parties that Murray, who had been the active manager of the company, was "no longer with the concern." Murray immediately filed a suit against Church for $450 in wages that he claimed were still owed him, plus various other amounts for services, expenses, and materials for which he claimed he should also be compensated. Church disputed some of the expense items submitted by Murray, but in particular objected to Murray's claim for $500 for his interest in a racing car he had built in the Church factory as the result of an arrangement with one of the company's officers, Charles G. Hart, despite the opposition of president Walter Clement, who apparently thought Murray was spending too much time on that project and not enough on the runabout. An out-of-court settlement was finally reached in the case after a jury, in June 1903, declared it was unable to arrive at a verdict. Ten of the members favored the Church company but two stubbornly held out for Murray. Meanwhile, Murray had gone off to Chicago, where he got a job with the Standard Motor Vehicle Company. A short while later, in 1904, he was listed as second vice-president of the American Motor League; if his residence was still Adrian, as listed, Murray was the only Michigan officer in this organization that Charles King had helped to found nine years earlier.[12]

Although the change in management that followed Murray's departure "caused some old employees to have a layoff," production of the Murray runabout continued in the fall of 1902 at its usual slow pace. In October, a car was shipped off to California, "neatly and firmly packed in a large box so no harm could come to it." In October and November, the Church company showed considerable imagination and foresight in making one of its cars available to the local postmaster for experimental use in rural mail delivery. Although the experiment, one of the first such in the country, was pronounced a success, it, like the earlier use of a Ford truck by the Detroit Post Office in 1900, had no visible effect on the sales of the vehicles.[13]

A driver and a mail carrier experiment with a Murray runabout on an RFD route out of Adrian in the winter of 1902. Note the chains on the rear wheels.
Courtesy Michigan Historical Collections

In February 1903, there was a flurry of excitement when it was announced that Charles G. Hart and E. S. Hamilton, vice-president and general manager, respectively, of the Church company, had signed a contract, with whom it was not stated, for the year's entire output of cars. The plant went on a full ten-hour day, ads were placed for more workers, and a relatively large number of men were hired in the next month, including a machinist from Detroit who was brought in as a foreman. Still unable to handle all of the work, however, Church farmed out some of its machine shop and blacksmith work to the Page Fence Company and the Bond Post Company. Although the struggling little Adrian automaker continued to be plagued by troubles — Hamilton resigned as manager, and a shortage of materials brought assembly operations to a standstill at the end of March — a month later Church reported its most impressive car shipments to date: two freight cars with six Murrays in each were sent off to Chicago, and an unspecified number of runabouts were shipped to a dealer in Liverpool, England.[14]

The record-breaking achievements of April 1903 seem to have reached the high-water mark for this company's automobile manufacturing. No further word concerning the Church Manufacturing Company appeared in the Adrian *Daily Times* until the following December, when it was announced the company was going into the business of manufacturing wire fencing, a product with which Walter Clement, Charles Hart, and most of the other officers and stockholders were more familiar than they were with motor vehicles. The company was not abandoning auto-mobiles, but work in that line would be continued "slowly" until addi-tional capital was secured. Instead of the Murray runabout, Church planned to produce a larger, five-passenger touring car, the Lenawee, named after the county in which Adrian is located. Work on the car had been underway for some time. The first tests were made the previous April, not long after the Olds Motor Works had announced its intention to come out with a bigger car. Church's move no doubt reflected some of the same thinking that lay behind the Olds decision (it is, of course, possi-ble that the legal problems that could have arisen out of continued pro-duction of a car designed by Willis Murray at a time when he had a suit pending against Church provided another reason for abandoning the Murray in favor of an entirely new car). How the Church officials, who had not had a resounding success manufacturing and selling the cheap runabout, could have expected to do better with a more expensive car that would be more difficult to manufacture is hard to understand. At all events, probably no more than a dozen Lenawees were produced, all of them in 1904. Grant Snedeker's father bought one of them for a thou-sand dollars, and paid the company in installments, an unusual arrange-ment in those days when cash-and-carry was the rule in the auto in-dustry.[15] By this time, the Church Manufacturing Company was doubtless glad to sell any of its cars on almost any terms. In the fall of 1904, it had only thirteen employees. The following year the *Michigan State Gazetteer* described the company's business as "automobiles, etc.," and a likely guess is that it was now producing a lot more "et cetera" than vehicles of any kind.[16]

Church's experience did not deter others in Adrian from venturing into the auto field. Late in 1906, the Page Woven Wire Fence Company took over the old Church factory and announced the formation of a new company to produce a light runabout, to be followed later by a touring car and possibly a truck. An elaborate set of photographs of the new Page automobile was prepared for promotional purposes, but it seems that few Page cars ever made it out of the plant. The subsequent location of the Lion Motor Car Company in Adrian in 1909 was a different story. It was formed by Detroiters who had experience and money. But even this ven-ture ended in failure as a fire in 1912 that destroyed the Lion factory dealt the company a blow from which it could not recover.[17]

A few years ago, Grant Snedeker discovered the remains of sev-eral Murray runabouts on a farm outside Adrian owned by the sons of Walter Clement. Snedeker managed to piece together two complete Mur-rays from the ruins. One of the restored vehicles was returned to the Clem-ent family, the other went to the Detroit automobile collector Jack A. Frost (who also owns the only Lenawee known to exist). These two run-abouts, plus one in Bellm's Car Museum in Sarasota, Florida, and another owned by the well-known Detroit collector Barney Pollard, are all that remain of the approximately 225 Murrays that were produced, and all that is left of the dreams of fame and fortune that Willis Murray and Walter Clement shared in 1901.[18]

* * *

As the automobile became increasingly visible and investors realized what money could be made by capitalizing on the public's mushrooming interest in these vehicles, the history of the Murray was repeated throughout southern Michigan. In a majority of cases, nothing at all came of the desire to manufacture automobiles. The lack of financial support was probably the primary factor. This seems to have been the case with M. Hendrickson of White Cloud, Michigan, who, in the summer of 1900, claimed to "have the right thing for automobile power," and advertised in *Motor Age* for a "Person with capital." Others, like the newly formed Regal Gasoline Engine Company of Coldwater, which, in 1901, was reportedly considering manufacturing automobiles as well as engines, apparently thought better of the idea and decided not to enter these uncharted waters. Still others, like the Alamo Manufacturing Company, an established producer of gas and gasoline engines in Hillsdale which, according to one compilation of automobile companies in the United States, produced the Alamobile in 1902, and the Hudson Auto Vehicle Company, formed in Hudson, Michigan, in 1903, seem never to have gotten much farther than the drawing board. Finally, however, there were the companies that took the plunge but who, after a few years, left or were forced out of the auto manufacturing business.[19]

A company that had a history typical of many such attempts was formed by Allie R. Welch and his younger brother Fred in the village of Chelsea, a community of less than two thousand inhabitants located a few miles north of Adrian. As a boy, Allie Welch reportedly had built a steam engine before going to work for a stove factory in Chelsea. There, he ultimately rose to the rank of superintendent. In 1895 he went east to take charge of a metal-working factory, and later established his own metal novelty shop in New York. In 1898, he moved his company back to Chelsea and took his brother, who had been operating a local bicycle shop, into the business.[20] In February of 1900, the brothers incorporated the novelty business as the Chelsea Manufacturing Company, with an authorized capitalization of $25,000, of which no more than $16,000 in cash was ever paid in, and began manufacturing small flashlights, pencil sharpeners, and other novelties invented by Allie Welch. At the same time, the two brothers, particularly Allie, were working on a twenty-horsepower, two-cylinder gasoline motor vehicle, which was completed and tested by April 1901. These experiments proved so costly that by the fall of 1902, in the plain words of a legal brief filed in subsequent bankruptcy proceedings, "this company was *Busted*." Seeking financial help, Allie Welch went to Battle Creek where he was introduced to Abram C. Wisner, who, in the words of the same legal brief, was "an exponent and devotee of the principles of high finance." (One source credits him with having organized the Malta-Vita Pure Food Company, one of Battle Creek's leading breakfast food processors.) Welch showed Wisner photographs and sketches of his automobile, which had certain unusual features such as a steering wheel, by itself something of a novelty in this day of the steering tiller, but a steering wheel that telescoped to allow passengers to enter and exit with greater ease — a real novelty. Wisner came to Chelsea, and after looking over the plant and the car he agreed to take charge of the company's reorganization. The enterprise was recapitalized at $200,-000. A fourth of the stock went to the stockholders in the old company, a fourth was set aside for future promotional purposes, and the remaining half went to Wisner and several of his associates. Welch and Wisner contended that this eight-fold increase in the stock of the company, when there was no visible increase in its physical assets, was justified by the value of Welch's ideas concerning automobiles (none of which he had yet patented, and some of which, one report charges, were based on features copied from a car produced in Massachusetts by the Holyoke Motor Works). When applied to the cars the company would manufacture, the ideas would make each share of stock worth its par value and then some. In addition, Wisner, besides demonstrating his knowledge of the finer points of "high finance," agreed to provide the company with funds up to $25,000; part of it was to be used to pay off the debts of the old company. Wisner regarded this money not as an investment but as a loan, which he expected to be repaid.[21]

At the time of the reorganization of the Chelsea Manufacturing Company in January 1903, it was announced that the firm would "launch out more extensively in the way of automobile manufacturing, having a thoroughly equipped and up to date touring car model (called the Welch Touring Car)." Materials for a hundred of these automobiles had been ordered, and fifteen were scheduled for completion by April. One was hastily completed in time to be exhibited at the Chicago auto show in February. At the show, a number of orders were received for the $2000 vehicle, including a carload ordered by a San Francisco physician who was so taken by the Welch that he signed up to be the company's Pacific Coast agent. Although the Welch brothers and their men completed at least two cars and managed to get ten others into various stages of completion, activity in the plant came to a halt in July when Wisner, who had debts of his own, was either unable or unwilling to continue to advance any more funds; he had thus far supplied less than half of the $25,000 he had promised the previous December. Allie Welch later testified that with as little as $10,000 more in the summer of 1903, the ten cars could have been completed and with the proceeds from their sale the company might have been saved. He also admitted, however, that he had underestimated the company's financial requirements when he asked Wisner for only

$25,000. In retrospect, he declared, twice that amount would have been a more realistic figure.[22]

With his Battle Creek source of funds drying up, Allie Welch sought new help in Pontiac, where, in the fall of 1903, interest that was shown in Welch's company by some carriage manufacturers seemed about to save the firm. However, a fire at the Pontiac Buggy Company, Welch claimed, upset these plans by diverting some of the promised funds into the rebuilding of the destroyed factory. Finally, in January 1904, upon the application of a group of creditors of the Chelsea Manufacturing Company, the federal district court appointed a receiver and the company was declared bankrupt. This was the first of many Michigan automobile manufacturers to end up in that fashion. Three appraisers, including John Dodge of Detroit, who, with his brother, was already a familiar name in the auto industry, were appointed to evaluate the physical assets of the Chelsea plant, which were then auctioned off on March 31, 1904. From the proceeds of the sale the receiver was able to pay the 123 approved creditors a small fraction of the more than $32,000 owed to them by the Chelsea firm.[23]

The fact that the Chelsea Manufacturing Company went bankrupt is not especially noteworthy. A number of commentators in this period remarked on the unusually high rate of failure among companies trying to get a toehold in this new industry. One compilation tallied 287 such bankruptcies between 1902 and 1907. Considering this national total, auto companies in Michigan in these years seem to have enjoyed a somewhat higher than average survival rate. The Chelsea bankruptcy proceedings, which dragged on until November 30, 1906, provide some significant insights into what went wrong in this particular case. One cause of the collapse, obviously, was the lack of substantial financial support. Chelsea was an unlikely place to secure the kind of investments needed to finance an automobile manufacturer, even in those early days. Lengthy examinations of the subsequent dealings with Abram Wisner raised serious doubts concerning Wisner's financial integrity and Welch's business intelligence. In addition, the proceedings raised questions regarding the merits of the 1903 Welch car; even if the necessary funds had been available to produce a few more of the cars, their poor quality might have led to the company's demise anyway.[24]

Apparently the Welch was largely an assembled job. In addition to the Dodge Brothers, who were one of the company's larger creditors, other parts suppliers with familiar names who were included among the Chelsea company's creditors were the Brown and Sharpe Manufacturing Company of Providence, Rhode Island, Brown-Lipe Gear Company of Syracuse, and the C. R. Wilson Body Company of Detroit. Welch had the usual problems with his suppliers, including one who deceived the company by shipping it malleable iron and labeling it as steel. But according to a mechanical engineer employed by the Chelsea company, it was "defective design," not defective parts, that proved to be the undoing of at least one Welch touring car sold in this period. Despite endless hours spent trying to make this vehicle operable, including installing a new engine, the car could never be driven any distance without breaking down, according to its owner, Daniel Gelder. A Chicago jeweler and a creditor of the Chelsea firm, Gelder declared in 1905 that his car was a "freak," and of dubious value even as junk. One of the company's Battle Creek investors had a similar experience with the car manufactured for him, one that was supposed to be a much better model than the one Gelder was stuck with. After spending $250 on repairs, this second Welch owner reported in 1905 that he had managed to sell the car for $425, "which was all that could be obtained for it, and all that it was worth." For a car that could not have been over one or two years old and was supposedly worth $2000 new, this represented an extraordinary rate of depreciation.[25]

The Welch brothers came through the collapse of their initial automobile venture in excellent shape. They eventually even got the court to accept their claim that their company owed them some $600, although, like the other creditors, they got only a few cents to the dollar in the final payoff. Allie Welch, meanwhile, had taken his $175,000 worth of ideas, an intangible asset that the court could not seize and auction off, to Pontiac, where the formation of a new company, the Welch Motor Car Company, was completed by March 1, 1904. Of the 450 shares of stock that were issued, Arthur Pack of Orchard Lake, just outside Pontiac, owned 447 shares. He had apparently supplied the Welch brothers with a factory valued at $20,000 and had put up $25,000 in cash, in return for this stock. Pack also served as the president and treasurer of the company, Allie Welch was vice-president and Fred Welch was secretary of the firm. Two cars that the brothers had apparently been planning to build were completed in time to be exhibited at the Detroit auto show in February, less than a month after the first Welch auto company went into bankruptcy and before the organization of the second company was completed. By April, production had begun on ten of these cars; it was a larger version of the old Welch touring car with a 36-horsepower, four-cylinder engine. All ten were completed and shipped by August, and by October, as the Welch company began work on fifty more cars and was reported to be looking for larger quarters for its operations, it was clear that this time the Welch brothers had found the right combination.[26]

The Welch car that was produced in Pontiac during the next half-dozen years was changed little, mechanically, from the 1904 model except for the addition of a six-cylinder, 75-horsepower engine. It was one of the largest American-made cars of the day, and also one of the most expensive. Rather than attempting "to put together a car to sell to the masses — a cheaply built car," the company declared, obviously referring to the kind of automobile more and more of its fellow Michigan auto manufacturers were turning out, the Welch brothers insisted on producing cars of the highest quality, with no compromises in standards; the resulting price tags ranged from $4500 to a whopping $9000 for the Welch touring coach.

An individual who could come up with $9000 in 1909 did get his money's worth from a vehicle that "contains sleeping, cooking, and dining accommodations for five. Ice box, storage for provisions, clothes, etc. It will seat nine people. Hot and cold water in lavatory." Naturally, for that kind of money one would expect the finest of materials to be used, and Welch obliged with such fine touches as using only steel that was imported from the Krupp plant in Germany. The same kind of snob appeal carried over to what the company had to say about its location in the "beautiful little city" of Pontiac, twenty miles removed from Detroit: its location enabled Welch to employ "a superior class of men attracted by the quiet suburban life," men who were "thoroughly in harmony with the conscientious work which is a fixture of the Welch construction."[27]

Eventually, Welch built about 250 cars each year and sold them to people who doubtless regarded such prestige cars as Detroit's Packard to be too common for their tastes. Then, in June of 1909, the Welch Motor Car Company was gobbled up by General Motors; this was just one of numerous acquisitions picked up in this period by William C. Durant, who wanted to gain control of as wide a variety of automobiles as possible. The high-priced Welch, however, never really fit into the plans Durant and his associates were developing, especially after they acquired control later that summer of Cadillac, a far more modestly priced car but a perfectly adequate entry in the fine car field. Durant sought to broaden the market for the Welch by purchasing the former Detroit plant of the Olds Motor Works from its owner, Samuel L. Smith, and setting up a Detroit branch of the Welch company. The Welch-Detroit was a less expensive car than the luxurious models produced in Pontiac, but, as in Packard's decision, later, to add a cheaper model to its line, the effect of this move probably was to cheapen the Welch label and to weaken its appeal as a rich man's status symbol. By the fall of 1909, General Motors was already having second thoughts about the Welch acquisition and was looking for ways to dispose of the Pontiac plant. Two years later, after this had been accomplished, an administrative reorganization resulted in shutting down the Welch-Detroit operations as well, and Welch became part of the new Marquette Motor Company, whose plant was located in Saginaw. Despite public statements by General Motors officials that the Welch car would continue being produced, it shortly disappeared entirely. The end officially took place in 1914, although no Welch cars had been produced for several years. Allie Welch, who, with his brother Fred, had continued to be involved in the Welch manufacturing activities after the General Motors takeover, did not live to see the end of his dream, for he died in a boating accident in November 1911.[28]

In recent years, the Welch has been rescued from complete oblivion by the auto writer and cartoonist, Ralph Stein, who found a 1907 Welch in Montrose, New York, in 1951, bought it for $500, restored it, and in several articles and books has sought to refurbish the car's reputation as one of the great automobiles in the history of the American automobile industry. A conflicting opinion of the car's merits is held by another automobile authority, Leslie Henry of the Henry Ford Museum, who declares that although the Welch engine was of superior design, other mechanical features of the car were decidedly inferior in character.[29]

Because of some industries already located there, Battle Creek, where Allie Welch had first sought help for his floundering company, would seem to have provided a likely spawning ground for auto manufacturing activities. In the nineteenth century it had grown to be a leader in the manufacture of steam-powered farm equipment, and by the 1890's one source declared that Battle Creek "made more traction engines and threshing machinery than . . . any other city in America." The Advance Thresher Company claimed to be second in the nation only to the J. I. Case Company in the production of threshers; the smaller Nichols & Shepard Company, manufacturers of the steam-powered road machine that caught Henry Ford's eye in 1876, was producing a thousand threshers a year. In addition, the fact that several other Battle Creek firms were manufacturing steam pumps would seem to have been still another reason for individuals interested in steam cars, at least, to locate in that city.[30]

Some slight stirring of interest in automobiles had been visible at least as early as 1898 when, as noted earlier, Henry W. Kellogg was assigned a one-third interest in the rights to William O. Worth's patented motor vehicle. The following year, Uriah Smith, also of Battle Creek, claimed to have invented an unusual device to reduce the fears that the sight of an automobile aroused in horses, fears that Smith believed constituted "the greatest impediment to the general use of motor vehicles." His novel idea was to attach a replica of a horse's head and neck to the front of the motor carriage so that an approaching horse would think he was coming upon a horse-drawn vehicle, "and before he could discover his error and see that he had been fooled, the strange creation would be passed, and then it would be too late to grow frantic and fractious." The horsey adornment, Smith pointed out, would also serve as a partial wind break for the passengers and could be used as "a receptacle for gasolene." Smith even succeeded in getting the Haynes-Apperson company of Kokomo to try out his idea. The office secretary recalled that the results were "not satisfactory"; after several months, Elmer Apperson ordered the horsehead attachment to be returned to its inventor, thereby ending Uriah Smith's career as an automotive designer.

Of a more practical nature was the report in 1901 that a steam carriage had been built in the shops of the Advance Thresher Company and was being operated on the streets of Battle Creek. A short time later, one of the local pump manufacturers added to his product line pumps that were specially designed to meet the needs of steam carriage manufacturers.

None of this activity, however, led to the development of any significant automobile manufacturing in Battle Creek. The reason is probably not hard to discover. The national automobile boom was paralleled in the first years of the twentieth century by a fantastic boom in the breakfast food industry in Battle Creek. With an occasional exception, such as Abram Wisner's ill-fated venture into automobiles, most of the energies and investment capital of businessmen with a speculative frame of mind in Battle Creek went into the establishment of new companies that hoped to make a fortune, as Charles W. Post had done in the late nineties with Postum and Grape-Nuts, by stealing some of Dr. John Harvey Kellogg's ideas. When one such firm, the exotically named Cero Fruto Food Company, was incorporated in February 1903, with a capitalization of $25,000,000, Battle Creek businessmen, who described this as "one of the biggest financial deals in the history of the city," could not be expected to pay much attention to the measly $200,000 stock deal that Wisner had engineered a month earlier.[31]

A similar preoccupation with another business activity may also explain the failure of automobile manufacturing to get a very strong hold in Battle Creek's neighbor to the west, Kalamazoo. Although celery was still its most famous product, the big economic development in the first decade of the century was a great expansion in Kalamazoo's paper industry. Much of the available local investment capital was no doubt tied up in this major economic effort. Nevertheless, there was enough flexibility and loose capital to foster the development of several automobile companies, none of which enjoyed lasting success. The most interesting aspect of this development is that three of the companies remained in business, giving up automobiles in favor of the production of automobile parts. Two are still producing today, with records of continuous production in the auto industry equaling or surpassing those of nearly all of the better known manufacturers in this field.[32]

The first automobile to be manufactured in Kalamazoo was the result of a rather curious wedding of divergent business backgrounds. In the summer of 1902, plans were unveiled by the Kalamazoo Cycle Company to put out an automobile that would weigh less than three hundred pounds and would sell for less than $400. It would carry two people at speeds of from five to fifteen miles an hour "over most roads." The vehicle had been designed and built by two brothers, Charles C. and Maurice E. Blood, who, since founding the Kalamazoo Cycle Company in 1891, had been manufacturing bicycles and bicycle accessories. This company, together with a small carriage firm, was absorbed by the Michigan Automobile Company, which was organized on December 30, 1902, to manufacture the lightweight, cheap car. Joining the Bloods in the company, and, indeed, controlling it, were members of the Fuller family, which had built up a highly profitable business making washboards. The Michigan Automobile Company was headed by Charles D. Fuller; Frank D. Fuller served as secretary, and Maurice Blood was treasurer. Significant local support for the venture was indicated by the presence on the board of Dr. William E. Upjohn, whose pharmaceutical company was already acquiring a national reputation.

The Michigan runabout, which the company began to manufacture in 1903, was, at 575 pounds, much heavier than originally anticipated, and its price of $450 was well in excess of earlier projections. Still, the little car, which prospective buyers were assured was "not a partly completed job," was one of the cheapest cars on the market. As such it was more typical of what would become the prevailing trend of thought among Michigan auto men than were the plans of the Welch brothers at this same time to put out a highly priced car. The Michigan Automobile Company continued to produce its car for several years, but never succeeded in parlaying the low price into a very sizable piece of the auto business. One apparent reason lay in the fact that although the company claimed that it made nearly all of its parts, the entire staff of the company in March 1904 consisted of only thirty-three men and two women. The announcement in October that because of its increased business the company was boosting its capitalization to $50,000 and was working until 10 or 11 p.m. three nights a week to try to keep up with the orders, was likewise not especially impressive. In 1905, following the industry-wide trend away from the light runabouts to heavier cars, the Kalamazoo company offered a touring car model, selling for a thousand dollars with tonneau.

Although the Michigan Automobile Company continued to be listed as a manufacturer of automobiles as late as 1909, it does not appear to have produced any cars after about 1906. Instead, it found its niche in the industry by turning to the production of clutches and transmissions for cars. In 1914, the automobile company was officially dissolved, and the transmission and clutch business continued as Fuller & Sons Manufacturing Company. After 1923 the company concentrated on transmissions and certain other parts for heavy-duty trucks. In 1928, the Fuller company was sold to the Unit Corporation of America, which also owned a plant in Wisconsin. By 1932, however, this corporation was forced into receivership, but through the efforts of the court-appointed receiver, J. Seton Gray, the Kalamazoo transmission works survived the disaster under the new name of the Fuller Manufacturing Company. In 1958, the Fuller company was acquired by the Eaton Manufacturing Company, and although the latter, when it became simply the Eaton Corporation, changed the name of the Kalamazoo operation to Transmission Division, the name of the founders of this pioneer Michigan auto parts manufacturer survives today through the continued use of the Fuller trade name.[33]

The Michigan Automobile Company should not be confused with the Michigan Buggy Company, the largest of several carriage manufacturers in Kalamazoo. Around 1909, after almost three decades of experience manufacturing carriages, the Michigan Buggy Company, while still continuing to make carriages, also began manufacturing a car called the Michigan. At first this was a high-wheeled buggy car, a type that enjoyed a brief popularity in the Middle West in this period. By 1911, however, the Michigan Buggy Company had switched to a more expensive touring car and a roadster model.

Based upon what happened in Flint and Pontiac, the two leading centers of the carriage industry in Michigan, many auto buffs and historians have concluded that the presence in Michigan of numerous successful carriage manufacturers who were readily able to convert to the manufacture of horseless carriages constitutes one of the major reasons why the auto industry was able to develop in Michigan to the extent that it did. However, examining the experience of the Michigan Buggy Company and carefully analyzing what happened to carriage manufacturers in other cities, including Flint and Pontiac, leads to a different conclusion — that there was little correlation between success in manufacturing horse-drawn vehicles and success in manufacturing the horseless variety.[34]

The Michigan Buggy Company made the mistake of assuming that such a correlation did in fact exist. In a January 1912 advertisement, the company declared that when it decided to enter the automotive field the building of a good automobile "had been reduced to an exact science," the principles of which were easily grasped by anyone familiar with factory operations. Furthermore, the company "knew that with our immense plant and thoroughly organized array of skilled mechanics, we could manufacture cars as economically as any concern in existence." An additional advantage it had over other auto manufacturers who had to start from scratch lay in its existing network of dealers — ten thousand of them, the company claimed — who had been selling its buggies and were now ready to sell its automobiles. "Before we built a car . . . these agents began to make demands on us for local territory. Letters came from all over the country, promising support. One agent came into our office with $10,000 in cold cash to deposit on the first machines we should turn out." As a result, the company declared that it had not had to budget large sums of money to promote sales of its cars since its "loyal agents have taken all the cars we could produce." These savings in advertising costs had been generously passed on to the public, who, it was said, would find that the "Michigan Forty," at $1500, sold for at least a third less than competitors with high advertising expenses could sell their comparable models. Then, to cap it all, the Michigan Buggy Company guaranteed its cars "for life . . . the fairest and squarest guarantee ever put on an automobile. If at any time you are dissatisfied — in one year, two years, five years, any time — go back to your local agent and he will make it right with you. If he doesn't, we will."[35]

It sounded convincing, but unfortunately for the owners of these Michigans, there was no guarantee that the Michigan Buggy Company would last as long as its cars. In August 1913, the company was declared bankrupt and its affairs placed in the hands of a receiver, the Detroit Trust Company. As Joseph Bower, vice-president of the trust company, began to report on his investigations into the affairs of the buggy company, the reverberations were felt not only in the Kalamazoo business community but in areas scattered across the state and nation. By the use of unorthodox, even fraudulent, accounting procedures, company officials had managed for several months to conceal the fact that the firm was insolvent. Under these false pretenses, officials had obtained credit from at least seventy-four banks, using as collateral so-called accommodation notes that it had received from some of its "loyal agents." The notes could be — and were — taken as legitimate orders for cars and parts, with the dealer's promise to remit payment upon delivery. Unknown to the banks, contracts between Michigan Buggy and these select dealers, who were nothing if not accommodating, made it clear that these notes were not a part of actual orders but instead were simply pieces of paper designed to keep the Kalamazoo firm afloat. In addition to the signed and dated notes the company had already taken to the banks, Bower discovered stacks of notes from sixteen dealers, awaiting only the insertion by the company of an appropriate date. These undated notes had a face value of over $2,462,000, including over a million dollars in notes signed by the company's dealer in the little town of Plano, Illinois.

Late in July 1913, with an army of creditors closing in, the company sought to keep some of its real assets out of the hands of these creditors by transferring most of its existing stock of automobiles to a Pennsylvania corporation. In the subsequent bankruptcy proceedings, this firm then submitted a bid on most of the remaining legitimate assets of the buggy company, a bid that the outraged creditors unanimously rejected. By the time some semblance of order began to emerge from the Michigan Buggy Company's jumbled records and a realistic appraisal of its assets was possible, it was clear that none of the creditors could hope to recoup a very large percentage of his losses.[36]

Indirectly, the defunct Michigan Buggy Company gave rise to what is possibly Kalamazoo's most famous automobile enterprise. The Kalamazoo Chamber of Commerce raised $5000 to persuade A. C. Barley of Streeter, Illinois, to move his auto company into the vacant buggy plant. Here, beginning in 1916, Barley's Roamer car began to be produced in the home of the old Michigan Forty. A flashy car that tried to incorporate Rolls-Royce features into a medium-priced car, the Roamer enjoyed a certain amount of success. The crunch of the fierce competition that developed in the twenties proved too much, however, and by the mid-twenties the Roamer and the Barley, another model that the company produced briefly, had suffered the same fate as the other Kalamazoo cars, including those of the Michigan Automobile Company.[37]

The decision, years earlier, of the Michigan Automobile Company to abandon automobile production may have stemmed from the fact that the Blood brothers, the designers of the Michigan runabout, left the company and, together with several other members of the Blood family and a New York investor, L. W. Wilson, organized their own company, the Blood Bros. Automobile and Machine Company, on March 2, 1904. In addition to "Manufacturing and selling automobiles and Sundry parts," the business of the new company also included "general repairing and job Machine Shop work." For a short time in 1905, the brothers put out the

Blood car, but when the universal joint in the vehicle proved defective they turned their attention to correcting it. So successful were they in accomplishing this objective that the brothers abandoned automobile production and concentrated on manufacturing the improved part, dropping the word "automobile" from the firm's name in 1906.

Subsequently the Bloods moved their company a short distance northwest to the town of Allegan, where in 1913 they re-entered the automobile field with a cyclecar, a lightweight automobile that enjoyed brief popularity in the period from 1913-15 when the auto industry was going through one of its periodic attempts to reverse the trend of sales away from bigger, more powerful vehicles. The Blood brothers' entry into the cyclecar field was called the Cornelian, the name resulting from the fact that Harold Blood had attended Cornell University and his wife's name was Cornelia. The Cornelian, priced at $410, or $435 if you wanted a top and a windshield, was advertised as being "mechanically perfect — A speedy, easy riding light car, *with the punch*." The car's speed was demonstrated in 1914, shortly after getting into production, at a 100-mile race in Kalamazoo. Despite the fact that its driver and mechanic had not even seen the car until a few minutes before race time, the Cornelian performed remarkably well in a field consisting mostly of much more powerful cars, including two Duesenbergs, a Marmon, a Benz, a Maxwell, a Mercedes driven by the great Ralph DePalma, and a Peugeot, the eventual winner of the race, driven by Bob Burman. The following year a Cornelian was driven in the Indianapolis "500" by no less a racing luminary than Louis Chevrolet, although valve problems forced the car's withdrawal after seventy-six laps.

About 120 of the Cornelian models were produced before September 1915, when the Blood brothers announced that they would again abandon auto production and devote their entire attention to the production of universal joints. Cyclecars in general passed from the scene around the same time, one prime reason no doubt being that the price of the roomier, more powerful and durable Ford Model T was by 1915 less than that of a car such as the Cornelian. The Bloods enjoyed success, however, with the manufacture of universal joints; they turned out as many as 3500 a month when they abandoned auto production for the last time in 1915. In 1934, Willard F. Rockwell bought the company and made it first a subsidiary, then a division of his Standard Steel Spring Company. Following successive mergers of the parent concern with Timken-Detroit Axle and North American Aviation, the Allegan plant, still in part occupying the factory originally built by the Blood brothers, is today known as the Universal Joint Operation of North American Rockwell's Automotive Products Division.[38]

A fourth car produced in Kalamazoo stemmed from the efforts of Warren Cannon and Frank Burtt who, beginning in 1904, managed to keep their Cannon Flyer in production for a couple of years before giving up. However, they may never have regarded automobiles as the major product of their small company, since the Burtt Manufacturing Company, which Cannon, Burtt, and several others organized in October 1902, listed its business interests in 1904 as including "the manufacturing and selling of all kinds of machinery, including cold tire setting machine, automobiles, gas engines, gasoline engines and tank lugs." After dropping automobiles from this diverse line of products, the Burtt company concentrated on the engine business.[39]

As for another company that was reported to have been formed in 1906, nothing more is heard from it or about its car, possibly because its founders, Dallas Boudeman, Jr., whose father was one of the original directors of the Michigan Automobile Company, and Harry Scott, boys described as being "of a mechanical turn of mind," were still in high school in Kalamazoo.[40]

Grand Rapids, to the north of Kalamazoo, was also the site of much activity, in the early years of the century, that seemed to be leading toward the production of cars. But despite many organizational attempts, the furniture manufacturers were seen to be in no danger of being toppled from their position of economic dominance in the community. Nevertheless, interest in automobiles was widespread in Grand Rapids and had been since the mid-nineties. One indication of this interest can be found in the formation of the Grand Rapids Automobile Club, the first one in Michigan, formed several months before a similar organization emerged in Detroit in June 1902. Among fifteen delegates from nine clubs in the country who met in Chicago on March 4, 1902, to organize the American Automobile Association, the only ones from Michigan were two members of the Grand Rapids club, Charles Judd of the Bissell Carpet Sweeper Company and Walter S. Austin, a businessman soon to become a manufacturer of automobiles. From the reports that appeared in automotive journals, the Grand Rapids organization was one of the most active clubs of its kind in the Middle West. Proportionately, the two hundred members who belonged to the club in 1908 represented a much more impressive showing for Grand Rapids than Detroit's two hundred and fifty members did for that city, whose population was four times as great. (Not everyone in Grand Rapids was as enthusiastic as club members about automobiles and auto drivers. In the fall of 1900 the city council was discussing the desirability of an ordinance to restrict the speed of motorists in the city, to which *Motor Age* responded tartly that if the city fathers "would adopt some means to prevent their women being so fast they would confer a greater boon on their constituencies.")[41]

In September 1902, *Motor World* reported that the Grand Rapids firm of Austin & Son had purchased a building on South Division Street in Grand Rapids in which it would begin the manufacture of automobiles. Although probably no more than three hundred of these Austins — not to be confused with the British Austin or the later American Austin produced in Butler, Pennsylvania — were manufactured, the company was in business for almost two decades, thus qualifying at least as one of the most tenacious of these early Michigan automobile companies. Austin & Son was an outgrowth of the activities of James E. Austin in the Michigan lumber industry beginning in the 1870's. Austin was from New York, where his son, Walter Scott Austin, was born in 1865. At the start of the twentieth century, the father and son had a machine shop in Grand Rapids specializing in the manufacture of shingle mill machinery. A shift in interest from the lumber industry was already evident, however, for they were also the Michigan agents for the U. S. Long Distance automobile, a one-cylinder runabout manufactured in Jersey City. In addition, they offered a general automobile repair service. Walter Austin had the inventive, mechanical abilities, and it was he who developed the car they would produce, although his father, who lived until 1936, continued to serve as "the prime consultant on all that his son did." Development of the car had begun in 1901, but production did not get underway until late 1902 or early 1903. The first Austin was a two-cylinder, sixteen-horsepower car selling for $2000. In the years that followed, the Austin, nicknamed the Highway King, became increasingly larger, more powerful, and expensive, competing with the Welch in the luxury field. One advertisement in 1906 described the Austin as "The Pullman of Motor Cars." Priced at $4500, it was "a distinctly beautiful car — finished in white and tan. Perfect in all mechanical details. 60 H. P. Seats eight persons." By 1907, when peak production of about fifty of the custom-built automobiles per year was achieved by Austin's tiny crew of workmen in the shop located almost in the Austin family's backyard, a six-cylinder, ninety-horsepower model was priced at $5000; the deluxe version cost $6000.[42]

Although the Austin automobile obviously had to appeal to a very prosperous clientele — William Randolph Hearst owned two of the Highway Kings, and the opera star, Emma Calve, stopped at the plant and took one of the cars back with her to France in 1915 — the Austin company itself was constantly, and not too successfully, struggling to achieve a degree of prosperity for its owners. In 1909, reports had Austin & Son planning to leave Grand Rapids for greener pastures in Shelbyville, Indiana, if the residents there would raise $180,000 for the necessary land and buildings for the company. Later in the year, Austin was looking at possible sites in Alma, Michigan. One reason given for the company's desire to leave Grand Rapids was the city's rigorous enforcement of the local speed laws which made it very difficult for the company to test drive its cars. Nevertheless, the year ended without a move. Again in 1911, Walter Austin was reported ready to move to Cambridge, Massachusetts, if residents there subscribed to enough stock in the company and the Cambridge industrial commission succeeded in obtaining a factory site. Once again, however, no move was made. It appears that the arrangement very likely was a ploy to gain support in Grand Rapids for the reorganization of the company that took place in 1912, with a capitalization of $500,000. The reorganization does not seem to have improved Austin's shaky financial status. Employment dropped from a peak of around thirty-five in 1908 down to twenty-three in 1912, eighteen in 1913, and thirteen by 1914. Further signs of the company's deteriorating financial condition are found in a legal action, prolonged for a year and a half in 1914 and 1915, that the Weston-Mott Company of Flint instituted in order to secure payment by Austin of an overdue bill for parts that amounted to about seven hundred dollars. In June 1914, Walter Austin admitted to Weston-Mott's lawyers that he owed the money but he simply could not pay it at that time. He told them he was leaving town for several days on a trip that he hoped would improve his company's finances sufficiently to enable him on his return to pay the bill in full. Otherwise, he proposed to turn over to Weston-Mott the full proceeds from a shipment of cars that he expected to make the following week. When this offer was relayed to the Flint auto parts manufacturer, a company official who had been trying to collect the money for many months before calling in the lawyers turned it down with the comment that "Mr. Austin is as slippery as an eel." After a suit was instituted against Austin, the Grand Rapids firm agreed to pay the bill in installments. Finally, in October 1915, after repeated proddings from Weston-Mott's lawyers, the account was closed.[43]

During 1915 Austin was also successful, however, in legal action of its own that it had brought against the Cadillac company in 1914 for patent infringement. The money that the court awarded the company must have been a welcome boost to its financial stability, a development which Austin also hoped to promote at this time by putting out a smaller, less expensive car. By 1917, the bigger Austin models followed the lead of Packard's famous Twin Six model by including a twelve-cylinder version. At the same time, however, the number of the company's employees had slipped to eleven, and in 1918 production of the Austin appears to have ended. Although the wartime shortage of materials was the immediate cause of the demise of this Grand Rapids company, the firm, despite the persistent efforts of the Austins, had obviously been living on borrowed time for many years. Although Walter Austin and his father went into other forms of business occupations, most notably real estate, Austin maintained his interest in automobiles, patenting a hydraulic transmission when he was nearly ninety years of age. He died in May 1965, at the age of ninety-nine, some thirteen years after he had been honored in 1952 as one of the two surviving founders of the American Automobile Association.[44]

Although it survived the longest, Austin & Son was not the only automobile company to start up in Grand Rapids, nor was it the first. In December 1900, Clark Sintz's Wolverine Motor Works obtained a three-story building in the city in which it reportedly intended to go into the production of automobiles. This goal, which Sintz had obviously had in mind since he and his sons had begun experimenting with gasoline-powered vehicles in the mid-nineties, was not achieved at this time. There were rumors of internal dissension in the Wolverine company that may have delayed the automotive effort and may explain the decision by Clark Sintz to sell his interest in the company to Charles Snyder and start up the Sintz Auto Gas Engine Company. This new firm did in fact produce a few cars, possibly a half dozen, in 1903 and 1904 before winding up in the hands of receivers. Sintz's son, Claude, meanwhile, had remained with Wolverine Motor until he too sold his interest to Snyder, who then moved the engine company to Bridgeport, Connecticut, where it was still in business as late as 1952. Claude Sintz planned to go to Guatemala and invest in the fruit business, but he made the mistake of allowing his father to persuade him to endorse some of his notes at the bank. When Clark Sintz's auto company went bankrupt, Claude was stuck with this debt, which took him fourteen years to pay off and forced him to abandon his Central American plans. The Sintz name, which had been on the periphery of automobile developments since before the Columbian Exposition of 1893, continued to appear in the industry, however. The Pungs-Finch Company, a Detroit firm, absorbed the old Sintz Gas Engine Company and in ads for the car it published in 1905 made the totally unfounded claim that in 1890 Clark Sintz had "built a practical and successful automobile that covered thousands of miles and was ten years in advance of times." Such a background of experience, Pungs-Finch declared, helped to explain "the secret of our ability to produce a reliable Touring Car for $1700." Five years later Pungs-Finch was out of business, thereby leaving unchanged the Sintz record of never having been part of a very successful automobile venture. Clark Sintz was killed in 1922 — in an automobile accident. Claude Sintz remained active in engineering work as late as the 1940's, turning his inventive talents to farm equipment. A nephew, Edward Clark Sintz, carried on in the automotive industry as an engineer with Cadillac.[45]

Late in 1900 another automobile company that seemed ready to emerge in Grand Rapids was linked with the bicycle industry. In other parts of the country the manufacturing of bicycles contributed greatly to the formation of the automobile industry, but in Michigan, where the manufacturing of bicycles had not been widespread, it played an insignificant role. In the 1890's Grand Rapids, however, had been the site of a thriving bicycle industry; in 1897 six factories had turned out thirty thousand bikes. But the activity was short-lived. One firm went into trusteeship in 1897, another was abandoned in 1899 by the American Bicycle Company, Colonel Albert Pope's national bicycle "trust." In 1900 the trust also shut down the most famous of these Grand Rapids firms, the Clipper Bicycle Company, which had once employed 250 men. In the winter of 1900-1901 an abortive effort was made by a local bicycle agent, W. S. Daniels, to form a company that would take over the Clipper factory to produce a car developed by Byron J. Carter of Jackson. A year later, hopes were still being expressed that Grand Rapids would "become an automobile manufacturing center of as great importance as it once was in the cycle trade." In part these hopes were based on rumors that Ralph B. Hain, builder of the first bicycle in Grand Rapids, organizer of the Clipper company, and at one time builder of the Monitor vapor engine, one of the better-known Grand Rapids gasoline engines, was connected with a proposed local auto venture. Instead, in the summer of 1902 Hain organized the Auto Vehicle Company of Los Angeles, California.[46]

Later in 1902, an automobile company was established in the Furniture City by the brothers Charles W. and Frank F. Matheson, who were associated with one of the city's leading furniture manufacturers, the Fred Macey Company. Although the Mathesons had purchased a Stanley Steamer, the Matheson Motor Car Company turned to manufacturing a gasoline car, reportedly designed by a French engineer. After turning out six cars in Grand Rapids, the Mathesons moved their operations to Massachusetts, probably in 1903, although an advertisement in January 1904 still listed them as based in Grand Rapids. In Massachusetts the Mathesons purchased the Holyoke Motor Works and acquired the services of its leading spirit, Charles R. Greuter. The Greuter, an expensive automobile designed by Greuter, was reportedly copied to a considerable extent by the builders of the Welch car. Now its design became the new Matheson. For a time in 1905 the Mathesons were talking of re-moving their plant to Detroit, but the Motor City, in this instance, lost out to the city of Wilkes-Barre, Pennsylvania, whose board of trade made the Mathesons a more attractive offer. The company was therefore located there permanently. About eighteen hundred of its costly, hand-made cars were produced before the company shut down in 1912. "Built for those who use the best," was the Mathesons' slogan, and they proved it in 1910 when a Matheson automobile was the only one of sixty-two entries in the New York to Atlanta reliability run that required no repairs, not even a flat tire. After competitive conditions forced them out of business, the Mathesons remained active in the auto industry for many years in other capacities, and Frank demonstrated the remarkable longevity that characterized so many of the automakers by living to the advanced age of ninety-five.[47]

In addition to the stimulus that came to the auto industry from its gasoline engine, bicycle, and furniture manufacturers, at least one of Grand Rapids' carriage manufacturers also sought to enter this new field. The Harrison Wagon Works, employing close to 150 workers at the start of the twentieth century, had been established by William Harrison in Grand Rapids in the mid-1850's. An Englishman who had learned the trade of wheelwright and joiner before emigrating in 1851 to the Kalamazoo area, Harrison got his start making wagon wheels before moving to Grand Rapids where he began manufacturing wagons and a few carriages. By 1881, Harrison was using a million feet of lumber a year to turn out three thousand of what he claimed was the "lightest-running wagon made," and he had diplomas awarded to him by county and state fairs as far distant as the San Joaquin Valley in California, attesting to the excellence of his product.[48]

At the start of the new century, the Harrison Wagon Works, now headed by the founder's son, William H. Harrison, became associated with Albert C. Menges, who reportedly had "spent much time in gasoline engine work," and now was working on the design of a gasoline-powered motor vehicle. Later, when it announced its entry into the automotive field, the Harrison firm declared that in Menges it had acquired the services of "one of the most *practical* and *original* mechanical engineers this country has ever known." By the latter part of 1904, Menges had nearly completed two models at the wagon works; *Motor Age* reported that "if the samples give satisfaction the concern may start to build." Harrison did not rush the road tests, however. For months the two cars were driven almost daily in the Grand Rapids area under the worst possible conditions, which, the company declared, were not hard to find, considering Michigan's notoriously bad roads. Finally, in 1906, Harrison was satisfied that the car was "as good as the most competent and skilled mechanics and the best of material can possibly produce."

The wagon manufacturer's debut in the automobile business was heralded by the exhibition of its car at the Chicago auto show in February. Observers noticed that Menges had indeed demonstrated considerable originality by the inclusion of a number of "very novel" features "in his motor as well as in many other parts of the car." These features included a method of reversing the rotation of the engine, and an air braking device to relieve strain on the regular brakes while going down hills. The most striking feature was a self-starter. "One does not have to crank a Harrison Motor Car," the company boasted. "A little knob is turned and the switch thrown on, and the engine starts. All this is done while sitting in the seat." Harrison guaranteed that the system worked "every time . . . on a cold morning as well as on a warm day. A Harrison car can stand idle for an hour, a day, a week, a month, or a year, and you will not have to crank it." Hence its slogan: "The Car Without a Crank."[49]

Assuming that the rest of the car was reasonably sound, the claim that the Harrison could be started without a crank would have been enough to assure the success of this car. It was generally agreed that the problems and even dangers involved in starting a car with a crank were one of the main obstacles to a more widespread adoption of the gasoline automobile, particularly by women. But in actual practice, as Alfred Reeves later joked, anyone who drove a Harrison *"was* a crank." Like several other self-starting devices that preceded the one developed by Charles Kettering and his staff at the Dayton Engineering Laboratories in 1910-11, Harrison's method, which employed a combination of acetylene gas and air with electric contacts on the commutator, apparently did not live up to the company's claims. In addition to problems with the car, Harrison may also have been beset with internal administrative problems. In November 1906, A. C. Menges left the company, announcing that he would try to start a company of his own in Grand Rapids. Fifteen months later he was reported to be associated with a company in Memphis, Tennessee, which planned to manufacture a medium-priced, four-cylinder car that Menges had designed. By that time, the Harrison Wagon Works had been declared bankrupt. It was one of many companies whose collapse may have been hastened in part by the panic of 1907. Although William H. Harrison stoutly insisted that his firm was solvent, the court, acting on an appeal from some of the company's 423 creditors who claimed the automaker owed them nearly $446,000, adjudged the company to be bankrupt on January 17, 1908. Later in the year a Nashville, Tennessee, company bought the Harrison plant, the land on which it stood and virtually everything else connected with the wagon business, including "two teams, with their harness," for slightly under thirty thousand dollars. After a half century of production, since the 1850's, the Harrison Wagon Works went out of business.[50]

Another veteran Michigan carriage manufacturer to fall by the wayside after it too had undertaken the manufacture of automobiles was a firm in Charlotte, a small town located a few miles southwest of Lansing. It was this company that had advertised: "If you want the car that satisfies get 'The Car John Dolson Built.'" The statement appears to have assumed that Dolson and his reputation were well known among automobile buyers. Whether this was a valid assumption is impossible to say, but the Dolson name no doubt had some market value in central Michigan where John L. Dolson had been making carriages since 1865.

At the start of the twentieth century Dolson had already achieved many years of success in the carriage business. He is remembered by one old-time resident as "a very stylish gentleman," who was never seen in anything but "a black suit and white shirt and black tie." His company, known as Dolson and Sons after he brought his sons D. Elmore (nicknamed Tom) and W. Elton Dolson into the firm, was Charlotte's largest manufacturer. It produced between four and five thousand carriages each year and employed a hundred workers. The Dolsons lived in affluence. Their fine Victorian homes were among the showplaces of the town, and Tom Dolson was able to send his son Gerald away to Culver Military Academy and later to Michigan Agricultural College.

Their success did not, however, blind them to the possibilities of greater rewards in another area. John Dolson had personal knowledge of Ransom Olds' successful automobile venture; Olds had paid a visit to Dolson at one time to urge him to come to Lansing and apply his carriage-making skills to manufacturing automobile bodies. The Dolsons had their eyes fixed on bigger things, however. "Realizing the colossal proportions the manufacture of automobiles is attaining and the importance of it among the manufacturing enterprises of this country," the Dolsons, according to a 1907 Charlotte booster publication, "decided to change their business from a carriage manufactory to that of a high grade automobile factory." The first Dolson automobile appeared in 1904, and by 1906 the Charlotte company was putting out several high-powered, relatively high-priced models: The sporty Dolson "Cannon Ball," a sixty-horsepower roadster, sold for $3250; the sixty-horsepower, seven-passenger Model F

Beside the Eaton County Courthouse in Charlotte, two men, well-protected against the elements, prepare to test a 1905 Dolson Model C; in appearance the Model C was little different from the later Model F. Tom Dolson, second from the left on the curb, keeps an eye on the trial run.
Courtesy David W. Dolson

touring car cost the same; and the Model H, a forty-horsepower touring car that could carry five passengers, sold for $2500. The Charlotte citizenry was assured that in the opinion of "disinterested experts . . . there is no automobile built in America, price considered, equal to that built in the Dolson factory." In particular, the company claimed that concerning ease of control and the transmission of power to the rear axle, the Dolson was ahead of all American cars, regardless of price. The demand for these cars in 1906 was said to have been "at least five times in excess of the number the company was able to supply." The following year, however, which began with optimistic predictions that at least 350 Dolsons would be produced, ended with the bankruptcy of the company.[51]

Mechanically there is evidence that John Dolson built well, and that deficiencies in the car were not a cause of the company's failure. In fact, three years after production of the cars had ceased, about 350 Dolsons were reported to be still in use; the average life of these cars is said to have been a very respectable five to six years, indicating that the term "Durable Dolson" was no mere advertising claim. Other evidence seems to indicate that the Dolsons underestimated the difficulties that their switch to automobile production would entail, and that this is what led to their downfall. It appears that they discovered that financing the manufacturing of high-priced motor vehicles was far more complex than what was involved in the production of horse-drawn vehicles costing less than a tenth as much money. In October 1905, the Dolson Automobile Company was incorporated, taking over the assets of the old family business, but now also able to obtain outside financial help. In January 1906, the Dolsons mortgaged various Charlotte properties in order to borrow a total of $30,000 from the three Charlotte banks. Later in 1906 these banks showed their interest in keeping this local enterprise on its feet by their willingness to loan the Dolson company additional funds of $25,000. However, to protect these loans, two bankers, J. M. C. Smith, president of the First National Bank, and H. K. Jennings, cashier of the Merchants' National Bank, joined the three Dolsons on the auto company's board of directors. At the same time, the capital stock of the company was increased from $150,000 to $300,000; in the early weeks of 1907 small amounts of this stock were sold to investors in Charlotte and other central Michigan communities. In most cases, however, the investors gave their notes, not cash, for this stock, and later, when the company was bankrupt, they objected to the receiver's request that they redeem their notes on the grounds that the Dolson company had fraudulently misrepresented the company's true condition when it sold them the stock.[52]

Despite the efforts that had been made to revitalize the company, at the end of 1906 the Dolson Automobile Company's accounts at the Merchants' National Bank and the First National Bank were overdrawn by $1200 and $2000 respectively. In the spring of 1907, an outside accountant was retained to straighten out the company's books and to install a better accounting system, which suggests that inadequacies in this area of the company's operations had contributed to its financial distress. The accountant's services were terminated in May 1907 as an economy measure. By June, Dolson's plight had become desperate. The company refused to accept the remaining engines that the Milwaukee Motor Company had contracted to build for the 1907 Dolsons, engines which, it was said, were of a design that could not be used in other cars. As a result, the failure of Dolson to pay for these engines left the Wisconsin firm itself in precarious financial circumstances.

In a last-ditch effort to get some money, a Dolson representative was dispatched east to try to sell a few cars, while W. Elton Dolson, company vice-president, went out to Seattle on a similar mission. In mid-July, his brother wrote to him that several of Dolson's creditors had agreed to withhold collection for a while. They intended to "stand back of us and see that we do go ahead and make this one of the big factories in the U.S., as they have faith in our car and believe that we are building a car second to none." But sales were crucial. Tom Dolson told his brother that if he could sell only five or six cars that would "help wonderfully." But Elton could sell only two cars, so at the end of July the Dolson directors agreed to let the creditors take control of the company. They had no better luck, and in November, on the petition of three Chicago creditors, the United States District Court in Grand Rapids declared the Dolson company bankrupt.

The Dolson factory in Charlotte was taken over by the Duplex Power Car Company, which in 1909 began to produce Duplex trucks. Trucks bearing this name are still produced in Lansing, where the company was later located and where it continues in operation as the Duplex Division of the Warner & Swasey Company. As for the Dolsons themselves, they showed great resourcefulness in bouncing back from their financial disaster. John Dolson and some associates went into the business of raising peppermint, a highly lucrative though specialized branch of Michigan agriculture, and he apparently did quite well. His sons continued seeking their fortune in the auto industry. In the spring of 1908, Elton Dolson was hired as the assistant sales manager of the Austin company in Grand Rapids. Tom Dolson went to Indiana, where the family had originally lived, and set up the Dolson Auto Supply Company in Muncie to furnish parts for the Dolson cars that were still on the road. The company also announced plans to produce a lightweight car, the Muncie Runabout, with a basic price of $500, but the car appears never to have gotten into production. Later, Tom and Elton Dolson returned to Charlotte to sell

Of the auto company that John Dolson and his sons built, little remains except worthless stock certificates.
Courtesy David W. Dolson

farm equipment produced by International Harvester. For a few years before his death in 1936 at the age of seventy-three, Tom Dolson was a salesman for a Charlotte monument dealer who had once worked for the Dolsons as a harness maker. In the 1970's, Tom Dolson's grandson, David W. Dolson, the last of the family, continues an association with the auto industry through his work as an executive of Leonard Refineries in Alma, Michigan.[53]

In Jonesville, the Deal Buggy Company, which had been in business since 1857, began producing motorized vehicles in addition to the horse-drawn variety in 1908, apparently undeterred by the collapse of the Harrison and Dolson automobile enterprises a few months earlier. The Deal motor vehicle continued to appear until 1911, when the company seems to have ceased the production of automobiles. The experiment was not quite as fatal for the Jonesville firm as it had been for some other Michigan carriage manufacturers. The Deal company stayed in business until at least 1916 by returning again to its old standby, the horse-drawn buggy.[54]

When the first Deal automobiles were appearing, in the summer of 1908, sixteen-year-old Miss Georgia Penrod took the advice of her high-school business teacher and accepted a job as stenographer-bookkeeper with the Dowagiac Automobile Company. Formed by Frank Lake and Doras Neff, two local machinists, the company was taken over by J. Victor Lindsley, eldest son of John A. Lindsley, a Dowagiac lumberman. Victor Lindsley had developed a small automobile company in Chicago which he now moved to his home town. Only a few of the Lindsley cars, a version of the high-wheeled-buggy type of vehicle, seem to have been produced in Dowagiac. Outmoded manufacturing ideas could have accounted for this low production; Lindsley told the local newspaper that it took two of his men two weeks to build one of the cars, and he was hoping soon to have forty men on the payroll. In addition, however, according to Miss Penrod, Lindsley was a "high-spender," and the company was soon in trouble. Many orders for cars were coming in, accompanied by cash deposits, but, Miss Penrod said, although some of this money was entered in the books, some of it was not. In December 1908, the company closed its doors — bankrupt. In 1971 Miss Penrod recalled: "It went kaflooey in a hurry! . . . It was my first job and quite an experience!" Victor Lindsley's father paid off his son's creditors and in the process was himself wiped out. Victor later joined with his three brothers in a highly successful revival of the family lumber business which they extended into the rich Florida market and ultimately sold in 1962 for nine million dollars. Frank Lake and several others bought up the Lindsley automobile enterprise and launched the Dowagiac Motor Car Company (sometimes referred to as the Dowagiac Auto-Car Company), with the intention of producing the Dowagiac car, designed by Lake. An accident in July 1909 on the Lake Shore interurban line in Indiana, which caused the death of Lake and Leon R. Lyle, another official of the Dowagiac firm, is believed to have caused the demise of this second auto company in a town that was then and would continue to be far better known as the home of the famed Round Oak Stove.[55]

So it went in the first decade of the twentieth century, and Adrian, Chelsea, Kalamazoo, Grand Rapids, Charlotte, Jonesville, and Dowagiac were only some of the towns in Michigan where citizens made the painful discovery that the chances of failure in this new automobile industry greatly exceeded those of success. Dundee, Constantine, Hillsdale, Muskegon, Saginaw, even Gaylord and Alpena in the more remote northern parts of the state, were among other communities whose townspeople came to the same realization through the sad experiences of local enterprises. Despite the failures, others kept trying, for if the prospects for success were slim, the profits for the few who made it in the auto game were also demonstrably great. As a Charlotte newsman commented at the time of Tom Dolson's death: "One more turn of the wheel of fortune and Tom Dolson might have been acclaimed today a great industrial genius. Too many successful men mistake luck for genius." Whether it was through luck or genius, the Olds Motor Works had proven by 1902 that success in the auto industry was possible and most rewarding. Within another half decade several other fortunate Michigan companies were demonstrating that their owners could match or surpass the triumphs of Olds. Of these, none was developing in as spectacular and far-reaching a way as that headed by William C. Durant. His enterprises were based in Flint, a carriage-manufacturing center already known as the Vehicle City, but which now saw that nickname given a new meaning as Durant, a consummate gambler, repeatedly hit the jackpot.[56]

CHAPTER 7

"EL CAPITAN DE INDUSTRIA"

Late in the 1950's, an official in the Oldsmobile public relations division discussed with the Michigan Historical Commission the possibility of placing in Lansing's Durant Park one of the state's new official historical markers in honor of the man after whom the park is named. For all the average Lansingite knew, the Olds official said, the park honored the popular historian and philosopher Will Durant, whereas in actuality it was intended to keep alive the memory of the founder of General Motors, who, in fact, had donated the land for the park in the 1920's. Since few markers had been put up that related to the automobile industry, reactions to the proposal were favorable. However, since state funds were no longer available to purchase markers, the Olds executive was advised that the two or three hundred dollars that a marker would cost would have to come from private sources. Whether he pursued the matter with his superiors in the Oldsmobile and G. M. hierarchy is not known, but the money was not forthcoming and a marker to William Crapo Durant was never erected.[1]

This incident is indicative of the low estate to which the fame of this American businessman had fallen scarcely a decade after his death in 1947. At the peak of his career it had been said that in the history of American industry Durant would probably be regarded as more important than Andrew Carnegie. But in the 1970's such a statement would have seemed ridiculous to most people. The name Carnegie still had some meaning, but that of William C. Durant meant nothing. To be sure, Durant's name still rang an occasional bell among members of an older generation, but even their recollections are not very clear or accurate. An elderly retired Detroit storekeeper in 1971 remembered Durant for his promotional activities, but the passing years had made these activities seem far more grandiose than even Durant could have envisaged them. An eighty-eight-year-old Buick retiree called to mind not Durant's triumphs but his failures. Durant, he said, had gotten mixed up with Wall Street bankers and had "lost his shirt, yeah, he lost his shirt."[2]

One man who was acquainted with Durant was Edward L. Bernays, the great public relations counsel, who, more than a decade after Durant was forced out of General Motors, had helped to refurbish that corporation's public image, but who earlier had enjoyed some purely social contacts with Durant. The two men had had summer cottages at Elberon, on the New Jersey coast, in the late 1920's. Recalling those days in 1971, Bernays wrote: "My first impression of Durant was the hugeness of the man. . . . No one could possibly be unaware that a commanding presence came into the room when he entered. My second memorable impression of him was his gentleness of speech and manner." Unlike most of the other big-businessmen of that day who, Bernays declared, "threw their weight around and unmistakenly wanted to create the impression of their prowess," Durant "acted like a beneficent giant . . . certainly in his social behavior." He seemed to get the most pleasure, Bernays recalled, from playing checkers with a small boy, the son of one of the other cottagers, and, Bernays declared, it was a sight he could never forget — "the huge Durant leaning over a checker board and playing . . . with the miniature little boy." Concerning Durant's interest in checkers there can be no doubting Bernays' recollections. Checkers were Durant's major diversion during any momentary lull in his heavy business schedule, and away from the office he carried a miniature set in his pocket. He became virtually unbeatable at the game. However, far from being a giant in size, Durant was actually quite small. When this was called to Bernays' attention, he checked with his wife, Doris Fleischman Bernays, whose recollections of Durant were quite different from those of her husband. "She remembers Mr. Durant as a quiet insignificant little man, who was socially not at ease at all. . . . His personality made no impression whatsoever on her." Puzzled over what had brought on his own "belief in the opposite of the reality," Bernays concluded: "It must have been that I equated in my mind his power and prowess in finance with his size — a type of Freudian transferring which occasionally does happen." Such a slip was especially appropriate in Bernays' case, since, as he pointed out, "Freud was my uncle."[3]

The almost complete lack — until 1973 — of any substantial biographical material on Durant has certainly helped to perpetuate such distortions, although Henry Ford is a classic example proving that the availability of such materials is no guarantee that the subject will be viewed in a more accurate light. The failure of writers, both those appealing to the general reader and those with more scholarly presentations, to be attracted to Durant is one of the most baffling observations in a study of the literature on the automobile industry. Here was a man whose business career spanned more than sixty years and was replete with drama, intrigue, and suspense. His was a life full of great achievements, prophetic insights, and remarkable comebacks from defeats that would have broken the will of lesser men.

One's first impression of Durant was apt to be similar to that of Mrs. Bernays — "a quiet insignificant little man." Durant, a Detroit *News* writer declared in 1909, was "the last man in the world you would guess" to be the head of a great industrial concern. "He is a man short of stature . . . who speaks a little above a whisper, and very slowly. . . . Thousands of his employes look more as one imagines an organizing genius should look." Genius — it was a term that was continually applied to Durant. A New York banker, after serving some years with Durant on the board of directors of General Motors, declared that Durant was "a genius and therefore not to be dealt with on the same basis as ordinary business men." If, as some insist, Ford and Olds were geniuses when it came to machines, Durant, who knew little about machines, was a business genius, whose mastery of the techniques of persuasion and promotion have rarely been equaled in the annals of American business. In the business world, which was the only world he cared about, the little man was transformed into a man of action, who worked incessantly, literally night and day, exhausting those whom he dealt with, who sometimes had to wait until after midnight to get in to see him. According to his daughter, two or three hours' sleep a night were sufficient for Durant. "Time to him was one of life's most precious elements. While he gave ungrudgingly of his time to those he felt deserved it, while he spent uncounted hours on any detail he thought important, the waste of a minute was in his eyes an affront to the Divine Creator." Durant's endurance was one of his greatest assets, and, his daughter declared, it was an "endurance that was not only physical but *spiritual*." When a friend asked him if he ever worried, Durant replied: "Never. . . . In the daytime I'm too busy. At night I'm too sleepy." But important as his untiring energy and cheerful optimism were to his business success, unquestionably the key to Durant's success — and ultimately to his failures — was his extraordinary imaginative power that enabled him to look ahead and shape his business policies according to what he saw to be the future demand for a product. "Durant sees — actually sees — 90,000,000 people just aching to roll along the roads of the

William Crapo Durant — *a photograph believed to have been taken in 1908. The photographer has captured the spirit of this eternal optimist, who was ever looking upwards and onwards to a more abundant future.*
Courtesy Flint Journal

country in automobiles, and he wishes to fill that aching void," commented a Detroit newsman in 1909. "To him," another wrote, "the immediate future was remote; the remote future near and vivid." Eventually this distorted vision would be the cause of Durant's downfall; but first it enabled him to place Buick and Chevrolet among the most popular cars of their day and then to bring them into his supreme achievement, General Motors.[4]

Yet despite the obvious importance of the man, aside from brief and relatively uncritical sketches in such biographical collections as the *National Cyclopaedia of American Biography* and the more specialized *Automotive Giants of America* by B. C. Forbes and O. D. Foster, the only book-length biography of William C. Durant for many years was Margery Durant's adoring portrait of her father, and since it was published in 1929, it failed to take him through the last climactic downturns in his mercurial career. The only objective treatment until recently has been a seventeen-page article by the automotive historian John B. Rae. Of course, Durant figures prominently in any treatment of the auto industry that claims to be comprehensive, but the emphasis on Durant as an uncontrollable promoter and one of the great stock market gamblers of the roaring twenties indicates the prevailing tendency among historians. They either ignore Durant entirely or dismiss him as an irresponsible speculator.[5]

If there is any place in America where one could expect to hear serious objections to such a characterization of Durant, it is Flint, Michigan. There was a time when hardly a resident of that community would have argued with Edwin O. Wood, a local historian, who wrote: "Without the foresight and genius and generalship of such a leader as Mr. Durant, Flint would not have been the manufacturing and commercial center that it is in 1916 when this book goes to press." Five years earlier, one hundred fifty of Flint's business leaders gathered in the Masonic Temple for an event they called "the wizard's banquet," at which they hailed Durant as the "master builder." Cigars made specially for the occasion, in boxes bearing a portrait of Durant, were labeled "El Capitan de Industria." But the memory of Durant dimmed with the passage of years even in this town where Buick and Chevrolet, among other industries, provide daily reminders of Durant's accomplishments as a creative industrialist. The city's leading hotel still bears his name, but until recently one could search there in vain for a portrait of Durant. Flint's new transportation museum is named after Alfred P. Sloan, Jr., who headed General Motors for so many years after World War I, a choice that overlooks Durant, without whom there would have been no General Motors. Similarly, the decision to name Flint's freeways after Chevrolet and Buick honors two other individuals who, even more than Sloan, owe their position in automotive history to Durant. Early in 1972, Lawrence R. Gustin expressed the belief that Durant had "been largely forgotten in Flint." As the Flint *Journal's* automotive editor, Gustin decided to do something about this. He prepared a series of ten articles on Durant's life that were published in the *Journal* in March 1972, on the twenty-fifth anniversary of Durant's death. Widespread reader response to the series indicated that Flint had not entirely forgotten its most important citizen, and this in turn encouraged Gustin to expand his series into a book, *Billy Durant: Creator of General Motors*, published in 1973. Additional evidence of a revival of interest in Durant came with the 1973 publication of an article in *American Heritage*, co-authored by the automobile historians Glenn Niemeyer and James Flink, who are reportedly also preparing a full-length biography of Durant.[6]

One Flint resident who did not forget Durant was Charles Stewart Mott, who up to the time of his death at the age of 97, in 1973, had only to consider his bank balance and his stock portfolio to be reminded of the debt he owed Durant for persuading him in 1905 to move his Weston-Mott plant from Utica, New York, to Flint. In the 1950's Mott insisted that something in the new Flint cultural center be named in memory of Durant. Recalling those efforts, Mott declared that when the center's Durant Plaza was to be dedicated, he told the sponsors of the event that he "would be as sore as a boil" if they did not allow him to say something about Durant. Mott then informed the audience that neither he nor they would have been there that day but for Durant, without whose efforts Flint "would have been a bush town." In 1971 Mott said of Durant: "He was a terrific man. Too bad he did not make a bright finish. Here are all these buildings Durant built. He was loyal to Flint and made Flint what it is." [7]

* * *

The story of William Crapo Durant's influence on Flint and the auto industry should start with his grandfather, Henry Howland Crapo. He was a remarkable businessman in his own right, from whom Durant may well have inherited his legendary drive and energy. Early in 1856, Crapo, who was then fifty-one years old, arrived in Flint from his home in New Bedford, Massachusetts, where he had grown modestly wealthy during the preceding three decades through such diverse activities as the whaling industry, insurance, a nursery business, and real estate speculation. It was real estate that brought Crapo to Michigan. Earlier he had invested in thousands of acres of land in the state. Now, employing promotional methods his grandson would have admired, he acquired an interest in and managerial control over twelve thousand acres of pine timber in Lapeer County — without putting up any of his own money. He had had no experience in lumbering, but learned quickly. Before long he was directing an increasingly complicated, far-flung operation. His timber was cut and floated down the Flint River to the small town of Flint. There the logs were run through one of three sawmills Crapo acquired. Soon he added another dimension to his lumber business by opening a sash, door, and blind factory, again in Flint. Not satisfied with local sales of lumber, which he soon virtually monopolized, Crapo sought outside markets. By 1857 he was hauling lumber south over plank roads to yards he had opened in Holly and Fentonville. These towns were on the line of the Detroit & Milwaukee Railroad, over which his lumber was shipped to more distant buyers. In 1863, he organized a corporation to build a rail link between Flint and Holly. When it opened in 1864, the Flint & Holly Railroad was an instant financial success. Four years later Crapo sold the railroad at a tidy profit to the Flint & Pere Marquette, and the stock interest he acquired in that major railroad subsequently led to Crapo's son, William W. Crapo, becoming the long-time president of the Pere Marquette.

Somehow, Henry Crapo also found time for Republican politics. Despite the fact that it was not till 1858 that he officially gave up his New Bedford residence and moved his family to Flint, in 1860 he was elected mayor of the city, and by 1862 he was a state senator. In 1864, his meteoric political career climaxed with his election to the office of governor, which he held for two terms. His numerous interests and the long hours that he gave to their furtherance eventually ruined his health and caused his death in July 1869. He was a victim, one newspaper observed, of "indulgence in that energetic industry which has marked his entire career." Starting at an age when many men are thinking ahead to retirement, Crapo amassed a fortune, the size of which is indicated by the report that in the last years of his life he paid between $38,000 and $50,000 annually in federal income taxes, even under the modest rates imposed at that time. At his death his estate was worth possibly a million dollars, at a time when millionaires were still a rarity in the Wolverine State. In the process of acquiring this wealth, Crapo had also been the principal cause of Flint's emergence as an early center of Michigan's booming lumber industry.[8]

Henry Crapo and his wife, Mary Slocum Crapo, had ten children. Their only son, William Wallace Crapo, managed the family's interests after his father's death, spending a good deal of time in Flint, but still maintaining his residence in New Bedford, where he began a distinguished career as a businessman, politician, and attorney. Eight of Crapo's daughters married, and several of the marriages turned out especially well. Such was not the case, however, with Rebecca Folger Crapo, who seems to have been a particular favorite of her father. A bright, lively, and attractive girl, Rebecca married William Clark Durant, a bank employee in Boston, in 1855. A daughter, Rebecca, was born to the couple in 1857, and four years later, on December 8, 1861, a boy, William Crapo Durant, was born.[9]

William Clark Durant's standing in Boston's financial world was apparently strong enough in the early 1860's for his father-in-law to think that Durant could be influential in raising money for some of Crapo's Michigan business ventures. But Crapo's opinion of his son-in-law was to change.

In June 1868, Rebecca Durant and her two children came to Flint to visit her parents. A close relationship developed between the grandfather and the grandson that had a lasting effect on Durant.[10]

Near the end of June 1868, Durant's father joined the family in Flint. The visit either climaxed or precipitated a complete deterioration in the relationship between William Clark Durant and his father-in-law. "I had no idea that he had got so low," Henry Crapo told his son William a few weeks later in an eight-page letter written immediately after the Durants left for Boston. Durant, Crapo said, had become addicted to alco-

hol to the point that it was completely ruining him. To Crapo, an unre-
lenting prohibitionist who had a standing order to fire any employee
found "guilty of intoxication," this alone would have been enough to
turn him against his son-in-law. "He can't get by a saloon or a drinking
hole, no matter how low, without a tip," Crapo reported. As a result, his
business career in Boston, Crapo had learned, "was going down fast."
Crapo and another son-in-law, a prominent local doctor, James C. Willson, had sought to help Durant get established in a business in Flint, "but
his appetite for intoxicating drinks is so strong, that I presume he had
not been here a week before every business man in Flint knew that he
was a *tipler*, & that he thought more of whiskey than any kind of business." On one occasion, Durant had "been so intoxicated here as to have
a regular drunken jab with Rebecca at the table before us all, so that we
felt it the best course to leave the table one by one to avoid a scene." Sixty
years later, Durant's son offered a prize of $25,000 "for the best and most
practicable plan to make the 18th [Prohibition] amendment effective,"
and in 1929 he went to the expense of publishing 102 of the resulting proposals in a large book. Although William Crapo Durant, who did in fact
occasionally have a drink to be sociable, denied that he was "a fanatical
dry," his expressed view of "liquor as a destroyer of the home," and the
support that he gave to eliminating the saloon from Flint may well have
originated with the unhappy experiences of his childhood. The depth of
his feelings and his generally Puritanical outlook were made painfully
evident to one of his California automobile dealers who threw a party for
Durant at which both liquor and women were dispensed with liberality.
The scandalized grandson of Henry Crapo acted in a manner that would
have been eminently satisfactory to his grandfather: the dealer's franchise
was immediately cancelled.[11]

    While experiences with his father may have started young Durant
on the paths of temperance, in other respects his father's ways may have
had a different influence. William Clark Durant, Crapo had to admit,
was possessed of "a peculiar kind of smartness," but he was "entirely"
lacking in "*judgment, principle,* or even *common sense.*" The clearest
evidence of this was that Durant "gambled in stocks." Henry Crapo had
shown himself to be a great gambler, also, but, to his mind at least, in
more tangible things than stocks. To be sure, Durant "made some money
by gambling in stocks, but having a mind without the least balance, he
has permitted himself, through flattery & whiskey, to be used by others as
a mere tool, until he is now 'used up,' both in character & means."
Although Crapo was unsuccessful in getting any information from his
son-in-law regarding his financial condition, Crapo inferred "that he has
nothing that he can really call his own. All his stock, &c. I presume is
pledged for more than it will bring, either now, or perhaps for a long
time to come." A few decades later, many questioned William Crapo Durant's judgment in a similar manner when he became one of the most
notorious Wall Street gamblers of his day; he too ultimately faced the

prospect of bankruptcy that his grandfather had declared would probably be the only way William Clark Durant would extricate himself from the financial quagmire into which he had blundered in the late 1860's.

Henry Crapo "talked very plainly & decidedly" with his daughter's husband in an effort to get him to straighten himself out, but Crapo saw little hope that Durant would be able to shake off his drinking or gambling habits. "He can't think of any business worthy of his attention, unless it has *speculation,* not to say *gambling* in it, or what is equally captivating to him — either Whiskey, Beer, &c. in some form." Unless Durant changed his ways, Crapo warned him, he could expect no help. Rebecca and the grandchildren would be provided for, but not the son-in-law.

In July 1869, upon the death of Henry Crapo, the Durants and their children came to Flint for the funeral. William Durant, apparently not yet estranged from the rest of the family, accompanied William Crapo, Dr. Willson, and some of his other numerous brothers-in-law on several trips concerning arrangements involving Crapo's estate. In August of the same summer, the Durant family returned to the east. When young Durant was about nine years old, sometime in 1871, the family moved to Flint to stay. Shortly after, William Clark Durant dropped out of sight. What happened to him has until recently been a mystery. His son is said to have spent a considerable sum of money in a vain effort to find out what had happened to his father. The elder Durant apparently died in 1883, and by 1888, at the latest, the family knew of his death.[12]

From the time that he was about ten, young William Durant was deprived of a father's companionship, and although Dr. Willson, with whom Mrs. Durant and her children lived during their first three years in Flint, was something like a father to Durant, the maternal influence became the dominant one in his life. Durant and his mother remained extremely close till her death in 1924 at the age of ninety-one. Durant's devotion to his mother is said to have been the trait most commonly remarked upon by his business associates. He lavished attention upon her, sometimes traveling for days by train in order to spend a few hours with her. In 1923, when Durant was in his sixties, tears welled up in his eyes when the subject of his mother came up in a conversation with the automotive writer, W. A. P. John. Mrs. Durant, the son said, had always thought of him as "a wonderful boy," and as an adult, he declared, he had always sought to do nothing that might in any way make her think less of him as a man. Upon her death, Durant "sobbed like a child," and he would not allow anything in the house in Flint to be touched for three years. Then he had everything shipped to his mansion in Deal, New Jersey, where he had the third floor fitted up "with the furniture, curtains, draperies, rugs and even chandeliers, that his mother had used for fifty years."[13]

Whatever emotional problems may have resulted from the disappearance of the husband and father from the Durant household, finances were not among the family's worries, for Henry Crapo had fulfilled his pledge to provide for his daughter and grandchildren in a suitable fashion. In 1875, Rebecca Durant purchased a large, sprawling house that was to be her home in Flint for the remaining fifty years of her life. "The rooms were furnished in the elegance of an era when furniture was hand-carved and upholstered in choice satin damasks and velvets," one woman later recalled. "The curtains of Brussels lace and other embellishments that gave luster to the surroundings were chosen with an eye to usefulness as well as beauty." Subsequently, the house was one of the first in Flint to have electric lights, a bit of home improvement that caused Rebecca's sister, Rhoda Willson, to remark: "I certainly hope I never become so lazy I can't strike a match."[14]

One day when he was seventeen, William Durant came home from the Flint high school and informed his mother that he was quitting school to look for a job. He was hired by the family-owned lumber company, now being managed by his uncle William, and remained with the Crapo lumber business for several years. It was characteristic of Durant, however, that he was never satisfied to confine himself to one line of work for very long. By the time he was in his twenties, therefore, he was seeking and getting other opportunities outside of the family interests.[15]

The prestige that came to one in Flint from being Henry Crapo's grandson undoubtedly helped open doors to these new opportunities, and throughout his life Durant constantly reminded people, as in his biography in *Who's Who in America,* that the "Hon. H. H. Crapo, gov. of Mich." was his grandfather. But in all fairness to Durant, at an early age he demonstrated remarkable talents as a salesman that soon showed him worthy of employment, regardless of family connections. He peddled patent medicines, went out on the road to sell cigars, and, like his grandfather before him, dabbled in insurance and real estate. One of his early business successes was an insurance agency which he and a partner, I. Wixom Whitehead, established in the mid-eighties. It was reportedly one of the largest agencies in central Michigan. His real estate venture was not as successful, but it proved to be useful to Durant in the long run. He and David D. Aitken were partners in this business, which ended, Durant later recalled, with him losing the few hundred dollars of his savings that he had put into the partnership. "They used to call me 'skinny' in those days," Durant said, "but Aitken called me 'skinned.'" Aitken, who was several years older than Durant, was a good person for Durant to know, one of many useful contacts Durant made in these years. A lawyer, Aitken served as city clerk and city attorney of Flint in the eighties, went on to serve two terms in Congress in the nineties, was mayor of Flint in 1905, was the first president of the Flint Chamber of Commerce, and had numerous interests in Flint business activities. Beginning in the early 1890's he and Durant served together as directors of the Citizens Commercial and Savings Bank.[16]

In addition to demonstrating his skills as a salesman, Durant also showed evidence of certain organizational talents. Although it was his inability or unwillingness to see the need for organizational changes that finally led to his downfall in the auto industry, in an earlier period he sensed that there was the key to success. "E. W.," he told Eugene Lewis around 1905, "they claim this motor car business is a mystery — has an electric plant, a water plant and a whole lot of other gadgets. But, after all, it is nothing but organiZAtion. . . . Bricks and mortar, men and machinery and organiZAtion. . . ." As a young salesman with the George T. Warren Cigar Manufacturing Company he was credited with a reorganization that made the firm one of the largest of its type in the state. More famous, however, is the job that he is reported to have done reorganizing and revitalizing the Flint City Water Works Company. Regarding the details of this accomplishment, however, the existing Durant biographies leave much to be desired. Confusion has arisen from Durant's connection with the gas company through his uncle, Dr. Willson, who was one of the organizers and at various times the president, and through Durant's mother, who was a stockholder. As for the water company, it was a private stock company, incorporated in 1883, which began to supply water to customers by the fall of that year. After some months of operation, the venture was not proving to be a success. At the same time, Durant came in as the new secretary. Margery Durant's account, apparently inaccurate, has Durant, a callow youth not yet twenty, taking the position in 1881. This was clearly not possible since the company was not organized until two years later. Although Durant no doubt did make some significant changes in company operations, as his daughter and others have asserted, the company continued to be plagued by difficulties, especially complaints from customers about the inadequate supply of water. The city finally took over the job of maintaining the waterworks in the second decade of the twentieth century, many years after Durant had gone on to other positions. But for Durant, the part-time job with the water company left him time to pursue his other interests, and was probably most important for the opportunity it provided him to further extend the circle of his acquaintances among Flint's older, more established business leaders.[17]

By the mid-eighties, Billy Durant, as his friends generally called him, although his family continued to call him Will or Willie, was becoming recognized as one of Flint's most promising and successful young men, one who was bubbling over with ideas and had proven he had the ability to put them across. His future did not, however, lie in the lumber business, patent medicines, insurance, real estate, cigars, or the waterworks. All this was only preparation for his big opportunity, which arrived, quite by accident, late in the summer of 1886.

One evening early in September, Durant later recalled, he came upon a group of people gathered around a new two-wheeled horse-drawn cart that its owner was proudly displaying. The unusual feature of this cart was its spring suspension system, which, as Durant discovered when he accepted the offer of a short drive in the vehicle, gave a remarkably smooth ride, in contrast to the bobbing, up-and-down motion that riders in earlier carts were accustomed to enduring. Durant could see that the merits of this cart were so apparent that it could virtually sell itself. This was the kind of product that best fit Durant's style of salesmanship, which he based on an assumption "that the man you are talking to knows as much or more than you do. Do not talk too much. Give the customer time to think. In other words let the customer sell himself." Recognizing that this road cart was a potential money-maker, Durant learned from the local agent that the vehicle was manufactured in Coldwater, Michigan. Two days after his ride, Durant had located the factory in Coldwater — "a small carriage shop of the old-fashioned variety converted into an assembly plant, having a capacity of two or three finished road carts per day," Durant reported. "There was no office, but opening a door, I found myself in a carpenter shop." Here he met one of the proprietors of the company, Thomas O'Brien, who had worked in Coldwater some years as a wagon-maker. In 1883 he had established with William H. Schmedlen one of the many small carriage and wagon companies scattered throughout Michigan at that time. In 1885 O'Brien had been granted a patent on a two-wheeled vehicle, with a half interest in the patent assigned to Schmedlen. A year later, on May 11, 1886, O'Brien and Schmedlen received a patent on the road cart that Durant saw in Flint a few months later. Basically, there seems to have been little difference between the two patented vehicles, but the terms of the 1886 patent appear to have applied more specifically to the suspension system used in the cart.

When young William Durant visited the shop in September 1886, he told O'Brien that he would like to invest a little money in the road cart business. "Why not buy it all?" O'Brien asked, meaning that Durant could buy the rights to manufacture the patented vehicle. O'Brien and Schmedlen had already sold the rights to the vehicle that had been patented in 1885. When Durant expressed doubts whether he could raise the necessary money, O'Brien replied: "It wouldn't take much." O'Brien conferred with William Schmedlen later that day, and the partners agreed to sell the road cart patent, all the finished carts that were on hand and everything else, except the tools, for $1500. Schmedlen even agreed to come to Flint and help Durant set up the business. "There isn't much to it," he declared. "You could learn all there is in 10 days."[18]

With a contract in his pocket, Durant returned to Flint to borrow $2000, enough to pay O'Brien and Schmedlen and have a little left to start the business going in Flint. To his credit, Durant did not turn to his relatives, though he could have. One of his uncles, Ferris F. Hyatt, who had married one of the Crapo girls, had been president of the First National Bank of Flint from 1875 to his death in 1883. Two other uncles, William Crapo and John Orrell, the husband of another Crapo daughter, had been among the organizers of the Genesee County Savings Bank in 1872. Orrell died in 1876, but his son, William Crapo Orrell, later took his father's place on the bank's board of directors with William W. Crapo and Dr. James Willson. Durant would call on these banks for financial help later when he was well established. In 1886, however, he went around to the city's third banking institution, the Citizens National Bank, where he had no relatives. Durant discussed his financial needs with the bank's president, Robert J. Whaley. "You think it's a good thing?" Whaley asked Durant when the latter told him about the road cart. "I surely do, Mr. Whaley," Durant replied, "or I wouldn't be here." Without further ado, Whaley directed the cashier, Henry C. Van Dusen, to make out a 90-day note for $2000 and deposit it to Durant's account. When Durant protested that he could not possibly pay the loan in such a short time, Whaley simply smiled to indicate that Durant need not worry about it and walked away. In later years, Durant gave Whaley full credit for having initiated, through the confidence he had shown in Durant's proposal in 1886, the developments that would ultimately lead to the foundation of General Motors. In turn, when Whaley's bank was reorganized in 1890 as the Citizens Commercial and Savings Bank, Durant was soon elected to the board of directors.[19]

Durant was now able to carry out the terms of the contract that he had signed with O'Brien and Schmedlen, who, in the meantime, had been congratulated by the Coldwater *Republican* on their astuteness in having "made no less than $5000 on their patents" in a year or so "besides the profits on their legitimate business which has never been stopped or curtailed on account of their road cart operations and which they still continue to conduct in the same thorough and satisfactory manner." Within a year or two Thomas O'Brien was no longer with the firm, and William Schmedlen carried on alone. In 1889 he patented still another road cart, by appearances little if any different from the one that Durant had bought the rights to in 1886. Schmedlen called it the Leader Road Cart and made it the specialty of his company for many years, although he also manufactured other carriages and buggies. In 1895 he advertised his carts as "the finest and most perfect line of speed and track carts made. . . ." Although the company, which eventually became known as W. H. Schmedlen & Son, seems to have tried to keep up with the times in the 1920's, when its business was listed as "auto trimming," in the early 1930's it had returned to a more familiar line of work — carriage manufacturing.[20]

Just as it is not entirely fair or accurate to place the blame for Durant's eventual downfall on Durant himself, it is also unfair to give Durant all the credit for his earlier triumphs. He had help from some exceedingly able associates. Within days, if not hours, after obtaining the loan that set him up in the road cart business, Durant ran into an acquaintance, J. (for Josiah) Dallas Dort, the manager of a local hardware store. Dort was a tall, slim, handsome man, a few months older than Durant. Dort was born in Inkster and as a boy attended the Scotch Settlement School, where one of his classmates was Henry Ford. Dort then attended Michigan State Normal School in Ypsilanti, began his business career there in 1876, moved on to other jobs in Jackson and Saginaw, and finally settled in Flint. After a brief discussion, Durant agreed to take Dort in as an equal partner in the business. The company was officially established on September 28, 1886, as the Flint Road Cart Company. Durant and Dort each put up one thousand dollars initially, adding an extra $3500 each shortly afterwards. For nearly two decades the two men were the very closest of business associates as well as personal friends. Later the business ties were loosened, although the friendship continued until Dort's death in 1925. Dort's personality was nearly the opposite of Durant's. Where Durant was the dreamer, the man with the ideas, Dort was the conservative, practical business type. Although quite often he would hold seemingly more important offices than Durant in the numerous companies in which they were associated, Durant got most of the publicity. Dort's importance in the success of these enterprises has been overlooked. Over the years in Flint he gained enormous influence and respect, and there is evidence that when some problem had to be resolved to clear the way for one of their developments, it was Dort who got the

The incredible duo — *William C. Durant, the gambler (left), and J. Dallas Dort, the stabilizing influence — outside their Imperial Wheel plant in Flint in 1908.*

thing done. Regarding Flint's emergence as an industrial center, Charles W. Nash, who also played a major role in the town's development, gave the credit largely to the efforts of Dallas Dort. Durant's troubles did not begin until his dreams took him beyond Flint. Durant's longtime attorney from Flint, John J. Carton, later declared that as long as Durant remained in Flint and was associated with Dort, the latter, along with some of their other associates, "could bring Billy down to earth." When Durant moved on to Buick and then General Motors, however, this restraining influence was removed. Carton said: "there were always too many yesmen around him for his own good." Away from Dort, Durant "soared high, wide, and handsome."[21]

Neither Durant nor Dort knew anything about manufacturing vehicles when they started out, but they had picked a good place to start such an activity, for, already in 1886, Flint was an important center of the vehicle industry. Although the last tract of virgin cork pine in the Flint area was not cut until January 1908, by that time, in the words of the Flint *Journal,* the event stirred up memories only among oldtimers "who were here in the early days when Flint was a 'sawdust' city." Those days were already approaching an end at the time of Henry Crapo's death in 1869, and by the 1870's the decline of the timber resources in the area was forcing a change of emphasis in Flint's economy. The growing importance of agriculture in the area led to the rise of numerous agriculture-related industries, some of which were based as well on the accessibility of lumber, which, if no longer so plentiful around Flint, could easily be brought in by rail from the booming lumber centers not too far north. The manufacturing of wagons and carriages, in this latter group, dated back to the 1850's when Abner Randall opened what is said to have been Flint's first vehicle factory. More important, however, were two companies established somewhat later by Canadians. W. F. Stewart of London, Ontario, established a plant in Flint in 1868 that soon specialized in making bodies for carriages and remained in business for 67 years, eventually becoming a manufacturer of automobile bodies. In 1869, William A. Paterson, a carriage-maker who had learned his trade from R. D. Scott of Guelph, Ontario, before working in New England and the South, came to Flint at the suggestion of Scott, who had established the first carriage factory in Pontiac. By the 1880's Paterson's company was the largest of its kind in Flint. Paterson, like Stewart, would later make the shift into the auto industry. He then manufactured one of the better-known of the strictly "assembled" cars, the Paterson, between 1908 and 1923. In 1882, the Flint Wagon Works, the company that would later be responsible for bringing the Buick auto manufacturing company to Flint, was organized. Josiah W. Begole, who became the second Flint lumberman to be elected governor of Michigan, was one of the principal owners of this wagon company, but the major force in the new firm, an outgrowth of Begole, Fox & Company, one of the larger lumber mills since 1865, was James H.

Whiting, who is credited with persuading Begole and his associates to launch the new venture.[22]

The Flint Road Cart Company, Durant's young firm, started out very modestly in the fall of 1886 in rented quarters, hoping to be able to produce carts initially with the advice and assistance of William Schmedlen, who spent a few days in Flint. Dort's responsibilities from the outset were to oversee production, while Durant went out to drum up sales. He exhibited one of the carts at a fair in Madison, Wisconsin, where it was awarded a blue ribbon. Capitalizing on the award, Durant gave the name "Blue Ribbon" to the best known of the various vehicles he and Dort manufactured. On his trip west Durant obtained orders for several hundred carts, although the plant of the Flint Road Cart Company had turned out only three handmade two-wheeled vehicles. So Durant and Dort turned to the largest of the Flint vehicle manufacturers, W. A. Paterson, and contracted for him to make a large number of carts for the Flint Road Cart Company. One source says the contract called for 10,000 carts, costing eight dollars each, which Durant then sold for $12.50. Another states that the contract was for 3200 carts, costing around twelve dollars, which the Flint Road Cart Company then retailed for about twice that amount. In any event, these were unheard-of production figures at that time in Flint and clearly indicated that the new company had its eyes set on a much larger business than the other Flint manufacturers had thus far achieved. Paterson apparently did not complete the contract, deciding instead to market his own road cart in competition with the Blue Ribbon line. But Durant and Dort got enough money from the sale of the carts Paterson did make to enable them to get more adequate plant facilities and equipment of their own, and to begin large-scale production of their vehicles.[23]

The development of the vehicle interests of Durant and Dort in the next few years can truthfully be described as astonishing. From a reported sale of four thousand carts in their first year of operation, they had by 1900 progressed to the point where they were turning out four hundred vehicles daily of all the varieties common to the carriage industry at that time, not simply two-wheeled carts. These production figures continued to rise in the early years of the twentieth century until a peak of about 150,000 vehicles a year (although some doubt exists as to the accuracy of that figure) was reached in 1905 and 1906. This represented the output of not just one factory or even that of the Durant-Dort interests in Flint, but that of more than a dozen companies they had established or acquired. In addition to four carriage companies in Flint, they owned at least one more in Michigan, two in Georgia, and one in Canada. Not content to depend entirely on outside suppliers, they also owned seven thousand acres of southern timber lands, several lumber mills, a spoke company in Arkansas, the Imperial Wheel Company in Jackson, Michigan (reportedly the largest wheel manufacturer in the world), the Flint Axle

Works, the Flint Varnish Works, a harness-making firm, and assorted other interests.[24]

The corporate control of this sprawling business domain rested with the Flint-based Durant-Dort Carriage Company. The new name had been adopted in 1895 to replace that of Durant and Dort's earlier Flint Road Cart Company, the name given to their company at its incorporation, September 9, 1893. At the outset, control of the company was held tightly by Durant and Dort, each of whom owned 6750 of the 15,000 shares of company stock. By the beginning of the new century, however, this control had been diffused somewhat to include some of the talented executives whom Durant and Dort had brought in. One of the key figures in the organization was Fred A. Aldrich, son of Almon L. Aldrich, a local newspaper editor who had also been Durant's predecessor as secretary of the local waterworks company. The younger Aldrich, who was the same age as Durant, went to work for the road cart company in 1889 at a salary of twelve dollars a week. His father wanted him to stay in the newspaper business but his mother wisely advised her son to "take the cash." Aldrich became secretary of the company when it was incorporated four years later, and continued in that role in the following years. In 1895, he was the only person besides Durant and Dort to own stock in the company, and later, when others became stockholders, Aldrich remained the third largest individual shareholder. He continued his association with Durant and Dort when they later branched out into automobile manufacturing.[25]

The vice-president's position with Durant-Dort came to be held by Charles W. Nash, who would ultimately enjoy much more lasting success in the auto industry than either William Durant or Dallas Dort. The story of Nash's boyhood years sounds much like a plot-line for a Horatio Alger novel, and there is some suspicion that later writers have exaggerated the rags-to-riches details. Nash was born in 1864 in DeKalb County, Illinois, although he had no birth certificate to prove it. (He once remarked to John Carton: "I never was born—I just sprung up and grew.") The Nash family moved to Michigan when Charles was one year old. At age six or seven he was bound out to a farmer in the Flint area. The reason for this court action is not clear. One report claims that Nash was orphaned. Another states that his parents separated. When he was twelve, Nash ran away from his new home and took various farming and carpentry jobs, at which he seems to have done fairly well. In 1891, he moved from the country into Flint so that his wife, who was ill, could receive better medical care. Both Durant and Dort later sought the credit for having spotted the future magnate hard at work in some menial job — the job varying according to who was telling the story — and immediately hiring him for their carriage company. Nash rose quickly in the ranks of the Durant-Dort organization, indicating at least that the hiring of Nash had been a wise move.[26]

In 1896, five years after Nash had been hired, Alexander Brownell Cullen (better known as A. B. C.) Hardy, who had been managing a carriage company in nearby Davison, was brought in as manager of one of

Durant-Dort's new Flint subsidiaries, and two years later Hardy briefly replaced Dort as president of the parent company. Hardy would later be the first in Flint to try to manufacture automobiles, and later still would be one of Durant's most loyal aides in the auto industry. After Durant made his final exit from General Motors, Hardy stayed on to run the Olds Motor Works division of G. M. in the 1920's.[27]

When Durant and Dort established the Imperial Wheel Company in 1899, they again sought out an experienced manager, in this case Clarence B. Hayes, an Ohioan who had been managing the Standard Wheel Company of Kalamazoo since 1890. Under Hayes' management, Imperial Wheel became one of the largest components of the Durant-Dort conglomerate, with plants in Flint and Jackson, the latter employing some seven hundred workers as early as 1901. In 1908, Hayes left the Durant-Dort organization to take over the National Wheel Company in Jackson, which he renamed the Hayes Wheel Company and which became one of the largest suppliers of wheels to auto manufacturers. At one time the Hayes company manufactured each month over a million dollars' worth of wheels for the Ford Motor Company alone, a figure that was about a third of the value of the entire annual output of Durant-Dort in 1900. In 1927, Clarence Hayes merged his company with the Kelsey Wheel Company of Detroit to form the Kelsey-Hayes firm that remains a familiar name in automotive circles to the present day. In 1935, Clarence Hayes organized Hayes Industries of Jackson, another auto parts manufacturer that continues in business today as the Hayes-Albion Corporation.[28]

Another top Durant-Dort executive was Charles H. Bonbright, an Iowan who had held sales positions in Des Moines, Muncie, and Chicago before coming to Flint to become general sales manager of Durant-Dort. In addition to organizing two auto parts companies in later years, Bonbright would also have financial interests in the other Flint automobile developments, and, with another old Durant-Dort associate, George E. Pomeroy, would profit from the huge housing shortage created by Flint's industrial boom by platting several new housing subdivisions.[29]

Two other Durant-Dort officials and stockholders were George C. Willson, who headed the Victoria Vehicle subsidiary, and William Crapo Orrell, who was comptroller of the Durant-Dort company and a member of the board of directors along with Durant, Dort, Nash, Aldrich, Bonbright, and Hayes. Both Orrell and Willson were cousins of Durant, and their presence was another indication that important as Dort or any of the others might be, the senior member of the business was William C. Durant, who was usually content with the position of treasurer, if he held any position at all.

Throughout the development of the Durant-Dort organization, one can see at work the same restless, innovative, gambling spirit that later characterized Durant's auto ventures. A newspaper report in 1891 that the Flint Road Cart Company was planning to move to Saginaw was certainly an early use by Durant of a technique he would later employ with great success to obtain more local support in Flint for his auto companies. An unsuccessful bicycle venture and the acquisition of a company that made revolving hat racks and other business display novelties reflected the same willingness to diversify that Durant later showed when he led G. M. into the tractor and refrigerator businesses. The constant expansion of the Durant-Dort interests and the proliferation of the companies they controlled were unquestionably Durant's, not Dort's work. In one specific case, Durant later recalled, Dallas Dort had been opposed to an idea Durant had gotten during the Christmas holidays in 1895 to establish a new carriage company (Diamond Carriage, which A. B. C. Hardy was brought in to manage) that would market a cheap carriage, to be sold for cash, not on time. For two solid hours Durant discussed the idea with Dort on the telephone. Durant, who would become famous as one of the telephone companies' best customers, with annual bills during the twenties that ran up into tens of thousands of dollars, declared that this was his longest telephone call and at the end he was so exhausted that he felt paralyzed. But he had succeeded in winning Dort's approval. One of Durant's later associates, Walter P. Chrysler, declared that Durant had "the most winning personality of anyone I've ever known. He could coax a bird right down out of a tree, I think."[30]

By 1900, William Durant, not yet forty years old, had become a millionaire, as had his partner Dort. The carriage industry was no longer the challenge to Durant that it had been. Increasingly, he seems to have looked around for something new to tackle. In 1902 he discussed with Whiting, Paterson, and other carriage manufacturers the possibility of a huge $50,000,000 consolidation of the major carriage companies, which, although it came to nothing, foreshadowed the kind of thinking that led Durant to establish General Motors six years later. Also at this time, Durant began to spend more and more time in New York, studying the stock market, and developing a taste for what he found there that finally proved almost as fatal for him as it had for his father. It is indicative of how Durant operated to observe that in these years when the auto industry was finally beginning to emerge as a really viable force in the economy, Durant seems to have shown little interest in this new development. Just as he had been a latecomer to the carriage industry in Flint, so too he would not be the one to pioneer the development of the auto industry there or anywhere else.[31]

As previously noted, the pioneer Flint automobile manufacturer was A. B. C. Hardy, who, exhausted by the demands that the Durant-Dort organization made on him, had resigned from the business in 1900. He went to Europe for eleven months, during which time his interest in automobiles is said to have been aroused. It is important to realize that at this time a number of European nations, particularly France, were well ahead of the United States both in regard to the manufacture of automobiles and in their acceptance by the public. Also, despite the achievements of such American-made cars as the Duryea Motor Wagon, which in competition in America and Europe in 1895 and 1896 had been proven to be at least the equal of European models of the day, there continued to be a widespread view held on both sides of the Atlantic that European cars were superior to American motor vehicles. As Hardy became more familiar with the subject, he is reported to have regarded his European stay as a great opportunity to absorb some of the advanced ideas of the European auto manufacturers. Interestingly, when Hardy returned to Flint in 1901, the car that he designed reflected the ideas not of the European automakers but of such thoroughly American builders as Ransom Olds. Hardy's experience in Europe had, however, convinced him that the vehicles for which Flint had become famous and which had caused the city by the nineties to dub itself "The Vehicle City," were certain to be bumped off the road by these new motorized vehicles in the not-too-distant future.

According to reports, Hardy attempted to persuade his former associates at Durant-Dort to go into this new field, but they refused. He then tried to borrow money from local banks to establish his own company, but they too turned him down. Since these same bankers in the next few years were notably generous in the credit they extended to similar companies promoted by James Whiting and William Durant, Hardy's experience suggests that it was the reputations and business connections of the persons involved, rather than their product, that dictated these decisions. Hardy finally went ahead with his own money, plus smaller amounts put in by three associates, Frank McPhillips, Irvil A. Harper, and Frank Dullam. In the fall of 1902, Hardy, Harper, and McPhillips incorporated the Flint Automobile Company, with a capitalization of only $5000. Hardy owned a majority of the stock and served as president and treasurer. Harper was vice-president and secretary. The legal work involved in the incorporation was handled by John J. Carton's law office, which was beginning an association with the Flint auto industry that would prove a lucrative one for the firm in the years ahead.[32]

Hardy had been developing his car for some months prior to this time, having first occupied part of the old Randall carriage factory and then moving into a former harness factory. By the end of 1902, *Motor Age* reported, Hardy had completed the "first batch of machines," although in its annual report filed with the state in 1903, the Flint company stated that on January 1 of that year it was only "getting ready to make and assemble and sell automobiles and automobile parts and specialties." Bodies for the cars came from the local W. F. Stewart Company, and Weston-Mott in New York supplied some other parts, but Hardy claimed that he built more of his parts than most of the early auto companies. The car he produced was usually called the Flint Roadster, perhaps in an effort to capitalize on the earlier fame of the Flint Road Cart. In some ads the vehicle was referred to as the Hardy. Whatever the name, the car was essentially a runabout, although it was said to be larger and more powerful than the average runabout, thereby leading to the claim that it combined some of the advantages of the larger touring cars with those of the better runabouts. Hardy's early background in the carriage industry probably accounts for the emphasis that appeared in ads for the car on the elegance and luxuriousness of the body and trimmings, "with her eighteen coats of paint and varnish and everything to match." The price of $850 "(with tools, not extras)" made the Flint Roadster considerably more expensive than such similar, but lighter contemporaries as the Oldsmobile and the Murray.[33]

The Flint Automobile Company, however, had a short life, even for one of these early auto companies. In January 1904, John Carton was recommending A. B. C. Hardy to a Cleveland auto company that was seeking to establish an agency in Flint. Hardy, Carton said, "was formerly in the business of manufacturing automobiles, but is now out of the business entirely." Hardy claimed that he was forced out of business when the Association of Licensed Automobile Manufacturers, the organization that was formed early in 1903 to license manufacturers under the Selden Patent, threatened to bring legal action against the small Flint company for failing to secure such a license. However, Charles Clifton declared, when he was president of the A.L.A.M., that Hardy's company had joined the association, but had then bolted, to avoid paying royalties. The real reason for the demise of Hardy's company may have been a lack of sufficient capital resources. The company had produced only fifty-two roadsters, hardly the kind of volume that the manufacturer of an inexpensive car needed to stay in business.[34]

Hardy later re-entered the auto industry as an aide to William Durant, but in his initial venture Hardy also had some links with the other important Flint auto pioneer, James H. Whiting. Whiting was nearly twenty years older than William Durant, having been born in Connecticut in 1842. He settled in Flint when he was twenty-one, and had worked in the hardware business before moving into the carriage industry with the Flint Wagon Works in 1882. Although it had been surpassed by the more widespread Durant-Dort interests, the company was still doing very well under Whiting's able leadership at the turn of the century. At that time, however, Whiting was investigating the auto industry, perhaps out of curiosity, or perhaps out of an awareness of what it would mean for the carriage industry. When A. B. C. Hardy was in New York in 1900 and 1901 attending the auto show, he found James Whiting there. In 1940 Hardy recalled:

> The French cars were an attraction. Their promoters were offering free rides to anybody who would go down to a place near Washington Square and lower Fifth avenue and apply. They wanted to lure the carriage and wagon makers. Mr. Whiting and I went down there and got a ride in one of those French cars. . . .

Whiting seems to have followed closely Hardy's efforts to establish an automobile company, but he was apparently not interested enough to provide Hardy with the kind of backing that might have made the venture a success. Instead, in 1903 while the Flint Automobile Company was

David Dunbar Buick *in 1908, the year that marked the end of his official connections with the auto company bearing his name.*
Courtesy Automotive History Collection

struggling to survive, Whiting cast his lot with a struggling Detroit company, the Buick Motor Company.[35]

David Dunbar Buick was born in Scotland on September 17, 1854. When he was two he was brought to Detroit by his parents. Three years later, Buick's father died, and at age eleven young David Buick was put out to work on a farm. In 1869, he went to work for the Alexander Manufacturing Company of Detroit, a firm that made enameled iron toilet bowls and wooden closet tanks. Eventually Buick became the foreman of the plant. Sometime in these years he reportedly also learned the machinist's trade in the James Flower & Brothers Machine Shop, where Henry Ford was an apprentice machinist in 1880. When the Alexander company failed in 1882, Buick and William S. Sherwood took over the business and built it into a successful plumbing supply house. One of the puzzling aspects of Buick's career is that while he demonstrated an abysmal lack of business sense later in life, his plumbing company was a success. Perhaps the managerial skills were provided by Sherwood. Buick's contribution, among other things, was his talent as an inventor, which resulted in his receiving a total of thirteen patents between 1881 and 1899. One was for a lawn sprinkler. The rest were for inventions more directly related to plumbing — various types of valves, a flushing device, water closets, and bath tubs. In particular, a new method developed by Buick for fixing porcelain onto metal was, one supposes, the principal reason for the popularity of the Buick & Sherwood line of bathroom fixtures. With the rapid growth of urban areas and the resultant great increase in the adoption of indoor plumbing facilities, David Buick's fortune would seem to have been assured. Instead he threw this away in favor of another interest that he had developed — gasoline engines and automobiles. Buick would probably not have been surprised at the report in the 1920's that a considerable number of families in Muncie, Indiana, who owned automobiles had not as yet had bathtubs installed in their homes. After all, as someone once remarked: "You can't ride to town in a bathtub."[36]

Few aspects of American automobile history have been so poorly recorded as that detailing the movement of David Buick from the plumbing business into the business of developing and manufacturing engines and automobiles. It would appear that the plumbing business was sold to the Standard Sanitary Manufacturing Company for $100,000 in December 1899, and that Buick used his share of this money to establish an engine company, which he named, rather imaginatively, the Buick Auto-Vim and Power Company. Although he held only one out of one thousand shares in the plumbing business, Buick was still serving as president of Buick & Sherwood, at the same time that he was president of the new engine company. But by January 1, 1902, Buick had severed his relations with the plumbing company and was able to devote full attention to his new interest.[37]

Much controversy surrounds the question of who was principally responsible for developing the advanced "valve-in-head" gasoline engine that would be the most distinctive feature of the early Buick automobiles. David Buick himself was undoubtedly involved in this creative process, as was perhaps his son, Thomas, who was at that time associated with his father's business. However, the early manager of the Buick Auto-Vim and Power Company, Walter L. Marr, has been credited by some as being the one who made the greatest contribution to the engine's development. Marr was a native of Lexington, in Michigan's Thumb region, who, like many other automobile men, moved from an enthusiasm for bicycles to an interest in motor vehicles. In 1898 he is said to have built such a vehicle powered by a four-cylinder gasoline engine that he had designed. This took place in Ohio, where Marr was then located. Somehow, Marr met Buick and joined the latter's new company. Buick could be a difficult man to work with, however. The Detroit businessman and politician, John C. Lodge, remembered Buick as "a crank, and a hard man to do business with." Marr and Buick apparently got into a fight, and Marr quit, formed his own Marr Auto Car Company in Detroit in 1903, failed in this independent venture, and finally rejoined Buick. Meanwhile, however, Marr's place had been taken by Eugene C. Richard, a Frenchman who had learned about engines in Philadelphia, and who is reported to have been employed by Olds before joining Buick sometime around 1901. Within three or four years, Richard was granted several automotive patents which he assigned to the Buick company, but the one that he received for an engine, apparently a version of the "valve-in-head" engine, was assigned not to Buick but to a Sarah L. Kneeland of Lansing, Michigan. Perhaps the Buick company obtained the rights to the engine from her, or perhaps Walter Marr perfected the engine when he returned to Buick. A contract between Marr and Buick in 1905 acknowledged certain engine improvements that Marr had invented, but which, for "business reasons," had not been patented.[38]

Whoever may have been responsible for the developmental work on the "valve-in-head" engine, David Buick's engine company was concerned, at the outset, with a gasoline engine of a more conventional design which would be sold for marine and farm uses. At least by April of 1901, efforts were being made to adapt these engines for use in automobiles. At that time, David Buick offered to sell to Walter Marr "the Automobile, known as the Buick Automobile, for the sum of $300.00." With the exception of six engines that were specifically excluded, Buick also offered to sell to Marr for an additional $1500 all other engines and "all patterns which we have on hand for making these engines, also delivery wagon body, two new carriage bodies, and runabout body." Whether Marr accepted this offer is not known, but Buick's willingness to sell suggests that financial problems were already beginning to plague him in his new field of endeavor. Buick soon seems to have run through the money he obtained by the sale of his plumbing business. In 1902 he reorganized the engine business, forming the Buick Manufacturing Company, which absorbed the Auto-Vim outfit. This move seems to have marked the abandonment of the earlier engine in favor of the experimental "valve-in-head" power plant. By the fall of 1902, the engine was being perfected and an automobile employing the new engine was being built, but Buick was also in serious financial difficulty.[39]

David Buick turned for help to Benjamin and Frank Briscoe, the brothers in the sheet metal business who a few months earlier had begun supplying parts to the Olds Motor Works and had then begun contributing parts and some money to Buick's infant automobile enterprise. In September 1902, the Briscoes agreed to write off Buick's existing debt to them and to supply him with an additional $650 in return for the car that Buick was building. When this car had been completed and successfully tested, early in 1903, the Briscoes allowed Buick to use it as a demonstrator to help him secure the financial backing needed to put it into production. By the spring of 1903, when David Buick had still made no visible progress in securing such backing, he and the Briscoes made a rather unusual arrangement. The brothers loaned him $1500 more, bringing to about $3500 the amount that Buick now owed them, and in return Buick agreed to another reorganization of his business. The Buick Manufacturing Company was replaced by the Buick Motor Company, with $100,000 in stock issued, of which the Briscoes took $99,700 and gave David Buick the remaining $300. Buick, who was the president of the new company, was given the option of paying back what he owed the Briscoes, in which case he would receive all their stock holdings, or, if he did not pay these debts by September 1903, the Briscoes would take over active control of the Buick company. Within a few weeks it was becoming clear that Buick was not going to pay off; the Briscoes began to have second thoughts about being stuck with the company, particularly when Benjamin Briscoe developed an interest in a new car that Jonathan D. Maxwell was designing. Maxwell had years of practical experience behind him, both in the designing and the manufacturing end of the auto industry. Little wonder if Briscoe judged his prospects of success to be far better if he backed Maxwell than if he continued backing David Buick. Compared with Maxwell, Buick was still a novice when it came to automobiles and, worse yet, seemed to have lost whatever aggressive, promotional talents he had displayed earlier when he was selling toilets and water closets.[40]

Sometime in the summer of 1903, one of the Briscoes visited a distant relative in Flint, Dwight T. Stone, a realtor. Out of the visit came a meeting between Benjamin Briscoe and James Whiting and other directors of the Flint Wagon Works. Stone apparently knew of Whiting's interest in automobiles, and suggested him as a likely prospect on whom Briscoe could unload the unpromising Buick venture. Whiting and his fellow directors were interested. They went to Detroit to examine the Buick operation and to see a demonstration of the one Buick automobile that had been built. The Flint businessmen decided to take over the Briscoes' interest in the company. Early in September, they paid the two Detroit brothers $10,000. On September 11, the Flint *Journal* gave front-page coverage to the announcement that "a splendid new manufacturing industry" was about to be established in the city. The five directors of the Flint Wagon Works — Whiting, Charles M. Begole, George L. Walker, William S. Ballenger, and Charles A. Cummings — had borrowed $10,000 to acquire the Buick Company rather than take the money out of their own funds, as they could easily have done. Apparently, they were anxious to keep their new business interest completely separate from their existing carriage and wagon business. At this time, sales of horse-drawn vehicles had not yet been seriously affected by automobile sales, and James Whiting had no intention of making the mistake that the Harrison Wagon Works of Grand Rapids and Dolson and Sons in Charlotte committed in this same period by prematurely abandoning a going business in favor of one that had not yet proven itself. Furthermore, there is considerable evidence that James Whiting and his associates, like Samuel Smith when he took over the major financial interest in the Olds business enterprises, were less interested in the automobile that David Buick and his men had built than in Buick's gasoline engine. It was announced that the products that the new company would manufacture would be "stationary and marine engines, automobile engines, transmissions, carburetors, spark plugs, etc." While the Flint *Journal* expressed hope that the Buick company would also manufacture automobiles, observing that Flint, as "the vehicle city of the United States," was "the most natural center for the manufacture of autos in the whole country," this apparently was not the goal of the new owners. Edwin Wood, a prominent Flint attorney, declared in 1916 that the Flint Wagon Works was interested in Buick because it saw "a market for stationary farm engines through their farm wagon agencies." As for the automobile market, the *Journal* reported on September 11, 1903, that the new company would "devote special effort to the manufacture of automobile engines and transmissions, for which there is a heavy demand all over the country." Beyond this, it would be many months before any complete Buick automobiles would emerge in Flint.[41]

By December 11, 1903, the Buick plant, begun only three months earlier next to the main plant of the Flint Wagon Works, was in operation, with twenty-five workers engaged in the manufacture of engines of varying degrees of power. At the same time, the existing Detroit plant of the Buick Motor Company was maintained, at least as late as the printing of the 1905 *Michigan State Gazetteer,* in which David Buick was listed as manager of this plant. He was reportedly reluctant at first to move from Detroit to Flint when the Whiting interests gained control of the company, but the latter, who were of course counting on Buick to run the business, made some special inducements to persuade him to agree to the change. The corporate arrangements, originally calling for a capitalization of $50,000, were completed in January 1904 with the incorporation of the Buick Motor Company, with a capitalization of $75,000. A report filed by the company later that year showed that James Whiting, the president, owned 1504 shares of the stock, and his wife, Alice, was listed as owning 367 shares. George L. Walker, the vice-president, had 725 shares, and his wife had an additional 25. William Ballenger, treasurer, owned 707 shares, and two other directors of the Flint Wagon Works, Charles Begole and Charles A. Cummings, controlled respectively 1068 and 492 shares. Whiting, Walker, Ballenger, Begole, and Cummings were on the board of directors along with David Buick, who was named secretary of the company, and his son, Thomas D. Buick. The two Buicks controlled 1500 shares of stock which they would actually receive only after their existing debts, which the Flint directors had paid, were repaid from the dividends these shares would earn. The purposes of the new company were listed as "the manufacturing of gas and gasoline engines, and their appliances; automobiles and their parts; operating foundries and machine shops; and manufacturing iron, steel, brass and metal works of all kinds, and dealing in same; and engaging in the manufacture and sale of machinery, appliances and accessories." These were definitely not objectives of a company interested only in automobiles.[42]

While the Buick workers were engaged in producing engines, David Buick and his assistants, including Walter Marr who had re-joined Buick late in 1903, continued their experiments with the valve-in-head engine and an automobile. Finally, by July 1904 they had completed a two-cylinder stripped-down model, which Marr drove, with Tom Buick riding along, from Flint to Detroit and back between July 9 and 12. The return trip, a distance of 115 miles by the round-about route Marr had taken, was completed in just over three and a half hours, "remarkable time," the Flint *Journal* noted, "a trifle less than a mile in two minutes." Marr reported that the car had performed with complete satisfaction. "We took hills handily with our high speed gear and the machine sounded like a locomotive. It simply climbed. In one place we raced with an electric car and showed them the way. We went so fast at another time that we could not see the village 'six-mile-an-hour' sign." The *Journal* wrote that the returning vehicle, with "its long rakish looking body, covered with mud," had "the appearance of a speeder and attracted much attention along the route of the run."[43]

The car that Marr and Tom Buick tested became the Buick Model B, which, with tonneau, it was announced, would sell for $950. On August 13, 1904, the first production Buick came out of the plant in Flint and was delivered to Dr. Herbert H. Hills of the Oak Grove Sanitarium in Flint. Hills was an automobile enthusiast who subsequently gave up the medical profession for a position with the Packard Motor Company in Detroit. In the next few weeks a number of other Buicks were produced — the exact number varying, depending on the source consulted, from seventeen to twenty-eight. Early in November, however, when a Buick agency was opened in Cleveland, *Motor Age* declared that the Buick was "a little machine which has attracted an immense amount of attention in the past few weeks, owing to high power and low price." By that time, the managerial control of the company had been removed from the hands of David Buick and turned over to William C. Durant.[44]

Up to this time, Durant had shown little interest in automobiles. In the summer of 1902 a school friend of Margery Durant, William's daughter, had taken her for a ride in her French-built Panhard. Afterwards, an excited Margery cried: "Pops, I've ridden in a horseless carriage." William Durant, "with deep emotion," scolded his daughter: "Margery, how could you — *how could you* be so foolish as to risk your life in one of those things!" By this time Durant had had at least a few rides in horseless carriages. His cousin, W. C. Orrell, had taken him out in his steam car, one of the first motor vehicles in Flint. He may also have ridden with Arthur Jerome Eddy, the noted automobile tourist, who had married Orrell's sister, Lucy, in 1890. Eddy had also driven from Chicago to Flint in addition to his epic Chicago-to-Boston journey of August 1901. In 1902, Judge Charles H. Wisner of Flint took Durant for a ride in the car that Wisner had built in 1900. Apparently Wisner was hoping to interest Durant in helping to manufacture the vehicle, but Durant was not impressed. Durant later declared that he had "thought it was terrible the way those noisy contraptions, especially the old steam engines, shocked people and startled horses." He was "mighty provoked" that his cousin, for example, "would drive around annoying people that way." But then on September 4, 1904, Dr. Hills took Durant for a ride in his new Buick, and finally Durant was impressed with the performance of an auto.[45]

Dr. Hills was apparently lending his assistance to an effort that was then underway to interest Durant in using his legendary skills to make Buick a financial as well as a mechanical success. It does not seem to have taken James Whiting long to realize what the Briscoes had found out earlier — the Buick company was not going to move as long as it remained under David Buick's direction. Although the details are not completely clear, it appears that by the summer of 1904 Whiting feared for the future of the company. Although a few engines had been sold, no automobiles had yet been sold, and the company was deeply in debt. To support the Buick company during its early months, the Flint Wagon Works had reportedly borrowed $25,000 from each of three Flint banks, a large amount for these institutions to lend at that time. The collapse of the Buick company could, therefore, have brought down the Flint Wagon Works and also have had serious repercussions upon the entire economy of the city.[46]

The previous winter, at a convention of carriage manufacturers in Chicago, Whiting had discussed his new company with Fred Aldrich of the Durant-Dort Carriage Company. Whiting told Aldrich of his growing doubts concerning Buick's abilities. Aldrich suggested that Whiting try to interest Durant in the auto company. The following summer, therefore, Whiting invited his old rival in the carriage industry to come back to Flint from New York, where Durant was then staying, to have a look at the Buick situation. Durant was apparently ready for a new challenge. He knew little about automobiles, or machines in general, but he had confidence in his ability to judge the worth of a product. Although he was favorably impressed by his initial experiences with the Buick car, he was not yet convinced. The demonstration rides he had been given had all been on good city streets. He wanted to make his own tests. For almost two months, Durant test-drove a Buick "with a thoroughness which to this day," Arthur Pound wrote in 1933, "is recalled in Michigan." Durant ran the car under the worst conditions he could find in the Flint area. In spite of the problems he encountered, Durant concluded that the Buick was a superior car for its day. It was a vehicle like the old Flint Road Cart — one that he could sell with a clear conscience, and one which would, in fact, sell itself. All that was needed was increased capital backing, more adequate plant facilities, and a strong sales campaign. Durant was sure he could handle all these demands, but before he would agree to undertake the task he insisted that Whiting and his associates give him complete control over the operations. He seems to have gotten little argument from Whiting and the other directors, and on November 1, 1904, management of the Buick company passed into the hands of William C. Durant.[47]

This action marked the beginning of the end for David Buick, although he continued as secretary of the company and Durant officially held no office at all aside from a seat on the board. Durant seems to have made a real effort to find a place in the company where Buick's talents could be utilized. He resisted pressure from some associates to have the name of the company's automobile changed to Durant, feeling that there was a certain appeal in the name Buick, although Durant did wonder if people would know how to pronounce it correctly. ("Would they call it Booick?" he wondered.) According to Margery Durant, he also felt that the retention of the name was only fair to the man who had originally conceived of the product Durant was now promoting. But unfortunately for Buick, Durant's concern had little effect on Buick's status in the company. At the end of 1905, David Buick, secretary of the company and a member of its board of directors, owned only one share of common stock. Further indication of David Buick's financial standing at this time can be seen in the difficulty he had in paying a bill of $92.58 from John J. Carton for legal services the latter had performed for Buick in connection with an automobile accident involving Buick's daughter. Finally Carton wrote to Durant, who saw that Carton was sent the money along with a letter on March 14, 1906, in which Durant reported: "Mr. Buick wishes me to say that until a few moments ago this [that is, the $92.58] was more money than he had in the world. He disliked very much to make this admission and possibly this is the reason why you have not heard from him before." Later in 1908, a news story described the "experimental room" at Buick, run by David Buick and Walter Marr, "whose inventive minds are constantly at work." By that time, although Buick remained a director of the company, and his holdings of common stock had increased to nearly 300 shares, he had been replaced as secretary. It was the last symbol of the dominant role he had held in the affairs of the company only four years earlier. By the end of 1908, Buick had resigned from the company completely. According to reports he had to surrender his Buick stock at this time since he had never paid off his debt to the Whiting interests. Durant, however, reportedly gave him a large sum of money — the most common figure cited is $100,000, but one source places the amount at a million dollars. Buick was free to do with the money whatever he chose, and he proceeded to squander it. He became involved in a shady California oil deal which failed, as did subsequent ventures into the manufacturing of carburetors with his son Tom, an attempted Grand Rapids automobile company, and a Florida real estate company. David Buick died, virtually a pauper, in Detroit's Harper Hospital on March 5, 1929.[48]

Durant fulfilled everything that had been expected of him when he was brought into Buick — everything and then some. Still only forty-two when he took over in November 1904, he was at the peak of his powers, and the manner in which he used them all in the next five years was a marvel to behold. During that half decade Durant established a record unmatched by any other single individual during a similar period of time in the entire history of the American automobile industry.

Durant's method of dealing with the financial problems of Buick was familiar to those who knew him. Just as he had increased the capitalization of Durant-Dort tenfold in a half dozen years and had proposed to finance his consolidation of major carriage companies by issuing $50,000,000 in stock, he now pushed through periodic increases in Buick's capitalization — from its original $75,000 in January 1904, up to $500,000 on November 26, 1904, up again to $1,500,000 (of which $900,000 was common stock and $600,000 preferred) on September 27, 1905, with a further increase on June 12, 1907, to $2,600,000 of which $2,000,000 was in common stock. Particularly regarding the threefold increase in 1905, Buick's attorney, John Carton, had difficulty justifying the change. After listing every conceivable asset that could be credited to Buick, he found himself still short $60,000. He proceeded to make this the value of an engine improvement "invented by Walter L. Marr, but on account of business reasons not patented." Secretary of State George A. Prescott, a Republican, approved the application as submitted by Carton, who observed: "The fact that I was very well acquainted at Lansing may have been beneficial in getting such a hazy item [as the Marr "invention"] passed." Carton was, in fact, one of the foremost Republican leaders in the state. He had been speaker of the house in the legislative sessions of 1901 and 1903, would later serve as president of the Constitutional Convention in 1907-1908, and would be seriously mentioned as a potential candidate for governor. The next session of the state legislature, incidentally, moved to prohibit the use in any incorporation applications made in the future of such intangible items as Carton had included.[49]

Durant's love for stock and stock dealings combined with his well-honed skills as a salesman made him hard to beat as a stock promoter. However, it should be kept in mind, as one reads of Durant's prodigious feats of salesmanship, such as the oft-repeated story that he went out and sold $500,000 in Buick stock in forty-eight hours, that he was not dealing with strangers. This was not the work of some outside drummer, new to the territory. This was the work of a businessman who was known throughout the community and was regarded with respect and a good deal of awe because of the magic touch he had demonstrated with almost every business venture he had undertaken. It was in this community and with this reputation that Durant raised the money that put Buick on the right road, building upon and greatly expanding the involvement of Flint residents with the company that had been initiated by the Whiting group.

On the face of it, James Whiting and his associates from the Flint Wagon Works continued to be, under the Durant regime, the dominant faction in the company. At the end of 1905, out of nine thousand shares of Buick common stock, Whiting, Begole, Walker, Ballenger, and Cummings controlled outright 1574 shares, along with 774 of the six thousand shares of preferred stock. In addition, Ballenger was the trustee of a block of five hundred common shares and two thousand preferred that had apparently been assigned to the Flint Wagon Works. Whiting stepped down as president of Buick, reportedly to devote more time to running the carriage business. In actual fact, however, Durant gave Whiting a large block of Durant's own Buick stockholdings in return for Whiting's help in managing the expanded Buick operations. Durant also assigned some of his stock to Charles Begole, who now replaced Whiting as president of the Buick company, in return for Begole's active participation in the management of the auto company. George Walker and William Ballenger continued in their positions as vice-president and treasurer, respectively, of Buick. Two years later, James Whiting and his wife had increased their holdings of Buick common until they owned nearly a seventh of the twenty thousand shares that had by then been issued. But although Begole and Walker still retained their offices at that time, Durant's decision to take over the post of treasurer formerly held by Ballenger was evidence of the diminishing influence of the Whiting interests in comparison with that of other interests that were by then represented among the stockholders.[50]

Those other interests had been brought in within a short time after Durant took over Buick. Although it is quite probable that James Whiting exerted a considerable influence in persuading Flint businessmen to lend their support to the auto company, it is probably fair to assign to Durant the major share of the credit for this development. At the very outset he is said to have gotten stockholders in the Flint Gas Light Company, who had just sold out to another group, to invest a large part of what they had realized from this sale in the new Buick stock issue. The fact that both Durant and his uncle, Dr. Willson, had been officers in the gas company helps explain this coup. As part of the deal that put him in charge of Buick, Durant had been given a large amount of Buick stock — reportedly as much as $325,000. He did not keep it, turning over about a third of these shares to Whiting and Begole and most, if not all, of the remainder to the Durant-Dort Carriage Company, of which he was, of course, still one of the two principal owners. Dallas Dort has been depicted by some as having had grave reservations concerning the wisdom of Durant's latest move. The Detroit writers, Norman Beasley and George Stark, declare that Dort's view was: "There will aways be horse and buggies," and they declare that he delayed following his partner's example until it was too late to make a success of his own automobile company. It is true that Dort told the Michigan Retail Implement and Vehicle Dealers' Association in 1909 that despite the "great progress" the automobile was making, "we still rally around the standard of the horse-drawn vehicle, for you cannot beat the horse. You can put anything you want parallel with the horse, but you can never put it ahead of him." Such a remark, however, was expected of a man, who just the previous year had been president of the Carriage Builders' National Association, addressing a group of men whose livelihood depended on the sales of horse-drawn vehicles. It is also true that the Dort Motor Car Company, which Dort did not establish until 1915, was liquidated only nine years later. But the cars that Dort put out were excellent vehicles. The failure of the business had less to do with Dort's late entry into the automobile field than it did with general financial conditions in the early twenties that closed up many automobile companies, including some, such as the Haynes and the Apperson companies, that had been in the business from the very earliest days. The truth is that Dort was deeply involved in the automobile developments in Flint at least from the time that Durant became involved. John Knapman, a retired Flint dentist who, as a young man, had worked in Flint's automotive plants and had become well acquainted with Dort, recalled in 1972 that he had once asked Dort: "Why did you get your start [in the manufacture of automobiles] so late?" "Well," Dort had replied, "I was so deeply mixed up with Durant." There is evidence that Dort had stuck by his old friend loyally, allowing Durant to get the headlines with Buick while he ran the carriage company, which was enjoying its best years ever in 1905 and 1906. His contributions included making the ample resources of the Durant-Dort organization available when Buick needed them. As a result, although the Durant-Dort Carriage Company was not as visible in the Buick company as the Flint Wagon Works, by the end of 1905 it controlled over a third of the Buick common stock, as well as a good chunk of the preferred stock. Behind the scenes Dort apparently lent his weight and talents to the efforts to make Buick a success. When John Carton was asked to do something about a problem that had arisen involving the new Buick plant being built in Flint at this time, he knew what to do. "I called up Mr. Dort," he reported, "who perhaps more than any other man, was instrumental in getting this thing started."[51]

Durant also secured the support of other big names in the Flint carriage industry. The two Canadians, W. A. Paterson and W. F. Stewart, had both bought small amounts of Buick stock and were serving as directors of Buick by 1905. Paterson did not retain his stock or his seat on the board, but by 1907 Stewart had substantially increased his investment and was continuing in the role of a director. Paterson's place as director was taken by another prominent Flint businessman, Flint P. Smith, whose father, Hiram "Hardwood" Smith, had been engaged in logging in the Flint area almost a decade before Henry Crapo commenced his operations. In addition to their other business interests, however, Flint Smith, Paterson, and Stewart, as directors of Buick, could also look after the interests of Flint's banks whose increased support Durant had also been able to obtain. Smith, Paterson, and Stewart were all directors of the Union Trust and Savings Bank, which had originally put up the money the Whiting interests needed to acquire control of Buick and which now pledged additional funds to support Buick, in return for which the directors of the bank received Buick stock to hold for the benefit of the bank's stockholders. The details and the exact amounts involved in these arrangements, made in 1905, are not entirely clear. The support of Flint's banking institutions seems to have resulted, however, from a multitude of links that joined leading figures in these banks with the Buick company. Durant, various members of the Whiting group, and Durant's old real estate partner, David Aitken, were or had been officers of the Citizens Commercial and Savings Bank. In 1905, this bank was still headed by Robert Whaley, the banker who gave Durant his first start toward success in 1886. The president of the First National Bank (one of whose earlier presidents had been an uncle of Durant's) in 1905 was none other than John Carton, while Buick's vice-president, George Walker, had been a director of that same bank for a number of years. Finally, the Genesee County Savings Bank was most closely linked to Durant through his uncles, William Crapo and James Willson, and his cousin, W. C. Orrell, all officers in the bank. One investment of about $20,000 in Buick stock that the Genesee bank made in 1905 is today still held by the bank's directors as a non-book asset for the benefit of bank stockholders. The General Motors stock, for which the original Buick shares were exchanged in 1908, is now worth around $8,000,000, and this figure would be much more if some of the stock had not been sold in recent years. Perhaps because of his family connections, the Genesee seems to have become Durant's favorite bank in Flint. "Billy always gets what he wants here," Arthur G. Bishop, cashier and, after Dr. Willson's death, president of the bank, once told Arthur Pound. Bishop showed Pound a spindle heavy with paper in his office. "Those are Billy Durant's notes, the ones that I thought it best not to put through the bank, so I let him have the money myself and just carry these along until it is easy for him to meet them." Durant in turn rewarded Bishop for his faithful service by naming him a director and vice-president of General Motors in 1915, positions which Bishop continued to hold long after Durant had departed for the last time from that corporation.[52]

At the same time that Durant was shoring up Buick's shaky financial underpinnings, he was tackling the problems involved in producing and selling the company's car. The latter job was the easier. Interest in the Buick Model B was already becoming widespread. To capitalize on this interest, Durant hired as Buick's sales manager Charles Van Horn, a a veteran of fourteen years experience in the bicycle industry, while W. L. Hibbard, manager of the Chicago office of the Studebaker company, was brought in as assistant sales manager. Durant, however, took a direct interest in this side of the business himself. He went to New York for the annual auto show at the end of 1904 and, according to a letter written by his wife a few weeks later, succeeded in getting orders for over a thousand Buicks. Durant was probably the best salesman the company had. Charles Mott relates how once he and Durant were going by train from Flint to Utica and had a one-hour layover between trains in Detroit. They went over to a nearby Buick agency, where the dealer told Durant of difficulties he was having with several prospective customers. Durant got the name of one of the prospects, hurried off and returned with the sale completed in time for the train departure. On another occasion, when the Buick agency in Chicago was doing poorly, Durant went and took charge personally and in five weeks had sold ninety-nine cars, a record for that agency to that time. Such actions no doubt helped to keep the Buick sales organization on its toes, but ultimately, as Durant's automobile interests grew ever larger, his apparent inability to leave minor details to the care of subordinates would infuriate some of these executives — most notably Walter Chrysler — at the same time that it prevented Durant from giving his attention to more important matters.[53]

Producing the cars to fill the orders that Durant had obtained in New York in 1904 was a more difficult problem. Thus far, fewer than forty Buicks, possibly as few as twenty-eight, had been produced at the plant in Flint. As Durant sized up the Buick operation in the fall of 1904 he had immediately concluded that a larger factory was essential. It just happened that the Durant-Dort organization had a vacant factory building in Jackson, formerly used by the Imperial Wheel Company, that was available. The Buick stock that was given to Durant at this time may have been given as much to insure the use of the vacant Jackson facility as it was to obtain Durant's services. By the end of 1904, plans were being implemented to move the Buick assembly operations to Jackson, although the production of engines continued to be carried on in Flint. In 1905, Buick production of the Model C, selling for $1250, at the Jackson assembly plant is variously estimated at from 627 to 750 cars.[54]

Jackson, in several respects, would seem to have been a better location for an automobile manufacturer than Flint. Its population, for one thing, was twice that of Flint at the beginning of the century, and many of Jackson's residents who worked in the city's eighty factories held jobs that would have qualified them to switch over to automobiles with little adjustment. There were nine companies in the city in 1901 making various kinds of horse-drawn vehicles. Although not as large as Flint's carriage industry, Jackson claimed that it, not Pontiac, was entitled to second place in the state in vehicle production.[55]

Parts manufacturers located in Jackson included not only the Imperial Wheel plant but the National Wheel Company, which, according to one report in 1904, was producing a fifth of all the automobile wheels in the United States. The Lewis Spring & Axle Company was another Jackson firm that could and later did produce parts for the auto industry. There were in addition four plants manufacturing agricultural implements, and several companies engaged in machine shop work and in making milling equipment, lathes, and steel tools. Even more important to the prospective manufacturer, Jackson was one of the major rail centers in the state. It was a main junction for several lines of the Michigan Central as well as for the Grand Trunk and the Lake Shore & Michigan Southern. Beginning around 1901, also, an extensive outstate network of electric interurban lines began spreading out from Jackson. Repair shops for these railroads and interurbans were among the city's largest employers. It may well be, however, that the seemingly overriding importance of this still expanding transportation industry in Jackson's economy served to deter the development of new industries. The columns of the Jackson *Daily Citizen,* for example, constantly were given over to news of what was going on with the railroads and interurbans, while, in contrast, very slight attention was paid to other business happenings in the city.[56]

Nevertheless, by the time William Durant moved the Buick assembly operations to Jackson, automobile manufacturing had been going on in the city for about three years. This work was an outgrowth of the efforts of one man, Byron J. Carter. Carter is possibly one of the more important of Michigan's auto pioneers, but he has not fared well at the hands of historians. Carter was born in Jackson in 1863 and was trained as a mechanic. In 1893 he developed an interest in bicycles and opened a shop where he sold and repaired the Columbia, Dayton, Eagle, and other popular bicycles of the day. By the mid-nineties he was also becoming interested in gasoline engines and automobiles. As related earlier, Carter bought one of Charles King's motor carriages in June 1899, paying $616.75 for the carriage, batteries, and spark coil. The deal did not include the engine. Oliver Barthel, that gadfly among these early Michigan auto mechanics, later recalled that he had been hired by Carter to design the engine, which, Barthel claimed, Carter then built in the machine shop that he was in charge of at the Jackson prison. Barthel may have been confused on the latter point since earlier contemporary accounts do not mention that Carter had held such a position. Carter also claimed that his engine, which he admitted was of Detroit origins, was not in satisfactory operating condition until he worked on it. In any event, he soon turned from gasoline to steam engines as the source of power for his vehicles. At the end of 1900, *Motor Age* reported that Carter had developed "a steam carriage of stanhope pattern," which, in its early tests, had demonstrated "satisfactory efficiency." Carter and W. S. Daniels of Grand Rapids announced they were forming the Michigan Automobile Company to manufacture this steam car, which would retail for as little as $750. They hoped to produce it in the vacant Clipper bicycle factory in Grand Rapids. The Studebaker company, the city of Elkhart, Indiana, and various Jackson businessmen were also reported to be negotiating for the rights to Carter's car. These plans collapsed, possibly because the announcement of Carter's success in building a steam car appears to have been premature. It was not until early August 1901 that one Jackson paper reported that Carter had "just completed" a steam-powered car containing several new features on which he subsequently was granted at least one patent. Carter, it was said, had driven the vehicle to Kalamazoo and back, "just for exercise." Later that summer, he and a friend tried to drive two of the steamers from Jackson to Buffalo for the Pan-American Exposition, but bad weather and bad roads were blamed for their decision to abandon the effort when they reached Painesville, Ohio.[57]

Carter's years of experimentation finally culminated on July 23, 1902, with the filing of articles of association of the Jackson Automobile Company. Joining Carter in this company, which was capitalized at $24,000, were two prominent Jackson businessmen, George A. Matthews and Charles Lewis. Matthews, who was born in Ohio in 1852, had worked for wheel companies in Ohio and New York before buying stock in the Fuller Buggy Company of Jackson in 1891. A year later he took over the ownership of the entire company, which became the largest of the carriage manufacturers in the city. Lewis, who was born in England, emigrated to New York in 1867, apprenticed as a machinist, and became superintendent of a carriage-spring plant in Amsterdam, New York. He later moved to Jackson and started the firm that became known as the Lewis Spring & Axle Company. Thus the new automobile company had substantial backing from the local business community. Byron Carter is the man, however, who was credited with being the most important figure in the establishment of the company. "For years past," the Jackson *Citizen* declared, "he has had unwavering faith in the auto as a modern vehicle for business and pleasure, and that faith leads him to the belief that in Jackson there is a splendid opening for one of the largest industries it has ever had." Carter, the paper said, was "no idle dreamer," and his company, it felt safe to assume, "has a great future."[58]

Of all the cars that have been produced in Michigan outside of either the Detroit area, Flint, or Lansing, the Jackson (or Jaxon, as the early models were called) probably came the closest to enjoying lasting success, despite the fact that two of the founders, Carter and Lewis, did not remain with the company very long. At the outset, however, these two were the most active. They went to Chicago to purchase machinery, and obtained the use of a former sash factory in Jackson. By December 1902, thirty workers under the management of Carter were "busy as a hive of bees" preparing "for an immense trade" the following year. Initially, the company received national publicity for its "good looking steam runabout," a three-cylinder car which Carter exhibited at the Detroit auto show in February 1903, and again at the Chicago auto show later that month. A number of these Jaxon steamers were produced and sold that year, virtually the only really production model steam cars ever manufactured in Michigan. Carter also exhibited a one-cylinder gasoline runabout at Chicago, where he observed that the gasoline car "seemed to be preferred" over the steamer. In March, it was reported that about two hundred cars would have to be produced to fill the orders that had been received. This was more than the company could handle, forcing it to sub-contract much of the work.[59]

Although production in 1903 was about equally divided between the steam and gasoline models, the emphasis seems to have switched entirely to the gasoline variety from 1904 on. The Jackson company followed the trend in the industry by moving from its lightweight, inexpensive model of 1903 to bigger, more powerful, and more expensive cars. By 1907, several models were offered, ranging from a two-cylinder touring car, priced at $1250, to a four-cylinder touring car that sold for $2500. By this time the company had adopted one of the most famous of the early automobile advertising slogans: "No Sand Too Deep — No Hill Too Steep." At about the same time, the Jackson, which used a picture of Andrew Jackson as its symbol, achieved fame as a campaign car for political candidates. Governor Fred M. Warner of Michigan, the first Michigan politician to make extensive use of an automobile in campaigning across the state, used a Jackson, although when he campaigned in Flint he diplomatically announced that he intended "to procure one of the celebrated

Buick cars for use during the balance of his trip." Others in both Michigan and Minnesota used Jacksons in their political travels.

Nevertheless, the Jackson seemed to lack that something extra that might have enabled it to stand out among others in its class, even though the company did have opportunities that others might have used to greater advantage in promoting their product. In 1906, for example, Bob Burman, a twenty-two-year-old driver from Imlay City, Michigan, persuaded the Jackson company to enter one of its cars in a fifty-mile race at Detroit. Burman drove the car to victory, winning over some of the leading drivers of the time. Next he drove a Jackson in a twenty-four-hour endurance race at St. Louis and won the event by 82 miles. But the company let Burman get away: William Durant signed him onto the team of racing drivers that he assembled to drive Buicks in competition throughout the country. Burman went on to become perhaps the greatest American driver of the day until he was killed in 1916 while driving a Peugeot in a race at Corona, California.

Another opportunity in the early history of the Jackson Automobile Company was missed when R. Samuel McLaughlin of Oshawa, Ontario, came to town looking for a car to manufacture in Canada. With his father and brother, McLaughlin had built up the largest carriage-manufacturing company in Canada, if not in the British Empire, prior to this time. McLaughlin purchased two Jacksons, but something in their performance seems to have disappointed him. On William Durant's suggestion, McLaughlin bought a Buick, liked it, and in 1908 secured the sole rights to manufacture the Buick in Canada. Thus began an association with Buick and General Motors that lasted until McLaughlin's death at the age of one hundred in January 1972. At his death he was still serving as board chairman of General Motors of Canada as well as having served on the board of the parent corporation longer than anyone except his contemporary, Charles S. Mott.[60]

Jackson cars were produced until 1923. By that time, however, the company had been absorbed by the Associated Motor Industries, a combination which, due to problems, was reorganized as the National Motors Corporation in 1923 and later that year went bankrupt. George Matthews was associated with the Jackson Automobile Company as president until his death in 1914, and three of his sons held offices in the company after his death. Charles Lewis withdrew from the company and devoted his attention to his spring and axle business which began supplying parts to the auto industry. At the time of his death in 1912, his company was occupying new, greatly expanded facilities, and seven hundred workers were engaged in making springs, axles, brake lever assemblies, transmissions, and forgings. It was in the production of parts, such as those Lewis and Clarence Hayes were manufacturing, that Jackson would make its lasting contribution to the auto industry. Other cars were produced in Jackson, most notably the Cutting, the Briscoe, and the Earl, cars that were, like the Jackson, reasonably good products, but like the Jackson, they would all be off the market by the early twenties.[61]

Byron Carter "severed his connection" with the Jackson company in May 1904. This followed his completion in the summer of 1903 of a light-weight little vehicle in which he replaced the geared transmission with a new friction-drive. He had begun experimenting with the model in 1901, and was ready to patent it. Apparently Carter or his partners in the Jackson Automobile Company, who had already made one transition from steam to gasoline engines, were not interested in subjecting the company to still another major change. Instead, Carter found the backing he needed in Detroit, where, late in 1905, the Motorcar Company was founded to manufacture the Cartercar, with Carter serving as a vice-president and manager of the firm. The Cartercar began to appear in 1906. Other friction-drive cars on the market included the Lambert and Simplicity. These two were produced in Indiana, and were on display with the Cartercar at the New York Auto Show in 1906. Carter's creation continued to appear until 1916, the longest life of any of the friction-drive models. The company that produced it had been taken over by Durant and General Motors in 1909, but the cars did not achieve lasting acceptance because of problems associated with the transmission. On the other hand, Byron Carter's original model was reported in 1910 to be still in good condition, ready for additional use after seven years and more than twenty-five thousand miles on the road.[62]

Byron Carter has come to be remembered, not for his friction-drive vehicle, but for inspiring the development of the first really practical self-starting device in a car. The story, as told by numerous writers, is that sometime late in 1910, while driving around Belle Isle in Detroit, Carter came upon a woman whose car had stalled. Carter gallantly came to the rescue by volunteering to crank the motor for her, a difficult and potentially dangerous task that few women liked to tackle. The motor backfired, however, and the crank snapped back, breaking Carter's arm and doing severe damage to his face and jaw. Two passers-by, officials of the Cadillac company, rushed Carter to the hospital, where he later contracted pneumonia and died. Henry Leland, head of Cadillac, and a friend of Carter's, reportedly cried out when he heard what had happened, "Those vicious cranks!" Determined that Cadillac would not cause such injuries in the future, Leland had Charles Kettering invent an electric self-starter. It was first used on the 1912 Cadillacs, and marked the beginning of the end for the hand-crank. It's a good story, although a tough way for Byron Carter to get his name in the history books. But there seems to be little truth to the tale. Carter did die of pneumonia, but at home, on April 6, 1908, more than two and a half years before the accident in which he was reputedly involved on Belle Isle. Accounts of Carter's death in 1908, furthermore, contain no mention of any such accident leading to his fatal illness. One can only wonder who it was that helped that woman in distress in 1910 and has been denied his rightful place in history all these years.[63]

The coming of the Buick assembly plant to Jackson early in 1905 brought to the city a car that would soon far outshine the Jackson, the first automobile to be produced there. Buicks continued to come out of the old Imperial Wheel factory until the summer of 1908. During those years William Durant and other Buick officials spent much of their time in Jackson. But it was apparent from the outset that the arrangements for manufacturing the Buick were only temporary. The division of the operations between Flint and Jackson was inefficient and expensive. The long-term solution was obviously to unite the manufacturing activities into new, larger facilities. There has been speculation that Durant would have been content to make Jackson the permanent home of Buick if local businessmen and bankers had made a determined effort to persuade him to do so by offering him money and land for the new plant. But this did not happen, perhaps because of an indifference in Jackson to the need for promotional efforts to keep the existing industries in the city and to entice others to come there. The Jackson *Daily Citizen* had noticed this attitude earlier in the decade, commenting on one occasion: "Jackson seems to be willing to fall into a soothing hypnotic sleep and dream of the possibilities which she might grasp, only to be aroused and discover the prize flown and all the greatness which was here, now merely a fleeting mirage." Whether Durant made any serious effort to find support for Buick in Jackson is not known, but if he did, Jackson lost the greatest opportunity for economic growth that it has ever had.[64]

The Flint businessman, George Maines, reported that Durant had really been interested in making Bay City the permanent location of the Buick plant. In 1940 Durant recalled:

> I walked all over Bay City. I talked with business men I had once sold cigars to. I talked with men who were working in lumber mills, and small factories. I called at some of their homes; visited the water front, and determined that the harbor was available for shipping in raw material, iron ore and steel, coal and metal products, and that finished automobiles could be shipped to distant places by barge and boat. The water supply was very adequate, and labor was available. I made an offer to the town that if the citizens would raise $100,000 I would match it and move the Buick Motor Company from Jackson to Bay City. That was in the winter of 1905. But the money was not raised, and Bay City lost the Buick Company.[65]

One suspects, however, that W. C. Durant was up to his much practiced trick of threatening to move one of his companies out of Flint to create a little more support; at the same time that he was offering to move Buick to Bay City, he was asking the four banks in Flint to underwrite $80,000 of Buick stock, which "amount of stock would insure the location of the works and business of the Company in the City of Flint." On April 24, 1905, the directors of Flint's Genesee Bank agreed to subscribe $20,000 for their share of this stock issue, the money to be paid into the Buick treasury by August 1, provided "that the Buick Motor Company will discontinue its Jackson plant and locate its entire business at Flint, commencing construction work upon its new buildings as soon as plants [plans] can be prepared and the weather will permit." Since the list of subscribers included Durant's relatives, Dr. Willson, George Willson, William Crapo, and W. C. Orrell, who together put up $8500 of the total, and Durant's partner, Dallas Dort, and friend, Arthur Bishop, each of whom contributed $2500, it is highly doubtful that Durant had to do much to secure their support. The fact that the Genesee directors supported the underwriting in turn may have helped Durant get the backing of the directors of the other banks, who, we are told, "promptly and cheerfully" made their contributions of $20,000 each. Later in the year when the capitalization of Buick was increased to $1,500,000, these bank directors turned in their stock for an equal amount of the new preferred stock issue, plus receiving free a twenty-five per cent common stock dividend.[66]

With the $80,000 in hand, Durant proceeded with plans to reunite all the Buick operations once again in Flint. Actually, it is unlikely that he ever had any intention of moving Buick out of Flint permanently. The site where the new Buick plant began to rise later in 1905 was on the northern edge of Flint, part of William Hamilton's farm that Durant had purchased in 1898. He had bought other property in the same area at least as early as 1895, and his intention all along was to make this a center of Flint's rapidly growing manufacturing economy. H. C. Spenser, another director of the Genesee bank, recalled that in the late nineties Durant "used to talk to me for hours" about his "idea of using the property known as the old Hamilton stock farm as a site for manufactures." In 1900, Durant and others platted these properties as the Oak Park subdivision. They set a third of the three hundred acres aside as sites for factories, and the rest was reserved for residential lots. By 1905, several plants of the Durant-Dort organization had been located in this subdivision. With this site already available and under development, it is hard to believe that Durant did not have in mind locating the new Buick plant there from the very outset. Rumors that he might instead choose a site in Bay City or Jackson may well have been simply added insurance that he would get his way with the money men in Flint.[67]

What began to happen on the north side of Flint by the summer and fall of 1905 quickly dwarfed anything the city had seen during the boom days of the lumber industry or during the industrial development of the city that followed the collapse of that boom. The pace of the construction work was astounding. Oak trees, which gave the subdivision its name, were felled, streets were laid out, and factories built, and by the fall of 1906 the new Buick plant was completed. With fourteen acres of space, it was claimed to be the largest automobile plant in the world. Although engine work continued for a time in the original Buick factory on Flint's west side, and auto assembly at the Jackson plant, their days were numbered as additional Buick buildings were completed at the Oak Park site. In the fall of 1908, with the completion of the Buick factory building No. 7 and a drop forge and foundry, Buick had achieved its goal of concentrating the entire operation in one complex of buildings. During September, twenty-four carloads of machinery were shipped in from Jackson as the operations there, which had employed about 450 men as late as March of 1908, were brought to an end. The plant in Jackson stood idle for some months before being reopened briefly in 1909 to make tools for various plants of the General Motors organization, of which Buick was by that time a part.[68]

Visits to Flint's great industrial district now became a highlight for visiting dignitaries, who almost invariably were reported as amazed at what they saw. Members of the Chicago Board of Commerce in May 1908 declared that the Buick plant "was a surprise party to all of us, as we had no idea that the saying that Flint had the largest automobile plant in the world was true, but it is for sure." Easterners in particular were astounded at the size of Buick. When the Boston financier, James Storrow, who was well acquainted with factories in the East, visited Flint in the fall of 1910, by which time the Buick plant had greatly expanded beyond what it was in 1908, he declared that this was the only factory that he had ever seen which made the big plant of the United Shoe Machinery Company in Beverly, Massachusetts, "look small."[69]

The aggregate financial rating of Flint's thirty-six leading business firms almost doubled between 1906 and 1908. In addition to the Buick plant in size and importance were plants of Imperial Wheel, the Flint Axle Works, Flint Varnish Works, the W. F. Stewart body factory (which Buick took over in 1908 when it decided to build its own bodies), the Michigan Motor Castings Company, and others — all straining to keep up with the demands of the automobile company. The most important of these suppliers was a company that was new to Flint and to Michigan, the Weston-Mott Company.[70]

In 1896, two brothers, John C. Mott and Frederick G. Mott, had bought I. A. Weston and Company, a firm in Janesville, New York, that had been making bicycle hubs and wheels since 1884. Late in 1896, the newly named Weston-Mott Company came out with "a new ball-bearing carriage wheel, which they have constructed specially for the motor trade." Several months later the company announced that it had received "a great many inquiries" regarding these wheels, and because the bicycle boom began showing signs of coming to an end, the company placed more and more emphasis on the automobile market. In 1898 the company moved to Utica, and John Mott's son Charles began to play an active role as a sales representative for the company. Charles Stewart Mott, who was born in Newark, New Jersey, on June 2, 1875, and had graduated as a mechanical engineer from the Stevens Institute of Technology, had just returned from service in the navy during the Spanish-American War. Within a year, Mott's father died, and shortly afterwards young Mott was moved up to the position of secretary and superintendent of the Weston-Mott Company. In 1903, when his uncle, who was president of the company, moved to the

Charles S. Mott of Flint. *Though in his nineties, he continued to be actively involved in the auto industry, as he had been during the preceding three-quarters of a century.*
Courtesy Charles Stewart Mott

West, his stock and other outstanding stock in the company were purchased by Charles Mott and William G. Doolittle, the company treasurer. Mott and Doolittle became equal partners, with Mott serving as president of the company and handling the manufacturing side of the business while Doolittle continued to be responsible primarily for company finances.[71]

By 1905 the Weston-Mott company was enjoying prosperous times as one of the leading suppliers of wheels and axles to the growing automobile industry. Its factory had twice been greatly enlarged since 1898 when the plant in Utica had been built. With the increasing shift of the auto industry from the East to the Middle West, one or two proposals had been received around 1903 that Mott and Doolittle locate their factory closer to their main customers, but they rejected the idea, Mott declared, because the offers were not "sufficiently attractive to offset the disadvantage of moving an established business to new territory." Among the less important customers of the company at this time was the Buick company, which used Weston-Mott axles on the handful of cars that were built in 1904. These parts continued to be purchased when Durant assumed direction of Buick and increased production. Durant's earlier experience in the carriage industry had taught him that it was vital to the success of a large concern to reduce the uncertainties and expense of buying from outside suppliers by getting as much control as possible over these sources of supply and locating them close to the assembly plants. Durant applied his experience to the auto industry, and one of the first targets of his attention was Weston-Mott. According to his daughter, Durant found that shipping axles from Utica to Flint by freight took too long, but when he had them sent by express, the shipping costs were far too great. Therefore, on June 4, 1905, Durant wrote to Charles Mott and asked the New York businessman: "Would you entertain a proposition of removing or establishing a branch factory at Flint, Michigan, provided the business of three or four large concerns was assured for a term of years? Flint is in the center of the automobile industry, a progressive city, good people, with conditions for manufacturing ideal."[72]

It is interesting that although Durant wrote this letter from the Buick sales office in Jackson, he directed Mott to reply to him not at that office or at the Buick office in Flint. Instead, he was to write to Durant in care of the Durant-Dort Carriage Company. A few weeks later, when Durant went to Utica, he was accompanied by Dallas Dort, a further indication of the important part that Durant's longtime partner in the carriage industry continued to play as Durant's interests shifted into the auto industry. Dort was very much in the forefront of the negotiations that led to Weston-Mott's removal to Flint. (As an example, when William Doolittle wrote to John Carton in June 1906 regarding some details about Weston-Mott's reincorporation as a Michigan firm, he suggested that Carton "go over this matter with Mr. Dort and whom ever he may suggest.")[73]

Mott expressed interest in Durant's proposition, but he declared that locating a branch plant in Flint would not be feasible and that it would take a very attractive offer to induce him and Doolittle to give up their Utica factory, which they owned, "free and unencumbered," and move their entire operation to Flint. Durant and Dort were fully capable of sweetening the offer, and did, enough so that Mott and Doolittle could not turn it down. After Mott had visited Durant in Jackson later in June, Durant and Dort visited Utica on September 1, 1905. The next day Mott and Doolittle returned with them on the train to Flint. In comparison with Utica, Flint impressed the two easterners as "a hick town," but with the help of such community leaders as W. F. Stewart, William Ballenger, John Carton, and Arthur Bishop, Durant and Dort convinced them of the advantages of moving to Flint. On September 9, 1905, Durant, Dort, Mott, and Doolittle entered into a contract whereby the two Flint businessmen agreed to furnish $100,000 of the capital in a reorganized Weston-Mott Company, the money to be used to build new manufacturing quarters for the company in Flint. The site of the Weston-Mott plant would be at the corner of Hamilton and Industrial avenues, next to the new Buick plant. Weston-Mott would then become the exclusive supplier of axles for the Buick automobile.[74]

Within a year, the Weston-Mott Company had been reincorporated in Michigan. Mott continued as president, Doolittle remained treasurer, John Carton, who handled the necessary legal arrangements, became vice-president, and Arthur Bishop, who personally handled the $100,000 building fund, was named secretary. The new factory was completed by the end of the summer of 1906, and by February 1, 1907, the very considerable task of moving machinery and employees from Utica to Flint was completed. On that same day in 1907 Charles S. Mott settled his family in the city, which remained his residence until his death in 1973, and which came to regard Mott as the community's greatest benefactor. On another level, the move had an even greater significance. Alfred P. Sloan, Jr., later expressed his belief that the transfer of Weston-Mott to Michigan marked

> the first step in the integration of the automobile industry. Thereafter, bit by bit, we were to see a constant evolution bringing the manufacture of the motorcar itself and the manufacture of its component parts into a closer corporate relationship. All were to cohere as if drawn together by some magnetic force.[75]

The Weston-Mott Company, of which Charles Mott became the principal owner following the death of William Doolittle in January 1908, prospered in its new home. It was soon necessary to enlarge the company's plant to keep up with the orders. In November 1909, a Connecticut banker inquired of John Carton, whom the easterner obviously did not know was connected with Mott, as to "the financial strength and responsibility of Weston-Mott." Carton replied that it was "one of the best institutions we have in our city." It had built up a surplus of $600,000, which had led to an increase in the capitalization from the original $500,000 of 1906 to $1,500,-000. The president of the First National Bank of Flint informed the president of the First National Bank of Hartford that Weston-Mott was "a very profitable business," and that notes endorsed by Charles Mott "would be a fine investment."[76]

The prosperous condition of Weston-Mott was in part due to the growth of its business as a supplier to the auto industry as a whole, but more specifically its prosperity was tied to the enormous expansion of the production of its chief customer, Buick. From the few hundred cars produced at the Jackson plant in 1905, production at Jackson and the new plant in Flint rose to 1400 in 1906, and up to 4641 in 1907. The financial panic of that year that was partially, if not entirely, responsible for the failure of a number of auto companies, such as Dolson and Harrison in Michigan, and which caused a temporary drop-off in auto sales, did not slow Buick. The new $900 Buick Model 10 runabout was the "sensation" of the New York auto show in November 1907, *Motor Age* reported, and the magazine predicted, quite accurately, that this would be the first car produced by a member of the Licensed Automobile Manufacturers Association that would provide "real opposition to some of the low-priced four-cylinder unlicensed cars." Durant, however, had no intention of abandoning Buick's other models, which ranged in price up to the Model 5, priced at $2500. Convinced that the economy would rebound quickly, with an accompanying sharp upswing in auto sales, Durant continued with the full-scale production of all the Buick models, storing the cars in every available space, and juggling the bills until money would begin to flow into the treasury again from renewed sales. (Mott, a major creditor of Buick, had to ask John Carton to wait several weeks in the winter of 1907-1908 for his annual retainer fee of $250 because of Weston-Mott's own cash shortage.) In 1908, business picked up, and Durant had the cars to meet the increased demand. "He was one hell of a gambler," Mott told Lawrence Gustin in 1972. "To this day, I don't know how he was able to handle it financially, but he did it."[77]

All this was only a prelude to 1908, when Buick production soared to 8820 units. Already in mid-January, Buick officials were reporting that prospects for the company had never been as bright at this time of the year. A night shift had been added to try to keep up with the demand for the new runabout. By the end of February, three eight-hour shifts were keeping the Buick No. 2 plant in Flint in operation around the clock, seven days a week, while other plants were working overtime until midnight every day. By the end of the following month, 2100 workers at the Flint and Jackson plants were turning out fifty cars a day, and 350 more men were to be hired by May 1 in order to increase the output to eighty a day. This was at least twice as many Buicks per day as were produced in all of 1904. On May 2, a special thirty-car freight train, carrying ninety Buicks, left Flint for Kansas City. Thirty-six-foot banners on each freight car proclaimed that it was carrying Buicks "made in Flint." To capitalize on the advertising value, the train was routed through a number of large cities, such as Saginaw and Grand Rapids, on its way to Chicago. From there it followed the Santa Fe route to Kansas City, but traveled only in the daytime. The shipment, which equaled a load of Buicks sent to Minneapolis in 1907, was believed to be the largest shipment of automobiles to one consignee in automotive history. But on July 13, a thirty-two-car Pere Marquette train left for the East, bearing an even larger number of Buicks, and on that same day, thirteen other carloads of Buicks left Flint on other rail lines.

By June of 1908, Buick production for the month in Flint amounted to 1409 cars, while an additional 245 Buicks came out of the Jackson plant.

Around this time, a reporter described with awe the basement of Buick plant No. 6, an area seven hundred feet long and seventy feet wide, with row after row of shelves and bins filled with frames, radiators, cylinders, axles, wheels, springs, tires, and other parts, with a value of about $2,500,000.

The following November, as orders picked up after the presidential election at an "unprecedented" rate, Buick announced that it would need another thousand workers, and even with these added men it would be mid-July 1909 before the company could be caught up with the orders. Within a day of this announcement, hundreds of workers from throughout southern Michigan poured into the city, which was already faced with a severe housing shortage and many other problems resulting from a fifty per cent increase in the city's population in only two years.[78]

Looking at these figures, William Durant had cause to be satisfied. Although production statistics in this period are open to much question, there is some evidence to indicate that by 1908 Buick was the top-selling car in the country. Almost certainly it was the best known. Durant had seized upon racing as a method of promoting interest in the car, and the Buick racing team of Bob Burman, Lewis Strang, and Louis and Arthur Chevrolet was perhaps the greatest ever assembled, winning half of all the road races in a two-year period and collecting over five hundred trophies. As the public's interest was aroused, it found that the Buick was one of

Dr. Frank Tinker and his wife Effie in their new Buick Model 10E, which Dr. Tinker had bought in 1909, the first automobile sold in the town of Clio, Michigan. (The other vehicle appears to be another, but far rarer Flint-made car, the Whiting.)
Courtesy Mrs. Lois M. Ridley

the most available cars to those who wanted to buy it. By May 1906, Durant claimed to have more than one hundred direct sales outlets for the car, and later on, after the 1907 panic, he made use of the widespread network of Durant-Dort Carriage dealers to show the Buick in many parts of the country where automobiles were still a rarity.[79]

What Durant and his associates had done since 1904 was indeed impressive. In looking back over his four decades of close dealings with the industry in 1940, Chris Sinsabaugh, the veteran automobile reporter, declared that with the exception of Olds, "Buick was the first real success of the automobile industry and did more to promote the industry's well-being, in terms of public education, engineering advancement, and manufacturing progress, than perhaps any other company." But Durant was not satisfied. Powerful competition was developing from other auto companies, and already by 1907 Durant was considering plans to blunt this competition by organizing a merger between Buick and several other companies. The companies he was most interested in were those led by such experienced automakers as Jonathan Maxwell and Benjamin Briscoe, Henry Ford, who was the fastest rising of all the automakers, and Ransom Olds, the veteran who had made a remarkable comeback.[80]

CHAPTER 8

"THE CAR THAT MARKS MY LIMIT"

Ransom E. Olds got up long before dawn on Friday, January 17, 1908, dressed, left his large new Lansing residence and went down South Washington Avenue a short distance to the Grand Trunk depot. There he boarded the 5:00 A.M. train to keep an appointment with William Durant, Benjamin Briscoe, and Henry Ford in Detroit. A week later, Olds was in New York, where he spent most of Friday and Saturday, January 24 and 25, closeted with these same manufacturers in the Wall Street offices of Herbert Satterlee, son-in-law and associate of the great financier, J. Pierpont Morgan. Negotiations were underway for a consolidation of the major automobile companies, and in addition to Durant's Buick, Briscoe's Maxwell, and Ford's Ford, the promoters hoped that the merger would include the company that Ransom Olds now controlled, and whose name had been formed by the initials of this pioneer automaker, R. E. O.[1]

* * *

When Ransom Olds was severing his ties with the Olds Motor Works early in 1904, he probably had no intention of getting out of the automobile industry permanently. The future of that industry, he told his Detroit broker, was limitless. "I believe that in five to ten years the horses will not be allowed on the streets in the larger cities. Did you ever stop to think what that means?" Each year, he said, over 200,000 carriages were manufactured in Michigan alone. (Actually, the figure was much larger than that. In 1898, forty-nine of the state's largest carriage companies had produced 371,769 vehicles.) Once horses and carriages were barred from city streets, automobiles would take their place. Olds declared:

> I have made a careful study of the business for a great many years, and predict that the Automobile business will be one of the greatest industries that this country has ever seen. Every successful Company will see its business multiplied many times in order to keep up with the demand.

Still, he kept insisting that he did not desire to get back into the industry. Although he did not realize as much as he had hoped from the sale of his stock in the Olds Motor Works, he got enough so that, when combined with his other business and real estate interests, he was left in excellent financial circumstances. In the early months of 1904, Olds, who did not reach the age of forty until June of that year, busied himself with these affairs from his office in Lansing's Hollister Building, which he owned. Among his business records at Michigan State University one can find this world-famous automobile innovator delving into such problems as the quality of the toilet paper that was being purchased for the Hollister's rest rooms. Although Ransom Olds was a man who did enjoy the luxury of not having to work any harder than he felt like working, the need for a more stimulating occupation must have occurred to him, especially in Lansing where so many of his acquaintances were now involved in the business that he had just abandoned, and which was rapidly displacing all other businesses in the city in importance.[2]

At one time, it would have seemed that there was little future for Lansing as an automobile manufacturing center. In 1899, the year the city lost the Olds automobile manufacturing operation to Detroit, George J. Bohnet, a young man who had run a bicycle shop before going into the music business, was inspired by the sight of a Locomobile steam car to try his hand at building a similar vehicle. In June 1901, Bohnet drove his first steam car on the streets of the city, and in a short time he joined with J. W. Post to form the Lansing Automobile Works to produce this vehicle. A local paper early in 1902 opined that Bohnet's venture "bids fair to become one of the representative industries in the field." In a sense this was true, for after producing possibly only one steamer, the Lansing Automobile Works folded up, which was indeed representative of what happened to most automobile manufacturers. Bohnet, however, stayed in the automobile business, hooking up with various dealers who sold Oldsmobiles, Cadillacs, and, later, Reos.[3]

Two other very abbreviated automobile ventures in these years also failed to add to Lansing's reputation as an automobile center. Nothing seems to have resulted from a report late in 1901 that the Prouty Motor

Company of Chicago was establishing a factory in Lansing "for the manu-facture of gasoline motors and automobiles." Little also is known of the origins or the fate of a Lansing-built car called the Greenleaf, designed by an engineer named Smith Clawson. One of the cars was exhibited at a Grange convention in Lansing in 1902, and an article in 1903 described it as a two-cylinder car selling for $1750. No records exist to show that any were sold at that or any other price.[4]

The year 1903 saw several Lansing businessmen who had had links with Ransom Olds' earlier engine and automobile businesses join in two new efforts. Bliss Stebbins, brother of the onetime secretary of the Olds Motor Vehicle Company, and others joined with former Olds associates, Madison F. Bates and James P. Edmonds, and the banker, J. Edward Roe, to form the Bates Automobile Company. They placed on the market a $2000 touring car, and described it as "The Most Up-to-Date and Efficient Car." However, only twenty-five of the cars were produced because the public just did not take to the product, whose slogan was: "Buy a Bates and Keep Your Dates." The company was an outgrowth of the successful Bates and Edmonds Motor Company, incorporated in 1899 with Bates, Edmonds, and Roe among its officers. The automobile venture was aban-doned finally in 1905 in order to save the engine company from going down with it. Roe remained the treasurer of the Bates and Edmonds Motor Com-pany, and at various times he also served as treasurer of the Auto Body Company and of the Reo Motor Car Company. His link with Ransom Olds was further cemented by the marriage of Roe's son Clarence to the youngest of Olds' two daughters, Bernice.[5]

Early in 1903 it was announced that Frank G. Clark, the carriage-builder who had sold his 125 shares in the Olds Motor Vehicle Company when he apparently lost faith in that enterprise, had completed a car of his own. Aping the popular automotive trend of the period, Clark's vehicle was a one-cylinder runabout which he called the Clarkmobile. The Clark-mobile Company was formed, with Frank Clark as secretary-treasurer and general manager. Arthur C. Stebbins, a colleague from the Olds Motor Vehicle Company days, served as president, and the vice-president was Harris E. Thomas, whose Auto Body Company supplied bodies for the new car. Despite the support of these and other prominent Lansing busi-nessmen, the Clarkmobile was not a success. After perhaps as many as a hundred Clarkmobiles were produced, the business was discontinued. In a sense, it was succeeded by the New-Way Motor Company, organized in 1905 and headed by William H. Newbrough, who had been associated with the Clarkmobile Company, and Harris Thomas was again the vice-president. The new firm attempted briefly to produce a car called the New-Way, a Mr. Way reportedly having been associated with Newbrough in the design. After no more than a half dozen or so of these cars had been turned out, the company concentrated its efforts entirely on the production of engines, and enjoyed considerable success. A segment of the old Clarkmobile Com-pany, meanwhile, seems to have been taken over by the John Deere farm equipment interests, which in 1906 and 1907 attempted an ill-fated effort in Moline, Illinois, manufacturing a car that was first called the Deere-Clark, then simply the Deere. Frank Clark switched to the production of a four-cylinder gasoline truck between 1905 and 1910 as well as continuing to try to put out an automobile. In the summer of 1909 he sold the family carriage business, but he never achieved any lasting success with his new motorized vehicle interests.[6]

More than offsetting the record of failure racked up by these other Lansing companies, however, was the record of the Olds Motor Works, which, within a few weeks after its new Lansing plant went into production early in 1902, was turning out more cars in a month than all the Bohnets, Greenleafs, Bates, Clarkmobiles, and New-Ways ever produced. By the beginning of July 1904, Fred Smith reported to Eugene Cooley, a member of the Olds board of directors, that Oldsmobile runabouts were coming out of the Lansing plant at an average of more than twenty a day. Total production for the year reached a new record of 5508, the bulk of this representing the output of runabouts from the Lansing plant. The Detroit branch had begun turning out the new two-cylinder Oldsmobile touring car. During 1905, when production reached 6500, the Olds Motor Works ceased all remaining activities in Detroit and concentrated all of its offices and manufacturing operations in Lansing. The decision seems to have been a rather sudden one. In the summer of 1904 the company had gone to considerable trouble to acquire a tract of land adjacent to its Detroit plant so that facility could be expanded. The move to Lansing, which came at a time when Edward W. Sparrow returned to the Olds board of directors, joining his old Lansing friend and business colleague, Eugene Cooley, was perhaps dictated by a desire to achieve the greater savings and efficiency in operations that could result from such a consolidation. Another reason cited a few years later was that the company feared that the rapid growth of other auto companies in Detroit would make it increasingly difficult to secure enough workers in the Detroit branch.[7]

Shortly after Fred Smith had written to Eugene Cooley in July 1904 regarding the glowing prospects of the Olds Motor Works, Cooley was being apprised of a move afoot to put out a new car bearing the imprint of Ransom E. Olds. On August 5, Cooley received a note from Benjamin F. Davis, executive head of City National Bank of Lansing, which he had helped to organize in 1886 with Cooley and Edward Sparrow, among others. Reuben Shettler had just been in to see him, Davis informed Cooley, "& here is his plan for building autos. He wishes me to lay the matter before you, but doesn't want a word to escape & only wants a few people in it." Shettler's plan called for the organization of a million-dollar corporation, with the stock divided equally into common and preferred shares. He proposed to do nothing with the preferred until a factory had been built and the machinery installed. Ransom Olds was to be given $260,000, or fifty-two per cent of the common stock, for his "genius, patents & realty for Plant." The rest of the common stock, with a par value of one dollar a share, would be sold for fifty cents a share, thus raising $120,000 in cash, of which amount Shettler would put up $37,500. "What do you think of it?" Davis asked Cooley. Whatever Cooley may have thought of the proposition, he did not invest in the new company. Davis did, however, becoming one of the new firm's major stockholders.[8]

Davis' letter helps to demonstrate that Reuben Shettler was again, as in the past, playing the role of the leg-man, organizing support for the latest Olds automobile development. His work had begun the previous winter when Ransom Olds, after being voted out of his job as general manager of the Olds Motor Works, had left Lansing late in January for a vacation on the West Coast. He had told his broker that he could be reached on February 6 and 7 in Los Angeles at the Oldsmobile Company, Shettler's agency in California. He met with Shettler at that time and, as Shettler later recalled, they had come to "an understanding that as soon as [Olds] could dispose of his Olds Motor Stock, we would organize a new automobile Company in the Spring, providing I would undertake the responsibility of financing it."[9]

The sale of Ransom Olds' stock, which Shettler, among others, sought to expedite, did not progress as rapidly as Olds and Shettler had hoped. Nevertheless, plans for the new company were being formulated at least by late March 1904. At that time Olds, who for several months after continued to disclaim any intention of getting back into the automobile business, wrote to Horace T. Thomas, outlining the discussions he had had with Shettler and expressing a desire to nail down Thomas' services. The thirty-year-old former engineer for the Olds Motor Works had quit that company about the time Olds was preparing to make his exit and was now working for the Electric Vehicle Company in Hartford, Connecticut. But in May he accepted a position as superintendent of a peat company that Olds had acquired. The job, Olds and Thomas frankly agreed, was intended only to tide Thomas over temporarily for "three or four months" until the new automobile company had been organized, at which time Thomas was hired as the firm's chief engineer.[10]

By July 5 at the latest, the sale of Olds' stock had been largely completed, for on that date he wrote to a New York newspaperman and friend, in confidence, that he was no longer a shareholder in the Olds Motor Works. Although still a member of the board of directors, he had practically severed his ties with that company, and there was "no arrangement that I will not go into [the automobile] business again." Olds declared that he had received "several propositions" whereby he could return to the industry on his own terms. "I say to them that I am not interested." But on the evening of that very same day, Reuben Shettler, who had arrived in Michigan in June, was scheduled to report to Olds on the progress he had made in working out the financial details for the company Olds and Shettler had discussed the previous winter.

Within about a month the final arrangements were completed, along the lines described by Benjamin Davis on August 5. The formal statement of the terms of the agreement were presented by Shettler to Olds in a document dated August 9. Officially, Olds took the position that he had not been a part of the negotiations leading up to the organization of the new company. He told the Olds Motor Works:

> Personally I can say that 30 days ago I never intended to enter the automobile business again; I have only done so because the trade in general requested me to do so; numerous friends of mine through out the U. S. have urged this upon me, while the people in my own town organized and had the stock all signed up before they submitted the proposition to me.

Olds continued to express this view in later years. In the 'twenties he related to the business writer, O. D. Foster, how he had been called back to Lansing from a northern Michigan vacation and had been met at the train station by a friend who presented him with "a very interesting looking paper" that set forth the business proposition. "To say that I was astounded would be putting it mildly," Olds told Foster. As a matter of fact, Olds *had* been called back suddenly from a vacation in the north in order to receive Shettler's proposal in its final form, but before leaving for the north, Olds had written to Ray M. Owen in New York, outlining the plans for the company and soliciting the New Yorker's financial support. Olds had, of course, been a party to, if not the originator of, the discussions leading up to his re-entry into the auto industry, but he liked to make it appear as though he had been drafted. On at least one occasion, however, he let down his guard, and in a biography published in a history of his own county in the mid-twenties, a biography that he undoubtedly saw and approved in advance, he allowed to pass a bald statement that he, Ransom Olds, had "organized the Reo Motor Car Company."[11]

Articles of incorporation for the R. E. Olds Company were registered on August 16. That same day, Ransom Olds notified Henry Russel, president of the Olds Motor Works, that he was resigning as a director of that company. In his new company, Olds served both as president and general manager, as well as having a controlling interest in the stock. It was the last feature that was particularly satisfying to Olds. As he had told Ray Owen on August 4, 1904, "had I never allowed the controlling interests of the Olds Motor Work's [sic] to get away from me, I know that the Company's matters would be going up the ladder instead of tumbling down the other side." Actually, the Olds Motor Works was still doing a booming business under Fred Smith's direction, but part of Olds' motivation in starting up the new enterprise probably stemmed from a desire to prove how much better his old company might have done had he remained in charge. This may also have been a factor in a decision he reportedly made turning down an offer from a New York syndicate worth about double what he got from Shettler's group. He may have felt that there would be greater satisfaction in out-performing the Olds Motor Works in face-to-face competition in the same town and with the same kind of Michigan-based financial support.[12]

In addition, Olds knew the people with whom he now became

involved, whereas the New York group was probably largely unknown to him. The original group of Reo stockholders was not as glittering an array of wealth and social prestige as had been found in the Olds Motor Works, but they did give the new company important ties to well-established Lansing banking and business institutions. Next to Olds, who, as had been planned, had fifty-two per cent of the voting stock, Shettler controlled the largest block of stock and was elected vice-president. The City National Bank was represented on the board by Benjamin Davis, and the American State Savings Bank of Lansing was represented by its cashier, J. Edward Roe, who had held this office since the bank's organization in 1892. William H. Porter, a prominent political figure in Lansing for many years, a realtor, and an officer of the People's State Savings Bank, controlled a block of shares equal to those of Roe. Porter's brother, Edgar S. Porter, another investor, had been a founder of the Auto Body Company, and earlier, as an outgrowth of his lumber interests, had established the Lansing Spoke Company. (This firm now began producing wheels for automobiles, and was one of three companies that merged in 1920 to form the Motor Wheel Corporation.) Two other investors were Elgin Mifflin, an officer in the firm of Hugh Lyons & Company, and Hugh Lyons, the head of this Lansing company that made showcases and that would soon branch out into making bodies for the Reo. Among other stockholders was Charles P. Downey, proprietor of the Hotel Downey, Lansing's foremost hotel, and a man with many and varied connections.

Ransom Olds was also well acquainted with many of the members of the staff of the new company. It quickly became populated with men who had been associated with him in his earlier businesses. Besides Horace Thomas, the chief engineer, Richard H. Scott, whom Olds had brought in as plant manager of the gasoline engine works in 1898, was now hired as the factory superintendent of the new auto company. Harry C. Teel, an Ohioan who had known Scott for years, had married his sister, and had followed Scott from Toledo to the Olds Gasoline Engine Works, now came into the Reo company in a supervisory capacity. He ultimately moved up to be factory manager when Scott advanced higher in the company hierarchy. Ray Owen, the man who had introduced the Oldsmobile in New York when he contracted for a thousand of the runabouts in 1901, now contracted with Olds to sell the entire output of the Lansing firm; it was an arrangement not entirely uncommon in this period of the auto industry's development and one that relieved Olds and his staff of the worry over sales and dealers. In the lower ranks of Reo employees one also finds a strong influence from the earlier Olds companies. Frank A. Stolte, in charge of construction at the new plant, was a Lansing contractor whose jobs in the past had included some of the other factories Olds built. William C. Walters, who started as a blacksmith at the Olds Motor Works in 1902, later became a supervisory employee at Reo. John Bohner, who had learned the upholstery trade with the Clark carriage company in Lansing and had then opened his own shop and gotten the contract to do the upholstery work for the Olds Motor Works, now did the same work for Reo. Others who joined Reo had not been associated with the earlier Olds automobile company, but nevertheless had a direct link with someone in the new company. The most notable example is Donald E. Bates, a native of Lansing who joined the Reo organization on January 1, 1905, and eventually rose to the presidency of the firm. His link with Reo was through Benjamin Davis of the City National Bank, where he had been employed for several years prior to 1905.[13]

The extent to which Ransom Olds' new company was an offspring of an earlier successful Michigan auto manufacturer demonstrates how important those early successes were to the subsequent enormous expansion of auto manufacturing in Michigan. The advantages of locating a new company such as Reo near a nucleus of knowledgeable investors, administrators, and workmen more than offset advantages that other locations elsewhere in the country might have possessed.

The R. E. Olds Company had some problems to overcome before it could get its car on the market in time for the 1905 season. The first source of trouble came from the Olds Motor Works, which immediately notified Ransom Olds and others, such as Benjamin Davis, who had been identified with the company, that it would take legal action if necessary to prevent the use of the Olds name as the name of the company or of its automobile; their claim was that such use was "clearly an infringement of the rights sold by Mr. Olds to the Olds Motor Works and the Olds Gasoline Engine Works." Although Olds denied that he had made any such assignment of the rights to his name, he decided not to press the matter. Ray Owen, for one, advised Olds that in the opinion of one lawyer he had consulted, the Olds Motor Works "would have a fair chance of getting an injunction against the use of this name." Someone then had the inspiration to use simply Olds' initials, and on September 27 the stockholders re-named the company the Reo Car Company, a name that was shortly changed to the Reo Motor Car Company. Legally, the three letters were to appear in capital letters, but common usage soon led to capitalizing only the first letter. The story that Olds claimed he was so famous that his initials were all that were needed to identify him with his car may be apocryphal, but there is no doubt that the connection was clearer and was more successfully used in the case of Reo than by many other automobiles adopting the same gimmick — automobiles such as the short-lived R.C.H. (for Robert C. Hupp), the K.R.I.T. or Krit (after Kenneth Crittenden), the R.O. (for Ralph Owen, Ray Owen's brother), or even the more popular E. M. F. (a combination of the last initials of the three owners, B. F. Everitt, William Metzger, and Walter Flanders).[14]

According to Reuben Shettler, there were also some financial and interpersonal problems facing the company. Shettler declared that he ended up contributing seventy-three per cent of the money received from the sale of common stock, since he not only had paid his own share but had loaned some of the other investors, including Richard Scott and

Edward F. Peer, who became the company's secretary-treasurer, the money they needed to pay for their stock. He received this money back eventually, and in addition Olds paid Shettler $5000, which Shettler said partly covered the expenses he had incurred in organizing the company, but he never could get Olds to turn over to him the two thousand shares of common stock that Shettler claimed Olds had promised him if he succeeded in getting the financing for the company. Worse yet, Shettler said, Olds refused to pay for five thousand shares of preferred stock for which he had supposedly subscribed at the time the company was organized. Olds' action jeopardized a loan of "several hundred thousand dollars" which Shettler said he had arranged with Alex McPherson of the Old Detroit National Bank. A banker noted for his generous treatment of the early Michigan auto companies, McPherson had, however, made the loan contingent on the successful disposition of all the Reo stock, both common and preferred.[15]

These problems were apparently resolved, but they were a fore-runner of serious internal difficulties that would plague the company in the next few years and would be climaxed by a blowup in 1910. At that time Shettler and Peer resigned their offices and sold their Reo stock after an unsuccessful attempt to get rid of Richard Scott, take away Olds' controlling interest in the company, and place Ray Owen in actual charge of affairs. Later discord eventually brought Scott and Olds into conflict over policy and finally led to the removal of both of them from any active role of leadership in the company.[16]

But late in the summer of 1904, the steps that were necessary to place the new company in operating condition proceeded with remarkable speed and efficiency. By September, construction of the factory had been started on the site adjacent to the Grand Trunk station, with access also to the tracks of the Lake Shore and Michigan Southern. The site was chosen mainly because Ransom Olds already owned part of the land, and he turned it over to the company in exchange for some of the stock he was given. The two-story brick buildings that comprised the Reo factory were nearly completed by the end of the year. Meanwhile, Horace Thomas, Olds, and Scott proceeded with the development of a car.[17]

By the end of August, the same month the new company was announced, over twenty draftsmen and mechanics were at work in temporary quarters, and by October 15 the first experimental Reo had been completed and tested. It was a two-cylinder, five-passenger touring car which would sell for $1250, the same price that was being asked for the new Oldsmobile touring car. The new Reo, which Thomas and Olds had worked on during the previous months when Thomas was theoretically running the peat factory, differed from Olds' earlier cars in that it looked like an automobile, not like a horseless carriage. The engine was still under the floor, but up front was a dummy hood, housing the radiator, gas tank, and batteries. Shortly thereafter, Olds and Thomas built a one-cylinder runabout, competitively priced with the Olds runabout at $650, and it too had the same distinctive automobile design as the Reo touring model. But it was the

heavier, higher-priced touring car that Reo chose to emphasize in its advertising. Now, once and for all, Olds abandoned his earlier commitment to
the low-priced field which he had first entered in 1896, and to which he
had returned in 1900 with his curved-dash runabout. The association of
the Reo with the medium-priced range of cars is but another indication
that it was not a dispute over whether the Olds Motor Works should produce that kind of car that led to Olds' departure from that company.[18]

While the factory was being completed and the design of the cars was
being finished in the fall of 1904, plans for advertising and selling the Reo
also progressed rapidly. Early in November, J. O. Powers of the Philadelphia advertising agency of Powers & Armstrong wrote Olds to tell him
how happy they were to be handling the advertising campaign. Powers
visited Lansing later in the month to secure more information on the
cars, but in the meantime he requested that good side-view pictures of the
models be sent as soon as possible. By December, ads for the Reo were
appearing. One full-page advertisement in *Motor Age* on December 22
contained several hundred words of text, a large number even in that day
when advertisers favored a lot of verbiage. A small side view of the Reo
touring car appeared against a background of a globe with wings on it.
Beneath this illustration appeared in large type the theme of the ad: "The
World Moves and the REO Motor Car moves with it." In the text that
followed, the Philadelphia copy-writer seized immediately on the most
recurring point in all of the early automobile advertisements — gaining the
public's confidence in a car by stressing who designed it and establishing
the superior credentials possessed by that designer.

> The world moves. You need no longer pay fabulous prices for intricate
> mistakes and doubtful experiments—Mr. R. E. Olds has built the Reo Car.
>
> His twenty years of practical experience, his inventive genius, mechanical
> skill, and thorough knowledge of American requirements have produced
> the best 16-horse power Touring Car that human brains and skill can
> conceive and put together — and the price is $1250.
>
> The principles which he was first to successfully demonstrate are now for
> the first time fully developed to meet the demands of present-day motorists.

The ad then describes, in smaller type, a few of the car's "Striking Features," including a radiator that was said to be "proof against freezing
and jarring." In addition, the Reo runabout, mentioned in passing at the
bottom of the page, was described as "equally wonderful in its way and
worthy of the inventor of the first practical gasoline Runabout."[19]

A few years later, the advertising campaign for the 1912 Reo came
into the far more capable hands of Albert Lasker's Chicago agency, Lord
& Thomas. The campaign featured one of the most famous automobile
ads of all time, written by Claude Hopkins, a Michiganian who is widely
regarded as the most influential and probably the greatest of copy-writers.
Hopkins had already achieved fame for the ads he had written for the
Bissell Carpet Sweeper Company of Grand Rapids, and for Schlitz beer,
before he came to work for Lord & Thomas in 1906. He quickly had even

greater success promoting Van Camp's beans and Palmolive soap, products that had previously had little public appeal. In his Reo ads, Hopkins used the standard device of playing upon the fame of the car's designer, but he went a step further by having Olds appear as the author, speaking of his creation in the first person. The ad copy itself was far wordier than that prepared by Powers & Armstrong for the 1905 Reo, but the layout was more attractive and easier to read. It was peppered with statements that the manufacturer might have regarded as unimportant or irrelevant, but Hopkins felt they would attract the reader's attention. Thus he had Olds saying such things as "I *analyze all my steel*," and "My carburetor is *doubly* heated." (One of his early Schlitz ads had been headlined: "Washed With Live Steam!" When the Schlitz executives pointed out that all breweries washed their bottles with steam, Hopkins replied that the public did not know this and no other brewery had made the claim before. Now any that tried to follow the lead of Schlitz would be branded as copycats.) The most famous gimmick that Hopkins used in his most famous Reo ad was to have Olds refer to the 1912 model as Reo the Fifth, thus establishing that it was in a long line of development; he then had Olds name it the best car he could ever build. "The Car That Marks My Limit," the ad was entitled.

> I have no quarrel with men who ask more for their cars — none with men who ask less. I have only to say that, after 25 years — after creating 24 models [a figure that Hopkins seems to have pulled out of the air] and building tens of thousands of cars — *here's the best I know.* I call it My Farewell Car. . . . Reo the Fifth marks my limit. Better materials are impossible, better workmanship out of the question. Better features or devices, if they exist, are still unknown to me. More care or skill or quality is beyond my capability. At twice the price I could build no better car. If others can, they are better men than I.

When Olds read over this copy, he told Hopkins, "But, I don't intend to retire." Hopkins replied that such a minor detail was of no importance. "Sarah Bernhardt made seven farewell tours. [Olds] could have two or three. Every farewell is subject to reconsideration." In the meantime, car buyers would have an added incentive to buy a new car designed by Ransom Olds while they were still available.[20]

According to Reo's sales agent, R. M. Owen & Co., this "farewell" ad appeared in magazines, weeklies, farm papers, and newspapers with a total circulation of thirty million copies, making this, the company told the Reo dealers, the biggest advertising campaign in automotive history to that time. It hailed the advertisement as "a sample of masterly salesmanship." A few years earlier, when Ray Owen was first trying to line up dealers for the new Reo, his experiences might have caused him to question the wisdom of basing the advertisements on the supposedly high reputation of Ransom Olds, as Powers did in December 1904, and Hopkins did in 1912. Near the end of September 1904, Owen told Olds:

> I find throughout the country the general impression is, that you are very

My Farewell Car

By R. E. Olds, Designer

Reo the Fifth—the car I now bring out—is regarded by me as pretty close to finality. Embodied here are the final results of my 25 years of experience. I do not believe that a car materially better will ever be built. In any event, this car marks my limit.   So I've called it My Farewell Car.

My 24th Model

This is the twenty-fourth model which I have created in the past 25 years.

They have run from one to six cylinders—from 6 to 60 horsepower. From the primitive cars of the early days to the most luxurious modern machines.

I have run the whole gamut of automobile experience. I have learned the right and the wrong from tens of thousands of users.

In this Farewell Car, I adopt the size which has come to be standard —the 30 to 35 horsepower, four-cylinder car.

Where It Excels

The chiefest point where this car excels is in excess of care and caution.

The best I have learned in 25 years is the folly of taking chances.

In every last part the alloy that I use is the best that has been discovered. And all my steel is analyzed to know that it meets my formula.

I test my gears with a crushing machine—not a hammer. I know to exactness what each gear will stand.

I put the magneto to a radical test. The carburetor is doubly heated for low-grade gasoline.

I use nickel steel axles with Timken roller bearings.

So in every part. The best that any man knows for every part has been adopted here. The margin of safety is always extreme.

I regard it impossible, at any price, to build a car any better.

Center Control, Finish, etc.

Reo the Fifth has a center, cane-handle control. It is our invention, our exclusive feature.

Gear shifting is done by a very slight motion, in one of four directions.

There are no levers, either side or center. Both of the brakes operate by foot pedals. So the driver climbs out on either side as easily as you climb from the tonneau.

The body finish consists of 17 coats. The upholstering is deep, and of hair-filled genuine leather. The lamps are enameled, as per the latest vogue. Even the engine is nickel trimmed.

I have learned by experience that people like stunning appearance. The wheel base is long—the tonneau is roomy—the wheels are large —the car is over-tired. Every part of the car—of the chassis and the body—is better than you will think necessary. No price could buy anything better.

Price, $1,055

This car—my finest creation—has been priced for the present at $1,055.

This final and radical paring of cost is considered by most men as my greatest achievement.

It has required years of preparation. It has compelled the invention of much automatic machinery.

It necessitates making every part in our factory, so no profits go to parts makers.

It requires enormous production, small overhead expense, small selling expense, small profit. It means a standardized car for years to come, with no changes in tools and machinery.

In addition to that, by making only one chassis we are cutting off nearly $200 per car.

Thus Reo the Fifth gives far more for the money than any other car in existence. It gives twice as much as some.

But this price is not fixed. We shall keep it this low just as long as we can. If materials advance even slightly the price must also advance. No price can be fixed for six months ahead without leaving big margin, and we haven't done that. The cost has been pared to the limit.

Catalog Ready

Our new catalog shows the various styles of body. It tells all the materials, gives all specifications. With these facts before you, you can easily compare any other car with this Reo the Fifth.

If you want a new car you should do that. Judge the facts for yourself. Don't pay more than our price for less value. After 25 years spent in this business, here is the best car I can build. And the price is $1,055. Don't you think you should know that car?

Write now for this catalog. When we send it we will tell you where to see the car. Address—

R. M. Owen & Co. General Sales Agents for Reo Motor Car Co., Lansing, Mich.

Canadian Factory, St. Catharines, Ontario

Reo the Fifth
$1,055

Center Control

Brake and Clutch Pedals

30-35 Horsepower Wheel Base

112 Inches

Wheels— 34 Inches

Demountable Rims

Speed— 45 Miles per Hour

Made with 2, 4 and 5 Passenger Bodies

One Front Door Open to Show Center Control

Top and windshield not included in price. We equip this car with mohair top, side curtains and slip-cover, windshield, gas tank and speedometer   all for $100 extra. Self-starter, if wanted, $25.00 extra.   (25)

One of several slightly varying ads prepared by Claude Hopkins for the "Reo the Fifth," which, he has Ransom Olds declaring, was as perfect as he could make it and, therefore, was his "Farewell Car."
Courtesy Motor Vehicle Manufacturers Association

much inclined to cut the material down on your cars. They cite an instance of the cast iron differential gears, the cast iron bearings in the transmission, and several well known weak points in the Oldsmobile, as being directly up to you. You will therefore, have this prejudice to overcome, and I would not hesitate, if I were in your place, to put in the best material obtainable in these cars, even at a slight additional cost.

This negative reaction that Owen found among many prospective dealers toward Olds, plus a natural hesitancy to sign up to sell a car that no one yet had seen, caused Owen no little trouble, but by the end of December he was stating publicly that upon his return to New York from a two-week tour of the west he was enthusiastic about the prospects for the new car. "The demand for agencies is something out of the ordinary," he stated. Reo agencies were now set up in Chicago, St. Louis, Cleveland, and Buffalo.[21]

The Reo touring car and runabout were exhibited at the major auto shows early in 1905, and were favorably received. *Scientific American,* which had been reporting on Ransom Olds' latest products since 1892, singled out the Reo as one of five cars — and the only Michigan-made car — it discussed in an article on "Some Leading Automobiles of the Present Year." "While this machine is new," the magazine commented, "there is every reason to believe that it will prove itself to be one of the finest light-weight touring cars for 1905." This prediction was borne out by the Reo figures, which showed that production for the fiscal year ending August 31, 1905, was a very respectable total of 864 cars. Production increased almost threefold in 1906 to a total of 2458, held up well during the panic of 1907 when production reached 3967, and showed a slight increase to 4105 in 1908 (part of this figure represents the output at the beginning of the fiscal year, which started on September 1, 1907, when economic conditions were the worst). Production figures indicate the return of better times for Reo during the fiscal year September 1, 1908, to August 31, 1909, when output reached 6592. These figures were paralleled by Reo's remarkable dividend record during these years. From a relatively modest dividend in 1905 of ten per cent cash on the $500,000 in common stock, the dividend in 1906 increased to thirty-seven and a half per cent in cash and a fifty per cent stock dividend, to eighty-six and a half per cent cash plus thirty-three and a third stock in 1907, dropping to eighty per cent cash in 1908, and to seventy per cent cash in 1909, with, however, a 100 per cent stock dividend. Pioneer auto historian James Rood Doolittle cited the Reo dividend record in 1907 and 1908 as an outstanding example of how successfully the auto industry weathered the economic buffetings of that period.[22]

As the president of the Reo Motor Car Company, Ransom Olds naturally received the major credit for guiding this new automobile company into a leading position in the industry within two years after its founding. In the process he had far outstripped the Olds Motor Works. After its record year of 6500 cars in 1905, the Olds company had abandoned its low-priced runabout in favor of ever-larger cars, introducing the first medium-priced four-cylinder car in 1906, followed by a six-cylinder model in 1907. Oldsmobile sales, however, plummeted to 1600 in 1906, and 1080 in 1908, only a quarter of the output of the rival Reo plant a few blocks away. In May 1907, the Oldsmobile-Reo rivalry received national attention when President Theodore Roosevelt came to town to participate in the fiftieth anniversary observances of Michigan Agricultural College. Word got out that Roosevelt would ride from the State Capitol in Lansing out to the college campus in an automobile, in recognition of Lansing's and Michigan's rising new manufacturing industry. A writer in *Motor Age* reported that

> Officials of [Lansing's] rival concerns laid plans for weeks, keeping the tele- graph wires hot, cornering the market on special delivery stamps and rail- roading special representatives to Washington all to the end that the president might not forget that there were two motor car factories in Lansing and that both were not only willing but anxious to furnish him a vehicle free during his entire stay in the Michigan state capital.

In the end, Roosevelt, "with his proverbial good judgment and good luck combined," availed himself of the services of both companies. He rode out to the college in a Reo, with Ransom Olds acting as chauffeur for the occasion, and then he returned to Lansing in an Oldsmobile. "At night- fall, when the nation's first citizen was well on his way eastward, the battle lines were withdrawn, and good judges and critics regarded the day's motoring engagement as a drawn battle."[23]

But in the overall context of the struggle between the two com- panies, there could be no arguing with the fact that Reo was winning the early rounds of the contest. Ransom Olds had demonstrated that whatever or whoever may have been responsible for the early success of the Olds Motor Works, he could repeat those same successes with a new company, built from scratch, of which he had, undisputed control. This achievement solidified his position as Lansing's foremost and most respected citizen. Until his death in 1950, the report that "Mr. Olds approved" or "Mr. Olds disapproved" was usually enough to decide the fate of any major civic development in Lansing. This prestige stemmed not only from the eco- nomic benefits that Olds' automobile companies had brought to the city, but also from the related activities of other companies for which Olds was wholly or at least partly responsible. Olds, like Durant and many other auto manufacturers, wished to have the suppliers for his auto company close at hand. Although the Auto-Body Company and the Prudden Wheel Company were already available to fill some of the needs of the new Reo company, Olds and various associates, including Richard Scott, Horace Thomas, Eugene Cooley, Edward Sparrow, and others, joined in 1906 to form in quick succession the National Coil Company, the Michigan Screw Company, and the Atlas Drop Forge Company — all Lansing businesses whose primary, although not sole, customer was Reo.[24]

On January 1, 1907, Olds noted in his diary that he was serving simultaneously as the president of the Reo Motor Car Company, the Atlas Drop Forge Company, the Michigan Screw Company, the National Coil

Company, the Capital National Bank, which he had also helped to organize in 1906, and the Bancroft Company, his peat company. As he surveyed his diverse and, on the whole, highly successful business interests, Olds seems to have lost his incentive to work hard. A study of his diaries beginning about 1906 indicates that, with the exception of his attendance at the annual stockholders' meetings, some directors' meetings, and the annual New York auto show, Olds' involvement in the business affairs of Reo becomes increasingly minimal. He spent long periods each winter in Florida, where he eventually had extensive real estate holdings. He satisfied an obvious love for travel by traveling extensively each year. Summers he spent much time vacationing in northern Michigan, and even when he was in Lansing his diary entries usually indicate that he was "at home," and only very infrequently does he say that he was "in the office." A few sketches and notations about automobile design indicate that this was one area of the business in which he maintained an interest, but even so, he seems to have been spending as much or more time in the design of his yacht. In a little over two decades he had built up a successful engine business, and had then gone on to play a major role in the success of an automobile company, had left that company and had now once again succeeded with another company. In the process he had become a wealthy man. Little wonder if he now decided to abandon the old grind in order to get more pleasure out of life.[25]

The job of running Reo was largely delegated to Richard Scott, a man of very considerable abilities, but a man who, for various reasons, was not liked by a number of the men in the organization. Some, like Reuben Shettler, resented what they regarded as Scott's unauthorized usurpation of the president's powers. There was also a feeling that Scott's prominent role in the affairs of the Anti-Saloon League was detrimental to the company's business. The late Herman Staebler of Ann Arbor once recalled how when he was handling sales for Reo in the Middle West he had just about completed a sale of a large number of vehicles to the Anheuser-Busch company of St. Louis when he was called into the office of the president, August Busch, Sr., who asked Staebler if it was not true that Richard Scott was a top executive with Reo. When Staebler replied that this was indeed the case, Busch tore up the contract, with the comment: "Do you think I'm going to buy cars from someone who's trying to put me out of business?" Whether the future development of Reo would have been different had Olds been more like Henry Ford in keeping a sharp eye on the business is impossible to say, but the fact is that as Olds seemed to lose interest in the company, Reo was not able to maintain the position it had originally seized among the producers of medium-priced cars. As it slid back, Reo's cross-town rival regained its former eminence and moved far ahead of the newer firm. Meanwhile, Olds formally relinquished the title of general manager to Scott in 1915, and then gave up the presidency to Scott in 1923 for the largely honorary post of chairman of the board, from which he resigned in 1936. In their place he busied himself with the design of a power lawn mower, real estate and hotel developments, a refrigeration company, service as a trustee of Kalamazoo and Hillsdale colleges and of the Edward W. Sparrow Hospital in Lansing, and with a host of other activities. Perhaps he concluded that he simply did not have time to be only an automobile magnate.[26]

In 1908, however, he was still one of the most famous names in the industry and his company ranked with Ford, Buick, and Maxwell as one of the four largest auto companies in the United States. It would have been inconceivable at that time to leave Ransom Olds out of any major automobile merger plans. Thus it was that he boarded the Grand Trunk train in the dark, pre-dawn hours on that January morning and headed for Detroit to meet with Durant, Ford, and Briscoe.

CHAPTER 9

"WATCH THE FORDS GO BY"

Henry Ford had only a short distance to travel across town from his home on Harper Avenue on January 17, 1908, to meet with his fellow automakers Durant, Briscoe, and Olds in the Penobscot Building. Nor was he far from the meeting place for later that same morning — Durant's suite in that favored gathering place of automobile men in Detroit, the Pontchartrain Hotel (a hostelry that was torn down in 1920, and is not to be confused with Detroit's present hotel of the same name). In a few months Henry, Clara, and Edsel Ford would be moving from their modest Harper Avenue residence into a big, red brick home that was being built for them at the corner of Edison and Second avenues, at a cost when completed of $283,253. For Henry Ford, who less than ten years earlier was drawing a monthly salary of $150, the new house, with its accompanying staff of servants, was visible proof that the farm boy from Dearborn had finally made good.[1]

*　*　*

The formal dissolution of the Detroit Automobile Company between November 1900 and January 1901 had seemingly put Henry Ford into the ranks of the unemployed, and these appearances were heightened early in the new year when the thirty-seven-year-old mechanic, his wife, and seven-year-old son moved in with Ford's father William, who had retired from the farm and come to live in Detroit. They remained with him much of that year. But actually, Henry Ford was never in any danger of becoming a charity case. William Murphy and possibly others from the old group of Detroit Automobile stockholders still had faith in him and supported him handsomely in his continued experimental work. Ford moved into a shop some three miles out Cass Avenue from downtown Detroit, although it is likely he worked at various locations during the year. Early in 1901, he spent some time on the further development of a marketable car, one of which he completed at least by April when he gave Murphy a demonstration ride. Coincidentally, when Roy Chapin and an Olds engineer had mechanical problems with a curved-dash Oldsmobile they were road testing, they stopped at a machine shop, Chapin recalled a few years later, and "found the 'Head' of the Shop. He was clad in blue overalls and fixed the spring for us in fine shape. His name was 'Henry Ford.' He was running an experimental shop then, trying to develop a motor car which would be commercially practicable." By May 1901, however, Ford was turning his attention largely to the construction of an automobile designed for racing.[2]

Automobile competition had improved immeasurably since the slow-paced events of the mid-nineties. The winner of the Tour of France race in 1899, a contest extending over 1428 miles, had averaged thirty-two miles an hour. By 1901, Henri Fournier, perhaps the most famous of the European drivers in this period, was averaging forty miles an hour in winning the Paris to Bordeaux road race. In a shorter time trial, a Belgian, Camille Jenatzy, in 1899 had set a record of 65.79 miles per hour in an electric car. In America, A. L. Riker also won races and set speed records with an electric car, while William K. Vanderbilt, Jr., achieved fame as a driver of an imported gasoline-powered Daimler. By 1901, however, the indisputable champion among American drivers was Alexander Winton of Cleveland, who, after effectively drawing attention to his gasoline automobiles by driving them cross-country, was now gaining new free publicity by entering and generally winning racing events. Ford, who was thoroughly familiar with the world of auto racing, was after the fame and reputation that racing brought to the successful designer and driver. The financial rewards would certainly also be welcome, as would the opportunity to try out ideas under the unusual and severe conditions provided in a race. William Murphy, who apparently shared the fascination with speed that most automotive buffs have always had, was persuaded to go along with this new project, which, according to one report, eventually cost over $5000 for just the materials used in the car.[3]

Ford did not work alone. In addition to William Boyer and Edward S. "Spider" Huff, who had been with him earlier in the Detroit Automo-

Alexander Winton, *prosperous and satisfied, some years after his pioneering days as a Cleveland automobile manufacturer and record-setting auto driver.*
Courtesy Motor Vehicle Manufacturers Association

bile Company, Ford was joined by Edward Ver Linden, a Detroit native who had apprenticed as a mechanic at the age of thirteen and had been a lathe operator in John Lauer's machine shop in the days when Charles King was building his experimental cars. Later, in 1910, Ver Linden became a plant manager with Buick, and then moved on to the Olds Motor Works, where he became president in 1917. In the shakeup that followed Durant's departure from General Motors, Ver Linden was fired from his job. Early in 1921, he moved on to head the new automobile company that Durant was establishing in Lansing. Today, a main street in Lansing is named after this son of a Belgian immigrant.

The men were also joined by an acquaintance of theirs, Oliver Barthel, who agreed to work part-time for Ford in May of 1901. Barthel had been running Charles King's pneumatic tool business after King became an engineer for Olds, but now he was trying to establish a business for himself as a consulting engineer since King had sold the tool business in May. Henry Ford had no visible financial resources of his own to pay these men, so it must be assumed that William Murphy took care of these expenses also.[4]

Once again the usual dispute arises over who was primarily responsible for the racing car that Ford and his little crew built in 1901. Relying
on his notoriously poor memory, Ford claimed in his autobiography that
he "designed a two-cylinder enclosed engine of a more compact type than
I had before used, fitted it into a skeleton chassis, found that I could make
speed, and arranged a race with Winton." However, since he also claimed
that this all took place in 1902, the statement cannot go entirely unchal-
lenged. Oliver Barthel, recalling these events at a much later date than
Ford did when he wrote his autobiography, declared that he had been responsible for designing the racing vehicle and superintending its construction. "I never knew Henry Ford to design a car," Barthel declared. In fact,
he said, "There was no possibility of Henry Ford sitting down and detailing a car." Such sweeping judgments may have been the result, partially,
at least, of envy and jealousy on the part of the old man who, although
possessed of undoubted mechanical abilities, had seen his own attempt to
establish an automobile company in 1903 (the Mohawk or Barthel Automobile Company) fail because of lack of interest among potential investors.[5]

By the summer of 1901, the Ford racing car, nicknamed "Sweepstakes," appears to have been completed. It was lighter and less powerful
than many other racing cars of that day, but it was fast. Barthel claims that
he got up to a speed of seventy-two miles an hour in a road test in July,
but this time remained unofficial since no observers were present with their
stop-watches. At any rate, the machine was good enough for Ford to enter
it against what promised to be some very stiff competition in races that
were to be held at a dirt track in Grosse Pointe on October 10.[6]

The afternoon of races, modestly billed as the World Championships, had been arranged by a committee headed by William E. Metzger,
the Detroit bicycle and automobile dealer. Serving with him, for obvious
reasons, was the president of the Detroit horsemen's club that owned the
track, Daniel J. Campau, a wealthy Detroit lawyer whose life centered
around two great loves, horse racing and the Democratic party. Also involved in the planning was Charles B. Shanks, sales manager for Alexander
Winton's company, who saw the event as another means of promoting sales
of the Winton car. In addition to Alexander Winton, whose presence was
assured, Metzger made a valiant effort to secure the participation of such
other racing luminaries as William K. Vanderbilt, Jr., and Henri Fournier. Although he was not successful in these two cases, he did get such entrants as Edgar Apperson from Kokomo (who, with his brother, was about
to split away from Elwood Haynes and form their own company), Windsor T. and Rollin H. White, with one of the splendid new steam cars that
these brothers had begun to produce at the White Sewing Machine Company plant in Cleveland, Gus Boyer from Reading, Pennsylvania, driving
a gasoline car that Charles Duryea was manufacturing in that city, and
Herbert H. Lytle of Toledo, driving a Pope steamer from that city. In
addition, there was the local talent: William Grant and William C. Rands

with steam cars, Roy Chapin and Jonathan Maxwell from the Olds Motor Works, and Henry Ford. The events at Grosse Pointe, if they were not the World Championships, were, *Motor Age* declared, at least "the first 'real thing' in the line of an automobile race meet held in the west."[7]

Enthusiasm for the auto races ran surprisingly high. Not only did the Olds Motor Works close for the afternoon (a Thursday) to allow its two hundred workers to attend the meet, but as a result of "several requests from attorneys and others," Detroit Recorder's Court Judge James Phelan announced in advance that "court will be adjourned for the day at one o'clock." Preceding the races, from sixty to one hundred automobiles, said to have been "more machines in line than had ever before been seen . . . in the west," paraded through Detroit's business district and on out to the track. Attendance swelled to a peak during the afternoon of seven thousand people, more than had ever attended any but the most important horse races at that track. The Detroit Street Railway Company ran cars to the grounds every thirty seconds to handle the local crowd, while from out of town a contingent had driven up from Toledo, and sixty to seventy enthusiasts had come by boat from Cleveland to witness the anticipated triumph of their home-town hero, Alexander Winton.

Although track conditions and the weather were pronounced to be ideal, the early events of the afternoon failed to excite the crowd. A five-mile race for steam cars was no contest as either Windsor or Rollin White (newspaper reports differed in identifying the driver) easily defeated Lytle, Grant, and Rands, the latter being forced out because of mechanical problems. The second race, described by one reporter as "a laughing farce," was a one-mile event for electrics that was won by another Cleveland manufacturer, Walter C. Baker of the Baker Motor Vehicle Company, with Fred Stearns of Detroit second. Baker's winning time of 4:49 was more than thirty seconds slower than the existing record for a man running the mile. Shortly afterwards, however, the crowd perked up and applauded Alexander Winton who, in a special exhibition feature, set a new record for a mile run by a gasoline-powered automobile with a time of 1:12.4. (It was later learned, however, that Winton's time was surpassed that same afternoon by Henri Fournier in an exhibition run in New York.) Windsor White won a ten-mile race for vehicles weighing less than a thousand pounds, defeating Chapin and Maxwell. In another ten-miler for cars under two thousand pounds, however, White came in second to Edgar Apperson, while the other participants, Gus Boyer and a Winton (not driven in this case by Alexander Winton) which developed a mechanical problem, trailed far behind.

The feature event of the day was supposed to have been a twenty-five-mile race open to vehicles of any classification. It had originally been hoped that this race would be a match-up between Winton and Fournier, and even after Fournier had decided to race elsewhere, excitement was generated by the entry of W. N. Murray of Pittsburgh, who, in his seventy-horsepower machine, had recently broken William Vanderbilt's mile

With Alexander Winton and his crippled racer far behind, Henry Ford charges to victory at Grosse Pointe on October 10, 1901.
Courtesy Ford Motor Company

record. But the luster of the afternoon's climactic event was greatly dimmed when, first of all, because of the amount of time consumed by the earlier races, Metzger had to reduce the distance from twenty-five to ten miles. Worse still, Murray's automobile developed a leaky cylinder, forcing his withdrawal. This left only Alexander Winton, with his record-breaking seventy-horsepower machine, opposed by Henry Ford, a novice who had never before driven in a race, driving a vehicle that was said to develop forty horsepower but in actuality was more correctly rated at around twenty-six horsepower. As the race began, Ford was more than able to hold his own with Winton on the straightaways, but the more experienced Scotsman pulled ahead on the curves. Ford, who was unsure of himself since he had never driven the car on a curve before, shut off power and went wide, while Spider Huff, who was riding with Ford as the mechanic, leaned far out of the car to help balance the light machine. But then Winton's car began to overheat, and the efforts of Charles Shanks, riding with Winton, to deal with the problem while the car was in motion, were to no avail; Winton, who had been well ahead, had to slow down. Ford, who was gaining confidence as he continued to circle the track, passed Winton on the eighth lap and finished the race almost a mile ahead of his crippled Cleveland opponent. Ford's time for the ten miles, 13:23.8, had reportedly been surpassed only twice before in the United States. It was almost four and a half minutes faster than Apperson's winning time in the preceding ten-mile event.

Ford's victory was, of course, as popular with the hometown crowd as it was unexpected. Clara Ford wrote to her brother,

I wish you could have seen him. Also have heard the cheering when he passed Winton. The people went wild. One man threw his hat up and when it came down he stamped on it, he was so excited. Another man had to hit his wife on the head to keep her from going off the handle. She stood up in her seat [and] screamed "I'd bet Fifty dollars on Ford if I had it." They were friends of ours.

Ford himself expressed his feelings about racing soon after the race: "Boy, I'll never do that again! That tight board fence was right here in front of my face all the time! I was scared to death." He announced to reporters that he was retiring from racing, and, although he would race against the clock, he never again raced in competition. He readily admitted his limited abilities when he declared that if Winton had been driving Ford's machine, no one could have beaten him.[8]

For his victory on October 10, 1901, Henry Ford apparently received the top prize of $1000, although one report states that the promoters had earlier cancelled this award. Ford also received a cut-glass punch bowl set that Charles Shanks had picked out as a prize "because he figured it would look well in the bay window of the Winton dining room." Instead it came to grace Ford's modest residence.[9]

Of far more lasting value to him than the prizes he had won was the publicity that Henry Ford gained from his triumph over Alexander Winton. For the first time, Ford became something of a national celebrity, a fame that for several years continued to center around his racing and speed-setting activities. On the local scene, too, Ford now had increased status as a result of his Grosse Pointe win. Among the spectators at the track that day were William Murphy, Mark Hopkins, Clarence A. Black, Albert White, and Lem Bowen, former stockholders in the Detroit Automobile Company. The men were highly pleased with the performance of Ford and his machine, which some of them had helped to finance. They immediately received offers from individuals in New York and Chicago who wanted to purchase the racer. Eventually, however, "Sweepstakes" was sold to the Detroiter, William C. Rands, who, in June 1902, was reported to have done a half mile in 26.2 seconds and was afraid to see how fast the car would go if he really "let it out."

Encouraged by the performance of Ford's racer and the interest it had aroused among buyers, Murphy and his associates regrouped and formed the Henry Ford Company, whose incorporation papers were filed on November 30, 1901. Black and White, whose names had no doubt occasioned some jokes as the old Detroit Automobile Company had gone deeper into the red, were president and vice-president of the new company, as they had been of the earlier Ford automobile venture. William Murphy regained his earlier position as treasurer, while Lem Bowen took the job of secretary that had been held in the first company by Frank Alderman, one of the Detroit Automobile investors who did not come into the new firm. The stockholders in the Henry Ford Company included the officers, Mark Hopkins, and Henry Ford, who was hired as the chief engineer and was given a sixth of the stock. The capitalization totaled $60,-000, with about half that amount paid in. A plant was obtained on Cass Avenue, and the company was in business, with the announced intention of producing a car designed by Ford which, it boasted, was entirely new and a "vast improvement" over any other car on the market. However, subsequent events did not bear out this initial promise, and on March 10, 1902, Henry Ford left the company, and the future of the Henry Ford Company became most uncertain.[10]

The reasons for this final break between Ford and Murphy and the others are in some doubt. One factor that led to dissension stemmed from Ford's continuing interest in racing. Although he had announced that he would not compete again against other drivers, he declared that he intended to practice almost every day for his assault on the timed speed record. He declared that he was also working on the development of an automatic timing device to ensure absolute accuracy in future time trials. Soon after the Grosse Pointe race, Ford asked Oliver Barthel to come to work full time for the new Henry Ford Company. Barthel consented, thinking that Ford wanted him to work on the design of a passenger car, but instead he found that Ford "talked mostly about wanting to build a larger and faster racing car." On October 28, Alexander Winton, a good loser if there ever was one, was offering Ford equipment and advice to help in the improvement of Ford's racing vehicle. In November 1901, Ford went to the auto show in New York, where he enjoyed his newly won fame as a champion racing driver. He met Henri Fournier, and, Clara said, "found him a fine young fellow." He also talked with C. H. Sieberling of the Goodyear Tire company. The talk apparently included a discussion of a new Ford racer, for later, on November 14, Sieberling wrote to Ford to remind him that when he finished his "new racing machine don't forget that you are to equip them with Goodyear detachable tires." By the beginning of the new year, Ford and his brother-in-law, Milton Bryant, who was acting as Ford's unofficial manager, were talking eagerly of challenging Fournier. Writing to Bryant on the letterhead of the Henry Ford Company, which was proclaimed to be "builders of high-grade automobiles and tourist cars," Ford declared that "there is a barrel of money in this business." He admitted that the officials in the company would "kick about me following racing but they will get the Advertising and I expect to make $ where I can't make ¢s at Manufacturing."

Ford was right. William Murphy, his principal backer, did kick. He had been perfectly willing to subsidize Ford's earlier racing venture, but now, with the Ford name's increased prestige, the time had come to market a car. To do so, Ford, the company's chief engineer, was expected to devote his complete attention to building and producing that car. At about the same time that Walter Clement in Adrian was seeking to prevent Willis Grant Murray from using company time to work on a racing car, William Murphy in Detroit was seeking to put an end to Ford's racing plans, which were jeopardizing the company's interest in a passenger car.

Ford, on the other hand, depicted Murphy's actions as an attempt to place obstacles in the way of his endeavor to implement new ideas. In his autobiography twenty years later, Ford declared that he resigned in March 1902, "determined never again to put myself under orders."[11]

Besides the rift that developed over the amount of time that Ford was devoting to a racing car, and possibly some dissatisfaction on Ford's part that he had only a sixth interest in the company, there is another possibility that Ford objected to outside interference and criticism of how he ran the plant. According to a story that has appeared in a variety of versions, Henry Ford did not really resign from the Henry Ford Company. He had, in effect, been fired by his backers, whose growing suspicions regarding Ford's capabilities had been confirmed by criticisms of various aspects of Ford's work. They received the evaluations from an unimpeachably qualified source, the brilliant mechanic, Henry M. Leland. Twenty years later, Henry Ford, by then the world's wealthiest and most powerful automobile manufacturer, purchased at a receiver's sale the Lincoln Motor Company, and, according to Henry and Wilfred Leland, the founders and owners of the bankrupt firm, made certain promises to them regarding the company which he then disregarded. Until a few months before his death at the age of eighty-nine in 1932, Henry Leland and his son were engaged in a protracted legal battle to force Ford to live up to his promises; but they lost, and this, it has been said, was Henry Ford's revenge for what Henry Leland had done to him in 1902.[12]

In the early 1950's, Allan Nevins was told by William W. Pring, who had worked for the Henry Ford Company as he had earlier for the Detroit Automobile Company, that William Murphy, who, Pring said, knew Henry Leland since they both went to the same church, had asked Leland for advice as to what needed to be done to prevent the Henry Ford Company from failing in the same way that the earlier Detroit Automobile Company had failed. Leland came into the plant and quickly saw much that needed to be changed. "He figured he could tell Ford what to do," Pring declared, "but Mr. Ford wasn't the type of man to take it." Later, in 1966, Henry Leland's biographers partially discredited Pring's reminiscences by demonstrating that Murphy and Leland did not attend the same church, as Pring had asserted, and by citing Wilfred Leland to the effect that neither he nor his father had been acquainted with Murphy and the other investors in the Henry Ford Company at the time Ford was with the firm. This may be true, given the size of Detroit at this time and the differing nature of the main business interests of the Lelands and Murphy and his associates, but it is almost impossible to believe, as Leland's biographers also maintain, that the Lelands did not know Henry Ford at this time either. For over a decade, Henry Leland had been the operator of one of Detroit's best known and most highly regarded machine shops. It seems unlikely that Ford, during the time that he was responsible for the machinery at the Edison Illuminating Company and during the more than six years that he had been working on the development of engines and automobiles, would not at some time have had jobs or problems that he would have taken to Leland, as Charles King, Oliver Barthel, and Ransom Olds had done. If we may credit the recollections of W. J. Moore of Caro, Michigan, this was apparently what Ford had in fact done in 1900. In the summer of that year, Moore claimed, he drove his DeDion-Bouton Motorette around to the Leland shop where he found Ford "working on the chassis of a vehicle he was building. . . . Ford showed Moore what he was doing to the chassis and in turn W. J. took Ford for a ride in the DeDion, and from this day on they became fast friends."[13]

Whatever the role of the Lelands may have been (and Henry Ford may very well have convinced himself later that on the basis of their subsequent associations with the Henry Ford Company the Lelands had had something to do with the events that led up to his departure from that company), it seems fairly clear that the break between Murphy and Ford stemmed from the latter's continued refusal to concentrate on the development and production of a commercially acceptable car. Ford's attempts to place the blame on Murphy and his associates cannot obscure the obvious fact that Ford had had at least six years to perfect his ideas. If after that length of time he was still not ready to produce a car, one can hardly blame his backers if they finally decided that they had had enough of his delays.

After Henry Ford left the company that bore his name, his duties were taken over by Oliver Barthel, who designed a four-passenger car, using a two-cylinder engine. Barthel, in his reminiscences a half-century later, declared that he took his plans around to Leland, who had advised Barthel earlier when he was working with Charles King on the engine for J. A. Vanderpoel's yacht. Barthel said that he never could understand why Ford disliked the Lelands, since, he said, they had had nothing to do with the company while Ford was with it. If anyone had cause to dislike Henry Leland, Barthel indicates, he did, for Leland and his aides vetoed Barthel's design in favor of a one-cylinder engine. This is substantially the same story as that related by Alanson Brush, an employee of Leland's at the time, in a letter to Frank Briscoe in 1950, although Brush recalled that it was Clarence Black and some of the other investors who came to Leland, not Barthel, and that they asked advice about using the two-cylinder engine, which Brush said had been designed by Ford, in a car. (It seems quite probable that the engine, as well as the car, that Barthel says he designed was one that he had been working on earlier with Ford.) Brush declared that it was decided to abandon this engine "due to Mr. Leland's suggestion that the Olds Company had demonstrated the sale-ability of a car using the less expensive single-cylinder engine." Still a third account, that of Wilfred Leland, declared that Leland was first visited in August 1902 by Murphy and Bowen, who "had come to ask my father to appraise their automobile plant and its equipment since they had decided to go out of business." The elder Leland made the requested appraisal, but when he returned to the Cass Avenue plant to present his report to Murphy and the other investors he brought along with him an improved version of the one-cylinder Olds engine that he and his men had developed. He then attempted to persuade Murphy and the others to stay in business and produce an automobile that Leland's staff could readily design, using their one-cylinder engine. A few days later, on August 27, 1902, Murphy, Bowen, Black, and White agreed to reorganize the Henry Ford Company. The capitalization was increased to $300,000, of which Henry Leland was given a small amount, as well as being named to the board of directors. The name of the new company was the Cadillac Automobile Company, after Antoine de la Mothe Cadillac, an appropriate choice for a Detroit company, as the bicentennial celebrations of the previous year would certainly have made clear. Murphy and his fellow investors would not regret their decision. In a short time there could have been no doubt in their minds that in Henry Martyn Leland they had found the man they had earlier hoped Henry Ford would turn out to be.[14]

Leland was born on February 16, 1843, on a farm near Barton, Vermont. His parents named him after the English missionary to India, Henry Martyn, and it proved an appropriate choice, for Leland was throughout his long life a God-fearing man. Of rather patriarchal appearance with his luxuriant Vandyke beard and his tall, angular figure, Leland was not only active in church work, but in his factory he held regular noon prayer meetings where he read from the Bible. In addition, in keeping with prevalent nineteenth-century Protestant attitudes, Leland was opposed to drinking and smoking, and he dealt sternly with any worker found guilty of either practice.[15]

Leland's father was a farmer, but not a successful one, and before Henry was very old, the large family had been moved to Worcester, Massachusetts, where manufacturing jobs were available for the father and his sons. By the late fifties, Henry Leland was an apprentice machinist with a company in Worcester that manufactured power looms. Here, and then at the United States Armory in Springfield, Massachusetts, during the Civil War, later at the Colt Revolver Factory in Hartford, Connecticut, and finally with the Brown & Sharpe Manufacturing Company in Providence, Rhode Island, Henry Leland learned the machinist's trade from the ablest, most experienced craftsmen in the country. In particular, he learned that to achieve the benefits of mass production through the use of interchangeable parts — a principle that the New Englander Eli Whitney had demonstrated as early as the 1790's — work of the greatest possible degree of precision was essential. This lesson would be the basis for Leland's greatest contribution to the manufacturing of automobiles. Brown & Sharpe, through the development and perfection of machine tools and measuring devices, was able to advance the standard of uniformity among machined parts from the 1/32 of an inch that prevailed in Whitney's day to 1/100,000 of an inch, and even on one occasion, declared Wilfred Leland, who also worked for this company, to a tolerance of 1/270,000 of an inch.[16]

Henry Martyn Leland, *the oldest of the major Michigan automobile pioneers, whose patriarchal appearance was sometimes matched by a suitably severe and unbending temperament.*
Courtesy Automotive History Collection

By the 1880's, Henry Leland had become one of the Rhode Island firm's top executives, and was handling sales of its tools in the Middle West. Eventually he decided he would like to establish his own shop in this area; his travels had made him aware of the great opportunities offered by the region's rapidly expanding manufacturing operations. The chance Leland had been looking for came in 1890 when Charles Strelinger, a prominent wholesaler of tools and hardware in Detroit, introduced Leland to Robert C. Faulconer, a lumberman from Alpena who was interested in investing in a business. Leland persuaded Faulconer to invest in a machine shop with him, and the firm of Leland, Faulconer & Norton was formed on September 19, 1890. Faulconer was elected president, and he put up $40,000 of the company's $50,000 in capitalization. Charles F. Norton, a machine designer for Brown & Sharpe, was brought into this new firm to serve a similar function, and was given a small amount of stock, as was Strelinger, who was elected secretary. But none of these men was the really important individual in the company. Norton went back east in 1894, and the company became simply Leland & Faulconer. Faulconer continued as president and as the principal financial investor in the company, but his health was not good, and he knew little about machines. He gladly deferred, therefore, to Henry Leland, who, although his investment in the firm was only a small fraction of Faulconer's, was, in addition to being vice-president and general manager, the real boss of the operation.

The business was a gratifying, if not spectacular, success. From a dozen employees at the outset, within three months the Leland shop was employing sixty workers. In November 1901, the state factory inspector found 160 employees on the job, working ten hours a day, six days a week. (The average pay of $2.10 a day was unusually high for that period.) Capitalization had been increased to $100,000 and would be boosted to $175,000 in 1902. Profits advanced, too, from $5434 in 1897, to $14,518 in 1901. Gear grinding and special toolmaking were the staples of the business for some time, but the company also designed and manufactured some machines, and did general jobbing work. Allan Nevins was certainly guilty of some exaggeration when he described Leland in 1902 as "probably the most experienced, farsighted, and successful director of a machine shop in America, if not in the world." As noted earlier, Charles King insisted that John Lauer's work was of equal quality to that of Leland, but nevertheless it was Leland's known reputation for gear work that caused Ransom Olds to come to him for help in eliminating problems with the curved-dash runabout's transmission. Similarly, it was the high quality of the marine engines that Leland & Faulconer had made for Charles Strelinger and others that led to the company receiving a contract from Olds for two thousand runabout engines in June 1901.[17]

For the fifty-eight-year-old Leland these contacts with Olds were apparently his first major introduction to the automobile industry. Leland had, however, been interested in and aware of the potential importance of the automobile for some time prior to his Olds contacts. Although he did not own a car at the time, in July 1900 Leland spoke to the delegates to the First International Good Roads Congress in Port Huron, Michigan, and declared that automobiles would be the chief means of bringing about road improvements in the future.

When he then became involved in manufacturing parts for automobiles, Leland admitted that he and his men were slow at first in producing the unfamiliar Olds engine, "but after we had gotten under way we delivered them so rapidly that Mr. Olds said we must have a motor incubator at our place." Not satisfied with the information that the Olds

Motor Works supplied regarding the engine, Leland decided to buy his first automobile — an Oldsmobile. Ransom Olds delivered the car personally, and as he demonstrated the vehicle for the family, gathered in front of the Leland residence for this exciting occasion, Olds had difficulty in getting the runabout started again. He commented that each of the little cars had "an individuality of its own." Although this Oldsmobile subsequently served the Lelands quite satisfactorily, Henry Leland's main interest at the outset was in taking out the engine, completely disassembling it, and then learning how to build these engines so that they would be of uniform quality, thereby eliminating the individuality that Olds had accepted as a trait of his cars.[18]

Among the members of Leland's staff who were assigned the task of ironing out the problems in manufacturing the Olds engine, the most important in the light of subsequent automotive history was Alanson P. Brush. According to Henry Ford's sister, Brush had been a schoolmate of Henry Ford's at the Scotch Settlement School, which, if true, would have made that little country school a hothouse of future automakers, since Brush, like Ford and J. Dallas Dort, another classmate, all produced cars bearing their own names. But since Ford attended the school from 1871 to 1873 and Brush was not born until February 10, 1878, this association of Ford with Brush can safely be labeled inconceivable. As a boy in Detroit and Birmingham, Michigan, where he actually did attend school, Brush manifested the same early interest in machines that seems to have been so common among automobile pioneers. He and an older brother built a tiny toy steam engine of their own design which actually ran and was still owned by Brush's sister in the early 1960's. After serving with the Thirty-first Michigan Infantry Regiment in the Spanish-American War, Brush went to work for Leland & Faulconer in 1899.[19]

Brush's first major job with Leland, he claimed, came when he was placed in charge of inspecting and testing the motors the company was making for Olds, although another long-time Leland employee, Charlie Martens, claimed in 1959-60 that this had been his job. Brush, however, recalled that when problems developed with the Olds engines, which, if not solved, threatened Leland's contract with Olds, Leland called him in. "You are a good mechanic," Leland had told him. "Can't you think of some way out of this difficulty?" Brush said that he thought he could, but it would take several days. "All right," Leland replied. "Go to it, boy! The shop is yours to command. Just get that machine to working right." Brush succeeded in overcoming the problem, and, according to Charles Strelinger, Henry Leland was heard to remark about Brush: "I've got a young fellow in my shop, in fact, I have a contract with him, who knows more about internal combustion engines than any one else in the United States." Strelinger, too, was impressed with Brush's work and commissioned him to design and build an inexpensive and small marine engine that Strelinger could sell. The financial security that Brush felt when he received a thousand dollars for this job led him to marry his girl friend, Jane Marsh, at the end of March 1902.[20]

By applying more precise standards in manufacturing the Olds engine, Leland and his staff not only made them uniform in quality, but also produced a more powerful engine than those of the same design that the Dodge brothers were producing for the runabout. But then someone in the Leland organization — one cannot be certain whether it was Henry or Wilfred Leland, Brush, or some other engineer — decided to go a step further. Keeping the basic features of the Olds engine, someone made certain improvements in it that changed the engine from about a three-horse-power engine to about ten horsepower. Evidence suggests that Brush carried through on this idea, completing the task sometime before the summer of 1902. Henry Leland then offered this improved engine to Fred Smith, pointing out that despite its increased power it would cost no more to manufacture than the existing runabout engine. According to Wilfred Leland, Smith rejected the idea because of the expense that would be entailed in redesigning the rest of the car to accommodate the new engine. (The fact that Leland consulted Smith, and that it was Smith, not Olds, who made the decision not to use the new engine, clearly indicates that by 1902 Fred Smith, not Ransom Olds, was the man actually running the Olds Motor Works.) It was this improved engine, then, that Henry Leland used to convince the investors in the Henry Ford Company to stay in the automobile business.[21]

Although Leland saw his long-range relationship with the new Cadillac Automobile Company as a supplier of engines and certain other parts, from the outset there were circumstances that foreshadowed the ultimate merger of Cadillac with Leland & Faulconer in 1905. According to Alanson Brush's wife, an "incompetent superintendent" at Cadillac was unable to handle the job of putting together a car, using the improved engine that Leland was supplying. He was fired, and Leland was asked by the other directors of Cadillac to assign Brush to this job. (Since Oliver Barthel was apparently no longer with the reorganized Henry Ford Company, the "superintendent" Mrs. Brush referred to may have been Patrick Hussey, who, in the early reports of the formation of the Cadillac company, was named as the manager.) Brush and other Leland staffers whipped the car together in quick order, building it, however, not in the Cadillac factory, but in the Leland & Faulconer shop. By October 20, 1902, a demonstration model had been completed and was driven by Brush, with Wilfred Leland as the first passenger. Four days later the Cadillac was exhibited at the second annual auto races held at Grosse Pointe. This Cadillac Model A, as it was dubbed, "evoked much favorable comment," according to one automotive reporter. "It is a handsome vehicle, substantial and yet trim looking, runs with absolutely no noise or vibration, starts without any grinding or noise of clutch engaging, and at the rumored price of $750 is likely to prove a sensation in the trade." The price, which held at $750 when the model went on sale in 1903, is of interest, considering Cadillac's later development as a manufacturer of one of America's most expensive cars. Initially, however, the Leland staff simply built a heavier copy of the popular Oldsmobile runabout. The one-cylinder engine used is said to have been the improved Leland version of the Olds engine, but this may not be strictly true, since the first Cadillacs were advertised as having a five-horsepower engine while the engine that Leland had offered to Fred Smith supposedly had more than ten horsepower. At any rate, *Motor World* declared that the car looked "like a winner and if present plans are carried out the company are [*sic*] bound to become big factors in the automobile industry."[22]

The accuracy of this prediction was soon borne out. To a great extent the car's success was the result of a vigorous promotional campaign launched late in 1902, long before any cars were yet available for purchase. The hiring of William E. Metzger as sales manager started the campaign off at a high level. In automotive circles, where Metzger's talents as a salesman were widely known, the announcement was hailed as a real coup.

Metzger had been born in 1868 in Peru, Illinois, but subsequently the family moved to Michigan, where Metzger graduated from high school in Detroit in 1884. In 1889 he began selling bicycles as a member of the Detroit firm of Huber & Metzger. Metzger withdrew from this partnership in 1895, establishing his own business in which he sold cash registers as well as bicycles, an early indication of a restlessness and a refusal to be tied down for long to any one product. It was also in 1895 that Metzger visited Europe and attended what was probably the world's first automobile show. His interest was aroused and within two years he was selling electric cars in Detroit. In 1898 he opened the first retail auto store in Detroit in the old Biddle House on Jefferson Avenue. Like most of the early auto dealers, he became the agent for more than one make of car. In the *Michigan State Gazetteer* for 1901, Metzger's was the largest ad of the six Detroit auto dealers whose notices appeared in the directory. Metzger, who always referred to himself as "the pioneer automobile dealer," was at this time the territorial agent for the steam Mobile, the Waverly Electric, the early Olds automobiles, as well as the Olds gasoline engines and the Lozier gas engines and launches from Toledo. In addition, he was a wholesale distributor of automobile "sundries" and tires. He still sold bicycles in a separate shop, and in a third shop nearby he sold furniture. In 1902, Metzger moved his auto dealership into a new two-story building on Jefferson Avenue, a building that *Motor World* called "one of the most thoroughly equipped establishments of the kind in the country." Within a year, Metzger, who continued to operate this business in addition to his new association with Cadillac, had expanded the facility to six floors. He devoted one department to custom body work, which, Metzger predicted, would be the next big development in the industry. "As a class," he declared, "automobilists are people who have the means and desire to have something distinctly their own. People are not going to be satisfied very long with machines which are just like every one else has or can buy."

In addition to his retail and wholesale automobile business, which he continued to run until he sold it to Cadillac in 1905, Metzger's interest in automobiles led him in other directions. After his success promoting the race at Grosse Pointe in October 1901, he became one of the organizers of Detroit's first automobile show early in 1902. He also had a hand in the organization of the Northern Manufacturing Company, an early and very promising Detroit automobile manufacturer. Later, in 1908, after leaving Cadillac, Metzger joined with Walter Flanders and Byron Everitt to form the E-M-F, and then in 1909, when this company was being taken over by Studebaker, he formed the short-lived Metzger Motor Company. Metzger continued in the automobile industry in various capacities, but the sight of the Wright brothers in action caused him to turn his attention more and more to aviation, a new field in which he helped to organize the Stinson Aircraft Corporation and a number of other aviation-connected firms.[23]

This was the man, then, who took on the job of selling the Cadillac in the fall of 1902, and during the short time that the job held Metzger's interest he did an outstanding piece of work. By November 1902, ads for the Cadillac in trade journals were advising dealers not to delay making their applications since "the CADILLAC agency is bound to be snapped up quickly." By September 1903, Metzger had signed up forty-eight agents, an impressive network of dealers in this early stage of automobile retailing. At the New York Automobile Show in January 1903, with four cars on display, including the Model A and the larger four-passenger Model B with tonneau, Metzger demonstrated his formidable abilities as a salesman by obtaining orders, with deposits, on over a thousand cars.[24]

To handle its advertising, Cadillac went straight to the top, signing up with one of the largest and best-known agencies in the country, N. W. Ayer & Son, a firm which had been the first to add a touch of dignity to this huckstering business by referring to its customers as "clients." In marked contrast, however, to the dignified, understated effect that the great Detroit adman, Theodore F. MacManus, would later seek to create in his Cadillac advertisements, the early Cadillac ads (which, of course, were not promoting the kind of luxury vehicle that MacManus would be dealing with) featured a hard-sell approach. They frequently revolved around stunts demonstrating the power of the little "one-lunger," as the Model A was popularly nicknamed. These stunts began when Alanson Brush drove a Cadillac with tire chains on all four wheels up the steps of the Wayne County building in Detroit and back down again. This feat was later repeated in Washington, D. C., on the steps of the nation's capitol. (In this case, the driver, who was arrested, had reportedly been gotten drunk, tied hand and foot to the steering mechanism, and sent on his way with the assurance that it was all part of a fraternity initiation.) On another occasion, a Cadillac runabout, carrying sixteen men who were sitting, standing, and hanging on for dear life all over the car, was pictured driving up a steep hill in Detroit. The origin of these hill-climbing exploits

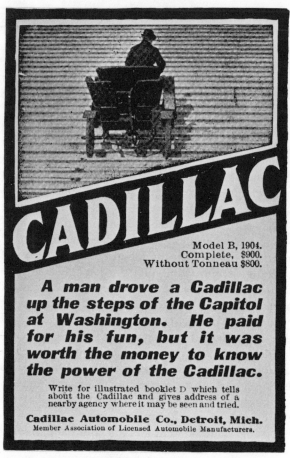

Model B, 1904.
Complete, $900.
Without Tonneau $800.

A man drove a Cadillac up the steps of the Capitol at Washington. He paid for his fun, but it was worth the money to know the power of the Cadillac.

Write for illustrated booklet D which tells about the Cadillac and gives address of a nearby agency where it may be seen and tried.

Cadillac Automobile Co., Detroit, Mich.
Member Association of Licensed Automobile Manufacturers.

A famous 1904 Cadillac ad.
Courtesy Eastern Michigan University Library

was undoubtedly the tests of various automobiles' ability to negotiate a steep wooden ramp that had been built on the roof of Madison Square Garden at the time of the first New York auto show in 1900. Joseph H. McDuffee, who became famous as the driver involved in these tests, subsequently became associated with Metzger in his Detroit auto dealership.[25]

The sales figures for the Cadillac soon indicated that the auto-buying public agreed with the advertising claims of excellence. The small plant that the company had inherited from the Henry Ford Company was totally inadequate for large-scale production, so an extensive plant expansion program progressed in 1903 simultaneously with the production of cars in the existing facilities. Manufacturing got underway by March of 1903, and the output for the rest of that year was at first reported to have been around 2500, well under the goal of three thousand cars announced at the beginning of the year. Later reports listed the total as 1895, but this apparently included production for the period March 1903 to March 1904. Nevertheless, the approximately 1700 Cadillacs that were produced by De-

cember 31, 1903, were enough to vault the new Detroit automobile manufacturer into second place in the country, behind the current leader, the
Olds Motor Works. After several profitless and frustrating years with
Henry Ford, William Murphy and his associates finally had something to
show for the thousands of dollars they had paid out. (Ironically, Henry
Ford's own Ford Motor Company, a late starter in 1903, was by the end of
the next year Cadillac's chief competitor for second place among auto
manufacturers.) That Cadillac's first-year performance had been no fluke
was amply demonstrated in 1904 when production was in the neighborhood
of 2500 cars, well above the first year's output, despite a fire that virtually
destroyed the entire factory on April 13 and forced a temporary suspension
of business. The ability of the company to rebound from this crippling
blow attested to its sound condition. Cadillac's strong position in the
industry, in turn, added mightily to the reputation Oldsmobile had given
Detroit earlier as a center of automobile production.[26]

Henry Leland's main relationship to Cadillac in this period continued to be that of a supplier of engines and transmissions. Even this relationship was threatened during the first year of operation when at least
one of the directors criticized the Leland & Faulconer engines as too expensive, raising the possibility that Cadillac might not sign a contract with
Leland for another year. Henry Leland overcame this opposition and
secured the renewal of the contract, but to protect his company he also
approached other Middle Western auto manufacturers, and received an
assurance from Studebaker of an order for three thousand engines at a
higher price than Cadillac was paying, just in case Cadillac did not renew
the contract. Then in 1904, as manufacturing problems arose from the
failure of other suppliers to deliver their parts as promptly and as well
made as those supplied by Leland & Faulconer, William Murphy and Lem
Bowen, who had always been strong supporters of Leland, approached him
about assuming the management of Cadillac. Leland demurred. As he
recalled later, "I never intended to get into the automobile business; there
was too much trouble in it." Murphy and Bowen were insistent, however.
"Either you fellows [meaning Leland, his son Wilfred, and some of their
chief assistants] come and run the factory for us or we will go out of business." Leland agreed, finally, and the arrangements were completed late
in 1904.

The following year, the next logical step occurred with the merger
of the Cadillac company and Leland & Faulconer. Cadillac was reorganized as the Cadillac Motor Car Company, with a capitalization of $1,500,000,
of which amount the assets of the old Cadillac company were assessed at
a million dollars and those of Leland & Faulconer at half a million. Henry
Leland, who was general manager of the company, and Wilfred Leland,
who held the title of assistant treasurer, were each paid salaries of $750 a
month, and in addition the two were awarded five per cent of the annual
profits of the company.[27]

Under Henry Leland's direction (with an increasingly large amount of assistance from Wilfred Leland), Cadillac sales continued their upward climb in 1905 and 1906. The company followed the trend in the industry toward bigger cars, introducing several four-cylinder models priced at $2000 or more, with a limousine available at $3600. Unlike the Olds Motor Works, however, Leland did not immediately abandon the low-priced one-cylinder runabout but kept it as a mainstay in the Cadillac line, along with the larger cars, until 1908. Sales declined sharply during the recession of 1907 and 1908, and Lem Bowen at one point despaired of the company being able to survive. The company was kept alive through the willingness of John T. Shaw, president of the First National Bank of Detroit, to advance the necessary funds. His confidence was validated by the remarkable recovery Cadillac made in 1909, due chiefly to the great popularity of the new four-cylinder "30" model introduced in 1908. From the time of its entry into the General Motors organization in 1909, Cadillac was for many years, along with Buick, one of the principal reasons why that vast assemblage of companies of widely disparate value did not succumb to the numerous problems that threatened it.[28]

But it is not for the cars that were produced under his direction that Henry Leland has been ranked as one of the three greatest individuals in the history of the American auto industry; auto historians Allan Nevins and Frank Ernest Hill rank Leland with Ford and Durant in importance. Leland's importance lies rather in the manner in which his cars were manufactured. When he took over as general manager of Cadillac he reportedly issued an order "that emery cloth and file should never be used in the assembly room of the Cadillac." The same precise, high-quality standards that Leland had learned in New England and which he had insisted on for the work done by Leland & Faulconer were now to be applied throughout the Cadillac operations. The most dramatic demonstration of the complete interchangeability of parts that resulted occurred on February 29, 1908, at the Brooklands race track near London, England. At the suggestion of Frederick S. Bennett, Cadillac agent in England, the Royal Automobile Club sponsored a Standardization Test for automobiles. Any manufacturer was free to enter, although Cadillac was the only one to do so. Three Cadillac "one-lungers" were supplied by Bennett out of the stock he had on hand. Under the supervision of observers appointed by the club, the three operable cars were completely disassembled, and the parts from the three cars mixed up. Then the observers removed eighty-nine parts, which Bennett replaced with identical parts he had in stock. The three cars were reassembled by workmen who could use no tools or other equipment except a wrench, hammer, screw driver, and pliers. The three cars they put together had a peculiar, patchwork appearance, since the original vehicles had had three different color combinations. But the three re-assembled cars worked perfectly and still worked perfectly after each had been driven for five hundred miles around the track. As a result, in February 1909, Cadillac was awarded the Dewar Trophy, regarded at the time as the highest award given in the auto industry, "in recognition of the most noteworthy performance of the year." Cadillac's reputation for excellence was now permanently established. In the process of achieving this reputation, it had also dealt a telling blow against those in England, elsewhere in Europe, and many still in the United States who continued to believe in the inferiority of the American-made car in comparison with those made in Europe.[29]

Alfred P. Sloan, Jr., once declared that nothing did more to establish the reputation of American cars than the Cadillac's perfect score in the Brooklands test. Sloan, however, did not have to wait until 1908 to have Leland's perfectionism brought home to him. Sometime after Leland took charge at Cadillac, Sloan received a call from his partner in the Hyatt Roller Bearing Company, Peter Steenstrup, asking Sloan to rush out to Detroit. "Old Leland's on the warpath," Steenstrup reported. "I'm no mechanic. I'm a salesman. We're not speaking the same language." When Sloan appeared in Leland's office, the bearded old Yankee showed him a collection of Hyatt bearings that were used in Weston-Mott axles purchased for the Cadillac. "Your Mr. Steenstrup told me these bearings would be accurate, one like another, to within one thousandth of an inch. But look here!" Leland said angrily as he fingered the bearings. "There is nothing like that uniformity." Sloan started to explain the great pressures that Hyatt, like all auto parts manufacturers, were under at this time from so many customers, but Leland cut him off. "You must grind your bearings. Even though you make thousands, the first and the last should be precisely alike." As the discussion progressed, Sloan declared, "A genuine conception of what mass production should mean really grew in me." He returned to the Hyatt plant in the east, "determined to be as fanatical as [Leland] in obtaining precision in our work."[30]

Eugene Lewis of the Timken Company told of a similar occasion when, while he was seated outside Leland's office waiting to see him, he heard Leland lecture a manufacturer of brass grease-cups about the inadequacies of his product. Leland intended to do no more business with the firm. At the conclusion of the meeting, the easterner got up and said, according to Lewis's recollection,

> Mr. Leland, I have been in this business for fifteen years. We thought we had it down pat. This trip has been worth thousands of dollars to me, personally, and to my company. I am going back home and tear that place apart, and we are going to make grease cups the Cadillac Company can use, and when we do, I am coming down, myself, and get an order.[31]

Ever on the lookout for ways of improving still more the accuracy of his company's work, Leland in 1907 or 1908 imported, at a cost of more than $1500, the first set of "Jo blocks" brought into the United States. These were a series of steel blocks developed by Carl Edvard Johansson of Sweden in 1896, the dimensions of which he was able to make "absolutely accurate" to millionths of an inch. These blocks, kept in velvet-lined boxes, became the universally accepted standard by which all gauges and other measuring devices were regularly checked. News of the receipt in America of these Jo blocks, as they came to be called, brought hundreds of engineers, mechanics, and others, some of them from distant locations, to the Cadillac plant to inspect this new standard of accuracy. Leland's set, which came to be preserved in a vault at the Cadillac plant, was the first of many that Johansson would make for the auto industry. The demand became so great by 1911 that he left his job with the Swedish armament works to devote his full time to the commercial production of his blocks.[32]

Thus in numerous ways did Henry Leland transfer his own, almost fanatical concern for precision in manufacturing work to the auto industry as a whole. So widespread was the resulting reputation of Leland's company for excellence, that by 1909 one trade journal declared that "Cadillac has been probably the most notable incubator of motor car genius of all the Detroit factories. Time and again other firms have hired away star members of the Cadillac staff but there has been always some one to fill the vacant place." To what extent Leland may have contributed to the desire of some of these employees to leave Cadillac is another question. It is certain, however, that not everyone in Detroit shared the views of Fred M. Zeder (who later became head of engineering for Chrysler) who said of Henry Leland: "He was a prince. We called him the Grand Old Man of Detroit. He was indefatigable and so patient in his directing and guiding wherever needed." On the other hand, Frank Briscoe, while recognizing Leland's "tremendous contribution," declared that Leland was a man "whom I never cared much for personally." Even the authors of the highly favorable biography of Leland note that some called him a "crackpot," an "autocrat," and a "scold," and they are forced to admit that at times he dealt with his associates in a rather high-handed fashion, particularly in the more complex business situations that arose when he and Cadillac became a part of General Motors. Ultimately, this attitude on Leland's part may have been the cause of his departure, and that of his son, from Cadillac and General Motors in 1917. In an interview in 1971, Charles S. Mott, a member of G. M.'s board of directors at the time, denied that Henry Leland had actually resigned, as has always been stated. "He didn't resign, he was fired!" Mott asserted, declaring that he himself was present at the board meeting when the action was taken. The action had resulted, according to Mott, from what the directors considered to be Leland's insubordinate conduct.[33]

Leland's attitude toward his workers was definitely a carryover of an older view of the proper relationship between employer and employee. Leland paid his workers well and saw that they were provided with comforts in the factory equal or superior to those offered in other plants at that time, but, although he vigorously denied that he was opposed to labor unions, after a brief strike at Leland & Faulconer, Leland took a leading role in the formation of the Employers' Association of Detroit in 1902. The association fought successfully to preserve and greatly strengthen Detroit's reputation as an open-shop city. Alanson Brush declared that Leland more than once told him: "Labor is a commodity, like any other commodity, to be bought in the cheapest market. In order to achieve this, we need, and should have at all times, a *pool of unemployment.*"[34]

It was Brush's distaste for what he regarded as Leland's reactionary economic ideas that was one cause of the friction that developed between them and caused the brightest star of Leland's staff to leave his position as chief engineer at Cadillac in 1905 after he had finished designing the first four-cylinder Cadillac. Leland, Mrs. Brush declares, had never been easy to get along with, but he seemed to become more difficult after he took over the management of Cadillac. He regarded Brush as his protégé, and although he recognized Brush's great talents, he expected Brush to be respectful toward him at all times. Mrs. Brush writes that Brush, on the other hand, resented Leland's efforts to tell him what to do, how, and when. When Brush finally quit his $10,000-a-year position with Cadillac, a dispute arose over the continued use by Cadillac of Brush's patents, which, Brush declared, were the basis of all the Cadillacs manufactured in this period. With Charles Strelinger's help, Brush secured the services of a leading Detroit attorney, Alexis C. Angell, and got a settlement whereby Cadillac paid Brush $40,000 for the use of his patents and designs for two years, during which time Brush was not to enter into any business that would put him in competition with Cadillac. At the end of that time Cadillac would have to pay Brush royalties on any patents it still wanted to use. Leland, Brush was told, assured the directors of Cadillac "that inside of those two years he would 'eliminate all the Brush' there was in their cars, thus relieving them from the necessity of paying royalties." But he was not able to do this, and Cadillac paid Brush royalties for the remaining years that some of the patents were in effect.[35]

Alanson Brush, who went on to have what was apparently a very satisfying career as an automotive designer and consultant with the Oakland Motor Car Company, Buick, and Marmon, spent the two years following his departure from Cadillac working on the development of a small car, the Brush Runabout, which Frank Briscoe would manufacture. Alanson Brush is remembered mostly for this car, overshadowing, Mrs. Brush notes with some dismay, the other, more important work that he did. In his leisure time, Brush sometimes chatted and played ball with his neighbors, Henry and Edsel Ford.[36]

* * *

When Henry Ford picked up his tools and left the Henry Ford Company in March 1902, thereby unwittingly paving the way for Henry Leland's entry into the auto industry, he was unperturbed by the fact that for the second time in a little over one year a group of Detroit's wealthiest citizens had lost faith in him. Ford's faith in himself was limitless, and once again he found others who shared that faith. In this case, support came from Tom Cooper, a Detroiter who had become a star on the bicycle racing circuit, winning the Bicycle Championship of America in 1899 and building up a tidy bank account from the purses that he had won.

At the Grosse Pointe auto races in October 1901, Cooper had given an exhibition of a motor-tandem cycle that he had purchased in England. With him on the tandem was another well-known bike racer from Toledo, the twenty-three-year-old Berna (Barney) Eli Oldfield. The Grosse Pointe crowd paid little attention to Cooper and Oldfield on that fall afternoon in 1901, however, and, like them, Cooper found his attention drawn instead to the automobiles and the speeds they were attaining. At this stage in the development of automobiles, a champion bicycle rider could have beaten most if not all of the motor vehicles that afternoon in a short race. Oldfield had done a mile in less than two minutes, and Charles M. Murphy had pedaled a bike in 1899 at a speed of a mile a minute, on a special wooden track, behind a train. But it was obvious to men like Cooper that a mechanically powered vehicle, when perfected, was certain to out-perform any man-powered racer. Prior to the big race of the day, Cooper had ridden with Ford for a couple of warmup laps, to give the nervous driver some advice on track conditions and how they might affect the speeds at which the Ford racing car could be driven. Cooper was apparently so impressed by this new sport that at the end of the day he announced he was retiring from cycling.[37]

Although Tom Cooper may have been thinking of entering the auto racing field, he gave no indication of it at the time. Instead, he dipped into his bank account, reportedly containing as much as $100,000, and invested in, of all things, a coal mine in Colorado, which he and Barney Oldfield now went out to take over. Within a few months the two men grew tired of the hard work involved in this venture and gave it up. Oldfield took Cooper's motorcycle to Salt Lake City, where he was soon setting records on the boards of the Salt Palace's indoor track. Cooper returned to Detroit, where, in March 1902, the Detroit *Free Press* reported that the ex-bike rider was about to launch a new career as an auto racer. By this time or perhaps even earlier, Cooper had discussed his plans with Henry Ford, and the understanding arrived at between them to work together on the construction of racing cars probably precipitated Ford's departure from the Henry Ford Company. In order to be rid of Ford, the company gladly gave him $900 and the uncompleted plans for the racing car that he and Barthel had been working on.[38]

At the beginning of April, *Motor Age* reported that Ford was building a racer that was to be completed by July and would be "much faster" than his first racing car. Shortly, however, Ford's association with Cooper was revealed, together with the news that they were building not one but two racing machines which would be "the highest powered yet produced in this country." In June a reporter found the two men, clad in overalls, busily at work on the vehicles. Cooper, "dirty and greasy from top to toe, but with the same old smile as of yore," declared he was "putting in his time trying to make something." Fourteen years younger than Ford, Cooper was apparently paying the bills for the project, although some who knew Ford in this period thought that other backers may have been involved as well. Cooper may also have contributed ideas to the project, since the wide wheel base and low center of gravity of the two finished racers were features credited to Cooper in the *Free Press* story in March announcing Cooper's intention to enter auto racing.

The cars themselves, however, were apparently built by another of the little crews of skilled workmen that Ford always seems to have been able to round up in these years. Oliver Barthel said he declined an offer from Ford to join him on this latest project in return for ten per cent of anything Ford would make in the future, which, if true, was a decision that Barthel must have regretted in later years when he compared his income with that of Ford the billionaire. In place of Barthel, Ford secured the services of Childe Harold Wills, a tall, strikingly handsome and talented young man. Despite his comparative youth — Wills was born in 1878 — he was a skilled toolmaker, draftsman, machine designer, and, through continued study, would eventually be generally recognized as the country's foremost practical metallurgist. There is evidence that Wills had worked for Ford prior to 1902 in his free time away from his regular job with the Boyer Machine Company. The work on the racing cars, however, began an association between the two men that lasted until 1919, and during much of that time Wills was perhaps the most valued of Ford's executives in the manufacturing end of the business. Much like such other gifted mechanics and designers as the Duryeas, King, Barthel, and Brush, however, Wills was less than successful on his own as an automobile manufacturer, although his Wills-St. Claire car of the 1920's was acclaimed as a technically superb piece of work. With the failure of the company that produced this car, Wills ended up back in a subordinate position, as chief metallurgist for Chrysler from 1933 to his death in 1940.

Joining Ford and Wills was Spider Huff, the most permanent member of what might be called the Ford racing team in the years 1901 to 1904; Huff had already demonstrated his racing proclivities in May of 1900 when he was arrested in Detroit for driving at a speed of twenty miles an hour and was fined two dollars. Another worker was August Degener, and later in the year, after the machines had been completed, John Wandersee, who, like Wills and the rest, would continue for many years with the Ford Motor Company. It is assumed that Tom Cooper paid for the services of the men who built the racers, as well as the rent on the shop building and the cost of tools and materials, although Wills, who, in 1902, signed an agreement to take a percentage of Ford's future profits, may have worked for nothing.[39]

By September 1902 the two racing cars were completed, in plenty of time for the second annual Grosse Pointe races the following month. They were monsters, "the materialization of a nightmare," in the words of one British journalist. They were, according to Leo Levine, historian of the Ford racing exploits, "perhaps the most stripped-down competition cars of all time." Barney Oldfield compared the stark chassis of the vehicles to "bedframes on wheels." Between the outer rails, everything — the four huge cylinders, developing from seventy to one hundred horsepower according to which source you accept, the wiring, the batteries — was completely exposed. In short, each car was, as one automotive magazine put it, "an engine on four wheels, a machine in which brute strength and a disregard for nearly all the essentials of modern [i. e. 1902] automobile construction are embodied." The driver sat in the single seat and steered with a two-handled tiller. Within a few laps, both the driver and the rails along the edge of the track were spattered with oil spewing from the open machinery.

In outward appearance, the two machines were virtually identical. To distinguish them from each other, one was painted red and was called the "Arrow," although later it would also be called the "Red Devil." The other, painted yellow, was named the "999." Its famous designation is said to have originated during an early test run when, as the enormous vehicle thundered around a curve, Tom Cooper yelled to Huff, who was driving, "Better slow down, Spider, or we'll go right through the damned fence!" "Yeah," Huff shouted over the roar of the machine, "she sure goes like '999.'" The reference, of course, was to the record-setting New York Central locomotive that had been exhibited at the Chicago World's Fair nine years earlier. Whatever the truth of this story, the "999" has remained the more famous of the two Ford speedsters, although some of the exploits credited to it should rightfully be accorded to the faster "Arrow."[40]

It appears that at the outset neither machine worked very well. Exactly what happened is, as is so often the case in Ford's career, not clear. From newspaper reports it is known that Ford ("Chauffeur Henry Ford," in the terminology of the day) tested one of the vehicles in mid-September. Although he did a mile in the very fast time of 1:08, it was apparently a frightening experience for a man whose one exposure to racing competition had taught him that he did not have the proper spirit for that sort of thing. "I cannot quite describe the sensation," he recalled later of this September 1902 test run. "Going over Niagara Falls would have been but a pastime after a ride in one of [these two racing cars]." Ford was not planning to drive either car in the auto races to be held at Grosse Pointe on October 25, and Tom Cooper seems to have had some momentary doubts about the wisdom of his taking the tiller. At any event, all accounts agree that, at Cooper's suggestion, a hurry-up call went out to Salt Lake City to Barney Oldfield. It was true that Oldfield had no auto racing experience, and, in fact, that he may never have driven a car before, but Oldfield, Cooper said, was "a man who lived for speed."

When the young Toledo daredevil arrived in Detroit and was shown the two cars, Cooper explained to him: "We didn't build these for looks." "You sure as hell didn't," Oldfield replied. "They're ugly as sin! You sure they'll even run?" Ford assured him that they would, but further tests seem to have uncovered serious problems in the cars' performance. Near the middle of October, as the day of the races drew closer, Ford, who, despite his seemingly unbounded confidence in his own abilities, always seemed to harbor doubts about the merits of the early cars that he built, became disheartened with the racers. Fearing that the machines would turn out to be monumental failures and the resultant bad publicity would ruin his reputation as an automobile builder, he decided to sell his interest in both cars to Tom Cooper for a reported figure of $800. Thus Ford apparently hoped to absolve himself from any responsibility for the future performance of the cars. In addition, in a letter to her brother Milton, who was still harboring visions of managing the racing team of Cooper and Ford, Clara Ford declared they were all lucky to have rid themselves of Cooper. Henry, she said, had caught Cooper "in a number of sneaky tricks," and Clara had never liked Henry or Milton to be around him anyway because, in her opinion, Cooper thought "too much of low down women to suit me."

But then after Ford had sold out to Cooper, the problems with the two racing machines were overcome, and they were launched on a spectacularly successful, record-setting career. Oldfield, who quickly mastered the art of driving the cars, Huff, whose services apparently went with the racers, and Cooper tinkered and experimented with the balky machines at Dayton, where Carl Fisher, future father of the Indianapolis 500, had invited them to take part in a race he was promoting, and at Toledo, where they finally got the "999" to work satisfactorily. The machine was brought by boat to Detroit, and was hauled by horse out to the Grosse Pointe track (considering the noise the racer made it would have been out of the question to drive it to its destination), where Cooper, Huff, and Oldfield had a full day to test the car before the race. It may have been at this time that Oldfield, who was determined he would drive the "999" in the race, said: "Well, this chariot may kill me, but they will say afterward that I was going like hell when she took me over the bank." The next day, on October 25, 1902, in the feature event at Grosse Pointe, thousands of spectators saw Barney Oldfield drive the "999" to an easy victory in the Manufacturers' Challenge Cup five-mile race in the record-setting time of 5:28. Alexander Winton, in his specially built "Bullet" racing car, was the only one of the other three entrants who had a chance of keeping up with Oldfield, but, just as in 1901, mechanical problems developed which forced the Cleveland manufacturer to drop out of the contest after the fourth mile.[41]

The race was important for two reasons. It marked the start of a fabulous new career for Oldfield that would make his name synonymous in the public's mind with fast, reckless driving. (There are doubtless still traffic policemen who begin their interrogation of a motorist with the remark: "Alright, who do you think you are, Barney Oldfield?") The victory of the rough-and-ready, hard-drinking, brawling Oldfield also brought an end to the domination that a wealthy, even aristocratic group such as

William Vanderbilt, Winton, and Foxhall Keene had previously held over the sport of auto racing.[42]

The other important result of Oldfield's victory was to solidify the reputation Henry Ford had gained the previous year as the builder of the fastest cars made. After the race, Ford, who only a few days earlier had been seeking to disown the car, once again sought the glory of being the builder of the winning vehicle. When Winton announced that he was going to build a car that would beat the time of the "999," Ford, ignoring the role that Wills, Huff, Cooper, and the others had played in creating this machine, declared: "If Mr. Winton does lower this time, I'll build another machine that will go him one better if I have to design a cylinder as big as a hogshead. I am bound to keep the record in Detroit." It was, of course, now beneficial to Ford's overall reputation and plans to have his name linked with the "999" and the "Arrow."[43]

In this he was successful, for despite the fact that Tom Cooper owned both cars, the press, in the months ahead as Cooper and Oldfield barnstormed over the country, referred to the cars they drove as "Ford racers." In the spring and summer of 1903, the two men went from one dirt track to another, treating thousands of spectators to exhibitions of daring and undreamed of speeds. Sometimes Oldfield drove the "999" and sometimes the "Red Devil," as the "Arrow" was now being called. The other car was driven by Cooper or, quite frequently, by his stand-in, Harry Cunningham. But the carefully prepared script called for Oldfield always to emerge victorious. Oldfield was the drawing card, especially after he became the first American to break the mile-a-minute barrier in a gasoline-powered car, a feat he accomplished in the "999" at Indianapolis on June 20, 1903. In mid-July, in one of a series of races in Michigan, Oldfield, driving the "Red Devil" this time, defeated Cunningham in the "999" at Jackson, setting what was claimed to be a new mile record on a half-mile track. (Such claims were part of the game. Whether it was true or not, the promoters figured nobody in Jackson, Michigan, would know the difference.) Then tragedy or near-tragedy began to dog the heels of the members of the Cooper-Ford racing team. After Oldfield left the team to become the driver of Alexander Winton's new Bullet No. 2, he beat Cooper, who was driving the "999," on August 30, in two out of three heats at Grosse Pointe. On September 9, in a ten-mile race at Grosse Pointe, Oldfield, who was driving a lighter Winton racing car, blew a tire, skidded, and smashed through the railing, killed a spectator, and landed himself in the hospital. Later that month, the "999" and the "Arrow" were at the fairgrounds in Milwaukee, with Spider Huff scheduled to drive one of the cars and Frank Day, an inexperienced auto racer from Columbus, Ohio, scheduled to drive the other. On the fourth lap of an exhibition warmup run, Day lost control of the "Arrow," which skidded through a railing, demolishing the car and killing Day. The wreckage of the "Arrow" was shipped back to Detroit, where it was rebuilt by Henry Ford. Although Tom Cooper still owned the car, Ford and the ever present Ed Huff used it to set a straightaway speed record of 91.37 miles per hour on the ice of Lake St. Clair on January 12, 1904, a hair-raising event that nearly cost them their lives. Tom Cooper subsequently sold both the "Arrow" and the "999," and went on to become general sales agent with the Matheson company, the automobile firm of Grand Rapids origins. Cooper was killed driving one of their cars on November 19, 1906, in a collision with another car in Central Park, New York. The "Arrow" ultimately vanished, but the "999" was found in a California junkyard around 1911, was restored, and is today one of the more awe-some exhibits at the Henry Ford Museum in Dearborn.[44]

Barney Oldfield is said to have remarked to Henry Ford in later years that they had "made" each other. Ford had made Oldfield famous by building the "999," while Oldfield had "made" Henry Ford through the fame he gained from Oldfield's driving exploits. "But," the great speedster added, "I did much the best job of it." On the other hand, it was on the occasion of Oldfield's first victory in Ford's "999" that the public was informed that Ford, whose "name has hitherto been connected with his fast speed freaks," had virtually completed a "family horse," and, with the backing of "a well-known Detroit business man," expected to have it on the market by the following spring. By the first of January 1903, *Motor Age* reported that Ford was working on a two-cylinder runabout that would sell for $650. Except for the price, this was an accurate descrip-tion of the car that Ford did indeed produce six months later.[45]

One can only guess why, in the fall of 1902, Ford did what William Murphy and the other investors in the Henry Ford Company had wanted him to do the previous winter, when he was much more interested in racing. Some have maintained that Ford had been interested all along in passenger cars and that his venture into racing with Tom Cooper was done only to interest the backers he needed to finance such a car. But of course he already had that kind of support behind him at the beginning of 1902 in the person of Murphy and his gilt-edged friends, and Ford had know-ingly thrown away their support by his insistence on devoting most of his time and that of his men to building a racing car. On the other hand, Ford began getting financial backing for his proposed commercial car by August 1902, about a month before the racing machines were completed and tested, and over two months before either of them had passed their first competitive test. Thus Ford's current racing project could not have been the main reason for the support he got in August, although it does make more understandable Ford's fears a few weeks later that a poor showing by these racers could have quickly cooled his new supporters' en-thusiasm. How relieved Ford must have been, therefore, when the "999" roared across the finish line a lap ahead of the next contestant's car, for this victory would certainly boost Ford's stock in the eyes of one of De-troit's leading coal distributors, Alexander Young Malcomson.

Malcomson, who was two years younger than Ford, having been born in Scotland in 1865, began his business career shortly after he settled

Alexander Y. Malcomson *in 1908, two years after his con-*
nections with the Ford Motor Company had been abruptly
severed. (Note the misspelling of Malcomson's name in the
hand-written inscription. Alfred O. Dunk, to whom the photo
is inscribed, was an almost legendary figure in Detroit who
made a career of acquiring the assets of bankrupt automobile
firms, including Malcomson's Aerocar Company, which folded
in 1907.)
Courtesy Automotive History Collection

in Detroit at the age of fifteen. He soon showed speculative instincts that
one would not expect of the typical thrifty Scot. His son Allan described
his father as one who was "the plunger type, a man who did not hesitate
to take chances." Starting out as a clerk in a grocery store, Malcomson
had gone on to establish a small grocery store of his own. Then in the
early 1890's he had switched over to the fuel business with one small coal
yard and one horse and wagon for deliveries. But he was aggressive and
determined. During a coal strike when most dealers, Malcomson included,
had cleaned out their yards, Malcomson kept his customers and gained
new ones by getting coal from the gas company, which still had surplus
stocks on hand. By 1902, Malcomson had what was probably the largest

coal business in Detroit with several yards around the city, plus a thousand acres of West Virginia coal land, while his customers included thousands of households and many businesses and institutions.[46]

Among Malcomson's customers in the nineties was the Edison Illuminating Company (apparently before the light company's enormous coal needs led it to deal directly with the mines). Here he had his first contact with Henry Ford. Later, when Ford left Edison, he still bought coal from Malcomson for his own home. Malcomson, who had become an automobile enthusiast, and owned a Winton, knew of the work that Ford was doing, of his racing success in 1901, as well as his failures with the Detroit Automobile Company and the Henry Ford Company. Sometime before August 1902 the two men began to talk about Ford's latest ideas for a car, a two-cylinder runabout. Ford was apparently persuasive, and on August 16 Malcomson and Ford went around to the law offices of John W. Anderson and Horace H. Rackham, two attorneys whose main business at this time lay in getting Malcomson's bad accounts paid up. A partnership agreement, dated August 20, was drawn up between Ford and Malcomson for the purpose of developing one Ford model car which could then be used to attract support to a manufacturing corporation, which would supersede the partnership. Ford agreed to turn over to the partnership all his tools, equipment, models, and drawings, and to devote his attention to the completion of the prototype car. He assigned Malcomson a half interest of all his patents, present and future, and agreed to turn over to the partnership one racing car when it was completed. The final provision was apparently not carried out, since both the racers Ford was working on wound up in the hands of Tom Cooper, who had been paying the bills for this work, and whose understanding with Ford preceded the new one with Malcomson by several months. For his part, Malcomson agreed to provide Ford with $500 for his work immediately and additional sums as they were needed, although Ford apparently assured him that the cost of building the model car would be no more than $3000. Both men agreed that in the manufacturing corporation that would be organized later they would hold a majority of the stock, split equally between them. Malcomson would handle the financial side of the business, Ford the manufacturing side.[47]

Although Malcomson had promised money to Ford, he had also borrowed large sums of money from several Detroit banks to expand his coal business, and was fearful that his credit would be threatened if the bankers learned of his new financial commitment. They quite possibly would not have viewed Malcomson's automobile speculation as favorably in 1902 as a short time later when Detroit banks became notorious for their generous treatment of motor car companies. Therefore, Malcomson had Ford's bills paid out of a new account which he opened not in his own name but in that of his trusted office manager, James Couzens. He also gave Couzens the job of keeping track of Ford's expenditures. Couzens, who knew nothing of automobiles, recalled later that when Malcomson took him out in his car and "turned something on the dash board," he thought that his employer, who explained that "he was changing the mixture . . . meant he was mixing water with the gasoline, and I continued to think so for a long time." Couzens was as knowledgeable in the ways of the business world as he was ignorant of the workings of gasoline engines. A native of Chatham, Ontario, where he was born in 1872, Couzens had gotten a job as a car-checker with the Michigan Central in Detroit in 1890, moving up quickly to be boss of the freight office. A man for whom the term "hard-headed businessman" might have been invented, Couzens was also a man of absolute honesty and integrity. Although he was ambitious to get a better job than he had with the railroad, he gave unstinting service to the company rather than currying favors from the businessmen who came to him with their complaints about freight charges. "The way Jim Couzens talked with these patrons on the telephone, giving them holy hell, was just astounding," one of his associates recalled. But it paid off for Couzens. In 1895, Malcomson, who had had numerous run-ins on freight charges with Couzens, hired him, apparently concluding from his experience with Couzens that he would be an employee he could trust. Now in the fall of 1902 a relationship of trust and somewhat grudging admiration began to develop between Couzens and Ford. Oliver Barthel once said: "In order to get along with Mr. Ford, you had to have a little mean streak in your system. You had to be tough and mean. Mr. Ford enjoyed that." And it does seem that most of the men who stuck with Ford for a long period of time fit that description. Couzens did, and his contribution to the success of the Ford Motor Company until 1915 would be more important than that of anyone save Ford himself.[48]

Initially, Malcomson may have thought that he could carry the financial burden of the new enterprise without outside help. Once they began to sell some cars the profits would take care of all expenses very nicely. But as Ford and his men devoted their full attention to putting their ideas into tangible shape (work that further explains Ford's desire to rid himself of any further responsibility for the racing machines in the early part of October), the expenditures rapidly mounted, as Couzens dutifully reported to his employer, until they topped $7000, well over twice the estimate Ford had given to his partner in August. By the end of the year one model had been completed, but Ford, as usual, was not satisfied with it. In 1903 work progressed on a second car, which, probably more through the efforts of the hard-driving Harold Wills than those of Ford, proved successful and became the basis for the Ford Motor Company's first production car. When outlays for an assembly plant, additional workmen, and parts became inevitable before any cars could be produced and income received, Malcomson, who was already strapped for cash, decided he would need assistance from other investors.

In November, therefore, the coal dealer had his attorneys convert the partnership agreement with Ford into a corporation. The company, variously styled Ford & Malcomson and Malcomson & Ford, was to issue

15,000 shares of stock, worth ten dollars each. Ford and Malcomson, between them, would receive 6900 shares as payment for the patents, designs, time, and money they were investing in the firm. In addition, they would pay cash for another 350 shares. The remaining 7750 shares were then to be sold, which, if accomplished, would pump $77,750 into the enterprise. It would be enough to insure success if the public liked the car. The division of stock is rather surprising, since it did not leave Malcomson and Ford with a control of the majority of the shares, as they had agreed earlier.[49]

It soon became apparent that selling stock in the company was not going to be an easy matter. The reasons are not hard to uncover. The automobile industry as a whole was still regarded by most investors, and rightly so, as a risky speculation. The number of companies that failed far exceeded those that succeeded, and even in the case of the companies that had survived, the history of the industry was still too brief to enable anyone to predict with confidence how long any of these companies might continue to make a profit. The local situation in Detroit could also have had an adverse effect on the market for Ford stocks. The competition for the available investment capital in the automotive field was becoming increasingly stiff in the city. In addition to Samuel Smith's group in the Olds Motor Works, and William Murphy's group in the new Cadillac company, a new Detroit auto company, the Northern Manufacturing Company, was financed in 1902. Employing such experienced automobile technicians as Jonathan Maxwell and Charles B. King, Northern was backed by a group of businessmen headed by William T. Barbour and G. B. Gunderson of the Detroit Stove Works. The trade journals predicted great things for the company's car, which was designed by Maxwell and King, and which, because of its remarkably noiseless operation, was dubbed the "Silent Northern." It was also in 1902-1903 that Henry B. Joy was funneling some of his ample funds and those of his friends from such leading Detroit families as the Newberrys, Algers, McMillans, and DuCharmes into the Packard Motor Car Company of Warren, Ohio, in a move that would result in the transfer of the company to Detroit in 1903. The Reliance Motor Car Company and the C. H. Blomstrom Motor Car Company, producer of the Queen automobile, also emerged in Detroit in 1903, as did the Buick Motor Company. The failure of Oliver Barthel's company that same year, despite the backing of the wealthy and highly successful young Detroit attorney, Alex J. Groesbeck, is an example of the difficulties that promoters now faced — many of the likely sources of investment were already committed to other automobile ventures. The major selling point in favor of the new Ford company was probably the association of its name with two victorious racing cars. More than offsetting this asset in the minds of many, however, was the knowledge that some of Detroit's wealthiest and most respected businessmen had been soured by their experiences with Henry Ford.[50]

To get the needed support, Ford reportedly approached his old boss, Alex Dow, on the matter of investing in the new company, but with no more success than he had had in 1899. James Couzens is said to have received so many rebuffs from prospects he had interviewed that he sat down on a curb and almost cried (a reaction so uncharacteristic of Couzens as to make the entire story seem suspect). However, the main job of finding investors fell on Alexander Malcomson, as one would expect, since he was the only one of the three with any independent standing in the business community. As a result, nearly every one of the individuals among the stockholders of the Ford Motor Company when it was incorporated on June 16, 1903, had been brought in through Malcomson. His biggest coup was in getting his elderly uncle, John S. Gray, to invest $10,500 in cash, the largest individual contribution. Gray, the president of the German-American Bank of Detroit, had been one of the principal arrangers of the credit Malcomson needed to finance a large-scale expansion of his coal business that he carried out in the winter of 1902-1903. Thus it was only in desperation that Malcomson went to his uncle again in the spring of 1903 and admitted that he was in need of still more money to finance an entirely unrelated business venture. Gray is said to have blanched when he learned that his nephew was involved with automobiles, but after Malcomson had shown his uncle the work that was already being done on the Ford car, he agreed to put up the money on Malcomson's guarantee to refund the entire amount anytime within a year if Gray was at all dissatisfied.[51]

Investments of $5000 in cash each were made by Albert Strelow and John W. Anderson, one of Malcomson's attorneys who had drawn up the original agreement between Ford and Malcomson. A struggling young graduate of the University of Michigan Law School, Anderson was convinced that here was his opportunity to make a fortune, and said so in a letter he wrote to his father on June 4, 1903. Wendell E. Anderson, a physician in LaCrosse, Wisconsin, was impressed by his son's detailed analysis of how this sure-fire venture would work and loaned him the $5000. Strelow, a Detroit contractor, became involved with Malcomson in December 1902, when a wagon shop that Strelow owned on Mack Avenue was part of some property that Malcomson had leased in connection with his coal business. Strelow agreed to remodel the shop so that it might be used as the Ford assembly plant, and Ford and Malcomson agreed to pay him $75 per month rent for three years. Although Strelow put between $3000 and $4000 into the remodeling, which was completed by April, he decided to invest $5000 more in the stock of the new company, apparently because he was impressed by banker Gray's willingness to back the company.

The other investments were either partly or entirely in the form of personal notes rather than cash. Horace H. Rackham, Anderson's law partner, later declared that he was sold on the soundness of the new company when Malcomson and Couzens showed him the stack of *bona fide* orders that had already been received for the car. Malcomson had begun to advertise early in 1903, long before any cars had been produced, and even before the prototype of the production model was completed. But on the basis of the sales, Rackham used some property he owned as security for a loan of $3500 that he obtained from the Michigan Savings Bank in Detroit, whose president, Rackham declared, strongly urged him not to throw his money away in such an unwise fashion. With this money, plus an additional $1500 in the form of a promissory note, Rackham obtained $5000 in stock.

Still another $5000 stock purchase, with $3000 in cash, was made by Vernon C. Fry, a cousin of Malcomson's who had a dry-goods business. Fry was finally won over by Malcomson after he was taken for a ride in the completed Ford model runabout.

Two of Malcomson's employees were the smallest investors. Charles J. Woodall, a clerk in Malcomson's office, gave his note for $1000, and James Couzens signed for $2500 in Ford stock, although he had only $400 in his own bank account. His mother-in-law agreed, reluctantly, to loan him the money he needed, but at the last moment Couzens decided it would be unwise to take money from his wife's mother. Then, although he and his father were barely on speaking terms, Couzens tried to borrow the money he needed from James Couzens, Sr., a soapmaker in Chatham, Ontario, but was quickly and decisively turned down. Couzens' sister, Rosetta, a Chatham school teacher, gave her brother a hundred dollars out of her savings, much to the disapproval of her father. Malcomson then advanced Couzens $500 of a bonus that Couzens was due to receive for his work, and also agreed to take Couzens' note for the rest of his $2500 investment.

There were three other investors, but none of them put up any cash at the outset for the stock they received. One, Charles H. Bennett, was an executive of the company in nearby Plymouth, Michigan, that manufactured that dream of every young boy in those years, the Daisy Air Rifle. Early in the spring of 1903, Bennett was in the market for an automobile. He was considering an Oldsmobile until one of Malcomson's cousins advised him to take a look at the new car Ford was building. Bennett approached Malcomson, who got Ford to take Bennett for a demonstration ride. Bennett forthwith put himself down for one of the cars when they were produced. His enthusiasm led Malcomson and Ford to try to interest Bennett's company into coming into the automobile venture. In discussions that apparently preceded the sale of stock to other investors, the proposal was made for the air rifle company and Ford and Malcomson to split the stock equally between them. Possibly the Plymouth factory could be used to assemble the car. There was even "some earnest talk" about calling the car "The Daisy." That brought an objection from Henry Ford, however, who insisted that the new automobile be called the Ford. Further obstacles were raised when the Plymouth firm's lawyers advised it that it was prohibited by law from investing in the stock of another company. These and other problems might have been overcome, but then one of the principal officials in the Daisy company vetoed the auto investment idea in favor of investing company funds in land in the South. Charles Bennett, however, went ahead on his own, and was awarded $5000 in stock in return for his note.

The two other $5000 blocks of Ford stock came into the hands of John and Horace Dodge. Although the two brothers had been making parts for the Oldsmobile since 1901, their rise to fame in the auto industry, which has kept their name on one of the more popular and most widely advertised cars of the present day, stems chiefly from their association with the Ford Motor Company in 1903. The brothers are perhaps remembered best for what are usually referred to as their "colorful" personalities. Their off-duty antics — usually attributed to John, the older of the brothers — included smashing all the light bulbs in the chandeliers of their banquet hall in Detroit's Book-Cadillac Hotel; on another occasion the drunken John Dodge pulled a gun and forced a saloon operator to dance while John smashed glasses against the bar mirror, and once John hauled the publisher of the Detroit *Times* out of the latter's house and knocked him unconscious in retaliation for criticisms of Dodge that had appeared in his paper. Joseph Thompson, one of the original dealers to handle the Dodge brothers' own car in 1914, declares that the pioneer automobile men were, as a group, "pretty crude." Men like the Dodges were unprepared for the enormous wealth they suddenly had thrust upon them. It took them some time to adapt their way of living to the kind of behavior that society, no matter how hypocritically, expects of men in their financial position. The Dodges never did quite make the adjustment, but money talks, and in the years after the death of the two brothers in 1920, their widows, both of whom lived to incredible ages, became accepted as the grand old ladies of Detroit society. The sometimes erratic, even scandalous behavior of their children and grandchildren was viewed as an amusing part of the lore of cafe society and, later, the jet set.

John F. Dodge was born in Niles, Michigan, in 1864. His brother, Horace E. Dodge, was born three and a half years later in the same southwestern Michigan town where their father had a blacksmith shop. In the 1880's the family moved across the state to Port Huron where the father opened a machine shop in which he repaired both steam and gasoline marine engines. With the background of the experience they had gained working for their father, the two brothers went to Detroit in the late eighties and became expert mechanics, Horace receiving some two years of training under Henry Leland. In 1894 the brothers, who, despite frequent heated arguments, were inseparable throughout their lives, went across the river to Windsor, Canada, and applied for work at the Dominion Typograph Company. When they were told there was only one vacancy, the older brother replied: "We're brothers and we always work together; if you haven't got room for two of us, neither will start. That's that!" Both were hired, and John was soon promoted to the position of superintendent of the plant. Later in the decade, while still in Windsor, John and Horace Dodge designed a bicycle which they then were able to manufacture with some success for two years, before selling the business to a Canadian bicycle manufacturer. With the money they realized from the sale, the brothers returned to Detroit, and at the beginning of the new century opened up a small machine shop. The business blossomed when they began making engines and transmissions for the Olds Motor Works in 1901.

On February 28, 1903, the Dodges, who had known Ford for some time, signed a contract to supply Ford and Malcomson with 650 chassis, including engines, transmissions, and axles to meet the new company's needs for the first year. They were to be paid $162,500, or $250 for each chassis. Ford and Malcomson agreed to pay the Dodges $10,000, in two equal installments, by April 15, to repay the brothers for the expenses involved in preparing the shop to produce the chassis, and another $5000 when the first chassis were delivered to the Mack Avenue assembly plant. After that, payments would be met as cash flowed in from the sales of cars. The contract, although an advantageous one, was something of a gamble for the Dodges, when safer contracts could be negotiated with the established Olds company. However, they hoped they would make more money with Ford in the long run — and they were quite right. However, later in the spring of 1903 the Dodges were not so sure of the wisdom of their decision. With the contracts that had been made with the C. R. Wilson Body Company of Detroit for the wooden bodies, the Hartford Rubber Company for the tires, and the Prudden Company of Lansing for wheels, the total financial obligations of the Ford-Malcomson company had mounted to a reported figure of $350,000, bills that were to be paid off with the profits from the hoped-for quick sale of the cars that were to be produced later in the summer. The Dodges, however, insisted upon the payment of the money owed to them at the times and in the amounts specified in their contract. John Gray's investment came in time to bail Malcomson out of the crisis. Further demands from the Dodges were then muted by an arrangement whereby they were awarded $10,000 in Ford stock, for which the brothers wrote off $7000 they had spent for materials needed to fill the Ford contract, and gave their note for the remaining $3000. Thus by April 15, the Dodges had received $10,000 in cash from the Ford contract and now they received, with no immediate outlay of cash on their part, $10,000 in stock that would bring them many millions of dollars in the next sixteen years. And yet John Dodge later grumbled that it was not a very good bargain. He maintained that he and his brother had had to invest far more than $10,000 of their own money to prepare for the Ford contract. "We were not as wise then as we perhaps should have been," he said in 1917.[52]

Finally, in June, the various stockholders who had been recruited were assembled, and, at Malcomson's suggestion, the name selected for the new company was the Ford Motor Company. Incorporation papers were filed in Lansing on June 16, 1903. Two days later the first stockholders' meeting was held in the Russel House, a Detroit hotel. The assets of the Ford-Malcomson association were officially transferred to the Ford Motor Company with an assessed valuation of $51,000, a highly inflated figure, but one which still was lower than the $69,000 figure that John Anderson claimed was originally sought by Ford and Malcomson. The latter were awarded $51,000 in stock, which they divided equally between themselves. Since only $100,000 of the company's total capitalization was issued at this time, the remaining $50,000 in stock being held back for future use, the two partners together controlled a majority of the Ford stock, as they had agreed the preceding August. Ford and Malcomson were also elected to the board of directors along with Anderson, John Gray, and John Dodge. Malcomson did not get the executive positions in the company that he had expected and which normally would have gone to the man whose efforts, entailing the expenditure of much money and time on his part, had been principally responsible for bringing about the organization of the company. Instead, for the post of president, which Malcomson apparently had thought he would receive, the stockholders chose John Gray, whose 105 shares of stock placed him next in stockholdings to Ford and Malcomson, each of whom had 255 shares. However, it was Gray's prestige as the head of a bank that apparently caused the other stockholders to vote for him. Ford, who never seems to have been considered for the top position, was elected vice-president and general manager in charge of production. Malcomson was elected treasurer, but James Couzens was elected secretary and business manager, again a responsibility that Malcomson had wanted to assume. His uncle, John Gray, however, insisted Malcomson give his undivided attention to running his coal business in order to make sure that the fuel company's numerous bank loans were repaid. Malcomson protested that Couzens was a man of great ability who could run the coal business very capably, leaving Malcomson free to handle the sales and financial side of the Ford Motor Company. John Gray ended the discussion by declaring: "If Couzens is so good, then you can send him to the automobile business. He can watch that for you."[53]

At the outset, the prospects for the Ford Motor Company could not have been called promising. Despite the $100,000 represented by the stock issued, only $28,000 in cash was immediately available. This compared favorably with the paid-in cash figures for the earlier Detroit Automobile and Henry Ford companies, but the crucial difference lay in the fact that in the Ford Motor Company there was no one, not even excepting John Gray, with the kind of standing in the community and the personal fortune that men like William Maybury, Frank Hecker, William McMillan, and William Murphy had. There was no one in the new company to keep the creditors from the factory door. As a group, the investors in the new Ford company were of a considerably lower class, both financially and socially. They could ill-afford even the small amounts of money they had scraped together or which they had obligated themselves to pay to the enterprise. There was little or no likelihood that any one of them would further jeopardize their financial standing by putting more money into the company. As it turned out, however, this fact was probably what saved the Ford Motor Company. The officers, knowing there were no more funds they could draw upon, fought all the harder to keep the company afloat until money from car payments began to flow into the treasury later in the summer.

Ads for the new Detroit-made automobile began appearing in such national, general-circulation magazines as *Harper's Weekly* and *Leslie's Weekly* as early as the end of June. The copy obviously had gone in before the Ford Motor Company had actually been organized. Initially called the Fordmobile, the car, as the name itself suggests, was another attempt to cash in on the widespread popularity of runabouts such as the locally produced Oldsmobile. In its price of $750 for the runabout model, however, Ford was seeking to be competitive with the Cadillac runabout which had been on the market for several months. Both the Ford and the Cadillac were somewhat heavier cars than the Oldsmobile, whose base price was a hundred dollars less than that of the two new 1903 runabout models. What set the Ford apart from the other runabouts, however, was that for his $750 the buyer got a two-cylinder engine, with somewhat greater power and speed than competing models which used the one-cylinder engine. Significantly, however, the Ford ads emphasized not the two-passenger runabout but the more expensive, $850 version of exactly the same car which, by adding a tonneau or extra seat at the rear, could seat four. By stretching a point, Ford was able to call this a "light touring car." Like Fred Smith of the Olds company and, a little later perhaps, Ransom Olds himself, Ford and his associates recognized that the public was increasingly going to demand something better than the little runabout. For driving comfort they wanted a heavier car and also a car that would carry more than two people. The Ford Model A (as the 1903 car was soon most commonly referred to) with detachable tonneau was the first step toward meeting that demand. In the next five years, instead of following the lead of the Olds Motor Works, Cadillac, and Reo, by providing the public with the kind of car it wanted at the expense of the runabout's cheap price, Ford sought to satisfy the public without at the same time sacrificing the advantages of the runabout's comparatively inexpensive cost.[54]

By the first part of July horse-drawn hayracks began to deliver the chassis from the Dodge plant to the little Mack Avenue shop. Crews of two or three men worked on groups of four chassis, attaching the wheels, the light wooden bodies, and the fenders, testing the car, then painting it, and moving on to another group. One worker later recalled: "We would work our hearts out to get out fifteen a day." (It is interesting to observe that Ford started out with an assembling method identical to that which Saab, the Swedish automaker [full name: Svenska Aeroplan A B], began to adopt in 1969 for certain assembling operations, and which has been hailed as a pioneering effort to eliminate the tedium and boredom associated with the kind of assembly-line operations for which Ford subsequently became so famous.)

On July 23, the first completed Ford Model A's were taken to the freight station, where Secretary Couzens, Vice-president Ford, and Chief Engineer Wills all helped in crating and loading the cars and seeing them off to fill orders in Indianapolis, Minneapolis, and St. Paul.

Although ads for the Model A bragged that it was "positively the most perfect machine on the market, . . . The Latest and Best, . . . Boss of the Road," it had its faults, as early owners soon discovered. When John Anderson's father came to town, Couzens, who knew enough about automobiles now to be able to drive one, took Dr. Anderson to the railroad station. On the way, the Model A stalled on a small hill, and after repeated unsuccessful efforts to get up the hill, Couzens had to back down and take a detour on more level ground. The doctor may have had doubts about his wisdom in loaning his son money to invest in the manufacture of such a vehicle. More serious, however, were the doubts that Henry Ford now felt about the car, doubts that led him to insist more than once in the early months of the company's history that shipments be halted until the defects in the car were corrected. A recurrence of the constant production delays that had proved fatal to Ford's earlier automobile ventures was avoided only by the even more determined insistence of James Couzens that the cars be shipped, defects and all, to save the company from bankruptcy. At one point in the first half of July, before any money from the sale of cars had come in, the company's bank balance was down to a mere $223.65. With a payroll to be met and suppliers to be paid, the company could not have long survived if there had been any delay in the shipment and sale of cars. As money from sight drafts that accompanied each shipment began to flow in, along with advance payments for cars that had been ordered, the situation quickly changed. By August 20, the company had a reasonably healthy balance of $23,060.67.[55]

As the Ford Model A began to emerge from the factory in what were for the anxious stockholders gratifying numbers (215 between July 23 and September 30, 1903), Couzens worked at signing up dealers to sell the cars. Fred Lockwood, who had been selling Oldsmobiles in Jackson, Michigan, came to Detroit on August 17, and drove one of the new Fords back to Jackson. He made the eighty-mile trip in the good time of five hours and fifteen minutes. On a stretch of good road between Ypsilanti and Ann Arbor, Lockwood reported that he easily achieved a speed of thirty miles an hour. The car, which Lockwood was now interested in selling in the Jackson area, was reported by the local paper to be "all that could be desired." Residents of southwestern Michigan who wanted to buy the car purchased it at first directly from the Mack Avenue assembly plant, as Lockwood had done. Later, in March 1904, the company opened a handsome new sales building on Jefferson Avenue, which in these early years was Detroit's first "automobile row." Outside of Michigan, Ford's agent in the crucial New York City market was the Duerr-

Ward Company, but in 1904 Couzens switched to the department store magnate, John Wanamaker, who also handled Ford sales in Philadelphia through his department store in that city. Agents were also appointed to handle sales in Chicago, Los Angeles, and, in fact, nearly all the larger cities. One shipment was sent off to Honolulu by the fall of 1903, and in October a New York agent was signed up to handle the export business.[56]

By November 21, 1903, the profits from sales led the directors to vote the stockholders dividends totalling $10,000. In January 1904, they distributed another $20,000, and on the anniversary of the company's incorporation, June 16, 1904, another $68,000, making a total of $98,000 in dividends in one year on a total capitalization of $100,000. Couzens, the Dodge brothers, and the others who had given their notes for part or all of the stock they had received were able to pay off their indebtedness from their dividends alone. Ford, who, as vice-president and general manager, was paid a salary of $3600 a year, received in addition $24,990 in dividends on stock for which he had to pay not one cent. Despite the large dividends, there was still ample money left in the company's treasury to pay for various improvements. At first there was an addition to the Mack Avenue plant, and then, in 1904, the company purchased land at Piquette and Beaubien avenues in Detroit for the construction of a new assembly plant. When the plant was occupied by early 1905, it provided ten times the space that had been available in the rented shop on Mack Avenue.[57]

The Ford, however, was a classic example of the assembled car. The company itself manufactured literally nothing, and its payroll was therefore very small. On May 9, 1904, as the company was in the middle of the busiest part of the year for the auto industry, the state factory inspector found the complete work force consisted of thirty-one people. Yet this handful of workmen established a new record that month, assembling and testing 299 cars. The real impact of Ford's success, in terms of the jobs that it created, was felt by the parts manufacturers. The Dodge brothers continued for a decade to turn out a very large share of the "vital parts," as they correctly put it, that went into the Ford. The Ford Motor Company in these early years contrasted sharply with other leading automakers. The Olds Motor Works, Buick, Cadillac, Reo, and Packard were increasingly manufacturers as well as assemblers, with a resultant great increase in the number of their employees.[58]

During the Ford Motor Company's first fifteen months, some 1700 cars were produced. Less than 600 of these appeared in 1903, a third of the output of the comparable Cadillac runabout for that same year. Cadillac, of course, had had a five-month jump on Ford and had had its cars ready for the peak buying period in May and June. In 1904, Ford introduced two new two-cylinder cars. The Model C replaced the Model A, with the price increased to $800 for the straight runabout and $900 for the runabout with detachable tonneau; the Model F, a touring car, was priced at a thousand dollars. In addition, a bigger four-cylinder Model B touring car sold for twice the price of the Model F. In the next three years, Ford continued on down through the alphabet, with the earlier production models being replaced by Models K, N, R, and S. These frequent model changes have been interpreted by some as further evidence of Henry Ford's inability in the early years of his automotive career to settle on one car, but it is more accurate to point out that these were transitional years in the industry. Most manufacturers were groping about to find the model or models that would satisfy the changing moods of the buying public. A list published in November 1907, for example, showed Ford with three different models on the market at that time, but it also showed Buick and Olds with five models each, and Cadillac with seven. To be sure, most of this diversity represented only different bodies on two or three basic cars that Buick, Cadillac, and the Olds Motor Works were producing, but by the same token, Ford's Models N, R, and S in 1907 were simply variations of the same four-cylinder, twenty-horsepower unit. If Henry Ford was, as his critics charge, finding it hard to make up his mind in these years, then so were Henry Leland, William Durant, Fred Smith, and many another automaker.[59]

During these years, the Ford Motor Company was beset by two major problems, neither of which was unique to that firm. An internal problem, which was solved more easily than the other, an external situation, was basically a power struggle between Alexander Malcomson and Henry Ford. The struggle probably originated with the disappointment that Malcomson felt at the failure of his fellow stockholders to give him the positions in the company that he felt he deserved. When it became clear that Couzens was not going to be simply a front man for Malcomson in the Ford organization, but that he would devote himself to serving the best interests of the company rather than those of his former employer, Malcomson sought to have Couzens removed so that he might take Couzens' place as business manager. But only John Anderson, among the other four directors, would support Malcomson's motion.

In another move, Malcomson sought to shift the emphasis in the company away from the inexpensive models to bigger, more costly cars. In this, Malcomson had support from what was happening in the industry. The trend away from the cheap car, away from runabouts such as the curved-dash Oldsmobile, was becoming clearly evident by 1905 as more and more expensive cars came on the market. In part the change was related to the higher profits that the more expensive cars promised, but more fundamentally the change resulted from the growing awareness that a bigger, more powerful car was essential to the motorist who wished to make more use of his vehicle than merely as a means of getting around town. Despite Ford's shifts on details, he rather consistently held to the principle that the company should concentrate on the production of low-priced cars. But Malcomson had enough support to secure the production first of the Model B, and then of the six-cylinder Model K, which sold for $2800. Neither car was a success. The failure of the Model K, which the company had to force on its reluctant dealers, was matched in the company's history only by that of the celebrated Edsel of a much later period.

There is an obvious parallel between the alleged difference of opinion between Ransom Olds and Fred Smith over the issue of cheap or expensive models and the fight between Ford and Malcomson over the kind of car their company should produce. There is a more critical parallel in that just as the real issue in the Olds Motor Works had been over who would have the final say in company affairs, so too the basic argument in the board meetings of the Ford company was the question of who would control the company. Ford was joined by Couzens in a fight first to reduce Malcomson's influence in company affairs and then finally in 1905 in a determination to rid the company of him entirely. In these efforts, they gained two powerful allies: the outspoken John Dodge, who, although he too supported the idea of an expensive car, had a personal dislike for Malcomson; and, surprisingly, Malcomson's uncle, John Gray, who, although he seems to have been personally fond of his nephew, still felt that Malcomson made a better coal dealer than automobile manufacturer. Ford, Dodge, and Gray constituted a majority of the board of directors. Including the stockholdings of James Couzens and Horace Dodge, who would undoubtedly support his brother, the Ford forces, in any showdown battle with Malcomson in a meeting of the stockholders, would start out controlling almost half of the stock that could be voted. Malcomson then lost whatever chance he had by announcing the formation late in 1905 of the Aerocar Company, a new motor car manufacturer which he controlled and which would produce air-cooled touring cars. For one man to have major interests in more than one automobile was not unheard of, but, coming at the time it did, Malcomson's action aroused general resentment among the Ford stockholders, who felt that Malcomson would be competing with their company. At almost the same time, Ford and some of his associates organized a separate Ford Manufacturing Company, which would make the parts for the popular new Ford low-price Model N and in the process could be used to siphon off most of the Ford Motor Company's profits. Naturally, Malcomson was not invited to join in the new venture. Faced by the prospect of a sharp decline in the value of his Ford Motor stock, Malcomson threw in the towel a few months later, selling his 255 Ford shares to Henry Ford on July 12, 1906, for $175,000. If he had held on to the stock until 1919, when Ford bought out all the remaining stockholders in the company, Malcomson would have made, through dividends and the selling price in 1919, about $100,000,000. To make matters worse, Malcomson's Aerocar Company was a failure, going under in 1907. He continued to have an interest in the coal business until his death in 1923, but in the Motor City being an important man in the fuel industry was, by then, of little consequence. When John Gunther came to Detroit to do research for *Inside U. S. A.,* which was published in 1947, he noticed Malcomson's name among the list of original Ford stockholders. He made some inquiries and reported his findings: "It seems that he was a coal dealer, and Couzens was a clerk in his office. Ford must, of course, have bought him out many years ago. . . . I was unable to find anybody in Detroit who knew further about Mr. Malcomson."[60]

Ford's control of his company was further solidified by other events in 1906-1907. In July 1906 John Gray died, and Ford was elected to his position as president; John Dodge moved up to the post of vice-president. By September 1907 the three stockholders who had supported Malcomson, Charles Woodall, Charles Bennett, and Vernon Fry, had all sold their stock, Woodall and Fry selling their shares to Ford, while Bennett sold thirty-five shares to Couzens and fifteen to Ford. (A by-law, adopted by the stockholders in 1903, forbidding them to sell to an outsider, foiled an attempt by Malcomson to make a comeback in 1907 by purchasing the shares of Fry and Bennett.) Albert Strelow also sold his stock in this period, disposing of his fifty shares to Couzens for $25,000 and forthwith losing it in a gold-mining venture in Canada. A few years later, Strelow was reportedly back at the Ford plant applying for a job on the line.[61]

As a result of the internal upheaval in the Ford ranks in 1905-1907, Henry Ford gained virtually complete control of the Ford Motor Company. Since that time, no matter how much one argues that someone else in the company was responsible for this or that development, the final decision has always rested with a Ford, and they have rarely hesitated in exerting that authority.

With Malcomson removed from the scene, Henry Ford was free to pursue his plans to build what he referred to as a "universal car," an inexpensive car that would be light in weight, yet durable, simple to repair, and simple to drive anywhere, regardless of road conditions. Under his watchful supervision, a number of staff men were assigned to design a vehicle that would fulfill these requirements. Ford decided his goal had been fulfilled when the immortal Model T first appeared late in 1908. But although the end of the serious internal divisions freed Ford to pursue the policies that he wanted, a bothersome external problem still required attention — the prolonged lawsuit filed against Ford by the owners of the Selden Patent.

This famous case has been the subject of one entire book, William Greenleaf's *Monopoly on Wheels,* and has been dealt with extensively not only in biographies of Henry Ford but in many other books on the automobile, since the case and the Selden Patent went well beyond the Ford Motor Company in the impact that it is alleged to have had on the development of the American automobile industry. In brief, it all started when George Baldwin Selden, a lawyer in Rochester, New York, applied in 1879 for a patent on a road vehicle powered by an internal combustion engine. The wording used by Selden to describe the vehicle was broad enough so that it could, and would, be said to cover any gasoline-powered motor vehicle. Selden, a man highly talented in the field of mechanics who had already patented several inventions, had not constructed a model at the time he made his application, but subsequent investigations conducted a quarter of a century later during the course of the Selden Patent litigation indicated that had Selden built a vehicle in 1879 according to the specifications he had set down, the vehicle would have been operable, although scarcely an outstanding success by later standards.[62]

Selden used his knowledge of patent law to keep his application from being acted upon until an increased awareness of the possibilities that lay in such a horseless carriage made it opportune to have the patent awarded. Since the life of a patent is only seventeen years, an inventor can achieve the maximum benefits only if there is considerable interest in manufacturing and buying his invention from the moment that his exclusive rights as a patent holder commence. Finally, in 1895, after keeping his application pending for over sixteen years, a record for any major patent, the publicity generated by the Chicago *Times-Herald* race, along with the work of such pioneers as the Duryeas and Haynes, apparently convinced Selden that the appropriate time had arrived. He therefore allowed his application to go through the final processing, and on November 5, 1895, Selden was granted patent No. 549,160.

Although the commissioner of patents at the time singled out Selden's patent as "the pioneer invention in the application of the compression gas engine to road or horseless carriage use," Selden's work was not taken very seriously by automobile pioneers. Charles Duryea prophetically dismissed the patent as one that applied only to vehicles using the two-cycle Brayton engine, which was the type referred to by Selden in his description of his vehicle. Although Selden attempted to make the principles embodied in his vehicle apply to vehicles using other types of gasoline engines, few of the early pioneers respected his claim. Alexander Winton took out an option on a license to manufacture automobiles under the Selden patent, but he allowed the option to expire after apparently concluding that the patent would not apply to the kind of automobiles he was going to produce. No one else showed any interest in being licensed, and Selden lacked the time and the resources needed to enforce his patent. Late in 1899, four years into the life of the patent, with nothing to show for it as yet, George Selden was glad to assign exclusive rights to the Electric Vehicle Company for the sum of $10,000 and a fifth of all royalties collected under the patent.

The Electric Vehicle Company was a New Jersey corporation that had originated with a company formed in 1896 by Henry G. Morris and Pedro G. Salom of Philadelphia, the operators of one of the electric carriages that had competed unsuccessfully in the Chicago *Times-Herald* race the year before. It was taken over in 1899 by a New York syndicate headed by William C. Whitney, a prominent financier and Democrat. Whitney's group had plans to establish a nation-wide network of electric taxicabs and delivery vans, and had acquired control of the motor carriage division of Colonel Albert Pope's great Hartford, Connecticut, bicycle manufacturing company. These plans did not work out, and in 1900, therefore, beset by financial difficulties, the Electric Vehicle Company sought to recoup its losses through its control of the Selden patent and the royalties it could extract from builders of gasoline automobiles. Notices were sent to the leading manufacturers in June 1900 warning them that they were guilty of infringement and would be subject to legal action by the holders of the patent unless they agreed to take out a license and pay royalties. Two suits were filed in mid-July, the most important of which was an action against the Winton Motor Carriage Company of Cleveland, the leading maker of gasoline automobiles in the country.

The Winton company, believing as strongly as Alexander Winton had in 1896 that Selden's patent was invalid, determined to contest the suit. Support for the company's stand came from some twenty other manufacturers of gasoline automobiles and engines who organized the Hydrocarbon Motor-Vehicle Manufacturers' Association, with Elmer Apperson of Kokomo, Indiana, as the president. Winton and the association first tried to get the case dismissed on the grounds that the patent was invalid since it contained nothing novel. In November 1900, however, the federal district court refused this request. This meant that hearings must be held to determine the merits of the infringement charges. Such proceedings were costly, and despite a general belief among the gasoline automobile manufacturers that the Selden patent did not apply to them, there was always the possibility that the courts would not share this opinion. The Electric Vehicle Company, with its impressive Wall Street connections and high-powered legal talent, was undoubtedly hoping that the less affluent young gasoline automobile companies would surrender to avoid a fight. Failing in this, the company then hoped that by winning its case against the most important of these companies, all the others would be forced to submit to paying royalties.

By the early part of 1902, as the proceedings in the Winton case dragged on, with no end in sight, increasing apprehension spread among gasoline car manufacturers. In 1901, the Selden forces had won widely publicized victories over two small eastern automobile companies that were too weak to contest the charges of infringement that were brought against them. The Hydro-Carbon Motor-Vehicle Manufacturers' Association, which had raised money to aid in the Winton defense, began to disintegrate, and the entire burden of the defense now fell upon Winton. At this time, in one of the earliest indications that the power center in the auto industry was shifting to Detroit, Frederic Smith of the Olds Motor Works took the leadership in negotiations with the Electric Vehicle Company for an arrangement that would be satisfactory to both sides and would be less costly than fighting the matter through to a conclusion in the courts. On May 17, 1902, Smith reported to Ransom Olds on a trip he had just made to New York "to see what sort of a deal we could get offered by the Electric Vehicle Co. & also what Winton & his attorney would do in the same matter of the Shelden [sic] patent." Winton's attorney, he had learned, was willing to advise his client to drop his defense, thereby agreeing to the validity of the patent, on several conditions: if the Electric Vehicle Company would make some agreement that would perhaps reimburse Winton for the $15,000 or $16,000 he had paid out already to defend himself from the suit; and if a reasonable license fee could be established that would not be too onerous for Winton to pay. For his part, George H. Day, the able president of the Electric Vehicle Company, indicated to Smith a willingness to meet the Olds company halfway, suggesting what Smith referred to as a "trifling" royalty of five per cent on gross sales. "If we can engineer the deal our own way we can share to a good big extent in the income from royalties paid in & make the thing healthy and lucrative," Smith told Olds. This was apparently the origin of the scheme that was ultimately arranged whereby in return for recognizing the Selden patent, companies such as the Olds Motor Works would have a portion of fees they paid kicked back to an association of such licensed manufacturers. Nothing definite could be settled at the preliminary talks in May, but Smith saw this plan as "the safety valve so we can come in out of the wet" if the Winton suit continued and the Selden forces won out.

Shortly afterwards, apparently, Fred Smith went to Cleveland to talk with the "Winton crowd," whom, he discovered, were initially opposed to any deal. Alexander Winton himself, Smith reported, "is hot foot (or blows off that way) to wipe the Electric Vehicle Co. of [sic] the globe." Smith, however, was more than ever in favor of a compromise settlement. His view was that if they waited for the matter to be settled in court and the Electric Vehicle Company won its case, the Olds Motor Works, to avoid another infringement suit, would have to pay royalties on the cars that it had produced earlier, possibly as much as $50,000, Smith estimated. The company would also have a heavy burden of fees imposed on it for its future production. To avoid this, Smith said, "I think we can handle it so we shall have to pay a nominal sum only for license and be co-owners of this patent . . . and can pretty near dictate terms for small fry like Spaulding, Jeffrey, Barbour [referring, no doubt, to Will Barbour of the new Northern company] and the rest." Thus, in addition to his original idea of devising a means of sharing the Selden royalty fees, Smith hoped to use this power as a means of establishing controls over who would be allowed into the elite circle of licensed auto manufacturers. Looking at this from the best possible angle, Smith's plan would be a means of regulating the new industry and eliminating the fly-by-night outfits that were giving the auto industry a bad name because of their shoddy products. Such firms, presumably, would not be licensed and would probably not be strong enough to contest infringement proceedings if they continued to manufacture gasoline cars without a license. On the other hand, Smith's proposal also raised the possibility that a handful of established manufacturers might use their power to eliminate perfectly reputable manufacturers who might offer a competitive threat to one or more of the licensed companies.[63]

Whether Smith first proposed these ideas, or whether they came from another source, by the summer of 1902, George Day was proposing the formation of just such a licensed, protective association of automobile manufacturers. He sent out an assistant, Hermann F. Cuntz, who, like Day, had been with the Pope company before that firm's automotive division was absorbed by the Electric Vehicle Company, to sound out individual manufacturers. He reportedly found general support for the idea of a protective association but strong opposition to the five per cent royalty fee Day was proposing to assess the licensed members of the association.

In the first part of October 1902, Fred Smith and Henry Russel went to New York to attend a conference that the Electric Vehicle Company had called with the Olds Motor Works and probably some of the other companies that had been approached by Cuntz. Smith told Olds before he left that he was not optimistic "of getting a very open deal with Electric Vehicle Co.," but at least he was hoping to "head off Winton from selling out to them." As long as the Winton case remained in the courts, Day and the Selden forces had as much cause as Smith and his fellow automakers to continue negotiations, since neither side could be certain of victory in the court. However, by the fall of 1902, Winton was wearying of the long legal battle it had been waging by itself. But, the other companies feared, if it now gave up the fight, the triumphant Electric Vehicle Company would have the upper hand and might impose much harsher terms on all of the automobile companies. Thus Smith and his cohorts felt that it was essential that the Winton case be kept alive, thereby keeping the pressure on the Selden forces to compromise.

On November 19, George Day came to Detroit from Cleveland to discuss with Smith his latest proposition, one which Smith declared "we could not in any way see to our advantage." Smith wrote to Ransom Olds in Lansing that he might be joining Henry Russel and Samuel Smith in New York to try to bring the negotiations with the Electric Vehicle Company "to a head one way or the other within the next 10 days." They had reached a point, Smith said, where "it looks to me now as though it were a case of settlement without cost to ourselves, or a case of standing pat and allowing them to bring suit if they wanted to."[64]

At this time another Detroiter, Henry B. Joy of the Packard company, took his place beside Fred Smith as a leader in the fight to obtain more favorable terms from the Selden forces. Joy was a man with a strong, decisive personality who could put starch in the ranks of the manufacturers who were wavering in the face of determined pressures from the Selden forces. A native of Detroit, where he had been born in 1864, Joy, like Fred Smith, had the added prestige that usually goes with being wealthy, and, also like Smith, Joy's wealth was the result of the efforts of his father, James F. Joy, a prominent lawyer and politician who had made his fortune and his reputation as one of the foremost railroad promoters in Michigan in the mid-nineteenth century. By the time Henry Joy began to take his place in the family business interests, the Joys had major in-

Henry B. Joy, *many years after he had retired from active management of the Packard company, posing in one of the Packard runabouts that had first attracted his interest in the firm.*
Courtesy Michigan Historical Collections

vestments in railroads, the Peninsular Car Company, mines in Utah, and real estate.[65]

In the mid-nineties Henry Joy had been interested in Charles King's work. Although his immediate interest, from the standpoint of an investment, was in marine engines, Joy also developed an early interest in automobiles. He had written the Duryea Motor Wagon Company in November 1895 inquiring if they could "furnish a good reliable wagon." Later in the decade, Joy is reported to have "tried to buy one of Henry Ford's experimental cars, but Mr. Ford had told him to wait for the next one, that it would be a better car." In 1901, Joy and his equally wealthy brother-in-law, Truman H. Newberry, were in New York for the automobile show. They were impressed with the performance of a one-cylinder runabout which they discovered was a Packard, manufactured in Warren, Ohio. Joy purchased the one model that was being exhibited at the show, and shortly after turned up in Warren to see if he might invest some money in the company that made the car.[66]

In Warren, Joy discovered that the Packard was manufactured by the Ohio Automobile Company, which was headed by James Ward Packard. Being a college graduate with a degree in mechanical engineering from Lehigh University in 1884 made Packard a rarity among early auto pioneers. In 1890, Packard and his brother, William D. Packard, formed the Packard Electric Company in Warren, an electrical equipment manufacturing business that proved to be quite successful. By 1893, the brothers, but principally James, were also working on a horseless carriage. Early in 1896 their work was sufficiently advanced for them to have some contact with Charles King in Detroit regarding an engine for the vehicle. Two years later James Packard bought the twelfth car that Alexander Winton manufactured. According to a well-known story, Packard supposedly complained so persistently to Winton about the car's poor performance that the Scotsman told the Ohioan to make his own car, if he thought he could do better. Apparently Packard thought he could, for in 1899 two of Winton's ex-associates, W. A. Hatcher and George L. Weiss, joined with the Packard brothers to form the Ohio Automobile Company. The Packard runabout, which Oliver Barthel states was actually the creation of Weiss and Hatcher, was a modest success, but the company lacked sufficient financial resources to enable it to became a bigger factor in the industry. James Packard then went shopping for new support. He is said to have asked the head of the Cleveland chamber of commerce if that city could provide some inducements in order to assist the Packard company in moving there. "Nothing doing," the Cleveland promoter replied. "We already have the Winton factory, and besides, we have just induced the largest clothes pin manufacturer in the country to build a local plant."[67]

A friendlier reception to Packard's bid for support came from Henry Wick, of Youngstown, Ohio, who offered to provide the funds Packard needed to expand. It was at this time that Joy apparently contacted the Ohio firm. He persuaded James Packard to delay a decision on Wick's offer until Joy could approach some of his wealthy friends in Detroit to see if they might be interested in investing in Packard. As a result, Truman Newberry, Russel A. Alger, Jr., son of the lumber millionaire and Republican party leader, Philip H. McMillan, son of millionaire Senator James McMillan, Dexter M. Ferry, Jr., son of the millionaire seed man and Republican stalwart, and two comparatively lesser lights, Joseph Boyer of the Boyer Machine Company (which subsequently became the Burroughs Corporation) and Charles A. DuCharme, son of one of the founders of the Michigan Stove Company, visited Warren and enthusiastically seconded Joy's desire to invest in Packard's company. Packard wanted $125,000, but Joy and his friends persuaded the Ohioans to accept twice that much, with an extra $125,000 held out as an inducement to build a new factory in Detroit "when indications and conditions should warrant it." Alger put in $75,000, Newberry, Joy, and McMillan $50,000 each, Boyer $25,000, DuCharme and Richard P. Joy, Joy's younger brother, $10,000 each, and Ferry $5000. The Warren firm was reorganized as the Packard Motor Car Company with James Packard as president. He and his associates held $150,000 of the stock, but the Detroit investors controlled $250,000 of the stock. By the end of 1902 it became clear that this group, under Henry Joy's leadership, was assuming active control of the company, while James Packard became little more than a figurehead. In 1903, the decision was made to build a new factory in Detroit, and the operations were transferred there from Warren by October. Joy assumed the position of general manager and, before long, the presidency. James Packard, who seems to have been too easy-going to fit in with the aggressive, demanding Detroiters, stayed behind in Warren with the excuse that his services were needed there at the Packard Electric Company. The Packard, which, before it left Ohio, was already becoming a bigger, more expensive car, was now developed under Joy's capable administration into Detroit's first and, for a good many years, most prestigious entry into the luxury car class. All of the city's cars prior to this time had started out in the low-price runabout field.[68]

Early in December 1902, Henry B. Joy, now firmly established as an executive in the auto industry, met with George Day for two days in New York. Apparently as a result of that meeting, Joy, upon his return to Detroit, worked out with Smith the plans for a meeting of the leading gasoline automobile manufacturers to be held in Detroit on January 2, 1903, to discuss Day's latest offer. But in addition, and Joy indicated in one letter that the suggestion came from James Packard, the meeting was also to consider the formation of an association, representatives of which would carry on further negotiations with the Electric Vehicle Company on behalf of the members.[69]

Those present at the January 2 meeting included both Henry Joy and James Packard from the Packard Motor Car Company and Fred Smith from Olds, plus representatives from the Haynes and Apperson companies of Kokomo, Indiana, the Peerless Manufacturing Company of Cleveland (Winton was purposely not asked to the meeting), the Autocar Company of Ardmore, Pennsylvania, the Searchmont Automobile Company of Philadelphia, the George N. Pierce Company of Buffalo, the Locomobile Company of Bridgeport, Connecticut, and the Knox Automobile Company of Springfield, Massachusetts. The leadership of Smith and Joy was quickly recognized, and their proposal to establish an association named the Manufacturers' Mutual Association was adopted unanimously; Smith was chosen to be the president and Joy the secretary-treasurer of the group. Smith and Joy were also designated as the committee that would conduct further negotiations with Day, whose proposals regarding the royalty fee were again rejected. Later, in Chicago in mid-February, representatives of the same companies signed a legal agreement officially establishing the association. Also at this time they agreed to contributions of $2500 each for a "fighting fund," heard from Joy on the results of his further talks with Day, and drafted counter-proposals to present to the Selden forces.[70]

Toward the end of February, George Day telegraphed Joy:

> We are ready to co-operate with you fully and create a situation that would be protective and surely profitable for all. Our people do not consider favorably the royalty offered, think it too small in view of expenses and obligation incurred. We believe we can prepare papers for mutual consideration by Friday, embodying substantial protection features on lines discussed with you. Important we should meet and come to a decision earliest date possible.

Throughout the negotiations, Day had had to contend with some of the backers of the Electric Vehicle Company who wanted to take a harder line toward the auto manufacturers. Joy, on the other hand, had to contend with the general willingness of the eastern manufacturers to concede more to the Selden forces than Joy and the western manufacturers were willing to do. As he told James Packard, "while they express great bravado yet I think their knees are somewhat weaker than the knees of the Western manufacturers."[71]

Finally, during a four-day bargaining session in New York which began on March 3, Day and Joy managed to bring their respective groups to a mutual understanding. The Association of Licensed Automobile Manufacturers was established, with the members of the Manufacturers' Mutual Association and the Electric Vehicle Company as charter members. Each licensed manufacturer paid a membership fee of $2500, plus $1000 advance royalty payments on cars produced since January 1. On the crucial issue of the amount of the royalty fee to be paid, Joy, Smith, and their fellow manufacturers had beaten the Selden forces down from their original five per cent figure to a fee of only one and a quarter per cent. Of that amount the Electric Vehicle Company, as the actual owner of the patent rights, kept three-fifths, and turned over the remaining two-fifths to the A.L.A.M. It was the association, however, and not the Electric Vehicle Company, that decided who would receive licenses under the patent and who would or would not be sued for infringement of the patent. Frederic Smith, who had been in the forefront of the fight to establish an association at least since the previous spring, was elected president of the A.L.A.M., and George Day, who, with Smith, had originally formulated the idea of a protective association, was named general manager. Joy was elected secretary-treasurer, and although he almost immediately submitted his resignation, claiming he could not afford to devote the time to the job that would be required on the voluntary basis that the members desired for the position, he apparently was persuaded to reconsider. He remained in the post, thus giving Detroit two of the most influential spots in the new organization's hierarchy. Two months later Joy expressed the opinion to James Packard that the A.L.A.M. was doing "good work. Our Association is, I believe, going to be felt, and I hope will be *the means of saving the trade to those who are now engaged in the business* [italics added]."[72]

This last statement of Henry Joy's, of course, expressed exactly what many at the time feared would happen, and many since that time have said did happen — namely, that the A.L.A.M. would be used as a means not simply of regulating the industry, but as a means of securing a monopoly for its members. To what extent this charge is warranted is a matter on which no agreement is ever likely to be reached.

At least at the outset, the association's original members seemed perfectly willing and, in fact, anxious to extend membership to other qualified manufacturers. By the end of April 1903, membership had been expanded to thirty companies, including Winton (the suit against that company being dropped at the same time), the several companies that Albert Pope was using to get back into automobile production, the Franklin company of Syracuse, New York, the E. R. Thomas company of Buffalo, and two more Michigan companies, Northern and Cadillac. There was merit in the assertion made by the association at this time that its licensed members were "the pioneers of the industry." There were, however, scores of companies that were not yet licensed but were producing and selling gasoline-powered cars and were, therefore, subject to prosecution for infringement, if the association so chose. As noted earlier, A. B. C. Hardy claimed that his Flint Automobile Company was driven out of business in 1903 by the A.L.A.M.'s threat of a suit against the firm, but whether this is true is another matter. Many automobile companies were closing down each year, and in most cases they were, like Hardy's company, too weak to survive under the most favorable of circumstances. On the other hand, there were a number of unlicensed manufacturers of gasoline automobiles who flourished in spite of the A.L.A.M.'s existence. The most notable of these in 1903 was Thomas B. Jeffery & Company of Kenosha, Wisconsin. The sales of this company's Rambler runabout, although down somewhat from 1902, were still good enough to make it probably the fourth best-selling car in America. In 1904 and 1905 strong gains pushed the Wisconsin company into third position. Jeffery simply ignored the licensed manufacturers' association. The latter, in turn, took no action to try to force Jeffery into line. Instead, on October 22, 1903, the A.L.A.M., acting through the agency of the Electric Vehicle Company and George B. Selden, filed suit against a much newer and, for the moment, much smaller company, Ford.[73]

Henry Ford had, of course, known, from his reading of the automotive trade journals, of the gathering storm regarding the Selden patent. In November 1900, a Detroit law firm had made a written report to him on the progress of the suit against Winton. In February 1903, Hermann Cuntz, aide to George Day, met with Ford in Chicago and talked with him about applying for a license for his new company. The discussions between Ford and Cuntz — and there were more than one — were, as Cuntz later recalled, quite pleasant, "and in fact it was considered that I was on such pleasant terms with him," Cuntz declared, "that I was given *carte blanche* to negotiate the purchase of a half interest in his business, for a sum which at the time was considered tremendous." Cuntz said that he did not follow this up because he understood, incorrectly it would seem, that Ford was not interested in selling any part of his business.[74]

Later, after the A.L.A.M. had been formed and about the time that the Ford Motor Company was taking shape, there were several contacts between Ford and his associates and Fred Smith regarding an application by the new company for a license under the Selden patent. A number of versions of these meetings have appeared, but all generally agree that Smith let Ford know that his application would probably not be approved at this time because the company's abilities were as yet untested, and that, in any event, the company would not be a manufacturer of automobiles but merely an assembler. Smith was apparently saying as politely as possible that, for all the A.L.A.M. knew, the Ford Motor Company might be one of those small, unscrupulous firms that were simply interested in making a fast buck — the very kind the association was hoping to eliminate in order to up-grade the reputation of the entire industry. It was, of course, unfair to brand the Ford company as nothing but an assembler when the same charge could be leveled at several members of the association and when none of the manufacturers produced all of the parts that went on their cars. On the other hand, Henry Ford's record as a producer of automobiles was certainly not a good one in the early summer of 1903 in view of the well-known results of his efforts with two earlier companies.[75]

But, according to William Greenleaf, there was more to Smith's reaction to the Ford company than his temporary doubts regarding the new company. Without citing any specific evidence, Greenleaf declares that both Smith and Henry Joy were opposed to considering an application from Ford because they saw "a threat to their own investments if the Ford Motor Company should succeed." Joy, Greenleaf asserts, "was inflexibly opposed to admitting Ford, and later threatened to withdraw Packard from the A.L.A.M. unless legal action was taken against the Ford Motor Company." Smith, Greenleaf writes, was opposed to licensing Ford because of the competition that the new Ford runabout, selling for $750, would offer to the curved-dash Oldsmobile. Such reasoning does not explain Joy's alleged opposition to Ford since his Packard company was now concentrating on the production of touring cars costing several times the price of the Ford Model A. But even if one grants that Fred Smith might have liked to see Ford out of the way as a competitor for the Oldsmobile, this does not explain why neither he nor Joy apparently exerted any appreciable pressure to sidetrack the admission to the A.L.A.M. of both the Cadillac and the Northern companies. These two Detroit automakers already had their own runabouts on the market selling for exactly the same price — $750 — that Ford had announced it would charge for its runabout model. It would have made even more sense for Smith to press an infringement suit against Thomas Jeffery, whose Rambler, likewise selling for $750, was in fact the Oldsmobile's chief competition in 1902 and in 1903 until the Cadillac began to get into real production later that year.[76]

One very good reason why Smith and Joy did not oppose the entry of Cadillac and Northern into the association may have had to do with the men backing these companies. William Barbour of Northern, and William Murphy, Lem Bowen, and their associates in Cadillac were part of the established aristocracy of wealth in Detroit to which Henry Russel, Fred Smith and his father, and the other Detroit investors in the Olds Motor Works, along with Joy, Alger, Newberry, McMillan, and Ferry in the Packard company all belonged. Not only did they all know and respect the wealth and influence that the others had, but the three groups of investors had numerous common business interests that linked various members together. For Smith and Joy to have opposed the admission of Cadillac or Northern would have been decidedly unwise, from both a social and business standpoint. There were no such factors to stifle any adverse feelings either Smith or Joy may have harbored about the Ford Motor Company. Men like Malcomson, Anderson, Rackham, Strelow, and even John Gray, head of one of the smaller Detroit banks, had little or no influence in the circles traveled by the McMillans, Algers, Joys, Russels, and Smiths. It is quite possible, even probable, that if Henry Ford had been speaking for the old Detroit Automobile or Henry Ford companies about a license in 1903, Smith's response would have been far more positive.

In the end, it seems most likely that the A.L.A.M. filed suit against the Ford Motor Company because, as Ford's biographer, Allan Nevins, puts it, Ford left the association no choice in the matter. Instead of ignoring the association and proceeding about its own business, as Jeffery and many other unlicensed manufacturers did at this time, the Ford Motor Company, stung by Fred Smith's implications that Henry Ford and his men had not demonstrated the ability or experience to produce a good automobile, threw down the gauntlet. In advertisements and public statements, Henry Ford's achievements as a pioneer builder of gasoline automobiles were recited, with considerable embellishment; the claims of Selden and the A.L.A.M. were thoroughly dissected and debunked; and finally, in reply to the association's open threat to sue the purchaser as well as the producer of unlicensed gasoline cars, Ford promised to defend anyone who was sued for infringement because he had purchased a Ford car. The Ford Motor Company, these statements declared, did not fear a court case over the validity of Selden's patent because the company was certain that the courts would find it not guilty of infringement. Ford was even quoted as taunting the association, saying he would pay it a thousand dollars to bring a suit against him, because the publicity he would gain thereby would be worth far more to him.[77]

Thus Fred Smith and his fellow officers in the A.L.A.M., much as they must have dreaded the idea of testing in court a patent which few of them, certainly not Smith and Henry Joy, believed had any real validity, had to take up Ford's challenge. As Nevins observes: "They would have been laughed out of the industry if they had not gone to court."[78]

During the years that followed, over five million words in testimony, exhibits, briefs, and other material were accumulated as attorneys

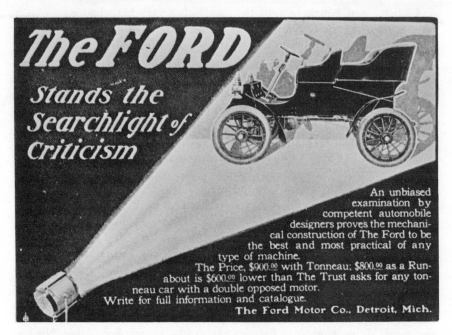

Ford admen spotlight the superior merits of the Ford Model C over those of comparable cars produced by members of The Trust, a term that knowledgeable buyers would recognize as referring to the Association of Licensed Automobile Manufacturers.
Courtesy Eastern Michigan University Library

for the various sides that became involved sought to support the case for or against Selden's patent. Finally, on September 15, 1909, Federal Judge Charles M. Hough of the Southern District of New York issued his opinion, upholding the Selden patent. It was an astonishing, if pleasant, surprise to the licensed manufacturers, and an equally surprising though dismaying turn for the many unlicensed manufacturers who had been confident of the patent's overthrow. After a brief flurry of activity as a great many of this latter group hurried to join the A.L.A.M., Henry Ford and his associates, after carefully considering a similar step, decided to appeal Hough's decision, and the trial resumed. On January 9, 1911, the three-man United States Circuit Court of Appeals for the Second Circuit unanimously ruled against the lower court's decision. The Selden patent, the appeals court declared, was valid only for vehicles powered by the two-cycle Brayton-type engine. It did not cover cars employing the four-cycle Otto-type engine that Ford and virtually all American manufacturers of gasoline automobiles were using. That ended the case, after more than seven years, since the executive committee of the A.L.A.M. quickly decided against making an appeal to the United States Supreme Court.[79]

In retrospect, it seems clear that the overall importance of the case has been greatly exaggerated. The greatest beneficiary of the whole affair was Henry Ford and the Ford Motor Company. As Ford had predicted, the case proved to be a God-send in terms of its publicity value. In an age when Teddy Roosevelt was whipping up public indignation against "trusts" and "monopolies," Ford was pictured by his publicity men as the little man doing battle against the A.L.A.M., which was seeking to monopolize the auto business and strangle those, like Ford, who refused to bow to their wishes. Meanwhile, after a slow start in its first three years, when Ford sales made only slight gains and actually declined in 1905-1906, Ford production and sales began to climb, pushing the Detroit firm to first place in the industry well before Judge Hough's adverse decision in 1909. By the time of the appeals court decision in 1911, Ford's output represented about twenty per cent of all the cars produced in America. By that time, it made no real difference how the courts ruled. Ford's strength was so great that even if the company had lost the case it would have had little difficulty securing a license under a patent that was due to expire on November 5, 1912, anyway.[80]

If Fred Smith, Henry Joy, and George Day had been hoping to use the A.L.A.M. as a monopolistic device, they were singularly unsuccessful. If, on the other hand, they regarded the association more as a trade association attempting to bring some order into the new industry, they were more successful. It is true that the manner in which the public bought the Ford and many other unlicensed cars indicates that the A.L.A.M. failed to sell the idea that its members had a monopoly on the production of high-quality automobiles. But within the industry, the A.L.A.M. did make great strides in advancing the concept of cooperation between auto companies, particularly in the pooling of patents and in the adoption of certain common sizes for basic parts such as spark plugs, wheel rims, and screw threads. This kind of cooperative effort was carried on in the various trade and professional organizations that succeeded the Association of Licensed Automobile Manufacturers after that organization ceased to operate when the patent that had sparked its formation no longer had any real meaning for the industry.[81]

The significant reduction in the number of automobile companies that have at some time made a more or less serious attempt to produce and sell cars (1008 such companies have been identified on a recent list) to the few that survive in America today has resulted not from the monopolistic efforts of an organization such as the A.L.A.M., but through a combination of competitive factors. There have been a multitude of weak companies that could not have survived under any circumstances. Other firms, small but well run, that produced quality cars, ultimately found it impossible to compete with the resources at the disposal of a few large and strong companies. The Ford Motor Company grew by developing one outstanding model, the Model T, and then concentrating all of its efforts from 1908 to 1914 on enlarging and improving the efficiency of its production facilities. Thus the company was able to turn out the car in ever larger quantities at ever lower prices and in this way rapidly increase its share of the market. In the long run, the Ford Motor Company was the only company to succeed and survive by this method. General Motors, Chrysler, and American Motors, on the other hand, survived through the processes of merger, combination, and acquisition, joining two or more companies together in a larger organization. These processes made possible (although the result was not guaranteed) the same competitive advantages of size and efficiency that Ford achieved through its single-minded approach.[82]

CHAPTER 10

"I WAS FOR GETTING EVERY CAR IN SIGHT"

At the time that the American automobile industry was just beginning to develop, consolidation of business activities through mergers and other methods was being conducted on a scale never before seen in the United States, leading to the creation of such giants of industry as the United States Steel Corporation. It was not surprising, therefore, that similar efforts were attempted in America's newest industry. One of the earliest consolidation efforts was represented in the Electric Vehicle Company, which was the result of the joining together of the resources of an electric cab company, a storage battery company, and Albert Pope's Motor Carriage Department. Colonel Pope, in turn, after failing in his effort to make his American Bicycle Company the great combination that would control the bicycle industry, attempted a consolidation in the auto industry. He acquired control of plants in Toledo, Indianapolis, and Hagerstown, which, with his existing plant in Hartford, became part of the reorganized Pope Manufacturing Company in 1903. It was an impressive business empire capitalized at $22,500,000, which produced several cars in several price ranges, bearing such names as the Pope-Toledo, Pope-Hartford, Pope-Tribune, and the Pope-Waverly, an electric vehicle. But this early-day General Motors failed to make it, partly because of a weak financial structure and partly because it lacked the talents of an able group of automotive experts. Pope had had such a group earlier in his Motor Carriage Department in the nineties, but it had gone with that unit when it was sold to the Electric Vehicle Company.[1]

In the spring of 1903, shortly after the formation of the A.L.A.M., a group of investors headed by Barclay H. Warburton, of the Searchmont Automobile Company of Philadelphia and vice-president of the licensed manufacturers' group, attempted to put together a combination. One company that was to be included was Packard, whose de facto head, Henry B. Joy, notified Warburton in May that he had secured from stockholders who held a majority of the Packard stock an agreement to sell their shares to Warburton's group for $200 a share, double their original value. "This is a close business proposition, and one which I myself am loth [sic] to make," Joy informed Warburton, ". . . but others, not so courageous perhaps, think it advisable to do so." Joy frankly stated that he hoped the sale would not go through, since he expected to do much better in the auto business than merely doubling his investment. "I do, however, realize the many, many advantages to be obtained through the proper management of the consolidated interests you have in contemplation." From what Joy says, Warburton had broached the subject earlier in New York, perhaps during the course of the negotiations leading to the formation of the A.L.A.M. in March 1903. Joy had told Warburton at that time that consolidation was bound to come to the auto industry, "but," he said in May, "I regret exceedingly that it has come so soon."[2]

Nothing is known of Warburton's overall plans aside from references in Henry Joy's papers, and even these contain only Joy's side of the correspondence. However, a letter from Joy to G. B. Gunderson of the Northern Manufacturing Company indicates that this Detroit automobile manufacturer was also to be a part of this consolidation. Warburton was unable to take advantage of the option he had been given on the Packard stock by Joy's July 1 deadline, his excuse being that the "monetary and general market situation" prevented him from doing so. He asked Joy if he might try again in six months, but Joy replied that this was a matter that would have to be renegotiated with the Packard stockholders at that later date. The bankruptcy a few months later of Warburton's own Searchmont company apparently killed all further hopes of carrying out this consolidation.[3]

If, as seems likely, Warburton's consolidation plans were an outgrowth of contacts between him and other members of the A.L.A.M., this was at that time a logical starting point for such plans. The detailed reports that members had to submit in connection with their royalty fees provided insiders in the association with a valuable body of information on which to assess the worth of these companies. In the course of his work as liaison between the New York office of the association and the individual members, Hermann Cuntz became thoroughly familiar with the strengths, weaknesses, and prospects of each of the licensed companies. In 1906 he discussed a plan to merge several of the firms with the well-known New York financier, Anthony N. Brady, who had been a member of the Whitney syndicate that took over the Electric Vehicle Company seven years earlier. Brady was impressed, and sent Cuntz out to secure agreements from several of the manufacturers to sell out to Brady. But Brady, who correctly foresaw the coming panic of 1907, decided to wait until the auto industry had faced the hardships of the financial panic. Brady anticipated that the asking prices for the several companies in Cuntz's combination would drop sharply, but the auto industry as a whole weathered the storm far better than anyone in Wall Street had expected. A good many weak companies were weeded out by the brief drop in auto sales, but the stronger companies came through the crisis with flying colors and greatly enhanced prestige. Although the names of the companies with which Cuntz and Brady had been in contact are not known, they obviously included some of the stronger firms, who now raised their prices rather than coming down, as Brady had hoped. Brady, who was an old hand at consolidations, had made his fortune consolidating utilities and traction lines, but he backed away from any further discussions of an automobile consolidation. Thus, as had happened several times earlier, a move that could have resulted in the establishment of a permanent control of the industry by eastern interests was thwarted.

In 1910, Anthony Brady became the principal backer of the ill-fated United States Motor consolidation, and from 1910 to 1913 he was also a director of General Motors. Neither of these combinations, however, had the A.L.A.M. origins that one can detect in Warburton's proposals in 1903, or Cuntz's in 1906.[4]

* * *

The historian who attempts to deal with the origins of the world's largest industrial corporation, General Motors, or with its subsequent development, works under the handicap of not having access to the records of General Motors. With very few exceptions, that corporation has chosen not to open its files to scholars. Eventually, as more and more substantial collections of the papers of leading G.M. executives become available, as in the case of the papers of Pierre S. DuPont and Charles E. Wilson, two men who headed the corporation in later years, it may become possible to piece together a more accurate and detailed history of the corporation than is now available in the company-sponsored history by Arthur Pound, *The Turning Wheel*, which covers only the first twenty-five years of the number one auto manufacturer. But if the papers of William C. Durant that were used by Lawrence Gustin in his recent biography of G.M.'s founder are all that survive of his records, then it appears likely that the story of how this most successful of all automobile consolidations got its start will always be wrapped in a certain amount of mystery.

Benjamin Briscoe, *the very image of a Detroit manufacturer pos-*
sessing Wall Street connections of the most impeccable order.
Courtesy Motor Vehicle Manufacturers Association

The evidence, including Durant's own testimony, indicates that the
initiative that led to the formation of General Motors did not come originally from Durant. Instead, the consolidation was an outgrowth of the
activities of Benjamin Briscoe. In 1888, Briscoe, who had been born in 1868
in Detroit, had, along with his brother Frank, established the Briscoe
Manufacturing Company. This small sheet metal establishment had developed into a substantial business by the time it began making radiators for
the curved-dash Oldsmobile in 1902. This in turn led the brothers to concentrate on the production of various other metal parts for cars, including
gasoline and water tanks, hoods (most commonly called "bonnets" at this
time in America, as they still are in Great Britain), and fenders. By the
end of 1903, the Briscoes were said to "virtually" control the local market
for these products. However, just prior to becoming manufacturers of auto
parts, the Briscoes had almost been forced out of business as a result of a
bank failure in 1901. Although Benjamin Briscoe got some temporary
relief from the Detroit banker, George Russel, he decided, as he later put

it, to "get money where money was." He went to New York, and unlikely as it seems, this small midwestern businessman claims that he went to the most illustrious of all American financial institutions, J. P. Morgan and Company, and got the senior J. P. Morgan himself to invest $100,000. "Mr. Morgan and myself became, therefore, the main owners of the Briscoe Manufacturing Co."[5]

As previously indicated, Benjamin Briscoe decided there was more money to be made manufacturing the entire car rather than just some of the parts, so after his brief fling at backing David Buick, he switched his support to Jonathan D. Maxwell. On July 4, 1903, Briscoe entered into a contact with Maxwell, and, with C. W. Althouse, agreed to supply the $3000 that Maxwell needed to build a prototype car. Althouse withdrew from the group shortly afterwards because of ill health. Maxwell built the car in John Lauer's Machine Shop in Detroit and on Christmas Day, 1903, Briscoe witnessed the successful test of the car. The Maxwell-Briscoe Motor Company was formed to produce the car, called simply the Maxwell. Jonathan Maxwell, who had earlier been involved in the development of the original Haynes-Apperson horseless carriage, the curved-dash Oldsmobile, and finally the Northern, had the satisfaction at last of seeing an automobile appear that bore his name. Although Briscoe, in keeping with the standard advertising practices of the day, would later be quoted in ads for the Maxwell saying that he considered Maxwell to be "the foremost automobile designer of the world," Charles King had a low opinion of the man's abilities. King claimed that the Northern, of which Maxwell had been the original designer, had not been a success until King was called in "to clear up a great many features of design," and that when Maxwell went with Briscoe he took with him King's chief draftsman, who, King thought, "was largely responsible for the Maxwell design." Be that as it may, Benjamin Briscoe, whatever his opinion of Jonathan Maxwell may have been (and Briscoe admitted that he and Maxwell later had some serious disagreements), never made Alexander Malcomson's mistake of letting his automobile designer-mechanic gain control of the company. Briscoe had found the money to put the company in business, and he kept the upper hand in running it.[6]

Although Briscoe succeeded in getting some financial support in Detroit, he claimed that the local capitalists turned down his request for the major amounts that he needed. The feverish automotive developments that had taken place in the city over the past year may have caused them to feel that it would be prudent to wait for awhile before supporting yet another company. Briscoe then went to his friends on Wall Street, and in 1904 the Morgan interests aided in raising the money the Detroiter needed through the sale of $250,000 in bonds. In return, probably because the eastern investors wanted to see what they were getting for their money, the Maxwell-Briscoe company moved into the Tarrytown, New York, factory of the recently defunct steam car manufacturer, the Mobile Company of America. Benjamin Briscoe went off to Tarrytown to run the company, leaving brother Frank behind to run the sheet metal company. (Before long, Frank Briscoe, too, developed what he called "an itch to get into the big tent" and in 1907 formed his own automobile company to produce Alanson Brush's runabout.) By 1905, the Maxwell was in full-scale production, and within a year it had become the best selling eastern-made car in America and was challenging the Michigan-made Ford, Buick, and Reo for overall leadership in the industry.[7]

The accounts that William Durant and Benjamin Briscoe left regarding how Briscoe became interested in the subject of a merger differ considerably. Briscoe claims that he originated the idea himself, while Durant asserts that the initiative came from J. P. Morgan and Company. Since Morgan was Briscoe's principal financial backer, and since even by Briscoe's account the Morgan interests came to dominate the merger talks once they had gotten underway, Durant's version has a ring of probability, at least. According to what Durant says and what is known from other evidence, sometime in 1907, though possibly earlier, George W. Perkins, a partner in J. P. Morgan and Company, talked with Briscoe about his interest in promoting a merger of some of the leading automobile companies. This was the type of activity for which J. P. Morgan had been famous since his well-publicized role in the creation of U. S. Steel. Perkins, a native of Illinois, may very well have heard rumors in Wall Street of Anthony Brady's interest in a similar merger, but if so, in working through Briscoe, Perkins was not approaching the subject through the medium of the A.L.A.M. as Brady was with Hermann Cuntz. Briscoe was a leader of the rival American Motor Car Manufacturers' Association that the unlicensed automobile companies had organized. Whether a company was licensed or not, however, was probably of little interest to Perkins and his Morgan associates whose attention may have been drawn to the auto industry by the fact that they were receiving, according to Briscoe, an almost usurious annual return of over twenty per cent on the money they had loaned to Maxwell-Briscoe.[8]

Durant, whose Buick company was a member in good standing of the A.L.A.M., first learned of the proposed merger when he received a telephone call in Flint from Briscoe, calling from Chicago. "Billy," Briscoe said, "I have a most important matter to discuss with you . . . it's the biggest thing in the country. There's millions in it." Briscoe wanted Durant to come to Chicago, but Durant, who was always up to his neck in work, replied that that was impossible, but that if Briscoe could take the evening Grand Trunk train out of Chicago, they could discuss Briscoe's proposal over breakfast in Flint the next morning. The following morning, therefore, in the dining room of Flint's Dresden Hotel and later at Durant's office in the Buick plant, Briscoe outlined Perkins' and his ideas. Briscoe may have explained what he later claimed was their major interest in promoting a merger of the industry's "principal concerns," which he said sprang not from "a desire to sell all of the automobiles that were to be sold," but a desire to create a giant automobile corporation that would be so large "that its influence would prevent many of the abuses that we believe existed" among some of the less respectable members of the industry. Briscoe, however, also declared that "at the bottom of every combination" proposal was the belief by some or all of the companies involved that this would be a means of obtaining more money and thereby improving their financial condition. "I believe the history of almost every combination will show that the principal motive comes from being hard up." This may have been what had motivated Barclay Warburton to propose a merger to Packard and Northern in 1903 in light of the bankrupt condition of his own company that came to light a few months later, and it may have had something to do with the interest of Briscoe and his Wall Street backers in a merger proposal in 1907 since there are hints that Maxwell-Briscoe, despite its high volume of sales, was in some financial trouble. However, it is difficult to see how the prosperous Michigan companies that Briscoe shortly approached with his merger plans could have been classified as "hard up."

Whatever may have been the origin of Briscoe's ideas, Briscoe, as Durant recalled, "had no well-conceived plans" as to how to carry them out. "He suggested calling a meeting of about 20 of the leading concerns, naming Packard, Peerless, Pierce-Arrow, Stoddard-Dayton, Thomas, etc. What did I think of it?" In reply, Durant said he did not think Briscoe's approach was practical since it would include too many companies whose interests, in terms of the kinds of cars they produced, were too diverse to be reconciled easily. Durant suggested instead that Briscoe broach the subject of a merger to Ford and Reo, which, with Buick and Maxwell-Briscoe, were the leading volume producers in the industry and which were all concentrating most of their efforts on cars in the medium- and lower-price ranges. "I suggested he first see Henry Ford," Durant said, since Ford "was in the limelight, liked publicity and unless he could lead the procession would not play." Briscoe followed Durant's suggestion and saw Ransom Olds in Lansing and Ford in Detroit. Both men showed some interest in a consolidation, so a few weeks later Briscoe invited Olds, Ford, and Durant to meet with him in the Penobscot Building in Detroit.[9]

In the memoirs that Durant wrote in the early 1940's, he cites May 16, 1908, as the date of Briscoe's initial visit with him in Flint. However, from an undated notation in a notebook that James Couzens kept during 1907, it is evident that some fairly explicit discussions of the possible terms of the merger had taken place with Ford and Couzens, at least, prior to 1908. Couzens had jotted down a series of figures, indicating that a consolidation with a capitalization of about $35,000,000 was contemplated. Ford, Reo, and Buick were each to receive $7,125,000, and Maxwell-Briscoe $6,125,000. The rest of the stock was to be sold or distributed as bonuses to the participants in the merger. From a diary that Ransom Olds kept, face-to-face discussions between the four principals in the merger can be dated as having begun in Detroit on January 17, 1908.[10]

When the four men and their top associates, whom Olds does not

name but whom Durant indicates were present, assembled in the public
reception room of the Penobscot building, Durant soon saw that this was
too open a meeting place to hold their discussions if they wished them to
remain secret. At his suggestion, therefore, they adjourned to his "commodious quarters" in the newly opened Pontchartrain Hotel where Durant
"had the unexpected pleasure of entertaining the entire party until mid-
afternoon." Briscoe opened the meeting by suggesting that they try to agree
upon a consolidation plan they might then present to the Morgan company. Although the notation in Couzens' notebook for 1907 indicates that
the financial arrangements had already been discussed, Durant's recollection was that there was considerable hassling concerning the values that
would be set on each of the four companies when they came into the
merger; nor do the figures that Durant mentions agree with those given
by Couzens. After further discussion they passed on to other questions
relating to the administrative relationship of the parts to the whole in the
new corporation. Briscoe favored consolidating the purchasing, engineering,
advertising, and sales departments of the four companies and having a
central committee to control operating policies. Durant, on the other hand,
favored simply a holding company arrangement, with the four operating
companies continuing to have complete autonomy over their own affairs.
"Ho! Ho!" Briscoe laughed, "Durant is for states' rights. I am for a union."
As it turned out, both men had a chance to try out their ideas and both saw
them fail. General Motors, under Durant's system of management, came
within a hair of a complete breakdown because of insufficient centralized
control; Briscoe's United States Motor combine was driven into an early
grave because, some analysts declared, he sought to achieve too much centralized control too soon.[11]

A week later, on January 24 and 25, all four of the auto leaders
reassembled to present their ideas, inconclusive as they were, to some of
the Morgan people. They met at 120 Broadway, New York, in the office of
Herbert L. Satterlee, J. P. Morgan's son-in-law and a member of the law
firm of Ward, Hayden and Satterlee. Further discussions were held in the
next few months. Olds recorded in his diary another meeting in Satterlee's
office on May 11, and in notes he set down on the memoranda page opposite the entry page for the week May 31 to June 6, 1908, he indicates that
further discussions may have taken place at that time.[12]

Throughout these discussions there was apparently never any question about the attitude of Briscoe and Durant toward the idea of a merger.
The very fact that Briscoe had first brought up the idea with his fellow auto
manufacturers suggests that he was eager for the merger, while anyone
familiar with Durant's previous career could have predicted that he, too,
would favor the proposal. Both men were firmly in control of their companies, and both were thinking of effecting the merger through an exchange
of their stock for that of the new corporation, with little or no cash changing hands. In April 1908, in an agreement signed by the individual Buick

stockholders, Durant had been authorized to act as the agent of the stock-holders in arranging for just such an exchange.[13]

But it had evidently not been entirely clear what Ford and Olds thought about the proposed merger or the method to be used to carry it out. Herbert Satterlee later recalled that he and his associates had been under the impression, first of all, that both Ford and Olds were interested in getting out of the auto business, and thus the merger would fit in with their plans. From the slight amount of time that Olds seems to have been giving to the day-to-day affairs of Reo by 1908 it is easy to believe that the right offer could indeed have persuaded him to retire from his company in order to be completely free to devote his full time to other interests. As for Henry Ford, he stood at the very threshold in 1908 of an immense fortune. Many have expressed puzzlement, therefore, at Ford's willingness even to consider the thought of merger and retirement. However, one must remember that the great success of the Model T was still in the future — in the winter and spring of 1908 — and no one yet knew how the vexing Selden patent case would come out. In addition, Ford was a moody man. Like Ransom Olds, he seems in this period to have become bored with the routine of the business, coming into the office for only brief periods. On one occasion he even suggested to Couzens that it might be a good idea if he stepped down from the presidency in favor of Couzens. Thus it is quite conceivable that Ford had told Briscoe when they first discussed the merger that he would welcome an excuse to retire.[14]

Where Satterlee and his associates had apparently been misinformed, however, was in their understanding of how Ford thought the merger would be accomplished. Satterlee was under the impression that Ford would agree to a simple exchange of stock, and that in addition he would make a sizable cash investment in the stock of the new corporation. At some point in the discussions that were held in Satterlee's office, arguments broke out again over the respective worth of the four companies. Briscoe was irritated at what he regarded as the undervaluation of his company. Ford or Couzens then spoke up and, according to Briscoe, said that the Ford Motor Company would have to be given at least $3,000,000 in addition to stock to be brought into the merger, at which point Ransom Olds declared that if Ford was paid cash, Reo would insist on receiving a like amount. Olds, in 1949, gave a somewhat different version of what had happened, recalling that he and Ford had agreed, in advance, "to hold out for $4,000,000," and that they made known their decision in the presence of J. P. Morgan himself. Morgan, Olds said, "threw up his hands and declared that it would be no go," although his reaction, Olds said, was based not so much on the amount of money that Ford and Olds were demanding as on their statement that they would retire from the business when the merger was completed. The accuracy of Olds' recollection is questionable since no other source indicates the direct involvement of J. P. Morgan in the negotiations. Morgan was in New York, attending to his various business interests, at the time of the January conference in Satterlee's office, but he was out of the country during the periods of the later, presumably more crucial, discussions. In his biography of his father-in-law, Satterlee makes no mention of the G.M. talks, let alone any involvement by Morgan in those discussions. Nevertheless, it would seem to make sense that someone in the Morgan organization, as Olds claimed, felt that the prospects for success in any consolidation would be reduced if the two men most responsible for the success of two of the components of the merger were not to continue to manage those divisions. The more usual interpretation, however, is that the money that Ford and Olds requested was the main cause of the breakup of the negotiations. To make matters worse, when Ford was asked how much stock in the new company he intended to purchase, he replied that he had no intention of buying any. As Durant recalled: "This was a great surprise and the bankers who were expecting a large subscription from Mr. Ford were quite disappointed." Satterlee then called Durant and Briscoe aside into an adjoining room and asked for an explanation concerning this sudden turn of events. Durant replied that he was as surprised by Ford's statements as Satterlee was. According to Durant, Briscoe then confessed that the position Ford had just taken was consistent with the views he had expressed earlier when Briscoe had first talked of a merger to him; since that time, Briscoe said, Ford had seemed so interested in the plans that Briscoe had allowed himself to believe that Ford had changed his mind about the financial arrangements, and that he would come around to accept the same kind of deal as the others were willing to accept. Satterlee, who was obviously quite perturbed at having been misled by Briscoe in this way, thought the matter over for a short time and then returned to the main meeting room where he "very diplomatically stated that there had been a misunderstanding, that the matter of finance was entirely up to the bankers and when they had perfected their plan, another meeting would be called."[15]

No further meeting of Ford, Reo, Buick, and Maxwell-Briscoe representatives seems to have been held after this dramatic session in Satterlee's office. It is not certain when the Ford and Reo companies were dropped from the consolidation plans, but in his diary notation, apparently written at the end of May or the first part of June 1908, Olds set down figures on the proposed distribution of stock that were essentially the same as those that Couzens wrote in his notebook sometime the previous year. This seems to indicate that at the end of May 1908 Ford and Reo were still being included in the discussions. In addition, *Horseless Age* in its June 3rd issue published unconfirmed reports of the consolidation talks, the first hints of which, it said, came in a dispatch from Flint on May 18. At that time rumors still included Reo at least as a possible participant in the merger. However, late in July, E. F. Peer, secretary of Reo, although admitting that "overtures" had been made to the company regarding a merger, denied that it had ever "seriously considered the proposition." In any event, *Horseless Age* indicated that by June talks had narrowed down simply to discussions between Buick and Maxwell-Briscoe involving a combination that would be headed by Satterlee, "the well known Wall Street man."[16]

In retrospect, of course, this failure to reach agreement with Olds and more especially with Henry Ford was a momentous mistake, although there is no way of knowing whether the Ford Motor Company would have developed as successfully as a member of a consolidated group of auto producers as it did as a completely independent manufacturer. In view of Ford's renowned aversion to bankers, particularly Wall Street bankers, it is possible that the site of the talks in New York made Ford less cooperative than he might have been in another location. Benjamin Briscoe, in fact, felt that the negotiations would have had a much different outcome if he had been able to follow Ford's suggestion to have the legal arrangements handled by Job E. Hedges, a New York attorney whom Ford and Briscoe had come to know when they were both members of the American Motor Car Manufacturers' Association and Hedges was the association's attorney. But since the Morgan interests were behind the proposed merger, Briscoe felt obliged to accept the services of a Morgan attorney.[17]

About this same time, Durant and Briscoe may have been encouraged to keep their merger plans alive, despite Ford's defection, by the announcement of the successful completion of another consolidation. On the evening of June 2, 1908, at a news conference in New York, the formation of the Everitt-Metzger-Flanders Company was announced. The new firm was the result of the merger of the Northern Motor Car Company, the old Northern Manufacturing Company, one of the companies involved in Barclay Warburton's abortive consolidation plan in 1903, and the Wayne Automobile Company, a Detroit concern that had been organized in 1903-1904 principally by Charles L. Palms, a Detroit capitalist.

Charles Palms' family had come to Detroit from Belgium in 1833, and his grandfather, Francis Palms, had become, according to one report, the largest landowner in Michigan, acquiring vast timber and mineral land holdings in northern Michigan along with considerable real estate in Detroit. He also became the president of a bank, a life insurance company, and the big Michigan Stove Company. Charles Palms, however, had been born in 1871 in New Orleans, where his father, Francis F. Palms, had taken up residence and had served in the Confederate army during the Civil War. His family returned to Detroit subsequent to Charles Palms' birth after his father inherited the vast Palms estate. Charles went on to college in Detroit and Washington, D. C., and spent a year in law school at Harvard, before turning to more esthetic interests. He became an accomplished performer on the violin-cello, and sought to pursue a literary career in Europe and Boston until his father persuaded him to return to Detroit to manage the family's real estate holdings. He was apparently a success in this job, and extended the family's business interests in the banking field and into newspapers, before entering the auto industry.[18]

Joining Charles Palms in providing financial backing for the Wayne company was his uncle, Dr. James B. Book. A native of Ontario, where he had been born in 1843, Book gave up his active medical practice in Detroit in 1895 to devote himself to his business interests. Although his practice had apparently been very lucrative, the Book family fortune was assured in 1889 when Dr. Book married Clotilde Palms, half--sister of Francis F. Palms and co-inheritor of the Palms estate.[19]

Through Charles Palms, who was its president and treasurer, and Dr. Book, the Wayne Automobile Company had access to personal fortunes and ties to the resources of banking and life insurance institutions that made the financial backing of such a contemporary company as the Ford Motor Company seem decidedly pale by comparison. Furthermore, the Wayne Automobile Company had as the man in charge of designing and building its cars William Kelly, who, if we believe all that was said of him, was the equal of any automobile designer of the day. Kelly, who is actually a very shadowy figure, was said to have worked with Henry Ford on Ford's first car, athough Ford biographies make no mention of him. Then, it is said, Kelly struck out on his own, building his own car and, friends said, developing the planetary transmission that Ford later made famous in his Model T. By the time a brochure was published announcing the 1912 Everitt, a Detroit car that Kelly was credited with designing, Kelly was being described as "nothing less than a genius," who had designed "at least a score of successful cars" since 1891, when he had "designed one of the first practical cars ever built."[20]

However, despite Palms' money and Kelly's alleged talents, the Wayne company was at best a modest success. In the summer of 1906, John H. O'Brien, former purchasing agent of the Ford Motor Company, was brought in as general manager, and in the weeks ahead the trade journals reported an unusual amount of activity by the company. Additional agencies for Wayne cars were signed up throughout the country, with a seemingly strong emphasis on locations in the South and West. Plans were announced for building a three-story addition to the Detroit factory. Then in the spring of 1908 came a major shakeup in the Wayne management as Byron Everitt, the veteran manufacturer of auto bodies and trimmings, took over as president of the company. He was joined by a number of top men from the Ford organization, most notably Walter E. Flanders, a big, tough, hard-living Vermonter who, during his year and a half at Ford, was credited with having started that company on the path toward the mass production methods for which it would soon become world famous.[21]

A few weeks later, however, it became evident that the developments at Wayne in March were but the prelude to bigger things. Everitt and Flanders teamed with William Metzger, who left his position as sales manager of Cadillac to purchase a large interest in the Northern Motor Car Company, which he now brought into the merger with Wayne. William Barbour, the original backer of Northern, was vice-president of the consolidated firm. Charles Palms was treasurer, and his uncle and fellow Wayne investor, Dr. Book, was on the board of directors, but the active management of the new concern was in the hands of the three men whose initials formed the name of the company. Everitt served as president, Metzger as sales manager, and Flanders as general manager. E. LeRoy Pelletier, the brilliant Ford advertising manager, joined the new company in a similar position, while another top Ford production man, Thomas S. Walburn, was brought in as general superintendent for E.M.F. With a capitalization of $1,000,000, E.M.F. announced that it would begin to manufacture a thirty-horsepower touring car that would probably be priced at $1200 and a roadster version at around $1150. Production was to begin by September 1908, with a goal of 12,500 cars the first year.[22]

At the Chicago auto show in February 1909 William Metzger admitted that the company's progress had been slow, "but that is due to our determination to have our cars right, and we closely scrutinize each machine before it goes on the market." But then a bewildering series of events began, with the result that the group that established the company was ultimately unseated. The first step, seemingly innocent enough, came in April 1909 when an agreement was reached with the Studebaker interests of South Bend, Indiana, whereby the latter contracted to sell the Detroit firm's entire output for three years. Studebaker had been dabbling in the automobile industry for several years, while continuing to concentrate on the carriages that had made the company famous. Those in the company who favored full-scale automobile development gained support for their view in 1907 when sales of Studebaker cars accounted for most of the increase in the company's sales during that panic year. With only limited auto production facilities of its own, Studebaker saw a chance to grab a larger share of the auto business in short order by contracting to sell the new E.M.F. Through this arrangement, Metzger and his associates were saved from the necessity of lining up agents for their cars, while Studebaker had an attractive new product for its extensive network of carriage dealers to market.

The next move, however, saw the Studebaker interests beginning to muscle in on the actual control of E.M.F. On May 3, 1909, it was announced that Clement Studebaker, Jr., and Hayden Eames, a veteran automobile executive with experience in the old Pope motor carriage division and the Electric Vehicle Company, who now became general manager of the Studebaker automobile operations, had purchased the stock of Everitt and Metzger and taken their places on the board of directors of E.M.F. Walter Flanders, the only remaining member of the E.M.F. trio, replaced Byron Everitt as president.[23]

Everitt, Metzger, and William Kelly, chief engineer of E.M.F., left and formed the Metzger Motor Car Company and took over a plant in Detroit formerly occupied by a truck company. In a rather unusual move, the founders of the new company called in "a select number of prominent retailers" and sought their views on the kind of car they would like the new concern to manufacture. The dealers who took part in this conference then divided up among themselves the initial run of 2500 cars, called the Everitt "30", that supposedly resulted from their suggestions. The philosophy of the Metzger company, as it was later explained, was in direct contrast to that espoused in an earlier day by the Olds Motor Works and that was now brought to its fullest fruition by the Ford Motor Company. Metzger professed to see a trend among the public "toward quality rather than quantity; that the production of a limited number of *good* cars was better business policy than a tremendous output of cheap cars." Asserting that "facts and figures" had already demonstrated that mass production could not produce "a really good car at a low price," but that instead it had been proven that good cars took time to build, Metzger, Everitt, and Kelly over the next three years produced limited numbers of Everitts, with, however, only indifferent success.[24]

The injection of Studebaker money, meanwhile, led to the rapid expansion of E.M.F. until by the end of 1909 it was, according to one report, Detroit's largest employer. The DeLuxe Motor Car Company of Detroit, which, since it opened in 1906, had failed to find much of a market for its expensive car, was purchased by E.M.F. in the summer of 1909. Its plant was converted to the production of the new Studebaker-Flanders runabout that was now added to the existing line of heavier E.M.F. "30" touring cars (although, at twenty horsepower, the new runabout was a far cry from the light cars to which that name had been applied a few years earlier). A Detroit company that had been making bathtubs was purchased, and with the addition of machinery it began making E.M.F. automobile stampings. Through the purchase of the Auto Crank Shaft Company, E.M.F. also began to make its own crankshafts. A brass foundry and iron works was built on land adjacent to the old DeLuxe factory. In Pontiac, the purchase of the Monroe Body plant enabled E.M.F. to make its own bodies, and the old Northern plant in Port Huron was converted to the production of rear axles and bevel gears. Across the border in Windsor, a vacant factory was acquired to enable the company to produce the E.M.F. and Studebaker-Flanders for the Canadian market. By December 1909, some ten thousand workers were employed at the several E.M.F. plants, with plans calling for the production in 1910 of 15,200 of the E.M.F. "30's," and 25,000 of the Studebaker-Flanders runabouts. Already in 1909, with an output of about 8000 cars, E.M.F. ranked second to Ford among Detroit auto producers, an impressive record for a firm that was only a year and a half old.[25]

On December 9, 1909, however, President Walter Flanders notified Studebaker that he was canceling the contract between E.M.F. and the Indiana firm, allegedly because Studebaker had refused to receive and pay for the number of cars specified in the contract signed in April. Studebaker immediately went to court with counter charges in an effort to force E.M.F. to go through with the contract, which still had over two years to run. Apparently, however, the arguments over the contract were only a blind for what was really at stake in the conflict: the desire of the Studebaker interests, controlling only thirty-six per cent of the stock, to gain outright control of E.M.F., and the effort of Flanders and the old Northern and Wayne interests to retain that control in the hands of the Detroit investors. When Walter Flanders won the preliminary rounds in the court fight and began to establish his own network of agencies to sell the E.M.F. models, the Studebakers began to dangle offers before the Detroit stockholders in order to secure all of the outstanding stock. On March 9, 1910, after weeks of "wild rumors," an announcement of what *Horseless Age* called "the most sensational deal in months in the automobile industry" revealed that Studebaker, through its agent, J. P. Morgan and Company, had purchased the remaining sixty-four per cent of the E.M.F. stock. The offer had been too good for the stockholders to turn down. One report declared that each investor received thirty-two dollars for every dollar put into the company in 1908. This may have been an exaggeration, but about $5,000,000 in cash changed hands. Dr. Book was said to have cleared about $1,250,000 on the deal, receiving $250,000 in cash at the time of the announcement of the deal, with equal payments to be made to him each month thereafter until the entire sum had been paid. Walter Flanders was reported to have made about $1,000,000, and he was kept on as president and general manager under a three-year contract. Charles Palms, Dr. Book, and William Barbour, however, retired from the company entirely to enjoy the handsome financial rewards of their adventure into automobile manufacturing. In addition to Flanders, another E.M.F. top official who was retained under the new management was E. LeRoy Pelletier, who, according to one report, conducted the negotiations that led to the sale and received $200,000 for his services in addition to continuing on in his $20,000-a-year post as advertising manager.[26]

In 1911, the various Studebaker-controlled enterprises, including E.M.F., were pulled together into the Studebaker Corporation. Automobiles were now the major product of the South Bend-based firm, although carriages continued to be produced until 1920. The E.M.F. name was soon superseded by the familar Studebaker label, but the Indiana corporation continued to turn out cars from its Detroit factory until 1925, when it concentrated its manufacturing activities in South Bend. Thus did Detroit, in this rare instance, lose an automobile manufacturing plant, which had begun over two decades earlier with the Northern and Wayne companies, to another city and another state.[27]

Walter Flanders became dissatisfied with his new role in the Studebaker-E.M.F. organization, so early in 1912 he pulled out to rejoin his old partners, Byron Everitt and William Metzger. In still another reshuffling of business holdings, the Metzger Motor Car Company combined with a truck firm that Flanders had founded to form the new Flanders Motor Company. This company came to an abrupt end later in 1912 when it was purchased by a group that was interested not in the company but in securing the services of Walter Flanders to make something viable out of the wreckage of Benjamin Briscoe's bankrupt United States Motor Company. At the time of his death in 1923 as a result of injuries suffered in an automobile accident, Flanders, although semi-retired, had rejoined his old friends Byron Everitt and LeRoy Pelletier in what was to be still another short-lived, ill-fated automobile venture, the Rickenbacker Motor Company.[28]

At the time of the announcement of the sale of all outstanding E.M.F. stock to Studebaker in March 1910, the press was full of reports that the move, which Morgan and Company had handled, was but part of a broad-scale scheme that the Morgan interests were seeking to carry out. The scheme would reportedly result finally in the formation of a huge "automobile trust" in which General Motors, United States Motor, and the new Studebaker combine would be joined together into a super-corporation. Such a development did not occur, but this did not obscure the importance of what was probably the most important development in the auto industry in the years from 1908 to 1911: the industry was becoming recognized in the financial centers of the country as a big business, worthy of the attention of such powerful institutions as the House of Morgan. The day was passing when men such as William Murphy, Samuel Smith, or Dr. James B. Book, big capitalists in their local community but only faces in a crowd among the financial giants of the country, could continue to finance and control the little companies they had originally organized. As the financial needs of the auto companies increased, so too did the interest of outside financiers. They were willing to make generous offers to the original investors in order to get control of these companies and thereby control the stock offerings that would finance further expansion. Their offers proved too tempting for anyone to turn down but an eccentric like Henry Ford, who in the mid-twenties would reject an apparently *bona fide* offer from a Wall Street firm of over a billion dollars for the Ford Motor Company. But in 1908 and again in 1909, even Ford would have sold out, if the price had been right.[29]

In the summer of 1908, Morgan and Company had backed off when Ford and Olds talked in terms of $6,000,000 for control of their companies, but Durant and Briscoe had kept the talks in New York going on the basis of a merger simply of Buick and Maxwell-Briscoe. Toward the end of June, "trustworthy sources" were reporting that the merger had been completed, that J. P. Morgan was "largely interested" in the financing of the consolidation, and that Durant would be the general manager. Throughout the discussions, Durant could either not be reached by the press or he refused to make any comment concerning the reports. However, on June 29, Briscoe gave an interview in which he admitted that the rumors of a Buick-Maxwell merger "were not altogether without foundation." As yet, he said,

> there has been nothing that could be called negotiations. There have been, however, a series of conferences in which was discussed the feasibility of the proposition in its many phases, financial and physical, all with the end in view to place the business of making and selling moderate-priced motor cars on a basis that will be attractive to the average buyer.

Expressing the approach he had always taken toward a consolidation, and not Durant's preference for a holding company composed of completely independent operating units, Briscoe emphasized the savings that would be possible in such a consolidation through the centralizing of such activities as the purchasing of raw materials. He even referred to "a centralization and greater harmony of the selling organization," although at the same time emphasizing that such "an amalgamation of manufacturing strength . . . would in no way eliminate the individualities of two or more motor cars."[30]

The discussions had in fact come much nearer to a conclusion than Briscoe was ready to admit. On July 1, the law firm of Ward, Hayden and Satterlee wrote to John J. Carton (in his capacity as president of the National Bank of Flint rather than as the attorney for Buick) informing him that incorporation papers for the United Motors Company, as the consolidated firm was then being called, had been filed, "and unless something unforeseen arises, its stock will be ready to be issued within a few days." Carton was requested to discuss with A. H. Goss of Buick the prearranged delivery and deposit of Buick common stock in Carton's bank, which would then arrange the subsequent exchange of this stock for the new United Motors issue. Six days later, Carton replied that he had carried out these instructions, and on July 8 Goss notified all Buick stockholders that arrangements had been completed for the exchange of Buick common stock for preferred and common stock "in the new company which has been organized in accordance with the agreement signed by you, dated April 30, 1908." The stockholder was directed to sign his certificate of common stock and deposit it with the National Bank, which would hold it until stock in the new company was issued.[31]

In a letter to John Carton on July 2 from New England, where he had gone to spend a few days relaxing with his daughter and her husband, Durant reported on events in the East:

> [After] a long hot session with our friends in New York . . . [he] was pretty nearly used up at the finish. If you think it is an easy matter to get money from New York capitalists to finance a Motor Car proposition in Michigan, you have another guess coming. Notwithstanding the fact that quoted rates are very low, money is hard to get owing to a somewhat unaccountable feeling of uneasiness and a general distrust of the automobile proposition.

Possibly it was on this occasion that Durant, arguing in favor of a large investment on the basis of the future increase in demand for automobiles, reportedly declared: "The time will come when five hundred thousand automobiles will be manufactured, and sold in this country every year." Some accounts have him specifying ten years as the time that it would take to achieve that volume, and some have him predicting sales of a million cars a year. At a time when annual sales were in the vicinity of fifty thousand, such remarks could well have created the shock that they are reported to have had in George W. Perkins, who scoffed at Durant as a dreamer and observed: "If he has any sense he'll keep those notions to himself if he ever tries to borrow money." It may have been some other member of the Morgan company who reacted in this way, if the story has any truth to it, because Durant, in his memoirs, does not mention the story. Instead, as noted, he credits Perkins with having thought up the idea of a Morgan-backed automobile consolidation in the first place, which would seem to make Perkins' reported reaction to the possibilities for growth in the automobile market seem unlikely. Further, Durant recalled a train trip from New York to Albany in this period during which he had a friendly and open discussion with Perkins of the proposed combination and of how Durant thought it should be handled, "and I think I sold him the 'holding company' idea." It was at this time that Perkins raised the idea of calling the new corporation the International Motor Company. Perkins was fond of the name, since he had engineered the highly successful merger a few years earlier of several farm machinery companies into the International Harvester Company. Durant said he liked the name, and with his consent, Perkins declared that upon his return from a business trip to Chicago, he would file for a New York charter under this name. The change from United to International had been effected before the end of July.[32]

Skittishness on the part of Perkins or other Morgan partners about the growth potential of the auto industry probably did not contribute to the derailing of the merger plans. Problems did arise, however, due to suspicions about how the Buick stock was being handled. According to Durant, after his talk with Perkins on the train to Albany, he had returned to New York. Upon going to the office of Ward, Hayden & Satterlee he was met by Curtis R. Hatheway, a junior member of the firm who now assumes increasingly the role of legal adviser played earlier by Herbert Satterlee, who would shortly depart for an appointment in the Navy Department in Washington. Hatheway told Durant that Francis Lynde Stetson, for many years J. P. Morgan's most trusted attorney, wanted to talk with him. When Durant got to Stetson's office, he found the 62-year-old New York lawyer in an apparently cordial mood. After some preliminary remarks about Buick, about which Stetson said he had heard some very favorable reports, Stetson inquired about the stock arrangements. Durant explained that, according to the agreement that the stockholders had signed several months earlier, he had complete control of the stock and had the authority to make the exchange for stock in the new corporation, if the terms of the exchange satisfied him. "Mr. Stetson asked if the depositors had knowledge of the new securities or any details regarding the new company, the size of the capitalization, etc. I told him the stockholders had confidence in me and that the matter was entirely in my hands." Stetson, Durant declared, then expressed his doubts "if a title of that kind would be sufficient and he said he thought it might be necessary to have the Buick stockholders execute a new set of papers." Durant expressed his opposition to any change from the existing agreement with the stockholders. According to the account of the meeting given in Durant's memoirs and additional information concerning the same meeting in

MacManus and Beasley's *Men, Money, and Motors,* Stetson was expressing a concern that the Buick stockholders may not have had any idea as to the magnitude of the plans Durant had in mind at the time he had obtained their permission to act as their agent. At the back of Stetson's mind was a suspicion that Durant, and possibly some other insiders, had taken advantage of the situation to increase their holdings of Buick stock. In July, as rumors of the Buick-Maxwell merger plans continued to circulate, it was noted that trade in Buick stock, which, like all automobile issues at that time, was not listed on an exchange, had been quite brisk in Detroit. During the past three months, the price of Buick common on the open market had gone from 90 up to 125. Although Durant's reputation for integrity in his business dealings is usually regarded as above reproach, there are occasional hints that he may not at all times have been completely deserving of that reputation. Stetson was apparently suggesting that this was one of the times, and that Durant should make a full disclosure to the stockholders of the planned merger and give any who had sold their stock since the past spring an opportunity to buy back their stock in view of the events, of which they had been ignorant, that had made their stocks more valuable. Durant objected, declaring that he was acting on the advice of his attorney, John J. Carton, who, Durant said in the account of MacManus and Beasley, "is an honorable man." "We are honorable, too," Stetson replied. Durant answered that he had no doubts about that, but nevertheless he would continue to follow Carton's advice.[33]

At this point, according to MacManus and Beasley, Stetson ended the conference, declaring, "I shall advise Morgan and Company to drop all negotiations." Durant's memoirs, however, indicate that matters did not terminate quite so suddenly, and the papers of John Carton attest to the accuracy of Durant's version. In a letter to Ward, Hayden & Satterlee on July 29, Carton discusses some of Stetson's questions about the Buick stock transfer procedures which Durant "has taken up with me." Carton wrote that Stetson's position, as he understood it, was "that the details of the organization of the International Motor Company be made known to the individual stockholders of the Buick Motor Company before the sale and transfer of their stock is made." Carton, on the other hand, declared that he could

> see no reason why the details of the organization should be voluntarily made known to the individual stockholders of the Buick Motor Company. If any of them should refuse to sell their stock without the knowledge of these details, then it would be a matter to be taken up with that individual stockholder but I do not think that will be required in view of the consent which they have already given to the sale and transfer.[34]

An impasse had now been reached between Durant and Stetson and the Morgan associates over the issue of full disclosure of the merger plans to the Buick stockholders. By this time, however, increasingly detailed reports of the proposed consolidation had appeared in various newspapers. On Saturday, July 25, the Flint *Journal,* in a story from Detroit, declared that formal announcement of a Buick-Maxwell merger was expected in a few days but that already the basic details of the merger were well known. The combined capitalization of the new concern, this story reported, would be $10,000,000, an increase of $6,000,000 over the present combined Buick and Maxwell-Briscoe capitalization. The underwriting of the merger would be handled by J. P. Morgan and Company. New York papers picked up this same story out of Detroit, but Morgan denied that his institution was involved.[35]

Then on Friday, July 31, the most complete account of the merger yet published appeared in the New York *Times*. Describing it as "the first big combination in the automobile world," that paper reported that the International Motor Company would have a capitalization of $25,000,000 of which amount $11,000,000 would be in common stock and $14,000,000 in preferred stock, which would be issued first. Although J. P. Morgan and Company, as an institution, was not involved, several members of the firm were, the paper declared. Among those who were interested in the merger besides Satterlee and his law firm, whose connection had already been publicized, the *Times* listed William P. Hamilton, a great-grandson of Alexander Hamilton as well as a son-in-law of J. Pierpont Morgan, of whose firm Hamilton had been a member since 1900. Also listed were W. P. Horn of the Morgan staff and a director of Maxwell-Briscoe, and Otto J. Merkle, another Wall Street financier. Preliminary estimates prepared to support the financing of the merger projected a total production of 13,000 cars for the current year (which was, in fact, almost exactly the total Buick-Maxwell output in 1908), with a modest increase to 15,000 in 1909 (which fell about nine thousand cars short of the actual figures for that year). On this basis, estimated earnings on the preferred stock would be seven per cent and on the common stock not less than twenty-five per cent. "If the negotiations under way are successful," the *Times* reported, "the company will be ready for operations by Sept. 1." Besides Maxwell-Briscoe and Buick, an unknown number of unidentified companies, including several producers of raw materials, were said to be scheduled to be added to the combination in a short time.[36]

This story, which was quickly spread across other papers and in automotive trade publications, apparently struck too close to the truth. Morgan and Company, although standing for the principle of full disclosure to the stockholders, was obviously angered by this kind of premature public disclosure of the plans and the involvement of its members in the plans. Curtis Hatheway wired Durant shortly after the *Times* article had appeared that the Morgan interests "now refuse to cooperate," although Hatheway was trying to persuade them to change their minds. Durant answered on Saturday, August 1, that he had not yet seen the story, "but I take it that it must have been very 'severe' to have so greatly disturbed our friends at this late date." Later that day when a reporter in Flint showed Durant the dispatch from New York summarizing the contents of the *Times* story, Durant refused to comment on the report or to either confirm or deny its accuracy. This was in keeping with his attitude throughout the negotiations, and the fact that the *Times* divulged specific financial arrangements for Maxwell-Briscoe's entry into the merger and not those for Buick suggests that the *Times'* source was someone in the former company, possibly Benjamin Briscoe himself, since he had not hesitated earlier to being quoted on the reports of a merger.[37]

On August 4, Briscoe, returning to New York, found that conditions were "in somewhat of a chaotic state." He could not "quite fathom," he told Durant, why "the people on the 'corner' " were so upset about the New York *Times* story, since numerous stories had been appearing earlier in Flint and Detroit papers "which have evidently emanated from Buick stockholders." Briscoe declared that he had always thought "that one of the surest ways to get publicity is to deny things, or to refuse to confirm or deny them, and this has been too much our attitude in regard to the publication of the matter." On the other hand, he recognized that Stetson's insistence on full disclosure of the merger details to all the stockholders "will, I imagine, somewhat interfere with your plans." Briscoe concluded that the time that had been wasted trying to resolve the problems with the New York financiers was "quite unnecessary," and that it would be entirely possible for Durant and him and possibly one or two others to take care of the financing by themselves without any help. "We have both concluded that a million dollars in cash would be enough to finance the proposition and I will eat my shoes if we can't raise a million dollars between us."[38]

But Durant and Briscoe did not proceed on their own. Briscoe probably soon realized that he was already so closely tied up with Morgan and Company that he could not dismiss that institution so cavalierly as he had suggested without jeopardizing his present and future business interests. Thus as the House of Morgan became disenchanted with Durant and backed away from further participation in the consolidation effort, so too Briscoe seems to have decided to break off discussions with Durant, for the moment at least, of a Buick-Maxwell merger.

By the end of August, the prospects for a consolidation, so close to realization a month earlier, had apparently faded completely, with only Durant still clinging to the idea. Durant recalled that Herbert Satterlee asked him what he would do now.

> I told him that I had come to New York several months earlier, and had been led to believe that the consolidation sponsored by the Morgan firm was being considered and had so informed my people; that the Buick stock had been deposited and if released could never again be collected in the same form — nor would I have the courage, or care, to make another attempt. I must have a consolidation.

When Satterlee pointed out that Durant could not have a consolidation if he only had Buick to bring into the new firm, Durant revealed an ace-in-the-hole he apparently had been keeping in reserve just in case the merger talks broke down.[39]

Some time in July, Durant had gone to Lansing to investigate the

Olds Motor Works as a possible member of the combine. According to Fred Smith, he arrived in town after midnight and roused company officials from their beds to take him on a whirlwind fifteen-minute tour of the factory at 3 a.m. In subsequent conversations with the Smiths, Durant found them not only willing but eager to unload their company, which had fallen on hard times. The four-cylinder and six-cylinder Oldsmobiles had failed to retain the market that the little runabout had built up, and by 1908 sales had plummeted to a mere thousand cars, in contrast to the more than six thousand vehicles sold only three years earlier. In the spring of 1907, Eugene Cooley had tried to sell his Olds stock for five dollars a share, a sixth of what some buyers had been willing to pay at the height of interest in the company in 1903, but he could find no takers. Cooley's Detroit broker advised him that he might find a buyer if he dropped the price to four dollars. Little wonder, then, that Samuel Smith, who had advanced the company over a million dollars to keep it going, and his sons were ready to jump at an opportunity to join in a merger and thereby bail themselves out of an increasingly embarrassing financial position. In a letter to Durant on July 21, Fred Smith agreed to turn over three-fourths of the 200,000 outstanding Olds shares whenever stock in the new firm became available.

Durant realized that at the moment the Olds Motor Works was a weak substitute for Ford or Reo, companies he had earlier hoped would be part of the consolidation, but to the public the Oldsmobile name was still well known. As Durant later told A. B. C. Hardy when he brought the company into General Motors, he was getting mostly a lot of road signs, but it was the reputation that these signs represented that Durant hoped to use in restoring the Oldsmobile to something like its earlier popularity among car buyers.[40]

After Durant had told Satterlee that he expected to make the Olds company a part of the merger along with Buick, Satterlee had some additional questions as to how Durant proposed to take care of the increased capitalization that would be needed for the merger. Durant expressed confidence that he could get Walter Marr to assign to him enough of his patents to cover this stock issue. As for the name to be used for the new concern, there are several stories as to how the name General Motors came to be selected. It appears, however, that Durant would have preferred to continue to use the name that had already been widely publicized that summer, but that George Perkins refused to relinquish his interest in the name International Motor Company in the belief that he might still be able to use it in some future combination. A letter from Ward, Hayden and Satterlee to Durant on September 10, 1908, suggested that he use the name General Motors Company, which the firm had determined was not then being used by any other automobile company. This account of the origin of what would become a universally recognized company name, although it is the correct version, does not have the flair of the MacManus and Beasley version. That less accurate account depicts Durant taking a piece of stationery on his desk and dramatically crossing out the word "International" and penciling in the word "General." Holding the paper up, he asks Benjamin Briscoe, who has just told him that Perkins did not want him to use the other name, "How does that look?" "Fine," Briscoe replies. "You mean you'll call your organization the 'General Motors Company'?" "Yes," was Durant's cryptic reply, according to MacManus and Beasley's script, which leaves Durant sitting at his desk, after Briscoe departs, "studying the sheet of paper on which he had written — almost carelessly had written — a name that has come to be familiar around the world."[41]

After checking with Henry Russel, president of the Olds Motor Works, to see if he and the Smiths still favored a merger, Durant told Satterlee to go ahead with the preparation and filing of the incorporation papers for General Motors. Durant was anxious that there be no leaks concerning this merger scheme, as there had been concerning the earlier one. Satterlee, therefore, made the arrangements and assured Durant on September 15 that "we have seen to it, as far as we were able, that no publicity will attend the filing of the papers." When Curtis Hatheway filed the company's articles of incorporation with the secretary of state of New Jersey, therefore, on September 16, 1908, the event — the birthdate of General Motors — seems to have gone totally unnoticed in the daily press and trade publications.[42]

The reason Durant chose to incorporate his new company in New Jersey, and not in Michigan, as had been the case with Buick, Durant-Dort, and most of the other companies with which he had been previously connected, was quite simple. Michigan placed strict limitations on the amount of stock that a firm incorporated in that state might issue. The state of New Jersey, on the other hand, since 1889 had eliminated virtually all restrictions on what a business incorporated under its laws might do. As a result, no other state had been as successful in attracting the business of the huge corporations that sprang up as the trend toward consolidation gained increasing favor with American business. All seven of the so-called "Great Industrial Trusts" of 1904, controlling over fifteen hundred plants throughout the country, with a total capitalization of over two and a half billion dollars, were chartered in the Garden State. No wonder Durant secured a New Jersey charter for General Motors, especially if John Carton was correct when he told Arthur Pound that Durant, in 1908, had had no idea that General Motors would become a great manufacturing concern. Instead, Carton declared, "what Mr. Durant desired most of all were large stock issues in which he, from an inside position, could dicker and trade."[43]

Initially, General Motors would have attracted little attention, in any event, since its capitalization at the time of incorporation was a mere two thousand dollars, and the three men who had signed the incorporation papers on September 15 were unknowns, fronting for the real organizer of the company, William Durant. (One of the three, George E. Daniels, who was elected interim president of the company on September 22, would later head up both the Cartercar and Oakland companies when these firms were acquired by G.M.) On September 28, the three incorporators met and were advised by President Daniels that "Mr. W. C. Durant is present and is prepared to make a business proposition to the company." Durant, continuing with this little charade, declared that since he had been "advised" that G.M. had been incorporated and that it was interested in automobiles, he proposed to sell his Buick company to the New Jersey firm. His suggestion met with a quick and favorable response, and the capitalization of General Motors was increased to $12,500,000 to facilitate the purchase. Three days later, on October 1, 1908, the Buick Motor Company became General Motors' first acquisition. In a complicated transaction, 18,870 shares of common stock of Buick, a company whose worth was listed as $3,417,142, were turned over to G.M. in exchange for $1500 in cash and G.M. preferred stock with a par value of $2,498,500, and common stock valued at $1,249,250.[44]

What happened to the Buick Motor Company on October 1, 1908, should not be confused with what happened to the Wayne and Northern automobile companies when they merged on June 2 of that year to form E.M.F. There was no merger of Buick with General Motors. The Buick company legally and in actual fact continued to exist after October 1 as an independent operating company. The General Motors Company of New Jersey now controlled Buick by the fact that it owned most, if not all, of the outstanding Buick stock. Legally, that was its only connection with Buick. A few months later, some little difficulty and confusion over the true nature of the Buick-G.M. relationship led the secretary of state's office in Lansing to send Arnold Goss of Buick some forms which he was directed to have General Motors fill out "in order to comply with the laws of that State, relative to foreign corporations doing business within the State." John Carton, in his blandest, most poker-faced manner, proceeded to explain to his friend, the newly elected Republican Secretary of State, Frederick C. Martindale, that the secretary did not "understand the exact position of the General Motors Company." It was true, Carton declared, "that it owns and holds the stock of several Michigan domestic corporations, but the General Motors Company itself is not transacting any business within this state." Thus, Carton concluded, G.M. was not subject to the regulations of the state of Michigan.[45]

Unlike the later General Motors Corporation which succeeded it in 1917 and which was, and is, a manufacturing business, the General Motors Company was a holding company, manufacturing nothing, but only controlling companies that were engaged in manufacturing. The holding company was a device that had originated in New Jersey when that state in 1889 made it legal for firms incorporated there to own stock in other corporations. Instead of forming trusts, a means of shutting off competition which had created a great outcry and had led to the passage of legislation such as the Sherman Antitrust Act of 1890, competing companies could now be linked together quite legally through a holding company. While one of the advantages of becoming part of such a holding company was the competitive edge that could be gained through the pooling of information and resources among the operating companies, it is quite likely, as Carton suggests, that Durant's interest arose more from the possibility of large profits. The experience of the preceding two decades had demonstrated the stock-buying public's willingness to pay far more for the stock of a holding company than the combined price of the stocks of the various operating firms that the holding company controlled. Thus there was big money to be made by the stockholder in Buick, who suddenly found himself the possessor instead of a more valuable block of General Motors preferred and common stock, and there was even bigger money to be made by the promoters of such holding-company combinations.[46]

At the end of October 1908, the veil of secrecy that Durant had tried to keep pulled down over his infant automobile combination began to lift with the publication in Detroit of the first reports of the formation of General Motors; it was a merger, stories claimed, that had been "fathered by J. Pierpont Morgan" and which would equal in importance Morgan's most famous offspring prior to this time, the U. S. Steel Corporation. The continued linking of the Morgan name to Durant's consolidation moves at this time and in the months ahead could have been simply a conclusion reached by the press, growing out of the known association of Morgan and Company with the earlier International Motor plans. But there may also have been more to it. On October 20, the by-laws of General Motors had been changed to provide for a board of seven directors, consisting of the three officers in the company and four other men. William M. Eaton, an officer with the Wall Street investment firm of Hodenpyl-Walbridge & Company, replaced George Daniels at this time as company president. Durant, who, as in his previous businesses, preferred to have someone else holding the top-rated job (although everyone recognized that he himself was actually in charge), took over the new position of vice-president of General Motors. Replacing Benjamin Marcuse, another of the original trio of G.M. incorporators, as secretary-treasurer was Curtis R. Hatheway, who held this key position until January 1911. The fact that Hatheway was the law partner of J. P. Morgan's son-in-law no doubt helped to keep alive the rumors that Morgan was the financial backer of General Motors. In addition, however, although Durant used the resources of Buick itself to underwrite the sale of some of the stock that was issued at the time G.M. acquired control of the Flint manufacturing firm, a suspicion lingers that one or more members of the Morgan company may still have been in the background lending their prestige and resources in carrying through the complicated negotiations and stock arrangements that were used to add more and more companies to the G.M. family throughout the remainder of 1908 and 1909.

Additionally, however, William Eaton's selection as president of General Motors, a position that he held from October 20, 1908, to November 23, 1910, provides a clue to Durant's efforts to secure financial support from another source, as well as indicating another indirect, but possibly significant link with the Morgan organization. Eaton, who has received only slight attention from previous automobile historians, had come to Jackson in the 1870's from Ohio, where he had been born in 1856. He probably first became acquainted with Durant in the 1880's when Eaton became the manager of the Jackson Gas Light Company at the same time that Durant had gotten involved with the gas company in Flint. At the beginning of the twentieth century, the two men probably became better acquainted when Durant was establishing the Imperial Wheel plant in Jackson. In 1903, Eaton left Jackson to become general manager of the Grand Rapids Gas Light Company, whose president was Henry Walbridge, a member of the Kalamazoo Walbridge family and a relative of George Walbridge Perkins, the Morgan partner. Walbridge, who had interests in several Michigan utility companies, now joined forces with a Grand Rapids financier, Anton G. Hodenpyl, to form Hodenpyl-Walbridge & Company, with offices in New York. By 1908 the new investment firm had organized or gained control of gas, electric, and traction companies in Michigan, Indiana, Illinois, Pennsylvania, and New York, beginning the development of the giant utility holding company that later became known as the Commonwealth & Southern Corporation. William Eaton joined the Hodenpyl-Walbridge organization as the manager of one of its properties in Rochester, New York. In 1907 he moved into Hodenpyl-Walbridge & Company itself, where he soon began selling gas and electricity to automobile companies. Eaton's election to the non-paying position of president of General Motors resulted, probably, less from his friendship with Durant than from Durant's hope that Eaton might help him to get support from the Hodenpyl interests. But as it turned out, Anton Hodenpyl, who had his eyes fixed on a utilities empire, was not to be diverted into what seemed at the moment to be the less secure prospects of the automobile industry.[47]

At the end of October there was considerable speculation about the full extent of the newly emerging consolidation. Some observers were of the opinion that the merger of Wayne and Northern and several other developments in recent months were related in some way to General Motors' activities. Maxwell-Briscoe, Pope-Toledo, and one or more Cleveland automobile companies would, it was reported, soon be taken over by G.M. The foremost candidate for immediate acquisition by General Motors, however, was stated to be the Olds Motor Works. A few days later, Fred Smith issued a denial of this report. "The story originated in New York," he said, "and there was no foundation for it. The Olds Motor Works is on a firm financial basis and is enjoying the best business in the history of the concern. The idea of selling the interests or joining with any combination," Smith declared, "has never been entertained." However, readers of the Flint Journal, which carried this statement by Smith, may have noticed a small item a week earlier that reported that Smith, Durant, Durant's son-in-law, Dr. Edwin Campbell, who had now given up his medical practice in Flint to become a kind of glorified errand boy for Durant, Charles P. Downey,

When it was acquired by General Motors in November 1908, the Olds Motor Works had come a long way from its curved-dash Oldsmobile days, as this 1908 Model M Oldsmobile "Toy Tonneau" clearly attested.
Courtesy Oldsmobile Division, General Motors

influential Lansing hotel man who had married the sister of Durant's first wife, and Curtis Hatheway were members of a weekend hunting party to Otisville, near Flint. It is quite likely that the talk centered around business matters, and that perhaps the objections that Smith had raised to G.M.'s first official offer for control of the Olds Motor Works, made on October 10, had been taken care of by the end of the hunting excursion. On November 12, the deal was completed and G.M. acquired control of the Olds firm.[48] Arthur Pound and Lawrence Seltzer, both of whom had access to G.M. records covering the purchase, are not in complete agreement as to the precise terms of the initial arrangement, but Olds stockholders received approximately $3,000,000 in stock plus $17,279 cash in exchange for the outstanding Olds stock that had a total par value of $2,000,000 but whose market value at the time was no more than half that amount. G.M. also agreed to assume the claims of Samuel Smith against his company that amounted to $1,044,173.89. In addition, Fred Smith and Henry Russel were named to the G.M. board of directors, bumping off Daniels and Marcuse, who had long since served their purpose. (The third member of the trio of incorporators, Arthur W. Britton, had been dropped from the roster earlier, on October 20.) G.M. retained the right to name three of the five members of the board of directors of the Olds Motor Works. The Smiths were able to deliver the huge block of Olds stock that they controlled, and by June of 1909, out of 200,000 shares of Olds stock, the holding company was lacking only the holdings of six individuals who opposed the settlement with G.M., and who controlled from ten to fifty shares each.⁴⁹

Frederic Smith and his brother Angus kept their executive positions with Olds Motor Works, just as Durant and his team of executives continued to run Buick after that company had come under the control of G.M. It was Durant's desire to maintain as much as possible the services of those who had been successful in running the firms that G.M. acquired. Since the Olds company had not been a notable success during the later years of Fred Smith's management, the announcement on September 2, 1909, that Fred and Angus Smith had resigned from the Olds company was probably not a matter of much regret to Durant, who may even have prompted the resignations. Fred Smith also left the G.M. board of directors at the same time. Although the Smith brothers were briefly connected with another automobile venture, their roles in the development of the auto industry were, for all practical purposes, played out when they severed their connections with the Olds Motor Works. Fred Smith later admitted rather sheepishly that in insisting on taking mostly G.M. preferred, rather than common, stock in 1908 the Smiths had acted foolishly, but they could scarcely complain of the generous nature of the financial returns they had received from the auto industry in a little over ten years' time. Nor could the auto industry complain about the contributions the Smiths had made in return for those rewards. When Samuel L. Smith died on May 7, 1917, just short of his 87th birthday, the Detroit *News,* strangely enough, made no mention at all of his connections with the automobile industry, but the *Free Press* eulogized Smith as the "father of the motor car industry in Detroit." The national trade publication, *The Automobile,* said of him: "He commercialized the automobile industry when it was in its infancy. He had the courage to spend millions on the industry."⁵⁰

The news of the acquisition of the Olds Motor Works did not reach the press until nearly the end of December 1908, leading to the first really extensive coverage of the appearance of a new automobile enterprise. *Horseless Age,* three and a half months behind in its coverage, headlined its December 30, 1908, story: "The General Motors Company Launched." When a Flint reporter questioned Durant about one of the reports on December 22, he replied: "I have no information on the subject that I can give out for publication. . . . So far as the Buick company is concerned, you may say, however, that it is still doing business and will keep right on doing business at the old stand." Six days later, the Flint *Journal,* publishing a dispatch from New York concerning the announcement of G.M.'s formation, headlined the story: "It Will Not Down. Report Concerning Merger of Auto Concerns. Understood in New York Automobile Circles That Buick Will Be in Consolidation." Stubbornly adhering to his noncommittal public stance, Durant again declared, when shown the latest report, that he could make no comment on the matter.⁵¹

The arrival of a new year soon demonstrated that the early rumors concerning the possible scope of General Motors' list of acquisitions had erred by being too conservative. In a bewildering series of maneuvers, the detailing of which would be a major research project in itself, Durant, through his holding company, gained control of all or a major share of the stock interests in over a score of companies, driving himself and his associates at a frenzied pace. In January, the acquisition of stock in the Oakland Motor Car Company of Pontiac was begun, and was completed later in the year. In view of the fact that this company ultimately evolved into the present Pontiac division, it must be viewed as one of Durant's more fortunate accessions. The Oakland company, which had been organized in August 1907 by Pontiac's leading carriage manufacturer, Edward M. Murphy, with Alanson Brush as the designer of its model — the Oakland — had actually built and sold only a few cars and was apparently in rather precarious financial circumstances. At the time, therefore, its possible contribution to the future prosperity of General Motors would probably have been deemed no greater than that of such long-forgotten G.M. acquisitions as the Cartercar Company, the Welch Motor Car Company, the Ewing Automobile Company, or the Elmore Manufacturing Company. Several truck companies and auto parts manufacturers also dotted the list of acquisitions, along with the mysterious decision to acquire the Heany Lamp companies, manufacturers of electric light bulbs that were based on patents that turned out to be fraudulent and the companies therefore worthless. Since Durant must have known this at the time, Lawrence Seltzer has surmised that the more than $7,000,000 in G.M. stock that was doled out for the Heany companies (including $5,908,500 in G.M. common, over two-thirds of all the voting shares in the company that were paid out in this way during this period) may have been part of an elaborate stock-watering scheme. In contrast, G.M. acquired forty-nine per cent of the stock in the eminently sound Weston-Mott Company (Charles Mott retained control of the remaining fifty-one per cent until 1913) for only $141,000 in stock plus $230,000 in cash.[52]

The most important addition to the G.M. group in 1909 was, without a doubt, that of Cadillac, which Durant almost lost more than once. In November 1908, Benjamin Briscoe, pursuing his own expansion plans, obtained an option on sixty per cent of the Cadillac stock at a price of $150 a share. He was unable to take advantage of this opportunity, however, so Durant approached the Lelands, who, he discovered, were interested in cash, not stock, for their company. Wilfred Leland later recalled that he and his father had been willing to sell for a total price of $3,500,000, giving Durant a ten-day option. Durant was forced to drop the idea for several months, but then, working through Arnold Goss, a little-known but close and trusted Durant aide throughout this period, resumed the negotiations in the middle of 1909. The Lelands now upped their asking price to $4,125,-000. Again Durant failed to act during the ten-day option period. Finally, on July 1, a contract was signed, and Durant had to come up with either $4,400,000 or $4,500,000 in cash (authorities disagree on the exact amount) plus $275,000 in G.M. preferred stock. On July 29, 1909, the Cadillac stockholders assembled at the National Bank in Detroit to receive their payment, amounting to some $300 a share. The total was the largest stock transaction in Detroit to that time. William Murphy had 3055 Cadillac shares, Lem Bowen and Clarence Black each had 2840, Albert White had 1607, and another investor who dated back to William Maybury's original group of Ford supporters, Everett A. Leonard, had 179 shares of Cadillac stock. In the long run, of course, these men would have profited far more if they had taken stock in G.M. instead of cash, but since they had reportedly put a total of only $327,000 in cash from all sources into the Cadillac venture, Murphy and his associates apparently decided that with the handsome dividends their stock had already earned, the payment they now received was ample compensation for the risks they had incurred when they first entered the business of automobile manufacturing in the late nineties. Some idea, however, of the riches that the Cadillac stockholders and their heirs might have had if they had decided to accept, instead of cash, G.M. stock valued at $4,500,000, can be seen in the experience of the step-mother of one of the early auto dealers of Ypsilanti, Michigan. In 1911 she sold $1500 in stock that she owned in a Battle Creek breakfast food company and invested the money in General Motors stock. During the next half century, through stock splits and by taking advantage of all the stock options she was offered, the woman saw her initial investment grow into a fortune of over $1,600,000 in G.M. stock by the time of her death in the 1960's.[53]

Wilfred and Henry Leland, who each owned 1340 shares of Cadillac, were called aside by Durant at the time that payment was made for the stock. He asked them to remain on as the managers of Cadillac. They replied that they would do so if they were left entirely free to manage the company along the same high standards that they had always sought to maintain. "That is exactly what I want," Durant replied. "I want you to continue to run the Cadillac exactly as though it were still your own. You will receive no directions from anyone." The good relationships that apparently existed between the three men at this time did not last very long, and when the Lelands left Cadillac and General Motors in 1917, for whatever immediate reason, they and Durant were unquestionably glad to be free of one another.[54]

Although Durant was probably not entirely clear in his own mind what he was after as he built up his collection of G.M.-controlled companies, two objectives clearly guided him. By acquiring as many auto parts manufacturers as possible he was attempting to end the uncertainties faced by the automobile company dependent on outside suppliers over whom it had no control. Durant had followed the same approach fifteen years earlier in developing his carriage interests. The other objective was one that placed him in direct opposition to the business philosophy of Henry Ford. Whereas Ford, in the spring of 1909, staked the entire future of the Ford Motor Company on the success of the Model T, abandoning all of his other models, Durant was not ready to take that kind of risk. Instead, he wanted to discount the sudden shifts in public taste by offering as wide a range of models, in as wide a range of prices, as possible. He expressed his philosophy to A.B.C. Hardy, who later recalled:

> Durant bought a lot of different companies, most of which were not much good; but he paid for them largely in stock. He didn't want the actual assets of these companies; most of them were head over heels in debt, anyway. He wanted a lot of 'makes,' so that he would always be sure to have some popular cars. I heard him explain this one day in this way:
>
> 'They say I shouldn't have bought Cartercar,' he said. 'Well, how was any one to know that Cartercar wasn't to be the thing? It had the friction drive and no other car had it [which was not actually the case]. How could I tell what these engineers would say next? Maybe friction drive would be the thing. And then there's Elmore, with its two-cycle engine. That's the kind they were using on motor-boats; maybe two-cycles was going to be the thing for automobiles. I was getting every car in sight, playing safe all along the line.'

Durant's idea, when it was carefully refined in the 1920's in the structuring of the General Motors Corporation's several automobile manufacturing divisions, became the basis for nearly all subsequent automobile development. It ultimately won the support of even the Ford Motor Company.[55]

Durant, however, did not succeed in "getting every car in sight." Some of the deals he worked on failed. In the fall of 1909, Arnold Goss had made arrangements for General Motors to buy all the stock of the E. R. Thomas Company of Buffalo. Little is known as to the reasons why this transaction was not completed, but, although the Thomas Flyer had been catapulted to fame by its victory a few months earlier in the New York-to-Paris (via Siberia) automobile race, neither the company nor the car could really be counted as a serious loss to G.M.[56]

Durant also renewed his efforts to add the three other companies which, with Buick, had been parties to the original merger talks in 1908. Ransom Olds jotted some notes headed "General Motors" in his diary in the fall of 1908, and on September 28, 1909, when he was in New York, his entry read: "Saw Durant." How far the talks progressed regarding an affiliation of Reo with G.M. is not known, but they came to nothing.[57]

On the day before Ransom Olds saw Durant in New York in September 1909 he had seen Benjamin Briscoe and Alfred Reeves, who was working with Briscoe on his renewed efforts to organize his own combination. Earlier in 1909 there had been persistent reports that Maxwell-Briscoe would enter the G.M. fold, and both Briscoe and Durant worked to bring this about. In July, Briscoe worked out a deal with Durant whereby General Motors would acquire control of the Maxwell company, the Briscoe Manufacturing Company, and Frank Briscoe's Brush Runabout, in exchange for $5,000,000 in stock. Briscoe went to Morgan and Company, whose approval of the deal, in view of the interest it held in Briscoe's enterprises, was required. The Morgan interests refused to approve the deal on the basis of a stock exchange. They would approve only if Durant paid $2,000,000 in cash. This Durant was either unwilling or unable to do. Thus, ironically, the acquisition of Maxwell-Briscoe was torpedoed by the

Morgans' insistence on the same kind of deal that supposedly was one of the main reasons for their refusal to support the acquisition of Ford and Reo in 1908. In 1921, Briscoe calculated that the $5,000,000 in G.M. stock that he and the Morgans could have had in 1909 would have been worth over $100,000,000.[58]

Later in the summer of 1909 when Briscoe was questioned about the continuing reports that G.M. might buy out Maxwell-Briscoe, Briscoe replied that it was much more likely that his company would buy out other companies, rather than the reverse. It was at this time that Briscoe got down to the serious business of organizing a rival automobile consolidation, if he could not be a part of Durant's. In January 1910 the United States Motor Company was organized with a capitalization of $16,000,000, backed principally by Anthony Brady. Maxwell-Briscoe was the first acquisition of the new combine, followed by the Columbia Motor Car Company, a company in which, as the successor to the old Electric Vehicle Company, Brady had a major interest. Soon other companies, including brother Frank Briscoe's Brush Runabout Company of Detroit, were added to what seemed to be an impressive list of acquisitions. But the Maxwell car was the only really strong entry. Without anything else to compete with Durant's money-making Buick and Cadillac cars, and his potentially valuable Oldsmobile and Oakland properties, the United States Motor Company succumbed to a multiplicity of financial problems in 1912. Walter Flanders salvaged the Maxwell car from the wreckage, and eventually in the 1920's the Maxwell company became the base on which Walter P. Chrysler built the Chrysler Corporation.

Benjamin Briscoe attempted a comeback in 1914 with his own Briscoe car, manufactured in Jackson; it was a low-priced car that is remembered chiefly because it had only one headlight. But when the war came, Briscoe turned his plant over to war production and then joined the navy, with the rank of lieutenant-commander. Shortly after the war he left the automobile business, dabbled in oil and in gold mining, and then in the last years of his life, before he died in 1945, he engaged in some agricultural experiments on three thousand acres of land he owned in Florida. Although his career in the auto industry had been somewhat abbreviated, his Maxwell-Briscoe company did in a sense remain in business, although under a different name, as the third member of the modern Big Three of the American automobile industry.[59]

The Big Three would not exist, at least with its present composition, if Durant had had his way in the fall of 1909. According to Theodore MacManus, he was in Durant's office in Flint late one Saturday while Durant was bemoaning certain difficulties he was having with General Motors. Other evidence indicates that the discussion must have occurred in the fall of 1909. Durant may have had an inkling of the problems that threatened the very life of G.M. a few months later in 1910. MacManus suggested that Durant's and G.M.'s standing would be helped immensely if they bought the Ford Motor Company. "Durant laughed in derision. 'I couldn't buy the Ford business.'" MacManus replied that he had been told the Ford company could be bought. "By whom?" Durant asked. "A name was passed. Durant grew excited. 'Can you make an appointment?'" MacManus said that he could, and a few days later Durant contacted Henry Ford and James Couzens at the Belmont Hotel in New York.[60]

MacManus' account is verified by evidence in Durant's memoirs and in the papers of James Couzens. Following Judge Hough's decision on September 15, 1909, upholding the Selden patent, James Couzens, confirming what MacManus had reported, told Durant that Ford was interested in selling his company. "General Motors, with its several companies holding licenses, would probably be able to make a very satisfactory adjustment with Selden if it owned the Ford Company." Durant, in turn, told Couzens before the latter went to New York with Ford to confer with their lawyers about the Selden decision, that General Motors would certainly like to purchase the company. It was arranged that the two would confer again in New York after Couzens had had an opportunity to talk more with Ford.[61]

In New York on October 5, Couzens and Durant met together to discuss a deal for control of the Ford Motor Company. Henry Ford, who, according to Couzens, was "sick in body and disturbed in mind," remained in his hotel room, letting Couzens handle the preliminary negotiations. It was agreed by the two other men that Henry Ford would be asked to sell the Ford Motor Company for $8,000,000. Couzens would pay Ford enough money to boost his own holdings of Ford stock to twenty-five per cent of the total. Couzens would retain that stock, and presumably continue to be active in the management of the company, while Ford was to retire from the automobile business. For the three-quarters of the Ford stock that was left, G.M. would pay $6,000,000, a third of which would be paid in cash at the time of the sale, and the rest to be paid off at five per cent interest over a three-year period. Couzens then carried the terms of this agreement upstairs in the hotel to Ford's room, where he found Ford, who was suffering an attack of lumbago, lying on the floor, since he could not get any rest in bed. There are two slightly differing versions of the ensuing conversation between Ford and Couzens. When Ford asked how much Durant would pay for the company, both accounts say that Couzens answered, "Eight million dollars," although Durant's account indicates that only $6,000,000 would come from G.M., the remaining $2,000,000 seemingly resulting in some way from the purchase by Couzens of the additional Ford stock. In any event, Ford, according to MacManus, responded: "All right. But — *gold on the table!*" Couzens asked Ford, "How do you mean that?" "I mean cash." The other version has Ford adding that if the payment was in cash, "Tell him . . . I'll throw in my lumbago!"

According to Lawrence Seltzer, the minutes of the board of directors of General Motors contain evidence that Durant received an option on October 5 to purchase all of the Ford stock for $8,000,000, with $2,000,000 down in cash, and the rest in one- and two-year notes. (The arrangement to allow Couzens to purchase and retain control of twenty-five per cent of the Ford stock was either arrived at later, or perhaps Henry Ford had already vetoed that idea.) On Sunday, October 24, Durant, Ford, and Couzens met together secretly in the Ford plant in Detroit and checked over the company inventory. Two days later, according to MacManus, the G.M. board of directors formally approved the purchase agreement. Ford had compromised on his demands for cash, so all that Durant had to come up with at the moment was $2,000,000. Frank A. Vanderlip, president of the National City Bank of New York, promised Durant the money, but then the loan committee of the bank, which had strong Morgan connections, vetoed the loan, and Durant's opportunity was lost.

Of course, the New York bankers were incredibly short-sighted — as any historian writing years later can safely assert. Benjamin Briscoe claims that he also was turned down when he was offered the same $8,000,-000 deal for Ford, suggesting that the bankers' refusal to loan money at this time reflected a skeptical view of the industry in general. On the other hand, there was some justification for the fears the bankers may have held that General Motors had expanded too quickly and that its resources were overextended. During the following summer of 1910, a slight drop in automobile sales in the country almost spelled disaster for General Motors, which was paying for an enormous expansion of some of the companies it controlled through the income from the sales of cars, largely the sales of Buick and Cadillac. Durant was able to save the company only by submitting to the severe terms imposed by the eastern syndicate that loaned G.M. the money needed to carry the company through the crisis. The added burden of the Ford indebtedness, had it been authorized in October 1909, might have been too much for G.M. to have handled as things turned out the following year.

Despite financial uncertainties, both Ford and General Motors survived the events of the fall of 1909. Ford was, by this time, securely established in first place in terms of automobile sales. It would continue to hold this position for almost twenty years, for several years dominating the industry to such an extent that the total sales of all other makes of cars in America were exceeded by those of the Model T. Without a strong competitor with Ford in the low-priced field, General Motors did not compare with the Ford Motor Company for many years in terms of total car sales, but its higher-priced Buicks, Cadillacs, Oldsmobiles, and Oaklands made the annual revenues of the company greater than those of the Ford Motor Company well before the rise of Chevrolet in the mid-twenties pushed the corporation ahead in volume output as well.

CHAPTER 11

"ARE YOU SATISFIED?"

The full flowering of the Ford Motor Company, which was becoming evident by 1909, and the obviously momentous nature of the General Motors developments at this same time simply served to emphasize and dramatize what had been happening in the automobile industry in the United States for several years. The events of 1908-1909 made these years the first major turning point in the industry's development.

By 1908-1909, the experimental phase of automotive development had about ended. The mystery that had surrounded the building of a horseless carriage in the nineties was gone. In place of the few mechanics and tinkerers who sometimes succeeded and sometimes failed to design and put together an operable vehicle, there now were a large number of individuals who were perfectly capable of building reasonably satisfactory automobiles without having to sweat out many months or years of trial and error before they finally achieved success.

In design and general appearance the automobile of 1909 had caught up with that of the Europeans. Although Alanson Brush's little one-

Ypsilanti, Michigan, about 1910. *For this proud owner of a new Reo touring car and his three companions the automobile had obviously become an accepted part of their lives. The courting stage in the affair between Americans and the automobile was over. The knot had been tied.*
Courtesy Ypsilanti Historical Museum

cylinder runabout and the high-wheeled buggy-type motor vehicle that enjoyed a brief popularity in the rural parts of the Middle West were a continuation of the popular models of the 1901 era, they were an exception that would soon pass from sight in 1909. In its place, the public was demanding and getting by that time a car which usually had four cylinders, with the engine in the front, under a hood. A steering wheel had long since replaced the tiller, and increasingly the steering was being done from the left-hand side of the car. Windshields, running boards, more commodious seating arrangements, electric horns, acetylene gas lights, and many less obvious mechanical improvements were accepted parts of the automobile world. The enclosed car was not yet a reality, but fabric tops and side curtains made motoring in bad weather considerably more practical and enjoyable. Many improvements now considered basic by automobile users were still in the future, but in contrast with the primitive vehicles that were being offered to the public in the early days of the industry, the automobile and its industry had come an amazingly long way in a very few years.

By 1908-1909, too, the heated debates that had been carried on a decade earlier between the proponents of the steam car, electric car, and gasoline car were at an end. Although the Stanley brothers were still producing their steamers, and although the Detroit Electric, the most popular of the electric vehicles, only began to appear in 1906, and was produced as late as 1940, the car driven by a gasoline, internal-combustion engine had long since won the day among automobile buyers. The Electric Vehicle Company, the most impressively backed manufacturer of the electric car, had gone bankrupt, and the White brothers in Cleveland, whose steam car was probably better than the more famous Stanley steamer, were about to abandon steam in favor of gasoline (the switch, which took place in 1910, undoubtedly accounts for the survival of this pioneer automobile company today as the largest independent manufacturer of trucks in America).[1]

The years from 1895 to 1909 were decisive not only regarding the type of automobile that would be produced, but also in determining what companies would be successful in manufacturing those cars in the years ahead. By the end of that era, the possibilities for successful and lasting entry into the industry were rapidly coming to an end, and the days when one could start to manufacture automobiles on a shoestring were definitely over. To be sure, hundreds of companies started up in the years following 1909, producing such famous or near-famous cars as the Saxon, the Jordan, the Duesenberg, the Cord, and the Kaiser, but none of them survived.

Of the cars that are still on the market today that date from the post-1909 era, only the Chevrolet, the Dodge, and the Lincoln can be called truly new developments, and even that is stretching the point. The Chevrolet was born in 1911, a creation of William C. Durant made possible by the resources he had accumulated in the industry prior to 1909. Whether Chevrolet could have survived without joining the General Motors organization, as it did a few years later, is at least debatable. The Dodge, which began to appear in 1914, was an outgrowth of the wealth and reputation the Dodge brothers had gained from their association with the older Ford Motor Company. Henry Leland's Lincoln was likewise made possible by the position Leland had gained earlier with Cadillac, and even then the car did not become a success until its manufacture was taken over by Ford. (The handful of Checker Marathon cars that are sold today should perhaps also be included in this list of successful surviving automobile makes developed after 1909, since the Kalamazoo taxicab company dates from the 1920's.)

As for the other surviving automobile manufacturers today, the Chrysler Corporation dates from 1925, but it was a direct outgrowth of two other models — the Maxwell, of pre-1909 origins, and the Chalmers, a Detroit car that began production in 1908. The American Motors Corporation, formed in 1954, was likewise the result of a merger of two companies which dated back to 1909 or earlier. One of these, Nash, was organized by Charles Nash in 1916, but that was simply a renaming and refinancing of the Jeffery Company of Kenosha, Wisconsin, which had been making cars since 1902. The other company involved in the 1954

A.M.C. merger was the Hudson Motor Car Company, a Detroit firm founded in 1909 by Roy Chapin, Howard Coffin, and several other former Olds Motor Works employees, with backing from the Detroit merchant, J. L. Hudson. Later, American Motors acquired the Kaiser-Jeep operation in Toledo, which was at the time the last surviving element of the post-World War II Kaiser-Frazer automobile venture, but which produced a vehicle that had originated with the older Willys-Overland company, a pre-1909 firm.

Although the Plymouth and the Mercury, among others, could be cited as automobiles on the market today that first appeared long after 1909, they were introduced by established companies; they were not the creations of new concerns organized to produce them, as were Ford, Buick, Oldsmobile, Cadillac, and Pontiac (the successor of the Oakland of 1907 origins).

No developments of this first era ending in 1909 were more striking or of more lasting importance than those affecting the geographical distribution of the manufacturers of automobiles. By 1909, Detroit's (or more correctly, Michigan's) domination of the industry had become a widely recognized fact. This dominance had been achieved in less than a decade. Only nine years earlier, in the summer of 1900, *Motor Age,* in attempting to list all automobile manufacturing activity in the country, could find only three Michigan companies that qualified for inclusion in a six-page report of its findings. Similarly, in 1901, the Michigan Bureau of Labor, surveying the 5572 business establishments in the state that it loosely referred to as factories, listed only three such firms as engaged principally in manufacturing or handling automobiles. Oddly enough, the Olds Motor Works, which was one of the three companies from Michigan included in the *Motor Age* survey, indicated to the state agency in 1901 that motors and gasoline engines, not automobiles, were the principal products of both its Detroit and Lansing plants. The *Michigan State Gazetteer* that year presented much the same picture regarding the extent of auto-related businesses in Michigan, listing only four automobile manufacturers, three of them in Detroit (including the Olds Motor Works) and one in Saginaw. A Detroit concern was reported to be repairing automobile motors, while six Detroit firms, together with one in Grand Rapids and one in Ionia, were engaged in selling cars.[2]

Within two years the situation was changing as first the Olds Motor Works and then the several new companies that successfully imitated Olds and its popular runabout shoved Michigan up toward the front in auto production. In December 1903, recognizing these developments, the trade journal *Automobile* devoted eleven pages to a discussion of the auto industry in Detroit, declaring that between them, Detroit and Cleveland produced more than half of all the cars produced in the country, "and of these two cities Detroit's output is easily first." Cleveland's automakers, such as the Winton company, would dispute Detroit's primacy for at least a year or two more, arguing that the touring cars on which the

Cleveland companies concentrated were a more significant contribution to the industry than the inexpensive runabouts that comprised the great bulk of Detroit's numerically larger output. But the special attention that the Michigan Bureau of Labor devoted to the state's auto industry in the bureau's annual report published early in 1904 was hailed by Detroit auto manufacturers as "official" recognition of the prominence the new industry had gained in Michigan's economy and, on a national scale, among American auto manufacturers. Commenting on these statements, *Automobile* in the spring of 1904 reiterated, without qualification, that Detroit "is today the greatest manufacturing center in this line in the United States. Throughout the West it is becoming known as 'The Automobile City.' "[3]

The year 1904 was to see the first really adequate and detailed statistics regarding the automobile industry when the federal census bureau conducted the Census of Manufactures which it carried out every five years. The publication of the results of this census effectively settled all arguments regarding where the industry was concentrated in the greatest degree. Prior to 1904, the Census of Manufactures had lumped statistics on automobile manufacturing activities in with those for the carriage and wagon industry. With the appearance of the manufacturing of automobiles and of auto parts as separate categories in the census for 1904, Michigan was revealed as being firmly ensconced in first place in both of these manufacturing operations.

In brief, at the end of June 1904 Michigan was reported to have twenty-two automobile manufacturing companies, employing 2123 wage-earners producing 9023 passenger vehicles and 102 commercial vehicles. The total of 9125 represented 42.1% of the motor vehicle production in the country, but the emphasis in Michigan on the production of low-priced cars was strikingly apparent. The value of the Michigan-made cars represented only 22.9% of the total value of all the automobiles produced in the country in 1904. Nevertheless, the figure of $6,876,708 which the bureau listed in its report of the 1904 census as the dollar-value of the Michigan auto production was more than a million dollars above the value of the second-place producer, Ohio, and far more than that of New York, Connecticut, Massachusetts, Wisconsin, Indiana, and Pennsylvania, the only other states with automobile production in the million-dollar range. Detroit, with twelve companies that together employed more than twice as many workers as the other ten automakers in the state, manufactured 78.3% of the Michigan cars, with the value of Detroit's output, $5,382,212, exceeding that of any state except Ohio. In the separate category of auto bodies and parts, Michigan was credited with about a third of the national product of $3,388,472, far ahead of Ohio, Massachusetts, and New York, which were closely bunched around the half-million-dollar figure. When added together, Michigan, with $7,996,534, contributed 26.6% of the total value of automobiles, including bodies and parts, that were produced in the United States in 1904.[4]

In a later report comparing the findings of the 1904 census with those of 1909 and 1914, the census bureau reduced the dollar value of Michigan's automobile production for 1904 by over $300,000, while it increased the value of the auto bodies and parts made in Michigan that year by a like amount, thus leaving unchanged the total value of automobiles and parts that had been given in the initial report of the 1904 census. Such a change is typical of the uncertain nature of so much of the information about the auto industry in this early period before the industry had developed reliable statistics for its own use. Contemporary observers of the industry, for example, recognized that 1904 was the year in which Detroit emerged as the unchallenged leader among American and, indeed, world automobile manufacturing centers, but they had some difficulty in accurately depicting the magnitude of this development. *Motor Age* declared that what was going on in Detroit, "when boiled down to cold, hard figures, seems almost incredulous." In an attempt to make the developments credible, the trade journal estimated that the horsepower represented in Detroit's auto production for 1904 would have been enough to run all the factories in many cities, or to pull a freight train that extended across the entire country, or to power all of the navy's battleships with enough left over to run a flotilla of torpedo boats. It credited Detroit with a production of over 9000 cars, an exaggerated estimate that may have resulted in part by crediting all of the Oldsmobile production to the Olds Motor Works' Detroit plant, whereas much of this production came from the Lansing plant. Even more inflated was the magazine's estimate that the Detroit companies employed 6000 workers, almost four times the total that the census bureau uncovered.[5]

Exaggerated or not, the statistics for 1904 soon paled by comparison with those of the months and years that followed. As they appeared in an ever widening circle of publications, the revised statistics simply added further confirmation of the pre-eminent position of the auto industry in the Wolverine state. The *Michigan State Gazetteer,* which in 1901 had located only thirteen automobile businesses in the state, in 1905 required some seven columns to list all of the Michigan firms that were selling or manufacturing automobiles or parts for such vehicles. It listed thirty-nine auto manufacturers in the state, in contrast with the four that had been listed four years earlier. As an example of both the rapidly changing character of the industry and the contradictory nature of much of the data in this period, Herbert N. Casson, surveying the growth of the industry in the country at this time, cited a lower figure — thirty-three — as the number of Michigan automobile manufacturers in operation. This was still eleven firms more than had been found by the census of 1904. Basing his figures on a survey of a hundred manufacturers, Casson likewise showed a substantial increase in the employment figures of the Michigan auto companies and the value of their auto production. Casson also reported that on a national scale the auto industry by 1905 was seventy times larger than the wheelbarrow industry, forty per cent ahead of sewing machine production, and on a par with the piano industry, and he declared that in Michigan the amount of money invested in this industry was "a million more than Michigan has invested in its famous breakfast foods." The auto industry was still, however, well behind a number of other established manufacturing activities in the state. In 1906, a special survey conducted by the Detroit Board of Commerce showed that Detroit automobile production was worth about $12,000,000, twice what it had been in 1904, but less than half of the value of the 1906 output of Detroit's leading industry, the railroad car manufacturers.[6]

Between 1906 and 1909, the auto industry forged ahead of all of its competition in Michigan's economy. It left behind not only the railroad car industry but such other entrenched interests as the furniture, paper, pharmaceutical, tobacco, and chemical industries, all of which had, nevertheless, continued to grow at an appreciable rate. The manufacturing census of 1909 showed that the total value of automobiles and auto parts made in Michigan that year was $96,651,451, about a seventh of the value of all manufactured products in the state. Five years earlier the same industry had contributed only 1.84% of the total value of Michigan manufactures. Within the auto industry, Michigan's production of 64,800 passenger and commercial vehicles represented 51.2% of the national total, up from the 42.1% of 1904, while the total value of vehicles and parts represented 38.8% of the national total, in contrast with the percentage of 26.6 of five years earlier. Ranking behind Michigan in total value of automobiles, including bodies and parts, were Ohio and New York, although their rate of increase was only about half that of Michigan for the 1904-1909 period. Indiana and Wisconsin moved into the fourth and fifth positions, replacing Connecticut and Massachusetts, which had held these positions in 1904. However, in the number of automobiles produced, Indiana, with a production of 17,253 vehicles, ranked ahead of Ohio and New York and was second, albeit a somewhat distant second, to Michigan.

By the time of the next federal census in 1914, Michigan automakers had widened even further the gap between them and other manufacturers in the state and the other auto manufacturers in the country. With a total production valued at $398,289,022, the Michigan automobile industry was contributing 36.7% of the state's total manufactured product value and 62.9% of the value of automobiles and auto parts in the entire country. By 1914 the 437,003 Michigan-made passenger vehicles and 5979 commercial vehicles represented 77.9% of the total American production of such vehicles.[7]

* * *

The preceding pages, of course, have been devoted to a survey of the events leading to the dominant position Michigan had attained in the auto industry by 1909 and which the census for 1914 further emphasized. The explanations as to why all this happened are a more complex matter.

First, it is important to realize that it took some time to achieve the concentration of control over the industry from Detroit that is taken for granted today. In 1909, the companies producing automobiles were still widely dispersed. One compilation for that year shows forty-four makes of cars produced in Indiana, only one less than in Michigan, while Ohio and several other states in the Middle West and Northeast also had large numbers of automobile companies and individual makes of cars. Some of the most fondly remembered American automobiles of the second and third decades of the twentieth century — the Pierce-Arrow, the Mercer, the Marmon, the Stutz, the Duesenberg — were products of non-Michigan companies. The competition of the giants — Ford, General Motors, and Chrysler — took its toll on the smaller companies outside Michigan in the 1920's, and the depression of the 1930's killed off most of the remainder. Studebaker of South Bend stubbornly hung on until December 1963, when this last surviving non-Michigan auto producer (excluding the small custom-car operations whose volume of production has never figured significantly in overall automobile production statistics) ceased automobile production. Of course, as John B. Rae has pointed out, with the development by the surviving big Detroit automakers of huge branch assembly plants across the country, more cars are being turned out of such plants in Buffalo, for example, in a few days than all the Pierce-Arrows and Thomas Flyers that their long-extinct Buffalo companies had been able to produce in an entire year. But the administrative control of these many diffuse assembly operations is now located in offices in metropolitan Detroit.[8]

At the start of automobile production in the United States there were no sure indications of what lay ahead. The activities of the Duryea Motor Wagon Company in Springfield, Massachusetts, in 1895-96, and of Pope's motor carriage division in Hartford, Connecticut, at the same time, gave New England an initial and apparently permanent lead in the new industry. New England had the longest manufacturing tradition and was acknowledged to have the finest collection of mechanical talents in the country.

But by the end of the century, the center of gravity in the industry was shifting from New England to New York, Ohio, and elsewhere in the Middle West. A glance at the map suggested that the more centralized location of these new companies gave them an advantage over the more remote New England plants in reaching the important automobile markets throughout the country.

Among the states of the Middle West, however, one is hard pressed to find any natural advantages in Michigan that explain why it soon outstripped the other states in the area, as well as those elsewhere in the country. Detroit's ready access to the cheap transportation facilities of the Great Lakes is sometimes mentioned, but aside from the obvious fact that the auto manufacturers in Kenosha, Milwaukee, Toledo, Cleveland, and Buffalo were similarly situated, little use was in fact made by these companies of Great Lakes shipping as a means of bringing in parts or shipping out the finished vehicles. Railroad sidetracks, run right to the

In January 1905, as bowler-hatted men and an occasional woman picked their way through the congested assemblage of exhibits at the national auto show in Madison Square Garden, the casual visitor would not have been able to predict that the Ford Motor Company was going to be a more important factor in the industry than its neighbors; the visitor certainly would not have predicted that Ford and Oldsmobile, the only Michigan-made cars on display in this view, would be the only automobile names seen here that would continue to appear after 1938, the final year of production for the Pierce-Arrow, which was the last survivor among these non-Michigan machines.
Courtesy Motor Vehicle Manufacturers Association

factory, were a much more convenient means of serving the transportation needs of the auto companies even in the lake ports, while flourishing Olds, Reo, Buick and Chevrolet operations in such inland cities as Lansing and Flint demonstrated how unimportant the Great Lakes waters were to successful automobile manufacturing.

The iron ore, copper, and wood for which Michigan was famous and which it was producing in record or near-record amounts at the time the auto industry began to develop is also cited as a factor favoring Michigan's emergence as a producer of automobiles. It is true that the automobiles of that day used great quantities of wood and some copper, in addition to iron, but it should also be pointed out that the bulk of Michigan's ores were unloaded at lake ports in Ohio, Indiana, and Illinois where the major steel and iron production of the Middle West was located. Thus this resource was more readily available and in greater quantities to the automobile companies in those states than to the companies in Michigan. In addition, the rapid depletion of Michigan's timber resources by the end of the nineteenth century was causing carriage manufacturers such as Durant and Dort to turn to the forests of the South in order to obtain the kinds of wood needed for some of their work; the same trend certainly carried over into the auto industry in its attempt to meet its requirements for wooden bodies and wheels.

Michigan's booming mining and lumber industries of the nineteenth century did, however, make one very major contribution to the state's subsequent auto industry — money. The leading financial backers of the Olds Motor Works, the Henry Ford Company and its successor, Cadillac, and the Wayne Automobile Company, and some of the major backers of the Detroit Automobile Company and Packard, had grown wealthy largely through their earlier success in exploiting Michigan's mineral and timber resources. The fact that the lumber industry was on the decline by 1900 while iron ore and copper mining had reached a stable, settled condition after the earlier period of rapid growth and development was probably a factor in creating a desire among those who had profited from these businesses to seek new speculative investment opportunities for their surplus capital. Manufacturing was, on the whole, not as far advanced in Michigan at this time as it was in some other states in the area. There still was, therefore, an above average number of wealthy individuals in Michigan who had not yet tied up most of their money in the manufacturing industries, which were just beginning to supplant the extractive economic activities that had dominated the state's economy prior to this time. There were, of course, great numbers of individuals elsewhere who possessed much larger fortunes, but it appears that few of them had much interest in automobile investments, at least in the formative stages of the industry. The Rockefeller, Carnegie, Mellon, Vanderbilt, and other fortunes of that magnitude were already committed to such economic areas as oil, steel, and railroads. In addition to such factors as have been mentioned, it seems likely, therefore, that in the further study of such men as Samuel Smith, Edward Sparrow, and William Murphy, we may find other clues to the causes for the rise of the Michigan automobile industry.

At the same time that Smith, Sparrow, Murphy, and the many others who had gained wealth through mining and lumber investments were interested in a new outlet for some of their uncommitted funds, likewise Detroit was going through something of a transitional phase in its economic development. Manufacturing was replacing the commercial activities that had been the basis for the city's earlier prosperity, but no single manufacturing interest had assumed dominance in the manner, as Merrill Denison has pointed out, that oil in Cleveland, steel in Pittsburgh, or railroads and meatpacking in Chicago had done. Despite the fame of Detroit's stoves and some of its other products, the city was, in the nineties, close to becoming stagnant economically. Some of the more aggressive and far-sighted of its business leaders were on the lookout for that something new which would give the city the boost it needed. The automobile, some of them recognized, could do just that. "We hope to make Detroit as prominent a manufacturing town for automobiles as it is for stoves," Henry Joy told the managing editor of the Detroit *News* in the spring of 1903.[9]

In the business world, one group that was repeatedly singled out in later years for its contribution to the establishment of the automobile industry in that city was the bankers. Several unidentified but "well-known manufacturers" told a correspondent for *Outlook* in 1915 that "much of the credit for the spectacular development of the Detroit automobile industry should be given to the bankers." Emory W. Clark, president of the First and Old Detroit National Bank, admitted that Detroit bankers had been more ready to take a chance on this new industry than bankers in Chicago and New York who had regarded the automobile initially "as only a luxury, and withheld their support until the industry had become firmly established." Eugene Lewis, whose business career encompassed both the auto industry and banking, agreed, declaring that bankers such as Alex McPherson of the Old Detroit National, William Livingstone of the Dime Bank, and John Thomas Shaw of the First National Bank had taken the long view and gambled on the young industry; they had approved some loans, Lewis declared in the 1940's, "which I doubt could be obtained today even from some of our progressive bankers." Roy Chapin was another who repeatedly indicated the importance of Detroit's bankers in the success that he and other pioneer Detroit automakers had enjoyed. These bankers, he said in 1924, were not prejudiced against the auto industry, as was the case in the East, and as a result they "were not afraid of our sight drafts."[10]

On another occasion, when asked by Peter Clark Macfarlane to comment on a novel about the Detroit auto industry that Macfarlane was writing, Chapin took exception to the actions of the bankers that appeared in Macfarlane's story. "No Detroit bankers, so far as I have ever heard, have squeezed the motor car manufacturers," in the manner that the novelist had the bankers in his story doing. "It was the New York crowd that has sometimes done this in the past." Chapin wanted Macfarlane to soften his treatment in order to "give credit to the Detroit bankers for their vision of the development of the industry." Significantly, however, Chapin was perfectly willing to allow Macfarlane to depict the bankers in a way which showed their actions to be motivated as much by the hope of personal gain as by the benefits that might accrue to the community. Macfarlane, Chapin suggested, could "indicate that these bankers want something extra for taking what they considered to be a very long chance. Of course no banker is warranted in taking long chances with money belonging to depositors, so why not for the 5% in stock that they each get, have them endorse the notes personally so that their banks are secure?"[11]

Not all Detroit businessmen were as optimistic about the new auto industry as were the bankers to whom Lewis and Chapin referred or as were such investors as Samuel Smith. In 1913 one observer reported a feeling "in some quarters that Detroit's banks are too intimately related to its automobile industry and that should the industry fail, it would carry with it many millions of dollars in banks." Although he reported that an average of twenty-five per cent of all the city's bank business was chargeable to the auto industry, the observer did not regard this as constituting too great a burden for Detroit's financial system to bear. Likewise, Alex Dow, Henry Ford's old boss at Detroit Edison, had been greatly concerned by the increased demands from the city's auto industry for electric power. By 1909, Detroit Edison's customers from this segment of Detroit's economy absorbed nearly ten per cent of the power company's effective capacity. By 1911, Dow feared, the auto plants' demands might be four times what they were in 1909, and he did not believe the industry could continue to grow at such a pace. If the automobile proved to be simply a passing fad, the power company could find itself greatly overextended. Fortunately for the future success of the industry, Miss Sarah Sheridan of Edison's sales department, a most remarkable woman in what was then exclusively a man's world, had greater faith in the future of the auto industry. She continued to seek more customers in the industry and thereby committed her company, despite Dow's misgivings, to further expansion in order to meet the needs of the booming auto plants.[12]

Some of the other manufacturing that had already arisen in Michigan also contributed to the establishment of an automobile industry in the state. Many have assumed that the carriage industry was of foremost importance, and it was a significant factor in the development of successful automobile companies when, as happened in Flint, those who had made money in the carriage industry used some of this money, plus the talents of some of their workers, to start up an automobile company; the carriage industry contributed most, however, when it continued to carry on the carriage business and used the profits from the latter to develop the automobile operation until it was firmly established. The experience of those carriage manufacturers in Kalamazoo, Grand Rapids, and Charlotte who assumed that it would be a simple matter to switch their plants over from carriage production to the production of horseless carriages demonstrated that that way lay disaster.

More significant by far than Michigan's carriage industry as a fertile ground from which successful automobile operations grew was the gasoline engine industry. Although the companies involved were small compared with the big carriage manufacturers in Flint, Jackson, and Pontiac, these companies by the mid-nineties had sold themselves and many Michigan mechanics on the gasoline engine as the power unit of the future. While highly talented mechanics and automobile experimenters elsewhere continued on into the twentieth century trying to work out the problems of developing road vehicles powered by steam or electricity, the same type of individuals in Michigan, almost without exception, were working with gasoline engines — first, perhaps, to develop small engines for marine uses (and here was an effect that can be directly attributed to the surrounding waters of the Great Lakes) but shortly to adapt the same engines for automobiles. Sintz, Worth, Olds, King, Ford, Brush, Murray, Buick, Joy, Dodge, Leland, Marr, Richard, Maxwell — the list goes on of Michigan men whose original interest in automobiles stemmed largely or entirely from an earlier interest in and work with gasoline engines. If they had any interest in other types of vehicles, they quickly decided against them and concentrated their efforts, and the money of their backers, on the production of gasoline cars. There was no wasted time getting to the kind of car which they saw would be the kind that the public wanted. Unlike Pope, who vacillated back and forth between gasoline and electric vehicles and bicycles, losing in the process what was probably the ablest group of automotive workers in America in the late nineties, or the Whites and the Locomobile company which made a late start with gasoline cars after first producing steam cars, the Michigan pioneers were working with a winner from the outset.

Observers at the time and in later years have thought they detected in Detroit's mechanics a greater willingness to experiment than was true of mechanics in New England, for example. The explanation, Eugene Lewis claimed, lay in the fact that most of the Michigan mechanics "had learned their trade the hard way and were not bound by orthodox mechanical training." This quality helps to explain why Detroit quickly developed a reputation for originality in its motor car design and construction, which helped to attract attention to its products. At the same time, one automobile writer declared in 1908, there was nothing frivolous about this quest for originality; the examples he had seen were "mostly sound as I have found any variation from the regular paths to be based wholly on good engineering practice." On the other hand, Roy Chapin did not agree with the claim that the availability of "desired types of skilled labor" in the area affected the location and growth of the auto industry in Detroit. As a matter of fact, he declared, "we had to import our really skilled labor from the east in the early years." Thus if one of the strengths behind the early automotive developments in Michigan had been the flexibility of the mechanics, this strength was diluted at least somewhat by the importation of eastern mechanics who, if Eugene Lewis is correct, were more hidebound in their procedures.[13]

In two other respects the character of the laboring force and the conditions governing these workers in Michigan may have had an important influence in making the area appear to be a favorable place for launching a new industry. Michigan's, and particularly Detroit's, reputation for open-shop, anti-union attitudes was vigorously promoted and fostered, most notably by the Employers' Association of Detroit, and was primarily responsible, some business leaders claimed, for the move to Detroit of Packard and certain other automotive concerns. In addition, the arrival of such non-automotive firms as the Burroughs Adding Machine Company, which moved to Detroit from St. Louis in 1904, was cited as evidence that others shared the automakers' attitudes regarding the open-shop atmosphere in that city as reason enough for transferring their operations to that location.[14]

In addition, however, and no doubt related to the generally unorganized character of Michigan's factory workers at the start of the century, the wages of these workers seem to have been lower than those in other manufacturing states. A comparison of the wages listed as having been paid to Michigan's auto workers in the 1904 Census of Manufactures shows a rate very appreciably less than the average wage not only for the comparable group of employees in such eastern states as New York, Connecticut, and Massachusetts, but also in Michigan's immediate neighbor to the south, Ohio. Further investigations would be needed to determine the actual wage differential between cities in these states and in Michigan, but the overall figures for these states at least suggest that cheaper labor costs could have been an important consideration in the decision of Henry Joy and his associates to move Packard from Warren, Ohio, to Detroit in 1903, or of Charles Mott to agree to Durant's proposal to move Weston-Mott from Utica to Flint in 1905.

Although the conditions in Michigan appear as though they would not have appealed to the higher-paid workers, some of whom were also dues-paying union members, from other parts of the country, the increasing emphasis on mass production decreased the auto industry's need for such skilled labor while it increased its need for unskilled or semiskilled workers. These positions could be and were readily filled by surplus labor from rural areas in the country or increasingly by immigrants from eastern and southern Europe. This unskilled labor pool was thus made up of men who had had no experience with unions, nor with factories, and were delighted to find a job, regardless of the wage, where their lack of industrial experience was not an impediment to employment.

Inevitably, the scarcity of labor to meet the insatiable demands of

Michigan's major auto companies forced the wages in the industry to go up. By 1914, the manufacturing census figures show that the earlier disparity between the industry's wage rates in Michigan and those in other auto-producing states had disappeared. Henry Ford's startling announcement at the beginning of 1914 that he would raise his daily pay scale to $5, double what he and others had been paying, arose from a variety of motives; its effect, probably intended, was to undermine any support that was developing for a union among the workers already employed in the industry, while attracting new hordes of untrained laborers, who now saw an opportunity not only to get a factory job, despite their lack of training, but also to be paid more than most of them had ever hoped to receive.

Thus Michigan's auto industry had benefited, when it was young and relatively weak, from the labor conditions that it found existing in the state. Later, when it had attained a stronger, more secure level of development, it maintained the open shop while attracting the labor forces it needed through the high wages that its financial position now enabled it to pay out.

In the final analysis, no single factor was responsible for the origins of the auto industry in Michigan or for the way in which it then developed. Instead, an explanation must be sought through a study of a combination of factors. The combination of Samuel Smith's money, the Olds gasoline engine, and an idea that Ransom Olds had in 1896 to build a light, inexpensive gasoline-powered motor vehicle led to the production of the curved-dash Oldsmobile. None of the ingredients of this particular combination was unique, but when brought together with an able team of workmen and a well-managed promotion and selling campaign, that organization's little car became a big success. When it was quickly followed by such other successes as the Cadillac, Ford, and Buick, which were in varying degrees inspired by the Oldsmobile, Detroit's and, to a somewhat lesser degree, Michigan's reputation as an important center of auto production was established.

From 1903 onwards a snowball effect was underway that probably made inevitable the complete dominance that was in sight by 1909 and that had become an obvious fact a few years later. New automobile manufacturers were spawned by former executives or backers of the earlier firms — such companies as Reo, Chalmers, E.M.F., Hudson, Chevrolet, and Dodge. In addition to generating more activity internally, within the framework of what had already developed, the growing Michigan auto industry also drew companies from elsewhere to Michigan. Packard is the major example of an established automobile manufacturer that moved to Michigan, and the control that Detroit investors had obtained over this Ohio firm no doubt largely explains the location they selected for the company's new home. Packard's move was not widely duplicated, as was demonstrated in 1908 by the failure of efforts to persuade the Moon company of St. Louis to move to Detroit and the Fiat company of Italy to establish an American branch in Detroit.[15] Furthermore, the loss of control of the E.M.F. company to the Indiana-based Studebaker interests is another reminder that the traffic between Michigan and the outside world during these formative years of the auto industry was not entirely a one-way affair. However, a glance at the auto parts industry demonstrates that the demands of the big Michigan automakers did exert a kind of magnetic force on many of those engaged in that kind of activity.

Five years before Weston-Mott's celebrated decision to move from Utica to Flint, Michigan's appeal was being recognized by other suppliers of auto parts. The Fisk Rubber Company of Chicopee Falls, Massachusetts, for example, opened its western office in Detroit for the specific purpose of serving the automobile and carriage trade. Three years later, H. Jay Hayes, a native of Muir, Michigan, who had gone into business in Cleveland where he pioneered in the building of steel automobile bodies, moved his company to Detroit; by 1909 it had two plants and had orders for over 100,000 automobiles for the coming year. Shortly after 1904, George Holley, who was getting orders for carburetors from Olds and Ford, moved his business from Pennsylvania to Michigan. In 1905, the Continental Motor Manufacturing Company of Chicago was persuaded to relocate its engine manufacturing business in Muskegon, and three years later, another Chicago firm, McCord & Company, an established supplier of railway equipment, opened a subsidiary plant in Detroit which by 1909 was producing 75,000 automobile radiators, in addition to such other parts as lubricators, fans, pumps, and gaskets. The same year saw the establishment of the Timken-Detroit Axle Company in the factory formerly occupied by the Standard Sanitary Manufacturing Company (the firm that had bought out David Buick's plumbing business a decade earlier) to manufacture a part that had previously been produced by the Timken Roller Bearing Axle Company of Dayton, Ohio. The fact that New Jersey's Hyatt Roller Bearing Company, when it moved its sales office to Detroit in 1909, kept its manufacturing operations in the East is a reminder that many auto parts manufacturers resisted the temptation to move to Michigan; this, of course, enabled the non-Michigan segment of the auto parts industry to retain a greater degree of importance in that industry than was the case among the non-Michigan assemblers of automobiles. Nevertheless, the companies who moved to Michigan, when added to such home-grown firms as the Fisher Body and Briggs body manufacturers, the Hayes, Kelsey, and Prudden wheel companies, Lewis Spring and Axle, and a host of others, were enough to make Michigan almost as much the center of the auto parts industry as it was of the larger and more famous automobile industry.[16]

Thus did the automobile industry — including the making of parts — grow in Michigan in an almost Topsy-like fashion from its timid beginnings in the nineties to the lusty adolescent of 1909. What would have happened if Samuel Smith had turned down Ransom Olds' plea for more money in the spring of 1899 or if Olds had received the support he had supposedly been promised earlier by New York financiers? What would have happened if Olds had persisted in his efforts in 1899 to develop a high-priced vehicle, instead of going on to build a little runabout? Would local support for Ford, Buick, Maxwell, and other Michigan automobile developers have been so readily forthcoming if the Oldsmobile had not already demonstrated the success that a locally owned and managed automobile venture could enjoy? No one knows. But what did happen is now clear. Michigan found the major new economic activity it needed to resume its growth in the twentieth century on a scale equaling and ultimately far surpassing that which mining and lumbering and farming had made possible in the preceding century.

Was it worth it? One recalls the question that the aged Charles S. Mott, who lived through it all, asked his visitors in 1971: "Are you satisfied with what happened?" Despite complaints about congested traffic, pollution, the horrible reality of highway traffic casualties, and finally, in 1974, the view of many that the auto industry, if not the automobile, was perhaps the main villain of the energy crisis — despite all this, one suspects that a majority of Michiganians, thinking of the jobs and the wealth that the auto industry has provided to the state, would agree that what Mott and his colleagues accomplished was of enormous benefit. But when one compares the descriptions of a town like Flint in the 1880's, with its tree-lined streets and its leisurely small-town atmosphere, with the reality of Flint, the factory town of today, one cannot help but wonder what history's final judgment will be.

Significant as the automobile's effect was on communities such as Flint, Lansing, and Pontiac, however, most attention has been given to what it did to Detroit. Detroit's image in the nineties as a staid, slow-moving community was rapidly erased by the new industrial stirrings of the early years of the following decade. In place of the older view, one visitor in 1903 was impressed by the "sense of hustle and activity" that he found in the historic old City of the Straits. A stranger to the town "soon falls into line with the rest of the folk and sets his watch a half-hour ahead of standard time to keep ahead of the outside world." Before long, the motto "Detroit the Dynamic" was adopted by city promoters as more appropriate to the new conditions than the earlier designation "Detroit the Beautiful." By 1915, a correspondent for *Outlook* was told by a taxi-cab driver: "There's always got to be something doing in Detroit." The reporter agreed that this seemed to be expressive of the new spirit that one encountered — "the spirit of do and dare to accomplish things, the intense desire for activity, the penetrating belief in the great destiny of Detroit, and the supreme joy of achievement."[17]

In the first two decades of the new century, Detroit, which had just celebrated its two hundredth birthday, was literally reborn and virtually rebuilt all over again. A boom-town atmosphere prevailed as the population exploded from slightly more than a quarter of a million in 1900 to the million people that the census bureau counted in 1920. Enormous

In 1907, the date of this postcard view of the main street in Milan, Michigan, the horse-and-buggy still ruled supreme.

Within a half decade, the rapidly changing character of the highway vehicular traffic was obvious in even the smallest communities, including Maple Rapids, Michigan.

difficulties and adjustments were forced on the city by that kind of overnight growth, but with it all there was a throbbing sense of excitement and of participating in a great technological revolution that was not only upsetting traditional transportation patterns but effecting numerous other social and economic changes. The reactions of Sidney Corbett, who grew up in Detroit during these years and became an executive with Chevrolet, probably typified those of most Detroiters of his generation, at least, to what was happening.

> Not for us was any delight in our lovely old town. Tree-shaded streets, flagged walks, quiet lawns, the all-too-slow moving street cars and the leisurely pace of our parents were a pain in the neck to us. We found no music in the plodding clop-clop of horses' hooves. Even our stout young legs couldn't spin the two wheels of a bicycle fast enough. Ho, for a Brave New World — on four wheels — whizzed along by gasoline.[18]

There were, naturally, those who viewed the developments in these years in quite a different, and less favorable light. They viewed with dismay the impact that the automobile industry and its satellites had on such fine old residential areas as Jefferson Avenue and such newer areas as Woodward Avenue. In 1911 it was reported that

> more than one palatial home has been razed to make room for the show palace of the automobile. Garages have been sandwiched in between some of the finest of the old Woodward Avenue homes, and one Detroit millionaire was recently compelled to purchase a square block on the avenue to protect his costly home from their unwelcome encroachment.

Some of the older families stuck it out in their old homes, but others, including the burgeoning new class of millionaires created by the auto industry, began the exodus to such suburban enclaves as Grosse Pointe and Birmingham. In 1916 one reporter found some of Detroit's older residents contradicting another familiar chamber of commerce slogan of the period stating that "In Detroit Life is Worth Living." Critics declared that "with smoke and street-cars packed to suffocation and the streets themselves crowded with automobiles, life in Detroit has ceased being worth living." Four years later another journalist, in what was now becoming a familiar assignment from the editors of national magazines, came to take a look at Detroit and was duly impressed: "tremendous . . . almost overpowering . . . one of the great cities, not only of the United States, but of the world." Among other developments, he reported efforts that were being made to give the city more of the appearance befitting its new status as a large metropolis. Plans were underway to build a symphony hall, and Detroit's *nouveaux riches*, the automobile millionaires, were leading the drive to make the hall and the orchestra it would house better, at the very least, than those of Cleveland or Cincinnati. A fine ambition, "and yet," one woman told him, "I would rather do without our fine new orchestra and have our nice old town back again."[19]

An impossibility. That nice old town's fate had been sealed when

348 A MOST UNIQUE MACHINE

Ransom Olds and his wife and two young daughters settled down in their new Detroit home late in 1899 and on New Year's Eve saw the old year, and the old life, pass into history.

BIBLIOGRAPHICAL ESSAY

The resources available to the student of the American automobile industry are voluminous, rich, and quite varied, much more so than one would gather from the narrowly limited kinds of material that have been the basis of much of the writing on this subject. Rather than repeating the bibliographical information about each specific source cited in the footnotes, I will confine myself to a discussion of the major sources that were consulted in the preparation of this volume and which are available to anyone interested in the topics I have discussed.

Manuscript collections of the papers of individuals, companies, and organizations involved with the auto industry are becoming increasingly numerous. The best known of these is the Ford Archives, now located in the Henry Ford Museum at Dearborn. Since the materials in this collection are extensively quoted and cited in the authoritative three-volume study of Ford and the Ford Motor Company that was prepared by Allan Nevins, Frank Ernest Hill, and associates, as well as in Sidney Olson's less heralded but very fine work, *Young Henry Ford,* I confined my research in these records to several of the oral interviews conducted at the time of the Nevins project, particularly the interviews with Oliver Barthel and Claude Sintz, and relied on the published work of Nevins and Olson as my basic guide to the contents of these archives.

The Historical Collections of Michigan State University has the papers of Ransom E. Olds and a massive collection of the business records of the Reo Company. The latter are extraordinarily rich but nearly all of the material falls into the period after 1909 and was therefore of little immediate value for this volume. Such was not the case with Olds' own papers, which were my single most important manuscript source. Glenn A. Niemeyer used the Olds papers in preparing his biography of Olds, which was published in 1963, but within the past three years Olds' family deposited additional materials, including not only Olds' correspondence but some correspondence of his associates, including Fred Smith and Reuben Shettler, and a complete run of pocket diaries kept by Olds over a forty-year period. This new material adds significantly to the knowledge of the Olds activities particularly for the years 1901 to 1904 and forces some of the traditional interpretations to be altered or abandoned. Unfortunately, Olds' papers as yet contain virtually nothing for the earlier years of Olds' life and business career, although some new insights into those years were gained through interviews with Olds' two daughters, Mrs. Gladys Olds Anderson and Mrs. Bernice Olds Roe. Also helpful were two interviews with Olds' grandsons, R. E. Olds Anderson and Woodward Roe, and an examination of certain materials in the office of the R. E. Olds Company in Lansing, particularly a typescript entitled "That Boy Ranny," which Olds wrote, or had written, concerning his childhood and early adulthood.

The papers of another major Michigan pioneer, Charles B. King, are in the Automotive History Collection of the Detroit Public Library. The King Papers are a very large and diversified collection consisting of King's correspondence, scrapbooks, photographs, plans, and other materials, including some correspondence of other individuals which King, an avid collector, drew together as he became increasingly interested in the early history of the automobile in America. He was using these materials in his later years for an uncompleted autobiographical work that would, from the portions of the manuscript that are in his papers, have covered considerably more than what is in his two privately published memoirs, *Psychic Reminiscences,* published in 1935, and *A Golden Anniversary,* published in 1945.

Three major collections of papers for the early development of the auto industry are to be found in the Michigan Historical Collections of the University of Michigan, located since the fall of 1973 in the new Bentley Historical Library on the university's North Campus in Ann Arbor. Two of these are well known to automotive historians from the use that earlier writers have made of them. The Roy D. Chapin Papers contain only a limited amount of correspondence or other materials from the period in which Chapin was with the Olds Motor Works, but Chapin's subsequent activities with Thomas-Detroit, Chalmers, and then Hudson are presented in great and extremely informative detail, making this one of the most important of all manuscript collections for the serious student of the industry, although its chief value lies in the period after 1909 until Chapin's death in 1936.

The Henry B. Joy Papers, also at Ann Arbor, although concentrated on the last years of Joy's life after his retirement from an active role in the Packard company, include some significant materials on his earlier business career, particularly a letterpress book for the years 1902 and 1903 that is full of correspondence documenting Joy's role in bringing Packard to Detroit and in leading the movement to form the Association of Licensed Automobile Manufacturers.

The third collection at the Michigan Historical Collections, consisting of the office files of the Flint attorney, John J. Carton, from 1900 to his death in 1920, is a relatively unknown source as yet to automobile historians, and because of the mass of material involved, most of which has nothing to do with the auto industry, it may never attract much interest among these specialists. However, for those who take the time to wade through the files, there is some choice material, particularly for the years 1905 to 1910, pertaining to the development of the auto industry in Flint and the early development of General Motors. This material results from Carton's position as a leader in the community and as an attorney for Buick and other business firms.

A more direct source of information on W. C. Durant opened up during the course of the research on this book when Lawrence Gustin obtained access to the papers of Durant, about whose location and very existence little information had previously been available. Mr. Gustin generously shared with me many of the new insights into the events of the period through 1909 that emerged from his examination of these papers and which were the basis for his biography, *Billy Durant: Creator of General Motors,* published late in 1973. There are plans to deposit Durant's papers in Flint and to make them, along with the papers of the late Charles S. Mott, which have likewise not been generally available to researchers, the heart of a collection that would make such a depository, if the plans are carried out, one of the major automobile history research centers.

Although I did not have direct access to the Durant and Mott papers, I was fortunate in obtaining new information on the career of another major pioneer, Alanson P. Brush, and on his relationship with Henry M. Leland and others, from an unpublished biography, written by Brush's wife, Jane D. Brush, entitled "Without Benefit of College: the Story of Alanson P. Brush." This typescript, together with some accompanying correspondence of Brush, was on loan to the Division of Michigan History, Michigan Department of State in Lansing, and was used by permission of the owner of the material, the late Mrs. Brush's brother, Harry Marsh.

A number of other groups of manuscripts were consulted which, although not of the overall importance of those already mentioned, added significant information on specific points. These include the William C. Maybury Papers at the Burton Historical Collection of the Detroit Public Library, which also has a collection of Henry B. Joy Papers, the papers of Joy's brother, Richard, and of his brother-in-law and business associate, Truman H. Newberry, which contain important information on the Packard company but, for the most part, for the period after 1909. At the Automotive History Collection in the Detroit Public Library, the H. Jay Hayes Papers are important regarding the activities of that pioneer auto parts manufacturer. At the Michigan Historical Collections, the

Eugene F. Cooley Papers contain several letters that throw new light on some of the Olds business operations, while the Henry H. Crapo Papers are essential to an understanding of Durant's family background and his childhood. Important sources of information for the early development of automobile dealerships are the records of the Ann Arbor auto dealer, Staebler & Sons, and the Charles Tyler Newton Papers, both in the Michigan Historical Collections, the records of the Wiedman Auto Company of Ypsilanti, Michigan, in the Ypsilanti Historical Museum, and the Carlton R. Mabley Papers in the Automotive History Collection. The scope of the present study did not permit the use of these sources that had originally been envisaged.

Two groups of governmental records yielded important new information on a number of Michigan automobile firms. The annual reports of those companies incorporated in Michigan and which were filed in Lansing with the state government are found in the Records of the Corporation and Securities Commission in the State Archives, which is part of the Division of Michigan History of the Department of State. Information regarding the officers, stockholders, assets, and capitalization of these firms is provided in these reports which I sampled, particularly for the first two categories of information. The papers filed at the time of the incorporation of these firms, however, are not in the State Archives but are retained by the Corporation and Securities Bureau of the Michigan Department of Commerce.

The Selden Patent case long ago made automobile historians, who have mined this massive court record, aware of the potential value of this type of archival material. One group of court records that has been neglected, however, are those dealing with bankrupt firms. A systematic survey was made of all the available records of bankruptcy proceedings under the federal bankruptcy laws that involved Michigan automobile companies down to the period of the 1920's. These cases were handled in the federal courts for the Eastern and Western Districts in Michigan, with the files now deposited in the Regional Archives of the National Archives, located in the Federal Records Center in Chicago. Although much of the material in these files is repetitious and routine in character, the records, aside from documenting the actual processing of the cases by the court and the court-appointed receiver, sometimes include copies of correspondence and transcripts of hearings as well as detailed statements of assets and liabilities that can provide clues into the operation of these companies and suggest reasons for their failure. Some 1500 or more pages from selected portions of these cases that I was able to have copied with funds provided by the Ford Motor Company have been deposited in the Automotive History Collection of the Detroit Public Library.

Another fruitful source of information, despite the length of time that has elapsed since the period covered in this book, is in interviews with individuals who possess first-hand knowledge of the formative years of the auto industry. An interview with Charles S. Mott in 1971, a highlight for both me and my wife in our research for this book, was one of the last opportunities anyone will have had to talk with a major industrial leader whose career extended back to the very beginnings of the industry. However, there are a good many people of a later generation who have clear recollections of those years from their childhood and early adult experiences. Interviews with Herman Staebler and Joseph Thompson, pioneer auto dealers in Ann Arbor and Ypsilanti, respectively, provided valuable background on the operations of the early dealerships and on their impressions of the automobile leaders of those years. An interview with Grant A. Snedeker of Adrian clarified a number of points regarding the Murray and subsequent Adrian-produced cars. Some of the materials that Snedeker showed me at the time of the interview have since been deposited with the Michigan Historical Collections. Some sense of what it was like to live and work in Flint in the early boom days of the auto industry there was conveyed in interviews with John Knapman of Flint, who worked at the Weston-Mott plant beginning in 1908, and with Waldo Culver of Owosso, who was an employee at Buick, although at a slightly later period than that covered in this book. David W. Dolson of Mt. Pleasant, although too young to have first-hand knowledge of the Dolson company of Charlotte, was able to explain what had happened to the family after the collapse of its automobile venture, as well as providing additional documentary material relating to the venture.

Newspaper inquiries were the means of getting in touch with several of those whom I interviewed. Such inquiries also brought additional information from a number of other people in the form of written communications.

Newspapers from the period of the 1890's and early 1900's constituted one of the principal contemporary sources of primary information for this study. The volume of the available Michigan newspaper sources is such that a sampling technique was the only practical method of making use of these materials. Michigan papers that were examined for particular events and dates or for blocks of time of several months or years in extent included the Adrian *Daily Times*, Benton Harbor *Palladium*, Detroit *Free Press*, Detroit *News*, Flint *Journal*, Grand Rapids *Democrat*, Jackson *Daily Citizen*, Lansing *Journal*, and Lansing *State Republican*, in addition to the historian's old standby, the New York *Times*. The superb collection of Michigan newspapers on microfilm that can be readily borrowed on inter-library loan from the Michigan State Library in Lansing makes it impossible for historians to ignore this material on the grounds of its relative inaccessibility.

Automotive trade publications that were examined for this period included *Motocycle, Horseless Age, Motor Age, The Automobile, Motor World, The Hub,* and *Motor*. At least one and usually two of these journals were carefully scrutinized, page-by-page, for every year between 1895 and 1910. Use was made of the exceptionally fine and complete files of these journals that are found in the Transportation Library at the University of Michigan and in the Automotive History Collection of the Detroit Public Library. The latter's extensive files of automotive company publications were also consulted, along with a modest but very valuable collection of such materials found in the Michigan Historical Collections at the University of Michigan.

Among magazines with a more general circulation, *Scientific American* was very useful for its coverage of automotive developments in the nineties and early twentieth century. The *Reader's Guide to Periodical*

Literature was used to locate significant articles in other popular journals of the time. Issues of *Harper's Weekly, Collier's, Saturday Evening Post, Scientific American,* and a number of other magazines were also scanned for the automobile advertisements that they carried.

No attempt will be made to list the books and articles that were consulted in the course of research for this book, but attention needs to be drawn to several important series. The manufacturing census reports of the Federal Census Bureau provide a solid statistical foundation for studies of the auto industry, at least for the years in which the census was conducted. The annual report of the State Inspection of Factories, initially appearing as a separate publication and then incorporated with the annual report of the Michigan Bureau (later the Department) of Labor, furnishes a continuous record of employment figures, wages, and certain other information for Michigan auto companies from the very beginning of the industry. The biennial *Michigan State Gazetteer and Business Directory*, together with local directories when they are available, furnish additional clues to the corporate development of Michigan companies. The *Official Gazette* of the United States Patent Office and the annual reports of the Commissioner of Patents are a definitive record of the technological contributions of Michigan auto pioneers, the dates of these developments, and the objectives of the inventors. Finally, for biographical information, the *National Cyclopaedia of American Biography*, when combined with *Who's Who in America* and the more localized biographical compilations and "mug" books, provides essential information, albeit in an uncritical fashion, on the lives of a great many of the lesser known, as well as the more familiar figures connected with the origins of the auto industry in Michigan.

ACKNOWLEDGMENTS

During the four years that this book was in preparation, many individuals and organizations provided assistance in a variety of ways to the project. It is a pleasure to acknowledge this help.

The following institutions, and especially the indicated staff personnel, assisted in obtaining information from the sources under their control.

Automotive History Collection, Detroit Public Library: James J. Bradley, head, and George W. Risley.

Burton Historical Collection, Detroit Public Library: Mrs. Bernice Sprenger, head, and members of her staff.

Detroit Historical Museum: Solan W. Weeks, director.

Federal Archives and Records Center, Chicago: Bruce C. Harding, chief, Archives Branch, and Elizabeth Trimmer.

Ford Archives, Henry Ford Museum, Dearborn: Henry E. Edmunds, director, Dave Crippen, and Win Sears.

Henry Ford Museum, Dearborn: Leslie Henry, curator of transportation.

Historical Collections, Michigan State University, East Lansing: William H. Combs, director, and his staff.

Michigan Historical Collections, University of Michigan, Ann Arbor: Robert M. Warner, director, and the members of his staff, particularly Mary Jo Pugh, Tom Powers, J. Fraser Cocks, III, and Ken Scheffel.

Michigan History Division, Michigan Department of State, Lansing: Dennis R. Bodem, Mrs. Geneva Kebler Wiskemann, and Mrs. Elizabeth Rademacher of the State Archives, Donald Chaput and William L. Lowery.

Michigan State Library, Lansing: Richard C. Hathaway, head of the Michigan section.

Ypsilanti Historical Museum, Ypsilanti: Mrs. Dorothy Disbrow.

The staffs of the Business Administration Library, Graduate Library, and Transportation Library of the University of Michigan, Ann Arbor; the University Library, Eastern Michigan University, Ypsilanti; the Michigan State University Library, East Lansing; and the public libraries of Ann Arbor, Dearborn, Grand Rapids, Lansing, and Ypsilanti.

Thanks are due also to the following individuals who supplied information and materials by mail or in conversations, in addition to those persons who were interviewed and whose names appear in the Bibliographical Essay.

Howard L. Applegate, George Arents Research Library, Syracuse University, Syracuse, N.Y.; W. J. Banyon, Benton Harbor *News-Palladium,* Benton Harbor; Katherine F. Beaver, Baker Library, Harvard University, Cambridge, Mass.; Edward L. Bernays, Cambridge, Mass.; Charles E. Bierwirth, Flint; Ronald G. Bean, Saginaw; John D. Briscoe, Lakeville, Conn.; Mrs. Carl Burgtorf, Cheboygan; Robert G. Carroon, Milwaukee County Historical Society, Milwaukee, Wis.; Bruce Catton, New York; Ford Ceasar, Lansing; John C. Chapin, Jr., Farmington, Conn.; Everett Claspy, Dowagiac; Mrs. Doris Eddy, Afton; Dr. and Mrs. Julius Fischbach, Lansing; Ron Graybill, Ellen G. White Publications, Washington, D.C.; Harvey Harmon, Charlotte; Mrs. Harriette F. Henderson, Long Beach, Wash.; L. Gaylord Hulbert, Detroit; Mrs. Joseph Klimkowski, Brooklyn; K. Raymond Lake, Flint; David H. Langeland, Transmission Division, Eaton Corporation, Kalamazoo; James LaParl, Lansing Business University, Lansing; Victor F. Lemmer, Ironwood; Dale A. Lyons, Dowagiac; Wayne C. Mann, Regional History Collections, Western Michigan University, Kalamazoo; Mrs. Linda Maurer, Michigan Center; Kenneth J. Mead, Lansing School District, Lansing; Morris Peilet, Detroit; Kenneth E. Peters, formerly of Ann Arbor, now of Columbia, South Carolina; John B. Rae, Harvey Mudd College, Claremont, Cal.; Richard W. Schwarz, Andrews University, Berrien Springs; Byron Spence, Penfield, N.Y.; Donald C. Stinedurf, Ypsilanti; William R. Sturgis and D. F. Wilbur, Universal Joint Operation, North American Rockwell, Allegan; Alex Toth, Flint Community Schools, Flint; Roger Van Bolt, Sloan Panorama of Transportation, Flint; C. Warren Vander Hill, Ball State University, Muncie, Ind.; Thomas C. Walsh, Lansing; Cecil Waltz, Flint.

The editors of the Adrian *Daily Telegram,* Charlevoix *Courier,* Charlotte *Republican-Tribune,* Flint *Journal,* Fowlerville *Review,* and New York *Times Book Review,* by publishing inquiries from me, helped materially to put me in touch with new sources of information.

Roy D. Chapin, Jr., of Detroit, gave me permission to use the papers of his father at the Michigan Historical Collections. Henry B. Joy, Jr., of Detroit, gave me permission to use his father's papers, some of which are at the Michigan Historical Collections and others at the Burton Historical Collection.

Patricia J. Johnston, Lenawee County Clerk, gave me permission to examine the records of the case of Willis Grant Murray vs. Church Manufacturing Company, filed in the courthouse in Adrian.

Lee Katz, director of Special Projects and Research Development, Eastern Michigan University, assisted me by arranging, through Jack Minzey, director of the Center for Community Education at Eastern, for the interview with Charles S. Mott, and through Richard Ruddell, manager of the Educational Affairs Department, Ford Motor Company, for a grant that enabled me to photocopy a large amount of material in the Federal Archives and Records Center, Chicago.

Additional help in obtaining illustrations was provided by Ty Cross, Consumers Power Company, Jackson; Joseph Klima, Jr., Detroit; the photographic labs at Eastern Michigan University and the University of Michigan; Mrs. Lois M. Ridley, Clio; Jerry T. Robbins, Oldsmobile Division, General Motors, Lansing; and particularly the Motor Vehicle Manufacturers Association, Detroit, which permitted me to make a generous selection of photographs from the association's collection and to use them, at no cost, in the book.

My department head at the start of this project, R. Neil McLarty, and his successor, Ira M. Wheatley, helped greatly by arranging my teaching schedule and departmental duties in a way that gave me large blocks of time for uninterrupted research and writing. Most particularly do I owe a debt of appreciation to Dr. McLarty and to the administration at Eastern for providing me with a sabbatical leave in the first half of 1973 which enabled me to complete most of the work on this book.

There would have been no book, of course, without the interest and assistance of William B. Eerdmans, Jr., Roger Verhulst, Marlin J. Van Elderen, and finally my editor, Joel Beversluis, whose work greatly improved the readability of my manuscript.

My wife, Tish, in addition to helping with the research and typing involved in this project, is responsible for the happy choice of the book's title.

NOTES

Introduction

1 Clarence M. Burton, editor in chief, *The City of Detroit, Michigan, 1701-1922*, 1:572 (Detroit, 1922).

Chapter 1

1 Details about the events of March 6, 1896, including reproductions of newspaper stories, are in Charles B. King, *A Golden Anniversary, 1895-1945*, 15, 44-46 (Larchmont, New York, 1945).

2 John B. Rae, *The American Automobile*, 1-8 (Chicago, 1965).

3 *Harper's Weekly*, 37:442 (May 13, 1893); *Scientific American*, 68:291 (May 13, 1893); Bessie Louise Pierce, *A History of Chicago*, 3:501-512 (New York, 1957); J. C. Furnas, *The American: A Social History of the United States, 1587-1914*, 761-67 (New York, 1969).

4 Charles E. Duryea, "It Doesn't Pay to Pioneer," *Saturday Evening Post*, 203:102 (May 16, 1931); Charles E. Duryea, "The American Motor Car Industry . . . ," *Motor*, 11:126 (March, 1909); Richard Crabb, *Birth of a Giant: The Men and Incidents that Gave America the Motor Car*, 3-14 (Philadelphia, 1969). It is now clear that other Americans developed gasoline cars before the Duryeas completed their first car, but the Duryeas were the first to effectively publicize and promote their vehicle.

5 John B. Rae, *American Automobile Manufacturers: The First Forty Years*, 7, 30 (Philadelphia, 1959).

6 There is much dispute concerning which motor vehicles were exhibited at Chicago. See Rudolph E. Anderson, *The Story of the Automobile*, 49-52 (Washington, D.C., 1950); Duryea, "The American Motor Car Industry . . . ," 126; David T. Wells, "The Growth of the Automobile Industry in America," *Outing*, 51:207 (Nov. 1907); Editors of Automobile Quarterly, *The American Car Since 1775*, 47, 65-67 (New York, 1971); correspondence in April 1940 between Theodore Steinway and Charles B. King; and an interview with King in Jan. 1940, by Dr. Milo M. Quaife, both in the Charles B. King Papers, Automotive History Collection, Detroit Public Library.

7 Furnas, *The American*, 761-67; *American Car Since 1775*, 47; George S. May, *Pictorial History of Michigan: The Later Years*, 90 (Grand Rapids, 1969).

8 *Scientific American*, 68:294-95 (May 13, 1893), and 69:195, 198 (Sept. 23, 1893); Chris Sinsabaugh, *Who, Me? Forty Years of Automobile History*, 39 (Detroit, 1940).

9 Alan Ominsky, "A Catalog of Minnesota-Made Cars and Trucks," *Minnesota History*, 43:94 (Fall, 1972); Pierce, *A History of Chicago*, 3:511n; I. M. Weston, ed., *Report of the Board of World's Fair Managers for the State of Michigan*, 190 (Lansing, 1899); William A. Simonds, *Henry Ford: His Life, His Work, His Genius*, 44-45 (Indianapolis, 1943); *Scientific American*, 68:294-95 (May 13, 1893), and 69:305-306 (Nov. 11, 1893).

10 King, *A Golden Anniversary*, 11; Brendan Gill, "To Spare the Obedient Beast," *New Yorker*, 22:31 (May 18, 1946); Peter Clark Macfarlane, "The Beginnings of the Automobile," *Collier's*, 54:47 (Jan. 9, 1915).

11 King interview of Jan. 1940, in the King Papers; Weston, *Report of the Board of World's Fair Managers,* 110; King, *A Golden Anniversary,* 13.

12 King interview of Jan. 1940, King-Steinway correspondence of April 1940, and King to M. J. Duryea, Feb. 16, 1940, all in the King Papers.

13 File on the Sintz Gas Engine Company in the Grand Rapids Public Library; *Scientific American,* 69:212 (Sept. 30, 1893); *National Cyclopaedia of American Biography,* D:158; *American Car Since 1775,* 55; Robert G. Carroon, Milwaukee County Historical Society, to the author, May 11 and 23, 1973; interview of Claude Sintz by Owen Bombard, Mar. 11, 1952, an uncompleted oral history project in the Ford Archives, Henry Ford Museum, Dearborn, Michigan.

14 King interview of Jan. 1940 in King Papers; King, *A Golden Anniversary,* 12, 14; *Headlight,* vol. 2, no. 17, p. 49 (ca. 1897); *Detroit, Its Points of Interest,* 56 (New York, 1896). King received his patent on the pneumatic tool and the brake-beam on the same day, Jan. 30, 1894. See *Annual Report of the Commissioner of Patents for the Year 1894,* 179.

15 Narrative of Oliver E. Barthel addressed to King, April 10, 1940, in the King Papers; Reminiscences of Oliver E. Barthel, July 1952, in Ford Archives.

16 King interview of Jan. 1940 in King Papers; King, *A Golden Anniversary,* 9.

17 Two-page account written by King, summarizing and quoting the correspondence with Cheminais, and King interview of Jan. 1940, in King Papers; King, *A Golden Anniversary,* 14.

18 Wallace S. Phinney, ed., "J. F. Duryea Letters," *Bulb Horn,* 31:46-47 (Nov.-Dec. 1970); King interview of Jan. 1940; Rae, *American Automobile Manufacturers,* 28.

19 Letterbook for period July 1895 to Dec. 1895, in King Papers.

20 The most thoroughly researched account of the *Times-Herald* competition is Russell H. Anderson, "The First Automobile Race in America," *Antique Automobile,* 35:51-56 (July-Aug. 1971). See also *American Car Since 1775,* 69-93; Anderson, *Story of the American Automobile,* 55-71; H. H. Kohlsaat, "America's First Horseless Carriage Race, 1895," *Saturday Evening Post,* 196:21, 89 (Jan. 15, 1924); *Scientific American,* 73:82-83 (Aug. 10, 1895).

21 King, *A Golden Anniversary,* 18; Anderson, *Story of the American Automobile,* 58.

22 *Scientific American,* 73:66 (Aug. 3, 1895), and 73:242-43 (Oct. 19, 1895); New York *Times,* Oct. 22, 1895.

23 *Scientific American,* 73:242-43 (Oct. 19, 1895); King, *A Golden Anniversary,* 26; J. P. Edmonds, *Development of the Automobile and Gasoline Engine in Michigan,* 10 (Lansing, 1942); Kohlsaat, "America's First Horseless Carriage Race," 89.

24 King to F. A. Adams, Aug. 15, 1895; King to Pneumatic Wagon Wheel Co., Oneida, N.Y., Sept. 5, 1895; King to Morgan & Wright, Sept. 17, 1895; King to C. Sintz, Sept. 12, 1895; King to Indianapolis Chain and Stamping Co., Aug. 17, 1895; King to J. & H. Duckworth, Springfield, Mass., Aug. 21, 1895; King to editor of Chicago *Times-Herald,* Sept. 11, 1895; King to F. A. Adams, Sept. 25, 1895, and King interview of Jan. 1940, all in the King Papers; King, *A Golden Anniversary,* 12.

25 Advertising brochures for the King Motor Car Company in Pamphlet Box 3, Michigan Historical Collections, University of Michigan; King interview of Jan. 1940; Barthel Narrative, 1940; Barthel Reminiscences, 1952; Macfarlane, "The Beginnings of the Automobile," 47.

26 *National Cyclopaedia of American Biography*, 30:559; King, *A Golden Anniversary*, 18-19; Sinsabaugh, *Who, Me?*, 39.

27 See the accounts of the *Times-Herald* competition cited earlier, plus New York *Times*, Nov. 16, 1895, for the departure of the Macy-Benz from New York.

28 King, *A Golden Anniversary*, 31, 35; *National Cyclopaedia of American Biography*, 30:559; and the accounts of the race cited earlier.

29 Benton Harbor *Palladium*, Nov. 29, 1895.

30 Hiram Percy Maxim, *Horseless Carriage Days*, 3 (New York, 1937).

31 *Motocycle* lasted for only a couple of years, while *Horseless Age*, originally a monthly and then a weekly, lasted until 1918 when it was merged with *Motor Age*, another automotive journal that started publication in September 1899.

32 King, *A Golden Anniversary*, 41. The copy of the letter reproduced in this book is addressed to the *Times-Herald*, but another copy in the King Papers is addressed to the editor of *Electrical Engineering*, while the same letter was also published in the November 1895 issue of *Horseless Age*.

33 *Horseless Age*, 1:15 (Jan. 1896); King, *A Golden Anniversary*, 41-43.

34 King to Maxim, Dec. 7, 1895, and list of members in the league as of Mar. 16, 1896, in the King Papers; *Horseless Age*, 1:23 (Mar. 1896).

35 King to J. Frank Duryea, Jan. 4, 1896; King to Edward Locke, Toledo, Dec. 13, 1895, in the King Papers.

36 *Horseless Age*, 1:4 (Nov. 1895); King to Shaver, Nov. 26, 1895; King to Maxim, Dec. 13, 1895, in the King Papers.

37 Rae, *American Automobile Manufacturers*, 25; King to "Dear Friend" Duryea, Jan. 4, 1896. In King's letterbook this letter is dated 1895, but the placement of the letter in the book makes it clear that the year 1896 was intended.

38 Copy of the agreement of Jan. 18, 1896, is in the King Papers, together with a manuscript written by J. Frank Duryea that is included with correspondence between King and Arthur Pound in 1943.

39 *Horseless Age*, 1:24-25, 34 (Feb. 1896); King to Shaver, Jan. 26, 1896; King to Wayne Sulkeyette and Road Cart Co., Jan. 28, 1896; King to Packard, Feb. 15, 1896; King to Frazar & Co. of Japan, New York, April 6, 1896, all in the King Papers.

40 King to Charles Duryea, April 7, 1896, and an account of the events at the horse show, written by King on Nov. 11, 1943, in the King Papers.

41 "The Duryea-King Motor Becomes a Circus Attraction," mss. account written by King in about 1942, and a typed copy of an undated letter from King to "My Dear Fletcher," evidently written in April 1896, in the King Papers.

42 Gill, "To Spare the Obedient Beast," 34; King, *A Golden Anniversary*, 45.

43 Barthel Reminiscences, 1952; *Horseless Age*, 1:32 (April 1896); King to Walton, Aug. 14, 1896; King to Ingersoll, Aug. 20, 1896, in the King Papers; Allan Nevins, *Ford, The Times, the Man, the Company*, 165 (New York, 1954).

44 *Horseless Age*, 1:19 (Sept. 1896), 2:9 (Nov. 1896), 2:6 (Feb. 1897); King interview of Jan. 1940, in the King Papers.

45 *Horseless Age*, 1:27 (June 1896), 1:27 (Aug. 1896), 2:4 (Feb. 1897), 2:21 (Mar. 1897); King's letter to Walker is in *Horseless Age*, 1:23 (Mar. 1896); King to Mueller, Aug. 22, 1896, in the King Papers.

46 *Horseless Age*, 2:2 (June 1897), 2:7 (Oct. 1897); Barthel Reminiscences, 1952; *Scientific American*, 78:53 (Jan. 22, 1898).

47 King to H. MacLaury of Philadelphia, Jan. 25, 1898; King to Martin

Motor Wagon Co., Feb. 28, 1898, in the King Papers; Barthel Reminiscences, 1952.

48 King, *A Golden Anniversary*, 14-15; King to Mrs. Vanderpoel, Jan. 29, 1900, in the King Papers.

49 King to Ingersoll, undated, but probably Feb. 1900, in the King Papers; Barthel Reminiscences, 1952; Gill, "To Spare the Obedient Beast," 30.

Chapter 2

1 Benton Harbor *Palladium,* Nov. 26, 1895.

2 *3rd Annual Report, Michigan Factory Inspectors,* 84-85; *4th Annual Report, Michigan Factory Inspectors,* 74-75; *14th Annual Report of the* [Michigan] *Bureau of Labor,* 181-82.

3 U. S. Patent Office *Official Gazette,* 74:668 (April 27, 1897); Benton Harbor *Palladium,* Feb. 8, 1896; *Horseless Age,* 1:17 (Jan. 1896); *Motocycle,* 1:17 (Jan. 1896).

4 Benton Harbor *Palladium,* Nov. 26, 1895; Grand Rapids *Democrat,* Nov. 27, 1895; W. J. Banyon, president, Benton Harbor *News-Palladium,* to the author, Nov. 16, 1971.

5 Chicago *Times-Herald,* Nov. 29, 1895, reproduced in King, *Golden Anniversary.*

6 The Detroit *Journal* story was referred to in the Benton Harbor *Palladium,* Dec. 5, 1895, and on Jan. 31, 1896, the *Palladium* referred to stories that had appeared in other unnamed newspapers. *Horseless Age,* 1:17 (Jan. 1896), and *Motocycle,* 1:17 (Jan. 1896).

7 Benton Harbor *Palladium,* Nov. 29, 1895.

8 *Ibid.,* Dec. 4 and 5, 1895.

9 *Ibid.,* Dec. 17 and 20, 1895.

10 *Ibid.,* Jan. 31, 1896.

11 *Ibid.,* Feb. 8, 1896.

12 W. J. Banyon to the author, Nov. 16, 1971.

13 U. S. Patent Office *Official Gazette,* 74:668 (April 27, 1897), and 84:264 (July 12, 1898); James T. Allen, *Supplement to the Digest of United States Automobile Patents, July, 1899, to January, 1902,* 1461 (Washington, n. d.); *American Car Since 1775,* 371, 442, 452; information regarding Henry Kellogg and William Worth was generously supplied to the author by Richard W. Schwarz, Andrews University, Berrien Springs, Michigan, from material in the S. N. Haskell Papers in that institution, and by Ron Graybill of Ellen G. White Publications, Washington, D. C. For a more complete examination of the career of William Worth see George S. May, "William O. Worth: Adventist Auto Pioneer," *Adventist Heritage,* 1:43-53 (July 1974).

14 Earl G. Fuller, "The Automobile Industry in Michigan," *Michigan History,* 12:282 (April 1928); *Horseless Age,* 1:15, 32, 36, 51 (Nov. 1895), 1:33 (Dec. 1895), 1:16 (May 1896), 2:3 (Aug. 1897), 2:4 (Sept. 1897), 20:282 (Aug. 28, 1907); G. N. Georgano, ed., *Encyclopaedia of American Automobiles,* 167-68 (New York, 1971).

15 Folder on Sintz in Michigan Room, Grand Rapids Public Library; interview with Claude Sintz, in Ford Archives; *Horseless Age,* 1:36 (Nov. 1895).

16 Charlevoix *Courier,* Feb. 10, 1972; *Horseless Age,* 1:51 (Nov. 1895), 2:7

(Mar. 1897); U. S. Patent Office *Official Gazette,* 78:782 (Feb. 2, 1897); Rae, *American Automobile Manufacturers,* 39-40.

17 *Horseless Age,* 1:51 (Nov. 1895); Mrs. Joseph Klimkowski, Brooklyn, Mich. to the author, Feb. 10, 1972, and an undated note from Mrs. Klimkowski in the same month.

18 *Horseless Age,* 1:33 (Dec. 1895); U. S. Patent Office *Official Gazette,* 86:1085 (Feb. 14, 1899).

19 Duane Yarnell, *Auto Pioneering: The Remarkable Story of R. E. Olds,* 25, 35-36 (Lansing, 1949).

20 Henry Ford, in collaboration with Samuel Crowther, *My Life and Work,* 22-25 (Garden City, N.Y., 1923); Sidney Olson, *Young Henry Ford: A Picture History of the First Forty Years,* 23-24 (Detroit, 1963).

21 Publication of Ohio Historical Society, reprinted in *Lake Front News* (Port Clinton, Ohio), Aug. 12, 1972; Arthur Pound, *The Turning Wheel: The Story of General Motors through Twenty-five Years, 1908-1933,* 32-33 (New York, 1934); Dorothy Marie Mitts, *That Noble Country: The Romance of the St. Clair River Region,* 246-47 (Philadelphia, 1968); *American Car Since 1775,* 41.

22 Glenn A. Niemeyer, *The Automotive Career of Ransom E. Olds,* 215 (East Lansing, 1963).

23 David J. Wilkie, *Esquire's American Autos and Their Makers,* 25 (New York, 1963); Ford, *My Life and Work,* 22; New York *Times,* Aug. 27, 1950; *Newsweek,* 36:53 (Sept. 4, 1950); Yarnell, *Auto Pioneering,* 26-27. In addition to the published accounts of Olds' life, I have used a typed manuscript entitled "That Boy Ranny," a copy of which is in the office of the R. E. Olds Company, Lansing. This is an account that Olds had prepared for his family and in it the details of his childhood experiences differ in some respects from other versions. This material, plus other previously unused material in the Olds papers at Michigan State University and information provided in interviews with Olds' daughters and grandsons, were also used by me in preparing a new biography of Olds that is to be published by Eerdmans.

24 R. E. Olds Anderson to the author, July 31, 1972, reporting information supplied by his mother, Gladys Olds Anderson; B. C. Forbes and O. D. Foster, *Automotive Giants of America: Men Who Are Making Our Motor Industry,* 226-27 (New York, 1926).

25 *Michigan State Gazetteer for 1881,* 743-56.

26 Forbes and Foster, *Automotive Giants of America,* 226-27; in a letter to the author, July 18, 1973, Kenneth J. Mead of the Department of Child Accounting, Lansing School District, reported that a search of school records failed to provide any evidence that Olds was ever enrolled in the city schools; Ford Ceasar, a local Lansing historian and long-time teacher in the city's schools, reported in a letter of Nov. 8, 1973, a similarly negative result of his search of certain other records. Records of the Lansing Business University have not survived from the period in which Olds is said to have been enrolled in that institution, according to James L. LaParl, Director of Education at that institution, in a letter of Aug. 17, 1973.

27 Sales figures of the Olds enterprises are included in a typed memorandum in Box 1, R. E. Olds Collection, History Collections, Michigan State University; employment figures are from the annual reports of *Inspection of Factories in Michigan,* 1893-97; Lansing *State Republican,* Aug. 2, 1890; *Scientific American,* 70:357 (June 9, 1894); Niemeyer, *Ransom E. Olds,* 6-7.

28 *Ibid.,* 11-12; Lansing *State Republican,* Aug. 2, 1890; annual reports of

P. F. Olds & Son, 1892-98, in Corporation and Securities Commission Records, State Archives, Michigan History Division, Michigan Department of State, Lansing, Michigan.

29 *Ibid.;* listings for P. F. Olds & Son in *Michigan State Gazetteer* in the 1880's and 1890's; Yarnell, *Auto Pioneering,* 41-45; R. E. Olds Anderson to the author, Oct. 17, 1972; obituary of P. F. Olds in Lansing *Journal,* July 1, 1908.

30 The evidence regarding the date of Olds' first horseless carriage is evaluated in Niemeyer, *Ransom E. Olds,* 1-2.

31 Frank N. Turner, *An Account of Ingham County From Its Organization* (vol. III, *Historic Michigan,* George N. Fuller, ed.), 341 (n.p., [1928]); Yarnell, *Auto Pioneering,* 31.

32 *Scientific American,* 66:329 (May 21, 1892); Yarnell, *Auto Pioneering,* 36; Ransom E. Olds, "The Horseless Carriage," *Michigan Engineers' Annual, Containing the Proceedings of the Michigan Engineering Society for 1898,* 93-94 (Battle Creek, 1898); interview with Mrs. Gladys Olds Anderson and Mrs. Bernice Olds Roe, June 28, 1973.

33 Yarnell, *Auto Pioneering,* 35-36; Frank Luther Mott, *A History of American Magazines,* 2:316-24 (Cambridge, Mass., 1938); advertisement for *Scientific American* in Benton Harbor *Palladium,* Dec. 6, 1895.

34 Yarnell, *Auto Pioneering,* 36; *Scientific American,* 64:285 (May 2, 1891), 66:268 (April 23, 1892), 66:332 (May 21, 1892), 68:396 (June 24, 1893), 70:191 (Mar. 24, 1894), 70:366 (June 9, 1894), 73:286 (Nov. 2, 1895); E. H. West, "The Meteoric Rise of the Automotive Industry," *American Review of Reviews,* 42:583 (Nov. 1910).

35 Niemeyer, *Ransom E. Olds,* 9-10; James J. Flink, *America Adopts the Automobile, 1895-1910,* 17 (Cambridge, Mass., 1970).

36 U. S. Patent Office *Official Gazette,* 56:495 (July 28, 1891), 67:1510 (June 19, 1894), 74:1780 (Mar. 31, 1896), 77:555-56 (Oct. 27, 1896).

37 *Ibid.,* 76:921 (Aug. 11, 1896); Niemeyer, *Ransom E. Olds,* 10.

38 *Horseless Age,* 1:26 (Mar. 1896); *Scientific American,* 74:167 (Mar. 14, 1896), 74:206 (Mar. 28, 1896).

39 Sales figures from typed note of sales from 1890 to 1904 in R. E. Olds Collection; *Scientific American,* 76:285 (May 1, 1897); annual reports of P. F. Olds & Son and the Olds Gasoline Engine Works in the 1890's in Corporation and Securities Records; Niemeyer, *Ransom E. Olds,* 20-21; Edmonds, *Development of the Automobile,* 3-4.

40 *Ibid.;* 2nd Annual Report of the [Michigan] *Department of Labor,* 158-61.

41 Niemeyer, *Ransom E. Olds,* 13; Yarnell, *Auto Pioneering,* 13; *Horseless Age,* 1:26 (Mar. 1896); *Scientific American,* 77:416 (Dec. 25, 1897).

42 An Oldsmobile brochure, reproduced in Q. David Bowers, *Early American Car Advertisements,* 129 (New York, 1966), referred to Olds' 1887 vehicle as "the first American vehicle driven by a gasoline motor." See also R. A. Parker to Olds, Nov. 23, 1904, in R. E. Olds Collection; Yarnell, *Auto Pioneering,* 54; Edmonds, *Development of the Automobile,* 10; Pound, *The Turning Wheel,* 49; Anne Jardim, *The First Henry Ford: A Study in Personality and Business Leadership,* 9 (Cambridge, Mass., 1970); Olds, "The Horseless Carriage," *Michigan Engineers' Annual,* 94.

43 Niemeyer, *Ransom E. Olds,* 13-14; Samuel W. Durant, *History of Ingham and Eaton Counties, Michigan,* 135 (Philadelphia, 1880); George W. Stark, *City of Destiny: The Story of Detroit,* 448-55 (Detroit, 1943).

44 Lansing *State Republican,* Aug. 12, 1896, quoted in Niemeyer, *Ransom E. Olds,* 15. See also Yarnell, *Auto Pioneering,* 52; *Horseless Age,* 1:18 (Oct. 1896); *Scientific American,* 75:380 (Nov. 21, 1896); and Wells, "The

Growth of the Automobile Industry in America," *Outing,* 51:212 (Nov. 1907).

45 *Scientific American,* 74:164 (Mar. 14, 1896); Yarnell, *Auto Pioneering,* 52-53; *National Cyclopaedia of American Biography,* 39:480; *Motocycle,* 1:20-21 (Nov. 1895), 2:14 (Dec. 1896); James T. Allen, *Digest of United States Automobile Patents from 1789 to July 1, 1899,* 501 (Washington, 1900); U. S. Patent Office *Official Gazette,* 89:614-15 (Oct. 20, 1899).

46 Niemeyer, *Ransom E. Olds,* 14-15; Detroit *News,* Aug. 13, 1896; *Horseless Age,* 1:27 (Aug. 1896), 1:18 (Oct. 1896).

47 Allen, *Digest of United States Automobile Patents,* 501.

48 Detroit *News,* Aug. 13, 1896; Grand Rapids *Democrat,* Aug. 14, 1896; King to W. G. Walton, Aug. 20, 1896, in the King Papers; *Motocycle,* 1:16 (Sept. 1896); *Horseless Age,* 1:18 (Oct. 1896); *Scientific American,* 75:380 (Nov. 21, 1896); U. S. Patent Office *Official Gazette,* 81:1398-99 (Nov. 23, 1897).

49 Niemeyer, *Ransom E. Olds,* 15, 17-18, 20. Niemeyer states that he found a copy of the early Olds ad in the Roy Chapin Papers at the Michigan Historical Collections, University of Michigan. I have been unable to find the ad in these papers, however. It is possible that the term used in the ad was not Motor-Cycle, as Niemeyer has it, but Moto-Cycle, which was a term still used in 1896 for what had previously been called a horseless carriage.

50 *Horseless Age,* 2:13 (Jan. 1897).

51 *National Cyclopaedia of American Biography,* 49:298; Mrs. Franc L. Adams, *Pioneer History of Ingham County,* 511 (Lansing, 1923); Yarnell, *Auto Pioneering,* 57-60; Niemeyer, *Ransom E. Olds,* 18-19; John K. Barnes, "The Romance of Our Automobile Makers," *World's Work,* 41:561 (April 1921).

52 Turner, *An Account of Ingham County From Its Organization,* 342-43; typed copies of correspondence of Eugene Cooley for May and June 1884, in the Eugene F. Cooley Papers, Michigan Historical Collections; George N. Fuller, ed., *Michigan: A Centennial History of the State and Its People,* 5:491 (Chicago, 1939); Niemeyer, *Ransom E. Olds,* 18-19.

53 *National Cyclopaedia of American Biography,* 11:235; Burton, *The City of Detroit, Michigan, 1701-1922,* 4:647; C. M. Burton, *History of Wayne County and the City of Detroit,* 4:9 (Chicago, 1930); Samuel L. Smith, "Pre-Historic and Modern Copper Mines of Lake Superior," *Michigan Pioneer and Historical Collections,* 39:137n; *Michigan Biographies,* 2:306.

54 Niemeyer, *Ransom E. Olds,* 18-20.

55 Yarnell, *Auto Pioneering,* 60-61.

56 *Motocycle,* 3:21 (Oct. 1897); Edmonds, *Development of the Automobile,* 12; Niemeyer, *Ransom E. Olds,* 17, 22. Late in 1897, Olds seemed to indicate that no vehicles had yet been completed. See Olds, "The Horseless Carriage," *Michigan Engineers' Annual,* 96.

57 Rae, *American Automobile Manufacturers,* 6-44; P. M. Heldt, "Rise and Decline of the American Steam Car Industry," *Horseless Carriage Gazette,* 8:25 (Dec. 1946).

58 Niemeyer, *Ransom E. Olds,* 21-23.

59 Typed note on sales from 1890-1904 in R. E. Olds Collection; *15th Annual Report* [Michigan] *Bureau of Labor,* appendix, 81; *16th Annual Report* [Michigan] *Bureau of Labor,* appendix, 70; *17th Annual Report* [Michigan] *Bureau of Labor,* appendix, 58; annual report of the Olds Gasoline Engine Works for 1899 in Corporation and Securities Records; Turner, *An Account of Ingham County From Its Organization,* 682.

60 F. L. Smith, *Motoring Down a Quarter of a Century,* 16 (Detroit, 1928);

Niemeyer, *Ransom E. Olds*, 24-25; *Michigan State Gazetteer for 1899*, 610 and 652; "That Boy Ranny," in R. E. Olds Company office.

61 Ray Stannard Baker, "The Automobile in Common Use," *McClure's Magazine*, 13:195 (July 1899); Niemeyer, *Ransom E. Olds*, 25; Pound, *The Turning Wheel*, 51.

62 Niemeyer, *Ransom E. Olds*, 25-26; Burton, *The City of Detroit, Michigan*, 4:647.

63 Niemeyer, *Ransom E. Olds*, 27; *Men of Progress*, 220 (Detroit, 1900).

64 Smith, *Motoring Down a Quarter of a Century*, 16; annual report of Olds Motor Works, 1900, in Corporation and Securities Records.

65 *Ibid.; National Cyclopaedia of American Biography*, 19:249; *Compendium of History and Biography of the City of Detroit and Wayne County, Michigan*, 253, 271, 388, 390 (Chicago, 1909); Melvin G. Holli, *Reform in Detroit: Hazen S. Pingree and Urban Politics*, 200-201 (New York, 1969).

66 Detroit *Free Press*, May 14, 1899; annual report of Olds Motor Works for 1900, in Corporation and Securities Records.

67 Niemeyer, *Ransom E. Olds*, 27-28; *Horseless Age*, 4:24 (April 19, 1899).

68 Crabb, *Birth of a Giant*, viii.

Chapter 3

1 Stephen B. McCracken, ed., *Detroit in Nineteen Hundred*, 64-65 (Detroit, 1901); Anne Mathewson, "The Detroit Bicentennial Memorial," *Century Magazine*, 60:709 (Sept. 1900).

2 Norman Beasley and George W. Stark, *Made in Detroit*, 174-75 (New York, 1957).

3 *The Bi-Centenary of the Founding of the City of Detroit, 1701-1901*, 292-94 (Detroit, 1902); Milo M. Quaife, *This is Detroit: 1701-1951, Two Hundred Years in Pictures*, 70 (Detroit, 1951).

4 *Bi-Centenary of the Founding of the City of Detroit*, 81-82; *Historical Art Souvenir, Detroit and Her Bi-Centenary ...*, n.p. (Detroit, 1901); Detroit *News*, July 26 and 27, 1901.

5 Information on the fate of Cadillac's Chair was supplied by Solan W. Weeks, director of the Detroit Historical Museum, in a letter to the author, April 4, 1972.

6 Arthur Pound, *Detroit: Dynamic City*, 243-49 (New York, 1940), is the source for much of the information in this and the following paragraphs on Detroit's population growth and the nature of that population in the nineteenth century. See also Holli, *Reform in Detroit*, for useful comments on Detroit's population and leadership in the late nineteenth century.

7 Henry M. Utley and Byron M. Cutcheon, *Michigan as a Province, Territory and State, the Twenty-Sixth Member of the Federal Union*, 1:321 (New York, 1906).

8 *Fortieth Annual Meeting of the National Educational Association, at Detroit, Michigan, July Eighth to Twelfth, Nineteen Hundred and One*, 9-10 (Detroit, 1901).

9 *Souvenir of Detroit*, n.p. (Detroit, 1891).

10 Michigan Secretary of State, *Michigan and its Resources* . . . [fourth edition], 282-83 (Lansing, 1893).

11 Detroit *News*, Aug. 9, 1896.

12 Raymond C. Miller, *Kilowatts at Work: A History of the Detroit Edison*

Company, 3-40 (Detroit, 1957); Stark, *City of Destiny: The Story of Detroit,* 396-98.

13 Pound, *Detroit: Dynamic City,* 255-57.

14 *Detroit, the Beautiful,* edited and compiled by S. F. Houghton and J. F. Walsh, 9 (Detroit, 1902?); *Michigan and its Resources,* 281; Silas Farmer, *All About Detroit ...,* 108-12 ([Detroit], 1899).

15 Stark, *City of Destiny: The Story of Detroit,* 434-37; Farmer, *All About Detroit,* 68, 82; Holli, *Reform in Detroit,* 24-26; "That Boy Ranny," in office of R. E. Olds Company.

16 J. Horace McFarland, "'In Detroit, Life is Worth Living,'" *Outlook,* 91:210 (Jan. 23, 1909); F. H. Walker, Walkerville, Ontario (his business address), to an unnamed woman, Aug. 5, 1898, copy in the William Maybury papers, Burton Historical Collection, Detroit Public Library; Nevins, *Ford,* 122.

17 *Fortieth Annual Meeting of the National Educational Association,* 37; the basic information on Detroit manufacturing activities used for this and the following paragraphs is drawn from *Michigan and its Resources,* Farmer, *All About Detroit,* and L. V. Spooner, "Detroit, the City Built by the Automobile Industry," *Automobile,* 28:791-97 (April 10, 1913).

18 Report on the stove industry in *18th Annual Report of the* [Michigan] *Bureau of Labor,* 177-78.

Chapter 4

1 *Motor Age,* 1:44-45 (Sept. 26, 1899).

2 King to Ingersoll, Sept. 25, 1897, in King Papers; Barthel Reminiscences, 1952.

3 Olson, *Young Henry Ford,* 112; Allen, *Digest of United States Automobile Patents from 1789 to July 1, 1899,* 502; *Horseless Age,* 3:7 (June 1898), 3:19 (Oct. 1898), 3:18 (Feb. 1899); Detroit *Free Press,* Aug. 19, 1899.

4 Ford, *My Life and Work,* 33; Nevins, *Ford,* 167; *Motor Age,* 1:45 (Sept. 26, 1899), 4:n.p. (June 6, 1901). See Detroit *News,* June 15, 1941, for reference to Annesley as the first used-car buyer.

5 Detroit *News,* July 16, 1899; *Horseless Age,* 3:26 (Oct. 1898).

6 *Ibid.,* 3:22 (Nov. 1898); Detroit *News,* July 16 and 30, 1899; Detroit *Journal,* July 29, 1899, as reproduced in Olson, *Young Henry Ford,* 105.

7 Unless otherwise indicated, the source relied upon for the basic biographical details on Ford's life in these years is Nevins, *Ford: The Times, the Man, the Company.* For Ford's attempt to obtain the superintendency of the municipal power plant, see Miller, *Kilowatts at Work,* 38.

8 *Motor Age,* 5:n.p. (Oct. 17, 1901); *Automobile,* 9:616 (Dec. 12, 1903); Wells, "The Growth of the Automobile Industry in America," *Outing,* 51:209-10; *Cycle and Automobile Trade Journal,* 14:126 (Dec. 1909); James Rood Doolittle, ed., *The Romance of the Automobile Industry,* 23 (New York, 1916); Macfarlane, "The Beginnings of the Automobile," *Collier's,* 54:47; Eugene W. Lewis, *Motor Memories ...,* 8 (Detroit, 1947); E. D. Kennedy, *The Automobile Industry,* 4 (New York, 1941); Oliver Barthel to Charles King, Oct. 3, 1941, in King Papers; Simonds, *Henry Ford,* 52; John Burchard and Albert Bush-Brown, *The Architecture of America, A Social and Cultural History,* 154 (Boston, 1966).

9 William Greenleaf, *Monopoly on Wheels: Henry Ford and the Selden Automobile Patent,* 117, 139 (Detroit, 1961); John B. Rae, ed., *Henry*

Ford, 13 (Englewood Cliffs, N. J., 1969); Ford, *My Life and Work*, 29-33.

10 Greenleaf, *Monopoly on Wheels*, 117, 139; Nevins, *Ford*, 113, 148, 156n.

11 Jardim, *The First Henry Ford*, 38-39; Rae, ed., *Henry Ford*, 15; Nevins, *Ford*, 154, 159; Barthel Reminiscences, 1952.

12 Nevins, *Ford*, 142-43, 146-48, 607n; King interview of Jan. 1940 in King Papers; Barthel Reminiscences, 1952.

13 *Ibid.;* Nevins, *Ford*, 156-57.

14 A. H. C. Dalley to King, July 8, 1896, and King to Ingersoll, Aug. 22, 1896, both in King Papers; Simonds, *Henry Ford*, 54; Gill, "To Spare the Obedient Beast," *New Yorker*, 22:39-40; Nevins, *Ford*, 159-60.

15 Olson, *Young Henry Ford*, 89; Jardim, *The First Henry Ford*, 168.

16 Olson, *Young Henry Ford*, 85-87.

17 For the work of David Bell, see Nevins, *Ford*, 158-59.

18 For examples of Maybury biographies, see *Compendium of History and Biography of Detroit and Wayne County*, 503-504; Burton, *The City of Detroit*, 4:783; *Who Was Who in America*, 1:793.

19 Olson, *Young Henry Ford*, 114-15; Nevins, *Ford*, 135n; *Compendium of History and Biography of Detroit and Wayne County*, 493, 503.

20 Olson, *Young Henry Ford*, 91; Simonds, *Henry Ford*, 55; Nevins, *Ford*, 161, 172; Ford, *My Life and Work*, 33; *Compendium of History and Biography of Detroit and Wayne County*, 503.

21 Olson, *Young Henry Ford*, 92, 115. Early in 1896 Maybury owned 769 shares in the Detroit Motor Company, according to the company's annual report as of Jan. 1, 1896, in Corporation and Securities Records.

22 Nevins, *Ford*, 171; Olson, *Young Henry Ford*, 103.

23 Miller, *Kilowatts at Work*, 32, 48.

24 Nevins, *Ford*, 171-72; Olson, *Young Henry Ford*, 103.

25 Nevins, *Ford*, 171.

26 This and other Garfield letters referred to in the following paragraphs are in the Maybury Papers.

27 See Olson, *Young Henry Ford*, 98, for excerpts from the report.

28 Detroit *Free Press*, Aug. 1, 1899.

29 Detroit *News*, Aug. 5, 1899; Olson, *Young Henry Ford*, 110-117; Nevins, *Ford*, 175; *National Cyclopaedia of American Biography*, 18:103.

30 Olson, *Young Henry Ford*, 188; Ford, *My Life and Work*, 36; Simonds, *Henry Ford*, 60-61.

31 *National Cyclopaedia of American Biography*, 39:344-45; Miller, *Kilowatts at Work*, 9-10.

32 *National Cyclopaedia of American Biography*, 21:190-91; Olson, *Young Henry Ford*, 115-17; Nevins, *Ford*, 174-75; J. Bell Moran, *The Moran Family: 200 Years in Detroit*, 79-80, 126 (Detroit, 1949); Silas Farmer, *The History of Detroit and Wayne County* . . . (3rd ed.), 514-15 (Detroit, 1890).

33 Nevins, *Ford*, 176; Detroit *Free Press*, Aug. 19, 1899; Olson, *Young Henry Ford*, 104-105; Jardim, *The First Henry Ford*, 42.

34 Nevins, *Ford*, 178-79; *Motor Age*, 1:280 (Dec. 14, 1899); Olson, *Young Henry Ford*, 118-21.

35 *Motor Age*, 1:373 (Jan. 11, 1900), 2:58-59 (Mar. 22, 1900); Nevins, *Ford*, 179-80, 184.

36 *Ibid.*, 184-85, 190-91; Olson, *Young Henry Ford*, 123; *18th Annual Report of the* [Michigan] *Bureau of Labor*, 28.

37 Ford, *My Life and Work*, 36. The experiences of Preston M. Hulbert are from his manuscript "Recollections of Sixty Years of Patent Practice," prepared in 1947, a copy of which was kindly supplied to me by Hulbert's son, L. Gaylord Hulbert, who, in 1921, followed his father into the

patent law firm of Whittemore, Hulbert & Belknap, with which he has been associated ever since.

Chapter 5

1 Pound, *The Turning Wheel,* 51; *Motor Age,* 1:440 (Feb. 1, 1900), 2:58 (Mar. 22, 1900).
2 Forbes and Foster, *Automotive Giants of America,* 230; *Motor Age,* 2:652 July 19, 1900), 3:113 (Sept. 27, 1900); Niemeyer, *Ransom E. Olds,* 35.
3 See Philip Hillyer Smith, *Wheels Within Wheels: A Short History of American Motor Car Manufacturing* (second ed.), 191-275 (New York, 1970), for a convenient listing of cars and production dates; *Detroit Directory for 1900,* 884; Floyd Clymer, *Treasury of Early American Automobiles, 1877-1925,* 11 (New York, 1950); Kennedy, *The Automobile Industry,* 19; Smith, *Motoring Down a Quarter of a Century,* 16; Forbes and Foster, *Automotive Giants of America,* 230; Niemeyer, *Ransom E. Olds,* 29; typed listing of sales of Olds Motor Works in R. E. Olds Collection; *Automotive Industries,* 46:249 (Feb. 2, 1922).
4 Niemeyer, *Ransom E. Olds,* 30; Forbes and Foster, *Automotive Giants of America,* 230-31.
5 Niemeyer, *Ransom E. Olds,* 30-31; Olds to W. B. Chenoweth, Palestine, Texas, Nov. 28, 1900, in R. E. Olds Collection; Olds Motor Works brochure, 1900, in Automotive History Collection; *Motor World,* 1:316 (Feb. 7, 1901); *Horseless Age,* 7:13-14 (Feb. 20, 1901); *Motor Age,* 3:1197 (Mar. 6, 1901).
6 Niemeyer, *Ransom E. Olds,* 31; *McClure's Magazine,* 18:880 (ad section, 1902); T. R. Nicholson, *Passenger Cars, 1863-1904,* 142 (New York, 1970); Clymer, *Treasury of Early American Automobiles,* 11; *Detroit Directory for 1900,* 884; Allen, *Supplement to the Digest of United States Automobile Patents,* 1197, 1238.
7 C. F. Caunter, *The Light Car,* 18-19 (London, 1970); Nicholson, *Passenger Cars, 1863-1904,* 124; Ralph C. Epstein, *The Automobile Industry: Its Economic and Commercial Development,* 27 (Chicago, 1928); for examples of the various runabouts, see *Motor Age,* 3:3 (Sept. 30, 1900), 3:171-73 (Oct. 4, 1900), 3:232 (Oct. 18, 1900), 3:366 (Nov. 1, 1900), 3:592 (Dec. 6, 1900), 4:n.p. (Mar. 13, 1901), 4:n.p. (Mar. 21, 1901), and 4:n.p. (June 27, 1901); *Scientific American,* 85:224 (Oct. 5, 1901), 86:153-54 (Mar. 1, 1902), and 89:112 (Aug. 8, 1903); see Willis F. Dunbar, *Michigan: A History of the Wolverine State,* 556 (Grand Rapids, 1965), as an example of a source for the statement that the Oldsmobile was the first cheap car.
8 Detroit *News,* Mar. 9-10, 1901; *Motor Age,* 4:n.p. (Mar. 13, 1901), 4:n.p. (Mar. 21, 1901); Niemeyer, *Ransom E. Olds,* 32-33; Pound, *The Turning Wheel,* 53.
9 For examples of the prevalence of this story, see Rae, *American Automobile Manufacturers,* 31; Pound, *The Turning Wheel,* 53; Reginald M. Cleveland and S. T. Williamson, *The Road is Yours . . . ,* 178 (New York, 1951); Automobile Manufacturers Association, *Automobiles of America,* 25 (Detroit, 1968).
10 Detroit *Free Press,* Mar. 10, 1901; *Motor Age,* 3:936 (Jan. 30, 1901), 4:n.p. (Mar. 21, 1901); Niemeyer, *Ransom E. Olds,* 34-36; *Historical Art Souvenir, Detroit and Her Bi-Centenary,* 20.
11 *21st Annual Report of the* [Michigan] *Bureau of Labor,* 212; *Motor Age,* 3:1212 (Mar. 6, 1901), 4:n.p. (Mar. 21, 1901).

12 *Motor Age,* 2:3 (Mar. 15, 1900); Lewis, *Motor Memories,* 187-89; "A Reprint of thirty-six advertisements in *Collier's* special Automobile supplement of January 6, 1912," an unpaged publication sent out to auto dealers, copy in University of Michigan Graduate Library.

13 *Motor Age,* 2:652 (July 19, 1900); Alfred P. Sloan, Jr., in collaboration with Boyden Sparkes, *Adventures of a White Collar Man,* 27-32 (New York, 1941).

14 *Motor Age,* 3:84 (Sept. 20, 1900); Clarence H. Young and William A. Quinn, *Foundation for Living: The Story of Charles Stewart Mott and Flint,* 21 (New York, 1963); Weston-Mott to Olds, Dec. 29, 1902, in R. E. Olds Collection; see Charles King letterbook for Feb. 1899 for an order that he placed with Weston-Mott at that time for a set of wheels.

15 Mrs. Wilfred C. Leland, with Minnie Dubbs Millbrook, *Master of Precision: Henry M. Leland,* 61-62 (Detroit, 1966); Niemeyer, *Ransom E. Olds,* 36-38; T. R. Nicholson, *Passenger Cars, 1905-12,* 6 (New York, 1971).

16 Detroit *News,* Mar. 9, 1901; *Automobile,* 9:617-18 (Dec. 12, 1902); Niemeyer, *Ransom E. Olds,* 37; Forbes and Foster, *Automotive Giants of America,* 17-18; H. Jay Hayes Papers, Automotive History Collection; Benjamin Briscoe, "The Inside Story of the Rise of General Motors," *Detroit Saturday Night,* 15:9 (Jan. 15, 1921).

17 *Ibid.;* Niemeyer, *Ransom E. Olds,* 37; William C. Redfield of J. H. Williams & Co., Brooklyn, N. Y., to James Whittemore, Detroit, an attorney for the Olds Motor Works, Oct. 21, 1901, in R. E. Olds Collection; see Rae, *American Automobile Manufacturers,* 31, and Beasley and Stark, *Made in Detroit,* 49, for examples of two different types of works that both place the same emphasis on the importance of the Olds fire in forcing Olds to turn to outside suppliers.

18 *Motor Age,* 4:n.p. (Mar. 28, 1901).

19 *Ibid.,* 4:n.p. (Mar. 28, 1901), and 4:n.p. (April 4, 1901).

20 Niemeyer, *Ransom E. Olds,* 40; Edmonds, *Development of the Automobile,* 14-15; "R. Shettler's Efforts — The Growth of Lansing," a typed manuscript, copies of which are in the Historical Collections of Michigan State University and the Michigan Historical Collections at the University of Michigan.

21 *Ibid.;* Shettler to Olds Motor Works, Aug. 14, 1901, in R. E. Olds Collection; B. F. Davis to Eugene Cooley, Aug. 5, 1904, in Eugene F. Cooley Papers.

22 "R. Shettler's Efforts"; Shettler to Olds Motor Works, Aug. 14, 1901; and a fragment of a letter from Fred Smith to Olds, apparently dating from the latter part of 1901, in the R. E. Olds Collection.

23 Smith to Olds, July 19, 1901, in R. E. Olds Collection.

24 "R. Shettler's Efforts"; Shettler to Olds Motor Works, Aug. 14, 1901, in R. E. Olds Collection.

25 Niemeyer, *Ransom E. Olds,* 42-43; Birt Darling, *City in the Forest: The Story of Lansing,* 159-62 (New York, 1950); *Motor Age,* 5:n.p. (Sept. 12, 1901); Jackson *Daily Citizen,* Oct. 10, 1901.

26 *Motor Age,* 4:n.p. (Aug. 21, 1901), 5:n.p. (Sept. 12, 1901); Niemeyer, *Ransom E. Olds,* 43.

27 *18th Annual Report of the* [Michigan] *Bureau of Labor,* 23, 64; *19th Annual Report of the* [Michigan] *Bureau of Labor,* 248-49, 292-93.

28 *Motor Age,* 4:n.p. (Aug. 21, 1901), 5:n.p. (Nov. 14, 1901); *Horseless Age,* 8:715 (Nov. 13, 1901); Niemeyer, *Ransom E. Olds,* 43.

29 Pound, *The Turning Wheel,* 54; *Horseless Age,* 8:709 (Nov. 13, 1901); *Motor Age,* 4:n.p. (Mar. 21, 1901); Niemeyer, *Ransom E. Olds,* 44; typed statement of sales of the Olds Motor Works in R. E. Olds Collection.

30 *Motor Age,* 4:n.p. (June 13, 1901), 4:n.p. (July 31, 1901).

31 *Review of Reviews,* 23:90 (advertising section bound with issues for Jan.-June 1901).

32 Lou [?] Baker to Olds, May 31, 1901, in R. E. Olds Collection.

33 *Ibid.; Motor Age,* 4:n.p. (April 4, 1901).

34 Detroit *Times,* Feb. 17, 1936, clipping in Roy D. Chapin Papers; J. C. Long, *Roy D. Chapin,* 33 (n.p., 1945); Roger Burlingame, *Henry Ford,* 55 (New York, 1955). For an over-all account and assessment of Chapin's trip, see George S. May, "The Detroit-New York Odyssey of Roy D. Chapin," *Detroit in Perspective,* 2:5-25 (Autumn 1973).

35 Long, *Roy D. Chapin,* 30-31; Niemeyer, *Ransom E. Olds,* 44-45.

36 One of the more extensive accounts of the trip is in Crabb, *Birth of a Giant,* 60-67.

37 Sinsabaugh, *Who, Me?* 325, and Crabb, *Birth of a Giant,* 66, are examples of writers who have credited Chapin with having set a long-distance record. For the Davis trip, see *Scientific American,* 81:26 (July 8, 1899), 8:153 (Sept. 2, 1899), and 81:299 (Nov. 4, 1899).

38 *Ibid.,* 81:92 (Aug. 5, 1899), and 81:139 (Aug. 26, 1899); *Horseless Age,* 8:530 (Sept. 18, 1901); J. A. Kingman, "Automobile-making in America," *Review of Reviews,* 24:297 (Sept. 1901), and Nevins, *Ford,* 195.

39 *Motor Age,* 3:558 (Nov. 29, 1900); "Chauffeur," *Two Thousand Miles on an Automobile: Being a Desultory Narrative of a Trip Through New England, New York, Canada, and the West,* 20, 317, and *passim* (Philadelphia, 1902).

40 *Horseless Age,* 8:711 (Nov. 13, 1901); New York *Times,* Nov. 5, 1901; Niemeyer, *Ransom E. Olds,* 46; *Motor World,* 3:164L (Nov. 7, 1901); *Motor Age,* 5:n.p. (Nov. 7, 1901); *Outing,* 39:494-98 (Jan. 1902); *Scientific American,* 85:314-16 (Nov. 16, 1901), and 85:331-32 (Nov. 23, 1901).

41 *Motor World,* 3:157, 164c (Nov. 7, 1901); *Horseless Age,* 8:697 (Nov. 13, 1901); Alexander Schwalback, "The Mechanical Side of the Show," *Motor Age,* 5:n.p. (Nov. 7, 1901).

42 Niemeyer, *Ransom E. Olds,* 46-47.

43 Long, *Roy D. Chapin,* 10, 24; Smith to Mrs. E. C. Chapin, June 6, 1902, in Roy D. Chapin Papers; Smith to Olds, July 9, 1902, in R. E. Olds Collection.

44 *Motor Age,* 4:n.p. (Mar. 21, 1901); Olds Motor Works annual report for 1902 in Corporation and Securities Records; Smith to Olds, July 19, 1901, in R. E. Olds Collection.

45 *National Cyclopaedia of American Biography,* 25:28, 30:3-4, 40:184; Harry W. Purcell, to Olds Motor Works, Mar. 13, 1901, in response to an Olds ad for workers placed in a Toledo paper; T. L. Elliott, Wheeling, to Olds Motor Works, Sept. 21, 1901; and Dow to Olds Motor Works, Aug. 22, 1901, all in R. E. Olds Collection; *Cycle and Automobile Trade Journal,* 14:135 (Dec. 1, 1909); Long, *Roy D. Chapin,* 35.

46 Davis & Deyo, Binghamton, to Olds Motor Works, Sept. 1, 1902, in R. E. Olds Collection.

47 Fred Smith to Olds, May 17, 1902, undated letter, *circa* July 1902, and April 22, 1903; Samuel L. Smith to Olds, Aug. 8, 1902, all in R. E. Olds Collection; Pound, *The Turning Wheel,* 56-57; Niemeyer, *Ransom E. Olds,* 54.

48 *Motor World,* 5:204 (Nov. 13, 1902).

49 "Chauffeur," *Two Thousand Miles on an Automobile,* 81; Sinsabaugh, *Who, Me?* 222; Harry Wilkins Perry, "Why Automobile Prices Remain Up," *Harper's Weekly,* 54:33 (Jan. 8, 1910); undated letter from Seager

to Smith in R. E. Olds Collection; interview with Olds' daughters and R. E. Olds Anderson, June 28, 1973.

50 H. H. Westinghouse to M. F. Loomis, April 19, 1902, in Roy D. Chapin Papers; Pound, *The Turning Wheel,* 54, cites both figures for the 1902 Oldsmobile production, while [Beverly Rae Kimes and Richard M. Langworth], *Oldsmobile: The First Seventy-five Years,* 70 (New York, 1972), gives only the 2500 figure, based, the authors say, on original Oldsmobile production records; *Harper's Weekly,* 46:1004 (July 26, 1902); *Motor World,* 5:302 (Dec. 4, 1902); Jackson *Daily Citizen,* July 14, 1902, Jan. 10 and 17, 1903.

51 *Saturday Evening Post,* 173:24 (Feb. 23, 1901), 174:16 (Feb. 15, 1902); Edmonds, *Development of the Automobile,* 16; Niemeyer, *Ransom E. Olds,* 50; Beasley and Stark, *Made in Detroit,* 83-84.

52 Niemeyer, *Ransom E. Olds,* 51; Pound, *The Turning Wheel,* 57-58; *Scientific American,* 88:295 (April 18, 1903). It has been claimed, in the passage cited above in Niemeyer's biography, for example, that Thomas and the *Pirate* were the first in the United States to break the mile-a-minute barrier. This is totally erroneous.

53 *Motor World,* 5:103 (Oct. 23, 1902); Barnes, "The Romance of Our Automobile Workers," *World's Work,* 41:564-65; Tom Mahoney, *The Story of George Romney, Builder, Salesman, Crusader,* 139, 255 (New York, 1960); *Horseless Age,* 8:709 (Nov. 13, 1901); Leland and Millbrook, *Master of Precision,* 72; Nicholson, *Passenger Cars, 1863-1904,* 124; Nicholson, *Passenger Cars, 1905-12,* 6-7.

54 Typed statement of sales of Olds Motor Works, Olds to Delano, Jan. 15, 1904, Fred Smith to Olds, June 22, 1903, in R. E. Olds Collection; King, *A Golden Anniversary,* 15; *Scientific American,* 90:29-30 (Jan. 9, 1904).

55 For the traditional view of the cause of the split between Olds and the Smiths, see, for example, Pound, *The Turning Wheel,* 62; Rae, *American Automobile Manufacturers,* 31; and Niemeyer, *Ransom E. Olds,* 54-55, although the latter does stress that several issues were involved in the dispute.

56 Annual report of Olds Motor Works for year ending Dec. 31, 1902, in Corporation and Securities Records; Niemeyer, *Ransom E. Olds,* 54; Henry Russel to Olds, April 19, May 9, and Aug. 20, 1903, and Olds to F. M. Delano, Jan. 28, 1904, in R. E. Olds Collection.

57 Niemeyer, *Ransom E. Olds,* 54, 57-58; annual report of Olds Motor Works for year ending Jan. 1, 1904, in Corporation and Securities Records; Olds to Smith, May 1, 1903, and Reuben Shettler to J. B. Bartholomew, Nov. 3, 1904, in R. E. Olds Collection.

58 Niemeyer, *Ransom E. Olds,* 55; Fred Smith to Olds, May 17 and Nov. 27, 1902, and Russel to Olds, April 19, 1903, in R. E. Olds Collection.

59 Niemeyer, *Ransom E. Olds,* 55-57; [Kimes and Langworth], *Oldsmobile: The First Seventy-Five Years,* 70; Fred Smith to Olds, April 22 and Sept. 3, 1903, in R. E. Olds Collection; Fred Smith to Eugene Cooley, July 1, 1904, in Eugene F. Cooley Papers.

60 Niemeyer, *Ransom E. Olds,* 58-65; Russel to Olds, April 19, 1903, in R. E. Olds Collection.

61 See Charles B. Wilson to Roy D. Chapin, *circa* July 1913, and Chapin to Wilson, July 8, 1913, in Roy D. Chapin Papers, for discussions of a reunion at that time.

Chapter 6

1 Adrian *Daily Times,* Nov. 23 and Dec. 23, 1901; *Official Gazette of the United States Patent Office,* 91:950 (May 1, 1900).
2 Adrian *Daily Times,* Feb. 28 and Aug. 1, 1903.
3 Adrian City Directories for 1890-91, 1894-95, 1900-01, and 1903; *Michigan State Gazetteer* for 1901; *19th Annual Report of the* [Michigan] *Bureau of Labor,* 298-99.
4 *Motor Age,* 3:813 (Jan. 9, 1901); *Michigan State Gazetteer* for 1901, 162 and 164.
5 Deposition in the records of the case of Willis Grant Murray vs. Church Manufacturing Company, filed in the Circuit Court for the County of Lenawee, Lenawee County Courthouse, Adrian, Michigan.
6 *Motor Age,* 5:n.p. (Sept. 12, 1901) and 5:n.p. (Oct. 10, 1901); Adrian *Daily Times,* Oct. 5, Nov. 16 and 23, Dec. 23, 1901.
7 Interview with Grant A. Snedeker, Oct. 27, 1970; Murray advertising brochure in Snedeker's private collection; Adrian *Daily Times,* Dec. 23, 1901, Aug. 9 and 23, 1902; *Motor Age,* 1:7 (Mar. 6, 1902).
8 Adrian *Daily Times,* Dec. 20 and 23, 1901; court records in the case of Murray vs. the Church Manufacturing Co.; Adrian City Directory for 1903, and *Michigan State Gazetteer* for 1905.
9 Adrian *Daily Times,* Dec. 7, 1901, Jan. 25, Feb. 22, Mar. 15 and 29, April 5 and 19, 1902; *Motor Age,* 1:7 (Mar. 6, 1902).
10 Adrian *Daily Times,* April 26, May 10 and 17, June 7, July 26, and Aug. 9 and 30, 1902.
11 *Ibid.,* May 3 and 24, June 7, 14, and 21, 1902.
12 Court records in the case of Murray vs. the Church Manufacturing Co.; *Motor World,* 4:739 (Sept. 25, 1902); Adrian *Daily Times,* June 5 and 9, 1903; *Motor Age,* 3:21 (April 9, 1903), 6:23 (Dec. 29, 1904).
13 Adrian *Daily Times,* Oct. 11 and 18, Nov. 8 and 29, 1902, and Jan. 14, 1903.
14 *Ibid.,* Feb. 21 and 28, Mar. 7, 14, 21, and 28, April 25, 1903.
15 *Ibid.,* April 4 and Dec. 10, 1903; Grant Snedeker interview.
16 *22nd Annual Report of the* [Michigan] *Bureau of Labor,* 92.
17 *Motor Age,* 10:33 (Nov. 8, 1906), 16:44 (Sept. 30, 1909); *Adrian City Directory for 1907,* 237; *Horseless Age,* 24:331 (Sept. 22, 1909); materials on Page and Lion automobiles in Snedeker collection.
18 Snedeker interview. Georgano, *Encyclopaedia of American Automobiles,* 140, states that "about 1,000" Murrays were built, but a careful examination of the files of the Adrian *Daily Times* for the period 1901 to 1903 would seem to support Jack Frost's estimate of 227. See Jack A. Frost, "The Lenawee," *Bulb Horn,* 26:24 (May-June 1965).
19 *Motor Age,* 2:629 (July 12, 1900), 5:n.p. (Oct. 3, 1901), 3:20 (April 9, 1903); C. B. Glasscock, *The Gasoline Age: The Story of the Men Who Made It,* 296 (Indianapolis, 1937).
20 Article from Oct. 1904 issue of *Cycle and Automobile Trade Journal,* reprinted by Welch Motor Car Company, in Charles Tyler Newton Papers, Michigan Historical Collections, University of Michigan.
21 News clippings, early 1903, in Thomas Shaw Scrapbook, Michigan Historical Collections, University of Michigan; Records of the Chelsea Manufacturing Company, Ltd., bankruptcy case, Case No. 764, District Court of the United States for the Eastern District of Michigan, Southern Division, in Regional Archives, National Archives and Records Service, Chicago; Mina Belle Wurster, "The Welch Tourist," *Washtenaw Im-*

pressions, 11:1 (June 1954), copy of publication in Michigan Historical Collections; Obituary of Frank F. Matheson in *Horseless Carriage Gazette,* 29:31 (March-April 1967).

22 News clipping, dated Jan. 15, 1903, in Thomas Shaw Scrapbook; *Motor Age,* 3:13 (April 9, 1903); Chelsea Manufacturing Company bankruptcy records.

23 Chelsea Manufacturing Company bankruptcy records.

24 Wells, "Growth of the Auto Industry," 213; Henry Jay Case, "The Rise of the Motor-Car," *Harper's Weekly,* 50:50 (Jan. 13, 1906).

25 Chelsea Manufacturing Company bankruptcy records.

26 *Ibid.;* Annual report of the Welch Motor Car Company, as of March 1, 1905, in Corporation and Securities Commission Records; Welch brochure in the Newton Papers; *Motor Age,* 6:21 (Oct. 20, 1904); Georgano, *Encyclopaedia of American Automobiles,* 205.

27 *The Book of the Welch Car,* in Pamphlet Box 3, Michigan Historical Collections; Georgano, *Encyclopaedia of American Automobiles,* 205; Flint *Journal,* June 1, 1909; Ralph Stein, "I Just Lost My Head," *Argosy,* page 76 (Dec. 1953), clipped copy in Michigan Historical Collections.

28 In the John J. Carton Papers, Michigan Historical Collections, there is correspondence in June 1909 regarding the acquisition of Welch, and on the organization of the Welch Company of Detroit in Carton to A. H. Goss, Dec. 28, 1909; *Motor Age,* 18:37 (Dec. 15, 1910), 20:43 (July 20, 1911), 20:23 (July 27, 1911), 20:40 (Sept. 21, 1911); Pound, *The Turning Wheel,* 122, 128, 132, 134; Wurster, "The Welch Tourist," 11:3.

29 In addition to the *Argosy* article by Stein referred to in a previous footnote, see Ralph Stein, "I Fell for America's Craziest Hobby," *This Week* magazine supplement, Sept. 13, 1953, copy in the Michigan Historical Collections; and Ralph Stein, *The Treasury of the Automobile,* 232-35 (New York, 1961). Comments by Leslie Henry in a conversation with the author, Nov. 1972.

30 *Headlight,* 2:5, 36, 39, 40 (May 1895).

31 *Horseless Age,* 4:8 (April 26, 1899); Stanley K. Yost, *They Don't Build Cars Like They Used To!* 9-10, 17 (Mendota, Ill., 1963); *Motor Age,* 3:943 (Jan. 30, 1901), 3:1096 (Feb. 20, 1901); Gerald Carson, *Cornflake Crusade* (New York, 1959); Adrian *Daily Times,* Feb. 2, 1903.

32 Willis F. Dunbar, *Kalamazoo and How It Grew,* 129-32 (Kalamazoo, 1959).

33 Information supplied to the author by David H. Langeland, employee relations manager, Transmission Division, Eaton Corporation, Kalamazoo, in letters of October 11 and 26, 1972; Dunbar, *Kalamazoo and How It Grew,* 131-32; *Motor World,* 4:405 (July 3, 1902), 5:443 (Jan. 8, 1903); *Motor Age,* 4:34 (Oct. 22, 1903), 6:20 (Oct. 6, 1904); *Horseless Carriage Gazette,* 9:16 (Dec. 1947); *22nd Annual Report of the* [Michigan] *Bureau of Labor,* 79; *1st Annual Report of the* [Michigan] *Department of Labor,* 83.

34 *1st Annual Report of the* [Michigan] *Department of Labor,* 83; Georgano, *Encyclopaedia of American Automobiles,* 133.

35 Michigan Buggy Company ad in "A Reprint of Thirty-six Advertisements in *Collier's* Special Automobile Supplement of January 6, 1912."

36 Records in the Michigan Buggy Company bankruptcy proceedings, Case no. 1200, U. S. District Court for the Western Division of Michigan, Southern Division, Regional Archives, National Archives and Records Service, Chicago; Bower, *Early American Car Advertisements,* 122-23; Dunbar, *Kalamazoo and How It Grew,* 132.

37 Dunbar, *Kalamazoo and How It Grew,* 132.

38 Annual report of the Blood Bros. Automobile & Machine Co., as of Feb.

23, 1905, in Corporation and Securities Commission Records; Dunbar, *Kalamazoo and How It Grew,* 131-32; *Motor Age,* 10:11 (Oct. 18, 1906); *Automobile,* 33:626 (Sept. 30, 1915); D. F. Wilbur, plant manager, Universal Joint Operation, to the author, Nov. 21, 1972; William P. Sturgis, sales engineer, Universal Joint Operation, to the author, Jan. 5, 1973.

39 Annual report of the Burtt Manufacturing Company, as of Dec. 31, 1904, in Corporation and Securities Commission Records; Dunbar, *Kalamazoo and How It Grew,* 132; Smith, *Wheels Within Wheels,* 201; *25th Annual Report of the* [Michigan] *Bureau of Labor,* 77.

40 *Motor Age,* 9:29c (Mar. 15, 1906).

41 Frank B. Woodward, *We Never Drive Alone: The Story of the Automobile Club of Michigan,* 6-7 (Detroit, 1958); Doolittle, ed., *The Romance of the Automobile Industry,* 210-11; Flint *Journal,* Feb. 26, 1908; *Motor Age,* 3:158 (Oct. 4, 1900).

42 *Motor World,* 4:709 (Sept. 18, 1902); Georgano, *Encyclopaedia of American Automobiles,* 22; Grand Rapids *Press,* May 10, 1965; *Michigan State Gazetteer* for 1903; *Motor Age,* 10:82 (Dec. 27, 1906); Stanley K. Yost, *The Great Old Cars . . . Where Are They Now?* 47-50 (Mendota, Ill., 1960).

43 *Motor Age,* 15:38 (May 6, 1909), 16:38 (Sept. 9, 1909), 20:41 (Sept. 21, 1911); Z. Z. Lydens, ed., *The Story of Grand Rapids,* 281 (Grand Rapids, 1966); Flint *Journal,* Sept. 30, 1956, in automobile clipping file, Michigan State Library; the number of Austin employees is given in the annual reports of the Michigan Bureau of Labor, later the Department of Labor, for the years 1907 through 1914; correspondence of John J. Carton, counsel for Weston-Mott, with Kleinhaus, Knappen & Uhl, Grand Rapids firm retained to handle the suit against Austin, and additional correspondence with H. J. Mallory, Weston-Mott comptroller, between June 1914 and Oct. 1915, in the Carton Papers.

44 *Automobile,* 32:92 (Jan. 14, 1915), 34:107 (Jan. 13, 1916); Georgano, *Encyclopaedia of American Automobiles,* 22; *37th Annual Report of the* [Michigan] *Department of Labor,* 118; Flint *Journal,* Sept. 30, 1956; Grand Rapids *Press,* May 10, 1965.

45 *Motor Age,* 3:719-20 (Dec. 26, 1900); Smith, *Wheels Within Wheels,* 247, 255; Claude Sintz interview in 1952; *Motor,* 3:73 (Feb. 1905); Robert G. Silber to James R. Hooper, June 24, 1946, in Sintz file in the Grand Rapids Public Library.

46 Lydens, *Story of Grand Rapids,* 287-88; *Motor Age,* 3:693 (Dec. 19, 1900), 3:810 (Jan. 9, 1901), 5:n.p. (Dec. 5, 1901); *Motor World,* 4:387 (June 26, 1902).

47 *Horseless Carriage Gazette,* 29:3-4 (Mar.-April 1967); *Motor World,* 4:587 (Aug. 21, 1902), 4:709 (Sept. 18, 1902); Yost, *The Great Old Cars,* 152-53; Automobile Manufacturers Association, *Automobiles of America,* 194.

48 *History of Kent County, Michigan,* 921, 1024 (Chicago, 1881); *19th Annual Report of the* [Michigan] *Bureau of Labor,* 328-29.

49 *Motor Age,* 6:19 (Nov. 17, 1904), 10:18-21 (July 26, 1906); Yost, *They Don't Build Cars Like They Used To!* 110-11; *The Harrison Motor Car,* brochure published by the Harrison company, in Pamphlet Box 2, Michigan Historical Collections.

50 Sinsabaugh, *Who, Me?* 222; T.A. Boyd, *Professional Amateur: The Biography of Charles Franklin Kettering,* 68-71 (New York, 1957); *Motor Age,* 10:22 (Nov. 1, 1906), 13:27 (Feb. 6, 1908), 12:18 (Dec. 19, 1907); Records in the Harrison Wagon Company bankruptcy proceedings, Case no. 619, U. S. District Court for the Western District of Michigan, Southern Division, Regional Archives, National Archives and Records Service, Chicago.

51 Durant, *History of Ingham and Eaton Counties,* 392; Harvey Harmon,

Charlotte, to the author, April 7, 1973; *19th Annual Report of the* [Michigan] *Bureau of Labor,* 300-301; *Charlotte, Michigan, The Maple City* (n. p., 1907), a brochure with no pagination, copy in the Michigan State Library; Dolson advertising brochure and clippings in the possession of David W. Dolson, Mt. Pleasant and made available to the author; *23rd Annual Report of the* [Michigan] *Bureau of Labor,* 367.

52 The information for this paragraph and the two that follow is from the records in the Dolson Automobile Company bankruptcy proceedings, U. S. District Court for the Western District of Michigan, Southern Division, Regional Archives, National Archives and Records Service, Chicago.

53 *American Car Since 1775,* 417; *Motor Age,* 13:25 (May 7, 1908); Harvey Harmon to the author, April 7, 1973; discussions between the author and David W. Dolson, May 22, 1973, and information in material in his possession.

54 The years of production of the Deal automobile are given in Smith, *Wheels Within Wheels,* 210; information about J. J. Deal & Sons and the Deal Buggy Company as it was later called is taken from the annual reports of the Michigan Bureau of Labor and its successor, the Michigan Department of Labor, for the years 1899 to 1916.

55 Most of this information is drawn from news clippings and other information supplied to the author by Everett Claspy of Dowagiac in letters of Oct. 21, 1970, and Oct. 30, 1971. Miss Penrod's reminiscences are contained in a letter from Dale A. Lyons of Dowagiac, to David A. Kolzow of Sandwich, Illinois, July 29, 1971, a copy of which was included in Claspy's materials. Permission to use this letter was granted by Mr. Lyons in a letter to the author, Jan. 27, 1972. See also *The Hub,* 51:17 (April 1909).

56 The sources dealing with the companies in the cities mentioned are too numerous to be given here, but the names of the companies can be found by consulting the list in Smith, *Wheels Within Wheels,* 191-275; the quotation regarding Tom Dolson is in an obituary in David Dolson's collection of materials.

Chapter 7

1 Based upon the recollections of the author, who was at the time in charge of the commission's historical markers program.

2 Reprint of a biographical sketch of Durant in the New York *Evening Mail,* June 3, 1916, copy in Michigan State Library; Morris Peilet to the author, April 10, 1971; interview with Waldo Culver, Owosso, Michigan, Jan. 31, 1972.

3 Edward L. Bernays, *Biography of an Idea: Memoirs of Public Relations Counsel,* 541-55 (New York, 1965); Bernays to the author, April 8, 20, and 28, 1971; Lawrence R. Gustin, *Billy Durant: Creator of General Motors,* 203 (Grand Rapids, Mich.; 1973); James J. Flink and Glenn A. Niemeyer, "The General of General Motors," *American Heritage,* 24:86 (Aug. 1973).

4 Flint *Journal,* Nov. 25, 1909, quoting an article from the Detroit *News;* Henry G. Pearson, *Son of New England, James J. Storrow,* 138, 139 (Boston, 1932); Margery Durant, *My Father,* vi, vii, 63-64 (New York, 1929).

5 *National Cyclopaedia of American Biography,* 36:16-17; Forbes and Foster, *Automotive Giants of America,* 44-60; John B. Rae, "The Fabulous Billy Durant," *Business History Review,* 32:255-71 (Autumn 1958).

6 Edwin O. Wood, *History of Genesee County, Michigan,* 1:779 (Indianapolis, 1916); Flint *Journal,* Nov. 29, 1911, copy of the article supplied to the author by George Bierwirth of Flint; Gustin's series, entitled "Billy Durant and Flint: The Beginnings of General Motors," appeared daily in the Flint *Journal* from March 19-28, 1972. I wish to thank Gustin for giving me access to the manuscript of his Durant biography, which was published after my manuscript had been completed. Although I have added references to Gustin's book in a few footnotes, I have retained my earlier references both to his newspaper series and to his manuscript copy, especially since both these sources differ to some extent from the final published biography.

7 Interview with Charles S. Mott, Feb. 11, 1971; Gustin, Flint *Journal,* Mar. 19, 1972.

8 The best source on Crapo is Martin D. Lewis, *Lumberman from Flint: The Michigan Career of Henry H. Crapo, 1855-1869* (Detroit, 1958). See also Wood, *History of Genesee County,* 1:507-508, and Carl Crow, *The City of Flint Grows Up: The Success Story of an American Community,* 22 (New York, 1945).

9 H. H. Crapo, *The Story of William Wallace Crapo, 1830-1926* (n.p., 1942); Gustin, Flint *Journal,* Mar. 21, 1972; H. H. Crapo, *The Story of Henry Howland Crapo,* 98, 229 (n.p., 1933).

10 Lewis, *Lumberman from Flint,* 132; Crapo's journal for 1868, in the Henry H. Crapo Papers, Michigan Historical Collections, University of Michigan; Gustin mss.

11 Crapo to William W. Crapo, July 30, 1868, in Crapo Papers; W. C. Durant, ed., *Law Observance: Shall the People of the United States Uphold the Constitution* (New York, 1929); Durant, *My Father,* 303; Flink and Niemeyer, "The General of General Motors," *American Heritage,* 24:86; Gustin, *Billy Durant,* 204.

12 Crapo to William W. Crapo, July 30, 1868, and Crapo's journal for 1868 and 1869, in Crapo Papers; Gustin mss.; *National Cyclopaedia of American Biography,* 36:16; Joyce Slocum Cook, *Vignettes of Early Flint* (Flint, 1962), a collection of articles reprinted from the Flint *Journal,* with no pagination.

13 Durant, *My Father,* 290-97; Gustin, Flint *Journal,* Mar. 21, 1972; Gustin mss.

14 Cook, *Vignettes of Early Flint.*

15 Durant, *My Father,* 23-26; Gustin mss.

16 *Who's Who in America,* 11:831; Durant, *My Father,* 21-31; *National Cyclopaedia of American Biography,* 21:269 and 36:16; Flint *Journal,* Nov. 29, 1911.

17 Lewis, *Motor Memories,* 67; Wood, *History of Genesee County,* 2:33-34; Crow, *The City of Flint Grows Up,* 30; Gustin, Flint *Journal,* Mar. 19, 1972; *National Cyclopaedia of American Biography,* 50:674-75; Cook, *Vignettes of Early Flint;* Durant, *My Father,* 28-31; *Michigan State Gazetteer for 1887;* George Bush, *Future Builders: The Story of Michigan's Consumers Power Company,* 141 (New York, 1973).

18 Gustin, Flint *Journal,* Mar. 19, 1972; Henry P. Collins, *A Twentieth Century History and Biographical Record of Branch County, Michigan,* 117 (New York, 1906); the listings for Coldwater in the *Michigan State Gazetteers* for the 1870's and 1880's; U. S. Patent Office *Official Gazette,* 31:585 (May 5, 1885), and 35:648 (May 11, 1886).

19 Wood, *History of Genesee County,* 1:521-37; Gustin, Flint *Journal,* Mar. 19 and 20, 1972; Flint *Journal,* Nov. 29, 1911.

20 Coldwater *Republican,* Sept. 14, 1886, quoted in Gustin, Flint *Journal,* Mar. 20, 1972; *Coldwater Illustrated,* 62 (Coldwater, 1889); *Michigan State Gazetteers* from the 1880's to 1931-32.

21 Gustin, Flint *Journal,* Mar. 19, 1972; *National Cyclopaedia of American Biography,* 36:405; Nevins, *Ford,* 47; John J. Carton to F. W. Brooks, Dec. 26, 1905, in Carton Papers; William V. Smith, ed., *An Account of Flint and Genesee County from Their Organization,* 217 (vol. 3 of *Historic Michigan,* edited by George N. Fuller) (n.p., [1924]); Arthur Pound, "General Motors' Old Home Town," *Michigan History,* 40:90-91 (Mar. 1956).

22 Flint *Journal,* Jan. 24, 1908; Wood, *History of Genesee County,* 1:511-13; Gustin, Flint *Journal,* Mar. 20, 1972; Pound, "General Motors' Old Home Town," *Michigan History,* 40:83-84.

23 Gustin, Flint *Journal,* Mar. 20, 1972; Pound, *The Turning Wheel,* 78-79.

24 *Men of Progress,* 525 (Detroit, 1900); *National Cyclopaedia of American Biography,* 36:405; Gustin, Flint *Journal,* Mar. 20, 1972; Detroit *Free Press,* Aug. 6, 1899, reported acquisition by Durant of the Ionia Wagon Works, one not otherwise listed in the usual compilations of Durant-Dort holdings.

25 Gustin, Flint *Journal,* Mar. 20, 1972; Cook, *Vignettes of Early Flint; Who's Who in Commerce and Industry,* 6:34; Wood, *History of Genesee County,* 2:63; annual reports of the Durant-Dort Carriage Company, giving the condition of the company as of Sept. 5, 1895, and Aug. 15, 1902, in Corporation and Securities Records.

26 Charles W. Nash to John J. Carton, May 18, 1920, in Carton Papers; Mahoney, *The Story of George Romney,* 136-37; Rae, *American Automobile Manufacturers,* 90; *National Cyclopaedia of American Biography,* 36:50; Gustin, Flint *Journal,* Mar. 20, 1972.

27 Gustin, Flint *Journal,* Mar. 20, 1972; Pound, *The Turning Wheel,* 233-34.

28 *National Cyclopaedia of American Biography,* F:489; Jackson *Daily Citizen,* July 20, 1901; Flint *Journal,* Sept. 5, 1908.

29 Wood, *History of Genesee County,* 2:265; Gustin, Flint *Journal,* Mar. 20, 1972.

30 Gustin, Flint *Journal,* Mar. 20, 1972; annual report of Durant-Dort Carriage Company for 1903, in Corporation and Securities Records; Walter P. Chrysler, in collaboration with Boyden Sparkes, *Life of an American Workman,* 143 (New York, 1950); *Headlight Flashes,* vol. 2, issue no. 12, no pagination (Aug. 1896), has details regarding several of Durant's companies in Flint.

31 Gustin mss.

32 Gustin, Flint *Journal,* Mar. 20-21, 1972; Julian Street, "The American Car to Date," *Collier's,* 44:18, sec. 2 (Jan. 15, 1910); statement of the Flint Automobile Company, Oct. 28, 1902, and Fred M. Warner to Everett Bray, Nov. 3, 1902, in Carton Papers; annual report of the Flint Automobile Company for 1903 in Corporation and Securities Records.

33 Gustin, Flint *Journal,* Mar. 21, 1972; *Motor Age,* 3:27 (Jan. 1, 1903), 3:43 (April 2, 1903), 4:40 (July 2, 1903); annual report of the Flint Automobile Company for 1903 in Corporation and Securities Records.

34 John J. Carton to Cleveland Motor Company, Jan. 23, 1904, in Carton Papers; George Humphrey Maines, *Men, a City, and Buick,* 4 (Flint, 1953); *Motor Age,* 15:10 (May 6, 1909).

35 Maines, *Men, a City, and Buick,* 1-2, 19.

36 *National Cyclopaedia of American Biography,* 34:368-69; Nevins, *Ford,* 81; *Michigan State Gazetteer* for 1897 and 1899; *Annual Reports of the*

Commissioner of Patents for the years 1881-1899; Beverly Rae Kimes, "Wouldn't You Really Rather be a Buick?" *Automobile Quarterly,* 7:80 (Summer, 1968); Robert S. and Helen M. Lynd, *Middletown: A Study in American Culture,* 256 (New York, 1929).

37 *National Cyclopaedia of American Biography,* 34:369; Rae, *American Automobile Manufacturers,* 18-19; *Michigan State Gazetteer* for 1899, 1901, and 1903; annual reports of Buick & Sherwood for 1901 and 1902, in Corporation and Securities Records.

38 Pound, *The Turning Wheel,* 69-71; Kimes, "Wouldn't You Really Rather be a Buick?" *Automobile Quarterly,* 7:80-82; *National Cyclopaedia of American Biography,* 34:369; John C. Lodge, *I Remember Detroit,* 148 (Detroit, 1949); *Annual Reports of the Commissioner of Patents* for 1904 and 1905; U. S. Patent Office *Official Gazette,* 116:1488-89 (June 6, 1905).

39 *Buick's First Half-Century,* 19 (n.p., Buick Motor Division, General Motors Corporation, 1952); Kimes, "Wouldn't You Really Rather be a Buick?" *Automobile Quarterly,* 7:80-81.

40 *Ibid.,* 80-81; Gustin, Flint *Journal,* Mar. 21, 1972.

41 *Ibid.;* Wood, *History of Genesee County,* 1:774.

42 Gustin, Flint *Journal,* Mar. 22, 1972; *Michigan State Gazetteer* for 1905; report of the Buick Motor Company, Nov. 1, 1904, in Corporation and Securities Records; Maines, *Men, A City, and Buick,* 3.

43 Gustin, Flint *Journal,* Mar. 22, 1972.

44 *Ibid.;* Maines, *Men, A City, and Buick,* 3; *Motor Age,* 6:18 (Nov. 3, 1904).

45 Durant, *My Father,* 3-9; Gustin, Flint *Journal,* Mar. 21-22, 1972; *Who's Who in America,* 11:848-49.

46 Gustin, Flint *Journal,* Mar. 22, 1972.

47 *Ibid.;* Pound, *The Turning Wheel,* 76-80; Maines, *Men, A City and Buick,* 4.

48 Durant, *My Father,* 59-60; annual reports of Buick Motor Company for 1906 and 1908 in Corporation and Securities Records; Durant to Carton, Mar. 14, 1906, in Carton Papers; Flint *Journal,* June 27, 1908; *Horseless Age,* 26:752 (Nov. 30, 1910); Kimes, "Wouldn't You Really Rather be a Buick?" *Automobile Quarterly,* 7:84; Maines, *Men, A City, and Buick,* 10. An obituary in the New York *Times,* Mar. 19, 1947, gave the highly unlikely figure of ten million dollars as the amount that Buick received from Durant.

49 John Carton to Durant, June 11, 1908, in Carton Papers; Pound, *The Turning Wheel,* 81.

50 Annual reports of the Buick Motor Company for 1906 and 1908, in Corporation and Securities Records; Gustin, *Billy Durant,* 70-71.

51 Gustin, Flint *Journal,* Mar. 23, 1972; Pound, *The Turning Wheel,* 84-85; Beasley and Stark, *Made in Detroit,* 56; *The Hub,* 51:321 (Dec. 1909); annual report of the Buick Motor Company for 1906, in Corporation and Securities Records; Carton to F. W. Brooks, Dec. 26, 1905, in Carton Papers.

52 Annual reports of the Buick Motor Company for 1906 and 1908, in Corporation and Securities Records; Wood, *History of Genesee County,* 1:525-39; Gustin, Flint *Journal,* Mar. 23, 1972; Pound, "General Motors' Old Home Town," *Michigan History,* 40:90.

53 *Motor Age,* 6:17 (Dec. 1, 1904); Kimes, "Wouldn't You Really Rather be a Buick?" *Automobile Quarterly,* 7:78; Gustin, Flint *Journal,* Mar. 23, 1972; Durant, *My Father,* 130.

54 Gustin, Flint *Journal,* Mar. 23, 1972; *Motor Age,* 6:19 (Dec. 15, 1904).

55 Jackson *Daily Citizen,* June 22, 1901.

56 Jackson *Daily Citizen,* June 22, 1901, and April 28, 1904, and a review of the issues for 1901 and 1902 for the paper's coverage of local business interests.

57 *Horseless Age,* 21:450 (April 15, 1908); Detroit *News,* April 6, 1908; Detroit *Free Press,* April 7, 1908; Ronald G. Bean, Saginaw, to the author, May 31, 1973; receipt, dated June 15, 1899, in King Letterbook in King Papers; Barthel Reminiscence in Ford Archives; Jackson *Daily Citizen,* May 11, Aug. 5, 1901, Mar. 11, 1903; *Motor Age,* 3:593 (Dec. 6, 1900), 3:692 (Dec. 19, 1900), 3:810 (Jan. 9, 1901).

58 Jackson *Daily Citizen,* July 24, 1902; *National Cyclopaedia of American Biography,* 18:94 and 146.

59 Jackson *Daily Citizen,* July 28 and 30, Aug. 12 and 23, Dec. 10, 1902, and Feb. 3 and Mar. 4, 1903; *Motor World,* 5:420 (Jan. 1, 1903); Georgano, ed., *Encyclopaedia of American Automobiles,* 105; W. O. MacIlvain, "Jackson Automobile Co. Jackson, Michigan," *Bulb Horn,* 13:14-15, 25 (Oct. 1952).

60 *The Automobile,* 17:793-94 (Nov. 28, 1907), 34:675 (April 13, 1916); miscellaneous material in a folder of Jackson Automobile Company publications in Pamphlet Box 3, Michigan Historical Collections, University of Michigan; Flint *Journal,* June 29, 1908; Gustin mss.

61 Smith, *Wheels Within Wheels,* 83; *National Cyclopaedia of American Biography,* 18:94-95, 146.

62 Jackson *Daily Citizen,* Sept. 12, 1903, May 11, 1904; *Scientific American,* 102:64 (Jan. 15, 1910); *Motor Age,* 8:26 (Dec. 14, 1905), 10:n.p. (Dec. 6, 1906).

63 Leland, *Master of Precision,* 129-33; Boyd, *Professional Amateur,* 68-69 (which places the date of Carter's alleged accident in the summer of 1910); and Rae, *American Automobile Manufacturers,* 109, are among the sources assigning the accident to Carter and labeling it the immediate impetus to the development of Kettering's self-starter. Pound, *The Turning Wheel,* 272, says simply that "an elderly friend" of Leland (and Carter could scarcely have been regarded as elderly) was fatally injured. Obituaries of Carter are in *Horseless Age,* 21:450 (April 15, 1908); Detroit *News,* April 6, 1908; Detroit *Free Press,* April 7, 1908.

64 Jackson *Daily Citizen,* Feb. 20, 1902.

65 Maines, *Men, A City, and Buick,* 8-9.

66 Details of the underwriting plan are given in a carbon copy of a letter, apparently from Durant, to the directors of the First National Bank of Flint, Oct. 25, 1905, in Carton Papers. The agreement signed by the Genesee Bank has been reproduced in several publications, most recently in Gustin, *Billy Durant,* 76.

67 Wood, *History of Genesee County,* 1:775; Maines, *Men, A City, and Buick,* 13-14; Flint *Journal,* June 6, 1908.

68 Gustin mss.; Flint *Journal,* Mar. 28, Sept. 2 and 14, 1908; *Horseless Age,* 24:179 (Aug. 18, 1909).

69 Flint *Journal,* May 21, 1908; Pearson, *Son of New England,* 131.

70 Flint *Journal,* Feb. 5 and 13, July 18, and Aug. 21, 1908.

71 Young and Quinn, *Foundation for Living,* 8-25; *Horseless Age,* 2:14 (Nov. 1896), 2:13 (April 1897).

72 Young and Quinn, *Foundation for Living,* 1-7, 27-29; Durant, *My Father,* 130-31; Mott interview, Feb. 11, 1971.

73 Young and Quinn, *Foundation for Living,* 1-7; Doolittle to Carton, June 11, 1906, in Carton Papers.

74 Young and Quinn, *Foundation for Living,* 2-7; Gustin mss.; John Carton to William Doolittle, Oct. 25, 1905, in Carton Papers.

75 Gustin mss.; Young and Quinn, *Foundation for Living,* 28-29; Sloan, *Adventures of a White-Collar Man,* 44.

76 Flint *Journal,* Jan. 29, 1908; Gustin mss.; John Carton to James H. Knight, Nov. 17, 1909, in Carton Papers.

77 Gustin mss.; *Motor Age,* 13:16 (Jan. 30, 1908); folder for Mar. 1-8, 1908, containing notice of Mott's payment of his retainer's fee to Carton, in Carton Papers.

78 Flint *Journal,* Jan. 17, Feb. 28, Mar. 28, May 1, June 27, July 2 and 13, and Nov. 9 and 11, 1908; Gustin mss.

79 Gustin mss.; for evidence that Ford out-produced Buick in 1908, see *American Car Since 1775,* 138; W. C. Durant form letter, dated May 7, 1906, in Carton Papers.

80 Sinsabaugh, *Who, Me?* 193.

Chapter 8

1 Entries in pocket diary of R. E. Olds for 1908, in R. E. Olds Collection.

2 Olds to F. M. Delano, Jan. 15, 1904, Olds to W. J. Morgan, July 5, 1904, and other business correspondence in Olds Letterbook in R. E. Olds Collection; report on the carriage industry in *17th Annual Report of the* [Michigan] *Bureau of Labor,* 65.

3 Darling, *City in the Forest,* 157-58; Lansing *State Journal,* Jan. 1, 1950, clipping in automobile file in Michigan State Library.

4 *Motor Age,* 5:n.p. (Nov. 28, 1901); Lansing *State Journal,* Jan. 1, 1950.

5 *Ibid.;* Darling, *City in the Forest,* 158-59; *Motor Age,* 3:16 (Jan. 4, 1903); Turner, *An Account of Ingham County From Its Organization,* 634-35.

6 *Motor Age,* 3:14 (Mar. 15, 1903), 3:16 (May 7, 1903); Darling, *City in the Forest,* 159; Lansing *State Journal,* Jan. 1, 1950; Turner, *An Account of Ingham County From Its Organization,* 580-81; form letter from Clark & Company to "Our Patrons," July 25, 1909, copy in author's possession.

7 Lansing *State Journal,* Jan. 1, 1950; Fred Smith to Cooley, July 1, 1904, and July 19, 1905, in Eugene F. Cooley Papers; *Cycle and Automobile Trade Journal,* 14:124 (Dec. 1, 1909); *American Car Since 1775,* 138-39.

8 Davis to Cooley, Aug. 5, 1904, in Eugene F. Cooley Papers.

9 Niemeyer, *Ransom E. Olds,* 58, 66; Olds to F. M. Delano, Jan. 28, 1904, in R. E. Olds Collection; "R. Shettler's Efforts."

10 Niemeyer, *Ransom E. Olds,* 66-68.

11 Olds to W. J. Morgan, July, 5, 1904, Olds to R. M. Owen, Aug. 4, 1904, and Olds to Olds Motor Works, Aug. 19, 1904, in R. E. Olds Collection; Niemeyer, *Ransom E. Olds,* 68-74; Forbes and Foster, *Automotive Giants of America,* 235; Turner, *An Account of Ingham County From Its Organization,* 590.

12 Niemeyer, *Ransom E. Olds,* 72-80; Olds to R. M. Owen, Aug. 4, 1904, in R. E. Olds Collection.

13 Information on Reo stockholders from Corporation and Securities Records; Turner, *An Account of Ingham County From Its Organization,* 349-50, 356-57, 402, 456, 569-70, 607-608, 634-35, 677-78, 681, 764.

14 Olds Motor Works to R. E. Olds, Aug. 18, 1904, and R. M. Owen to Olds, Sept. 27, 1904, in R. E. Olds Collection; Olds Motor Works to Benjamin

F. Davis, copy in Eugene F. Cooley Papers; Niemeyer, *Ransom E. Olds*, 73-74.
15 "R. Shettler's Efforts."
16 *Ibid.*
17 Niemeyer, *Ransom E. Olds*, 76; *Motor Age*, 4:9 (Sept. 15, 1904); Turner, *An Account of Ingham County From Its Organization*, 384-85.
18 Niemeyer, *Ransom E. Olds*, 76-78; Georgano, ed., *Encyclopaedia of American Automobiles*, 169.
19 Powers to Olds, Nov. 9, 1904, in R. E. Olds Collection; *Motor Age*, 6:37 (Dec. 22, 1904).
20 Frank Rowsome, Jr., *They Laughed When I Sat Down*, 128-38 (New York, 1959); John Gunther, *Taken at the Flood: The Story of Albert D. Lasker*, 84 (New York, 1960). The ad has been frequently reprinted. See, for example, Clymer, *Treasury of Early American Automobiles*, 162.
21 "A reprint of thirty-six advertisements in *Collier's* special automobile supplement of January 6, 1912," no pagination; Niemeyer, *Ransom E. Olds*, 80-81; *Motor Age*, 6:19 (Dec. 29, 1904).
22 *Scientific American*, 92:83 (Jan. 28, 1905); *American Car Since 1775*, 138-39; Doolittle, *The Romance of the Automobile Industry*, 290; Niemeyer, *Ransom E. Olds*, 111.
23 Pound, *The Turning Wheel*, 63-64; *Motor Age*, 11:14 (June 6, 1907).
24 Niemeyer, *Ransom E. Olds*, 94-95; Darling, *City in the Forest*, 164-65.
25 R. E. Olds diaries, 1906-1909, in R. E. Olds Collection.
26 "R. Shettler's Efforts"; interview with Herman Staebler, July 28, 1971; *National Cyclopaedia of American Biography*, 39:480-81.

Chapter 9

1 Nevins, *Ford*, 372-74; Gustin mss.
2 Nevins, *Ford*, 192-93; Chapin to Stanley L. Otis, June 17, 1916, in the Chapin Papers.
3 Nevins, *Ford*, 194-95, 203; Leo Levine, *Ford: The Dust and the Glory, a Racing History*, 3 (New York, 1968).
4 Nevins, *Ford*, 192-93; *National Cyclopaedia of American Biography*, 36:376; Barthel Reminiscences, 1952.
5 Ford, *My Life and Work*, 37; Barthel Reminiscences, 1952.
6 *Ibid.;* Detroit *Free Press*, Oct. 11, 1901.
7 *Motor Age*, 5:n.p. (Oct. 17, 1901); Detroit *News*, Oct. 10, 1901; Detroit *Free Press*, Oct. 11, 1901; Nevins, *Ford*, 202-203; Lodge, *I Remember Detroit*, 159.
8 See the accounts of the race in the issues of *Motor Age* and the Detroit *News* and *Free Press*, cited in the previous footnote, and Nevins, *Ford*, 202-205; Olson, *Young Henry Ford*, 146; and Levine, *Ford: The Dust and the Glory*, 3-5.
9 Olson, *Young Henry Ford*, 146; Levine, *Ford: The Dust and the Glory*, 5; Simonds, *Henry Ford*, 69.
10 *Motor Age*, 5:n.p. (Oct. 17, 1901), 5:n.p. (Nov. 28, 1901), 5:n.p. (Dec. 5, 1901), 1:1 (June 26, 1902) (*Motor Age* began renumbering its volumes in 1902); Nevins, *Ford*, 206-13; Detroit *Free Press*, Oct. 11, 1901.
11 Detroit *News*, Oct. 11, 1901; Nevins, *Ford*, 207-11; Olson, *Young Henry Ford*, 153; Barthel Reminiscences, 1952.

12 See MacManus and Beasley, *Men, Money, and Motors*, 1-4; Cleveland and Williamson, *The Road is Yours*, 36; Rae, *American Automobile Manufacturers*, 147.

13 Nevins, *Ford*, 212; Leland, *Master of Precision*, 66-68; Barthel Reminiscences, 1952; Charles E. Hulse, "Michigan's Pioneer Tourist," *Bulb Horn*, 14:5 (April 1953).

14 Barthel Reminiscences, 1952; Jane D. Brush, "Without Benefit of College, The Story of Alanson P. Brush, Automotive Pioneer," mss. on loan to the Division of Michigan History, Michigan Department of State, and used by the author with the permission of the owner, Harry Marsh; Leland, *Master of Precision*, 66-69.

15 The details of Leland's early life here and in the following paragraphs are drawn from Leland, *Master of Precision*, the only full-length biography of Leland that has been published.

16 For this last detail, see Nevins, *Ford*, 212.

17 *19th Annual Report of the* [Michigan] *Bureau of Labor*, 244-45; Nevins, *Ford*, 211.

18 Leland, *Master of Precision*, 62, 65; Kenneth E. Peters, "The Good-Roads Movement and the Michigan State Highway Department, 1905-1917," 139 (Ph. D. dissertation in American Culture, University of Michigan, 1972).

19 Nevins, *Ford*, 47; *National Cyclopaedia of American Biography*, 40:529; Brush, "Without Benefit of College."

20 *Ibid.;* Leland, *Master of Precision*, 62.

21 *Ibid.,* 62-63; *National Cyclopaedia of American Biography*, 40:529; Brush, "Without Benefit of College."

22 *Ibid.; Motor World*, 4:701 (Sept. 18, 1902), 5:135 (Oct. 30, 1902).

23 *Ibid.,* 4:658 (Sept. 4, 1902), 5:163 (Nov. 6, 1902); *Motor Age*, 5:n.p. (Oct. 17, 1901); Burton, *History of Wayne County and the City of Detroit*, 3:157-59.

24 *Motor World*, 5:281 (Nov. 27, 1902); *Motor Age*, 3:4 (Jan. 22, 1903); Leland, *Master of Precision*, 69.

25 Ralph M. Hower, *The History of an Advertising Agency: N. W. Ayer & Son at Work, 1869-1936*, 117 (Cambridge, Mass., 1939); Rowsome, Jr., *They Laughed When I Sat Down*, 92, 110-11; Leland, *Master of Precision*, 76; Clymer, *Treasury of Early American Automobiles*, 157; *Motor Age*, 3:980 (Feb. 6, 1901).

26 Leland, *Master of Precision*, 72; *Motor Age*, 5:17-18 (Jan. 7, 1904); *American Car Since 1775*, 139; Pound, *The Turning Wheel*, 104.

27 Leland, *Master of Precision*, 71-74.

28 *Ibid.,* 88-91; *American Car Since 1775*, 138-39.

29 Leland, *Master of Precision*, 12, 15-17; Pound, *The Turning Wheel*, 106-107; *Cycle and Automobile Trade Journal*, 14:132 (Dec. 1, 1909).

30 Sloan, *Adventures of a White Collar Man*, 37-39.

31 Lewis, *Motor Memories*, 59-61.

32 Christy Borth, *Masters of Mass Production*, 129-38 (Indianapolis, 1945); Leland, *Master of Precision*, 113-14.

33 *Cycle and Automobile Trade Journal*, 14:133 (Dec. 1, 1909); Leland, *Master of Precision*, 92, 114, 152; Frank Briscoe to Alanson Brush, Feb. 24, 1951, in correspondence accompanying Brush, "Without Benefit of College"; Mott interview, Feb. 11, 1971.

34 Leland, *Master of Precision*, 167-69; Nevins, *Ford*, 377-78; Brush, "Without Benefit of College."

35 *Ibid.*

36 *Ibid.; National Cyclopaedia of American Biography*, 40:530.

37 Nevins, *Ford*, 204-205; William F. Nolan, *Barney Oldfield: The Life and Times of America's Legendary Speed King*, 21-39 (New York, 1961); John Woodforde, *The Story of the Bicycle*, 161-63 (London, 1970).

38 Nevins, *Ford*, 213; Nolan, *Barney Oldfield*, 39-43.

39 *Motor Age*, 1:32 (April 3, 1902), 1:1 (June 26, 1902); Nevins, *Ford*, 213-15; Jardim, *The First Henry Ford*, 47; *National Cyclopaedia of American Biography*, 30:502-503; Beasley and Stark, *Made In Detroit*, 82.

40 Nevins, *Ford*, 215-17; Nolan, *Barney Oldfield*, 44-50; Levine, *Ford: The Dust and the Glory*, 8.

41 Nevins, *Ford*, 215-18; Ford, *My Life and Work*, 50-51; Nolan, *Barney Oldfield*, 44-49; Levine, *Ford: The Dust and the Glory*, 8-9; Jardim, *The First Henry Ford*, 47-48.

42 Nolan, *Barney Oldfield*, 50.

43 Nevins, *Ford*, 218.

44 *Motor Age*, 3:6 (Mar. 12, 1903), 4:9 (Sept. 3, 1903), 10:11 (Nov. 22, 1906); Jackson *Daily Citizen*, July 17, 1903; Nolan, *Barney Oldfield*, 50-59; Levine, *Ford: The Dust and the Glory*, 9-17.

45 Nevins, *Ford*, 218-19; *Motor Age*, 3:14 (Jan. 1, 1903).

46 *National Cyclopaedia of American Biography*, 22:190-91; Harry Barnard, *Independent Man: The Life of Senator James Couzens*, 29-30 (New York, 1958); Nevins, *Ford*, 225.

47 Barnard, *Independent Man*, 35-36; Miller, *Kilowatts at Work*, 265-66; Nevins, *Ford*, 225-26.

48 Barnard, *Independent Man*, 11-37; Barthel Reminiscences, 1952.

49 Barnard, *Independent Man*, 37-39; Nevins, *Ford*, 226-29.

50 *Cycle and Automobile Trade Journal*, 14:122; *Motor World*, 4:4-5 (July 3, 1902); Henry B. Joy letterbook for 1902-1903, in the Joy Papers; Barthel Reminiscences, 1952; Nevins, *Ford*, 222.

51 Information on the original Ford Motor Company stockholders has been drawn principally from Nevins, *Ford*, 229-38; Barnard, *Independent Man*, 39-43, and Olson, *Young Henry Ford*, 176-81.

52 Other sources on the Dodges that were used in addition to those cited in the previous footnote are Crabb, *Birth of a Giant*, 342-47; Lodge, *I Remember Detroit*, 149; Malcolm W. Bingay, *Detroit Is My Own Home Town*, 42-46 (Indianapolis, 1946); interview with Joseph Thompson, Ypsilanti, May 10, 1971.

53 Nevins, *Ford*, 237-39; Barnard, *Independent Man*, 42-43.

54 *Harper's Weekly*, 47:1079 (June 27, 1903).

55 Nevins, *Ford*, 240-46; (London) *Sunday Times*, Mar. 11, 1973; Detroit *Free Press*, April 1, 1973; Barnard, *Independent Man*, 46-47; MacManus and Beasley, *Men, Money, and Motors*, 19-20.

56 Jackson *Daily Citizen*, Aug. 19, 1903; Nevins, *Ford*, 250.

57 *Ibid.*, 262-65.

58 *Ibid.*, 251; *22nd Annual Report of the* [Michigan] *Bureau of Labor*, 138.

59 Nevins, *Ford*, 260, 275, 333-34; *Automobile*, 17:792-95 (Nov. 28, 1907).

60 Nevins' biography of Ford has the greatest detail on the Ford-Malcomson fight. See also Barnard, *Independent Man*, 59-64; Wilkie, *Esquire's American Autos*, 54; and John Gunther, *Inside U. S. A.*, 403 (New York, 1947). Epstein, *The Automobile Industry*, 55-101, has the most detailed analysis of the changes in the market for low- and high-priced cars.

61 Nevins, *Ford*, 331; Barnard, *Independent Man*, 64.

62 The basic source used in this account of the Selden controversy is Greenleaf, *Monopoly on Wheels*. Rae, *American Automobile Manufacturers*, 72-

79, is a good brief summary that differs in some of its interpretations from those of Greenleaf.

63 Smith to Olds, May 17, 1902, and two additional pages, signed by Smith, that are apparently the last pages of another letter to Olds in this same period, in the R. E. Olds Collection.

64 Smith to Olds, Oct. 11 and Nov. 19, 1902, in the R. E. Olds Collection.

65 See biographies of James and Henry Joy in *Compendium of History and Biography of the City of Detroit*, 272-75, and *National Cyclopaedia of American Biography*, 27:396-97.

66 Mss. account by J. Frank Duryea in the King Papers; John K. Barnes, "The Men Who Created 'Cooperative Competition,'" *World's Work*, 42:60-64 (May 1921). The story of Joy's visit to the New York auto show has been related many times, as, for example, in Rae, *American Automobile Manufacturers*, 35-36. This author can recall running across an account of these events written by Joy which he found in the Joy Papers in the course of other research some twenty years ago. A search of these voluminous records for this account in the course of research for the present book, however, failed to turn up this version.

67 *National Cyclopaedia of American Biography*, 20:15-16; Rae, *American Automobile Manufacturers*, 35; Barthel Reminiscences, 1952; *Detroit Times*, Nov. 6, 1949.

68 Memorandum in Joy letterbook inserted after a page dated June 25, 1903, and other letters in this letterbook for 1902-1903 in the Joy Papers; Rae, *American Automobile Manufacturers*, 36-37; *Automobile*, 9:609 (Dec. 12, 1903).

69 Joy to James Packard, Dec. 29 and 30, 1902, and Jan. 9, 1903; Joy to Day, Dec. 23, 1902; Joy to S. T. Davis, Dec. 30, 1902, all in the Joy Papers.

70 Joy to James Packard, Jan. 4 and Feb. 12, 1903; Joy to Day, Jan. 5 and 8, 1903; Joy to S. T. Davis, Feb. 21, 1903, all in the Joy Papers.

71 Day to Joy, telegram enclosed in a letter from Joy's secretary to Joy in Warren, Ohio, Feb. 25, 1903; Joy to James Packard, Feb. 12, 1903, both in the Joy Papers.

72 Joy to Smith, Mar. 7, 1903; Joy to James Packard, May 4, 1903, both in the Joy Papers.

73 Details on the early membership in the A.L.A.M. are in Epstein, *The Automobile Industry*, 369-71.

74 Herman F. Cuntz to Charles B. King, Aug. 11, 1936, in the King Papers.

75 Greenleaf, *Monopoly on Wheels*, 107-10, summarizes the information relating to the discussions between Smith and the Ford officials.

76 *Ibid.*, 107.

77 Nevins, *Ford*, 284-301. Much of this account is the same as that found in Greenleaf's work, Greenleaf having originally begun his research as a member of the team of researchers that worked with Nevins in the preparation of the Ford biography.

78 *Ibid.*, 301.

79 The reader is again referred to Greenleaf, *Monopoly on Wheels*, for the details of the case.

80 Seltzer, *Financial History of the American Automobile Industry*, 97.

81 Rae, *American Automobile Manufacturers*, 78-81.

82 The list of automobile manufacturers referred to is in Smith, *Wheels Within Wheels*, 191-275. There have been much higher estimates of the total number of American automobile manufacturers, and of course the number of different automobiles that have been produced is much higher still, since many companies have produced cars of more than one name.

However, Smith's list appears to be one of the most satisfactory efforts to list those firms that have made a serious attempt to produce cars, in contrast with such paper firms as the Benton Harbor Motor Carriage Company, which have been included in some lists but which never produced anything but talk.

Chapter 10

1 Rae, *American Automobile Manufacturers,* 49, 61-62, 67-69.

2 Joy to Warburton, May 12, 15, 18, and 19, 1903, in the Joy Papers.

3 Joy to Gunderson, May 22, and Joy to Warburton, July 2, 1903, in the Joy Papers; Greenleaf, *Monopoly on Wheels,* 110.

4 Pound, *The Turning Wheel,* 111-13.

5 *Automobile,* 9:617 (Dec. 12, 1903); Benjamin Briscoe, "The Inside Story of General Motors," *Detroit Saturday Night,* 15:2 (Jan. 15, 1921).

6 *Ibid.,* 15:9 (Jan. 15, 1921); *Horseless Age,* 22:21 (Dec. 30, 1908); interview of Charles B. King by David Beecroft, Sept. 24, 1924, in the King Papers.

7 Briscoe, "The Inside Story of General Motors," *Detroit Saturday Night,* 15:4 (Jan. 22, 1921); Rae, *American Automobile Manufacturers,* 52-54, 94; Glasscock, *The Gasoline Age,* 98-99; *American Car Since 1775,* 138-39.

8 Gustin mss.; B. C. Forbes, *Men Who Are Making America,* 282-85 (New York, 1919); Rae, *American Automobile Manufacturers,* 94; Briscoe, "The Inside Story of General Motors," *Detroit Saturday Night,* 15:7 (Jan. 22, 1921). The interest Perkins had in an automobile combination may have been minor in terms of his overall business concerns. No mention of General Motors or of the talks leading up to its formation appears in the principal biography of Perkins, John A. Garraty, *Right-hand Man: The Life of George W. Perkins* (New York, 1960).

9 Gustin mss.; Briscoe, "The Inside Story of General Motors," *Detroit Saturday Night,* 15:2 (Jan. 15, 1921), and 15:4 (Jan. 22, 1921); Epstein, *The Automobile Industry,* 223-24.

10 Gustin mss.; Barnard, *Independent Man,* 72-73; R. E. Olds Diary for 1908 in the R. E. Olds Collection.

11 *Ibid.;* Gustin mss.; Briscoe, "The Inside Story of General Motors," *Detroit Saturday Night,* 15:4 (Jan. 22, 1921); Pearson, *Son of New England,* 135.

12 Olds Diary for 1908 in R. E. Olds Collection.

13 A. H. Goss to Buick stockholders, July 8, 1908, in Carton Papers.

14 Barnard, *Independent Man,* 72-73, 76.

15 *Ibid.,* 73; Gustin mss.; Lansing *State Journal,* June 2, 1949, clipping in Olds biographical file, Michigan State Library; Herbert L. Satterlee, *J. Pierpont Morgan: An Intimate Portrait,* 494-500 (New York, 1940).

16 Olds Diary for 1908 in R. E. Olds Collection; *Horseless Age,* 21:671 (June 3, 1908); Lansing *Journal,* July 25, 1908.

17 Briscoe, "The Inside Story of General Motors," *Detroit Saturday Night,* 15:4 (Jan. 22, 1921).

18 *Horseless Age,* 21:671 (June 3, 1908); *National Cyclopaedia of American Biography,* 22:222; Lodge, *I Remember Detroit,* 152-53, 159-60.

19 *National Cyclopaedia of American Biography,* 18:81-82.

20 *Cycle and Automobile Trade Journal,* 14:123 (Dec. 1, 1909); *Advance Catalog 1912 Everitt,* in Pamphlet Box 3, Michigan Historical Collections, University of Michigan.

21 *Motor Age*, 10:29 (July 12, 1906), 10:33a (July 26, 1906), 10:28 (Aug. 30, 1906), 10:31 (Oct. 25, 1906), 13:23 (Mar. 19, 1908); Nevins, *Ford, The Times, the Man, the Company*, 334-35, 364-65.

22 *Horseless Age*, 21:671 (June 3, 1908).

23 *Motor Age*, 15:36-37 (Feb. 11, 1909), 15:10 (May 6, 1909), 17:40 (Jan. 13, 1910).

24 *Ibid.*, 16:9 (Dec. 23, 1909); *Advance Catalog 1912 Everitt*.

25 *Motor Age*, 16:22 (July 22, 1909), 16:8 (Dec. 23, 1909); *Cycle and Automobile Trade Journal*, 14:142 (Dec. 1, 1909).

26 *Motor Age*, 17:40 (Jan. 13, 1910); *Motor*, 112a (April 1910); *Horseless Age*, 25:412 (Mar. 16, 1910); *The Hub*, 51:446 (Mar. 1910).

27 Rae, *American Automobile Manufacturers*, 93; Stephen Longstreet, *A Century on Wheels, The Story of Studebaker, A History, 1852-1952*, 70-71 (New York, 1952).

28 Rae, *American Automobile Manufacturers*, 93-94; Nevins, *Ford*, 365; Glasscock, *The Gasoline Age*, 189-90, 256-58.

29 *The Hub*, 51:446 (Mar. 1910); Seltzer, *Financial History of the American Automobile Industry*, 5.

30 Flint *Journal*, July 3, 1908, quoting a report from Detroit of an agreement reached on June 27; *Motor Age*, 14:17 (July 2, 1908).

31 Ward, Hayden & Satterlee to Carton, July 1, Carton to Ward, Hayden & Satterlee, July 7, and Goss to Buick stockholders, July 8, 1908, in the Carton Papers.

32 Durant to Carton, July 2, 1908, and Carton to Ward, Hayden & Satterlee, July 29, 1908, in the Carton Papers; MacManus and Beasley, *Men, Money, and Motors*, 4-5; Epstein, *The Automobile Industry*, 4; Gustin mss.

33 Gustin mss.; MacManus and Beasley, *Men, Money, and Motors*, 104-105; Flint *Journal*, July 25, 1908; Seltzer, *Financial History of the American Automobile Industry*, 35, 158; Pound, "General Motors' Old Home Town," *Michigan History*, 40:91.

34 MacManus and Beasley, *Men, Money, and Motors*, 105; Gustin mss.; Carton to Ward, Hayden & Satterlee, July 29, 1908, in the Carton Papers.

35 Flint *Journal*, July 25, 1908; *Horseless Age*, 22:146 (July 29, 1908).

36 New York *Times*, July 31, 1908.

37 Gustin mss.; Flint *Journal*, Aug. 1, 1908; *Horseless Age*, 22:146 (July 29, 1908), 22:181 (Aug. 5, 1908).

38 Gustin mss.

39 *Ibid.*

40 *Ibid.*; Smith, *Motoring Down a Quarter of a Century*, 36-37; *American Car Since 1775*, 138; J. L. Carleton to Eugene Cooley, April 10, 1907, in E. F. Cooley Papers; Lansing *Journal*, July 25, 1908; Seltzer, *Financial History of the American Automobile Industry*, 156.

41 Gustin mss.; MacManus and Beasley, *Men, Money, and Motors*, 106.

42 Gustin mss.

43 Thomas C. Cochran and William Miller, *The Age of Enterprise: A Social History of Industrial America*, 190 (New York, 1943); Pound, "General Motors' Old Home Town," *Michigan History*, 40:88.

44 Gustin mss.; Pound, *The Turning Wheel*, 114, 137; Seltzer, *Financial History of the American Automobile Industry*, 151-52, 154.

45 Carton to Martindale, April 30, 1909, in Carton Papers. Martindale was not so easily persuaded, however, as further correspondence between Carton and Martindale's office on this question indicates.

46 Frederick Lewis Allen, *The Big Change: America Transforms Itself,*
    1900-1950, 75-77 (New York, 1952).
47 Flint *Journal,* Oct. 31, 1908; Pound, *The Turning Wheel,* 115; Seltzer,
    Financial History of the American Automobile Industry, 151-52; Bush,
    Future Builders: The Story of Michigan's Consumers Power Company,
    115-20, 141-42, 472-73.
48 Flint *Journal,* Oct. 31 and Nov. 6, 1908; Pound, *The Turning Wheel,* 65.
49 *Ibid.,* 65; Seltzer, *Financial History of the American Automobile Industry,*
    156; *Horseless Age,* 22:943 (Dec. 30, 1908); Curtis R. Hatheway to John J.
    Carton, June 16, 1909, in the Carton Papers.
50 Flint *Journal,* Sept. 2, 1909; Smith, *Motoring Down a Quarter of a Cen-*
    tury, 22; Detroit *News,* May 8, 1917; Detroit *Free Press,* May 9, 1917;
    Automobile, 36:894 (May 10, 1917).
51 *Horseless Age,* 22:943 (Dec. 30, 1908); Flint *Journal,* Dec. 22 and 28, 1908.
52 Pound, *The Turning Wheel,* 93-94, 121-23; Seltzer, *Financial History of*
    the American Automobile Industry, 154, 158-60.
53 *Ibid.,* 153-55; Pound, *The Turning Wheel,* 109-10; *Motor Age,* 16:22
    (July 15, 1909); Leland, *Master of Precision,* 95-96; interview by the author
    with Joseph Thompson, May 10, 1971.
54 Leland, *Master of Precision,* 96-97.
55 Seltzer, *Financial History of the American Automobile Industry,* 157.
56 Pound, *The Turning Wheel,* 120.
57 Olds Diary for 1908 and 1909 in the R. E. Olds Collection.
58 *Ibid.; The Hub,* 51:18 (April 1909), and 51:174 (Aug. 1909); Briscoe,
    "The Inside Story of General Motors," *Detroit Saturday Night,* 15:4 (Jan.
    29, 1921).
59 *The Hub,* 51:174 (Aug. 1909); Rae, *American Automobile Manufacturers,*
    94-96; Briscoe obituary in the New York *Times,* June 28, 1945.
60 MacManus and Beasley, *Men, Money, and Motors,* 69-70.
61 Details of the Ford-G.M. negotiations are drawn from MacManus and
    Beasley, *Men, Money, and Motors,* 70-72; Barnard, *Independent Man,* 74-
    75; Seltzer, *Financial History of the American Automobile Industry,* 36.

Chapter 11

1 *Automobiles of America,* produced and periodically up-dated by the Motor
   Vehicle Manufacturers Association (formerly the Automobile Manufacturers Association), is a convenient guide to the technological and design
   changes in these early years.
2 *Motor Age,* 2:558-64 (June 28, 1900); *19th Annual Report of the* [Michi-
   gan] *Bureau of Labor; Michigan State Gazetteer for 1901,* 1732.
3 *Automobile,* 9:609 (Dec. 12, 1903), 10:460 (April 23, 1904); *21st Annual*
   Report of the [Michigan] *Bureau of Labor,* 211-13.
4 Bureau of the Census, *Manufactures, 1905,* Part I: *United States by In-*
   dustries, 80-81; Part II: *States and Territories,* 500, 510, 520-21 (Washington, 1907); *Census of Manufactures, 1914,* vol. I: *Reports by States . . . ,*
   670, 692-93 (Washington, 1918). Actually, two years before the 1904
   manufacturing census figures for Michigan appeared in the Federal Census
   Bureau's report, these same figures appeared in volume 2 of the *Census*
   of the State of Michigan, 1904, compiled by the secretary of state and
   published in Lansing in 1905. By prior agreement the Federal Census

Bureau and the state cooperated in carrying out a manufacturing census
for the period ending June 30, 1904, as part of Michigan's regular mid-
decade census-taking operation, with the federal census agency accepting
these figures from Michigan, although in other states the manufacturing
census covered the year ending Dec. 31, 1904. Thus the comparisons that
were made between the development of the auto industry in Michigan
and in other states were not entirely valid since the statistics for Michigan are for a period that ends six months earlier than the period used in
Ohio, New York, Indiana, and the other auto-producing states. Had the
census in Michigan also been over the period ending December 31, 1904,
Michigan's production would have bulked even larger in the overall
picture, due to the rapid growth that occurred in the state in the last half
of that year.

5 *Census of Manufactures, 1914,* vol. 1: *Reports by States . . . ,* 692; *Cycle
and Automobile Trade Journal,* 14:123 (Dec. 1, 1909); *Motor Age,* 7:13-14
(Jan. 5, 1905).

6 *Michigan State Gazetteer for 1905,* 1923-25; *Review of Reviews,* 33:621
(May 1906); Albert Nelson Marquis, ed., *The Book of Detroiters,* 15
(Chicago, 1908). *Review of Reviews,* which summarized Casson's article
from *Pearson's Magazine,* where it originally appeared, was apparently
guilty of a misprint when it reported that Casson estimated the value of
Michigan-made cars in 1905 to have been $80,000,000. Since it reported
that Casson's estimate of sales in the country as a whole was only about
$36,000,000, we may assume that the figure for Michigan that Casson in-
tended to give was $8,000,000, which would have roughly accorded with the
rate of increase that he was showing in the industry in 1905 over the figures
assembled by the census bureau for 1904.

7 *Census of Manufactures, 1914,* vol. 1, 692-93; vol. II: *Reports for Selected
Industries,* 733, 739 (Washington, 1919).

8 "Motor's Historical Table of the American Car Industry," *Motor,* 11:36-
42 (Mar. 1909). The observation attributed to John B. Rae is one that
I read in one of Rae's publications but which I failed to make a note
of, as to precise location, at the time.

9 Denison, *The Power to Go,* 74; Joy to P. C. Baker, April 4, 1903, in Joy
Papers.

10 " 'F. O. B. Detroit,' The Romance of the Wonder City of the Magic
Motor," *Outlook,* 111:983 (Dec. 22, 1915); Lewis, *Motor Memories,* 190-
91; Seltzer, *Financial History of the American Automobile Industry,* 30.

11 Chapin to Macfarlane, Mar. 8, 1921, in Chapin Papers.

12 Spencer, "Detroit, The City Built by the Automobile Industry," *Automobile,* 28:797 (April 10, 1913); Miller, *Kilowatts at Work,* 163-64.

13 Lewis, *Motor Memories,* 189; *Motor Age,* 13:21 (April 16, 1908); West,
"The Meteoric Rise of the Automobile Industry," *American Review of
Reviews,* 42:583; Barnes, "The Romance of Our Automobile Makers,"
World's Work, 41:560; Seltzer, *Financial History of the American Automo-
bile Industry,* 30.

14 Nevins, *Ford,* 512-16.

15 *Motor Age,* 13:30 (April 23, 1908); *Horseless Age,* 22:946 (Dec. 30, 1908).

16 *Motor Age,* 2:690 (July 26, 1900), 15:44 (Jan. 21, 1909), 15:38 (June 10,
1909); *Cycle and Automobile Trade Journal,* 14:150-52; *National Cyclopaedia of American Biography,* 43:545; Lewis, *Motor Memories,* 202, 211-
13; Muskegon *Chronicle,* Sept. 27, 1952, clipping in Automotive Industries file in Michigan State Library; *The Hub,* 50:328 (Dec. 1908).

17 Mott interview, Feb. 11, 1971; *Automobile*, 9:609 (Dec. 12, 1903); " 'F. O. B. Detroit,' " *Outlook*, 111:979.

18 Lucy and Sidney Corbett, *Pot Shots from a Grosse Ile Kitchen*, 141 (New York, 1947).

19 I. T. Martin, "Where Woman Runs Her Car," *Harper's Weekly*, 55:12 (May 6, 1911); John Ihlder, "Booming Detroit," *Survey*, 36:449 (July 29, 1916); Edward Hungerford, "America Goes Back to Work: Detroit, the Fourth City," *Harper's*, 141:235-36 (July 1920).

INDEX

A. Baushke & Bros., Benton Harbor, entry in *Times-Herald* race, 26, 41, 43; attempt auto manufacturing, 40-45

Adams, Frederick Upham, and *Times-Herald* race, 25, 26, 27

Adrian, automobile work, 26, 143-51; manufacturing in, 144

Advance Thresher Co., Battle Creek, leading thresher producer, 156

Advertising, Oldsmobile ads, 125, 136; Reo ads, 230-31, illus., 232; Cadillac ads, 253-54, illus., 254

Aerocar Co., Detroit, Malcomson and, 266, 279

A. G. Spaulding and Co., New York, and Oldsmobile, 130

Ainsley, Charles, *see* Annesley, Charles G.

Aitken, David D., Durant partner, 183, 205

Alamo Manufacturing Co., Hillsdale, automobile produced by, 151

Alamobile, automobile, production, 151

Albion, auto experiments in, 48

Alderman, Frank R., and Detroit Automobile Co., 102, 104, 106, 243

Aldrich, Almon L., father of Fred A. Aldrich, 190

Aldrich, Fred A., and Durant-Dort, 190; and Buick, 201

Alexander Manufacturing Co., Detroit, Buick and, 195

Alexandre Darracq, auto production, 137

Alger, Russel A., Jr., and Packard, 286

Allegan, automotive work in, 161

Alma, and Austin, 163; Leonard Refineries in, 172

Althouse, C. W., and Maxwell, 299

American Automobile Association, organized, 162, 164

American Bicycle Co., bicycle trust, 165, 295

American Brake Beam Co., Chicago, and King, 21

American Car and Foundry Co., absorbs Detroit firms, 82, 102

American Motor Car Manufacturers Association, Briscoe and, 300, 305

American Motor League, formation of, 31-32; Murray and, 148

American Motors Corp., organized, 132-33, 331-32; acquires Kaiser-Jeep, 332

Anderson, Gladys Olds, daughter of R. E. Olds, on Olds move to Detroit, 71-72

Anderson, John W., and Ford, 267; and Ford Motor Co., 270, 274, 276, 278

Anderson, Wendell E., father of John W. Anderson, 270, 276

Angell, Alexis C., Brush attorney, 259

Ann Arbor, Howard Coffin and, 132

Annesley, Charles G., and King, 36; and Ford, 85, 95; auto pioneer, 84, 85-86

Anti-Saloon League, Richard H. Scott and, 235

Apperson, Edgar, and Haynes, 24; manufacturing efforts, 66, 137; races at Grosse Pointe, 240-42

Apperson, Elmer, and Haynes, 24; manufacturing efforts, 66, 137; and Uriah Smith, 156; and auto manufacturers group, 282

Apperson Automobile Co., Kokomo, Ind., and Selden Patent, 287

"Arrow," Ford racing car, 262, 264-65

Associated Motor Industries, and Jackson Automobile Co., 210

Association of Licensed Automobile Manufacturers, Olds and, 139; and Flint Automobile Co., 194, 289; and Buick, 218; origins, 282-84, 287-88; and Ford Motor Co., 289-93; alleged monopolistic intent of, 293; and auto mergers, 296-97, 300

Atlas Drop Forge Co., Lansing, and Olds, 234

Austin, James E., father of Walter S. Austin, 163-64

Austin, Walter S., and American Automobile Association, 162, 164; career, 162-64

Austin, automobile, produced in Grand Rapids, 162

Austin & Son, Grand Rapids, history, 162-64

Auto Body Co., Lansing, Olds supplier, 123; Reo supplier, 234

Auto Crank Shaft Co., Detroit, purchased by E. M. F., 308

Auto Vehicle Co., Los Angeles, organized, 166

Autocar Co., Ardmore, Pa., and Selden Patent, 287

Automobile, experimental period, 329; design features by 1909, 329-30; problems created by, 345; *see also* names of individual makes and companies

Automobile industry, histories of, 11; in Europe, 16; Michigan's emphasis on mass-produced vehicles, 27, 61; early U.S. production, 66-67; early leaders, 142, 336; superiority of European over American, 192-93, 257; Olds on future of, 222; reduction in companies in, 293-94; consolidation in, 295-97; concentration in Michigan, 332-36, 343-45, reasons, 336-43; *see also* names of companies and localities

Automobile parts industry, importance in